Children's
Literature
Review

Guide to Gale Literary Criticism Series

For criticism on	Consult these Gale series
Authors now living or who died after December 31, 1959	*CONTEMPORARY LITERARY CRITICISM (CLC)*
Authors who died between 1900 and 1959	*TWENTIETH-CENTURY LITERARY CRITICISM (TCLC)*
Authors who died between 1800 and 1899	*NINETEENTH-CENTURY LITERATURE CRITICISM (NCLC)*
Authors who died between 1400 and 1799	*LITERATURE CRITICISM FROM 1400 TO 1800 (LC)* *SHAKESPEAREAN CRITICISM (SC)*
Authors who died before 1400	*CLASSICAL AND MEDIEVAL LITERATURE CRITICISM (CMLC)*
Black writers of the past two hundred years	*BLACK LITERATURE CRITICISM (BLC) AND BLACK LITERATURE CRITICISM SUPPLEMENT (BLCS)*
Authors of books for children and young adults	*CHILDREN'S LITERATURE REVIEW (CLR)*
Dramatists	*DRAMA CRITICISM (DC)*
Hispanic writers of the late nineteenth and twentieth centuries	*HISPANIC LITERATURE CRITICISM (HLC)*
Native North American writers and orators of the eighteenth, nineteenth, and twentieth centuries	*NATIVE NORTH AMERICAN LITERATURE (NNAL)*
Poets	*POETRY CRITICISM (PC)*
Short story writers	*SHORT STORY CRITICISM (SSC)*
Major authors from the Renaissance to the present	*WORLD LITERATURE CRITICISM, 1500 TO THE PRESENT (WLC)*
Major authors and works from the Bible to the present	*WORLD LITERATURE CRITICISM SUPPLEMENT (WLCS)*

ISSN 0362-4145

volume 55

Children's Literature Review

Excerpts from Reviews,
Criticism, and Commentary
on Books for Children
and Young People

Deborah J. Morad
Editor

The Gale Group
DETROIT • SAN FRANCISCO • LONDON • BOSTON • WOODBRIDGE, CT

STAFF

Deborah J. Morad, *Editor*

Sara Constantakis, Catherine Goldstein, Holly Griffin, Alan Hedblad, Motoko Fujishiro
Huthwaite, Arlene Johnson, Paul Loeber, Thomas McMahon, Malinda Mayer, Adele Sarkissian, Gerard J. Senick,
Kathleen Witman, Renee Wrublewski *Contributing Editors*

Karen Uchic, *Technical Training Specialist*

Joyce Nakamura, *Managing Editor*

Maria Franklin, *Permissions Manager*
Sarah Chesney, Edna Hedblad, Michele Lonoconus, *Permissions Associates*

Victoria B. Cariappa, *Research Manager*
Corrine A. Stocker, *Project Coordinator*
Barbara McNeil, Cheryl D. Warnock, *Research Specialists*
Patricia Tsune Ballard, Wendy K. Festerling, Tamara C. Nott, Tracie A. Richardson, *Research Associates*
Phyllis J. Blackman, Tim Lehnerer *Research Assistants*

Mary Beth Trimper, *Production Director*
Cindy Range, *Production Assistant*

Gary Leach, *Graphic Artist*
Randy Bassett, *Image Database Supervisor*
Robert Duncan, Michael Logusz, *Imaging Specialists*
Pamela A. Reed, *Imaging Coordinator*

Library of Congress Catalog Card Number 76-643301
ISBN 0-7876-2901-4
ISSN 0362-4145
Printed in the United States of America

10 9 8 7 6 5 4 3 2 1

Contents

Preface

Literature for children and young adults has evolved into both a respected branch of creative writing and a successful industry. Currently, books for young readers are considered among the most popular segments of publishing. Criticism of juvenile literature is instrumental in recording the literary or artistic development of the creators of children's books as well as the trends and controversies that result from changing values or attitudes about young people and their literature. Designed to provide a permanent, accessible record of this ongoing scholarship, *Children's Literature Review (CLR)* presents parents, teachers, and librarians—those responsible for bringing children and books together—with the opportunity to make informed choices when selecting reading materials for the young. In addition, *CLR* provides researchers of children's literature with easy access to a wide variety of critical information from English-language sources in the field. Users will find balanced overviews of the careers of the authors and illustrators of the books that children and young adults are reading; these entries, which contain excerpts from published criticism in books and periodicals, assist users by sparking ideas for papers and assignments and suggesting supplementary and classroom reading. Ann L. Kalkhoff, president and editor of *Children's Book Review Service Inc.*, writes that "*CLR* has filled a gap in the field of children's books, and it is one series that will never lose its validity or importance."

Scope of the Series

Each volume of *CLR* profiles the careers of a selection of authors and illustrators of books for children and young adults from preschool through high school. Author lists in each volume reflect:

- an international scope.

- representation of authors of all eras.

- the variety of genres covered by children's and/or YA literature: picture books, fiction, nonfiction, poetry, folklore, and drama.

Although the focus of the series is on authors new to *CLR*, entries will be updated as the need arises.

Organization of This Book

An entry consists of the following elements: author heading, author portrait, author introduction, excerpts of criticism (each preceded by a bibliographical citation), and illustrations, when available.

- The **Author Heading** consists of the author's name followed by birth and death dates. The portion of the name outside the parentheses denotes the form under which the author is most frequently published. If the majority of the author's works for children were written under a pseudonym, the pseudonym will be listed in the author heading and the real name given on the first line of the author introduction. Also located at the beginning of the introduction are any other pseudonyms used by the author in writing for children and any name variations, including transliterated forms for authors whose languages use nonroman alphabets. Uncertainty as to a birth or death date is indicated by question marks.

- An **Author Portrait** is included when available.

- The **Author Introduction** contains information designed to introduce an author to *CLR* users by presenting an overview of the author's themes and styles, biographical facts that relate to the author's literary career or critical responses to the author's works, and information about major awards and prizes the author has received. The introduction begins by identifying the nationality of the author and by listing the genres in which s/he has written for children and young adults. Introductions also list a group of representative titles for which the author or illustrator being profiled is best known; this section, which begins with the words "major works include," follows the genre line of the introduction. For seminal figures, a listing of major works about the author follows when appropriate, highlighting important biographies about the author or illustrator that are not excerpted in the entry. The centered heading "Introduction" announces the body of the text.

- **Criticism** is located in three sections: **Author's Commentary** (when available), **General Commentary** (when available), and **Title Commentary** (commentary on specific titles).

    - The **Author's Commentary** presents background material written by the author or by an interviewer. This commentary may cover a specific work or several works. Author's commentary on more than one work appears after the author introduction, while commentary on an individual book follows the title entry heading.

    - The **General Commentary** consists of critical excerpts that consider more than one work by the author or illustrator being profiled. General commentary is preceded by the critic's name in boldface type or, in the case of unsigned criticism, by the title of the journal. *CLR* also features entries that emphasize general criticism on the oeuvre of an author or illustrator. When appropriate, a selection of reviews is included to supplement the general commentary.

    - The **Title Commentary** begins with the title entry headings, which precede the criticism on a title and cite publication information on the work being reviewed. Title headings list the title of the work as it appeared in its first English-language edition. The first English-language publication date of each work (unless otherwise noted) is listed in parentheses following the title. Differing U.S. and British titles follow the publication date within the parentheses. When a work is written by an individual other than the one being profiled, as is the case when illustrators are featured, the parenthetical material following the title cites the author of the work before listing its publication date.

    Entries in each title commentary section consist of critical excerpts on the author's individual works, arranged chronologically by publication date. The entries generally contain two to seven reviews per title, depending on the stature of the book and the amount of criticism it has generated. The editors select titles that reflect the entire scope of the author's literary contribution, covering each genre and subject. An effort is made to reprint criticism that represents the full range of each title's reception, from the year of its initial publication to current assessments. Thus, the reader is provided with a record of the author's critical history. Publication information (such as publisher names and book prices) and parenthetical numerical references (such as footnotes or page and line references to specific editions of works) have been deleted at the discretion of the editors to provide smoother reading of the text.

- Centered headings introduce each section, in which criticism is arranged chronologically; beginning with Volume 35, each excerpt is preceded by a boldface source heading for easier access by readers. Within the text, titles by authors being profiled are also highlighted in boldface type.

- Selected excerpts are preceded by **Explanatory Annotations,** which provide information on the critic or work of criticism to enhance the reader's understanding of the excerpt.

- A complete **Bibliographical Citation** designed to facilitate the location of the original book or article precedes each piece of criticism.

- Numerous **Illustrations** are featured in *CLR*. For entries on illustrators, an effort has been made to include illustrations that reflect the characteristics discussed in the criticism. Entries on authors who do not illustrate their own works may also include photographs and other illustrative material pertinent to their careers.

Special Features: Entries on Illustrators

Entries on authors who are also illustrators will occasionally feature commentary on selected works illustrated but not written by the author being profiled. These works are strongly associated with the illustrator and have received critical acclaim for their art. By including critical comment on works of this type, the editors wish to provide a more complete representation of the artist's career. Criticism on these works has been chosen to stress artistic, rather than literary, contributions. Title entry headings for works illustrated by the author being profiled are arranged chronologically within the entry by date of publication and include notes identifying the author of the illustrated work. In order to provide easier access for users, all titles illustrated by the subject of the entry are boldfaced.

CLR also includes entries on prominent illustrators who have contributed to the field of children's literature. These entries are designed to represent the development of the illustrator as an artist rather than as a literary stylist. The illustrator's section is organized like that of an author, with two exceptions: the introduction presents an overview of the illustrator's styles and techniques rather than outlining his or her literary background, and the commentary written by the illustrator on his or her works is called "illustrator's commentary" rather than "author's commentary." All titles of books containing illustrations by the artist being profiled are highlighted in boldface type.

Other Features: Acknowledgments, Indexes

■ The **Acknowledgments** section, which immediately follows the preface, lists the sources from which material has been reprinted in the volume. It does not, however, list every book or periodical consulted for the volume.

■ The **Cumulative Index to Authors** lists all of the authors who have appeared in *CLR* with cross-references to the biographical, autobiographical, and literary criticism series published by The Gale Group. A full listing of the series titles appears before the first page of the indexes of this volume.

■ The **Cumulative Index to Nationalities** lists authors alphabetically under their respective nationalities. Author names are followed by the volume number(s) in which they appear.

■ The **Cumulative Index to Titles** lists titles covered in *CLR* followed by the volume and page number where criticism begins.

A Note to the Reader

CLR is one of several critical references sources in the Literature Criticism Series published by The Gale Group. When writing papers, students who quote directly from any volume in the Literature Criticism Series may use the following general forms to footnote reprinted criticism. The first example pertains to material drawn from periodicals, the second to material reprinted from books.

[1]T. S. Eliot, "John Donne," *The Nation and the Athenaeum,* 33 (9 June 1923), 321-32; excerpted and reprinted in *Literature Criticism from 1400 to 1800,* Vol. 10, ed. James E. Person, Jr. (Detroit: Gale Research, 1989), pp. 28-9.

[1]Henry Brooke, *Leslie Brooke and Johnny Crow* (Frederick Warne, 1982); excerpted and reprinted in *Children's Literature Review,* Vol. 20, ed. Gerard J. Senick (Detroit: Gale Research, 1990), p. 47.

Suggestions Are Welcome

In response to various suggestions, several features have been added to *CLR* since the beginning of the series, including author entries on retellers of traditional literature as well as those who have been the first to record oral tales and other folklore; entries on prominent illustrators featuring commentary on their styles and techniques; entries on authors whose works are considered controversial; occasional entries devoted to criticism on a single work or a series of works; sections in author introductions that list major works by and about the author or illustrator being profiled; explanatory notes that provide information on the critic or work of criticism to enhance the usefulness of the excerpt; more extensive illustrative material, such as holographs of manuscript pages and photographs of people and places pertinent to the careers of the authors and artists; a cumulative nationality index for easy access to authors by nationality; and occasional guest essays written specifically for *CLR* by prominent critics on subjects of their choice.

Readers who wish to suggest authors to appear in future volumes, or who have other suggestions, are cordially invited to contact the editor. By mail: Editor, *Children's Literature Review,* The Gale Group, 27500 Drake Road, Farmington Hills, MI 48331-3535; by telephone: (800) 347-GALE; by fax: (248) 699-8065.

Acknowledgments

The editors wish to thank the copyright holders of the excerpted criticism included in this volume and the permissions managers of many book and magazine publishing companies for assisting us in securing reproduction rights. We are also grateful to the staffs of the Detroit Public Library, the Library of Congress, the University of Detroit Mercy Library, Wayne State University Purdy/Kresge Library Complex, and the University of Michigan Libraries for making their resources available to us. Following is a list of the copyright holders who have granted us permission to reproduce material in this volume of **CLR.** Every effort has been made to trace copyright, but if omissions have been made, please let us know.

COPYRIGHTED EXCERPTS IN *CLR,* VOLUME 55, WERE REPRODUCED FROM THE FOLLOWING PERIODICALS:

Appraisal: Science Books for Young People, v. 27, Fall, 1994. Copyright © 1994 by the Children's Science Book Review Committee. Reproduced by permission.—*The Book Report,* v. 5, November-December, 1986. © copyright 1986 by Linworth Publishing, Inc., Worthington, Ohio. Reproduced by permission.—*Booklist,* v. 76, March 1, 1980; v. 77, May 1, 1981; v. 77, July 1, 1981; v. 78, April 1, 1982; v. 78, July 1, 1982; v. 80, June 1, 1984; v. 81, March 15, 1985; v. 82, July, 1986; v. 83, September 1, 1986; v. 83, September 15, 1986; v. 83, August, 1987; v. 85, September 1, 1988; v. 87, September 1, 1990; v. 88, January 1, 1992; v. 88, June 15, 1992; v. 89, December 15, 1992; v. 90, December 1, 1993; v. 90, January 15, 1994; v. 90, June 1 & 15, 1994; v. 90, August, 1994; v. 91, October 15, 1994; v. 92, September 15, 1995; v. 92, January 1 & 15, 1996; v. 92, February 15, 1996; v. 92, June 1, 1996; v. 93, September 1, 1996; v. 93, February 1, 1997; v. 94, October 1, 1997; v. 94, November 15, 1997; v. 94, February 15, 1998; v. 94, June 1 & 15, 1998. Copyright © 1980, 1981, 1982, 1984, 1985, 1986, 1987, 1988, 1990, 1992, 1993, 1994, 1995, 1996, 1997, 1998 by the American Library Association. All reproduced by permission.—*The Booklist,* v. 62, December 1, 1965; v. 64, December 1, 1967; v. 65, June 15, 1969; v. 69, February 15, 1973; v. 72, October 15, 1975; v. 72, April 1, 1976. Copyright © 1965, 1967, 1969, 1973, 1975, 1976 by the American Library Association. All reproduced by permission.—*Books for Keeps,* n. 44, May, 1987; n. 105, July, 1997. © School Bookshop Association 1987, 1997. Both reproduced by permission.—*Books for Young People,* v. 1, December, 1987 for "Renaissance Man Donn Kushner a Delightful Challenge for Children" by Bernie Goedhart. Reproduced by permission of the author.—*Books in Canada,* v. XXII, February, 1993 for "Adventures with Colour" by Diane Schoemperlen. Reproduced by permission of the author.—*Bulletin of the Center for Children's Books,* v. XIV, March, 1961; v. XVI, April, 1963; v. XVII, May, 1964; v. XVIII, March, 1965; v. 20, April, 1967; v. 21, February, 1968; v. 24, April, 1971; v. 25, December, 1971; v. 26, February, 1973; v. 28, January, 1975; v. 29, May, 1976; v. 29, July-August, 1976; v. 31, February, 1978; v. 32, February, 1979; v. 34, June, 1981; v. 35, October, 1981; v. 35, June, 1982; v. 36, September, 1982; v. 36, January, 1983; v. 36, May, 1983; v. 38, March, 1985; v. 38, April, 1985; v. 39, December, 1985; v. 39, May, 1986; v. 42, October, 1988; v. 43, May, 1990; v. 44, October, 1990; v. 44, June, 1991; v. 45, October, 1991; v. 45, June, 1992. Copyright © 1961, 1963, 1964, 1965, 1967, 1968, 1971, 1973, 1975, 1976, 1978, 1979, 1981, 1982, 1983, 1985, 1986, 1988, 1990, 1991, 1992 by The University of Chicago. All reproduced by permission./ v. 46, September, 1992; v. 46, December, 1992; v. 46, January, 1993; v. 47, February, 1994; v. 48, October, 1994; v. 48, November, 1994; v. 48, May, 1995; v. 49, November, 1995; v. 50, November, 1996; v. 50, June, 1997; v. 51, November, 1997; v. 51, January, 1998; v. 52, September, 1998; v. 52, December, 1998; v. 52, March, 1999. Copyright © 1992, 1993, 1994, 1995, 1996, 1997, 1998, 1999 by The Board of Trustees of the University of Illinois. All reproduced by permission.—*Canadian Children's Literature,* n. 43, 1986; n. 49, 1988; n. 65, 1992; n. 71, 1993; n. 81, 1996. Copyright © 1986, 1988, 1992, 1993, 1996 Canadian Children's Press. All reproduced by permission.—*Canadian Literature,* n. 121, Summer, 1989 for "Dragon Wise," by Mary-Ann Stouck. Reproduced by permission of the author.—*Children's Book News,* v. 3, January-February, 1968. Reproduced by permission of Baker Book Services.—*Children's Book Review Service, Inc.,* v. 25, October, 1996; v. 26, December, 1997. Copyright 1996, 1997 Children's Book Review Service Inc. Both reproduced by permission.—*Children's Books,* June, 1986. © The British Council, 1986. Reproduced by permission.—*Children's Literature: Annual of the Modern Language Association Division on Children's Literature and the Children's Literature Association,* v. 15, 1987. Yale University Press. Yale University Press, © 1987 Hollins College. Reproduced by permission.—*Children's Literature Association Quarterly,* v. 21, Spring, 1996. © 1996 Children's Literature Association. Reproduced by permission.—*The Christian Science Monitor,* May 2, 1968; November 6, 1969. © 1968, 1969 The Christian Science Publishing Society. All rights reserved. Both reproduced by permission from *The Christian Science Monitor./* November 17, 1938; December 8, 1949. © 1938, renewed 1966; © 1949, renewed 1977 The Christian Science Publishing Society. All rights reserved. Both reproduced by permission from *The Christian Science Monitor.* —*CM: A Reviewing Journal of Canadian Materials for Young People,* v. XVI, May, 1988; v. XIX, March,

Children's
Literature
Review

Robert (Edmund) Cormier

1925-

(Also has written as John Fitch IV) American author of fiction.

Major works include *Beyond the Chocolate War* (1985), *Fade* (1988), *In the Middle of the Night* (1995), *Tenderness* (1997), *Heroes* (1998)

Major works about the author include *Presenting Robert Cormier* (by Patricia J. Campbell, 1985).

For information on Cormier's career prior to 1985, see *CLR*, Vol. 12.

INTRODUCTION

For over two decades, Cormier has been, and continues to be, one of the most controversial and widely read authors of young adult novels. His nontraditional subjects and uncompromising treatments of the relationship between good and evil have critics appalled at the dark and hopeless worlds he creates, yet enthusiastic about his ability to speak to adolescents from their own perspectives. Considered a skilled craftsman, Cormier presents his readers with fast-paced, gripping narratives and a clear prose style that relies on strong imagery and employs such literary techniques as interior dialogue, multiple narration, flashbacks, irony, and plot twists. High-school English teachers find reluctant readers enthralled by Cormier's novels, which require readers to think to comprehend the true voice of the author. Cormier crafts these mysteries to highlight his characters' moral dilemmas and coping skills, and to bring the reader closer to the moral issues being explored. Centering his plots around outside forces that challenge the integrity of the individual, Cormier's novels explore themes such as loyalty, independence, responsibility, guilt, revenge, and misuse of power. His strong realism, combined with his anti-authoritarian philosophy, defies stereotypes and speaks loudly to today's youth. Of his audience, Cormier once explained, "I write for the intelligent reader, and this intelligent reader is often twelve or fourteen or sixteen years old. A work of fiction, if true to itself, written honestly, will set off shocks of recognition in the sensitive reader no matter what age that reader is, and I write for that reader."

Much of Cormier's impact comes from the shock value inherent in the perspectives his characters bring to a given situation. His protagonists are usually teenagers grappling with unbearable conditions all too familiar in the twentieth century—physical and emotional abuse, negative peer pressure, broken trust, death, rape, and incest. These youth, often mentally unbalanced, are pitted against potent adversaries and come up with solutions for survival befitting their characters that often lead to tragic outcomes. Some reviewers denounce Cormier's novels as bleak and fatalistic, while parents are often disturbed by the sexual references, graphic language, violence, and genuinely evil personas. His stories typically lack happy endings; good does not always triumph over evil, and doing the right thing and following one's conscience may lead to one's destruction. In an interview with *Books for Keeps* in 1985, Cormier acknowledged, "All I'm doing is warning [young people] that when they get out into the world it's kind of tough out there, and that's something hardly any other book or TV show is doing for kids at the moment." While his no-holds-barred view of reality has caused some of his novels to be questioned as suitable for school libraries, it is also a welcome perspective for teen readers. In *Banned in the U.S.A.*, Cormier noted that young adults enjoy his works because they are tired of unrealistic books. He further questioned the idea that children's books should have happy endings, citing the many folk tales and nursery rhymes with disastrous endings. "You're not shocking the students, because the kids live with this. You're shocking the parents." Cormier has frequently found himself in the position of having to defend his writings. Although he resents this need, he feels a responsibility to support those who advocate his vision. He once stated, "I try to write realistic stories about believable people, reflecting the world as it is, not as we wish it to be." Noting the worldwide appeal of Cormier's works, Sylvia Patterson Iskander stated in *Concise Dictionary of American Literary Biography*, "Cormier has acquired these fans because of his sensitive awareness about what actually occurs in the lives of teenagers today and his abundant talent for conveying that awareness through fiction. He has brought controversy and, simultaneously, a new dimension to the field of young-adult literature. He has earned the respect of his readers, regardless of their age, because of his refusal to compromise the truth as he sees it. His superb craftsmanship, his ability to create suspense and to shock the reader repeatedly, and his forcing the reader to think are all qualities which make Cormier's works entertaining, unique, and, indeed, unforgettable."

Biographical Information

Cormier was born and raised in the French-Canadian sector of Leominster, Massachusetts. His childhood surroundings, such as the plastics factory, the Catholic school, and the large extended families who lived in the town, often appear, though disguised, in the settings and characters of his novels. In 1943 Cormier entered Fitchburg State College, where an art teacher took an interest in his writing and sold one of his stories to a national Catholic magazine—the budding writer's first publication. After graduation he began writing ads for a radio station in nearby Worcester. He later launched a career as a reporter for the *Telegram & Gazette* in Worcester, and then as a book reviewer and editor for the Fitchburg *Sentinel and Enterprise*. Using the name John Fitch IV, he wrote a human-interest column, "And So On," that presented an entertaining, humorous, and revealing glimpse of small-town life. He also worked as a freelance writer and published many stories in magazines such as *Redbook* and *Saturday Evening Post*. He never thought of himself as a writer for teenagers, but when he submitted the draft of *The Chocolate War* to his agent, she identified it as a young adult novel. Although publishers pressured Cormier to change the downbeat ending, he resisted, and when the book was printed in 1974, it became an instant sensation. Cormier has been a full-time freelance writer since 1978, working out of an alcove in his dining room. He credits his close relationship with his own children to his working late hours, which made him awake and available when his teenage children came home. Now a grandfather, he lives with his wife in Leominster.

Major Works

It took Cormier ten years to write a sequel to *The Chocolate War* (1974). The abuse of power and its ability to corrupt are once again explored in *Beyond the Chocolate War*. Many of the characters from the first book appear again in this one, including Jerry, who returns to Trinity High after recuperating both physically and psychologically, the villainous Archie, and the corrupt and authoritative priest, Brother Leon. In a frightening tale of revenge, Cormier tells how Obie, who was Archie's best friend and stooge in the previous story, turns against Archie. Obie falls in love with a girl, and when Archie attempts to rape her, Obie's eyes are opened to Archie's evil. Obie subsequently plots Archie's murder by rigging a guillotine in a magic act to actually kill him. Although it fails, the murder plot serves to free Obie from his bondage to Archie, if not from his guilt of acknowledged complicity in Archie's immoral acts. In the end, Archie leaves Trinity with his organization intact and a new commander and aide prepared to take over as he heads into the wide world to sell his peculiar talents. Mary M. Burns remarked, *"Beyond the Chocolate War* is remarkable for maintaining the balance between plot and philosophy characteristic of the most memorable novels. Quite simply, the work is one of Cormier's finest books to date: combining the sense of immediacy that a good newsman can convey with the psychological insight of a mature writer."

Fade is the story of Paul Moreaux, a typical resident of French Town, who discovers on his thirteenth birthday that he has inherited the ability to "fade," or disappear. Paul's discovery of the curse in this blessing and how he ultimately deals with it are the subjects of this novel. Combining beautiful descriptions of French Town with elements of magic, Cormier further complicates the story and increases the suspense when the reader discovers that the early part of the book is, in fact, a manuscript by a famous author left to his niece. Cormier uses multiple frameworks to tell the remainder of the story, including the voices of the niece, the literary agent she contacts, and an illegitimate and abused child, who has also inherited the fade. Cormier's compelling and complex story led Janet R. Mura to remark: "This is a wonderful story, the characters reach out and touch you. They seem like acquaintances who affect your life. Cormier takes situations and makes them believable and always with endings that ring true. . . . This is not a depressing novel, it is a thought-provoking one. Teens will enjoy."

Cormier explores guilt and responsibility in *In the Middle of the Night*. Inspired by the story of the 1942 Boston Coconut Grove Fire, *In the Middle of the Night* explores the aftermath of a disaster and its effects on the people who lived through it. In this story of vengeance and psychological turmoil, Cormier weaves an intricate tale about a teenager named Denny whose father, John Paul, was once blamed for the deaths of twenty-two children, who were accidentally killed in a movie theater fire. Denny's father, though exonerated from any wrongdoing, has lived for the past twenty-five years under the glaring and suspicious eyes of those who still blame him for the tragedy, specifically a survivor of the fire named Lulu. Lulu has been tormenting John Paul for years with late-night telephone calls and hate mail. When Denny picks up the receiver one day, he becomes Lulu's new target for her hatred. Events are recounted through various voices and points of view. Gary E. Joseph commented, "The reader is drawn in by the suspense, but it is the second level, the dark side of things, that keeps the reader hooked. Questions about life after death may raise some eyebrows, but as Cormier once said, 'We don't do these kids any service by writing namby-pamby, ride-off-into-the-sunset stuff.' We don't and he didn't. A must read."

Tenderness is a novel of obsession. Once again told from multiple perspectives, this story centers on a serial killer and a runaway girl, both from troubled backgrounds, who follow their obsessions in the search for love. Convicted for the murders of his mother and stepfather who were believed to be abusive, eighteen-year-old Eric Poole has just been released from a three-year prison sentence in a juvenile detention facility. He is being carefully watched by a police detective near retirement who has a hunch, but no proof, that Eric has killed other women. Eric finds himself matching wits with the detective to avoid another prison sentence. He eventually meets Lori, a fifteen-year-old girl who has been a victim of sexual abuse, remembers him fondly from a chance meeting long ago and is now fixated on him. As Eric tries to decide what to do about her, they develop a mutually supportive relationship that could be the salvation of both. In the ironic and tragic climax, Lori dooms Eric to life in prison when she accidentally dies while trying to save him from the detective's set-up. Robert Dunbar noted, "From their intertwining destinies Cormier shapes a narrative which, in its sheer power to hold a reader's attention, is tinglingly skilful. It has, additionally, the tantalizing merit of provoking questions about crime and responsibility, motive and manipulation, which threaten to dislodge even our most apparently secure assumptions."

In *Heroes*, Cormier explores the concept of heroism and the truth behind it. Francis Cassavant returns home from World War II with a Silver Star for heroism and a face that has been disfigured by a grenade blast. Living incognito, Francis plans his revenge on Larry LaSalle, his once-hero and mentor whom Francis discovers to be the man who raped his girlfriend. The story reveals in flashback Francis's growing up in French Town, learning to play Ping-Pong and gaining self-confidence under Larry's tutelage, and eventually dating the girl of his dreams. Distraught by guilt over his inability to prevent the rape, fifteen-year-old Francis joins the army as a suicide mission. Thinking all heroism a sham, Francis's own heroic act of throwing his body on a grenade to save his war buddies, was, in fact, an attempt to kill himself. The story of Francis's childhood and his betrayal is intertwined with the veteran Francis's vengeful search for Larry and his intent to kill him and commit suicide. When Francis finally finds Larry, he discovers a broken and bitter man. The meeting causes Francis to turn away from his revenge with thoughts of a new beginning for himself. Paula Lacey commented, "Cormier explores the meaning of heroism and the hidden motivations for what may appear to be heroic acts. . . . The theme of guilt and revenge is also powerful and readers will iden-

tify with Francis's final desperate attempt to assuage his guilt. . . . Once again Cormier has written a suspenseful novel that addresses serious questions of concern to most young adults."

Awards

Cormier has won a host of awards for *The Chocolate War*, including *The New York Times* Outstanding Book of the Year Award in 1974, an American Library Association Best Book for Young Adults citation in 1974, the Maxi Award from *Media and Methods* in 1976, the Lewis Carroll Shelf Award in 1979, and *School Library Journal*'s Best of the Best Books 1966-1978 award in 1979. *I Am the Cheese* received *The New York Times* Outstanding Book of the Year Award in 1977 and an American Library Association Best Book for Young Adults citation in 1977. *After the First Death* also received *The New York Times* Outstanding Book of the Year Award in 1979 and an American Library Association Best Book for Young Adults citation in 1983. These three books each earned a Best of Best Books 1970-1983 award in 1984. Cormier was honored with the American Library Association's Margaret A. Edwards Award for Author Achievement in 1991. An American Library Association Best Book for Young Adults citation was also awarded to *The Bumblebee Flies Anyway* in 1983, *Fade* in 1988, and *In the Middle of the Night* in 1996. *Eight Plus One* was selected a Notable Children's Trade Book in the Field of Social Studies from the National Council for the Social Studies and the Children's Books Council in 1980. It also won the Assembly on Literature for Adolescents Award from the National Council of Teachers of English in 1982. *The Bumblebee Flies Anyway* was nominated for the Carnegie Medal in 1983. *Beyond the Chocolate War* received a *New York Times* Notable Books citation in 1985 and a *Horn Book* Honor List citation in 1986. *Fade* received a Best Book for Young Adults citation from the American Library Association in 1988 and a nomination for the World Fantasy Award in 1989. *In the Middle of the Night* received a citation from the American Library Association's Quick Pick for Reluctant YA Readers in 1996.

AUTHOR'S COMMENTARY

Roger Sutton with Robert Cormier

SOURCE: "Kind of a Funny Dichotomy," in *School Library Journal*, Vol. 37, No. 6, June, 1991, pp. 28-33.

What kind of a world do you think you portray in your books?

Cormier: Well, I like to call myself a realistic writer. I think probably I could summarize it best by saying that

I take real people and put them in extraordinary situations.

Pretty scary situations.

Cormier: Yeah, they are. I mean, they're not scary in the way of spooky kinds of situations, but I'm very much interested in intimidation. And the way people try to manipulate other people. And the obvious abuse of authority. I guess I'm sort of an anti-authority figure. In my writing, that is, which is kind of a funny dichotomy, because in my life I'm a pretty ordinary person.

That's one of the legends of YA literature: Robert Cormier's a nice guy, *people say with surprise. But that darkness in your books has to come from someplace.*

Cormier: I suppose it has. Well, I think a lot of it comes from my adolescence. On the surface it looked like a very pleasant, ordinary one. I came from a warm and loving family, really, and I went to parochial school and on into high school. But between the lines there is the fact that I always felt that I didn't belong. I was easily intimidated: on my paper route, being chased by dogs or going into certain neighborhoods intimidated me. I was a pretty timid kid.

Were you writing then?

Cormier: I was writing. I always tell people I began in the seventh grade, when a wonderful nun by the name of Sister Catherine really discovered me as a writer, enabled me to write. But it began, I think, before then. I can't remember a time when I wasn't trying to get something down on paper. Just the way, I think, artists start early in life sketching. I can remember when I first started to read, the fascination of a book, and I can't remember a time, really, when I haven't been a writer. That was always my escape, you know; reading and writing. Those were the two great escapes of my life and I suppose they still are.

Do you surprise yourself by what you write?

Cormier: I do. Really. The characters take over, and they often do things that you don't anticipate, that you hope they don't do. In *After the First Death,* I could see doom descending on Kate, the bus driver. I hated to see it coming. But you have to follow the laws of inevitability. I thought it must end this way. Sometimes I'm really horrified, and yet I have to follow the seeds that I've planted in the stories and let them sprout.

They're dark seeds sometimes. Do you think of the world as a malevolent place?

Cormier: There's that dichotomy again. In my own life I don't see it, and yet I know it's out there. The strange thing is that I'm an optimist and I see that old cliché—I see the bottle half full rather than half empty. Do I really write pessimistically? I don't think I write pessimistically. I probably write—well, I suppose it is pessi-

mistically. I hate to talk in terms like "lessons" or "themes" because the characters and plots must come first. Still, I was kind of surprised at the initial controversy about *The Chocolate War,* because to me there was the implicit lesson. It was obvious to me that we all lose when the good guys don't do anything. I thought I was portraying what happens when good people don't come to the rescue. Which didn't mean that was the way life is all the time, just in that particular situation.

No, and you would never come away from **The Chocolate War** *thinking, "Boy, I want to be just like Archie." You know who to identify with, you know who to admire in that book.*

Cormier: No, I think people are fascinated by Archie just as we've always been fascinated by evil. That's why Stephen King is so popular. There's an attraction. Because you're sitting there nice and safe, reading or seeing a movie, and you have that safety of being distanced from what's going on. But I think evil can be endlessly fascinating. Archie still fascinates me as a character. Frankly, I've run into Archies all my life.

Snake in the garden.

Cormier: Yeah, they're there all the time. It is simply the guy you come across in straight-line parking who comes up and parks across the parking spaces. He's a little bit of an Archie who thinks the rules aren't made for him, who thinks he can bend them.

We think a lot of the same things Archie does; he acts out for us.

Cormier: You know, I think that's certainly in my work. My characters do things that I would never do, and yet I must admit that in writing certain parts of *The Chocolate War* and *Beyond the Chocolate War* I sat there with a gleeful look on my face. If I'm the good guy in my book I'm also the bad guy: we're sums of what we write about and I think a lot of it is vicarious. I know it's vicarious. If you live through the bad deeds, when the tragic things happen, they upset you too, like wanting good things to happen, and knowing they're not going to.

Patty Campbell calls it "implacability" [in her book Presenting Robert Cormier.]

Cormier: It's hard for me to articulate those things. The best kind of criticism is the kind that really illuminates your own work for you. And sometimes it amazes me how I'll read a critical essay, and even if it is critical in the sense of being critical of what I do, it's often illuminating. And of course that's what the best criticism does anyway.

With all the controversy that surrounds your books, one thing that sometimes gets overlooked is that you're first a good storyteller.

Cormier: The story comes first. If it doesn't succeed as a story, no one is ever going to get to the theme. If someone reads a book and just says "Gee, I loved it, what a story" that is terrifically pleasing to me, because we must succeed as storytellers first. I didn't sit down with **The Chocolate War** and say "Well, I think I'll explore the abuse of power in this book." As you write it, true, sometimes you say, "Ah, here's a chance for me to explore this particular thing I'm interested in" and then you create a character or situation in which you can explore it. I know there's a certain readership out there, very loyal, and I just hope that I don't let them down. And I realize what I'm hoping for is not to let them down as a storyteller. The rest really is a bonus, that people can find things in my books to argue about. Or to teach or debate. Or even to be upset about. That's all an extra richness for me. I just want to tell a darn good story.

Is the controversy that surrounded **The Chocolate War** *still going on, or do you find your work controversial in different ways?*

Cormier: Gee, it's amazing that it's still going on with **The Chocolate War.** There are cases of censorship that have come up just in the last year or so in which the same old—I'd say it hasn't changed that much.

I Am the Cheese *was a pretty risky book, too, just in terms of its structure.*

Cormier: **I Am the Cheese** was written almost in a sort of an innocence. It's hard to cast myself back to that time. I knew that I wrote **The Chocolate War** from a practical standpoint. It was the first really successful book I had done in terms of being critically received and also financially successful. And I thought, here's a chance to follow it up—the door is open now. God, when I sent **I Am the Cheese** to Fabio Coen, who had been so great to publish **The Chocolate War** at Pantheon after five publishers had rejected it, I sent it to him with an apology. First of all, I certainly didn't want to lose this young adult audience that I had just discovered, that I didn't even know was *out* there. Second of all, it was such a complex book, and I didn't know whether it had worked or not. But really, I did send it to him with an apology, saying "You've done this great thing in introducing me to this audience and now I'm letting you down." And I remember he called me up, and he was ecstatic. He said, "My God, I know it's complex and it's ambiguous and everything, but why not try to have young people reach?" I said "Young people?" And he says, "Oh, sure! We're going to publish this the way we did **The Chocolate War.**" And I've never looked back.

Several people have said that your books began a trend of downbeat themes, or downbeat treatment of themes, i.e. the good guy not winning, in young adult books, but I'm not sure that's happened. I think there you almost stand alone, still.

Cormier: I don't know. It's hard for me to talk in these terms because it sounds like I'm a trailblazer, or tried to be, or something. And I don't think of myself as that.

Well, nobody followed.

Cormier: That's right. The door was open but nobody came in. But maybe when they saw me getting away with it, there were books that tried other themes, that wouldn't be looked at as following in my footsteps, but as opening other doors. Just like *The Catcher in the Rye* was a door-opener for me. It made me see that adolescence could be something very dramatic to write about. Not that I sat down and said "I'm going to write an adolescent novel" at the time, but that was a book that opened a door for me. I didn't write another *Catcher in the Rye,* but it had a definite influence on me.

But I think you are writing about adolescents who face terrible things and sometimes lose, which happens to Holden Caulfield.

Cormier: It is such a lacerating time, and I probably forget the name of the guy I met last week, but boy, some of those adolescent experiences are still with me. Most of us carry the baggage of that adolescence with us all our lives. And I think that's why a lot of young adult novels jump over the borders of the genre and can be read by other people.

It seems that the town of Monument is a place and time that you are still living in.

Cormier: It's a thinly disguised Leominster, I suppose—the spirit of the city rather than the actual place. I've changed the name and everything and I've moved the streets around but it's the same. Yes, I'm lucky that I've got that place—that I can take a ride down to Frenchtown anytime and there it is.

Scary place.

Cormier: Well, any place is scary. All these small towns, there's a lot going on in them, I think. Do you think Monument is really scary?

Yes.

Cormier: You wouldn't want to live there?

It's a fascinating place to visit.

Cormier: Well, there again, there is something that's fascinating about the shadows. Every town has its shadows, and Monument certainly has its share. I've just written a novel [**In the Middle of the Night**] which will be published in November by Dell, and I've moved away from Monument in it.

Is this a story for young adults, or one that will have a young adult audience?

Cormier: It's about an act of violence and its effect on

two families, but principally a teenager in one family and a teenager in the other family. When violence happens to adults, it's bad, but when it happens to young people they're even more vulnerable, and I find it more intriguing to write about from that point of view. I'm hoping it's a successful psychological suspense story, a thriller.

Do you ever ponder why your stories take such a dark turn?

Cormier: I ponder it but I don't worry about it. This new novel has what I think of as my first love story in it. And although I didn't anticipate it, the book has that element in the midst of all this violence. There's that sort of a tenderness to it, I think.

I think there's a strong love story at the center of **After the First Death** *between the father and the son—it seems to go back to Abraham and Isaac.*

Cormier: Well, that was one of the inspirations for it. As a father I've always been conscious of wanting to always do the right thing for my kids. My great fear was that if they came to me for advice or if they were really concerned about something, I wouldn't give them good advice. Because the fact of parenthood doesn't confer wisdom upon you. So I've always prayed for it. And ultimately I always was afraid of doing anything that would disgrace me to them. And then how far would a father ever go for his family? I could never understand that Abraham and Isaac story in the Bible; it always stunned me that Abraham could go that far. I thought "My God;" and that was one of the principal catalysts for writing *After the First Death,* that story always bothered me. I wanted to see in modern terms how far a father would go.

How do you reconcile your Catholicism with your rather—apparently—grim vision of the universe in your books?

Cormier: Well, the universe can be grim and yet—if someone truly, truly believes this lifespan is but a wink in the eye of God—it doesn't matter a hell of a lot what happens, because this is just a preparation, a short term in the eye of eternity. Maybe we weren't meant to be that happy anyway. Long ago, I had a crisis in Catholicism back when I was—that again was part of my adolescence, because I went to a parochial school where everything is faith. You're brought up on faith, you don't question, you believe what the nuns tell you, and then suddenly you grow up, and you come upon Darwin's theory of evolution, and all these other things occur to you, as you meet new people and other faiths. It was a very oppressive faith that I had. It was a theology of fear rather than of love. I was good because I was afraid not to be. The nuns would tell us—at thirteen, or twelve, a nun is telling you—if you have bad thoughts today, going home you might be hit by a car and go straight to hell, at a time when bad thoughts were the greatest things of my life. It was that kind of

theology. Then when I was a young married man with kids being born we were in a parish and met a priest who was really a man of joy. This came about the time of John XXIII, Pope John, and the two things coincided, and it changed my belief to one of joy rather than fear.

Do you think that God is present in the world that you portray?

Cormier: Probably a silent watchful God who doesn't interfere, who probably hopes that people do the right thing. But we have free will to do what we want, even though God knows what the next step will be, just as the father who tells the kids not to do a certain thing and leaves the room knowing they're going to do it. . . . I get very self-conscious when I start talking this way. It's like looking in a mirror while you're writing. I find it difficult to be articulate about my own work.

Well, your job is to write it, not to talk about it.

Cormier: That's true. In fact, even coming to the defense when my books are attacked really gets irritating. I'll get a call from a reporter or an interviewer who wants me to give a defense of my novels. I'm glad that they give me the chance to tell them how I feel about things, but then I always go back to what you just said: Look, I wrote the book, why should I have to defend it? Or they'll call me and say, "Why do you think they're opposing *The Chocolate War?*" And I say "That's for them to say, not for me to say." So I do get a little irritated with people who want to put me on the spot when the books should speak for themselves.

The book is already on the spot.

Cormier: In fact, the funny thing about a book is, by the time it has appeared, you're usually onto another book, and you're all involved with other characters. I've been lucky that I've been able to keep most of my books fresh in my mind because I keep getting questioned about them by students.

Do you get impatient with that?

Cormier: No, not when it comes from students, because there I'm not being asked to defend the book. They're just asking about aspects of the book and aspects of writing it. "Why did you do this?"—something like that. And I love to talk about the writing itself, the techniques. The only time when I get defensive is when I'm asked to be defensive. If a reporter calls up looking for a story, you can't say—you don't want to say—"No comment." I was a reporter for too many years, so I do try to say something. But I still feel a little irritated.

It's too bad, when the questions of censorship obscure real questions about a book. Any literary discussion of Judy Blume, for example, has become almost impossible because if you say you don't like Judy Blume, people say "Oh, you're being censorious" when you could have other reasons.

Cormier: That's what happens. They assume right away that it's censorship of the subject matter or something when some people might say that they just don't like the book. That's why I think everything should be judged on the basis of the story: does the story work? And if the story works, that means the characters work. And that's the important element, of course. Your story isn't going to work unless the characters are real and you bring everything to a climax. Even though there's a degree of ambiguity in some of my books, I still try to satisfy the reader, to give him that satisfying click of a climax, the sense that something has happened. And then you can be ambiguous beyond that. But I'm always very conscious of telling that story. So all that controversial stuff, all the stuff that upsets people, is almost secondary in my mind as I write it. And yet there's always the qualifier there, you know the readers are out there. When I was writing *Fade,* I was conscious of the audience when I wrote a couple of scenes that the boy witnesses. As I wrote them, I knew that people would be upset about them. I modified, and I made sure that I wasn't being titillating or exploitive, that I didn't make the acts sound attractive. I wanted to make them sound sordid, and I tried to make them brief. So there is that consciousness there as you're writing all the time. But again it's all bent on the altar of storytelling. I just shook my head after that one; did I say that?

You said it, and it sounds like a great last line to me. Thank you—congratulations on your award.

John Cohen with Robert Cormier

SOURCE: "An Interview with Robert Cormier," in *Reading Time,* Vol. 37, No. 1, February, 1993, pp. 7-8.

Editor: Robert, I first came across your first major work for young people, *The Chocolate War,* in 1974 when I was in the United States. It had just been released and of course it was the talk of the town. What triggered that particular story off?

Robert: I woke up one day to find myself as a young adult author, but what triggered it really was a very personal thing. My son went to a Catholic private boys' school of 400 boys and they were having a chocolate sale. He came home one day with two shopping bags of boxes to sell, which dismayed me in a way because I went through a parochial school system in the depression where times were hard and we sold everything to help support the purchase of the basic needs of the school. I remember nuns even crocheting the edges of hankies for sale. Now here we are a generation later, times being pretty good to us, a middle class family, paying tuition at a school, and I thought "My God, what are we doing with a chocolate sale at this point?" The upshot of it all was that we made a family decision with my son, Peter, that he would not sell the chocolates. This is fine when you are talking about it but when it actually goes into practice it has an entirely different aspect.

I am an emotional writer in that I do not write emotionally but if something affects me emotionally then that sends me to the typewriter. I don't devise a plot and then start writing but the emotions with this issue were amazing because I took him to school the next day with his chocolates and a letter to his headmaster saying that he wouldn't be taking part in the sale as a matter of principle and he had the approval and support of his parents. When he got out of the car and went up the walk I realized the truth, first of all it was just before the bell rang and 400 athletic, energetic boys were jostling each other. Peter walked up with his bags and I realized he was 14 years old: this was the start of the school year; he was in a new school in a new city and he was virtually with 399 strangers. He looked so vulnerable and I wondered what is going to happen to him. I thought that they would probably kill him. These were the first words of *The Chocolate War,* "They murdered him", so it sent me to the typewriter. Peter had no problems. In fact we would not have allowed him to get into this situation if he was extra sensitive or an introvert, but he was an average kid who played football, was a B student, got along well and didn't seem to have any problems. I worried about it at first when he walked up that walk, thinking that we were going to ruin his high school career. Actually the kids were OK with him and they only kidded him a little bit. Ironically the brother who was in charge of the school was his home room teacher and everyday, just as was in the book, there was a roll call and everyday the teacher asked the students one by one, how many chocolates they had sold the day before. For five weeks Peter said, "None". He confessed towards the end that he thought the teacher was getting a little tense about it, but nothing more than that happened. However, as a writer, I started thinking what if there had been peer pressure and faculty pressure and so I began to write what became *The Chocolate War.* My agent called me to say she hadn't heard from me. I told her I was writing this crazy thing about chocolates and the sale and about a boy who goes to high school and she said it sounds like a YA novel and I asked her, "What's a YA novel?" She said "A Young Adult Novel, a wonderful new series of books coming out in the schools. It makes a nice bridge from the kind of books the kids brought into the class to the classics," and of course she scared me to death because I thought I would have to go back and see what I have been writing here. I hadn't been conscious of using anything that would affront anybody. I was writing about the way boys act and talk, think of girls and about masturbation. She said not to worry about all of that but just write this book as I saw it and let her worry about the publishing, so that is what I did. I found that the young people who were led to my books by teachers and librarians were a terrific audience and I could write for them with all the craft I could summon. I always had the very intelligent reader in mind who happened to turn out to be a 13-year-old reader sometimes. So that is the genesis.

Editor: I guess the book that has fascinated me the most is *Fade* and I am wondering what got you onto that?

Robert: I never thought that I would write a novel as the years went along but then *Fade* came along which presented a problem for me, both the writing and also the marketing side. *Fade* was based on something that happened in my family. Way back in the early part of the century my father's family did what a lot of families did in those days, they gathered on the front steps of the lawn and had their picture taken. When the picture came back, one of my uncles was missing, just as in the book. That picture had sort of been a hot joking legend in our family, a picture in which one of my uncles didn't appear and I had heard about it. In my later life when I started thinking about it I quizzed my aunts. My mother seemed to remember it but we didn't quite know what had become of it, but that wasn't important anyway. I didn't ever see it again. I started to write what became *Fade* because I wasn't quite sure what I would do with this and where I was going. I was interested in the theme of gifts that become curses, and I might have been feeling nostalgic at that time. I had been doing some writing on the depression and it has always tugged at me. I have a bunch of stories that I have written which are very nostalgic about a boy growing up in the depression. For ten years I wrote a newspaper column and a lot of them were about the depression so I started writing about this very nostalgic thing. I always thought that I was, in a sense, an invisible man, like G. K. Chesterton, as a reporter, being there but people not really seeing me. Also I had always been interested in the things that fade out of your life. There is always a fading going on like growing old photographs which are slowly losing their impact. All of this came together and I decided I would explore, "what would happen if." What if my uncle hadn't ducked down or played a prank, what if he had disappeared. But then I thought I do not want to write a Stephen King novel. I thought what I have to do is create a very real world so that people would think that they weren't reading a fantasy novel or a horror novel but reading about a real world and that is why this is the most autobiographical thing I have ever written. The town is real, the factories, the strikes that my father and brothers were involved in, the scabs that came in, the newspapers, there was a man who controlled all the newspapers in our section of town and I had a route exactly like Paul's. I wanted to make it so effective that when the fade happened, the people would just suspend disbelief and take it as a matter of course. Then I thought, invisibility is impossible and so I made a decision that after creating this real world I would then destroy it. I think it is the biggest risk I have ever done in writing, but I followed my instincts. It was a different voice, it was a different time I kept plunging with this idea of reality. I ended up with 600 manuscript pages, the longest I had ever written. My wife said she'd never seen me work so hard on a book. Whenever she turned around I was hunched over on a typewriter or at the table where I do editing. It was finally 499 pages when I sent it in to the Ark, my editors.

Editor: Have you had much of a problem with censorship in the States?

Robert: Yes, constant. We are in very conservative times now and the fundamentalists are very vocal. Censorship is such a many faceted thing and frankly I have sympathy with parents who are very upset when their child says he is going to study *The Chocolate War* at school because I know that there are sensitive kids and sensitive parents out there. That is alright with me and schools are willing to give them another book to read. The problem is when they say they don't want their child to do this, but they don't want any other child to read it. Often what happens in the States is that a parent will make an official protest about a book and then it is picked up by a group that supports that protest and then there are Letters to the Editors, editorials and public hearings and then it becomes an issue. The tragedy of this is that people start reading the book for the wrong reasons. My point has always been that if it is that controversial then it should be in the classroom where even a kid can get up and say "Look I don't like this book, I don't like the words in it" but it never gets to that stage if kids are reading it like this, looking for the bad words, and they are missing the whole point. In fact I purposely try in certain scenes to tone down because I don't want those to be the focus of the book. I want the book to be read in a context. There was a case in Massachusetts where a parent protested about *The Chocolate War.* The father said that while the book was being discussed he wanted his daughter to be out of the classroom, so she went to the library. I received a letter from one of her classmates who said this poor kid was being ostracized by the other students. The irony was that the letter had a P.S. on it saying she read *The Chocolate War* last year anyway. She was probably afraid to tell her parents, so the kids are the victims. You see the different levels of this whole censorship thing so it goes beyond whether a book should be printed. A lot of these people are trying to organize a text book committee so they are going to be censored before they get to the classroom. We are going to go back to *Jane* and *See Jane Run.* There was a case recently where Goldilocks was under attack because she wasn't punished for breaking into the Three Bears' house. She got away with a crime.

As a writer you cannot afford to sit there wondering if you are going to offend people. *The Chocolate War* is a case in point. Some people it doesn't bother them that the bad guy won in the end. What bothers them is the language. Other people aren't bothered by anything but that terrible reference to masturbation. With some people, it is the language. They couldn't care less who won. There seems to be something in there to offend anybody who wants to be, if you take it out of context. The whole censorship thing is always a constant thing with me because a teacher will call me or write to me, or a school librarian. I kind of ignore it because it is better to teach it rather than fight my battles, so I do come to the fore. I resent it. I wrote the book and why do I have to go off and explain it and yet how can you let these teachers be out there all by themselves. I try to support them. Some need more support than others, and sometimes appearing helps, of course.

Editor: What have you got in the pipeline for us?

Robert: I have a new book that will be out in October (1992) in the States called *Tunes for Bears to Dance To.* It is the story of communication between an 11-year-old boy and a survivor of the Holocaust, set right after World War II. There is a third man who is evil personified and the boy becomes a pawn between these two men with every act of corruption possible.

Robert Cormier

SOURCE: "Waxing Creative," in *Publishers Weekly,* Vol. 242, No. 29, July 17, 1995, p. 140.

In a single paragraph of an article dealing with *The Chocolate War, I Am the Cheese,* and *After the First Death,* a writer listed these topics as central to the books: brutality, sadism, corruption (religious and governmental), insanity, murder, torture, personality destruction, terrorism, child murder, and suicide.

What kind of person writes about those terrible things? And why?

The name on the novels is Robert Cormier, and my name is Robert Cormier. But sometimes I don't recognize myself, either in what others say about my work or when I face questions from an audience about the violent nature of the books that bear my name.

I am a man who cries at sad movies, longs for happy endings, delights in atrocious puns, pauses to gather branches of bittersweet at the side of a highway. I am shamelessly sentimental: I always make a wish when I blow out the candles on my birthday cake, and I dread the day when there may be no one there to say "Bless you" when I sneeze. Although I aspire to be Superman, I am doomed to be Clark Kent forever, in an endless search for that magic telephone booth. I wear a trench coat, but nobody ever mistakes me for Humphrey Bogart. I hesitate to kill a fly—but people die horrible deaths in my novels.

But, of course, it's easy to kill off characters in novels or assign them tragic roles, because they are only figments of the imagination. People in books are made of print and paper, not flesh and blood, after all. They are creatures who live and die only between the covers of a book. Right?

Wrong. They also live in my mind and imagination and have the power to disturb dreams and to invoke themselves at odd, unguarded moments. Kate Forrester in *After the First Death* was a very real person to me. I cheered her brave actions as they unfolded on the page. I was moved by her sense of responsibility toward the children who were hostages on that hijacked bus. I loved the way she refused to concede defeat. And yet, I sensed a doom descending on her, a foreshadowing of failure. She was an amateur at deceit and intrigue. And ama-

teurs often make mistakes, fatal miscalculations. In going to the limit of her dwindling resources to protect the children and then to escape, it was inevitable that she would go too far. I saw her moving in that direction with the horror that a parent feels watching a child dash into noonday traffic on a busy street, helpless to avert what must happen. Fiction must follow an internal logic. Given the circumstances I had created, Kate had to die. That doesn't mean I didn't mourn—or that I don't wish to write happier stories, with strolling-into-sunset endings, the cavalry arriving at the last minute. How I loved the sound of bugles and those thundering hooves at Saturday movie matinees.

But I've come to realize that Saturday matinees have nothing to do with real life, that innocence doesn't provide immunity from evil, that the mugger lurking in the doorway assaults both the just and the unjust.

It is possible to be a peaceful man, to abhor violence, to love children and flowers and old Beatles songs, and still be aware of the contusions and abrasions this world inflicts on us. Not to write happy endings doesn't mean the writer doesn't believe in them. Literature should penetrate all the chambers of the human heart, even the dark ones.

GENERAL COMMENTARY

Sylvia Patterson Iskander

SOURCE: "Readers, Realism, and Robert Cormier," in *Children's Literature: Annual of the Modern Language Association Division on Children's Literature and the Children's Literature Association,* Yale University Press, Vol. 15, 1987, pp. 7-18.

The young-adult novels of Robert Cormier—*The Chocolate War, I Am the Cheese, After the First Death, The Bumblebee Flies Anyway,* and *Beyond the Chocolate War*—have been criticized for the bleak, hopeless world they describe. Norma Bagnall says of *The Chocolate War,* "hopelessness pervades the entire story"; "there are no adults worth emulating"; "only the ugly is presented through the novel's language, action and imagery." Anne Scott MacLeod describes Cormier's work as "a world of painful harshness, where choices are few and consequences desperate." Robbie March-Penny states that *I Am the Cheese* depicts a "completely ruthless" system and *The Chocolate War* presents "a frightening universe."

Some of these comments have been answered in an article by Betty Carter and Karen Harris, who argue that "Cormier does not leave his readers without hope, but he does deliver a warning: they may not plead innocence, ignorance, or prior commitments when the threat of tyranny confronts them." Yet the objections point accurately to problems raised by these novels. The almost universal distress about Cormier's work springs directly from the power and consistency of his imagined world, which convinces readers that it bears a recognizable relationship to the "real world" and yet appears to leave no room for anything but pessimism about the survival of Cormier's protagonists. Because of this, several school boards and parental groups in New York, Massachusetts, South Carolina, and Arizona have tried to ban Cormier's novels from the classroom.

Agreement between author and audience is not always possible for readers of Cormier's novels. The conventions of the genre of the young-adult novel, according to MacLeod, may deal with harshness and stern reality, but they must offer some hope, "some affirmative message." She among others does not find any affirmation of the traditional adolescent "themes of adjustment, acceptance, and understanding" in any of Cormier's novels. She feels, for example, that when Jerry, the protagonist of *The Chocolate War,* is carried off the football field on a stretcher, Cormier "has abandoned an enduring American myth to confront his teenaged readers with life as it more often is—with the dangers of dissent, the ferocity of systems as they protect themselves, the power of the pressure to conform." She correctly states that the "discussion of political evil [in *I Am the Cheese*] is cast in fiercely contemporary terms" and that Artkin, Miro, and the general in *After the First Death* "disavow their humanity in the same moment that they seal their innocence by choosing never to question nor even to contemplate questioning." MacLeod does not, however, mention either Ben Marchand or Kate Forrester, who are positive role models in *After the First Death.* She comments on Cormier's powerful ability to reach the innermost thoughts of his readers and to make them question the contemporary systems within which they find themselves, but she does not explore this subject.

There are, it seems to me, three aspects of this problem. First, who is Cormier's reader, or what are some of the characteristics of young-adult readers? Teenagers stand at a threshold; not fully committed to the adult world, they are uncertain of their own strength, yet they clearly tend toward moral idealism. Second, what do adults consider appropriate reading for adolescents? Many parents and critics feel strongly that literature for teenagers at this vulnerable period in their lives should help them develop their sense of moral choice and responsibility by presenting clear-cut guidelines. Finally, what does Cormier require of his readers? The answer to this question touches on the concerns raised by the other questions, for, rather than asking his readers to endorse simple affirmations, Cormier demands that they respond to ironies and qualifications.

The reader—parent, school board member, or young adult—who rejects a Cormier novel as totally without hope has failed to recognize its positive elements because these are presented ironically and indirectly. The successful reader must recognize the various levels of reality present in these novels and extrapolate beyond

the novel's close to see an extended moral development. In *After the First Death,* Cormier holds out "the possibility that hope comes out of hopelessness and that the opposite[s] of things carry the seeds of birth—love out of hate, good out of evil. Didn't flowers grow out of dirt?" To the attentive reader, this irony and paradox offer a positive alternative to the bleaker vision of the novel.

Parents may justifiably ask how many teenagers are capable of so perceptive a reading, and yet adults often underestimate the teenage reader, who may understand the thrust of a Cormier novel in a practical rather than critical fashion. Some of the arguments between parents and children about the books have shown teenagers applying the received meaning of the book to constructive action in their own world. For example, consider the key passage in *The Chocolate War* where Brother Leon, the corrupt headmaster of Trinity High School, deliberately intimidates young Gregory Bailey, while waiting for some protest from Bailey's classmates, who know that he is innocent. When one voice finally protests, "Aw, let the kid alone," Brother Leon says it is "a feeble protest, too little and too late." Brother Leon teaches about the dehumanization of the Nazis by practicing it; he shows that this moral corruption occurred at least in part because there was not enough resistance to tyranny. Although Leon's motives are not entirely altruistic, the perceptive reader recognizes the author's message. When the protagonist of *The Chocolate War,* Jerry Renault, lies on the football field at the novel's close, crushed both physically and emotionally, the novel dramatizes the lesson and carries it to its conclusion. Who helped Jerry? Who resisted tyranny? No one. For nearly two hundred pages Jerry is a hero; in the final four pages he is defeated, at least for the present. In Cormier's sequel, *Beyond the Chocolate War,* Jerry returns to Monument after a lengthy recovery in Canada. He gradually regains his physical and mental strength until he is able to face, deflate, and defeat Emile Janza, his tormentor in the earlier novel. This might lead us to consider the two books as an extended version of the American myth of the victorious nonconformist in which a youngster surmounts physical and emotional obstacles to achieve a triumph that is more than just an athletic victory. The outcome of *The Chocolate War* must, however, be considered on its own merits, and it contains an apparent rejection of this myth. The question must be asked: does Jerry's crushing defeat leave the reader hopeless?

When their parents objected to the teaching of *The Chocolate War,* the students in a New York school petitioned to keep the book. In answer to one student who suggested that the signing of the petition be unanimous, a thirteen-year-old boy said no one should be compelled, as Jerry was, to join the majority. From the boy's statement the parents realized that the novel had provided an ethical example to their children; they voted to keep the book.

Why did this boy understand the message of the book

when others, including adults, failed? The answer, I believe, lies in his ability to perceive the different levels of meaning or "reality" in these texts. The complexity of Cormier's work challenges our notions of the proper relationship between events and their meanings. Tzvetan Todorov explains that "reality" or "verisimilitude" may be "the relation of a particular text to another general and diffuse text which might be called 'public opinion,'" "whatever tradition makes suitable or expected in a particular genre," or "the mask which conceals the text's own laws and which we are supposed to take for a relation with reality."

Jonathan Culler takes Todorov's three definitions of verisimilitude or *vraisemblance* a step further and distinguishes "five ways in which a text may be brought into contact with and defined in relation to another text which helps to make it intelligible."

> First, there is the socially given text, that which is taken as the "real world." Second, but in some cases difficult to distinguish from the first, is a general cultural text: shared knowledge which would be recognized by participants as part of the culture and hence subject to corruption or modification but which none the less serves as a kind of "nature." Third, there are the texts or conventions of a genre, a specifically literary and artificial *vraisemblance*. Fourth comes what might be called the natural attitude to the artificial, where the text explicitly cites and exposes *vraisemblance* of the third kind so as to reinforce its own authority. And finally, there is the complex *vraisemblance* of specific intertextualities, where one work takes another as its basis or point of departure and must be assimilated in relation to it.

The reader of a Cormier novel will experience no difficulty with the first level, the representation of the socially given world. The novels all appear to derive from a contemporary world, with a stress on its unpleasant aspects, such as corruption in a Catholic school (*The Chocolate War*), the murder and torture of innocents (*I Am the Cheese*) and (*After the First Death*), suicide (*After the First Death*) and (*Beyond the Chocolate War*), or teenagers who are terminally ill (*Bumblebee*). Cormier sets all his novels in a fictional Monument, Massachusetts, whose details, typical of small-town American life, reinforce the sense of relationship to the social world of his readers. (Monument also illustrates Culler's fifth level of *vraisemblance,* since these intertextual repetitions appear to offer external confirmation of the world that lies behind each novel.)

Similarly, Cormier's characters are plausible in the context of our social experience and expectations. Certainly the terrorists in *After the First Death* seem to fit a stereotypical portrait of terrorists; they believe that their cause is more important than human life. The teenagers in all the novels act like teenagers; for instance, Amy and Adam from *I Am the Cheese* are young adults and yet they pull off "numbers" or pranks in grocery stores and parking lots. Jerry Renault of *The Chocolate War* is atypical, however, in his total nonconformity, but

even such an unusual teenager appeals to the young adult's sense of uncertain identity and therefore seems valid and believable as a role model.

The second, cultural level of *vraisemblance* also presents only minor problems of recognition to the reader. The notions of innocence, betrayal, sacrifice, terrorism, death, love, and fear are intelligible as appropriate motives or products of actions and situations, given our cultural codes. At this level, Cormier's characters engage systems of values that readers can accept as plausible, whether or not they actually coincide with our own beliefs; however, it might be argued that Cormier violates our generally hopeful vision of the world by concentrating almost exclusively on the bleaker aspects of life.

Yet the third, generic level of *vraisemblance* will cause more adult readers to experience their first difficulty with Cormier's texts. At this level, literary norms govern the author's imaginative world. Two of the principal norms governing the structure of literature for children and adolescents are the identification of the protagonist with morality and the triumph of good over evil—in other words, a victorious protagonist. Hope in the novels of Cormier is both reinforced and shattered on this level. In *The Chocolate War,* Jerry Renault draws our moral admiration because he defies corruption and pressure from three sources, thus maintaining his individuality. He refuses to surrender to an inner desire to conform. He refuses to yield to peer pressure whether it be from the gang that tries to manipulate him or from his friend Goober, who worries about Jerry's nonconformity. And he refuses to submit to the tyranny of Brother Leon. Through this nonconformism, then, Cormier offers the reader a strong moral model that paradoxically conforms to narrative convention but does not meet our expectations in that good does not triumph over evil.

The structure of Cormier's plot, instead, shatters our expectations. Powerful American stereotypes insist that the good nonconformist must, in fiction, win at least a qualified victory. Cormier's testing of Jerry seems to prepare the way for a conventional reversal; readers anticipate a stunning last-minute victory by the hero. But when the hero is crushed and brutally beaten, his very survival in question, many readers feel betrayed and disoriented. The overthrow of the nonconformist protagonist at the close, like the killing of Kate in *After the First Death,* violates the anticipated outcome of the action; within the myth, the validation of nonconformity is victory. When readers complain about Cormier's hopeless pessimism, they mean that the novel's close defies their expectations. It is this deviation from narrative convention that repels some readers, who then protest at school board meetings or forbid their children to read Cormier's books. They prefer censorship to an examination of the social issues at stake in Cormier's novels or a reappraisal of American myths.

Yet Cormier deliberately violates our optimistic expectations in a strategy designed to convert the reader from a passive to an active role. He carefully develops, for example, the positive aspects of Jerry's home life, which was warm and loving before his mother's death and which can be so again when Mr. Renault recovers from his grief over his wife's death. In Jerry's "good" home he learned his values and developed the courage to fight back. Jerry's supportive friendship with Goober demonstrates the need of an individual to choose his friends, and it contrasts with the manipulation of an individual by the gang. Although Goober through human weakness fails Jerry, his guilt and anguish over his failure to help offer positive reinforcement to the adolescent reader who is struggling with his own problems of loyalty and betrayal. Although the novel does not resolve the social problems it raises, it does show how we can gain the moral strength to face them. Thus if—and it is a large if—one accepts the notion of a vital link between response to reading and behavior in the "real world," true hopelessness will result only if the reader concludes that people should not fight for their beliefs.

Cormier ironically calls upon our expectation that the author will finally reestablish moral order, and thus he employs Culler's fourth kind of realism. He forcibly reminds us that the reader cannot count on fictional escapes from the hard choices of life. The same message is evident to the receptive reader of *Beyond the Chocolate War.* Evil surrounds us and will continue to do so; when an Archie Costello graduates, a Bunting is waiting to take his place. Archie articulates Cormier's message clearly: "'Know what, Obie? You could have said *no* anytime, anytime at all [to joining the gang, to finding victims for them]. But you didn't.'" Obie's reaction dramatically reinforces Cormier's point: "A sound escaped from Obie's lips, the sound a child might make hearing that his mother and father had been killed in an auto accident on their way home. The sound had death in it. And truth. The terrible truth that Archie was right, of course. He had blamed Archie all along." Obie now understands that he should have taken a stand, that we have free choice; however, his first stand—an attempt to murder Archie to rid Trinity High of him forever—shocks the reader as it shocks Obie. Fortunately Obie's plan does not succeed, but Cormier succeeds in making his audience reevaluate the individual's response to evil and those who promote it in a way that overt moralizing would never do. He forces the readers into Culler's fourth and fifth levels of realism: those who have read *The Chocolate War* with its destruction of the American myth of the victorious nonconformist will no longer take for granted the myth's validity in the sequel. Even though the sequel reestablishes the myth, we no longer approach a Cormier novel with the same expectations that we have for other young-adult novels.

In *I Am the Cheese* the individual's stand against evil raises similar problems. A conscientious newspaperman, Mr. Delmonte, uncovering some corruption in government and believing in civic duty, testifies as a witness. The Department of Re-Identification relocates his family and gives them a new identity as "the Farmers," an ironically all-American name. At the novel's close this family is destroyed—the parents killed and fourteen-year-old Adam Farmer driven into amnesia, his only protection from "termination." Such pessimism conflicts with our social expectations, our myths of participatory democracy, of triumphant patriotism and civic allegiance. The defeat of these myths also defies our literary expectations, and we again feel shocked by Cormier's rejection of the conventions that we adhere to as "real."

But Cormier also incorporates positive materials that show his commitment to democratic values and that give grounds for hope. Mr. Farmer is a warm, concerned father, respected and loved by his son; he is what we expect a model citizen to be. Mrs. Farmer—a stereotypical "good wife"—does not criticize her husband's attempt to do the right thing, although his action vastly changes their lives and leaves her sad and disoriented. Remaining in seclusion much of the time, she tries desperately to maintain the unity of the family by refusing to obey the rules about what items they can keep from their former life or where they can speak without fear of being overheard. As complex and isolated as her life becomes, she remains clear-sighted about their fragile safety and says that the corruption they opposed is "like an evil growth: cut off one part and another part still grows. Your father's testimony killed one part, but who knows about the other parts?"

Cormier seeks to touch deep within his sensitive youthful audience their sense of right and wrong, of fair play, while he refuses to accept the literary and social stereotypes in which these values are so often delivered to the young. The reader's need for reaction depends upon his own ability to feel rage at the miscarriage of justice. As Wayne Booth has said, authors create images of themselves and their readers and "the most successful reading is one in which the created selves, author and reader, can find complete agreement." Teenagers, standing at the threshold between childhood and adulthood, face a world of computers, missiles, and terrorism; they depend less upon the reassurance of stereotypes and expect more moral complexity than did their elders, whose teenage years took place in more stable times.

Assumptions made by older readers about "appropriate" themes, moral values, and literary structures for teenagers lead them to misinterpret Cormier. Culler's last three levels of *vraisemblance* are at issue here. The reader of the young-adult novel does not bring to his reading the same assumptions about genre that, for example, the reader of an adult mystery story does. The former does not believe that information vital to the full comprehension of the book will be withheld from him until the very end as it is normally in a mystery and as it is in *I Am the Cheese,* whose final revelation smashes the reader's prior assumptions and crushes any hope for Adam Farmer.

By withholding information and by his fine craftsmanship, Cormier keeps the reader riveted to these novels. The withholding of information is particularly evident in *The Bumblebee Flies Anyway,* where the teen reader wants to believe what he has been told: Barney Snow, sixteen years old, lives in an experimental hospital for the terminally ill because he is to be the norm by which various treatments and medications for the sick are measured. The Complex, as Barney innocuously calls the experimental hospital, is a world few young-adult readers have experienced, so initially they accept the explanation for Barney's presence as truth in that world. They may not at first perceive the unreliability of a narrator unable to remember many facts about his life or to face certain fears, for instance, his trick of "providing a more suitable label for things that he feared or worried about. Like *merchandise* for drugs" or *invader* for disease. In other words, the reader unfamiliar with an experimental hospital relies on the narrator Barney to make the strange more familiar, and when Barney makes up names to mask unpleasant items and fears, the reader accepts both the names and Barney as a reliable spokesman.

This mistaken acceptance involves us in yet another kind of *vraisemblance*. At Culler's fourth level the author may ironically insist on or expose the improbability of his narrator's tale, thereby insuring the reader's acceptance of the fiction as a whole. Cormier not only violates the stereotypes of the young-adult genre but also forces his audience onto a new level of reality; Cormier does not allow Barney himself to realize that he is unreliable as a narrator. The truth is withheld from the protagonist as well as the readers, who finally learn that there is a very practical reason for Barney being in a hospital for the terminally ill, whether or not he can remember it; he too is terminally ill. Cormier has actually made the reader believe Barney's less probable story about being the norm, whereas Barney is a patient just like the others, although his disease is temporarily in remission.

At this point some readers may feel they have been tricked by Cormier, and indeed they have been, for they have failed to perceive the unreliability of the narrator or to recognize Cormier's ironic subversion of the conventions of the young-adult genre, a subversion which exposes their "nature" as mere literary "tricks." But Cormier has, at the same time, understood that a sense of being unable to see the full picture or of being deceived, kept from real knowledge, and fed on half-truths, is a powerful element in the teenager's picture of himself—one which may increase his sense of identification with the main character. Publishers of young-adult novels and others associated with the genre clearly recognize the identification of reader and protagonist in young-adult literature. Judy Gitenstein of Bantam Books says that the reader "learns and grows along with the adolescent narrator"; Beverly Horowitz of Putnam says of a teen series that the intent is "to interweave with the lives of teen readers"; and Ann Durell from E. P. Dutton comments on young-adult writers who "show kids a mirror into themselves." Since publishers seek this quality in the books they accept, characters with whom teens can identify are an institutionally imposed criterion of the young-adult genre; but the identification

is seldom in terms of such a bleak perception of the adult world.

In the case of Barney, such identification is rendered difficult for the adolescent reader through Cormier's ironic challenge to his teenage narrator's authority. This level of reality may present problems for less experienced readers because irony presupposes "operative expectations" at work, the contrast between the literal meaning of the text and an alternate ironic meaning or "the contrast between a protagonist's vision of the world and the contrary order which the reader, armed with foreknowledge, can grasp." As he seeks to make the world of the novel intelligible, the reader may not perceive the discrepancy between his view and the protagonist's because he may not be sufficiently conscious of his own expectations. We side with Jerry Renault and want him to be victorious. When he is crushed, we do not like to confront our own recognition that nothing else but defeat could be expected when one teenager stands alone against a large group of forces, all in opposition to him. It is so improbable for us to expect him to succeed against those odds that it would be ironic if he did win; yet the stereotypical hero of a young-adult novel does experience success in such a situation.

The same type of irony operates in the case of Ben Marchand in *After the First Death.* Ben believes that he is helping his father and his country, serving as a go-between for the United States government and the terrorists who have captured a busload of first graders, when actually he is betraying both of them and being betrayed at the same time. With the terrorists, his father and his father's secret organization counting on him to give in to torture, how can we expect him not to reveal the information about the planned attack? And then how can we expect such a sensitive young man to live with the fact that he has betrayed and been betrayed? But some readers are surprised by Ben's suicide—if indeed they can determine just when his death occurred, for can we trust this narrator? Ben seems to narrate the first few odd-numbered chapters; then his father takes over. However, the careful reader may discern some discrepancies that could be used to build a case that Ben is already dead and that his schizophrenic father is narrating all the chapters written from Ben's point of view.

Be that as it may, the general's schizophrenia is another rather obvious example of this situational irony; his attempt to save other children's lives costs his own child's life. Torn between love for his son and patriotism, the general chooses patriotism, a costly and useless error. He seems unable to question his own simple and rigid morality in sending his young, idealistic, inexperienced son to be tortured by terrorists, but the teenage reader questions it. Under the stress of what actually happens, as opposed to what he expected, the general's mind snaps. Cormier shows clearly what Millicent Lenz calls "loathing for the false god of blind patriotism." As Lenz points out, Cormier relies upon the reader—the idealistic teenager—to move from unreflective and absolute ideals toward a clearer yet more complex vision of good. The perceptive reader also is not completely surprised by the death of innocent Kate Forrester, the attractive eighteen-year-old bus driver, because of Cormier's earlier reversal of our expectations of a "happy ending" with the suicide of Ben and the deaths of two young children. The resilience of the teen reader is sometimes overlooked by adult critics, who may also fail to take into account the teenager's *continuing* identification of himself with the heroes about whom he reads, once or many times—a level of verisimilitude dependent on, but more powerful than, any of the others. Even those heroes who die remain alive in the book and in the reader's mind.

Cormier relies, then, on situational irony rather than verbal irony in his five young-adult novels. He forces us to contemplate such subjects as the death of innocent hostages, diseased teenagers, and civic-minded citizens, the defeat of the nonconformist, the suicide of several boys betrayed—all for the purpose of making the reader move beyond the close of the novels to a new sense of personal responsibility. For the reader, unlike the characters, has a second chance. From the defeat of the protagonists who struggle for right in an evil, corrupt, and convincingly real world, where no law of poetic justice prevails, can come the wisdom and understanding of the next generation of individuals who will fight tyranny, who will stand up for their principles, who will be the heroes trying to make the world a better place. Gregory Bailey's classmates learn that Nazism took hold because not enough people protested; Barney tells Billy the Kidney that the bad thing is not doing anything; Obie realizes he has a choice. Mr. Farmer, Ben, and Kate all took positive action. That some of these failed is more realistic than the myth that people courageous enough to stand up for their beliefs will automatically be victorious.

Cormier makes his readers think long after they have closed his novels because he chooses not to follow the literary norm of the happy ending. The climactic structure of his novels with their shocking, unhappy, but quite realistic endings reinforces not the temporary defeats or a bleak pessimism, but rather a longing for justice. His books "argue" for moral responsibility far more effectively than sermonizing or stereotypical formulas of virtue automatically triumphant. Cormier himself said in a letter to me (29 March 1985), "(The) message that I have always felt was implicit in the novels, [is] that evil only occurs when we allow it to occur, it does not blossom by itself." Hope for the future is in the minds of Cormier's more astute teenage readers as they recognize that in the "real world" as well as the literary world they themselves are the next generation of heroes.

Mike Peters

SOURCE: "*The Chocolate War* and After: The Novels of Robert Cormier," in *The School Librarian,* Vol. 40, No. 3, August, 1992, pp. 85-7.

The publication this year of Robert Cormier's latest novel,

We All Fall Down, is likely to renew the controversy that surrounds his work. Whether or not adults judge that his dark and relentless narratives of conspiracy and humiliation provide appropriate reading experiences for young people, few would deny that he is one of the most interesting and important writers of contemporary teenage fiction.

The extremism of his style and material are certainly shocking. Different forms of abuse, including torture and murder, are described in sharp focus, causing many librarians and teachers to worry about the possible harm such concentration on the worst side of human behaviour will do to young readers. In this context, it is worth remembering John Schostak's view [in *Schooling the Violent Imagination*] that the 'violent imagination' provides a way for adolescents to make sense of themselves and their world. Nor is the violence depicted superficial, for it seems to be the expression of deeper and darker forms of human cruelty and despair—the need to control and manipulate, and the fear of pain and death. To adolescents, caught between dependence and independence, and between innocence and knowledge, the dramatisation of these needs and fears will have a particular resonance.

Cormier's characters are always being tested, stripped of familiar illusions and protections, and pushed to their furthest limits—whether at school, in the midst of home and family, on a bus held up by terrorists, or in a hospice for the terminally ill; and continually present is an understanding of how vulnerable we all are. Parents age and die, bodies are hurt, love disappears, friends betray, death seems preferable to a defeated life of broken promise. Adolescent male readers, tough on the surface, fragile underneath, may find echoes here of their own realisations about themselves and their world. And who can the characters turn to when things get bad? Adults in these novels tend to be either well-meaning non-entities or corrupt. Here is a writer who can easily match the most disillusioned and cynical of teenagers.

Now often taught at GCSE, Cormier's stark representation of the nature and force of evil links **The Chocolate War,** published in the UK in 1975, with another postwar pessimistic fable about our fallen state, still popular with English teachers, William Golding's *The Lord of the Flies.* While, however, the message of Golding's story of greed and savagery can be diluted with the thought that his characters are children trying to survive in strange circumstances, no such reassurance is possible with Cormier. Here the adults in authority, depicted at their strongest and most charismatic in Brother Leon, underpin and legitimatise the corruption of the Vigils, led by Archie; one hierarchy mirrors the other. And instead of a remote desert island, the setting is a private school in the heart of America.

Beneath its team games and school spirit, Trinity, like other institutions, like society itself, is riven by spiteful rivalries, exclusive divisions, and multiple temptations and betrayals. No one is safe; anyone may be picked on, irrespective of virtue or innocence. To refuse to conform, to say no to the assignment to sell the chocolates and thus to challenge the twin authority of the Brothers and the Vigils, is to suffer the humiliation wreaked on Jerry in the closing stages of the novel. Adolescents accustomed by the narratives of much popular and much literary culture to the ultimate triumph of the lone individual against a malevolent order, will probably find Jerry's advice to his friend 'to play ball, to play football, to run, to make the team, to sell the chocolates, to sell whatever they wanted you to sell, to do whatever they wanted you to do', extremely unsettling. And yet, it is the absoluteness of the admission of defeat that convinces the skeptical adolescent reader that this novel is one which can be trusted.

Ten years later the sequel to **The Chocolate War** was published. While Jerry, Archie, and Brother Leon are significant presences, other characters now receive more attention, and the traumas are spread more widely. Although Jerry turns away from withdrawal, going back to school as a means of coping with his humiliation, and achieves a kind of victory, a fact regarded by some reviewers as a sign of Cormier's softening with the passing of the years, the narrative refuses the temptation of the happy ending. Obie's effort to break away from the Vigils and the role of tormentor through the love of a girl, and David Caroni's one chance of proving his worth through academic achievement, are both deliberately sabotaged, leading in the one case to a failed attempt to stage the murder of Archie and in the other case to a successful suicide. So, at the close of **Beyond the Chocolate War,** as Archie prepares to leave Trinity, instead of resolution, there are only the figures of his successors talking of their future plans. Archie rules, OK!

For his next two novels after **The Chocolate War,** published in the late 1970s, Cormier turned from the school story to the thriller genre. Corruption is no longer only a matter of individual psychology, but is entwined with the public world beyond family and school. Plots are no longer the product of Vigils' assignments, but are the stuff of political manipulation and ambition, in which ordinary people are caught up and exploited.

Whereas the structure of the Chocolate War books was relatively straightforward, Cormier now uses the conventions of the thriller to offer a more complex narrative form—a form that serves as a metaphor for his sense of how the world is. This is especially the case with **I Am the Cheese,** in which corruption at the highest levels of government and the consequent attempted cover-ups produce three interleaved stories of search and pursuit that resonate against one another. Central is the issue of trust. Overhearing conversations behind doors and on the telephone, Adam slowly begins to discover the dangerous truth his father possesses, becoming a spy in his own home. Faced with questions recorded in the transcripts of taped interviews, which are reproduced throughout the novel, both he and we struggle to interpret the signs correctly. No one and nothing can be taken at face

value; even his girlfriend, who seems to offer some refuge from the private bafflements he suffers, disappears.

The book certainly encourages paranoia, and in this lies its appeal to young readers. For Adam's situation may be read as a fictional representation of the situation of many teenagers, acutely concerned with who may or may not be relied upon, with what is being said in other rooms, and with whether what seems to be the case really is the case. Adolescents are likely to find the message that **I Am the Cheese** carries—that everyone tells lies—acutely appropriate.

Although not quite so intricate in its narrative as the earlier book, **After the First Death** also switches between various points of view as a means of giving greater richness and complexity to its handling of significant themes. No longer mainly seen within a family setting, the three main youthful protagonists of this novel, whether Kate, the female driver of a bus load of children held hostage, or Miro, the young terrorist eager to prove himself, or Ben, the son of the General in charge of solving the crisis, are all directly exposed to the manipulations, abuses, and deceits of adults.

Kate's situation, on the hijacked coach, is the most obviously vulnerable one; every move she makes has to be carefully calculated, and her last ends in her death. However, although more marginal, the stories of Miro and Ben are more subtly interesting, as each struggles to come to terms with his newly discovered failing—the former that he is capable of feelings of tenderness and desire for his enemy, and the latter, through being used by the General as a messenger to carry false information to trick the enemy, awareness of the limits of his own courage. As a result, divided by opposing cultures and values, one literally finds a father he never thought he had, and the other symbolically loses a father he always thought was his. Both characters, however, are used and betrayed in the name of a good cause—the terrorists' fight against American imperialism and the military's fight to defend American society.

Although the latter forces finally win, **After the First Death** is scored through with painful brutality, particularly the torture and murder of some of the small children held on the bus. The image of a drugged boy being swung around a terrorist's head most vividly reinforces a major theme in Cormier's fiction—the failures of parents, fathers especially, to take proper care of their children. The theme is present most sharply in one of the stories in **Eight Plus One.** 'Mine on Thursdays' describes how too frightening a fair ride, taken by a young girl out with her divorced father for the day, turns her against him; a minor treachery becomes a symptom of different and deeper treacheries. Other stories in this volume delicately register why such treacheries are common. Fathers are depicted as weak, narrow-minded, and fearful of growing old. Little wonder they can offer limited security to their offspring. Certainly, as the jacket blurb suggests, **Eight Plus One** shows a gentler side to Cormier, but some of the roots of his darker insights into human relationships can be traced to the ground covered in these deceptively simple tales, all of which are seeking, and usually find, to use the author's own words, a 'second level' of meaning.

Secondary levels of meaning are certainly present in Cormier's next novel, *The Bumblebee Flies Anyway,* published in 1983 and perhaps his most ambitious. Set in a surreal futuristic hospice, which is used to test out therapies on terminally ill teenagers, this book takes the closed setting of *The Chocolate War* to a horrifying extreme. Instead of a school regime of spoken and unspoken rules and assignments, there is a regime of drugs, in which the human being becomes a mere object for scientific experiment. Illness and the realities of death are drawn in cold and painstaking detail. Young readers need to be prepared for what the novel offers. Yet, the experience of reading the book is likely to be rich and memorable, for within this world of decay and suffering, alternatives, of a kind, exist. There is the friendship and loyalty between some of the adolescent characters; there is the inventive and resistant language of Barney, the protagonist, to the processes he observes and undergoes; there is his sexual longing for Cassie, sister of one of the patients; and most importantly there is his rebuilding of the model car he finds on the outskirts of the institution, to give Mazzo one last ride. Whereas in earlier novels, the symbolism of Cormier's writing is relatively muted, here it is loud and assertive, as if only symbolism on such a large scale is adequate for the terrible intensity of the writer's vision. As in previous books, but here with greater emphasis and concentration, readers are faced with the vulnerability and mortality of the body, the constant struggle to maintain a sense of the free and individual self against external pressures, the difficult effort to achieve an authentic identity, the awkward and uncontrollable lusts of the heart and, perhaps most significantly of all, the essential aloneness of adolescent life irrespective of the supposed protection of parents and adults.

That aloneness is taken even further in Cormier's next book—*Fade.* Here the customary conflict between the private self and the pressures exerted by various kinds of institution is translated into a volatile and eventually destructive inner conflict across the generations between two forms of identity: that of the normal world and that generated by the strange and frightening 'fade', a power inherited by certain individuals to disappear from view. The novel's combination of realistic family saga and supernatural thriller uses the device of the fade as a metaphor to explore the relationship of a sensitive adolescent to his surroundings, playing with the different meanings carried by the idea of fading, and with the complex relationship between fiction and truth. Once again, a boy becomes a spy in his own home and world, uncovering in the process a series of horrifying secrets, which disturb his mind and destroy his happiness. Growing to adulthood, he finds his secret power has been given destructive expression in the new generation, producing both a literal and metaphorical fight to the death.

As in previous books, the line between the reassuringly everyday and the terrifyingly nightmarish is finely drawn.

More intensely here than in any other novel so far, Cormier registers the strength of male adolescent sexuality, as Paul is compulsively attracted to his aunt and to voyeurism. Few adults, I suspect, will be able to read the relevant scenes without some anxiety concerning the suitability of the book for young readers—an anxiety that was expressed in some reviews. Yet, the force of the writing reinforces the author's own claim that he wrote 'unsensually, not to titillate or sensationalise'. What distinguishes Cormier's treatment of the topic is his willingness to take the sexual feelings aroused in the hero seriously, without reducing them to either simple romance or simple lust. If librarians and teachers really do believe in the value of teenage literature, then they have also to accept the challenges of such literature.

Such challenges may take different forms. In *Darcy* [published in the U.S. as *Other Bells Toll for Us to Ring*] readers are invited to accept the possibility of miracle, as its young heroine, after a kind of conversion to Catholicism, experiences the desertion and death of her best friend. Set among the anxieties created by the war in Europe, the first-person narrative registers with beautiful simplicity the bewildering confusions and joys of the passage from childhood to adolescence. As in other Cormier novels, parents, at best, offer only partial protection from the world's cruelties. Yet, unlike as in his other fiction, religion here plays a much more significant role, holding out the promise that the life we see around us is not the only one. The image of the crippled infant who starts to walk after being blessed by a nun, and the sound of church bells echoing the words of her dead companion in Darcy's head, may strike readers as excessively sentimental, straining credibility to breaking point. They confirm, however, the author's willingness to break new ground and take new risks, and his unwillingness to remain within the conventions of realism.

Cormier continues to write, and thus no assessment can be complete. There is little doubt, however, of the sustained quality of his work so far—work which helps to ensure that fiction for young people is treated with respect. Yet it would be wrong to ignore possible criticisms. Despite Darcy and some significant female characters in other books, this is a male-dominated fictional world, in which girls are as often as not viewed as objects of boys' desire. And even in *After the First Death,* which has a heroine at its centre, Kate is compelled by the situation in which she is placed, and implicitly by the narrative as well, to use her sexuality as her only means of potential escape. Female readers of much of Cormier's work are likely to find their relation to its main characters and concerns more problematical than that of their male counterparts.

Another criticism is the impression much of his fiction gives of pessimism and despair. Certainly it is worth remembering that there are alternatives to Archie Costello's belief, expressed in *The Chocolate War,* that 'nobody's innocent'; and each narrative calls variations of these alternatives into existence. For example, there is General Marchand's wish that his son will forgive him in *After the First Death;* Adam's puzzled love for Amy in *I Am the Cheese;* the glorious futility of Barney's passion to rebuild a car that will never be driven in *The Bumblebee Flies Anyway;* and Jerry's final recognition that you can lose a fight but still win in *Beyond the Chocolate War.*

However, these suggestions of the positive do not cut a way through the terrifying nets of deceit and brutality which the books spin, and do not make up for Cormier's own perception that " . . . the mugger lurking in the doorway assaults both the just and the unjust." Instead they are simply delicate and temporary breaks in the tightly woven skein, and as such are reminiscent of the small assertions of love and faith which lighten the darkness of another twentieth-century writer whose conception of human nature is also framed in terms of corruption and betrayal. Like Graham Greene, Robert Cormier was raised as a Catholic, and for both, evil, innocence, sin, confession, and death are haunting presences. The distance between Pinkie in *Brighton Rock* and Archie in *The Chocolate War* is relatively short.

Perhaps, then, it is Cormier's rejection of liberal solutions, premised on notions of reason and progress, a rejection that is most sharply underlined by the explicit spirituality of *Darcy,* rather than the overt sex and violence of his work, which is really shocking. Difficult questions follow—questions which Cormier himself voiced in a recent interview. Do librarians and teachers want young readers' sense of life's values and possibilities to be soured so early, or has such a souring already occurred? Can we ensure that other images of human nature and society are available? How do we compare the horrifying visions of serious texts with those of popular film and fiction?

Whatever the answers, it is important to recognise that while teenage literature may not change the world or change lives, it may play a part in shaping the developing moral perceptions of adolescents, who are still open to new and different influences. This is not to argue for censorship—a fate which *The Chocolate War* nearly suffered in American school libraries—but for a recognition of the powerfully disturbing meanings carried by Cormier's fiction.

Patricia Head

SOURCE: "Robert Cormier and the Postmodernist Possibilities of Young Adult Fiction," in *Children's Literature Association Quarterly,* Vol. 21, No. 1, Spring, 1996, pp. 28-33.

This study of Robert Cormier deals with a positive view of children's literature: its possibilities not its impossibilities. For Jacqueline Rose, the impossibility of children's literature stems from those adult readers and writers who desire a literature that returns us to "something innocent and precious which we have destroyed" and who, consequently, impose their wishes upon the literature they produce for children. Cormier's works challenge this imposition by denying his readership a romantic view of society and by subverting a unitary view of childhood through the content and form of his work. Fiction such as Cormier writes interrogates the boundaries of children's literature as a genre, and the presence of his adolescent audience brings a further challenge to any notion of a unitary childhood that is the "Other" of a unitary adulthood.

Peter Hunt's opening to "The Text and the Reader" provides a useful summary of the tradition of viewing children's texts as monological—interpretable on only one level. Hunt describes *First Term at Trebizon* as such a text: "It is very familiar, it is predictable; because it involves little deduction, it can be read easily . . . it is not so much implying a readership as prescribing the level of reading." He goes on to say that the problem with texts that "challenge these assumptions" is that they "commonly find themselves in the no-person's land between writings for adults (so-called) and writings for children (so-called)." This no-person's land often goes under the heading "Young Adult" or "adolescent" fiction. Adolescent literature often embraces cultural references that do not make for a safe read: violence, suicide, and sexuality, not conventional topics in the genre of children's literature. Moreover, the security of the text is often destabilized further by the narrative form, which tends to foreground the instability of the narrative through fragmented or cyclical narrative structures and multiple narrators. Nevertheless, it is important to align adolescent fiction with the genre of children's literature, rather than to discuss it on a purely literary and theoretical level as popular fiction, because it operates as a "supragenre" that at once moves beyond the generic expectations of much children's literature and is dependent upon it. If the term "children's literature" refers to a genre housing non-peer texts (that is, texts with an adult as implied author and a child as implied reader), Cormier, and other writers of adolescent literature, operate within this genre because even while they work on the cutting edge of children's literature, they still maintain a non-peer relationship with their readers.

Rose describes books written for the child-within-the-adult; what I am describing are books written for the adult-within-the-child. The latter type of writing challenges the construction of childhood that is the concern of Rose's book. Her depiction of the impossibility of children's fiction comes from a definition in which "children's fiction sets up a world in which the adult comes first (author, maker, giver) and the child comes after (reader, product, receiver) but where neither of them enters the space in between." The postmodernist features of Cormier's writing bring new possibilities to reader and critic, because the relationship between author and reader is foregrounded, and the implied adult author and the implied child reader can enter the space in between.

The name "Cormier" conjures up descriptions of violent acts, shifting narratives, institutional power, and lonely protagonists. Cormier's work interests me in two contexts. First, his writing of adolescent fiction extends the possibilities for fiction within the genre of children's literature. The challenging aspects of his stories are not just his coverage of taboo subject areas but also what may be called the postmodernist features of his writing: his uses of metafiction and multiple points of view, his destabilization of the reader, and his questioning of the boundaries between fiction and reality. Second, any extension to the genre of children's literature through adolescent literature extends the critical schools associated with that genre.

Cormier claims that he did not begin writing with a specific audience in mind and did not know that such a thing as a young adult audience existed until he discovered it through the success of *The Chocolate War* (1975). In an interview with Roger Sutton, Cormier admits that he was afraid his young adult following would reject the complexity of his second novel, *I Am the Cheese* (1977). From the start, he has received a mixed critical response. He is often viewed as a "conspicuous oddity in his chosen field," as Anne Scott MacLeod puts it, because he has "departed from standard models and broken some of the most fundamental taboos" of adolescent fiction. Cormier has been accused of brutalizing the hopefulness of children's fiction and at the same time been praised for his challenging use of form and his "new realism." Cormier accepts the uncompromising stance that has been articulated by these critics, stating that his books "are an antidote to the TV view of life . . . phony realism. As long as what I write is true and believable, why should I have to create happy endings?"

Cormier's early work would not have disturbed so many critics if those critics had not been working within a tradition of viewing children's literature as a sort of cultural touchstone that could, or should, comfort its readers or reinforce certain cultural codes. Such descriptive rather than analytic discussions of the genre of children's literature have played a role in mythologizing the genre and reinforcing notions of what children's literature should be like. For example, Sheila Egoff's book *Thursday's Child: Trends and Patterns in Contemporary Children's Literature* provides a perceptive commentary on the relationship between literature and culture in children's literature (each period, Egoff notes, has coded into its children's literature what may be described as a public or consensual view of the young and therefore their books), but subsequently fails to recognize the critical/cultural relationships present in specific texts. In her chapter on "Realistic Fiction," Egoff is critical of formal experimentation when it undermines content—but her criticism is often driven by an uneasiness with the content itself. In her discussion of *The Chocolate War,* Egoff falls back on a mythical rather than a theoretical articulation of the text when she writes that "the Devil is in control rather than God." Accepting Cormier means accepting two premises: that it is possible to present a

disturbing view of society's so-called secure institutions in a piece of children's fiction, and that the field of children's literature is one such institution.

On a superficial level Cormier's work is famous because it alerts readers to the presence of deception in the currently accepted strongholds of social morality: family, school, and government. But to restrict analysis of Cormier to the content and character of his stories would mean that his fiction has meaning only in a narrow, contemporary context. If a reader finishes a Cormier novel aware of the deceptive nature of fiction itself, however, this recognition would confirm the author's postmodernist stance. Cormier's work subverts the assumption that literature should present a straightforward, schematic view of the world. The contemporary world can only appear unified if discordant voices, those not representing the dominant ideological view, are marginalized. The foregrounding of the untrustworthy adult voice—for example, Brother Leon in *The Chocolate War,* Adam's interviewer "T" in *I Am the Cheese,* Artkin and the General in *After the First Death* (1979)—reinforces the manipulative power of fiction and implicitly inculcates the habit of asking the reader to question any authoritative narrative voice. In these early novels, Cormier also makes use of disrupted narratives to alert readers to the fictionality of their reading experience, and it is sometimes difficult to unravel the relationship between what is being narrated and who is in control of the narration. The confusion of viewpoint is used to greatest effect in *I Am the Cheese* and *After the First Death,* where Cormier presents a contemporary world that can no longer be conveyed through more ordered narratives. In the sense that Cormier's early novels try to articulate a world that comprises a multiplicity of interpretations, they can be said to be postmodern.

This same confusion about what is "real" occurs elsewhere in Cormier's oeuvre. In *The Bumblebee Flies Anyway* (1983), Billy the Kidney, a terminally ill hospital patient, has his own fiction of himself as a joyrider and car thief, and he constructs other fictions as he tries to escape the confines of his disease and his wheelchair. In this same novel the protagonist, Barney, finds a fake car, which he later names "The Bumblebee." Like fiction, the model car apes reality but is not real; it only operates when Barney's imagination turns it into a real car. Thus, like fiction, it is only credible because someone's imagination transforms it into "reality." The questioning of reality and fiction continues with Barney's dilemma about his own sense of self: "Sitting here in this forlorn room, he felt almost as if he didn't exist. But at least he could cling to his identity, his name, and do something about it. 'I am Barney Snow,' he said aloud, enunciating carefully. His voice echoed in the air. There was no answering voice to say: Yes, you are Barney Snow." This questioning of identity is a common theme in Cormier's narratives. As the identities of the characters are foregrounded, so the reader is encouraged to rethink the possibility (or the impossibility) that any unitary or stable sense of self can exist.

Metafiction is fiction about fiction, stories that reflect on the nature of story making itself and that, in doing so, draw attention to their fictionality. In *Postmodernist Culture,* Steven Connor defines metafiction as a "link between text and world." This link is forged not by masking a text's fictionality or by "an effacement of the text in the interests of a return to the real, but by an intensification of textuality such that it becomes coextensive with the real." Metafictional discourse manifests itself in several ways in Cormier's writing. First, his characters often construct stories about themselves within the novel as a whole, for example Adam's fictional journey within the mental institution in *I Am the Cheese,* or Ben's therapeutic writing of his experiences in *After the First Death.*

Fade (1988) is arguably the most metafictional of Cormier's novels to date. Metafictionality is made explicit here, as "fiction" is the central subject of this novel, which is structured so as to collapse the boundary between fiction and reality. The first 120 pages of *Fade* are about a young boy, Paul, who learns he has the power to become invisible—a familiar fantasy topos. But after this opening narrative, the Susan section of the novel begins, and the fictionality of the preceding story is thrown into question. Although the three fictional readers of Paul's story, Susan, her grandfather, and a literary agent, Meredith, agree that Paul's story must be a fantasy, by the end of the novel, Cormier has so successfully blended a fantasy-reality, a conventional fictional-reality, and transtextual references to his career as a writer and his fictional community of Monument and Frenchtown that the reader may be forgiven for beginning to believe that Robert Cormier, the real author, has Paul's power to "fade." Cormier alerts his readers to the unreliability of a notion of reality by foregrounding the unreliability of his fictional realities. In *Postmodernist Fiction,* Brian McHale states that it is a postmodernist tendency to write "fictions about the order of things, discourses which reflect upon the worlds of discourse." McHale goes on to say that postmodernism is about "unmasking the constructed nature of reality." This exposure is exactly what happens in *Fade.*

The initial narrative sequence of *Fade* is set in 1938. In 1967 its writer, Paul, dies, and his manuscript is passed to an attorney. The manuscript is kept, as per Paul's instructions, until 1988 when it is passed to Meredith Martin, Paul's literary agent. The manuscript is found by Susan, a distant relative of Paul's, in Meredith's apartment. Together they read the manuscript and analyze it, debating its validity as fact or fiction. The character Susan exists in the contemporary world, 1988. The temporal sequence crosses three generations of faders; in 1938, Paul, then 13, learns from his uncle that he is a fader; in 1967 Paul finds Ozzie, his lost nephew who is the fader of the next generation; and in 1988 Paul's manuscript is made public to Meredith and Susan, when the next fader, if there is one, is due to reach maturity. *Fade* is self-conscious in asserting itself as fact not fiction, in an attempt to make readers aware of the act of fiction in which they are participating.

Apart from the timescale, *Fade* self-consciously reinforces its own validity by returning to Frenchtown, the neighborhood in Monument, Massachusetts, that Cormier has established in his other books. Paul's father works in the comb factory, and his family is part of the Frenchtown community. This is the world of Cormier's short stories and the setting for *The Chocolate War, I Am the Cheese,* and *After the First Death.* Reading the embedded manuscript in *Fade,* Susan and Meredith reflect on Paul's use of his community in his writings: "Some critics accuse him [Paul] of being an autobiographical novelist, but he really wasn't. I mean, he employed his familiar surroundings, the Franco-American scene, but his plots were fiction." Although this comment is about the fictional author Paul, it reflects on the real world of Cormier's writing. Cormier admits that Monument is "a thinly disguised Leominster . . . I've changed the name and everything and I've moved the streets around but it's the same. Yes I'm lucky that I can take a ride down to Frenchtown anytime and there it is." This self-conscious insertion of autobiographical elements asks the reader to question the boundaries between fact and fiction.

In its multiple narratives and fictional readers, *Fade* also reflects on writing and reading as activities. Through the fictional writers we, as readers, can recognize often unreliable narrative perspectives, and through the fictional readers we can see into the process by which meaning is constructed by a reader and naturalized by that reader's previous experiences and expectations of reading. Paul writes from his own experience. This fact is foregrounded by his comments upon his initial efforts at writing: "I submitted the story I had written about the boy and his father and the shop to *The Statue,* leaving it on Miss Walker's desk. I had titled the story 'Bruises in Paradise,' pleased by the contrast of those two nouns linked uneasily by the plain preposition." This story, "Bruises in Paradise," resurfaces in the Susan narrative sequence as Paul's first successful novel. Paul reflects on how his own past seems to be a fiction: "With my Uncle Adelard gone, the events at Silas B. [Paul's school] consumed me completely and the fade became part of the past summer and its witchery, along with street games and garden raids and the battle of Moccasin Pond." Cormier's own assertion in *Eight Plus One* (1980) that the "stuff of actuality is transformed into the stuff of fiction" cannot be ignored. The dynamic of the "real author" is present here.

McHale's analysis of postmodern fiction has led him to conclude that it was a modernist tendency to make the author invisible: "The modernists sought to remove the traces of their presence from the surface of their writing, and to this end exploited or developed various forms of ostensibly 'narratorless' texts." This process seems to be what happens in *The Chocolate War* and *After the First Death* when the shifting first person narratives displace a dominant, potentially *author*ized, narrator.

Although *Fade* is far from the experimentality of more recognizable postmodern fictions that McHale describes, such as those by Donald Barthelme, Robert Coover, and Italo Calvino, Cormier has here performed the postmodernist exercise that McHale identifies: he has "brought the author back to the surface . . . free . . . to break in upon the fictional world." By advertising himself as author within the text, Cormier reminds readers that even an apparently real author is a constructed feature of fiction.

The metanarrative of *Fade* has metatheoretical implications, not just in the presence of the multiple critiques of Paul's manuscript (from Meredith, Susan, Jules, and the actual reader) but also in terms of the metanarrative's foregrounding of the theoretical continuum of Real Author/Implied Author/Narrator/Narratee/Implied Reader/Real Reader. The transfer between Paul's roles as Narrator and Real Author interrogates authorial intentionality and foregrounds the author as a controlling force. This issue of narrative power and the role of the author is particularly important in adolescent literature, for in this genre, we are dealing with non-peer texts and, therefore, a non-peer author/reader relationship is the norm. Hunt highlights the relationship between adult author and child reader when he states that in "peer-texts the adult reader (real or otherwise) can adjust to the degree of control which the author appears to be exercising." In children's, and I might add in adolescent, literature, however, "the audience is created by the writer much more directly than with a peer-text, in the sense that the text does more than display its codes, grammar, and contracts; it suggests what the reader must be or become to optimize the reading of the text." By exposing the roles of author and reader in *Fade,* Cormier allows the reader to interrogate the production of a fiction from both ends of the continuum, from the perspective of producer and from that of receiver. By making this transferral of textual responsibility explicit, Cormier may be developing a more mature and knowledgeable readership. The reader is not meant to be a passive receiver but an active and involved critic. If the supragenre of adolescent literature makes the adult-within-the-child a possibility, then postmodern adolescent novels such as *Fade* encourage the development of the critic-within-the-reader.

As Susan and Meredith become readers of Paul's story, they undermine its validity for the real reader, and, perhaps, challenge the construction of the implied reader. The initial Paul sequence is erased as part of the novel, instead becoming a manuscript that exists only within the frame of the novel as a whole. Ironically, the discourse of the Susan sequence positions itself within the conventions of young adult narratives by employing the first-person voice, by relying on phrases such as "Let me introduce myself," and by using slang and hesitant digressions:

> Shit.
>
> This isn't the way I want to begin. What I want to

do is keep things plain and simple and direct. Professor Waronski in Creative Writing 209 says that the best way is to plunge in, make a beginning, any beginning at all, as long as you start. Most of all, he said, be yourself.

Because Cormier does not frame the Paul story as a story within a story from the beginning of the novel, the reader has, by this stage, become comfortable in Paul's world. The effect of suddenly being catapulted into an apparently conventional YA novel is that "the reader clings to the 'lost' erased sequence as he or she might not to one less highly charged." Further the change in narrative voice from Paul to Susan allows the reader to evaluate the nature of the fictional act and the implications of relying on a single narrative point of view. The abrupt shift from Paul's narrative to Susan's section throws into relief the potential for any reader to settle into an unquestioning relationship with a prescribed narrator.

Thus far, I have established two discourse types in *Fade:* the magic realism of Paul's story and the YA new realism of Susan's story. Within the story, Susan and Meredith continue to evaluate the truth of Paul's manuscript, so they call upon Jules Roget, Paul's cousin and Susan's grandfather, hoping that he will be a reliable arbitrator: "He's a detective. An investigator. His job is finding facts, the truth. So, I went to Monument, two weeks ago. Took the manuscript with me. Asked him to read it, to give me an opinion." Jules's discourse is that of a third discourse type, the formal police report, and through it Jules mirrors all the episodes that have been described in the preceding narrative. Apart from Jules's personal knowledge of Paul's family and his alternative perspective on the events described by Paul's manuscripts, his overwhelming justification for not believing in the power to fade is the presence of such a power in other fictions:

> The fade—as Paul called it—is impossible to accept as fact. . . . Paul always dealt with realism in his novels and never showed any tendency towards science fiction or fantasy. However, he was addicted to the movies like so many of us who were members of the double-feature generation of the thirties and forties. There was a film that was impossible to forget, which had a definite impact on viewers, both young and old, of that era. The film—*The Invisible Man,* starring Claude Rains. It's possible, I believe, that Paul received the idea for the fade from the movie and waited several years before using the idea. The fade, all by itself, proves that the narrative is fiction.

I have quoted at length in order to exemplify the role of the reader that is being exposed here. In his roles as both narrator and narratee, Jules shows how fictions and interpretations are constructed. The assumption about the fictionality or unreality of the fade comes from Jules's own reading experiences. Jules is what Roland Barthes terms the "I that approaches the text," and he is influenced by the film-texts that he uses to make sense of the fictionality of the fade. His role in constructing an acceptable interpretation of the manuscript is undermined by his own exposure of how he believes fictions are created.

If Jules can be interpreted as an individual reader, he is also an unreliable narrator. Earlier in Susan's story, she has suggested that she has learned something from her grandfather, Jules: "something my grandfather had told me during one of my visits to Monument." Jules had admitted to an episode in a library as a child when Paul seemed to have disappeared. After reading her grandfather's critique of Paul's manuscript, she wonders why her grandfather hasn't mentioned this in his report to Meredith: "had he refused to acknowledge Paul's disappearance because it would lead him to enormous conclusions that he could not accept?" The potential unreliability of narrative is also part of Paul's story. Paul is fascinated by the idea of his Uncle Adelard, who is a traveller:

> "He's back," my father announced as he entered the kitchen in a cloud of celluloid and banged his lunch pail on the table. I leapt from the chair where I had been reading the latest issue of *Wings* magazine, eager for details. "When did she arrive?" my mother asked.
>
> *She?*
>
> I realized that my ears had fooled me into hearing what I wanted to hear.

The readers in the book—Meredith, Susan, Jules—all want to hear something that will give them more comfort than accepting the fade as fact. The fictional readers, in other words, are afraid of the potential reality of the apparently fantastic, a fear that forces the reader outside the novel to reexamine the possibility of achieving escape ("fading") through literature. Thus the self-reflexive Susan sequences undermine the escapist function of fantasy or science fiction, the genres that have most in common with the Paul and Ozzie sequences. Cormier's juxtaposition of two types of fiction draws attention to the possibility of fiction in general, as when Susan voices the cyclical impact of *Fade:* "'I have a theory,' I said, not certain whether I *did* have a theory at all. 'Maybe Paul had to create a real world so that the reader would be *forced* to believe the fantasy. But that doesn't mean the fantasy was real.'" Cormier layers fictional reality upon fictional reality, constructing a narrative world that relies upon increasingly distant and disappearing foundations. As the character Susan has suggested above, the truth or lack of it is not the real issue; what is significant is that the reader questions the construction of fiction. Cormier educates his readers, not by presenting a schematic view of their world, but by revealing its constructed nature.

Much of my preceding analysis has been devoted to the liberating qualities of Cormier's narrative forms, for it seems clear to me that narrative and critical advances are extending the possibilities of children's literature.

Although much of the preceding analysis has been devoted to *Fade,* the principles apply in one way or another to most of Cormier's novels. I am critical of Rose's insistence on the impossibilities of children's literature, but it must be said that her book does not deal with the new realist practitioners of children's literature, as she admits in her conclusion. Her work, however, is of direct relevance to my study, as she successfully articulates the limitations of the genre and the difficulties in defining and discussing children's literature. Rose views the appropriation of children's literature as a repository for an innocent, closed world as a form of colonialism: "childhood is seen as the place where an older form of culture is preserved." The desire for children's literature to be a safe haven from the cultural decay that surrounds us is reflected by some of the criticism that she notes:

> The development of children's fiction has followed that of the novel . . . but what seems to have happened in recent discussions of children's books is that, in response to the breakdown of the realist aesthetic in the modern adult novel, writers have been arguing with increasing vehemence for its preservation in writing intended for the child.

Rose claims that the commentaries of John Rowe Townsend, Marcus Crouch, and Geoffrey Trease, for example, situate "children's fiction [as] the chief battle ground in the attempt to preserve our culture from imminent decay."

Cormier is exactly the kind of author who disturbs a secure and conventional tradition of children's literature, and because of this challenge his work is marginalized, consciously or not, into a border country of children's literature called adolescent fiction. In refusing to be the kind of adult author that some critics of children's literature expect, Cormier also denies the construction of a conventional child (or adolescent) reader. Many negative critical readings of Cormier stem from an anxiety that the author as adult is absent from his more brutal and disturbing books. But in fact what Cormier does is to provide levels of narration that remove many of the constraints of children's literature, allowing the implied author to be mediated through the literariness of the disturbing narratives.

Earlier in this article, I mention critics who are disturbed by the content of Cormier's work. Any critical approach that privileges a discussion of the content of a text and does not deal adequately with the form of narration only tells half the story. What is positive and valuable about Cormier's adolescent fiction is that unlike more closed children's literature, the adult voice is not implied through reductive narrative forms (for example, with a plot of resolution) but through the polyphony of the text. What would seem to be the death of the author and the abandonment of the reader to a sometimes brutal fictional world is actually what liberates the adult author/child reader dynamic, allowing author, reader, and genre to mature into adolescence.

TITLE COMMENTARY

📖 *BEYOND THE CHOCOLATE WAR* (1985)

Sally Estes

SOURCE: A review of *Beyond the Chocolate War,* in *Booklist,* Vol. 81, No. 14, March 15, 1985, pp. 1048, 1050.

Cormier has not compromised **The Chocolate War** in a long-awaited sequel that is as grim if not grimmer as it completes the school year begun in the first book. The same insidious unrelieved tension pervades from the first sentence, "Ray Bannister started to build the guillotine the day Jerry Renault returned to Monument," to the last ironic chapter, which forebodes the next school year. Arch-Machiavellian Archie Costello, more devious than ever, operates at the hub of various subplots that all converge in a climactic blockbuster. With the exception of Ray, would-be magician and new innocent thrust into the morass that is Trinity High, the main characters will be familiar to **Chocolate War** readers. Obie, Archie's chief henchman, has fallen in love and is trying to draw away from the Vigils. He is eventually driven to a desperate act that forces him to confront his own turpitude. Jerry Renault's return not only pits him once again against the brutal Emile Janza but also puts his friend Goober's loyalty to the ultimate test. Even Brother Leon faces a deadly nemesis in the form of a maddened, suicidal, revenge-seeking David Caroni. The fact that Cormier's writing has matured since publication of **The Chocolate War** in 1974 shows up in the difference in literary style between the two books. At least twice, though, he employs a self-conscious but effective literary device designed to stun the reader momentarily, and it's almost as if he is manipulating his readers while similar manipulation goes on within the story. However, this novel is more complex in construction, style, theme, and characterization than its predecessor—indeed, the portrayal of Archie, in particular, is much more finely honed and convincing. Another disturbing look at the darker side of human nature and the misuse of power that is sure to provoke discussion.

Zena Sutherland

SOURCE: A review of *Beyond the Chocolate War,* in *Bulletin of the Center for Children's Books,* Vol. 38, No. 8, April, 1985, p. 143.

As he did in **The Chocolate War,** Cormier explores the motivations and the consequences, like a viscous ripple effect, of the combination of evil and power. Archie, leader of the Vigils, the secret society that dominates a Catholic high school for boys, is a senior now and has chosen his successor, a less subtle and more openly vindictive sophomore. Several of the Vigils rebel against Archie in this powerful sequel, but only Archie wins. This has diversity within the framework of Trinity High, with the despair and resentment of several students perceptively detailed and tied together by the inexorable momentum of events. Some readers may find the story depressingly somber; for others it may have the cathartic effect of Greek tragedy, evoking pity and fear.

Gayle Keresey

SOURCE: A review of *Beyond the Chocolate War,* in *Voice of Youth Advocates,* Vol. 8, No. 2, June, 1985, pp. 128-29.

Eleven years after the publication of the highly acclaimed and controversial **The Chocolate War,** Cormier continues the chronicle of the school year at Trinity after the chocolate sale. Jerry Renault has returned to town after recovering at his aunt and uncle's home in Canada but is not attending school. Archie Costello is still controlling the Vigils, but his right-hand man, Obie, is more interested in his new girlfriend, Laurie Gundarson, a senior at Monument High, and later avenging her attempted rape. Bunting, a sophomore, is desperately trying to replace Obie so that he can become the assigner after Archie graduates. Other subplots intricately interwoven with the main plot deal with Ray Bannister, a new student who is a magician who builds a guillotine; David Caroni, a suicidal student determined to make Brother Leon pay for the F he gave him; Carter, the president of the Vigils who makes the mistake of revealing Archie's plans; and the death of Brother Eugene, who had never recovered from one of the Vigil's assignments given to The Goober. Archie, always the mastermind, controls all activities at Trinity School, even at the conclusion of the novel, as he passes on his assigner duties. **Beyond the Chocolate War** will be controversial both because of its uncompromising view of human weaknesses, as well as its honest depiction of the language and personalities of male high school students. Readers will be riveted to this suspenseful novel. While it is possible to read this sequel without reading its predecessor, prior readers of Cormier will more fully enjoy this novel. However, after reading this sequel, readers will probably demand to read its predecessor if they haven't already read it. The best of Cormier's highly acclaimed novels, this book demands inclusion on the Best Books for Young Adults list.

Mary M. Burns

SOURCE: A review of *Beyond the Chocolate War,* in *The Horn Book Magazine,* Vol. LXI, No. 4, July, 1985, pp. 451-53.

The Chocolate War, published eleven years ago, was a milestone in the writing of fiction for young adults, for it translated the attitudes, concerns, and relationships peculiar to the microcosmic world of the private high school into symbols of a far larger universe—yet remained quintessentially a story about and for adolescents. When a book achieves such status, the evaluation of its sequel poses special problems. Often the second book, which in any other context would be superior, seems weaker in comparison with its predecessor; less frequently, the second becomes a logical extension of the first, rounding out the theme and bringing events to an aesthetically satisfying conclusion. *Beyond the Chocolate War* belongs in this latter category: first, because it fleshes out the pivotal characters into more complex personalities; and secondly, because it probes the effects of violence and the abuse of power on the victimizers as well as on the victims. "Power tends to corrupt and absolute power corrupts absolutely," the aphorism attributed to Lord Acton, is made concrete, ugly, and immediate—not in the weary world of politics but in the shelter of school and playground. But the sequel is not simply a continuation, for it introduces Ray Bannister, newcomer to Monument, who not only provides a new point of view as the bystander to whom events of the previous autumn must be explained but who also serves as the unwitting agent for the final confrontation between the manipulative, amoral Archie Costello and Obie, once one of his loyal satraps. Nearly four months have elapsed since the chocolate sale which precipitated Brother Leon into power as headmaster and established Archie, his mirror image, as the unofficial power among the students. On the surface the school is calm; in reality, tension—not resolution—supports the fragile facade. That revolution lies just beneath the surface is foreshadowed in the first gripping sentence, "Ray Bannister started to build the guillotine the day Jerry Renault returned to Monument." These two seemingly disparate events set in motion a chain of circumstances which move inexorably to their final, dramatic convergence as Obie, less blind than formerly to Archie's ploys, seeks to eradicate what he considers to be the source of all the school's problems. He does not succeed; but the attempt forces him to confront what few wish to acknowledge— that evil exists because it is tolerated. Curiously, but not surprisingly, it is Archie—cold, calculating, Mephistophelian Archie—who articulates the theological principle which is at once the glory and the price of being human: "You had free choice buddy. . . . free choice . . . and you did the choosing." And it is this principle, implicit in *The Chocolate War,* which is developed as the major thematic motif in the sequel, for each of the characters has the opportunity to find a solution to the problem, and each makes a choice appropriate to his personality: Carter, subterfuge; David Caroni, self-annihilation; Goober, retreat; Brother Leon, accommodation; Emile Janza, intimidation; Obie, vengeance. Only Jerry Renault elects to continue the battle, a choice which postulates change and offers hope, for in the larger world outside Trinity these are the choices made daily—and adolescents who adopt the fatalistic attitude that they are powerless need somehow to learn that despair often becomes a self-fulfilling prophecy. It is generally acknowledged that a profound theme is one of the elements separating genuine literature from simple entertainment; conversely, a dominant theme can overwhelm other considerations, transforming story into sermon. *Beyond the Chocolate War* is remarkable for maintaining the balance between plot and philosophy char-

acteristic of the most memorable novels. Quite simply, the work is one of Cormier's finest books to date: combining the sense of immediacy that a good newsman can convey with the psychological insight of a mature writer. Nowhere is this combination better evidenced than in the descriptions of Obie's first experience with love; suggestion instead of explicit documentation somehow touches the heart rather than titillates the senses. And it is this ability to suggest and ultimately to provoke response which raises Cormier's novels above the mass. Consequently, his are among the few books written for young adults which, in all probability, will still be discussed in the twenty-first century.

Marcus Crouch

SOURCE: A review of *Beyond the Chocolate War,* in *The Junior Bookshelf,* Vol. 49, No. 6, December, 1985, p. 274.

Robert Cormier has kept us waiting ten years for a sequel to his *The Chocolate War.* To be honest I would have been prepared to wait longer.

This is not to say that he is anything other than a writer of outstanding powers, master of a brutal and brittle style which crackles and spits out of the page like sticks on a fire, and ruthless in the completeness of his picture of a world. But surely I am not alone in finding that world totally repulsive and, thank goodness, far distant from reality, at least in this part of the globe.

Trinity High, like all schools, is a microcosm. Here are acted out the rackets, the feuds, the pursuit of power to be found on another scale in the adult world. The titular head of Trinity is Brother Leon—it is a Catholic school, but one would have to look hard to find any evidence of spirituality—but power in reality rests with Archie Costello, the Assigner of The Vigils, a Mafia-like secret society whose activities are not particularly secret. Archie is a strange character. He seems to get no satisfaction out of his position. He uses it for mostly quite futile ends, setting in motion activities which, apart from bringing a degree of humiliation and discomfort to those involved, apparently have no object other than a demonstration of Archie's pre-eminence. No one has seen Archie do any school work. He likes nothing and nobody, not even—one suspects—Archie himself. Cold, untouchable, even his sexual exploits appear to be more for prestige than pleasure. Like a spider Archie stretches his net over Trinity High, entangling not only all the boys from smallest to strongest but also Brother Leon and the rest of the staff. Archie calls the tunes, and pretty unmelodious they mostly are.

Mr. Cormier uses a large canvas, and there are a host of portraits, none of them particularly attractive but all crisply drawn. If only the reader could care about any of them, victims or victimizers. So, while admiring unreservedly the writer's skill, his mastery of every detail of the complicated plot, the building of climaxes, this reader at least passed from repulsion to indifference. A plague on all their houses!

Archie leaves school before the last chapter, but, *in absentia,* he still has the last word. He has chosen as his successor an ambitious weakling and saddled him with, as chief of staff, a sadistic Godfather-in-the-making. Archie has ensured that Trinity will look back to his reign as a golden age. Meanwhile there are opportunities for his talents in the larger world. As the pathetic and Christ-like Jerry says: 'How many Archie Costellos there are in the world. Out there. Everywhere. Waiting.' It is not a pretty thought, but then this is not a pretty book.

Val Randall

SOURCE: A review of *Beyond the Chocolate War,* in *Books for Keeps,* No. 44, May, 1987, p. 23.

Robert Cormier has, perhaps, the surest touch of any novelist I know in seeking out the worst in all of us and parading it before our horrified eyes. *Beyond the Chocolate War* clearly demonstrates that he has suffered no diminution of this skill.

Cormier makes double fools of us—he lets us believe that we have cracked the code of his book and then, at the last moment, twists it breathtakingly away from us. He places us in a position of superiority, only to demonstrate that the characters we have judged and found wanting are an undeniable part of us all.

Yet in all this fine writing there is a flaw—in his description of the sexual relationships of the two main characters, Archie and Obie. Obie's relationship motivates him to rid himself of Archie's domination and Archie's provides a further insight into his manipulatory powers. It is the unpleasant coyness of the description of the sexual act which shocks—not the act itself. Cormier has here failed to resolve the dilemma implicit in this area: it is not explicit language which is the issue but a failure to describe a sensitive subject in an acceptably honest way.

This aside, *Beyond the Chocolate War* is tailor-made for GCSE wider reading—offer it selectively to maturer fourth and fifth readers.

FADE (1988)

Robert Cormier

SOURCE: "Creating Fade," in *The Horn Book Magazine,* Vol. LXV, No. 2, March, 1989, pp. 166-73.

In my new novel, *Fade,* Paul Roget [Moreaux], the boy who grew up to be a novelist, looks back on his life and says, "I have fictionalized so much of what happened in those days that sometimes, re-reading my books and thinking of the past, I'm not sure what's real and what isn't."

This is sometimes the case with me. My memories do not always obscure reality, of course. There was a real photograph which provided the inspiration for *Fade.* The picture showed my father's family—himself, his four brothers and five sisters, and his mother and father. One of my uncles did not emerge in the picture. His place in the photograph was vacant, as if he had not existed, as if he had disappeared, vanished from sight.

The opening chapter of *Fade* shows the family picture being taken on the steps of a Canadian farmhouse to commemorate the departure of my father's family for a new life in the United States. Did it happen exactly like that?

Family legend is hazy, and so are my memories. The important thing is not whether it happened exactly that way but that it has become real to me—and, I hope, to the reader.

Fade actually answers a more important question, one that has haunted me for a long, long time. Why did my uncle's image fail to appear in the photograph even though he was posed there with the rest of the family? The next question is the key to all my writing: what if? The answer this time became *Fade.*

I have always wanted to write a book about "Frenchtown," and that picture opened the door. I wrote a great many short stories when I started out as a writer, and I sold them to a series of small magazines. Many of the stories were set in French Hill where I was born and grew up. I called it Frenchtown in my writings and still do.

In the fifties I wrote a three-generational novel whose events began in 1910, written from the point of view of a man who might have been my grandfather. I drew upon those old days, brought in the shops and unions and the fires. I cut my teeth on that novel. It was never published, but it proved that I could write a novel. I've been drawing on its background ever since. All of my novels have been different, but every one takes place around Leominster. As I got older, memories of my own childhood pulled at me more and more. I felt a need to look back.

I also had been writing grim novels reflecting what was going on in the world today, and I thought it might be different—and nostalgic—to capture French Hill and boyhood. I was thirteen in 1938 as Paul is in *Fade.* So I began to write the book to see what might have happened as a result of that photograph. Frenchtown was the centerpiece. I've always been interested in the French Canadian migration to Leominster, and this was my chance to portray an aspect of it. French Hill is only three miles away from where I live, and I drive there any time I need inspiration. Recently, after years of attending our neighborhood church, my wife, Connie, and I returned as parishioners to the church on French Hill where we were baptized and married. It was wonderful going back there while I was writing the Frenchtown scenes in *Fade.* I have been lucky to have my childhood so close by. I've never had to fly across the country to find it.

Before reaching midpoint in the novel, I slipped on the ice and broke a bone in my hand. My fingers of that hand were immobilized for a few weeks, and I wasn't able to type. I began writing in longhand, something I hadn't done since I was a kid. Thus, I was writing about childhood scenes in the way I used to write as a boy on the kitchen table at home.

I wrote very nostalgically and tenderly but knew a moment would come when the mood would change, and it would be a big jolt to readers. They would think they were reading one kind of book and suddenly find that the book had become something else. I realized I was taking a major risk at the point where the book changes from what seems to be a nice, docile, ethnic story. It was necessary to foreshadow that moment, to prepare readers. In the first version of the novel I didn't mention fading at all in the early scenes, and Paul was not aware of what was happening to him. For instance, when Paul witnessed the Ku Klux Klan ceremony, I did not mention that he had faded, merely showed the symptoms of the fade. But these were too vague and unrealized, and in the second version, the word *fade* is actually mentioned, although it is not fully explained.

The writing of *Fade* took about two-and-a-half years, but it seemed longer. It went through several versions. The first was about 600 manuscript pages long; the final one was 366 pages. It is my longest published novel. Connie says that she doesn't ever remember me being so wrapped up in a book. Day and night, either at the typewriter or with pencil at the table. That's probably because I was edging forward rather than running. Eventually, the inevitability of events overtook me, and the novel began to gallop. New characters evolved as the action unfolded. For instance, Ozzie did not exist at all when I started writing, although I knew that the fade, the family trait that is the heart of the novel, had to pass on to a new generation. This meant a new voice in the last section of the novel.

Voices are so important. In the early version three major voices carried the story: Paul, his cousin Jules, and Ozzie. We met the other characters through these people, and, in particular, we saw Meredith Martin, Paul's agent, through Jules's eyes. Somehow, the book seemed disjointed to me. When the book was accepted at Delacorte, I went to New York to confer with George Nicholson, head of Books for Young Readers, and Olga Litowinsky, who had been assigned as my editor. Olga had misgivings about the narration by Jules and suggested another voice, another viewpoint, perhaps a young woman. I immediately fell in love with the idea and created Susan who became the unifying character I had been seeking, someone who would be a bridge between the events of yesterday and today. The novel covers fifty years. She allowed me to bring it up to the present time. She is twenty years old, attending Boston University. My daughter, Renée, was twenty at the time, attending Regis College on the periphery of Boston. I was able to make use of her background. Susan leaped to life at the typewriter. The plot demanded that she be placed in a Manhattan apartment, and, here again, I found myself writing about a background I knew and loved. I have friends living in Peter Cooper Village in Manhattan, their windows looking out at the East River. I had always wanted to use that wonderful apartment in a novel, and Susan made that possible. Susan also became the key to cutting the novel, providing me with a perspective I had lost in the immediacy of writing.

Ozzie, who carries the final part of the novel on his shoulders, became a problem I had not anticipated. I wanted him to be a complete victim of the fade. In the first writing he turned out to be a monster with no redeeming qualities. His story was bloody and violent. I realized Ozzie would be entirely unsympathetic to readers. Olga agreed with my doubts, suggesting that he should be softened. I rewrote much of his section, humanizing him. For instance, in the first version, he is without any feelings toward Sister Anunciata, the nun who was his friend. This was changed. Ozzie brought her flowers, wilted and straggly, perhaps, but he was expressing an emotion that was beginning to awaken inside of him.

Ozzie is a completely invented character. I don't know where he comes from. I was sitting in my writing room one day when I heard his voice in my mind. His voice was lyrical, because of the bit of Irish he absorbed from his adoptive mother. There are no seeds of him in anybody I know, although he's like some of my fictional characters taken to a greater degree—an Archie Costello but with a different shade.

People who don't go by the rules have always interested me, terrified me, and astonished me. When I see someone who has parked a car across three or four parking spaces or has cut in front of other people in line, I wonder what kind of person does that, what kind of person doesn't have any regard for anyone else. Carry this further, and you have someone like Archie Costello. Archie has no rules, and neither did the terrorists in *After the First Death.* Ozzie is a direct descendant of that kind of character.

I've always been fascinated by another kind of character, too: the rowdy young woman with hidden depths. Susan has seeds in her of Amy Hertz from *I Am the Cheese* and Cassie from *The Bumblebee Flies Anyway.* I can see Amy Hertz-like things popping up in Cassie and Susan. Of course, I wanted Susan also to be a sharp contrast to Paul and a distinctive new voice.

Paul, on the other hand, is the most autobiographical character I've ever created. Adam in *I Am the Cheese* had a lot of my characteristics. He wanted to be a writer, lived on his bike, and was chased by dogs and bullies. So was I as a kid. Paul—up to a point, of course—pretty much reflects how I felt as a boy growing up. Even his relationship to religion, agonizing sometimes, is much like mine was.

When I went to confession as a boy, I tried to state my sins to the priest so that I wouldn't have to go into detail, and he wouldn't have to ask me questions. I was always aware of that thin curtain separating me from others nearby in the pews, fearing that someone would hear my innermost secrets. In the novel Paul is trying to figure out how he is going to tell the priest what happened to his aunt Rosanna. The priest would know by Paul's voice that a boy was confessing. If he confessed that a woman and not a girl was involved, it would have raised all kinds of questions with the priest. After much thought I came up with the word *female* instead of *woman* or *girl*. That scene was a delight to write because it reflected so much of what I felt as a young boy at that terrible age, burdened by a terrible sense of sin.

There was also a major bully in my life, this older kid who used to chase me. Somehow the first time I looked at him, I knew he was my enemy. I had a paper route just as Bernard did. I had about twelve customers, and the route was about two miles long and ended at the cemetery like Bernard's. I also certainly had my share of crushes as Paul had on Rosanna. I guess I was exorcising some of my ghosts in this book.

The shop scenes also come from my own life, although I never had an uncle involved with union activities. But I worked in a shop similar to the one in the book, and my father worked in a comb shop a good many years during the Depression. He worked in the factories for forty-two years. I tried to capture the feeling of life in the shops. Paul, of course, wants something else, and he doesn't even know what it is. That was also me, although I knew I wanted to write. Working in a factory, I could see how people could be seduced by that kind of life. It was a family business; very nice, located right near my home. One of the owners said I had potential if I wanted to stay, and I even had a date with the owner's daughter. Shop life was not all bad. There's the camaraderie of working together, shop picnics, and holidays. But I knew it was not for me. I left, looking for a job where I could write. I found a job writing commercials for a radio station and then worked for newspapers.

Paul also reflects the guilt I have always felt. I think the idea of goodness, of trying to be good has always haunted me. *Now and at the Hour,* my first novel, had a line that I truly believe, to the effect that many people are good because they never had an opportunity not to be. I am always striving to be good and never feeling that I am. Maybe that comes from a Catholic upbringing. You always have a sense of not doing enough, not being good enough, and even if you think you have done something good, you then feel the guilt of pride.

Usually I write out of strong emotions, like my feelings about terrorism which gave birth to *After the First Death.* But there wasn't a compelling emotion that sent me to the typewriter when I began *Fade.* It was mostly nostalgia and wanting to write about my childhood and to explore several themes: the impossibility of the fade; the fading that goes on in life; Catholic guilt; and the gifts that become curses. I am reminded of Truman Capote's *Answered Prayers: The Unfinished Novel;* more harm has been done, perhaps, by answered prayers than those that are not answered. The book explores the whole idea of life fading and people fading, love fading. That's why I never resolved the problem of Paul's love for Rosanna. She just faded from his life. Paul also fades away. Susan says, toward the end, that he really becomes a true fader, after all.

All the time I am writing I am haunted because I don't know whether the novel is working or not. That is what keeps me at the typewriter and at the table where I edit every night. In some ways *Fade* was more difficult than the other books. It didn't have a straightforward, natural story line in the way *The Chocolate War* did. Even though *I Am the Cheese* was complex, there was a sense of forward movement in the bike scenes, and I knew where it was going. I knew from the outset in *Fade* that I was writing about something that was impossible. It is impossible to be invisible. I wanted to write a realistic novel. I didn't want to write a horror story or a fantasy. I wanted the book to be convincing. That's why I took a long time writing about Frenchtown and the people and the shop, to provide the reader a very clear, realistic background so that when the fantasy did occur, the story would not seem to be a fantasy—even though people would say, "This is impossible." I was trying to do something that wasn't possible. There are not a lot of antecedents for the book I wanted to write. Stephen King lurked in the background. His secret is creating people you care about, so when these terrible things happen to them you really feel it. Yet I wasn't trying to write a Stephen King novel.

I really felt I was breaking new ground for myself. My big dread in life has been rewriting the same novel; that's why I resisted a sequel to *The Chocolate War* for ten years. I want to use my strengths, yet so often those strengths lead a writer to repetition. There's a danger of becoming slack and doing the easy thing. But that certainly wasn't the case with this novel—it was a struggle.

People, of course, don't see what you've left out of the novel. Readers won't know what has been deleted. Knowing the novel was too long and leisurely and realizing that I had consciously let it grow, I asked Olga for suggestions. She came through beautifully, not only pointing out where cuts could be made but providing perspective. It's easy to lose your perspective when writing a novel, and a good editor can restore it. In fact, that's what makes an editor great. I really believe in editors and try to put their suggestions to good use. Fabio Coen did so much to launch my career with *The*

Chocolate War, I Am the Cheese, and *After the First Death.* He was the old-fashioned kind of editor who revered writers, who did not think in terms of one book but of an entire career. Olga is a marvelous editor with a keen eye, almost a sixth sense. One of my strengths has been my willingness to be guided by editors, to rewrite and listen to editorial suggestions. Once I've had the joy of writing the book, then I want it to be the best book possible for the reader. Of course, I do disagree with some suggestions. You must be careful that the novel remains your own, that the integrity of the book, what you set out to do, is not lost in the rewriting.

Despite the problems, I loved writing *Fade,* especially Frenchtown and the family scenes. Writing them brought back things I had forgotten—like the wakes that went on for three days and nights. Writing about them brought back the smell of flowers and food, the fatigue, the endlessness of it all, the memories flowing as I wrote. Yet memory sometimes distorts. At one point Paul mentions reading the Superman comic strip and also Batman and Robin. Someone at Delacorte checked and found out that Batman and Robin weren't around in 1938. Memory, however, doesn't distort the emotions. These do not vary. I have total recall of my boyhood emotions, and a wrong date can always be corrected.

In cutting a novel, you are always dealing with choice and selection and whether to take out huge chunks of prose to save wordage. I decided against hacking away at the book. I began with the first page and rewrote the entire novel, page by page. Tightening, refining, searching for the perfect word or phrase. Yet, I was also adding, in particular, the confessional scenes. I felt a bit like Thomas Wolfe. When Maxwell Perkins sent him home to rewrite a brief chapter, Wolfe would return with one hundred thousand additional words. At one point I thought maybe *Fade* would become a monster. But as I rewrote, I saw the benefits. In the 1963 section I had gone into great detail about Paul's relationship with his father. I loved writing about this because it was a re-creation of my relationship with my own father. But that chapter, while pleasant to write and read, did not provide forward movement, did not add momentum to the story. So I cut it drastically although it hurt. You have to be ruthless with yourself and avoid self-indulgence. You have to remember the reader, always. The books I don't enjoy are the ones in which the writer neglects the reader and indulges himself or herself.

Cutting is not all negative. For instance, I wanted to show that Omer LaBatt did not bully Paul exclusively but picked on other kids. Originally, I had him assaulting Paul's brother, Bernard, at the end of a long paper-route scene. Paul followed Bernard customer by customer, and I relived my own paper-route days in that scene. Then I realized the important thing was to show Omer with another kid. It didn't have to be Bernard; I didn't have to explain the anatomy of a paper route. I rewrote

the scene. The first version was about fifteen pages; the final version was three pages long, much sharper, more vivid, and with a greater effect on the reader.

Meredith Martin voiced one of my tenets: an author is allowed one coincidence in a book. The death of Adelard's brother and the death of Bernard could be a coincidence. Adelard contributed to his brother's death, but not in the way the reader thinks or that Paul thinks. It was really a coincidence that both brothers died. Yet, was it? Was the fade involved? How I love ambiguity. Thus, the book is open-ended with plot twists that allowed me to explore also the guilt that the fade always brought. It never brought happiness.

There is a very dark side to writing. I love writing, but it has its nightmares. A lot of things that you need to convey in your writing you have to experience yourself. You go through the agonies that your characters go through. It really affects me emotionally. When I was younger, I had some nervous problems right after a tonsil operation. I went through several months of nightmares. Later I talked to a doctor about my feelings, and he said, "Never let yourself be psychoanalyzed; don't take the machine apart that makes you write. You might not put it back together again. You are lucky if you can make use of the hurts and sensitivities of childhood." Maybe I have.

You experience a lot of extremities in writing. Insomnia, restless nights, nerves, guilt. Sometimes I get tired of looking at things with a third eye, a writer's eye. When you are writing, you are constantly looking, looking, and it becomes compulsive. In many ways writing is a gift that is not always a gift, like the fade, perhaps. Some days I soar. On days that I don't put something down on paper, I feel as if I have committed a sin. Of course, I might have been sensitive to all these things without being a writer. That is terrible to contemplate. Fortunately, I can put all my sensibilities to work in books like *Fade.*

Publishers Weekly

SOURCE: A review of *Fade,* in *Publishers Weekly,* Vol. 234, No. 14, September 30, 1988, p. 69.

Much of Cormier's fiction poses a paradox: you are most alive just as outside forces obliterate your identity. Cormier's protagonists want to be anonymous, and their wishes are fulfilled in nightmarish ways. In *Fade,* which encompasses three stories in three decades, 13-year-old Paul discovers an incredible secret gift: he can become invisible. His long-lost uncle appears, to tell Paul that each generation of the family has one fader, and to warn him of the fade's dangers. Paul, however, abuses his power and quickly learns its terrible price. Twenty-five years later, Paul, a successful writer, confronts the next fader, his abused nephew Ozzie, whose power is pure vengeance. And 25 years after that, in 1988, Paul's distant cousin Susan, also a writer, reads his amazing story, and must decide if Paul's memoir is fact or fiction.

Fade is an allegory of the writer's life. Paul's actions stem from his compulsion to understand the behavior of the people around him; Susan's questions and her awful dilemma, which concludes the book, result from her near-pathological writer's focus on other persons, a purpose her unreachable late cousin serves well. Omniscient power—Paul's invisibility and Susan's access to his unpublished work—leads to identity-consuming responsibility. At its best, *Fade* is an examination of the writer's urge to lose identity and become purely an observer. As in all Cormier's novels, the protagonists are ciphers whose only affirming action seems to be to assert, however briefly, that they exist.

The story is gripping, even when it approaches melodrama, and Cormier concentrates on each action's inner meaning. *Fade* works better as allegory than as fantasy; this is Cormier's most complex, artful work. He seems to challenge himself as a writer, and in doing so, offers a respectful challenge to his readers. Through him, they will discover the extremes of behavior in the quietest human soul.

Robert E. Unsworth

SOURCE: A review of *Fade,* in *School Library Journal,* Vol. 35, No. 2, October, 1988, p. 160.

Those who find Cormier's novels bleak, dark, disturbing, and violent will not be disappointed with his latest. And true to his past, he has given readers a story with more twists and turns than a mile of concertina wire. The first half is set in Frenchtown, a working-class section of a Massachusetts town. The time is the 1930s, and the evocation of life among the French-Canadians (with marvelous names like Omer LaBatt and Rudolphe Toubert), who toiled in sweatshops where celluloid combs were made, is the best thing about the novel. Not that the story line doesn't work. Cormier uses an old device that guarantees attention—a lead character who can make himself invisible. The rules for fading are as complicated as a missile defense treaty. Paul Moreaux is the teenage fader who narrates the first section, an autobiographical account written after he has become a famous novelist. Readers learn early on that there is a grim side to this gift of fading and that Cormier intends it to represent a potentially evil force within us all. Subsequent sections include a narration by a present-day female cousin, which throws into question the truth of the entire first section, and a concluding section that features another cousin who can fade but who is certainly mad and possibly possessed. So the novel has a bit of many things: magic, murder, mystery, history, romance, diabolical possession, sex (not a lot, but what there is is explicit), and even a touch of incest. The character of Paul is developed especially well. The story is too long, and the plot is too contrived to be taken seriously, but *Fade* is riveting enough to be appreciated by Cormier fans.

D. A. Young

SOURCE: A review of *Fade,* in *The Junior Bookshelf,* Vol. 52, No. 6, December, 1988, p. 299.

Robert Cormier has taken a traditional theme—the fabled magic cloak of invisibility—tied it in knots, twirled it round before our very eyes and, like the brilliant conjuror he is, left us wondering if we know what really happened. As happens in all the best stories such magical gifts bring their owners not the hoped for benefits but a string of disasters.

It would seem that the gift for 'fading' is passed down in the Moreaux family from uncle to nephew. The problem is which nephew. A strange set of circumstances always seems to bring about a meeting when the ability to 'fade' is making itself felt in the life of the nephew. The uncle is able to explain and warn of the consequences—sometimes in time and sometimes too late.

In 1938 Paul Moreaux uses it to satisfy his fourteen-year-old preoccupation with the charms of the opposite sex and commit a murder. In 1963 Ozzie destroys his brutal step-father with a rain of hammer blows.

At this point we are informed that the evidence for these violent events and indeed the phenomenon of 'fading' itself is from a manuscript by Paul Moreaux who grew up to be a famous writer. The manuscript reaches his literary agent some years after his death. Is it autobiographical or just another example of his brilliant imagination? Investigations are carried out but are inconclusive. The literary agent decides the MS is fiction but the reader may think otherwise.

This remarkable novel is presented in the manner of a series of Chinese boxes and confusing voices. The cleverly convoluted plot with its jolts and sudden changes of direction will appeal to readers who are prepared to live with uncertainty and enjoy the tricks played upon them by the author. The writing is compelling enough to guarantee the turning of pages in the hope of discovering what it is really about. It is such a treat for the experienced reader that it would be a pity for it to languish on a shelf where adults do not normally browse. This is clearly a case for both children's and adult sections to shelve their own copy. I think I know which will be the most popular.

Janet R. Mura

SOURCE: A review of *Fade,* in *Voice of Youth Advocates,* Vol. 11, No. 5, December, 1988, pp. 235-36.

First, what I disliked was the cover. It is a close-up of a young boy's face, he could be as young as ten or 11, and this is not the intended audience.

Now, for the good stuff. It is 1938 and Paul Moreaux, an average 13 year old of French-Canadian background, thinks his family is very ordinary and average (except for Uncle Adelard). But, into this ordinary life come feelings that are unaccountable and inexplicable. Uncle Adelard arrives to explain that Paul has inherited the ability to "fade," to become invisible. Paul learns that this gift/curse passes from uncle to nephew and that the uncle can always tell which nephew by a certain glowing of the skin and the feeling that someone is calling for them. This ability comes when wanted, but fading, also, comes on its own volition often surprising the fader. Paul is excited and scared of this power. He learns quickly how to fade and investigates private situations, including two sexual situations, which target the book for grades 10-12. Later, after the death of his younger brother, Paul swears he will never again fade deliberately. The next chapter is set in 1988: Paul is dead, but had become a famous novelist, an eccentric who stayed away from everyone but family and refused to have his photo taken. Susan, Paul's cousin, narrates this part during her stay with Meredith, Paul's agent. Meredith has let Susan read Paul's last effort (the first part of this book) and they try to decide if it is true or just the marvelous invention of an imaginative writer. Chapter 3 takes us back to Paul and his search for the gifted/cursed nephew and what happens when he finds him. The last chapter returns to 1988 with Susan still questioning herself while reading a newspaper story about a young man seen disappearing.

This is a wonderful story, the characters reach out and touch you. They seem like acquaintances who affect your life. Cormier takes situations and makes them believable and always with endings that ring true. Paul aroused the same feelings in me that Adam Farmer did in *I Am the Cheese*. This is not a depressing novel, it is a thought-provoking one. Teens will enjoy.

Ann A. Flowers

SOURCE: A review of *Fade,* in *The Horn Book Magazine,* Vol. LXV, No. 1, January, 1989, p. 77.

In a book that feels like a nostalgic memoir in the beginning and a Greek tragedy in the end, we follow the destiny of Paul Moreaux, a French-Canadian boy living in a mill town in Massachusetts. Paul seems to be an ordinary boy, living in a well-defined milieu, where the adults work in the mill manufacturing celluloid objects under terrible working conditions and the children go to parochial school. He is a member of an extended family with five siblings and numerous aunts and uncles. He suffers from a confusing and mortifying sexual attraction to his Aunt Rosanna and is intrigued by the family mystery of why his uncle Adelard fails to appear in a photograph when he is known to be present. Adelard has always taken a surprising interest in Paul; when Paul is about thirteen Adelard tells him why. Adelard is a "fader," a person who can become invisible at will and sometimes unexpectedly—a family trait that passes from generation to generation. Paul is the new "fader," a fact that explains some heretofore puzzling episodes in his

life. Adelard warns Paul that the fade will cause complications and disappointments, that it is a difficult burden to bear. When Paul cautiously tries out his fade, he observes his Aunt Rosanna going to a distasteful assignation. Finally, while in a fade, Paul accidentally kills the small-town crook responsible for his Aunt Rosanna's unhappiness and for his father's injuries during a violent strike. He determines never to fade voluntarily again and is forced to live a discreet and quiet life, which severely restricts him when he becomes a famous novelist. After his death his distant cousin Susan finds the manuscript in which Paul tells about his life and discovers another manuscript telling further adventures with his sister's illegitimate son, Ozzie, who has inherited the fade. Ozzie, a sadly abused child, uses his fading ability to avenge all the misery he has undergone and has become crazed and a killer on a rampage. Paul is forced to kill Ozzie to save his own life. Susan is in doubt as to whether Paul's story is true but is horrified at the end of the manuscript to find newspaper stories indicating the existence of a new fader. The form of the novel is rather complex, with four narratives—Paul's, Ozzie's, and two of Susan's—all doubling back on each other. There is a certain ambiguity in the meaning of the novel. Perhaps we are meant to understand that extraordinary abilities, good or bad, always bring unhappiness and even exclusion from normal life. But the story itself is gripping, leading every reader to imagine what he or she would do with such an ability, and the factory-town setting is permeated with an atmosphere of gritty struggle and gray hopelessness that is very realistic. Despite the violence and overt sexual episodes, the book is another thought-provoking and endlessly debatable novel by an outstanding author.

OTHER BELLS RING FOR US TO RING (1990; British edition as *Darcy*)

Mary M. Burns

SOURCE: A review of *Other Bells for Us to Ring,* in *The Horn Book Magazine,* Vol. LXVI, No. 6, November, 1990, pp. 742-43.

Although intended for a younger audience than others of his works, such as *The Chocolate War* and *Fade,* this latest of Cormier's books is no less thought-provoking, no less intense in its emotional impact, no less remarkable for carefully honed phrases and an unfailing sense of the right detail to convey an idea—the inspired use of Kenneth Patchen's haunting poem "At the New Year" as a preface and as the source for the title, for example. The pre-World War II poem sets tone and theme for the chapters that follow and reverberates like a descant in the development of plot and characters. The narrator is eleven-year-old Darcy Webster, newly transplanted to Frenchtown "in a lonesome place called Monument near Fort Delta in Massachusetts." Because of the Depression, Darcy's family has never stayed long enough in any one place for her to put down roots. But now the United States has moved from the throes of the Depression into World War II, and her father has enlisted in the army. Neither French-Canadian nor Roman Catholic, Darcy feels isolated until she meets Kathleen Mary O'Hara, also an outsider in the tightly knit community. Daring, iconoclastic, and, like Darcy, a lover of poetry, Kathleen Mary turns daily life into a series of adventures, particularly with her intriguing interpretation of Catholic rituals—an interpretation filtered through her own vivid imagination. Her descriptions of organizations such as the Children of Mary, of the dire consequences attending the eating of meat on Friday, and of the nuns as "brides of Christ" both mystify and enthrall the fascinated Darcy. But then Kathleen Mary impulsively sprinkles her friend with holy water and declares that she is now a Catholic—"forever and ever, world without end, Amen." Dismayed, Darcy tries to resolve the dilemma. Must she now follow Catholic practices? Could a few drops of water have so irrevocable an effect? But she has to act alone, for Kathleen Mary unexpectedly disappears after a serious family altercation, failing to honor the promise that she would never desert her friend. And then Darcy's gentle, haunted father is reported missing in action. Recalling Kathleen Mary's comments about an elderly nun whose prayers were said to bring miracles, Darcy turns to this unexpected source of comfort and learns the true nature of religion, love, and prayer. And indeed there is a miracle—not exactly what Darcy had expected, but nonetheless an answer, marking her transition into adolescence. The bittersweet ending is both aesthetically and emotionally satisfying. Like Patricia MacLachlan's *Sarah, Plain and Tall,* this is a transcendent, multi-layered story that defies simplistic categorization by the age of the audience. It is truly one of those rare and brilliant gems for all seasons and for all those who would be possessed by its honest poignancy and superb craftsmanship.

Janice M. Del Negro

SOURCE: A review of *Other Bells for Us to Ring,* in *School Library Journal,* Vol. 36, No. 11, November, 1990, p. 137.

Darcy is having a tough time. Her father is missing in action, her mother retreats into migraines and silence, and her best friend Kathleen Mary disappears overnight. Also, Darcy, a Unitarian, has a crisis of faith that she attempts to resolve with a secret visit to an elderly, miracle-wielding Catholic nun. While Cormier effectively evokes the streets and tenements of Darcy's World War II Frenchtown, the characters he places there never come to life. Flat and two-dimensional, they fail to engage readers' sensibilities. The most "alive" vignettes in this low-key title are the most sensational—the suicide leap of a disturbed young woman and the violent outbursts of Kathleen Mary's alcoholic father stand out with shocking clarity. The least affecting moments are those that are supposed to be the most touching; Darcy's visit with the elderly, dying nun and the return of her father are so understated they elicit little or no sympathetic response. As Darcy's voice does not mesh with her char-

acterization as an 11-year-old innocent, it is never bright enough to light the dark environs in which Cormier places her. The news of Kathleen Mary's death and the "miracle of the bells" that accompanies it have no spiritual resonance—there is little in the characterization or plot to make this Christmas miracle real for readers. Kathleen Mary's climactic miracle message to Darcy is unfortunately unbelievable, and, symptomatic of this book, without emotional impact.

Kirkus Reviews

SOURCE: A review of *Other Bells for Us to Ring,* in *Kirkus Reviews,* Vol. LVIII, No. 22, November 15, 1990, pp. 1599-600.

By the author of *The Chocolate War* (1974) and other YA fiction renowned for its fiercely astringent posing of tough questions, a gentler story for younger children, depicting a lonely 11-year-old's qualms and wonderment concerning her neighbors' Catholicism.

Darcy's father is a rolling stone; shy Darcy has never had a chance to make friends. "Delta," Massachusetts, where the army has now assigned her father, is even more isolating: the neighbors are mostly "Canucks," Catholics who speak only French. Then Irish Kathleen Mary makes Darcy her best friend, insists that she demonstrate her approaching adulthood by giving away the doll that has long been Darcy's only confidante, earnestly instructs Unitarian Darcy on Catholic observances and the perils of sin, privately sprinkles her with holy water and declares her a Catholic—and then disappears forever with her deeply troubled family, leaving Darcy to puzzle about her own status and beliefs during a time when her father is declared missing in action in WW II and her mother, always frail and withdrawn, is exhausted by factory work. A saintly old nun helps Darcy to understand that, eclipsing denomination, "Loving God is the first thing."

Superbly crafted, the story concludes with some trademark Cormier ambivalences: Though Darcy is the only one to hear a glorious peal of bells on Christmas Eve, and though Dad's safety is reported, by miraculous-seeming coincidence, just as Sister Angela prays for him, Kathleen's story has a tragic end that Darcy is unable to share with her reserved parents. How Darcy will deal with these conflicting experiences is left open— a disturbing but realistic conclusion to a book remarkable for its evocation of the milieu and anxieties of the era. [Deborah Kogan] Ray's soft-pencil illustrations beautifully reflect the story's pensive mood. A provocative look at the meaning of belief.

Patty Campbell

SOURCE: A review of *Other Bells for Us to Ring,* in *The Five Owls,* Vol. V, No. 3, January-February, 1991, p. 57.

A new book from Robert Cormier is always a surprise package. Now, following the monumental intricacies of *Fade,* this finest of all young adult novelists has written a gentle, charming novella ostensibly for middle readers. Although the large type and many illustrations of *Other Bells for Us to Ring* do seem aimed at middle grades, the nostalgia of its World War II home front setting and the darkness of its mystic conclusion would also seem to point to that sometimes imaginary readership designated by publishers as all ages.

Those familiar with Cormier's work will recognize the setting in Monument, New England, among the Frenchtown tenements. Although this is the first time that Cormier has written for this age level or used such a young female protagonist, the tone is not entirely new. It is reminiscent of the style of his earlier short stories, but while in those pieces he occasionally teetered on the brink of sentimentality, here the sweetness is balanced and given depth by the shadowing of his dark vision.

Desperately worried about her father, who is missing in action overseas, eleven-year-old Darcy struggles to find a way to ask God for help. Her best friend, spunky redheaded Kathleen Mary O'Hara, is an Irish Catholic, and her naive explanations of the practices of that faith both fascinate and repel Unitarian Darcy. When Kathleen Mary sprinkles her with holy water in the church vestibule and declares her a Catholic, Darcy runs home in horror and watches herself worriedly for "Catholic symptoms." In the end the ancient nun Sister Angela helps her to understand that loving God is all that matters, in spite of the hard truth that miracles sometimes happen but sometimes are denied—an insight that helps Darcy to accept both the miraculous return of her father and the tragic death of Kathleen Mary.

Spiritual questioning is rare as a theme in fiction for young people, although the experience is nearly universal with adolescents. In clumsier hands, this story might have been a religious tract, but Cormier's delicate skill has made it a tender and sometimes funny book that belies his reputation for hopelessness.

Susan Derren

SOURCE: A review of *Other Bells for Us to Ring,* in *Quill and Quire,* Vol. 57, No. 2, February, 1991, p. 25.

Robert Cormier's novels are notable for their darkness, their depth, and their male protagonists. His newest, *Other Bells for Us to Ring,* is different. It has been written for a younger audience, perhaps of the same age as its 11-year-old heroine, Darcy Webster, and while it has Cormier's characteristic depth and certainly deals with dark themes, its treatment of these themes results in a piece of fiction that is suffused with light. This is a wonderful book, and though less controversial than its predecessors, it could be Cormier's most lasting achievement.

Darcy Webster tells her story, which takes place after the Americans have entered the Second World War, in a bleak town in Massachusetts populated largely by French Canadians and poor Irish. Darcy, an only child, and her parents have wandered around a lot and have ended up in Frenchtown, where, as she says, "Kathleen Mary O'Hara altered the events of my life when she sprinkled me with holy water in the vestibule of St. Brendan's and pronounced those terrible words: 'Now you're a Catholic, Darcy Webster. Forever and ever, world without end, Amen.'" To the nominally Unitarian Darcy this baptism feels like an imprecation, one that fills her with a kind of holy terror. But Catholicism also holds out the potential for solace and miracles, and Darcy needs both when her father is pronounced missing in action and her friend Kathleen Mary O'Hara unaccountably disappears. With both longing and dread, Darcy goes to an old nun; at her side, she learns what it is to believe and what it is possible to know—at any age—of love, faith, and miracles.

Kenneth Patchen's poem "At the New Year," positioned opposite the opening page of the novel, informs everything that follows. The poem is an incantation both plain and beautiful; it introduces and mirrors a novel that is plainspoken, authentic, deep, and lovely. What a pleasure to have a book for this age group that achieves so much.

WE ALL FALL DOWN (1991)

Michael Cart

SOURCE: A review of *We All Fall Down,* in *School Library Journal,* Vol. 37, No. 9, September, 1991, pp. 277-78.

After the benignities of his last novel, *Other Bells for Us to Ring,* Cormier returns to the gritty form that made him famous. His new novel is sure, accordingly, to inflame the same parental passions and excite the same critical controversies that visited the publication of *The Chocolate War* (1974) and *After the First Death* (1979). It is also sure—like those books—to find a devoted following among the kids themselves, who will recognize and embrace the authenticity of the achingly awful adolescent world that Cormier has created. It is a world in which emotions are raw, evil exists, and violence—both studied and offhand—is an everyday occurrence. The book begins, in fact, with overt violence—the trashing of a suburban house by a group of teenage boys—and ends with a more subtle kind of violence—the trashing of love and the destruction of hope. If this looks like familiar territory, look again. Cormier is gingerly exploring some new terrain here, both literally (by moving his setting from the familiar confines of Monument to the neighboring community of Burnside) and figuratively (by counterbalancing the emotional aridity of evil with a genuinely moving and nurturing love story). More familiar territory is a suspenseful subplot involving a character called "The Avenger," whose goal is to exact revenge for the trashing. Although it certainly will keep readers turning the pages, this may be the weaker part of the novel, particularly its resolution, which seems somewhat glib. Other considerations, however, of character, setting, and the complexity of family interrelationships are richly realized. And the overriding thematic treatment of the dialectics between good and evil and free will vs. predestination is sure to stimulate discussion and vigorous dialectic of its own.

Betsy Hearne

SOURCE: A review of *We All Fall Down,* in *Bulletin of the Center for Children's Books,* Vol. 45, No. 2, October, 1991, p. 35.

"They entered the house at 9:02 p.m. on the evening of April Fools' Day. In the next forty-nine minutes, they shit on the floors and pissed on the walls and trashed their way through the seven-room Cape Cod cottage." So begins this story about revenge and victims of revenge, about the violence of misdirected anger and its effects on random targets. After the trashing, the four boys assault fourteen-year-old Karen Jerome, coming home early from a friend's. As she lies in a coma, her sister Jane falls in love with Buddy, one of the unidentified vandals, who uses gin to ease the pain of his parents' divorce. Stalking them all is The Avenger, a secret witness determined to dispose of the villains the same way he murdered a classmate and his own grandfather. The real villains here seem to be fathers: Buddy's father, who deserts his family and neglects his embittered son; the father whose disappearance seems to have left The Avenger a psychotic killer; gang leader Harry's father, who, by paying all the damages his son inflicts, buys off publicity. Harry is an Archie-like character—right out of *The Chocolate War.* In true thriller tradition, each character here has a role to fulfill, no more and no less, and each does it with pared-down efficiency. The action is compelling enough to buoy readers across frequent transitions in point of view, which in fact serve to heighten the suspense. Signature Cormier, with calculated impact, sinister implications, and inevitable appeal.

Nancy Vasilakis

SOURCE: A review of *We All Fall Down,* in *The Horn Book Magazine,* Vol. LXVII, No. 6, November, 1991, pp. 742-43.

In the bold and unsentimental style for which he is so well known, Robert Cormier has written a gripping page-turner told from the point of view of three disparate characters whose lives converge in violent confrontations. All of them are introduced in the riveting first pages of the novel. Buddy Walker is one of four boys who vandalize a suburban house and attack fourteen-year-old Karen Jerome. The second major character is Karen's older sister, Jane, whose lucid, intelligent voice

serves as the novel's moral center. And the third is the mysterious Avenger. Obviously psychotic, this unidentified character has committed murder twice in his life, one of his victims his own grandfather. He witnesses the trashing and sets out to avenge Jane, for whom he feels a voyeuristic fascination—attracted by her wholesomeness, disturbed by her sexuality. The black hole down which the novelist draws the reader is both repellent and enthralling. Buddy has turned to alcohol to numb the pain of his parents' impending divorce and long years of paternal neglect. His addiction leaves him vulnerable to the machinations of Harry Flowers, a corrupting evil force much as Archie was in *The Chocolate War.* When Buddy and Jane meet and fall in love, Buddy cannot muster the courage to admit his participation in the vandalism of her home. A sense of doom descends, for violent and bleak as it is, the world of Cormier's novel is a moral one. The Avenger, feeling betrayed, turns on Jane and abducts her. Unlike Buddy, however, Jane is not a helpless victim, even when bound and confronted by a madman with a knife. Although Cormier clearly understands that he is writing for an audience reared on the novels of Stephen King, this sensationalistic episode with the killer clouds over some important issues raised in the novel—questions of the dissolution of family and societal violence, of personal responsibility and guilt. The tender love story between Jane and Buddy is a sweet interlude in the midst of unflinching revelations. And the final scene, when the reader learns for certain that Jane is saved and Buddy doomed, leaves an unforgettable impression.

D. A. Young

SOURCE: A review of *We All Fall Down,* in *The Junior Bookshelf,* Vol. 56, No. 5, October, 1992, pp. 214-15.

Harry Flowers, a senior at Wickburg Regional and son of the influential architect Winston Flowers, likes to set up for himself and his fellow bloods 'a bit of fun'. He gains access to the Jerome house when the family are out where he and his mates set out to vandalise the place. They smash all that is breakable, vomit in a bedroom and pee on the walls. Karen, the 14-year-old daughter, returns in the midst of this chaos and is set upon with intent to rape but escapes to be pushed down the flight of steps to the cellar resulting in a coma lasting to the end of the book.

The first half of the book deals with the traumatic effect on the Jerome family of this meaningless and motiveless intrusion of violence into their hitherto normal American lives. Sixteen-year-old Jane bears the brunt of the burden. Her younger brother has nightmares and parents struggle with the redecoration of the house and the daily attendance at the hospital where Karen lies unconscious in the Intensive Care Unit. We meet also Buddy Walker, the desperately unhappy victim of a broken marriage, in the grip of alcoholism and the latest addition to Harry's group of bloods who wreaked havoc on the Jerome house. Then there is the mysterious "eleven-year-old Avenger" responsible, it seems, for the undetected murders of a school bully and his grandfather, who is playing peeping Tom in the Jerome's garden and is a witness to the vandalism. It is some way through the story before the reader picks up the connection between the Avenger and Mickey Stallings—otherwise known as Mickey Looney, the local simpleton, odd job man and general do-gooder for all and sundry concealing a psychotic killer. Harry is tracked down as the perpetrator of the damage but a combination of lies, trickery and family influence gets him off with probation and manages to keep his 'bloods' out of the messy business.

In the second part of the book we read of the unlikely but intense love affair between Buddy and Jane who is totally ignorant of Buddy's part in Harry's 'little bit of fun'. Only when 'the Avenger' steps in and attempts his third murder does Jane learn the truth about Buddy. 'The Avenger' in a fit of jealousy lures Jane into a lonely hut where he chloroforms her, trusses her in a chair and explains why she must die for loving the boy who vandalised her home. She talks fast and furiously to The Avenger/Mickey until he turns the knife upon himself and her rescuers arrive.

Robert Cormier continues his dalliance with the evil side of human nature. His young adults are more adult than young. They are over the threshold of innocence and are fully fledged participants in the fallen world of adult selfishness, vandalism, violence, lies and deceit. The vivid portrayal of the sleazy side of human nature allied with the convolutions of the tightly drawn plot makes riveting reading and the interest is held throughout. The world Robert Cormier creates is full of fascinating detail and the characterisation is brilliantly presented. It just so happens to be a world closer to the cynicism of the old than the optimism of the young and in which the book's title seems only too true.

📖 *TUNES FOR BEARS TO DANCE TO* (1992)

Hazel Rochman

SOURCE: A review of *Tunes for Bears to Dance To,* in *Booklist,* Vol. 88, No. 20, June 15, 1992, p. 1825.

In a stark morality tale set in a gray Massachusetts town after World War II, 11-year-old Henry is tempted, corrupted, and then redeemed. The "snake" is a racist grocer, Mr. Hairston, for whom Henry works after school, glad for the money since his depressed father can't get a job. At the same time, Henry gets close to a Holocaust survivor, Mr. Levine, who's carving a miniature village out of wood, recreating the home the Nazis destroyed. The climax comes when the diabolical grocer threatens and bribes Henry to destroy the model village. Cormier's a compelling storyteller, and the pace is inexorable. Will Henry "follow orders"? Will he smash Mr. Levine's world in a second holocaust? ("Do it," the grocer whispered.) Since Archie in *The Chocolate War,* Cormier has been interested in satanic figures of pure,

calculating evil. But the conflict here is set up for the message. Unlike Slepian's *Risk 'n' Roses,* where the girl is tempted to hurt a Holocaust survivor, Cormier doesn't root corruption in personality. Not only is the bad guy dehumanized, but so is the victim. We're told Mr. Levine is crazy, but we see only gentleness, innocence, creativity—a survivor drawn with such sweet reverence that he's not a person.

Roger Sutton

SOURCE: A review of *Tunes for Bears to Dance To,* in *Bulletin of the Center for Children's Books,* Vol. 46, No. 1, September, 1992, p. 8.

Henry, eleven, longs to give his dead older brother a fitting marker for his grave, but since Eddie died last year, their father, depressed, has been unable to work and their mother barely makes enough money for the family to get by. But the bigoted, evil grocer Mr. Hairston promises Henry the gravestone and more if he will perform one task: destroying an exquisite toy village carved by Mr. Levine, a refugee of the Holocaust. Henry has befriended the old man, so Hairston's proposal should engender a profound dilemma as well as a great temptation; unfortunately, Cormier stacks his story in a way that allows little real examination of ethical questions. Hairston is a monster who hates all foreigners and beats his daughter Doris; his evil is unrelieved and unreal, his smile "like the smile on a Halloween mask." Henry never has to make a decision about wrecking the woodcarvings: at the moment of truth, Henry holding mallet high, a rat runs over his foot and turns a moral quandary into a slapstick accident. The compression of evils—"*Deliver us from evil.* From Hitler, yes, from a grocer too"—does justice to neither, and Hairston's fadeaway from ogre to coward ("Your father's weak, Doris. And he's afraid") dilutes both the character and the theme. This novel is written in a simpler style (bar the title, an elliptical quote from Flaubert) and at a younger reading level than most of Cormier's other books, and the suspenseful storytelling may pull readers to their own consideration of the questions Henry faces. Let's hope they know that the answers aren't so easy.

Ruth Cline

SOURCE: A review of *Tunes for Bears to Dance To,* in *Voice of Youth Advocates,* Vol. 15, No. 4, October, 1992, p. 222.

In true Cormier style, the reader is introduced in a quiet way to the neighborhood grocery store run by Mr. Hairston, who appears to have an interest in Henry, the young boy who works for him. Henry is trying to deal with the sadness and loneliness in his family life, including his father's depression over his son Eddie's accidental death and their poverty which denies even a grave marker. Henry's mother works hard hours at a diner and Henry contributes his pay to help the family. Because they moved from Frenchtown after Eddie's fatal accident, they have no friends or support group. Mr. Hairston is an evil man who tries to use his money and position to get Henry to do something he knows is wrong. Henry's conscience nags him and even though the event was an accident rather than an intentional act, Henry is able to live with himself only by refusing to take the "rewards" that Mr. Hairston promised him. The family moves back to Frenchtown in the end and the reader feels there is some optimism about their future.

A powerful book for discussion with readers of all ages. Henry's loss of innocence is a dramatic event, but how he reacts to this event is thought-provoking. Readers should consider what alternatives were available to Henry, both before the event occurred and its aftermath. How do people use power? Can we buy morality? The use of prayer, the insidious results of child abuse, and the effect of evil on good are topics appropriate to any grade level.

D. A. Young

SOURCE: A review of *Tunes for Bears to Dance To,* in *The Junior Bookshelf,* Vol. 57, No. 4, August, 1993, p. 161.

One does not have to turn many pages of a story by Robert Cormier before the unmistakable whiff of sulphurous fumes can be detected. He has an enormous capacity for evoking the positive force of evil. *Tunes for Bears to Dance To* may be short but it is a powerful distillation of his favourite theme—the corruption of the innocent.

The innocent in this case is eleven year old Henry. It is the sudden death of Eddie, his brother, which has traumatised the family. His father is swallowed up in his sorrow. They moved house in an effort to get back to normality, but memories of Eddie still flood in incessantly. Henry has made the acquaintance of Mr. Levine who lived in a village devastated by the Nazis and turned into a concentration camp. Scarred by this bitter experience his therapy is to work away at creating a model of the one-time happy village in the municipal Art and Craft Centre. It wins the First Prize at the City Hall Exhibition.

But Henry also works after school in the Corner Market for Mr. Hairston who is charming to his customers when he serves them but turns to character assassination once they are out of earshot. Henry sometimes gets a glimpse of Doris whose sad eyes and bruised body hints at rough treatment from Mr. Hairston, her father.

Can Mr. Hairston persuade eleven year old Henry to destroy his friend's model village just as the Nazis destroyed the real village all those years ago? The persuasive tongue of the serpent is once more at work. The resolution of this frightening dilemma makes compulsive reading.

Robert Cormier must surely write to please himself. His central character may be eleven years old but his theme adult. What is it in human nature which makes some people so determined to drag the innocent down to their own squalor? Why do we need so often to pray that we be not led into temptation and be delivered from evil?

This is a book more suitable to provoke discussion at the sixth form level than be passed round a class of eleven year old children without comment.

IN THE MIDDLE OF THE NIGHT (1995)

Roger Sutton

SOURCE: A review of *In the Middle of the Night,* in *Bulletin of the Center for Children's Books,* Vol. 48, No. 9, May, 1995, p. 302.

In three narrative threads that twist into each other, a woman nurses her rage over a childhood accident that "killed" her many years ago, a man still wrestles with his guilt over that tragic event, and his son Denny finds himself drawn into the pain of them both. Lulu was thought dead after the balcony in the Globe Theater crashed to the ground (and killed twenty-two children), but, revived by doctors, she lived again to focus her revenge on the boy she thought responsible: John Paul, a teen-aged usher who had been sent up to the balcony to investigate strange noises and who inadvertently started a fire when he lit a match for light. Despite John Paul's official exoneration, Lulu has been tormenting him with phone calls and letters ever since, and Denny has grown up with the family rule that he must never answer the telephone. One day, though, as the twenty-fifth anniversary of the tragedy approaches, he cannot resist, and Lulu finds a new victim for her rage. Morally, this is less complicated than much of Cormier's work and in fact less complicated than the book seems to want to be: while Lulu, John Paul, and Denny each wrestle with demons, their struggles fail to parallel or meet on any plane more than the narrative. Lulu's fear of the death she got a glimpse of, Jean Paul's private atonement, Denny's fear of involvement with anything that might be trouble—each is compelling, but none have enough to do with one another. As far as storytelling goes, though, it's classic Cormier. Relatively speaking, however, it's *easy* Cormier, and kids who find themselves at a loss with the narrative intricacies of *After the First Death* or *Fade* should have no trouble following the plot and its suspenseful turns.

Joel Shoemaker

SOURCE: A review of *In the Middle of the Night,* in *School Library Journal,* Vol. 41, No. 5, May, 1995, p. 118.

When a balcony collapsed during a special magic show in a rundown, neighborhood movie theater, 22 disadvantaged children died. Although he was never charged with any wrongdoing, John Paul Colbert, who was 16 at the time, was working as an usher and accidentally caused a fire that contributed to the tragedy. He resolutely refused to comment on what happened even after the theater's owner committed suicide and the public clamored for someone to be held responsible. Many of the victims' relatives blamed John Paul for the incident and tormented him into adulthood. Years later, his son Denny, now 16, begins to receive the same harassing phone calls. Resentful of his father's long passivity, Denny resolves not to follow in the man's footsteps. Intersecting plot lines rush together in an exciting climax that reveals the relationships between some key characters. Parallel in plot elements and themes to Cormier's previous YA titles, especially *We All Fall Down* (1993) and *Tunes for Bears to Dance To* (1992), this book seems more accessible, especially to horror/mystery fans. While grim and terrifying in some respects, this is not, in toto, a bleak novel. Its style is reminiscent of Jay Bennett's, with fairly long passages of dialogue that are heavy with foreshadowing. Unresolved details detract only slightly from the power of the prose to address the painful process of maturing and of beginning to understand and accept adult roles. Readers experience several time shifts and must discern the identity of several narrative voices while grappling with complex themes concerning tragedy, guilt, responsibility, and expiation. YAs willing to invest some intellectual effort will be amply rewarded by this sophisticated psychological thriller.

Patty Campbell

SOURCE: "The Sand in the Oyster," in *The Horn Book Magazine,* Vol. LXXI, No. 3, May-June, 1995, pp. 365-69.

A new book by Robert Cormier is an exciting event—both for readers and for critics. What dreadful happenings and dark corners of the mind will he explore this time, and how will he lead us, protesting all the way, to another grim but utterly inevitable conclusion? For readers, there is the pure joy of abandonment to a gripping story, and for critics, the even purer pleasure of peeling the plot down to its gleaming bones of structure and plucking out the metaphors and hidden resonances.

In the Middle of the Night is Robert Cormier's devastating new study of the nature of guilt. With Cormier there is always the precipitating event, and in this case it was the Boston Coconut Grove fire of 1942, in which 490 people were burned to death in an overcrowded nightclub. A busboy was at first blamed for lighting a match, but he was later exonerated. As Cormier watched the newspaper re-creations of this disaster each year on its anniversary, a "what if" grew in his mind. What if that boy had grown up and had a son? How would the annual orgies of finger pointing and the assumption of guilt affect their lives? And what if it had been not a nightclub full of adults but a theater full of little children? What if the balcony collapsed on them just before

the fire broke out? What if a young usher had been sent up to the balcony without his flashlight to investigate the strange creaking noises, and had lit a match, burnt his fingers, and dropped the matchbook just as the balcony lurched and made a screeching groan like a ship pulling away from the dock?

But Cormier is too subtle to make the disaster the center of his novel. Although the story of the catastrophe is told three times—once in a prologue, by two children, Dave and Lulu; once by John Paul, the young usher; and once, briefly, many years later, by John Paul's wife—it is the far more penetrating drama of John Paul's guilt that holds center stage. The torturing nature of this guilt is its ambiguity: "Am I to blame?" he asks himself in the hospital afterwards. "Did I do something wrong?" And although it is obvious that the fire did not cause the collapse, and a court clears him of responsibility almost immediately, he continues to probe his conscience.

Cormier is always most interested in sins of omission, and so John Paul almost eagerly seeks guilt by wondering if he should have overcome his fear of the rats and spiders to explore the strange noises in the balcony earlier; if he should have pressured the owner to do something to repair it. The public, too, is eager to blame him, even though he has been officially cleared, and after the theater owner's suicide, there is no scapegoat left but John Paul. Year after year, there are hate letters and anonymous phone calls, no matter how often the family moves, and eventually he comes to accept them as his penance.

Denny, John Paul's son, has grown up against this background of silent guilt, often seeing his father listening quietly to hate phone calls in the middle of the night. At school he is uninvolved, both because the family has moved so often and because he fears taunts about his father's crime. One day, in a scene that recalls Emile's attack on a nonresistant Jerry in *Beyond the Chocolate War,* John Paul sees a boy being pushed around by three others and accepting their blows with complete passivity. Later, the boy explains, "I didn't figure I was the victim that day. They were." Denny has the key to his father's behavior, and when he confronts him, John Paul's explanation reveals the Christlike nature of his suffering: "The pain stays, and it has to go someplace. It comes to me. . . . So. Let them use the telephone, let them write me letters. Let them accuse me. . . . It makes them feel better. I offer myself up to them."

The question, of course, is whether John Paul is a positive or a negative example. Guilt must be accepted to exist, and there is something unhealthy in his pursuit of it in the face of facts. In a life spent drenched in guilt, the sins of the father have been visited upon the son: their family life is hidden and silent, and Denny has learned not to reach out or intervene. He respects his father's commitment to nonviolence and says "no comment" to the reporter who wishes to clear the record. Yet part of him yearns to take action, to "do *something.*" When he meets Dawn (a name that means "sunrise, full of hope" to Denny), she encourages his impulses for positive action; but in the end he rejects her for the seductiveness of another woman, Lulu, as his father has rejected life for the seductiveness of guilt. Here Cormier returns to the theme of the stifled potential of individual action against evil, a theme that he explored so effectively in *The Chocolate War* and attempted to resolve with Jerry's pacifism in *Beyond the Chocolate War.*

A second level of the story focuses on Dave and his sister Lulu, who are victims of the disaster. Lulu nearly dies, and she returns to life disabled and bitter. She and Dave grow up twisted around one another like stunted and distorted plants, and she becomes the malevolent presence who seduces Denny on the phone and finally tries to kill him as vengeance for the theater catastrophe. Lulu is one of Cormier's strangest creations. The name— and names are often the source of secrets in his work— evokes the nineteenth-century avant-garde: artists' models, modistes, the demimonde, the feverish excesses of Alban Berg's opera *Lulu.* For much of the book she is seen obliquely through Dave's eyes as an avenging fury skulking in the night, or through Denny's ears as a voluptuous voice on the telephone. In a classic case of Cormier misdirection, we are led to suppose (cleverly, we think) that Lulu has actually died and has become a voice in Dave's head, a voice that makes him disguise his own voice on the phone to entice Denny. . . . When Lulu finally does appear in the flesh, we mourn the loss of the illusion along with Denny.

The relationship between Dave and Lulu is claustrophobic, almost incestuous, and reminiscent of other pairs of too-close brothers and sisters in *Fade* and *The Bumblebee Flies Anyway.* Lulu calls Dave "Baby," and as children they reenact a scene from *Wuthering Heights,* Heathcliff carrying a dying Cathy to the window. Dave is in remission from cancer, and the wig and false teeth he wears are symbols of the false personality he presents to everyone but Lulu. She has taken care of him in his "dark days," and he takes care of her in "her own darkness."

Dave grieves that Lulu has been changed by her "death," become cold and withdrawn. She refuses to talk about her experience in the beyond until the very end, when she reveals the "glimpse of horror" that has frozen her soul and driven her mad with the desire for revenge. "A terrifying blank! Unable to think and yet aware . . . knowing that I would be like this forever, for an eternity." In a telephone interview, Cormier revealed that he actually underwent such a horrifying ordeal himself one morning three years ago when he awoke to find that his mind and vision had become like a television screen full of snow—continued awareness but with no content. It lasted less than a minute, but the memory still chills him. Ever the craftsman, he decided to use his own terror to explain Lulu's transformation.

In the Middle of the Night, like all Cormier stories, needs at least two readings. The first time through it seems rather bare and deceptively simple, although pow-erful emotions are produced in the reader. On a second reading, what originally appeared to be casual references and random phrases are now heavy and fragrant with the resonance of coming events. Every detail, every choice of wording, is there to produce a considered effect. The language is almost as clipped and spare as in *The Chocolate War,* but occasionally Cormier allows himself one of those gorgeous metaphors that gladden readers' hearts: "Small and dark and energetic, she was like a hummingbird, going sixty miles an hour while standing still."

The structure, which seems quite straightforward at first, proves inordinately complex on analysis. There are three narrators: Dave, who speaks in the first-person present tense, and Denny and John Paul, who both speak in the third-person past tense. Each chapter has only one voice, but it is immediately clear from internal clues who is speaking. The chapters are grouped into four sections and prefaced with a prologue in which Dave tells the story of the day of the catastrophe. The first section introduces Denny and the effect of his father's guilt (although we do not yet know who the father is), and in the last chapter of that section, Dave resumes the story of the aftermath of the disaster. The second section takes place in the late sixties and is told by John Paul as he remembers the events that led up to the balcony collapse, his time in the hospital, and his realization of the consequences of his guilt. The third section focuses on the effects of that guilt on Denny's life and his ambivalence about his father, and the last section concerns Lulu's telephone seduction of Denny, leading up to a dramatic scene of attempted murder and double suicide.

Cormier aficionados will find *In the Middle of the Night* very Cormieresque, not only in style and content, but in the many characteristic details and references to his life and other works. Although the story is not set in Monument, Massachusetts, where most of his previous young-adult novels take place, the city of Wickburg is familiar from *Tunes for Bears to Dance To.* As in *The Chocolate War,* there is the shy young man who meets the girl of his dreams at the bus stop. But in this story, Denny realizes "he was always drawn to impossible loves, those always out of reach," and when the girl responds to him, he rejects her in favor of a different impossible love. There are young lovers who tryst at the public library, a familiar place of comfort and refuge in times of distress. There are nurses gliding in silent hospital corridors as in *Bumblebee,* and a gray woman who personifies guilt, just as Mr. Grey personifies faceless menace in *I Am the Cheese.* There is the Jewish girl who expands Denny's horizons, a direct excerpt from Cormier's own life. There is even a sly reference to Trinity high school, when Denny sees "guys who want to take over, pushing people around, intimidating young kids. It happens at other schools, too."

But most of all there are references to old films. The disaster occurs in Cormier's place of ultimate childhood happiness—a movie theater. In it is an ornate chandelier drawn directly from the original version of *Phantom of the Opera,* a lighting fixture that is the cause of Dave and Lulu's exquisitely ironic change of seats from under its imagined danger to under the balcony's real danger. Denny names the rowdy little kids at the bus stop "Frankenstein" and "Dracula." Dave and Lulu drive up to capture Denny in "an old car, four doors, black, like a car in an old gangster movie." In their house is an empty interrogation room with "an unshaded bulb in the ceiling filling the place with naked light." And the melodramatic climax recalls a dozen old movies with the last-minute struggle over a poisoned hypodermic needle.

And, of course, there is the ending. Cormier cannot allow us the luxury of a happy conclusion even if he has set it up himself. In this case, several friends and editors pleaded with him to let Denny and Dawn go off happily together, but he held firm. "Life's just not like that," he insists. *In the Middle of the Night* is pure Cormier, a tight and spare construction of amazing complexity worthy of a place among his best works.

Gary E. Joseph

SOURCE: A review of *In the Middle of the Night,* in *Voice of Youth Advocates,* Vol. 18, No. 2, June, 1995, p. 92.

"The opposite of peace was war. Maybe that's what he wanted—a battle against whatever or whoever had thrown a shadow over his family." For Denny Colbert, the shadow had been over him for all of his sixteen years, but it was approaching twenty-five years for his father. It was his father who opened the hate mail, read the accusations in the newspapers and answered the telephone in the middle of the night. When Denny's father was sixteen years old, he had a job working as an usher at the Globe Theater, an old theater well past its prime. During the annual magic show, with an auditorium filled with children, the balcony collapsed, killing twenty-two children. When the owner of the theater committed suicide, Denny's father was the only employee left to receive the sorrow and anger of the community. So the nightmare begins, along with the accusations, pranks, and calls. Though Denny has been insulated by his father, he feels compelled to do something. Told never to answer the phone, Denny decides one day to get involved, and that decision starts a war that engulfs him in a way he could never imagine. The caller, someone injured in the accident, has decided that "the sin of the father will be visited upon the son."

Like the spider to the fly, few writers can weave a web of intrigue that captures readers as well as Robert Cormier. Superbly written, with characters well developed and a tight, fast moving plot, *In the Middle of the Night* is what you would expect in a Newbery quality book. Cormier's stories always exist on two levels, and this one is no exception. The reader is drawn in by the suspense, but it is the second level, the dark side of things, that keeps the reader hooked. Questions about life after death may raise some eyebrows, but as Cormier once said, "We don't do these kids any service by writing namby-pamby, riding-off-into-the-sunset stuff." We don't, and he didn't. A must read.

D. A. Young

SOURCE: A review of *In the Middle of the Night,* in *The Junior Bookshelf,* Vol. 59, No. 4, August, 1995, pp. 151-52.

Robert Cormier was thirty years a journalist which gave him all the time he needed to collect the hard-nosed seamy characters and their victims who proliferate in his novels.

The nub of *In the Middle of the Night* is the collapse of the balcony of the Globe Theatre in which 22 children died. John Paul Colbert at the age of 16 worked at the Globe as an usher and was investigating strange noises in the balcony at the time. The inquiry exonerated him from all responsibility but many thought otherwise. John Paul himself was haunted by the possibility that he might, in some way, have contributed to the disaster and made no attempt to defend himself from those who over the years tracked him down with persistent accusations and threats of vengeance. He changed jobs and addresses when he could but he was never able to escape from them.

Twenty-five years later, his son Denny takes up the story and becomes the target for revenge by one of the survivors. How he is lured to a place of execution and escapes by a hairsbreadth makes exciting reading.

The author does not, of course, lay out these events in a straightforward fashion. He hands readers the bits of the jigsaw and leaves them to fit the pieces together to reveal the whole picture. It may be that the technique of the storytelling will appeal to some readers more than the events or characters so depicted. The writing is as brilliant as ever. The loneliness and longing for acceptance and recognition suffered by Dennis and his father are portrayed with painful clarity.

It is a book which, by some, will be admired rather than enjoyed, touched more by November's cold wind than May's burgeoning warmth.

📖 *TENDERNESS* (1997)

Kirkus Reviews

SOURCE: A review of *Tenderness,* in *Kirkus Reviews,* Vol. LXV, No. 1, January 1, 1997, p. 57.

A serial killer; an aging cop with a hunch; an impulsive 15-year-old runaway: Three familiar characters are spun by a master of suspense into another disturbing study in emotional dysfunction.

Convicted in the less punitive juvenile court—just as he had planned—for the murder of his mother and stepfather, Eric Poole has served his three years, and is slated for release on his 18th birthday. Outwardly guileless and extremely charming, he has convinced everyone that he was a victim of abuse (with self-inflicted scars as evidence) who struck back. Only Lt. Jake Proctor, who suspects Eric in the unsolved murder of two teenage girls, is skeptical. Enter Lori, a rootless girl with scars on her wrist, a woman's body, and the memory of a clean-cut boy who was nice to her years ago. Both she and Eric are searching for "tenderness"—which means, for her, safety and respect, and for him, the fierce inner response after he holds a life in his hands and then takes it. Cormier draws the strings taut as Eric decides what to do with Lori, and Proctor watches and waits for a chance to get Eric back behind bars before he can kill again. In a devastatingly ironic climax, Lori helps Eric evade Proctor's trap, then dooms him by dying under suspicious but entirely accidental circumstances. Almost everyone here is a victim; one is a monster.

Stephanie Zvirin

SOURCE: A review of *Tenderness,* in *Booklist,* Vol. 93, No. 11, February 1, 1997, p. 935.

Cormier's latest is a mesmerizing plunge into the mind of a psychopathic teen killer that is both deeply disturbing and utterly compelling. Eighteen-year-old Eric Poole, handsome, clean cut, and with a vulnerability that plays well before the cameras, is about to be released from the juvenile facility where he has spent three years for killing his mother and stepfather, who were believed to have abused him. That he murdered his parents without provocation and is a serial killer (who sexually assaults his girl victims) is known only to Eric himself, though it is a virtual certainty as far as veteran cop Jake Proctor is concerned. When Proctor's covert endeavors to obstruct Eric's release fail, the teen walks out of the facility, glorying in his cleverness and in great anticipation of renewing his obsessive search for "tenderness." Then the chase begins, with Eric carefully avoiding controversy until he can escape to another town and Proctor anxiously watching and waiting for the young man to make a mistake. Neither villain nor cop suspects that Eric's undoing will come in the form of 15-year-old runaway Lori, who sees her own desire for affection mirrored in Eric's haunted eyes.

This edgy thriller isn't textured enough to satisfy YAs who are already reading substantial adult true-life accounts of sociopaths by authors such as Ann Rule or psychological thrillers by the likes of Ruth Rendell. There are, however, a number of intriguing psychological underpinnings to attract teens who haven't made the leap. Foremost are the murky psychosexual nuances related to Eric's fixation: his young victims have long, dark hair, just like his mother's. The suggestion of incest is strong. In fact, although Cormier deserves a lot of credit for eschewing grisly sexual specifics (even an early scene in

which Lori hitches a ride with a strange man and lets him kiss and fondle her is cleverly managed, with things set up so that the reader's imagination easily fills in most of the blanks), the sexual component here is far stronger than in Cormier's earlier books. And it factors as prominently in Lori's behavior as it does in Eric's. A victim of sexual harassment and abuse, Lori blatantly and aggressively uses her sexuality to get what she wants. Like Eric, she is obsessed with a search for genuine affection, and she's every bit as committed to pursuing it.

Good characterizations make up for the slender background, with both main characters revealed with equal finesse. Cormier introduces them first in alternating chapters, later smoothly entwining their perspectives after they meet and the circle of violence begins to tighten. Lori is a complicated blend—at once a selfish, vulnerable child; a sexy tease; and an intuitive young woman. Surprisingly, Eric turns out to be nearly as complex. Certainly he's a monster, but he's also cast as a victim and, finally, as a hero of sorts. He can't simply be dismissed as the stereotypical villain who gets what he deserves. His relationship with Lori (whom he tries unsuccessfully to kill and later tries to rescue from drowning) results in the final irony: he becomes human despite himself. It is the idea of Eric's humanity that is the most disquieting aspect of the novel. It is also what ultimately makes the book so seductive. That's the operative word in Cormier's dark world: seductive.

Barbara Harrison

SOURCE: A review of *Tenderness,* in *The Horn Book Magazine,* Vol. LXXIII, No. 2, March, 1997, p. 197.

In juxtaposing a sexually precocious, obsessive runaway and a psychopathic murderer, each seeking a kind of tenderness, Robert Cormier creates a lurid, violent, grating world not fit for the tender-hearted. Lori Cranston is fifteen years old. Her father is dead, and her mother's an alcoholic. When she finds herself in a caressing embrace with her mother's latest boyfriend, she leaves home to protect her mom. She also leaves home to fulfill her obsession with Throb, lead singer in a heavy metal band whose voice fills her ears and the inside of her head: "I got fixated on him, staring at the black cave and knowing that I had to press my lips against his lips and put my tongue through that hole in his mouth." No sooner has she satisfied this obsession than she becomes fixated on Eric Poole, a psychopathic serial killer who has murdered his mother, stepfather, and three teenage girls whom he sexually assaulted after strangling. While tenderness for Lori equals gentleness, tenderness for Eric is the ecstasy he feels as he murders his teenage victims. Lori's tenderness finally transforms Eric, but it leads to her demise and his undoing. The style is vintage Cormier: short pithy sentences and bends in the text that take the reader along startling paths. The author is a master of irony, but the basic premise—that there will be a serious exploration of tenderness—is unfulfilled, and the characterization of Lori (with her bizarre compulsions, and contradictions of naiveté and savvy, morality and immorality) stretches credulity. It's a jolting, unsettling novel, lacking the thematic depth of Cormier at his best, but still suspenseful and chilling.

Florence M. Munat

SOURCE: A review of *Tenderness,* in *Voice of Youth Advocates,* Vol. 20, No. 1, April, 1997, pp. 27-8.

The two main characters in this novel are Eric Poole, an eighteen-year-old psychopath who has just been released from a juvenile detention facility where he was sent after murdering his mother and stepfather, and Lori Cranston, a sexually active fifteen-year-old runaway who has developed a "fixation" on Eric. The only other character of note is a police lieutenant nearing retirement who is keeping a close watch on Eric, because he suspects Eric murdered two teenage girls before his incarceration. In fact, Eric has gone unpunished for murdering three girls, all of whom had long dark hair that reminded him of his sexually abusive mother. He believes Lori (who is blonde) may have witnessed one of these murders three years earlier. As he drives her through the back roads of New England in his van, he begins to plan Lori's murder.

Cormier's vivid characterizations highlight this book in which action is secondary. While depicting Eric as an emotionally remote, monstrous murderer, and Lori as a girl who deceives her mother and trades sexual favors for money, Cormier performs literary magic by making us empathize with these two teenagers who live at society's far edges. He gets inside the heads of a precocious runaway and a psychopath—no easy feat—and reveals both Eric's and Lori's great need for love. The words "tender" and "tenderness" occur dozens of times as the story unfolds in alternating points of view (Eric's third-person and Lori's first-person). Both characters are desperately seeking tenderness, and in a way they end up providing it for one another.

Robert Dunbar

SOURCE: A review of *Tenderness,* in *Books for Keeps,* No. 105, July, 1997, p. 27.

There is a moment early on in this powerful but extremely disturbing novel when reference is made to 'that terrible world out there'. This is the bleak contemporary landscape familiar to us from previous Cormier books, a terrain in which the values of what might be called 'the system' (invariably perceived as corrupt and dehumanising) are challenged by youthful protagonists in search of their own dreams and fulfilment. Here, the youthful protagonists come in the form of Eric, an eighteen-year-old serial killer, and Lori, a young woman of fifteen, who introduces herself in the novel's opening line as a person who gets 'fixated on something', someone who 'can't help' herself. Both have a history of

societal and sexual abuse, resulting in a compulsive need to experience the 'tenderness' of the book's title. From their intertwining destinies Cormier shapes a narrative which, in its sheer power to hold a reader's attention, is tinglingly skilful. It has, additionally, the tantalizing merit of provoking questions about crime and responsibility, motive and manipulation, which threaten to dislodge even our most apparently secure assumptions.

HEROES (1998)

Jennifer A. Fakolt

SOURCE: A review of *Heroes,* in *School Library Journal,* Vol. 44, No. 8, August, 1998, p. 160.

Francis Cassavant, now 18 and the recipient of the respected Silver Star for heroism, returns to the Frenchtown section of Monument following World War II intent on murdering his former mentor and fellow Silver Star winner, Larry LaSalle. With a face ravaged by shrapnel from the grenade he fell on—ostensibly to save his comrades, but in reality to take his own life—Francis walks the streets of his old hometown. Wearing a silk scarf to mask his disfigurement, he remembers his childhood in the prewar days and searches for his nemesis, whom he feels sure will also return. Memories of his innocent years at St. Jude's Parochial School are sardonically juxtaposed with the present horror of his desolate existence. Expert at nothing as a boy, Francis was empowered by the encouragement of Larry, the acrobat, dancer, teacher, and coach at the town's recreation center. Francis's dreams and youth were shattered when the man, home on leave, raped Francis's girlfriend, and he failed to intervene. Disillusioned, the boy forged his birth certificate, enlisted to die an honorable death, and ended up living a nightmare. Cormier takes the notion of heroism and deconstructs it. The hero is epitomized by Francis: a white scarf, no more than a veneer, hiding an appalling reality of hypocrisy and betrayal. The thread of Catholicism is woven throughout the narrative. Characters are not absolutes, but capable of great and evil acts. This lean, compelling read may not rank among the most popular of Cormier's works, but it is a powerful and thought-provoking study.

Paula Lacey

SOURCE: A review of *Heroes,* in *Voice of Youth Advocates,* Vol. 21, No. 3, August, 1998, pp. 198-99.

Eighteen-year-old Francis Joseph Cassavant returns to Frenchtown, hideously wounded after falling on a grenade in World War II. His face has been destroyed and he awaits reconstructive surgery that may not be successful. Cormier's dark, mysterious style projects a sense of impending doom, and the reader soon learns that Francis has returned in order to carry out a mission involving the talented, handsome founder of Frenchtown's recreation program, Larry LaSalle, and Francis's young girlfriend, Nicole Renard. LaSalle, already considered a hero for his dedication to the town's youth, has earned a Silver Star for bravery at Guadalcanal.

Through flashbacks, Cormier reveals that it was Larry LaSalle who helped Francis overcome his shyness and gave him the self-confidence to win the love of the beautiful Nicole. However, Larry, the shining hero, is a tragically flawed human being. After a party celebrating his heroic return from the war, Larry rapes Nicole, and Francis, hiding nearby, is too frightened to intervene. Overwhelmed by guilt and shame, Francis fakes his birth certificate, enlists in the Army, and finally attempts suicide by falling on a grenade. This desperate act saves the lives of his company and earns Francis a Silver Star.

Cormier explores the meaning of heroism and the hidden motivations for what may appear to be heroic acts. Teens will understand Francis's adulation of Larry, who helped Francis realize his potential, and then his bitter feelings of betrayal when Francis learns the truth about his idol. The theme of guilt and revenge is also powerful and readers will identify with Francis's final desperate attempt to assuage his guilt by killing Larry LaSalle. But when the two "heroes" finally come face to face with each other after years of war, death, and despair, the answer is not so simple. Once again, Cormier has written a suspenseful novel that addresses serious questions of concern to most young adults.

Elizabeth Bush

SOURCE: A review of *Heroes,* in *Bulletin of the Center for Children's Books,* Vol. 52, No. 1, September, 1998, p. 11.

Cormier returns to familiar turf in the Frenchtown section of fictional Monument, Massachusetts, with this tale of eighteen-year-old Francis Cassavant, who has returned from World War II with a Silver Star for heroism and a face hideously deformed from a grenade blast. Readers follow Francis on his real-time mission to kill Larry LaSalle, another decorated Frenchtown hero, while reconstructing through Francis' flashbacks the events which brought him to this pass. Struggling to maintain his anonymity, Francis finally tracks down and confronts LaSalle, the town's former social director, who once nurtured the talents and confidence of Frenchtown youth—and, as is eventually revealed, raped Francis' girlfriend. Guilt over not preventing the rape had driven Francis to suicidal enlistment at fifteen, and now he seeks revenge. While neither plot nor structure is particularly innovative, the pacing is meticulous, the mood is tense, and the climactic confrontation between Francis and Larry is charged with ethical ambiguity, as LaSalle challenges Francis to consider, "Does that one sin of mine wipe away all the good things?" Young adults struggling with their own moral choices may be sparked to discussion by the novel's ambivalent conclusion.

Additional coverage of Cormier's life and career is contained in the following sources published by The Gale Group: *Authors and Artists for Young Adults,* Vols. 3, 19; *Contemporary Authors New Revision Series,* Vol. 23; *Contemporary Literary Criticism,* Vols. 12, 30; *Dictionary of Literary Biography,* Vol. 52; *Junior DISCovering Authors; Major Authors and Illustrators for Children and Young Adults;* and *Something about the Author,* Vols. 10, 45, and 83.

(Cassia) Joy Cowley

1936-

(Born Cassia Joy Summers) New Zealander author of picture books, fiction, nonfiction, and retellings; scriptwriter and editor.

Major works include *The Duck in the Gun* (U.S. edition, 1969; New Zealand edition, 1984), *The Silent One* (1981; British edition, 1982), *Bow Down Shadrach* (1991; U.S. edition, 1996), *The Mouse Bride* (1995), *Singing Down the Rain* (1997), *Starbright and the Dream Eater* (1998).

INTRODUCTION

One of New Zealand's most highly respected writers for children, Cowley is a prolific and popular author who is recognized for the variety of her works, the quality of her writing, and her insight into human nature. Cowley's books, only a handful of which have been published in the United States, cover a wide range of genres. She has written picture books for children from preschool through the middle grades, fiction for primary graders and young adults, short stories, nonfiction, and retellings. She is also a well-known author of fiction and short stories for adults and is the editor of a collection of works by twentieth-century New Zealand women writers. In addition, Cowley has written more than five hundred readers for classroom use as well as scripts for New Zealand radio. Her books for children, primarily categorized as realistic fiction, fantasy, and a combination of the two, feature both human and animal characters and are set in such places as the South Pacific, New York City, and Arizona as well as in imaginary lands.

Although many of her works are filled with warmth and humor, Cowley also addresses serious themes, such as the uselessness of war, the power of both faith and superstition, and the value of community. Several of her books blend humor and social commentary, while others contain ironic or satiric undercurrents. Often including multicultural and multigenerational characters in her works, Cowley is further recognized for featuring the disabled as protagonists or secondary characters. As a literary stylist, she is praised for the lyricism of her prose and for her skill as a storyteller. Her books, illustrated by artists such as Val Biro, Jan Spivey Gilchrist, and Edward Sorel, are often regarded as excellent for reading aloud. Writing in *Twentieth-Century Children's Writers,* Tom Fitzgibbon commented that Cowley "has established herself as one of New Zealand's finest writers for children. . . . As a writer she is gifted and committed. Her imagination, her depth of understanding, her sense of fun, and her exhilaration give her books lasting qualities."

Biographical Information

Cowley was born in New Zealand to a Scottish father—a deaf, partially blind man with a heart condition that kept him an invalid for most of his life—and a mother, mostly of Scandinavian descent, who suffered from schizophrenia. Cowley has described her parents as having a volatile, though loving, relationship. She first began to express her creativity in drawing. "Neither of my parents' families valued books," she wrote in her essay in *Something about the Author Autobiography Series (SAAS).* "Books were not a part of my preschool years, but drawing was. . . . I couldn't help myself. A blank surface triggered automatic behaviour." When she started school, Cowley had difficulty learning to read from texts with lists of words and sounds; however, she took solace in art and in friendships with her classmates. She became an avid reader when she discovered Marjorie Flack's picture book, *The Story about Ping.* She wrote in *SAAS,* "That book was a doorway into another world, and I entered joyfully. . . . I had found that reading accessed story. As often as I picked up a book, I could take that journey to other worlds and have safe adventures. My appetite for story and my fascination with it became limitless." When she was nine, Cowley joined the local library and discovered authors such as Charles Dickens, Jules Verne, the Brontë sisters, and Mark Twain. Although her Scottish grandmother warned that "so much reading would make [her] soft in the head," Cowley wrote in *SAAS*: "[t]he library became my other home." She also began telling her sisters stories to escape their parents' frequent arguments.

When she was twelve, a teacher told Cowley that she was a good writer, a discovery that led to the next stage of her development. She began writing stories and poems, first for herself and then for the children's page of the *Wellington Southern Cross* newspaper. When she was sixteen, Cowley took an after-school job as the editor of the children's page of the *Palmerston North Daily Times* newspaper. Although she was offered a full-time position with another newspaper after graduation, Cowley refused, at the wishes of her parents. She became a pharmacist's apprentice for four years before joining a writing group. In the mid-1960s, Cowley published two short stories in *Short Story International,* an American reprint magazine; the stories caught the attention of Anne Hutchens, an editor at Doubleday, who suggested to Cowley—at that time a farmer's wife and mother of four—that she write a novel. Eighteen months later, Cowley's first adult novel, *Nest in a Falling Tree,* was published; later, author Roald Dahl acquired the film rights for the novel as a vehicle for his wife, actress Patricia Neal. After her marriage broke up when she was thirty, Cowley worked in a pharmacy during the day and wrote in the evening. She penned adult fiction, humorous children's stories, and short pieces for the school magazine of the New Zealand Educational Department. When her son Edward had difficulty with reading, Cowley began tutoring him; their sessions included reading stories that Cowley had written for Edward about things he liked. She eventually tutored more children in a similar way, both from Edward's school and others. As Cowley noted in *SAAS,* she wrote "funny little stories that made children laugh and forget that they hated reading"; these stories became the first of her series of early readers.

In 1970, Cowley married Malcolm Mason, a writer and accountant; their marriage lasted until 1985, when Mason died of cancer. Before his death, Cowley converted to Catholicism and traveled extensively throughout places such as India, South America, and the United States. With her teacher friend June Melser, Cowley founded the Story Box Reading Programme, an approach to reading in which, as Cowley wrote in *SAAS,* "Story was the thing." Originally intended for use by New Zealand schools, the program became popular internationally. In 1989, Cowley married Terry Coles and began concentrating on writing picture books and stories for children and young people and on holding writing workshops. Cowley stated in *SAAS,* "For me, writing is always a leaning of the heart towards a reader, and an unread story, like an unsung song, is only half alive. . . . At its best, creative writing involves some metaphysical process which taps into a cosmic voice, new and sur-

prising to the writers." As Cowley told *Something about the Author,* "Writing for young people requires a memory; more than that—before starting a book it's necessary to peel away years of adult experience like the layers of an onion, and expose a self that's of an age corresponding with character and reader. Only by being once more ten or fourteen or whatever age I'm writing for, can I evaluate the work. I can 'live' with my characters and understand them as equals."

Major Works

Cowley's first book, *The Duck in the Gun,* is also one of her best known. An antiwar fable in picture book format, the story describes how a duck prevents a war by nesting in a general's cannon to lay her eggs. Stuck in the town that he is besieging, the general ends up working with its Prime Minister and marrying his daughter; at the wedding, the duck and her eight ducklings are in attendance. An antiwar message also underscores another of Cowley's picture books, *Salmagundi* (1985). This satire outlines how two rival arms manufacturers, sentenced to work in each other's factories after committing individual crimes, blow up the factories and then turn to building peace factories that make items like bread, candy, and sun umbrellas. Although the factory owners are jointly awarded the Peace Prize, the pair begins devising plans to build new and improved weapons. Marcus Crouch called *Salmagundi* an "extraordinary and remarkably entertaining tale. . . , rich in irony as well as good jokes. A joyous frolic which is much more."

Cowley's novel, *The Silent One,* is considered one of her signature works. Set on a tropical island in the South Pacific, the tale features a native boy, twelve-year-old Jonasi, who is both deaf and mute. Ostracized by the villagers because he is considered possessed, Jonasi is accepted only by his stepmother and the village chief and his son, who has attended school off the island. Jonasi spends most of his time fishing in the lagoon, where he befriends an albino turtle that is also mistrusted by the villagers. Jonasi and the turtle are blamed for a drought, a hurricane, and a fatal shark attack. After Jonasi gets the chance to leave the island to attend a school for the deaf, a hunter threatens the turtle. Jonasi jumps into the ocean to save his friend and is never seen again; however, the owner of a cargo ship later reports that he has seen two white turtles swimming together. Described as "a forceful lesson in values" by a critic in *Publishers Weekly, The Silent One* was praised by Virginia Haviland for containing prose that is "brilliantly evocative of the physical background as well as of the emotional atmosphere."

Cowley has also achieved success for her works published in the 1990s. *The Mouse Bride,* a picture book retelling of a traditional folktale, describes how a mouse desires to marry the strongest husband in the world so that her children will not be small and weak. Her search takes her to the sun, a cloud, the wind, and finally, back home, where she meets the mouse who becomes her husband. Cowley frames the tale by paralleling the mouse and a powerless little girl who is directed to go to bed by a commanding adult. Susan Dove Lempke noted that "Cowley relates the story with enough wit and energy that it could stand alone for telling. . . ." With *Gracias, the Thanksgiving Turkey* (1996), Cowley tells the story of Miguel, a small Puerto Rican boy living in Manhattan with his grandparents and aunt while his truck-driving father is on the road. When Miguel's father sends him a turkey for Thanksgiving dinner, the boy, who names the turkey Gracias, adopts it as a pet. As the holiday approaches, Gracias follows Miguel to church, where the priest blesses both boy and bird. As a result, Miguel's relatives decide to have chicken for Thanksgiving. Linda Nelson commented, "Multicultural influences . . . deepen the realistic tapestry of this multi-generational story."

Singing Down the Rain is a picture book that treats one of Cowley's most consistent themes: the power of faith and community. The story, set in a farming town beset by drought, describes how young Brianna meets a tiny woman with a big smile who specializes in rainsongs. At first, only the community's children and Brianna's mother believe the woman's claim that she can bring rain by having the community join her in song. However, when the rain begins to fall, the entire town joins in; at the end of the story, only Brianna notices when the rain-maker leaves. Of *Singing Down the Rain*, Elizabeth Burns stated, "The textual crescendo . . . and the resultant welcome rains . . . are almost palpable, and storytime audiences may be happy to echo the refrain, 'Sweet wonder'." *Starbright and the Dream Eater* is considered somewhat of a departure for Cowley: a fantasy novel for young adults that incorporates such elements as the para-normal, prophecies, and alternate universes. The story describes how Starbright, a child born to a brain-dam-aged fifteen-year-old who passes herself off as the girl's sister, realizes that her destiny is to save the world from an alien life force that has caused spindle sickness—a plague that puts people to sleep permanently. Trevor Agnew concluded, "Joy Cowley draws a nice line be-tween credulity and scepticism, leaving readers to make their own minds up. This is a satisfying page-turning novel, rich in ideas. . . . "

Awards

Cowley has received three New Zealand AIM Children's Book Awards: for *The Silent One* in 1982, for *Bow Down Shadrach* in 1992, and for *The Cheese Trap* in 1996. She also won two Children's Book of the Year Awards, for *The Silent One* in 1983 and for *Bow Down Shadrach* in 1993. In 1985, Cowley was presented with the Russell Clark Award for *The Duck in the Gun*. She also received the New Zealand Buckland Literary Award for *Man of Straw,* an adult novel, in 1970. *Ticket to the Sky Dance* was shortlisted for the *New Zealand Post* Children's Book Awards, junior fiction category, in 1998, as was *Starbright and the Dream Eater* in 1999. Cowley

has been given several awards for her body of work, including the New Zealand Literary Achievement Award in 1980; the New Zealand Commemoration Medal in 1990; the Order of the British Empire in 1992, for services to children's literature; and the Margaret Mahy Lecture Award in 1993. She was also presented with the Women's Suffrage Centennial Medal in 1993 as well as an honorary doctorate in literature from Massey University in 1994.

AUTHOR'S COMMENTARY

Trevor Agnew with Joy Cowley

SOURCE: "Know the Author: Joy Cowley: Toad in a Tiger Moth Meets Icaraus," in *Magpies, New Zealand Supplement*, Vol. 14, No. 1, March, 1999, pp. 1-5.

[Trevor Agnew] *I like that passage about the motorbike* [in **The Machinery of Dreams**] *because of its very spe-cific details. In your writing, the descriptions of things like eel catching are often detailed. Do you do this in order to convince readers? Does it involve you in lots of research? Or do you keep one of those mysterious note-books?*

[Joy Cowley] Writers seem to work mainly one of two ways. Some are auditory. They write as though they are taking dictation. Others, like me, are visual. I spend a lot of time with plots and characters, expanding them, asking questions of them until I know them so well that I can see the details. Writing, then, is simply a matter of describing what I can see in my mind.

I like reading stories with specific detail. I think that it is detail which connects with our own experiences and hooks us into a story. I also try to be selective with description, using it for pacing, for light and shade in a work, and for general leitmotif effect.

Do I keep a notebook? Yes. New ideas will gatecrash a work in progress, and without consideration or respect, yell, "Look at me!" I have found that the most effective way of getting rid of them is to jot them down in my notebook. The idea might still be active a year later but then again, they might be dead. It doesn't matter. My notebook serves as a clearing station for intrusive mate-rial rather than a source of inspiration.

Is humour an important part of your writing/story-telling? I notice the almost slapstick humour of much of your writing, like in **Starbright and the Dream Eater**, *Starbright's taking a solo bungy jump without working out how to untie her feet. How do you feel humour should be used in writing? Especially writing for chil-dren?*

You bet! It is an important part of life. Yet few writers

take humour seriously! I am appalled at the lack of humour in most of my early adult short stories and novels. I can only say that I am glad these works were aimed at adult readers who have choices, and not young people. In real life the masks of comedy and tragedy are rarely far apart.

It sounds flip to say "the darker the shadow, the brighter the light" but life really is a oneness and the balance seems always there. Some of the funniest things happen at funerals. That is the wholeness of being. Look at Frank Court's book *Angela's Ashes*. But, for some reason, most writers for young readers tend to focus on problems in a humourless way that presents an incomplete picture.

Does the humour sometimes conceal pain? The joke about cutting off fingers in **Gladly Here I Come** *made me wonder. Is black humour an effective tool for your style of writing?*

I am not aware of using "black" humour or employing humour to cover pain. I simply try to reflect the world I live in. At the same time I am very aware of laughter as therapy, especially for children whose authority is not always recognised in an adult world.

Humour has been an important ingredient in my early reading books. These stories began in the 1960s, when I was working with my son Edward and then other children who could not read. Many were arbitrarily labelled dyslexic but I noticed that their right/left confusion and disability did not extend to those activities they enjoyed. Most had simply "switched off" learning to read, unwilling to put themselves at risk of further failure. Their body language was explicit of a frozen attitude to the printed word.

These children taught me that early reading materials need to be easy, exciting, meaningful. They taught me that an engaging story was important, even at the lowest levels, and they showed me that no one can be tense while they are laughing. With the all-important humour, there developed a tendency to put a twist at the end of a story. This was a bit like pudding after vegetables. It encouraged a child to read to the end of the book.

Do you have anyone in mind when you write? In other words, do you write for a particular, person, audience, reader, when you are working on something?

Not any one person. I am keenly aware of the age and reading level of my intended audience and this awareness tempers my writing.

For beginner readers, the focus is the acquisition of reading skills. This means a very simple graded text with much of the plot detail going into the illustrations, so the page-by-page notes to the illustrator are very important, especially if the illustrator has not had a lot of experience in working at this level.

Books for fluent readers have more language content and here is where I try to push the limits in expanding a young person's awareness of the richness of the English language and ways in which it may be used. ("Once upon a mousetime, two little squeaks went cheesing . . .")

It is always a delight to find that teachers have used the books as a springboard for the student's own creative writing.

The spiritual as a part of everyday life seems a regular theme in your work. I am thinking of the mussels on p. 24 of **Bow Down Shadrach** *or the trees in* **Gladly Here I Come.** *Then there's your hymn* **Sacrament of the Seasons** *(No. 77 in Alleluia Aotearoa) "Jesus comes to me as a springtime tree . . ." Your characters even discuss religion, and have spiritual beliefs (e.g.* **Starbright and the Dream Eater***). What are your views on the mysterious behind the mundane?*

What is mundane? Everything has a particular beauty. Everything is a facet of the mysterious.

I have always known an "otherness". Most children have that knowing. I am sure they bring it into the world with them. For me, at a young age, the knowing had simple self-evident truths: that everything was connected to everything else; that good and bad described how we thought about things and not the things themselves; that there was no such event as death—things simply turned into other things.

There was also a strong sense of another greater reality somewhere very close. It was as though this life was a dream and I was very close to wakening. I remember that as a young child I felt very old. Not just parent-old or grand parent-old, but as old as a mountain. I have spoken with my children who have the same feelings.

Naturally, when I was young, I tried to place these feelings where they could be affirmed, but there was no explanation for them in the religious or scientific beliefs of my childhood. My views earned me beatings from my mother who believed the devil was in me.

These days there have been huge shifts in spiritual awareness as people discover the metaphysical outside of the old religious structures. Part of this shift is supported by new physics and the sudden expansion of knowledge that has come with microchip technology. But we still tend to talk to children about religion in demeaning and meaningless ways, which are remote from their own spiritual experiences. So, yes, I do write about child-centred spiritual experience. I believe it is not separate from other life experience, merely an extension of it.

I was interested in your views on fantasy in the Introduction of **Beyond the River**, *where you wrote, "Since the beginnings of communication, people have used fantasy to express truths which could not be contained in a factual account." Are you myth-making for the 20th Century? Are you entering a new science fiction-fantasy field* *with* **Starbright and the Dream Eater** *and* **Ticket to the Sky Dance**?

I don't see myself as myth making for the 20th Century, although I am aware that I belong with a number of writers who are exploring myth. The stories in **Beyond the River** were largely inspired by the New Zealand landscape which seems to dictate ongoing legend.

Starbright and the Dream Eater and **Ticket to the Sky Dance** were inspired by quantum physics, and they did involve a bit of research.

I'm a lover of plots. I like stories to work like intricate well-oiled machines.

Fantasy is not apart from reality. It is reality pushed to the edge, and it must work logically. I like to read science fiction, but am disappointed when plots are illogical or when they rely heavily on coincidence.

What are your views on settings of children's fiction? Your New Zealand settings and descriptions in, for example, **Gladly Here I Come** *are very sharp, right down to, say, the smell of eels. There seems to be an American setting in* **Starbright and the Dream Eater**. *Was this your idea, or the publisher's?*

I believe that every work needs a sense of place and, because I'm a visual writer, place is always specific and important. Much of my writing has been set in New Zealand. Some books have been located in Australia and could not be anywhere else. The two fantasy novels are set in the USA. In both **Ticket to the Sky Dance** (California) and **Starbright and the Dream Eater** (Wisconsin) we have situations which could not have taken place in a country with a small population and as the only densely populated country, that I know reasonably well, is the United States, I chose localities there.

You were once the editor of the Children's Page of a newspaper. What did you discover about children's reading and writing interests from this experience?

In 1935 I was the children's page editor, known officially as the NFC lady (News for Children), for the *Manawatu Daily Times*. There is a pre-story to this. My parents suffered poor health. My mother had schizophrenia and my father's heart condition prevented him from working. I was the eldest of five and it was always understood that I would leave school and work to help the family. We lived at Foxton at the time and I travelled by bus each day to Palmerston North Girls' High School, where a wonderful group of teachers conspired to keep me this wonderful job at the paper, plus board with a family near the school. Half of my wages paid for my board, the rest was taken home to my parents at the weekend. This was a very happy arrangement. Every day after school I spent two to three hours in Broadway at the *Manawatu Daily Times*.

I had an office typewriter on a small table, in a window-less room that smelled of old smoke and printers ink, and as long as I got my copy to the typesetting room by Friday afternoon, I could do what I liked with the Children's Page. Under a bare, fly-specked light bulb, I hammered out an identity for myself as a self-important, middle-aged, world-travelling editor who had a dog called Crackers. When I was out of the country, Crackers took over the typewriter and gave the readers another, less dignified image of me. We became popular, Crackers and I.

This was heady stuffy for a sixteen-year-old. At the end of the year, I was offered a cadetship with the paper, a position usually reserved for males. More heady stuff. My rejoicing was short-lived, however, when my parents refused permission. Reporters were a lot of heathens, as far as Mum and Dad were concerned, and I had already been too much under their influence. No, I would be apprenticed to our local pharmacist and that was that.

The last day of school was a sad affair but, as I was walking out the gate, my English teacher ran after me. She had a favour to ask. Would I please give her my essay book? She wanted me to promise her that I would keep on writing. I promised. And it was largely that promise that made me buy an old typewriter three years later and start writing short stories. It was another three years before I had anything published.

Why do you visit schools, and take part in workshops? Is it after-sales service?

It's not so much "after-sales" as a matter of keeping in touch with source and resource. My own inner child is overlaid with so much adult that I need to maintain contact with the unadulterated—the children out there. When I am researching a book, I talk over issues with school classes. The results are almost always different from what I anticipate. For example, before writing **Bow Down Shadrach** I put this question to children: "If your family pet was very old or sick and had to be killed, would you want your parents to tell you the truth? Or would you like them to tell you that the animal had run away, or maybe gone to a lovely home where it would be looked after for the rest of its life?" I imagined that all children would opt for the truth, but only older children wanted that. Almost all five-to-seven year olds wanted the nice story.

Generally, when I am researching likes and dislikes, or anything to do with feelings, I ask questions of children older than the reading age of the intended work. If I'm writing early reading books for five and six year olds, I interview seven and eight year olds and begin, "When you were five. . . ." I find that children are not usually able to reflect on their immediate situation but will readily give information from the past.

Also all my manuscripts are trialled in schools before they are submitted to a publisher. I have a team of great teachers who help me with this. Almost always, rewriting needs to be done as a result of the trialling. Sometimes the story is discarded. I'm never sure of the final seasoning until the dish has been tasted in this way.

How do you keep in touch with the way children speak, their styles of speech and language? Also, how do you make up languages like Starbright's private language?

I realize there is such a thing as style but, all the same, I try to give each story an original and authentic voice. Very often this means leaving behind everything I've been taught about "writing" and simply telling the story on paper in a conversational way. I suppose writers are a bit like actors in this.

Dialogue? It's a matter of listening to young people, noting vocabulary, speech patterns and inflections. Young children are still engaged with the novelty of language. They enjoy taking words to bits and reassembling them in different ways. They experiment with language and, often, when they haven't the right word will invent one—as Starbright does. I confess that I too enjoy inventing words. A recent addition is "flumsy" which is a combination of flimsy and flummery. Very useful.

Dreams play a part in some of your stories. Are dreams important to you?

Dreams are sometimes important to me; more often unimportant. I do remember them whereas many adults don't. Children always remember their dreams and they are always important. They always want to discuss their dreams. Which is why dreams play a bigger role in my children's writing than in my adult works.

*You often mention your own animals (cats, goose, dog, etc) in biographical notes. Your stories often deal with animals in trouble (Shadrach, or the turtle in **The Silent One**). How do you feel about animals?*

I have great respect for the intelligence of animals and am grateful for their companionship when it is offered. Quite frankly, I don't see a lot of difference between them and me. I like Mark Twain's statement: "Man is the highest creation. Now I wonder who found that out?" and I feel deep regret at the way humans see other species through the eyes of their own comfort. For example, save whales. Kill rats. It is the selective attitude that bothers me. Rats are highly intelligent animals, natural survivors. Cockroaches, snakes, sharks all have bad press yet all are very beautiful. Where do adults find such unreasoning hate for some of their fellow species? Not from their childhood, that's for sure. But they are usually successful in passing their attitudes on to their children.

Many children bond with animals. Pets in a home are as important as parents and siblings. Sometimes, more so, judging from the letters I receive from children. I don't underestimate the love that a child can feel for a pet. In a world weighted with adult authority and expectation,

it can be a great comfort to have a companion who accepts you exactly as you are.

Maurice Gee once said that writing children's novels is easier than writing adult ones. Is this your experience?

I do not find writing for children easier than writing for adults. It would be true to say that I write for children as I write for adults, doing the best that I am capable of, but at the same time staying with the child's experience of life and language. In that last point lies the challenge. Writing for children means being true to readers of a certain age group. It involves disciplines that don't come into adult writing.

When I write an adult story or novel, I can stretch the wings of language to their fullest extent and soar like an Icarus. With writing for children, there are limitations that tether me to a particular audience. No ego trips permitted.

On the other hand, a novel for a young reader is usually less than half the length of an adult novel, so it is a shorter course.

I must say that I enjoy the challenges of writing at all levels, but find writing for early emergent reading the most difficult. Trying to make an engaging story out of a vocabulary range of some twenty words can be like trying to create a crossword puzzle with no black squares. This year [1998], the writing of an adult novel **Classical Music** was luxuriously easy, compared with the work that went into some emergent readers written the previous year.

How do you feel about the illustrations for some of your books? Do they reflect how you see the characters?

Most often I am delighted with the illustrations, although there have been a few disappointments. Availability of a suitable illustrator is an ongoing problem for writers and publishers. Many illustrators are booked up five years ahead. I waited for six years to get the Mexican illustrator Joe Cepeda for *Gracias the Thanksgiving Turkey*. Problems also arise when an artist is not available to do a second or third book in a series. We have four different sets of characters depicted on the covers of the two Shadrach novels. The third book in the trilogy will probably bring more changes. Young readers find this disappointing and confusing.

In early reading books, much of the story is contained in the illustrations and I need to write full illustrator briefs for each page. Both the illustrator and I are under the same constraints. We are helping the child to learn to read. But when I write picture book texts for established readers, I do not dictate to the illustrator in any way. Rather, I view the illustrator as a co-author who can expand my original idea into something much bigger and better.

Did you ever get that motorbike? When I first asked you

that, in Winton in 1984, you were still rueful about the Royal Enfield 147cc your dad had bought you, thirty years earlier.

No. The year after my father bought me the miserable little Royal Enfield (aye, but he was a canny man) I discovered a new interest which consumed every penny I could earn. The spluttering bike became a means of transport to the Middle Districts Aero Club at Palmerston North, where I fluttered over the city doing circuits and bumps in Tiger Moths. Like Toad, my passion changed overnight and two wheels on the ground could not compete with a love affair with flying.

Marriage and children soon grounded me but, even now, I ache at the sight of an old DH-82. I am filled with nostalgia for a contraption of wood, wire and canvas, with a 48 mph cruising speed, just fast enough to whistle the wind under your goggles, slow enough to fill the open cockpit with smoke from the crematorium.

But I should add that there is a postscript to the motorbike era. My son James has a beautiful Harley, which I may occasionally ride.

TITLE COMMENTARY

📖 *THE DUCK IN THE GUN* (U.S. edition, 1969; New Zealand edition, 1984)

Kirkus Reviews

SOURCE: A review of *The Duck in the Gun,* in *Kirkus Reviews,* Vol. XXXVII, No. 16, August 15, 1969, p. 853.

"Please, sir, we can't shoot at that town. We would spoil the new paint"—and the gunner's plea, seconded by the other men ("We've worked for two weeks on those houses") cancels the long-postponed siege; besides, the attacking General has become rather fond of the resident Prime Minister's daughter. It all began with the duck nesting in the gun who wouldn't be lured out and couldn't be shot out; proceeded with the egg-hatching armistice arranged by General and Prime Minister; and became a working partnership when the General's idle, unrecompensed troops undertook to repaint the town for pay. At the close, the General and the Prime Minister's daughter are wed; with the duck and her eight ducklings in attendance. Edward Sorel's sly contours and moody cross-hatchings make the most of the cockaded mockery and give this a reach beyond the picture book brigade.

Margaret Riddell

SOURCE: A review of *The Duck in the Gun,* in *School Library Journal,* Vol. 16, No. 3, November, 1969, p. 110.

The General finds a duck nesting in his cannon, and so is unable to begin the attack. He goes to the Prime Minister of the besieged town to beg for more artillery and is politely refused. However, the opposition does offer to help the General pay his men by having them paint the town, and by the time the ducklings hatch and the gun is free, the newly painted houses are so beautiful that the war is called off. These overly simplified episodes are accompanied by pen drawings accented with blue and gold water color. Such delight as is forthcoming from the book is implicit in the funny, satirical illustrations which depict toy soldiers playing with toy guns; the only real character is the duck, who accomplishes her task quietly and efficiently.

The Christian Science Monitor

SOURCE: A review of *The Duck in the Gun,* in *The Christian Science Monitor,* Vol. 61, No. 291, November 6, 1969, p. 8B.

The toughest gold-braided, cocked-hatted, beplumed toothy general will balk when it comes to firing off a gun with a nesting duck in the barrel. Joy Cowley's pleasant and ridiculous fable of how a mother duck stopped a war is illustrated by Edward Sorel with suitably pretentious drawings of fully-rigged generals and regiments of hussar-like soldiers. Not of course that anything about *The Duck in the Gun* can match war itself for sheer unlikelihood.

📖 *THE SILENT ONE* (1981; British edition, 1982)

Publishers Weekly

SOURCE: A review of *The Silent One,* in *Publishers Weekly,* Vol. 219, No. 3, January 16, 1981, pp. 77, 80.

[Hermann] Greissle's wood engravings are the work of a master, creating authentic scenes of the people and locales in Cowley's haunting story. Hurt at the snubbing of his tribe, deaf-and-dumb Jonasi paddles his raft to the reef, where he finds solace, and there he is startled by a big, white turtle. Jonasi abandons plans to capture the creature and, instead, keeps the find a secret during days when he and the albino form a close relationship. They are threatened, however, by superstitious people on the boy's South Sea island, who believe he is possessed and blame him for a hurricane that destroys their crops. Both Jonasi and the white turtle become targets for vengeance in the fearful climate, described clearly and compassionately by Cowley. What happens is ineluctable, a resolution that brings both rejoicing and tears plus, not incidentally, a forceful lesson in values.

Denise M. Wilms

SOURCE: A review of *The Silent One,* in *Booklist,* Vol. 77, No. 17, May 1, 1981, p. 102.

This story of a deaf-mute South Sea island boy shunned by his people is involving but has a troublesome mixed message that some will find intriguing and others frustrating. On one hand, the villagers' view that Jonasi's disability is a sign of evil possession is firmly countered by the enlightened rationality of Chief Taruga Vueti and his son Aesake, who protect Jonasi. Yet plot development bears out the villagers' view: when Jonasi discovers and tames an albino sea turtle, the village is plagued by drought, hurricane, and death. And Jonasi himself dies when he tries to steer the turtle from hunters. With both Jonasi and the turtle gone, prosperity returns to the village. It is the latter two elements that are most problematic, because a heretofore realistic story reaches for mythic proportions. Whether one finds this appealing or contrived is a matter of preference.

Zena Sutherland

SOURCE: A review of *The Silent One,* in *Bulletin of the Center for Children's Books,* Vol. 34, No. 10, June, 1981, p. 189.

A story set in the South Pacific by a New Zealand author has a haunting quality that is due in part to the grave simplicity of the writing style, and in part to the touching picture of the plight of a deaf-mute in a rather primitive island society. Jonasi, the hero, doesn't understand his own condition; he only knows that the others of his island community move their mouths. In his silent world, he cannot comprehend the superstitious fear with which the people of his village regard him; he knows that they want to get the albino turtle that has become his pet as they swim together, but not that his neighbors think the creature is magical and evil. The few people who love him are taking him to a school for the deaf in another community when, with the tragic inevitability of mythic events, the boy jumps from the boat to save his turtle—and is never seen again.

Virginia Haviland

SOURCE: A review of *The Silent One,* in *The Horn Book Magazine,* Vol. LVII, No. 3, June, 1981, pp. 301-02.

A strong, haunting story about the force of superstitious belief, which on a South Seas island caused people to reject a boy called "The Silent One." His mother Luisa always had to defend Jonasi from accusations based on fear and ignorance. Jonasi, a mute, was believed by the islanders to be possessed by a demon; they feared him even more when he found and became devoted to a shining white turtle. Aesake, the chief's son who had been educated at school, was aware that the turtle was merely an albino and not an evil creature. While trying to save the turtle from a greedy hunter, Jonasi disappeared. The prose is brilliantly evocative of the physical background as well as of the emotional atmosphere, including the palpable tension caused by the coming of a hurricane. More important than all the fear and dev-

astation, however, is the islanders' perception of Jonasi. "People chose to forget about Jonasi and the white turtle. But beyond the village . . . stories of the white turtle multiplied like fire." And the crew of a cargo ship reported sighting two turtles that "gleamed like stars in all that dark blue water."

Kirkus Reviews

SOURCE: A review of *The Silent One,* in *Kirkus Reviews,* Vol. XLIX, No. 19, October 1, 1981, p. 1235.

The Silent One is deaf, twelve-year-old foundling Jonasi—a pariah on his South Pacific island because the superstitious local folk ascribe sinister powers to him. His comfort is the sea, and now he has a second: a white turtle—a "demon" too?—that has taken to following him. Chief's son Aesake, who has been away to school, knows that deafness is a natural condition and that the white turtle may be an albino; but he recognizes that the danger to Jonasi is also real (once, the islanders are about to use him for bait to catch the turtle)—so it's arranged for Jonasi to be sent away to a school for the deaf. Aboard the departing ship, however, the Native Affairs officer spies the white turtle following and wants it caught for its monetary value. As the man rages, Jonasi jumps overboard, and turtle and boy disappear. Some sense of locale (Cowley is a New Zealander), but otherwise totally flat—conventionally lyrical and conventionally maudlin.

Chris Brown

SOURCE: A review of *The Silent One,* in *The School Librarian,* Vol. 30, No. 2, June, 1982, p. 128.

The story revolves around the innate superstitions of the people of a South Pacific island village. A deaf and dumb boy, Jonasi, is supposed to be the instrument of misfortune and as his isolation leads to friendship with anti-nature itself, in the form of a white turtle, the villagers' worst fears seem confirmed. A quaint colonial flavour which appears with the largesse of a Native Affairs officer in the wake of a hurricane ought to be disquieting, but as the events inhabit a misty hinterland hovering between reality and myth the context seems appropriate. The mystique is made plausible by the quality of the writing which is at its best in sparse passages of strikingly realised description, yet it is this very quality which makes a brief list of one man's fatal injuries quite appalling. The people, the setting and the occurrences all contribute to the enigmatic feel of the book.

SALMAGUNDI (1985)

Marcus Crouch

SOURCE: A review of *Salmagundi,* in *The Junior Bookshelf,* Vol. 50, No. 2, April, 1986, p. 60.

According to the Concise Oxford Dictionary 'salmagundi' is a 'dish of chopped meat, anchovies, eggs, onions, etc.' or alternatively a 'general mixture, miscellaneous collection, of articles, subjects, qualities, etc.' In Joy Cowley's extraordinary and remarkably entertaining tale, it can also mean 'salad' or 'spying' or 'fighting' or anything else at the whim of the speaker. The book is a fine salmagundi of sense and nonsense which blends knockabout farce and social comment, always with a flavouring of good humour and high spirits.

We are in the town of Garpen Flat, but we can't see it for the covering of smog which comes from its two factories. The factory owners are respectively Doctor Foster who makes 'missiles to blow up tanks' and Major Brassblow who makes 'tanks to shoot down missiles'. Because they are very wealthy, both tycoons (Dr. Foster is a woman, by the way) live in style, well away from the smog, and are able to indulge their fancies, for peacock feathers and liquorice of all sorts. However, by a happy chance, the Doctor and the Major both fall foul of the law and are sentenced to hard labour in each other's factories! Each devises a fiendish plot to blow up the factory. They go up together, much to the long-term benefit of Garpen Flat (no more smog). All comes out in the end. After characteristically hypocritical performances by the precious pair, they turn to alternative, but still profitable, activities, building peace factories for making bread and buns, sweets and sun umbrellas. No wonder they win the Peace Prize.

Of course a great deal of this fun is for adults only, but enough is left to please the whole family. Joy Cowley's story is rich in irony as well as good jokes. Philip Webb's pictures which sprawl over every page are as full of fun as of exuberance. Clearly he has enjoyed making them as much as we enjoy being at the receiving end. A joyous frolic which is much more. Don't be misled by the picture-book format. There is no upper age-limit for its appeal.

Beverley Mathias

SOURCE: A review of *Salmagundi*, in *Children's Books*, June, 1986, p. 12.

Salmagundi is a heavy-handed attempt at ridiculing industrial society and its values, thus showing the virtues of harmonious living within an urban environment. The text is laboured and difficult to read for all except the better under-ten reader. The illustrations are distorted and Lowry-like, yet lacking definition as characters within the book.

Mary Lourde

SOURCE: A review of *Salmagundi*, in *The Book Report*, Vol. 5, No. 3, November-December, 1986, p. 54.

This is a brief satire on war, dedicated to "all those who work for peace in the world, and for all those who don't." On one side of town, Major Brassblow owns a factory that makes tanks that shoot down missiles. On the other side of town, Dr. Foster makes missiles to blow up tanks. The story points up the stupidity of believing that weapon proliferation will bring peace. It shows the greed of factory owners and the plight of the workers. After blowing up each other's factories, the owners "reform" and plan a new town where peace factories turn out good things for people. At the end, their reform has worn off and the factory owners are again plotting new, improved weapons. The writing and the illustrations are excellent. Even 10-year-olds will see the main point without help and older readers will see the United States and the USSR in the two main characters. It may take some nudges from the librarian to get the more sophisticated teenagers to pick up the book since the cover looks like a child's book. The timely theme is anything but childish.

THE MOUSE BRIDE (retold by Cowley, 1995)

Kirkus Reviews

SOURCE: A review of *The Mouse Bride*, in *Kirkus Reviews*, Vol. LXIII, No. 19, October 1, 1995, pp. 1425-26.

A mouse, tired of being small and weak, decides to find herself the strongest husband in the world. First, she proposes to the sun, but he informs her there is someone even stronger—a cloud; the cloud, in turn, sends her to the wind, the wind to a house (that he can't blow down), and the house directs her to the cellar, where "there is a creature who nibbles and gnaws at my timbers."

Cowley renders a delightful story from the traditional elements of its structure; the text does not ignore the absurdity of the situations—such as the mouse's proposal of marriage to the sun—but warmly mocks them. The pictures—pencil and sturdy, solid watercolors—play up the comic aspects of the story. [David] Christiana gives the enormous sun, cloud, and wind sympathetic human features; the tiny mouse, comically foreshortened and in her wedding gown, is heroically awkward to the end.

Susan Dove Lempke

SOURCE: A review of *The Mouse Bride*, in *Bulletin of the Center for Children's Books*, Vol. 49, No. 3, November, 1995, p. 87.

Illustrator Christiana provides a wordless prologue for the story: an adult arm is shown directing a little girl off to bed on the title page, and on the following pages, the girl scolds the dog, the dog trees the cat, and the cat chases the mouse. As the text begins, the mouse cries, "Small and weak! How I wish that I were strong!" and she sets off to find a strong husband, so that her children will be more powerful than she is. First, she proposes to the sun, but he points out that a cloud can completely cover him. The cloud in turn reminds her that the huffing wind can blow him across the sky. By the end of this (unsourced) traditional tale, the mouse has discovered an appropriate mate. Cowley relates the story with enough wit and energy that it could stand alone for telling, but Christiana's watercolors add a special dash of humor. Often giving the mouse's perspective, with objects looming above her, Christiana uses color and brushstroke to create different textures, and gives the sun, the cloud, and the wind each its own distinct personality. Unfortunately, he does undercut the final page's revelation ("And, yes, you have guessed it: Out from the depths of the cellar came another little mouse") by showing the male mouse on the previous spread, but this is a slight misstep in a storyhour book that will particularly satisfy its audience of small people.

JoAnn Rees

SOURCE: A review of *The Mouse Bride,* in *School Library Journal,* Vol. 41, No. 11, November, 1995, p. 89.

Another version of the folktale about the mouse who tries to marry varying powerful beings, like the sun, a cloud, and the wind, and ends up marrying the strongest of all—another mouse. Cowley's retelling is competent, but is overwhelmed by Christiana's large, eye-catching paintings. Unfortunately, in trying to show the enormity of the potential suitors and the smallness of the mouse, the illustrator has made the rodent so small that she's very hard to see, especially for a story time group.

April Judge

SOURCE: A review of *The Mouse Bride,* in *Booklist,* Vol. 92, Nos. 9-10, January 1 & 15, 1996, p. 843.

Feeling "small and weak," a tiny mouse sets out on a journey to find a strong husband. She asks the sun, the clouds, and the wind to marry her, but they all turn her down, disclaiming their strength. She proposes to a very old house, who tells her that the ideal husband is living in the basement. If this strong creature continues to nibble and gnaw on my beams and timbers, "I shall collapse in a heap of dust," he says. The tiny mouse scurries to the basement, where, to her surprise, she discovers another mouse, her future husband. Drawn from a mouse's perspective, the soft, unfocused illustrations sweep across each double-page spread. The exaggerated—almost cartoon-like—features of the mice, who are not portrayed as cute, cuddly animals, add a touch of whimsy to this playful tale. Amusing fare for young listeners.

Linnet Hunter

SOURCE: A review of *The Mouse Bride,* in *Magpies,* Vol. 11, No. 1, March, 1996, p. 28.

In this traditional folktale, a search for a strong husband is made for a small weak mouse, so that she might rear children who would not also be small and weak. The sun, the cloud, the wind, all are proposed to, but all can nominate someone stronger then they. In this version the mouse carries out the search herself (rather than her father), in modern day farmland. The author has made some interesting choices in her retelling. She has framed the tale so that a connection may be made between the powerless mouse and a child and she has kept the mouse small to highlight her lowly position in the world. Christiana has cleverly used broad shapes upon the page—the great, gentle semi-circular face of the bespectacled sun almost touches the green semi-circle of the grassy hill which the mouse perches upon, for example—to keep the mouse the focus of the story.

His watercolours make abundant use of white paper left uncoloured to dapple the effects of his dabbling brush. Every page is full of light, swirling movement, even the air is alive with subtle pattern and shade which make the illustrations a pleasure to dwell upon. It was difficult for me to engage with the mouse herself as she was so shiny and pink, her eyes so protuberant and her nose so bulbous. She almost appeared to have been skinned. This, and the way the twist in the tale (tail) was forestalled in the illustrations a page before the text revealed it, undermined the overall attraction of the book.

📖 **GRACIAS, THE THANKSGIVING TURKEY (1996)**

Carolyn Phelan

SOURCE: A review of *Gracias, The Thanksgiving Turkey,* in *Booklist,* Vol. 93, No. 1, September 1, 1996, p. 136.

Little Miguel lives in a New York City apartment with his grandparents and his aunt, while his truck-driving father is on the road. Papá sends Miguel a turkey to fatten for Thanksgiving, but the boy names the bird Gracias and loves him as a pet. As the holiday approaches, Gracias' fate looms darkly over the festivities. However, when Gracias follows Miguel to church and receives Padre Jaime's blessing, even Abuelo and Abuela concede that they must have chicken for Thanksgiving, because "no one can eat a turkey that's been blessed." Cowley creates a distinctive, modern setting for the old theme of a turkey who sits *at* rather than *on* the Thanksgiving table. Although city life is not idealized (at one point a thief steals Gracias), most of the neighbors in Miguel's multiethnic community take a friendly interest in the boy and his bird. The inclusion of Spanish words within the text is handled well, with most meanings evident from the context, but a short glossary also appears on the last page. [Joe] Cepeda's oil paintings, reminiscent of Ezra Jack Keats' illustrations, vividly create Miguel's colorful, sympathetic community as well as individual characters.

Linda Nelson

SOURCE: A review of *Gracias, The Thanksgiving Turkey,* in *Children's Book Review Service, Inc.,* Vol. 25, No. 2, October, 1996, p. 14.

The name Joy Cowley will be familiar to just about any child in a primary grade whole language classroom, but this story is very different from her usual entries. Miguel's truck-driving father sends him a live turkey with advice to "fatten him up before Thanksgiving," but Gracias, of course, becomes an endearing pet. Multicultural influences, including a sprinkling of Spanish names and phrases and the blessings of the Padre deepen the realistic tapestry of this multi-generational story.

Janice Del Negro

SOURCE: A review of *Gracias, The Thanksgiving Turkey,* in *Bulletin of the Center for Children's Books,* Vol. 50, No. 3, November, 1996, p. 90.

[In *Gracias, The Thanksgiving Turkey*] Miguel goes to the train station with his Abuela and Tía Rosa to collect a Thanksgiving present from his truck-driver father. No, it's not roller blades or a baseball glove—it's a live turkey. The note says, "Fatten this turkey for Thanksgiving. I'll be home to share it with you. Love from Papá." Miguel's Abuelo wonders where they'll keep a live turkey in a NYC apartment, Tía Rosa declares her brother is crazy, and Miguel says, "I love my turkey. I'm going to call her Gracias." Gracias becomes Miguel's *amiga,* and her Thanksgiving fate becomes a source of worry. When Miguel lights two candles at church, "one for his father and one for Gracias," Tía Rosa knows they have a problem. But Cowley saves the day. Late for church, Abuela forgets to tie up Gracias, and in the middle of mass the turkey gobbles her way down the aisle looking for Miguel. "Padre Jaime smiled. 'God made small boys and God made turkeys. Stand still while I give you both a blessing.'" Well, you can't eat a turkey that's been blessed, says a laughing Abuelo. A petting zoo and Papá's eagerly anticipated homecoming tie this one into a fulfilling Thanksgiving package.

Selene S. Vasquez

SOURCE: A review of *Gracias, The Thanksgiving Turkey,* in *School Library Journal,* Vol. 42, No. 12, December, 1996, p. 91.

Miguel, a Puerto Rican boy in New York City, receives a surprise package from his absentee truck-driving father—a gigantic wooden crate with the message: "Fatten this turkey for Thanksgiving. I'll be home to share it with you. Love from Papá." What ensues is a humorous story of Miguel's increasing attachment to the bird he nicknames *Gracias.* His new *amiga* follows him everywhere, even to Mass. Will Miguel be able to save Gracias from being seasoned and cooked? Can Papá make

it home in time for the holidays? This picture book, illustrated with colorful oil paintings, offers a heartwarming narrative that captures the boy's close-knit sense of community and family.

SINGING DOWN THE RAIN (1997)

Kirkus Reviews

SOURCE: A review of *Singing Down the Rain,* in *Kirkus Reviews,* Vol. LXV, No. 18, September 15, 1997, p. 1455.

The declaration "Sweet wonder!" ends this book—an apt assessment for an uplifting story from Cowley and [Jan Spivey] Gilchrist (*Madelia.*) Drought has struck Brianna's town, and the grown-ups gathered on the porch of Mr. Williams's store, usually "good and kind neighbors," are "getting real scritchy with each other." Something's got to change or the corn will die. The possibility of that change roars into town in a pickup truck, a woman with a "smile so big, it used most of her face," who specializes in rainsong. The adults don't take her seriously, but Brianna can smell the coming rain. She joins the woman in singing; the other children follow, as does Brianna's mother. The rain begins, and only Brianna notices the woman leave. A universal message reaches out of this warmhearted book.

Lisa Falk

SOURCE: A review of *Singing Down the Rain,* in *School Library Journal,* Vol. 43, No. 10, October, 1997, p. 95.

In the depressing heat of an extended drought, Brianna notices that "good and kind neighbors were getting real scritchy with each other." Until, that is, a mysterious "fine small woman with bangles on her arms, painted parrots in her ears, and a smile so big, it used most of her face" arrives. The stranger explains that she specializes in rainsongs. She begins her chanting, begging the children and skeptical, uninterested adults to help by joining in. One child, then a few at a time, join her, and finally the adults do, too, once the welcome rain begins to fall. Gilchrist's full-page, full-color illustrations face small vignettes and text that is set like verse. The soft, impressionistic paintings depict the general store and open landscape of a farm community. This beautiful, quiet book may be a shelf-sitter, but with a little pushing, it will certainly inspire cool relief for hot readers in warm climes.

Publishers Weekly

SOURCE: A review of *Singing Down the Rain,* in *Publishers Weekly,* Vol. 244, No. 45, November 3, 1997, p. 85.

Cowley's narrative voice and Gilchrist's sun-touched faces are the high points of this picture book about the power of community and faith. A blue pickup truck enters young Brianna's town during a heat spell that has "gone on so long/ that good and kind neighbors/ were getting real scritchy with each other." Out jumps "a fine small woman/ with bangles on her arms,/ painted parrots in her ears,/ and a smile so big,/ it used most of her face." The woman announces that she "felt a praying and a needing" as she rode past and that she "specializes in rainsongs." At first, everyone laughs when she asks them to join her in singing and dancing—"Oo-sha-la! Bo-ba-lo-lee!" Then one by one, led by the children, the entire town begins "dancing wet to the skin, face up,/ drinking all that mighty good rain" and only Brianna notices the mysterious woman driving off. Gilchrist's country scenes and characters can be a bit static and inconsistent, but at times her multiracial cast of children lights up the page with their rapt expressions. Cowley's chanting narrative fairly sings, and by packing her storytelling with homespun images and repetitive phrases, she makes her fanciful tale almost believable.

Stephanie Zvirin

SOURCE: A review of *Singing Down the Rain,* in *Booklist,* Vol. 94, No. 6, November 15, 1997, p. 565.

Brianna watches as the adults in her community grow impatient and apart as the hot, rainless days go on without end. A tiny woman, a rain singer, comes to town promising relief, but it isn't until Brianna joins the woman in song that the community draws together once again and the rain comes. In rich colors and broad, sure strokes, Gilchrist perfectly catches the shifting moods and the changing landscape as the story blends fantasy and reality. A tale about "sweet wonder" that speaks to the possibility of miracles.

Arlene Wartenberg

SOURCE: A review of *Singing Down the Rain,* in *Children's Book Review Service, Inc.,* Vol. 26, No. 4, December, 1997, p. 37.

Delightful! Cowley's prose reads like poetry in this tale of a town suffering from intense heat and severe drought. Things had gotten so bad that "neighbors were getting scritchy with each other." It takes a stranger; frogs, crickets and birds; and the children who "believe" to end the drought. Each of Gilchrist's paintings clearly portrays the emotions and actions of the town's people.

Elizabeth Burns

SOURCE: A review of *Singing Down the Rain,* in *Bulletin of the Center for Children's Books,* Vol. 51, No. 5, January, 1998, p. 157.

The air was so thick, you had to "cut it up to breathe it," and the heat had lasted so long, "even polite conversation was drying up." As the adults of the town gather on the porch of the grocery store to fan themselves and complain, little Brianna and her friends witness the arrival of a small, wild-haired woman with dangling parrot earrings and a "smile so big, it used up most of her face." The woman promises to bring the rain down by leading the community in song, but the skeptical adults turn away in embarrassment. The children, affected more by the music itself than by faith in its efficacy, sing along, and as their efforts bring results, the adults wholeheartedly join in while the rainmaker quietly slips away. Gilchrist's figures are unevenly rendered and awkwardly drafted, the faces poorly articulated and unexpressive. The textual crescendo of "Oo-sha-la! Bo-ba-lo-lee's," and the resultant welcome rains, however, are almost palpable, and storytime audiences may be happy to echo the refrain, "Sweet wonder!"

THE BUMP (1998)

Margaret Kedian

SOURCE: A review of *The Bump,* in *Magpies,* Vol. 13, No. 1, March, 1998, pp. 7-8.

> My mother has a bump in her tummy. It's because she eats heaps of pickled onions and cheese. She says there's a baby inside, but I don't think that is true. No baby could live in all that squished up cheese and pickled onion.

This provocative beginning goes right to the heart of any child who is wondering where babies come from. Told from a first child's point of view, this cleverly crafted story skilfully handles the biting jealousy and demanding behaviour of Anna coming to terms with her mother's pregnancy and the birth of a new baby into the family.

Linda McClelland of *Why Nana* and *Pavlova and Presents* fame, adds warmth to Joy Cowley's story with her paintings of round children and muted colours which enhance the characterisation and take the reader beyond the text. Successful use of thought bubbles and reflections allow us to see what is actually happening as well as the thoughts and emotions going on inside Anna. The delightful twist in the end makes the story completely satisfying.

Joy Cowley, as a storyteller, never disappoints her readers. Her talent, combined with Linda McClelland's illustrative skills, has produced a book that is a must for any child expecting a new sibling and every parent anxious about coping with sibling rivalry. The story is quite long and is best used as a read-aloud story for young children.

THE WILD WEST GANG (1998)

John McKenzie

SOURCE: A review of *The Wild West Gang,* in *Reading Time,* Vol. 42, No. 3, August, 1998, p. 31.

When Michael's very middle-class parents (he is an only child) decide to go off on a golfing weekend and his Aunty Rosie, Uncle Leo and five cousins (new[ly] arrived in the neighbourhood) welcome him to stay at their place, the stage is set for Michael to have adventures. If *Keeping Up Appearances* appeals to the adult audience who enjoys the send up that Mrs. Bucket gets, then younger readers will enjoy the send up of niceties in this humorous tale of young Michael's fortunes and misfortunes with the Wild West Gang. It's less the comic adventure (rafts and mudfights and grisly tales) that captivates and more the sense of human warmth in the midst of chaos. Michael desperately wants to be told off by Auntie Rosie with her colourful and irreverent language for that would signal acceptance in this family of seeming misfits. The cartoon style of [Trevor Pye] matches exactly the tone of this story.

For children who are about to go camping, or the teacher who wants a good read aloud for the junior school, this book is highly recommended.

📖 STARBRIGHT AND THE DREAM EATER (1998)

Trevor Agnew

SOURCE: A review of *Starbright and the Dream Eater,* in *Magpies,* Vol. 13, No. 5, November, 1998, p. 8.

I first saw Joy Cowley in action, talking to a group of teachers in Winton (a town equally off the beaten track in Australia and New Zealand). She was enthusiastic, modest, giving her time freely, and showing a brilliant ability to turn a dry anecdote into a real story, one with characters, motives, plot and action. Joy Cowley is never dull and never repeats herself either. So *Starbright and the Dream Eater* is quite unlike *The Silent One* or *Bow Down Shadrach,* except that it has characters, motives, plot and action. In other words, it's a Joy Cowley novel. The birth of a child to a brain-damaged fifteen-year-old may not seem a promising start to a novel, but the heightened descriptions, hints of foretold events and flawed predictions, create a dramatic arrival for Starbright. She grows up as a lively girl in a normal American town, until the moment of crisis arrives, with a plague—the spindle sickness—which puts people into a sleep from which they never wake. Then we have a double narrative, an overview from the mysterious Nurse Tietz who sees her twin brother's prophecy unfolding, and an underview from Starbright who finds her own family and friends threatened by the 'disease'.

Without giving too much of the plot away, it is fair to say that, while descriptions of dreams can be very boring, Joy Cowley has managed to avoid this trap. She has also managed to include spiritual elements, an awareness of the importance of the different outlook of the mentally handicapped ('special' people), shrewd observation and gentle fun. There is a tiny comic gem when Star-

bright decides to do a solo bungy-jump and realises, too late, that she has no way to untie herself.

The prose of *Starbright and the Dream Eater* has a rich texture; Starbright makes up her own vocabulary ("I swim too good to deadydrown") just like the author who has created the *breathsmoke* of a frosty night. In handling such themes as secret powers, the paranormal, prophecies and alternate universes, Joy Cowley draws a nice line between credulity and scepticism, leaving readers to make their own minds up. This is a satisfying page-turning novel, rich in ideas, and my only reservation is that it never really comes to grips with the situation of a child discovering that her sister is her mother. Perhaps this may become another Joy Cowley story?

Jilaine Johnson

SOURCE: A review of *Starbright and the Dream Eater,* in *Reading Time,* Vol. 42, No. 4, November, 1998, p. 32.

This is a rattling good yarn with interesting characters. The story is set in a rural community, possibly in middle America, in 'now time' with the protagonist, Starbright, twelve and a half years old. Starbright is the child of a prophecy, born to face a universal danger. In 1986 a meteor lands in a tiny farming community in South America, an alien life force is released in an explosion by a scientist's experiment, and the future confrontation between the child without fear and the Dream Eater is set. A mysterious sleeping sickness, called Spindle sickness, (as the afflicted go to sleep and do not wake up) was first noticed in the South American farming hamlets. Few tie it in with the meteor. A scientist, Jacob and his twin sister, Lena, believe. Jacob unravels a message about the dangerous Dream Eater, sent by a friendly alien race light years away. When the sickness, some years later, hits Clairbourn, the area where Starbright lives, Lena knows that the Dream Eater is tracking the one person who can save the world. She informs Starbright of the prophecy, hands her all the scientific evidence and the struggle for earth begins. This novel is well written, although I did find the made-up exclamations of Starbright—especially 'whodiddly' rather grating. I found the ending where the previous 13 years of the world's history was 'overlaid' taxed my sense of belief in the story somewhat. However the child readers—10-12 years olds may well enjoy the special made-up words and accept the ending as part of this pacy story.

📖 BIG MOON TORTILLA (1998)

Roxanne Burg

SOURCE: A review of *Big Moon Tortilla,* in *School Library Journal,* Vol. 44, No. 11, November, 1998, p. 7.

A picture book set on a Tohono O'odham (Papago) reservation in southern Arizona. When the aroma of Grandmother's fresh tortillas fills her room, Marta Enos begins to daydream about them. Her toes twitch and her legs just can't wait to run to the cookhouse. She hurries off for a sample, but knocks over a table on the way. The wind picks up her homework papers and scatters them. The dogs outside think it's a game, and they eat her assignment. As Marta tries to regroup, her glasses fall off, she steps on them, and they break. Grandmother is sympathetic and offers the child a tortilla as "big and pale as a rising full moon" as well as wise words of advice from a Native American proverb about dealing with adverse situations. Watercolor illustrations [by Dyanne Strongbow] in muted tones enhance this sweet tale.

AGAPANTHUS HUM AND THE EYE-GLASSES (1998)

Kirkus Reviews

SOURCE: A review of *Agapanthus Hum and the Eyeglasses,* in *Kirkus Reviews,* Vol. LXVI, No. 23, December 1, 1998, p. 1732.

Agapanthus Hum is always in motion, a packet of energy who also happens to wear glasses, which cause her no end of trouble. When she smothers her parents—called good little Daddy and good little Mommy—with kisses, her glasses come off and swing from one ear. When doing a handstand, the glasses drop off entirely and get crushed when Agapanthus crashes down upon them: "Her hum puffed out like a birthday candle, and her head went quiet," but only briefly. Her parents are sweet and kind and utterly forgiving (absurdly so, as Cowley makes clear) and mention that she is one fine acrobat all the same. The ultimate solution is for good little Mommy to hold Agapanthus's glasses during practice. When Agapanthus attends an acrobat show and learns that at least one professional acrobat who wears glasses gives them to her mother when she performs, one little girl's fate is sealed. This story is just like Agapanthus, full of beans, song, and heart; she's so disarming in both text and [Jennifer] Plecas's comic illustrations that readers will hope for an encore.

THE RED-EYED TREE FROG

Janice M. Del Negro

SOURCE: A review of *The Red-Eyed Tree Frog,* in *Bulletin of the Center for Children's Books,* Vol. 52, No. 7, March, 1999, p. 235.

When evening comes to the rainforest, the red-eyed tree frog wakes up hungry and begins its search for sustenance. The frog eyes a succulent black ant, a fierce-looking katydid, and an exotically colored caterpillar; it escapes a hunting boa, eats a tasty moth, and "shuts its eyes . . . and goes to sleep . . . as morning comes to the rainforest." Cowley's spare but attractively declarative text is set in a sans serif font against grass green panels which feature gloriously sharp color photographs of said tree frog and other rainforest creatures it encounters in the search for food. [Nic] Bishop . . . is just as impressive here with his intimate close-up photographs of tropical flora and fauna. The book's involving design displays an attention to detail that pays off with a subtle visual feast (for example, as the evening dark deepens, so does the color green that serves as the background; as the morning lightens, so does the green). The photographs practically drip with color, and the crystalline focus results in precise, articulated images. A concluding double-page spread entitled "Did You Know?" gives additional information about the life cycle of the red-eyed tree frog. The combination of high photographic action and lively text makes this a *ribbet*ing adventure for beginning readers.

THE RUSTY, TRUSTY TRACTOR

Janice M. Del Negro

SOURCE: A review of *The Rusty, Trusty Tractor,* in *Bulletin of the Center for Children's Books,* Vol. 52, No. 7, March, 1999, p. 236.

Micah's farmer grandfather considers his old tractor to be an old friend, and he resists the blandishments of tractor salesman Mr. Hill and refuses to buy a new machine. The salesman bets the farmer a box of jelly doughnuts that the tractor won't make it through harvest. With a lot of coaxing and gentle handling, the old tractor wins the old man and his grandson a box of jelly doughnuts--after which they pull the salesman's car out of the mud with the rusty tractor. Cowley's easygoing storytelling style makes the most of the simple story: "When Mr. Hill saw Granpappy's tractor, he laughed fit to bust his britches. 'Woo-oo!' he cried, slapping his knee. 'You call that a tractor?' Micah looked at Granpappy to see what he was thinking, but Granpappy was not letting on." [Olivier] Dunrea illustrates this satisfying little farm story with low-key gouache art that, despite the occasionally awkward drafting of the characters, offers a comfortable rusticity. Cowley's old-fashioned story has charm, and it will make a successful group read-aloud and maybe even a read-alone for those beginning readers ready to tackle a little more text-intensive literature.

Additional coverage of Cowley's life and career is contained in the following sources published by The Gale Group: *Contemporary Authors First Revision Series,* 25-28; *Contemporary Authors New Revision Series,* Vols. 11, 57; *Something about the Author,* Vols. 4, 90; *Something about the Author Autobiography Series,* Vol. 26.

Karen Cushman

1941-

American author of fiction.

Major works include *Catherine, Called Birdy* (1994); *The Midwife's Apprentice* (1995); *The Ballad of Lucy Whipple* (1996).

INTRODUCTION

Considered one of the most accomplished authors of juvenile literature to have emerged in the 1990s, Cushman is praised for creating accurate, fascinating historical novels for young adults that feature appealing female protagonists in medieval England and Gold Rush-era California. In contrast to the dry, antiseptic tomes on long-ago times that are sometimes directed to the young, Cushman's novels are acknowledged as graphic, even earthy portrayals of historical people and periods as well as moving coming-of-age stories. She is also noted for updating traditional views of history with her subjects and themes. In Cushman's books, young women struggle to establish their identities in male-dominated, often oppressive cultures. Her teenage protagonists find the strength to survive, and even thrive, in their particular situations. In Cushman's first book, *Catherine, Called Birdy,* the heroine, who lives in relative luxury as the daughter of a nobleman during the reign of Edward I, resists her father's attempts to sell her into marriage. Cushman shows the other side of medieval life in her next book, *The Midwife's Apprentice,* which describes how an orphaned, homeless peasant girl rises from sleeping on a dunghill to becoming a respected member of her village. In her third novel, *The Ballad of Lucy Whipple,* Cushman features a young woman who, taken from the civilized comforts of Massachusetts to the rough-and-tumble life of the American West, learns to make a home in her new environment. Often noted for her success in evoking atmosphere, Cushman is credited with providing her audience with thorough renderings of social history and insightful portrayals of human nature. She is further lauded for including a wealth of information about the daily lives of her characters—their lifestyles, beliefs, practices, and habits—as well as the cruelty, faith, duplicity, kindness, and strength of their personalities. Cushman is especially well regarded for creating rounded, engaging protagonists with whom contemporary readers can easily identify. In addition, she is acclaimed for the realism of her stories: her works include death, racism, and domestic violence as well as waste elimination, swearing, flatulence, and other gritty details of life. Although Cushman deals with serious subjects and themes, she fills her books with humor and wit as well as colorful supporting characters. As a literary stylist, she favors first-person narratives, often in diary or letter formats, and is often celebrated for her

craftsmanship and ability to sketch characters in a few strokes. She also includes an afterword in each of her books that provides historical facts about medieval peoples, midwifery, and women during the Gold Rush, respectively. Although some reviewers note that Cushman sacrifices historical facts to reflect contemporary feminist concerns and depends too much on plot conveniences, most observers see her as a writer whose views of history are authentic, relevant, and entertaining. Writing in *The Lion and the Unicorn,* Joseph Zornado claimed that Cushman challenges "our notions of historical fiction, history, and how we make meaning of and from the past. . . . Cushman sets out to challenge traditional notions of historical fiction by writing a new kind of historical fiction."

Biographical Information

Born in Chicago, Cushman was an avid reader from an early age. She told *Something about the Author* (*SATA*), "Once I discovered the library, I discovered books. Fiction was my favorite, but I would get these wild passions and read all there was on the Civil War for instance, or on the physiology of the brain. I guess this kind of curiosity explains my later fascination with the Middle Ages." She enjoyed books such as *The Story of Ferdinand, Homer Price, Cotton in My Sack,* and *Caddie Woodlawn* as well as the Bobbsey Twins series, *Mad* magazine, and the comics of Little Lulu and Donald Duck. In addition, she remembers liking books such as *Microbe Hunters, Triumph over Pain,* and *The Rise and Fall of the Third Reich.* Her working-class family often did not know what to make of her. In her Newbery Award acceptance speech, Cushman recalled that she used to imagine that she "was the only child ever kidnapped *from* gypsies and sold to regular people." Cushman's rich fantasy life found an outlet in neighborhood plays and imaginary adventures on her brother's scooter. She told *SATA,* "I used to borrow that scooter and take off and imagine myself going all around the world, which is sort of what I do now, only I travel backwards in time in my writing." At ten, she moved with her family to Tarzana in southern California; at around the same time, she began to write poems, stories, and plays. "Recently," she told *SATA,* "I came across a play I wrote in junior high—'Jingle Bagels,' a sort of multicultural Christmas story. I also wrote several possible plots for new Elvis movies." Once her teachers and classmates discovered her talent, Cushman was often tapped to write everything from valedictory speeches to submissions for writing contests.

After graduating from high school, Cushman won a scholarship that allowed her to attend any college in the United States; she decided to attend Stanford in her home state of California, where she became an English major. Cushman soon discovered, as she recalled in *SATA,* that she "liked the wrong kinds of books"; she began studying Greek and dreaming of a career in archeology. At the time, she never thought about writing as a profession and only used it, as she noted, to "ventilate my feelings or to celebrate." After graduating from Stanford with a double major in English and Greek, Cushman wanted, as she told *SATA,* "to dig for treasures on the Acropolis by moonlight." Instead she took on a series of administrative and customer service jobs, including one at Hebrew Union College in Los Angeles, where she met her husband Philip, then a rabbinical student. The couple moved to Oregon, where they lived for two years and had a daughter, Leah. After returning to California, both Karen and Philip earned master's degrees in counseling and human behavior; Philip also received his doctorate in psychology and became a professor and psychotherapist. Karen received a second master's degree in museum studies and became an adjunct faculty member at John F. Kennedy University in Orinda, California, where she taught classes in museology and material culture, coordinated the master's project program, and edited the *Museum Studies Journal.* She also began to read children's books, both to and with her daughter. Cushman told *SATA,* "When we got to young adult literature, I just stayed there while she went on to adult books. There is something about the themes of these books that appeal to me—coming of age, the acceptance of responsibility, and the development of com-

passion." She began to come up with ideas for a book of her own; in 1989, she formed the genesis of a story that would tell young people what life was like for a girl during the Middle Ages. This became her first published work, *Catherine, Called Birdy.*

Written after three years of research—including finding a thirteenth-century book on manners that advised readers not to blow their noses on the tablecloths—*Catherine, Called Birdy* was published when its author was fifty-three. Called "the love child of Rosemary Sutcliff and Adrian Mole" by Cushman in *Booklist,* the book was written, according to the author in her Newbery acceptance speech, "because I needed to find out about things, about identity and responsibility, compassion and kindness and belonging, and being human in the world. How could I learn about them if I didn't write about them?" During the process of writing her first novel, Cushman came up with the title for her next book, *The Midwife's Apprentice.* Using the background information she had gathered for *Catherine, Called Birdy,* Cushman wrote, as she called it in her acceptance speech, "a celebration of rebirth and renewal. . . . " She told *SATA,* "I could see this girl crawling out of the warm spot she had created for herself in the heap, sort of exploding out of it like she herself was being born." Cushman added in her acceptance speech, "I knew this girl and her longing for a place, her feelings of unworthiness, her fear of trying and failing, and her fragile confidence." She was inspired to write her third novel, *The Ballad of Lucy Whipple,* by a book on the California Gold Rush that stated that ninety percent of the people involved in the movement were men. Cushman began to wonder about the women and children who came to the tent cities in the wilds of California. In addition, she began to see the parallels between her protagonist Lucy and herself, a young girl transplanted from Chicago to California. "So, again," Cushman noted in a *Booklist* interview, "I think my own life is sort of playing out with somebody else's in this story."

Major Works

Cushman's first book, *Catherine, Called Birdy,* is set in 1290 in the village of Stonebridge, Lincolnshire, England, in the small manor house of an impoverished nobleman. Hoping to receive a large profit, the lord attempts to arrange a marriage for his fourteen-year-old daughter, Catherine, who is nicknamed Birdy because she loves animals and keeps a caged bird in her room. In order to fulfill an assignment issued to her by her brother, a monk, Birdy keeps a journal throughout the year in which she describes daily events at home, her family, and her fellow villagers as well as her own thoughts and feelings. Birdy emerges as a bright, feisty girl with a pronounced social conscience and a strong sense of independence. Attempting to foil her father's plans, she scares off several suitors—for example, she pretends to be mad and sets fire to a privy that one is using—and is consequently beaten by her father. Throughout the year, Birdy grows and changes. She finally realizes that her only option is to go ahead with a marriage that her father has arranged with a boorish middle-aged man she calls "Shaggy Beard"; however, when the man dies suddenly, Birdy becomes engaged to his son, an educated youth who promises to be a better match. A critic for *Kirkus Reviews* wrote of *Catherine, Called Birdy,* "The period has rarely been presented for young people with such authenticity. . . . [Birdy's] tenacity and ebullient naivete are extraordinary; at once comic and thought-provoking, this first novel is a delight." Bruce Anne Shook called the book "[s]uperb historical fiction" and commented, "Birdy lays before readers a feast of details about medieval England. . . . A feminist far ahead of her time, she is both believable and lovable."

Cushman's next book, *The Midwife's Apprentice,* is set in fourteenth-century England among the lower classes. In just over a hundred pages, Cushman outlines how a nameless waif finds her place in the world. The girl, who is called Brat and is about twelve or thirteen, is rescued from her dunghill by the irritable local midwife, Jane Sharp, who takes her in as a servant and names her Beetle, short for Dungbeetle. Proving herself a hard worker, Beetle is entrusted with some of the secrets of Jane's profession. Gradually, the girl begins to develop self-esteem; for example, she rescues a cat, helps a boy to deliver twin calves, and renames herself Alyce. Jane Sharp becomes jealous when a woman in labor asks for Alyce; however, the girl's confidence is shaken when the labor becomes difficult and Jane is called in to save the mother. Humiliated, Alyce runs away and gets a job in an inn; however, she comes to realize that midwifery is her destiny and returns to Jane to become a full-fledged apprentice. A critic in *Kirkus Reviews* called *The Midwife's Apprentice* "a gripping story about a time, place, and society that 20th-century readers can hardly fathom. Fortunately, Cushman does the fathoming for them, rendering in Brat a character as fully fleshed and real as Katherine Paterson's best. . . . [T]his is not for fans of historical drama only. It's a rouser for all times." Robert Dunbar added, "Cushman brilliantly incorporates . . . themes of personal growth within a fascinating frame of medieval social and medical history."

In her third novel, *The Ballad of Lucy Whipple,* Cushman describes how twelve-year-old California Morning Whipple unwillingly travels to Lucky Diggins, a hard-scrabble mining camp in the California gold fields in 1849. California, who has come from Massachusetts with her mother, brother, and sisters after the death of her father, rebelliously changes her name to Lucy because it sounds more "eastern." Feeling homesick and out of place, Lucy starts saving her gold dust and money earned from baking for a trip back East. She also writes complaining letters to her grandparents back in Massachusetts about life in the camp. Even though Lucy misses civilization—especially books—she learns to survive in her new home. She makes friends and deals with floods, fires, and an array of eccentric characters, some of whom, to her dismay, want to court her mother. Lucy also experiences the loss of her brother, who becomes ill and dies from a lack of medical treatment. When her

mother falls in love with a traveling evangelist and prepares to move to Sandwich Island for missionary work, Lucy decides to stay in California and become the town librarian for Lucky Diggins; she also changes her name back to California Morning. Linda Perkins wrote of *The Ballad of Lucy Whipple,* "Lucy's story is packed with more history than many textbooks. . . . Karen Cushman takes the reader inside Lucy's heart and mind." Writing in *Kirkus Reviews,* a critic noted, "Lucy is an irresistible teenager. . . . With a story that is less a period piece than a timeless and richly comic coming-of-age story, Cushman remains on a roll."

Awards

Catherine, Called Birdy won the Carl Sandburg Award for Children's Literature and the Golden Kite Award in 1994. In the same year, it won the Cuffie Award from *Publishers Weekly* and was named a Newbery Award Honor Book and a Best Book of the Year by both *School Library Journal* and *Voice of Youth Advocates* (*VOYA*), as well as a *VOYA* Editor's Choice, Books for Youth. In 1995, the Young Adult Library Services Association named *Catherine, Called Birdy* a Best Book for Young Readers and a Recommended Book for Reluctant Young Readers, and in 1996, the novel appeared on the Honour List of the International Board on Books for Young People. *The Midwife's Apprentice* was awarded the Newbery Medal in 1995; in the same year, it won the *Booklist* Editor's Choice Award and was named to the Best Books lists of both *School Library Journal* and *VOYA*.

AUTHOR'S COMMENTARY

Hazel Rochman

SOURCE: An interview with Karen Cushman, in *Booklist,* Vol. 92, Nos. 19-20, June 1, 1996, p. 1700-701.

BKL: How did the museum scholar come to write children's books?

CUSHMAN: I think it was the story. I didn't start out to write a book. I just started thinking of this story about somebody who was faced with what looked like no choices or options, and I wondered, what could she do about her life? Then I thought, well, how much more would that have been true in the Middle Ages, when people had less power and less value. But I think my interest always (even though I never thought I was going to be a writer exactly) was communicating with children.

BKL: Have you always been interested in medieval history?

CUSHMAN: I remember years ago I had these charts of kings and queens all over my walls, and I was reading a lot about medieval Europe and was interested in the music of the time. But every time I looked at academic programs in medieval history, I was turned off by their narrowness and by their focus, which was always on great events and great people and great movements. I was more interested in the ordinary. So I came to it through museums and material culture, the stuff of everyday life—what we can find out about ordinary people at another time. I had written a grant to the National Endowment for the Humanities about doing research in the history of childhood, so I was looking at the subject more academically. I didn't get the grant, and I was doing some research on my own. But once I got the idea for the story, I had to write it down, no matter what I was going to do with it.

BKL: Writing historical fiction is like writing about a foreign country. How do you get an authentic sense of thirteenth-century England and at the same time make us care about your characters?

CUSHMAN: It's all subconscious, but I've been trying to put it into words. Imagination and the facts and empathy have to all come together, and none of them must overpower anything else. If empathy overpowers the facts, then you're not going to have people who are realistic to their era. But if the imagination doesn't come in, then you just have a textbook. So it really is a combination of all of those things. The way I seem to do it is to get the idea for the story first, and then do a lot of reading in the time and place. I know the kind of interesting things I'm looking for, the kind of background that I need, and then I go back and forth from the story to the research.

BKL: You feel so comfortable in that world that you can relax.

CUSHMAN: Yes, that's what happened with the second book. I was very comfortable in that time and place. I knew that village and that place so well from all the research I had done for *Birdy* that I could put more emphasis on the story.

BKL: Could your two characters, Catherine and Alyce, have known each other?

CUSHMAN: They certainly could have lived in the same village. And given the way Catherine liked to go down and muck around with the villagers, they could have known each other. Someone told me that a school in Britain is using the two of them together to look at the two halves of the village, comparing the different ways of life. Catherine, you know, has this over idealized view of what it's like to be a peasant, sort of frolicking in the hay and eating apples. The other book is a bit more realistic.

BKL: Both books are funny. How did you avoid being too reverential or too romantic?

CUSHMAN: The way I got away from the reverential

was to read a lot of primary sources. Luckily, there's a lot that's been reprinted. So I could read the diaries and etiquette books from the Middle Ages. And these were not people for us to revere. Those were very earthy, direct people, and I found that I could really relate to that. People say to me, How could you use words like piss and fart? Did you do that just to appeal to modern kids? And I say, no, in fact those were the least offensive words that I found. I cleaned it up for you, and now you're complaining.

BKL: Are kids embarrassed?

CUSHMAN: Not usually. I think these are words they hear before they even start school. It's not that I go that far beyond where they are. I think they're surprised that somebody is writing it in a book. They read about her hiding in the dung heap, and they know what dung is. At one school, a kid said, "How come, you write so much about dung?" And I said, "Because there was so much there."

BKL: One thing you bring out so strongly in Catherine is her longing for privacy. Were people aware of it then, or is this you looking back?

CUSHMAN: Well, I refuse to believe that because medieval women were supposed to be a particular way that all of them were the same. So when people say to me, oh, but those weren't real characters because medieval women weren't like that, I say, well how do you know? I don't think Eleanor of Aquitaine, for example, was a retiring woman who spent most of her time on her embroidery. I think that at all ages and in all places there have been women—and men—who were not content with their lot.

I think of the Middle Ages moving into the Renaissance as like a child growing into adolescence. A lot of scholars have written books about the development of the sense of privacy and identity. People started to pay attention to how they looked to someone else. They started to have books of etiquette. I have one book that has a section on how to share a bed with somebody else. You come to the inn and you pay your pennies and you get a third of a bed; so you can't knock the guy out of bed or steal the covers or stab him; there are all these rules. Catherine, whenever there were visitors, had people not only in her room but in her bed.

There was much less privacy then than we have now. Everybody lived in one room. I talk about that when I visit schools, because it is so hard for kids to understand. I mean many of them have their own rooms, their own TVS, their own bathrooms, and they can't imagine a more communal life. On the whole, most medieval people were used to it. I think that some people really liked it that way, not everybody mourned the lack of privacy, but Catherine was a little idiosyncratic and already moving more toward a modern person in that she noticed it and sometimes even complained.

BKL: What connects us with Alyce?

CUSHMAN: I think that Alyce in *Midwife* lived in a world that was all about place. Even people's names, Thomas At-the-Bridge or Robert Weaver, everything was all about their place, in the culture, in the society, or geographic place. And here was this child without place. She wasn't willing to be just a placeless, nameless child; she wanted an identity and to belong. I think that's what I related to as I wrote her story. I never was homeless or hungry, but I could understand that search to know where I stand and who I am. Kids can relate to that.

BKL: How do kids respond to Catherine and Alyce's stories?

CUSHMAN: I get a lot of feedback from kids. Much more about Catherine, because the book is being used in so many classrooms in the seventh grade when they do medieval Europe. They all seem to get caught up in the story, and they all want to know how her father could do this and why her friend would marry somebody she didn't want to. I bring up the idea of attitudes changing, about what we think is right. We talk about the bear-baiting and the public executions. You know, they can't imagine it, but they side with Catherine, and so they get very involved in her story and much more as a group. The kids who prefer Alyce seem to be quieter, and they come up to me afterwards. They say they are so happy she got to go back to the midwife, that she found this place.

BKL: Was it hard to get published?

CUSHMAN: People said nobody wants historical fiction, children don't like diaries, the Middle Ages are dead. But I had this idea for the story, and I wanted to write it down no matter what happened, so before I did anything, I had the whole book written. Then I thought, well, what am I going to do with this? I didn't want to go to a writing class because I was almost 50 at that point, and I thought I don't want to sit and hear other people talk about their stuff. I only want to talk about my stuff. So I called a woman who teaches writing classes locally and arranged to meet with her. I needed to get outside my family and get more objective feedback. My husband took the manuscript, and he says he sold it to Dorothy Briley (editor-in-chief at Clarion) in the elevator of their apartment building. He gave her the manuscript in the elevator, and a couple of days later, she said, "We'll take it." So that's the story. I don't know if it's apocryphal or not.

BKL: What about *Midwife?*

CUSHMAN: With *Midwife,* I wrote the first half just in this fury, very quickly, and sent it to my editor, Dinah Stevenson, and she reminds me that I said, "I don't know if this is a writing exercise or a book. What do you think?" Then I wrote the second half, and I had Alyce leaving the village and going off on this series of picaresque adventures. I sent it in, and I said I wasn't

happy with it. Dinah agreed that it was not right. I couldn't figure out what was wrong, and I had my father read it and all sorts of people, and what I finally decided, with their help, was that what Alyce really needed to do was to complete the circle and to go back. So I kept her closer to home, took out all of these adventures and all these other characters, and then sent her and the cat back to the Midwife.

BKL: And then it won the Newbery.

CUSHMAN: It's still hard for me to believe it most of the time. I haven't made my Newbery speech yet and gone to all the cocktail parties; maybe it will be more real then. While I was in New York (in April), Paula Quint gave me a copy of a poster that the Children's Book Council had done for the first 75 years of the Newbery Award. Luckily, I won it this year, so there I am in the lower right-hand corner, along with all of these other people. And when I saw that, it just blew my mind. I couldn't believe it.

BKL: I heard that when your first book received the Newbery Honor, you had to go to the library to find out what the award meant. Do you read a lot of children's books?

CUSHMAN: I do. One of the things that I tell librarians is that I think of *Birdy* as the love child of Rosemary Sutcliff and Adrian Mole. I love Sutcliff's books and was very much inspired about reading and then writing historical fiction from her books. The *Adrian Mole Diaries* are very funny, and I like the way that we can see him through our own eyes and also through his eyes, and how different it is. I love *Sarah, Plain and Tall* and *Missing May* and books with that clear, clean prose.

BKL: What's your next book?

CUSHMAN: It's called *The Ballad of Lucy Whipple.* . . . It's set in the California gold rush. I think two things pulled it together for me. First, I was looking at the back of a book in a bookstore in California, and it said that the gold rush was a movement of men, that fully 90 percent of the people who came to California to search for gold were men. I thought, okay, so what about the other 10 percent, who were probably women and children who didn't choose to come, who weren't marching across the country strumming "Oh, Susannah" on their banjos? They came because of the men. And some of them were happy to do it, but some were unsure, and some were downright reluctant. What about a young girl who was moved from her home in Massachusetts, where she had indoor plumbing and a favorite tree and a public library and her grandparents and a dog, and who came to a tent city in the wilderness in California? And as I was starting to write about it, talking about it, telling my husband (you know, she had to leave her grandparents and her dog and her library and blah blah blah . . .), he said, "That sounds just like you when your folks moved to California from Chicago." I think that's very true. I'm still dealing with that. It wasn't my choice. I was 10 years old. The reasons that they gave me, like picking oranges all year round and eating Christmas dinner outside in your shorts, didn't seem good enough reasons to me. So, again, I think my own life is sort of playing out with somebody else's in this story.

Karen Cushman

SOURCE: "Newbery Medal Acceptance," in *The Horn Book Magazine,* Vol. LXXII, No. 4, July-August, 1996, pp. 413-19.

[*The following excerpt is Karen Cushman's acceptance speech for the 1996 Newbery Medal for* **The Midwife's Apprentice,** *which she delivered at the American Library Association annual meeting in New York City on July 7, 1996.*]

Among a native Australian people, it is said, when the rice crop shows sign of failure, the women go into the rice field, bend down, and relate to it the history of its origins; the rice, now understanding why it is there, begins again to grow.

Aha, I thought, as I read this passage, Such is the importance of stories. This is why I write.

I don't start a book by thinking of the listener or the reader; I just climb inside a story and write it over and over again until I know what it's about. Then I try to write as clearly and honestly as I can.

But when the book is finished and I hold it in my hands, I can see myself bending down to whisper it into the ear of a child. You are there, too—you writers, illustrators, booksellers, publishers, and librarians, all whispering away. And the child, now understanding, begins to grow. This is why I write—so children can begin to grow, to see beyond the edges of their own experience.

There are other reasons, also, why I write—not quite so philosophical and high-minded. I write because it's something I can do at home barefoot; because I can lie on my bed and read and call it work; because I am always making up stories in my head anyway and I might as well make a living from them; because I am fifty-four years old and I just figured out that I am not immortal. Like Jacqueline Woodson, I want to leave a sign of having been here. I have ideas, opinions, things to say, and I want to say them before I go. I want to take sides, to argue from my own passions and values and beliefs. I have questions I want to explore in an attempt to find, with Herb Gardner, "the subtle, sneaky important reason" I was born a human being and not a chair.

But maybe, most of all, I write because when I relax and trust myself, it feels so right to be a writer. Writing is my niche, my home, my place in the world, a place I finally found, just as Alyce, the midwife's apprentice, found hers, and, in my next book, Lucy Whipple finds hers.

And my place is full of words, of settings real and pretend, of people I have never met but know as well as I know myself, of events that never happened but have changed me in the imagining. This is why I write.

I write for the child I was and the child I still am. Like countless other lucky adults, I have much in common with children. We daydream, wonder, exaggerate, ask "what if?"—and what we imagine sometimes is more true than what *is*. We like to play with squishy things—mud, clay, dough, words—and we make stuff out of them. We like kids, animals, rain puddles, and pizza, and dare to love silly things. We don't like Brussels sprouts, the dentist, or books with great long passages of description, flashbacks, or dream sequences. We like happy endings—or at least, hope. And we love stories.

There is a Hasidic story (there is always a Hasidic story):

> Some followers go to their rabbi.
>
> "Rebbe," they ask, "what is heaven like?"
>
> "In heaven," answers the rabbi, "they sit at a table with all sorts of delicacies and good things. The only problem is, their arms do not bend."
>
> "And what is hell like?"
>
> "In hell they sit at a table with all sorts of delicacies and good things. The only problem is, their arms do not bend."
>
> "Then, Rebbe, what is the difference between heaven and hell?"
>
> "Ah, my children," said the rabbi, "in heaven they feed each other."

Writing for me is us feeding each other—writer and reader—fifty-four-year-old me and the young people who pick up my books. Me whispering in their ears and them talking back. They read and I am nourished, and my book becomes something richer and more profound than ever I hoped.

After *Catherine, Called Birdy* was named a Newbery Honor Book last year, a number of interviewers remarked that I had come out of nowhere. I didn't. I always knew where I was. I just hadn't started whispering to the rice yet.

As a child I wrote constantly but never thought about growing up to be a writer. I come from a working-class Chicago-area family that loved me dearly but often didn't quite know what to make of me. I used to imagine I was the only child ever kidnapped *from* gypsies and sold to regular people. I didn't know writing was a job, something real people did with their lives, something like being a secretary, or a salesman, or a school crossing guard, like my Grandpa.

With school, writing became hard work—homework, assignments, term papers. Like many other students, I procrastinated, suffered, and counted words.

Besides, my greatest passion was not for writing but for reading: *Uncle Wiggily's Storybook;* Little Lulu and Donald Duck; *The Story of Ferdinand; Rufus M.; Homer Price* and *Caddie Woodlawn; Blue Willow* and *Strawberry Girl;* the Bobbsey Twins books; *Kristin Lavransdatter; Microbe Hunters; Triumph over Pain; The Rise and Fall of the Third Reich; Mad* magazine. We didn't own many books; in school I suffered through basal readers, but before long I discovered the library. Then chances were if I could reach it, I would read it.

Writers, I began to think, were people who had all the answers. I didn't have all the answers; I didn't even know all the questions. So I stopped writing, for a very long time, and for years endured the painful search for a place to belong. Some times were great, some empty and awful, but there was always something missing.

Finally, the day my daughter began filling out college applications, I sat down to write, for myself. I still didn't have the answers, but I began to know some of the questions: why? what for? what if? how would it be?

Writing was still hard work—hard to begin, hard to stop. But it also became a passion, and that made all the difference. "To sum it all up," Ray Bradbury said, "if you want to write, if you want to create, you must be the most sublime fool that God ever turned out and sent rambling . . . I wish for you a wrestling match with your creative muse that will last a lifetime. I wish craziness and foolishness and madness upon you. May you live with hysteria, and out of it make fine stories . . . Which finally means, may you be in love every day for the next 20,000 days and out of that love, remake a world."

I read that, and I said, "Yes." And out of my passion came **Catherine, Called Birdy,** my first book. I wrote it despite my own doubts and the "don'ts" of others, because I needed to find out about things, about identity and responsibility, compassion and kindness and belonging, and being human in the world. How could I learn them if I didn't write about them?

Sometime during the process of writing **Catherine,** I thought of the title "The Midwife's Apprentice." I liked it. So I made a file. I wrote "The Midwife's Apprentice" on the tab. Inside I wrote on a slip of paper, "Possible title—Midwife's Apprentice." And I filed it.

After I mailed **Catherine** off, I sat for hours looking at that file. I had a title. The research I had done for **Catherine** gave me a firm place to stand: I knew that village and those people so well. But I had no story, until finally I saw in the unrelieved darkness of a medieval dawn a homeless child sleeping on a dung heap, longing for a name, a full belly, and a place in the world. Although we were separated by geography, circumstances, and hundreds of years, I knew this girl and her longing for a place, her feelings of unworthiness, her fear of trying and failing, and her fragile confidence. The story poured out of me: the girl rising from her nest in the dung heap, the cat escaping from the bag, Alyce coming clean and shining from the river, the blossoms bursting forth on the trees, a celebration of rebirth and renewal as Alyce grew from waif to midwife's apprentice. Still, Dinah Stevenson, my editor and often my pipeline to reality, reminds me that I sent the manuscript to her with a note that said: "I don't know if this is a book or a writing exercise. What do you think?"

After we decided it was indeed a book, and it was written and published, I worried about Alyce the way I would the plain younger sister of a popular girl. *The Midwife's Apprentice* was quieter, more subtle than **Catherine.** Would anyone love Alyce as I did? Would anyone even find her among the thousands of books published each year? What about the many images of Alyce being born or the ways she is like the cat? The importance of her owning a name or her profound wounds and prosaic but effective tenacity? Would anyone notice or care? Would adults think her story too disturbing for children, and children think it too serious and dull? I took the risk and whispered the story of Alyce. And so many people have listened, noticed, and cared.

Children ask me who Alyce is—is she me or someone I know? Alyce is Alyce, a girl with no place in a world all about place, a girl who has to give birth to herself. And I am Alyce, who becomes truly alive only when she learns to smile and sing and tell stories to the cat. You are Alyce, if only in the way that all of us are, born cold and nameless, in search of a full belly and a place in this world. And Alyce is every child who is parentless, homeless, and hungry, who lives on the edges of our world, who is mocked or excluded for being different.

With the exception of this lovely noisy bunch of people down front here, I have in my life loved books more than anything. Writing is my way of honoring and sharing that.

"There's worms in apples and worms in radishes," says Arvella Whipple in my newest book. "The worm in the radish, he thinks the whole world is a radish." Those of us who read books know the whole world is not a radish. It is a crabbing boat in the Chesapeake Bay, the walls of medieval Krakow, twenty-first-century Zimbabwe, and the place where the wild things are. It is Narnia and Brooklyn and Gold Rush California. It is the glory of the whirligigs in May's garden, the lonely anger of Heidi's grandfather, the warmth of the wind blowing through the willows, and the terror of a Nazi death camp.

As children are what they eat and hear and experience, so too they are what they read. This is why I write what I do, about strong young women who in one way or another take responsibility for their own lives; about tolerance, thoughtfulness, and caring; about choosing what is life-affirming and generous; about the ways that people are the same and the ways they are different and how rich that makes us all.

Katherine Paterson, whose books, both fiction and non-fiction, have inspired me more than I can say, wrote, "It is not enough simply to teach children to read; we have to give them something worth reading. Something that will stretch their imaginations—something that will help them make sense of their own lives and encourage them to reach out toward people whose lives are quite different from their own."

I remember an eight-year-old Karen, shy and dreamy and in love with books, running home from the library, flinging herself still in coat and woolen leggings onto the floor to read Lois Lenski's *Cotton in My Sack.* And I remember realizing with a pain in my heart that this book about sharecroppers in Arkansas was not a fairy tale, with trolls hiding under the bridge and a guaranteed "happily ever after." These were real people who had lives and dreams and troubles so real and so different from mine. I came back from the cotton fields of Arkansas to suburban Chicago a little different myself, a little changed.

"The goal of storytellers," Russian poet Kornei Chukovsky wrote," . . . consists of fostering in the child, at whatever cost, compassion and humaneness—this miraculous ability of man to be disturbed by another being's misfortunes, to feel joy about another being's happiness, to experience another's fate as one's own."

Such is the importance of stories. This is why I write. And what can be more important in this world?

Although I write my books upstairs, alone except for an elderly cat with a gleaming patch of white in the dusty orange of her fur, I know that writing, like living, is a communal act. For helping me to this moment I would like to thank:

Dinah Stevenson and everyone at Clarion, the world's greatest publishers, for their genius, their faith, and their devotion;

Ginee Seo and the HarperTrophy folks for their enthusiasm, support, and all those flowers;

James Levine, Dan, Arielle, and Melissa, for doing what agents do so well and with such good will;

Jack Hailey, my West Coast agent, who generously shares his investigations, inspirations, and exuberant friendship;

Trina Schart Hyman for using her talent to make my girls live and breathe;

the Newbery Committee for seeing what I was trying to do with Alyce and honoring it;

the Lipskis, who were kings in Poland—especially my parents, Arthur and Loretta Lipski, for loving me and giving even when they didn't have;

Frances and Alvin Cushman, who have taught me the meaning of generosity, honesty, and humanity;

my daughter, Leah, who shows me every day how strong and independent yet gentle and compassionate a young woman can be;

and most of all, Philip, my husband, inspiration, love slave, and most ardent fan, who always believed I could do it; no matter what it was, he believed I could. So usually I did.

It was Philip who slept with the phone by his pillow on January 21st and so answered it at dawn. He handed it to me, whereupon I heard, sounding like the voice of God in a medieval mystery play, "Karen Cushman? This is Mary Beth Dunhouse from the American Library Association in San Antonio, Texas."

What does one say to that?

I said, "Yes." And it was the right response. *Yes* to writing without having all the answers, *yes* to Ray Bradbury and Alyce and the Newbery Committee, *yes* to compassion and humanness, to being disturbed and feeling joy, to life and passion and love and remaking a world. God made people, says Elie Wiesel, because He loves stories. Such is the importance of stories.

GENERAL COMMENTARY

Philip Cushman

SOURCE: "Karen Cushman," in *The Horn Book Magazine,* Vol. LXXII, No. 4, July-August, 1996, pp. 420-23.

By now, at the time of her Newbery award, my time on earth with my wife Karen has been longer than my time on earth without her. I've gotten to know her pretty well. And there is something I can tell you that you won't find by reading about her on the inside flap of dust jackets: before she began to devote most of her work week to writing, there was always about Karen the sense of something desperate trying to come out. This wasn't usually a noisy or panicky desperation, and in fact one had to know Karen pretty well in order to notice it. It didn't so much appear as a disturbance as it did an absence: Karen was like an ear waiting for a song. In retrospect, we should have realized what was missing, but sometimes the most important things are the most difficult to see.

Karen grew to womanhood and set out to find a job in

the years when the word *career* was still reserved for men. She graduated from Stanford with a degree in classics and no money for graduate school; in those days, job opportunities for female liberal arts grads pretty much revolved around two possibilities: stewardess or secretary. She hated the thought of being a waitress at thirty thousand feet, and she saved herself from the fate of being a secretary by her first "career" strategy: she refused to learn how to type. The strategy worked, sort of: she was hired at several low-level, low-paying administrative, clerk-type jobs—but at least they weren't (too) secretarial.

We found each other in graduate school, me as rabbinical student, Karen as assistant-clerk-administrator. There was from the first moment I talked to her the sense of a special and remarkable person imprisoned inside the deeply sad and wary blue-gray eyes that were so stunningly intelligent and beautiful. Yes, she was physically beautiful, but her beauty was more than that; it was the kind that shone forth from a deep warmth and intelligence.

We were strange, similar, different, and very bonded very fast. It was the winter of 1968 in Los Angeles; we have been together ever since.

We made many plans about the life we would make, in the world we would have a hand in shaping, after the revolution. We dreamed about babies and organic corn, apple trees and wild blackberry jam, political sanity, rainy Oregon days, and peaceful snug nights with warm wood stoves. First we dreamed about it, and then we made it (well, some of it) come true. We built a big, beautiful dining-room table out of hardwoods from the four corners of the earth, around which all our children, students, and friends could sit while eating and arguing and making music together. Needless to say, the dreams weren't quite as great in reality as they were in the planning. The revolution failed, and political sanity—even in Oregon—continued to evade us, but the corn grew sweet and the jam was spectacular. Also, however, the baby was expensive, and teaching jobs dried up. We reevaluated, made new, slightly more realistic plans, clung to each other, and tried again.

The baby grew into a wonderful young girl, dogs and cats came and went, and my hair grew increasingly thin. Finally, we found Berkeley, learned to live with disappointment and without the revolution. We made new friends, and struggled to become reconciled, reluctantly, to being adults in a permanently unredeemed world.

But even these many changes could not shake from Karen the sense that something was not right. Many jobs, many graduate schools, many new ideas, new plans, new starts. Even our child, smart, beautiful, and much loved, could not allow Karen to shake the sense of something not yet expressed, not yet done. Over the years she tried many different careers, from organic gardening to a job as administrator of a community arts program, from two masters degrees to a position as editor of the *Museum*

Studies Journal. These were all interesting and informative to her, and she was an engaged, conscientious, and remarkably efficient worker. But with all the variety and action, something still was not right.

The quiet torment and absence is gone now, as long as Karen has time to write. The stories that used to intrude, unbidden and unwanted, into her consciousness can now be researched, written out, crafted, sculpted, and gifted to others. They are no longer something to be avoided or put away, but joyfully embraced.

Now we know why good jobs and respected graduate degrees, friends, family, and good times were not enough. It was not as though the jobs were bad; they just weren't the job she was born for. She was destined for a different kind of work, and she had the honesty and integrity to face her despair until she figured out what that was. In our world today, it is not easy to choose to be an artist. Innumerable seekers read do-it-yourself job-change books and see career counselors and go to informational interviews until they are blue in the face, but rarely does the pilgrim "realize" she is a novelist. Karen did. And thank God she did.

Karen did not, of course, proclaim herself a novelist. She just found the courage to let herself try what she knew she was meant to do from her first breath: write. It is one thing to write when one is a child, before one knows the risks. It is quite another, at fifty, to take up what one has been longing to do all of one's life, and do it publicly. To write, instead of just dream of writing, to actually put the words on paper, for everyone to see and evaluate—that is difficult.

Pretty much everyone tried to dissuade Karen from trying. They told her that history books do not sell, that adolescents are not capable of understanding the concept of the past, that boys would never read a novel with a female protagonist. They told her that she would never find an agent, and if she did, the agent would never find her a publisher. They told her to write cutesy little books about boring subjects, or vulgar little books filled with action and violence. They told her to write what would sell, what would not offend, what would be marketable and merchandisable. No one told her to write what was in her heart; no one told her to search her soul and write what she saw there; no one told her to listen to her voices, and bring them to life. No one, that is, except Ray Bradbury. Once, in the mid-seventies, we traveled to a big book fair, not sure why we were going except that we loved books, and there he was making the most inspirational speech I have ever heard. I watched Karen as he talked, and I've never seen anyone absorb the spoken word quite like she did that day. She never forgot what he said (and in fact tells you in her Newbery speech)—it just took her a while to know what to do with it.

Well, Karen didn't listen to "them," thank God; she listened to Ray instead. A dozen or so years later, she decided to write, and write from her heart. She decided to write what wanted—no, demanded—to be written. Now that she writes each day, it is easy to see the difference it makes in her life. But of course it was not simply a matter of deciding, or of finally realizing something relatively easy. To write the way Karen writes, about the issues Karen writes about, one has to be wise and courageous. It takes time to learn all the things that go into making up one of Karen's novels, and I don't just mean the painstaking historical research. Writing takes living, and soul-searching, and a deep love of humanity. Karen's writing is also motivated by sadness and anger, responses to the greed and deceit and mean-spiritedness that often overwhelm our meager attempts at kindness and political change.

Through a lot of hard work, and despite a sizable amount of self-doubt and fear, Karen Cushman found the courage to let herself write. Fortunately for us. Now, the whole world, not just me, can get a sense of the compassion and intelligence that lie deep in those blue-gray eyes. She deserves to be known by you, and you—children, parents, teachers, and librarians—deserve to know her and her stories. I am glad to share her with all of you. In fact, I am relieved to do so. I have been waiting for so long to tell you about her. Now you, and she, can take it from here. Enjoy.

Joseph Zornado

SOURCE: "A Poetics of History: Karen Cushman's Medieval World," in *The Lion and the Unicorn,* Vol. 21, No. 2, April, 1997, pp. 251-66.

Historical fiction occupies an uncertain space in the field of children's literature. Offer a teacher or scholar a work of historical fiction in any genre, from picture book to novel, and you are sure to get a varied, contentious response about what makes historical fiction work. Why? Because historical fiction has ambitious, ambiguous aims. For instance, should historical fiction be good history, even if this means the story might be, say, a little dull? Or, on the other hand, should the author take liberties with setting, dialogue, and character in order to provide the audience with "a good read?" What happens when a historical fiction contains no "famous" historical personages, or no clear identification as to when in history the story takes place? In short, what are we supposed to experience when we read historical fiction? History? Fiction?

Karen Cushman's Newbery Honor book *Catherine, Called Birdy,* and her Newbery Award-winning *The Midwife's Apprentice* are no exceptions to this debate. Though honored by the Newbery award committee, Cushman's *Catherine* and *Apprentice* nevertheless draw mixed opinions about the books' merits as historical fiction from teachers and scholars alike. Those who favor the books praise the main characters, young women who discover within themselves the strength and confidence to survive, even thrive, in a brutal and unforgiving medieval world. Skeptics charge that Cushman's work is not "real"

historical fiction, but rather, simply "fiction" because her work sacrifices historical "facts" in order to tell what amounts to contemporary stories about female adolescence. Alyce, the main character in *Apprentice,* does, says, and thinks in a way young women in the fourteenth century simply could not. In Cushman's first book set in medieval England, Catherine, the daughter of a knight—and by rights a "lady"—develops a keen sense for the logical inconsistency that surrounds and makes up her life, and grounds her demands for fair treatment on this way of seeing the world. Some argue, then, that the history in these novels reflects more of Cushman's late twentieth-century concerns about women that it does historical truths of English medieval culture and countryside. And worse still, Cushman's work has been labeled by some as "politically correct."

Yet, to my mind, those critical of Cushman's work rely on a too rigid sense of history and historiography. To dismiss Cushman on the grounds that her work violates traditional notions of historical fiction blinds us to Cushman's larger project: *Catherine, Called Birdy* and *The Midwife's Apprentice* challenge our notions of historical fiction, history, and how we make meaning of and from the past. Cushman's first two novels reveal a passion for the *process* of history-making rather than the product produced by the historian—which is why she populates her texts with marginalized, heretofore unexamined characters from medieval England. No kings or bishops take center stage in her first two novels. Rather, young girls with no power, no voice, and little or no future are her protagonists.

Cushman sets out to challenge traditional notions of historical fiction by writing a new kind of historical fiction. . . .

[According to Anita Silvey in *Children's Books and Their Creators,*] "Setting must be integral to the plot, otherwise the tale is simply a 'costume romance' that exploits rather than explores history. . . . Whether a picture book, a book for beginning readers, or a novel, the historical story is composed of two elements. To be taken seriously, it must fulfill the requirements for both good history and good literature." . . .

In *Metahistory: The Historical Imagination in Nineteenth-Century Europe,* Hayden White offers an analysis of . . . historiography. . . .

> It is sometimes said that the aim of the historian is to explain the past by "finding," "identifying" or "uncovering" the "stories" that lie buried in chronicles; and that the difference between "history" and "fiction" resides in the fact that the historian "finds" his stories, whereas the fiction writer "invents" his. This conception of the historian's task, however, obscures the extent to which "invention" also plays a part in the historian's operations.

It is at the level of "metahistory" that the historian and fiction writer share the will to invent, to order, and to discriminate among the countless historical moments that each considers as resources for their work. White "postulates a deep level of consciousness on which a historical thinker chooses conceptual strategies by which to explain or represent . . . data. On this level," White writes, "the historian performs an essentially *poetic act,* in which he prefigures the historical field and constitutes it as a domain upon which to bring to bear the specific theories he will use to explain "what was *really* happening" in it. This act of prefiguration may, in turn, take a number of forms, the types of which may be characterized by the linguistic modes in which they are cast. And what was really happening in history is not so much a collection of facts, but rather, White suggests, it is the process of history making that *is* at the bottom of every written history. "The dominant tropological mode and its attendant linguistic protocol comprise the irreducibly 'metahistorical' basis of every historical work." . . .

I cite Hayden White's work on metahistory at length because it offers a particularly useful way of seeing Karen Cushman's medieval world and the kind of historical fiction she is writing, especially in the case of *Catherine, Called Birdy.* White describes the trope, "Irony" as a notion that grows directly out of the Satirical mode. He describes it in terms that are reminiscent of a "postmodern" analysis of language. . . .

In *Catherine, Called Birdy* Cushman moves the reader through a narrative that, among other things, plays out in fiction a number of the tropological modes [Irony, Satire, Romance, Comedy, and Tragedy] White identifies in *Metahistory*. It is no accident, I think, that Cushman's protagonist, Catherine, discovers the limits of particular modes of thinking and abandons them only to settle on a kind of Satiric mode of self-reflection, adopting as she does an ironic turn of mind. Catherine discovers her ability to doubt even as she discovers the ability to trust her own instincts. As a result of this peeling-away of narrative modes, Catherine discovers her own capacity to suffer, and at the same time to doubt the cultural constructs that inflict that suffering; Catherine discovers the process of life, and as a result, she grows from seeing herself as someone else's property to seeing herself as self-possessed.

Yet, even Cushman herself seems a little uncomfortable with this idea. At the end of *Catherine* Cushman writes in an Author's Note, "our ideas of individual identity, individual accomplishments and rights, individual effort and success did not exist. . . . No one was separate and independent, [not] even the king." Still, this begs the question, does the medieval life of the community necessarily exclude any hope of self-consciousness? Self-consciousness is a large part of what makes humans human, even in the thirteenth century. And from self-consciousness comes the possibility of self-awareness and from self-awareness comes the possibility of doubt. And from doubt, or "aporia" as White terms it, grows that Ironic turn of mind known so well in the post-modern age, which "tends to dissolve all belief in the possibility of positive political actions." But for Catherine (and Alyce in *Apprentice*) the possibility of *personal* action—

however politicized and anachronistic it might appear to be to us—opens before her and she saves herself.

This might sound as if I am suggesting that Cushman has written a radical, proto-feminist novel. When, in fact, Catherine's story could easily be read as a subversive tale bent on maintaining the oppressive status quo. Again from White: he writes that "inasmuch as one can legitimately conclude from a history thus construed that one inhabits the best of possible historical worlds, or at least the best that one can "realistically" hope for, given the nature of the historical process as revealed in her account of it." One might conclude from all of this that Catherine—and women and children in general—already inhabit the best world that they can "realistically" hope for—they just need to learn how to make the best of it. Catherine's betrothal to Shaggy Beard, her escape from this betrothal because of his death and her subsequent marriage to Stephen, Shaggy Beard's fair-haired son might not be the stuff of medieval feminism, but rather, as sentimental propaganda: make the best of it and things will work out in the end. Which means that one might read *Catherine* in this way: paternalistic betrothals designed only for political and economic gain of the Father can work out in the end, if the daughter knows her place.

Because Cushman is a fiction writer as well as a historian in this case, she has at her disposal all of the tools White describes in his *Metahistory*. As a result, Cushman does not confine her story to merely the Romantic/Comic modes of employment, but rather, she also employs the Satirical mode in her narrative and by doing so subverts a strictly conservative ideological reading. Cushman's manifestly Romantic/Comic plot is undercut by the content of Catherine's chronicle. This undercutting of conservative ideological implications works in two ways: first, Catherine's interest in the lives of the saints compels her to begin each day's journal entry with a small fact from a saint's life celebrated on that day. So, for instance, on the twelfth of July Catherine notes the "Feast of Saint Veronica, who wiped the face of the suffering Jesus with her veil, where His image remains to this day" is undercut by Catherine's mundane journal entry. "It is too hot to write. Too hot even for the cats to chase mice." As Catherine's journal entries continue one is bombarded by an almost unending list of violence and cruelty in a majority of the lives of the saints that Catherine notes. As a result, the distance between the theological history of the church and Catherine's own experiences grows greater and greater until, finally, Catherine begins to question quietly the broader cultural history that shadows her own sense of time and place. Or, in other words, this is one of the ways Catherine learns to doubt, to look for multiple meanings, to find shades of gray rather than black and white.

Second, Cushman's historical fiction employs—and perhaps even relies on—the reader's own doubt as a part of the reading experience. Much of Cushman's audience is well aware of the plight of women over the past seven hundred years. As late twentieth-century readers raised in an age of irony, skepticism, and resignation, we bring to the text the knowledge that for women and children—the marginalized—things have not improved very much at all for most of this past millennium. So that if Catherine *were* to transcend her historical moment somehow in her story, we know that it is only for one moment, and as such it remains anachronistic, conservative fantasy.

Still, the self-conscious Satirical mode of *Catherine,* combined with the reader's own doubt about the "truth" of the history presented destroys any effort on the part of her audience "to use history as a means of comprehending the present world in anything but Conservative terms" [according to White]. In other words, because the Satiric mode undermines the Comic and Romantic modes also employed in the novel, Catherine's story calls attention to itself as a necessarily provisional mode of truth-making; the provisional nature of the textual form unravels in a way that calls attention to the provisional nature of the content. Further, it is precisely because her audience questions the history of Cushman's fiction that we participate in a new kind of historical fiction. Simply put, we doubt that it is true. We ask of Cushman's medieval world questions like: could a young woman have been as brave, strong and true to herself as Catherine was in the *thirteenth century*? This must be an anachronism. Women did not have a sense of themselves as anything more than property for hundreds of years after that, right? From this critical question some dubious conclusions have been drawn, among them the claim that the novel simply does not work as historical fiction because Catherine (or Alyce) could not have existed *because Cushman's characters violate our notions of medieval England.* This perspective reduces Cushman's two novels to political tracts and maintains notions of historical fiction as the domain of places and dates rather than the interpretive process it is.

But what if I could invent a history where Catherine and Alyce did "exist"? How might that version of history shape the present moment? By refusing to consider the possibility of Catherine's existence we fall prey to another kind of conservatism, one which maintains *today's* status quo, for if we change our view of women in history, perhaps we will have to change our view of women (and children) *right now.* The writing of history and the reception of it share something in common: both are largely determined by what White calls "Ideological implications."

I call Cushman's work historical fiction precisely because she calls attention to the provisional, slippery nature of storytelling, the writing of history, and the nature of the self. Catherine develops a sense of self—something that is, according even to Cushman, beyond the medieval mind set. Nevertheless, Catherine's growth and development falls along poetic—rather than scientific or historic—lines. Catherine's growth comes as a result of her brother Edward's encouragement to keep a journal. She does, and her writing grows stronger, and so too her vision. She becomes, by all rights, a writer, a poet

and, finally, a character possessed of an "ironic" mind-set.

For instance, late in the novel Catherine takes tentative steps in distinguishing ideological traces in the lives of the saints from the so-called "facts" in religious history—itself a small step to philosophical and religious skepticism. Catherine notices "how many male saints were bishops, popes, missionaries, great scholars, and teachers while female saints get to be saints as a result of giving birth to a male saint, or refusing to marry some powerful pagan. *It is plain that men are in charge of making saints.*"

Though this remains only a short entry in Catherine's chronicle, it speaks loudly to her skeptical point of view. What this entry of July twenty-sixth does not say speaks even louder: there is no mention of God, divine forces, the infallibility of popes or any other theological construct, though in past entries she has shown the intelligence to tackle theological issues in her own way. No, by July twenty-sixth Catherine recognizes however implicitly that culture—be it secular or religious—is created by men for men.

Even in her role as Lady and as caregiver she finally abandons much of the superstition and ignorance of medieval medicine and resorts to what feels right: when her mother's legs have swelled late in her pregnancy, Catherine first tries "a paste of bean meal, flour, vinegar, and oil, but the dogs kept trying to eat it. So I washed her off and have been rubbing her legs with sweet-smelling oils and singing her sweet songs and it seems to help."

Later, in an entry from the twelfth of September Catherine reveals a decidedly ironic—even postmodern—notion of people. "I think sometimes," she writes, "that people are like onions. On the outside smooth and whole and simple but inside ring upon ring, complex and deep." And like her entry about the creation of saints, what Catherine does not say implies the depth of her ironic turn of mind: onions have no inside, only ring upon ring of outside. Catherine's onion metaphor is a self-consuming one from which nothing is left when the last skin has been peeled. Catherine might also have written it this way: people (and the history they write) have no essence; we are only our clothes, our occupations, and the expectations the community and culture place on us. Perhaps this is a crisis or perhaps this is an opportunity.

Because Cushman is not writing straight history or traditional historical fiction she has the freedom to draw on aspects of both genres and reject others. She employs multiple tropological modes as a historian and avoids "real" historical figures so that she might concentrate on the simple, plain, and powerless in her two novels. For some this is a problem in Cushman's work, but White's analysis of historiography reminds us that scientists and historians have never agreed on what makes history a good account of reality. . . .

The Midwife's Apprentice is another successful example of Cushman's challenging historical fiction precisely because it approaches the same kind of tension between fact and fiction, history and story that *Catherine, Called Birdy* explores. Some have criticized the novel as anachronistic because Cushman tells a tale of a young female orphan who, with luck and help, leaves the dung heap on the fringes of society and begins a process that, ultimately, leads her to a more secure, and most importantly, meaningful existence. What in this bare outline is anachronistic? Did young girls starve and sleep in dung heaps during the Middle Ages? If a second daughter was lucky enough to survive her initial birth during the Middle Ages, she very well may have been abandoned afterwards, and yet lived somehow. Did young girls desire a meaningful existence even though born and raised in a dung heap? Probably not, if only because they lacked the emotional and intellectual integrity to ask for more from life. Might it be possible to imagine a situation where a young girl does somehow manage to ask more of herself, her village, her life? Yes. Karen Cushman's novel is proof of this. What I am driving at is this: Historical fiction like Cushman's *The Midwife's Apprentice* does not examine a different medieval history, but rather, organizes the parts in a way that speaks to our concerns today. This is not anachronistic. This is simply the process of interpretive meaning-making at work.

For instance, Alyce stumbles into a similar crisis of meaning when, in a scene reminiscent of Catherine's onion-skin metaphor about the nature of people, Alyce attempts to help an orphaned boy called "Runt." Alyce first encourages the boy to change his name, knowing from her own experience how humiliating and debilitating names can be. Runt and Alyce then discuss names and naming in some detail.

"What then is the king's name?"

Alyce did not know, so she hid the boy in the chicken house and went about the village asking folks what was the king's name.

"Longshanks," said the baker.

"Hammer," said Thomas At-the-Bridge.

"The Devil Hisself," said Brian Tailor, who was a Scot and so had reason to feel that way.

"Just 'the king' is all," said several.

"Edward," said the bailiff. "The king's name is Edward."

"Edward," said Alyce to the boy.

"Then Edward is my name," said Edward, who used to be called Runt. Alyce nodded.

Two things strike me about this passage: first, as already noted, the power of names and the power of naming

takes center stage. And second, Cushman suggests that those who live on the fringes of society see (and know) only what their position in life allows them to see. So few of the villagers know the king's "Christian" name, though they have their own name for him drawn from their own or their community's experience with him. So, the bailiff—a kind of medieval law enforcement officer—knows the King's name to be "Edward" because he draws his authority, ultimately, from him. On the other hand, the Scot knows the king as "The devil hisself." How we name others, it seems, speaks as much about who we are as how we name ourselves.

By the time Alyce names Edward she has already gone through her own similar naming experience in which she chooses a new name, and in the process draws herself out of the dung heap and into the human community. With luck and a bit of mistaken identity, the young girl called "Dung" and "Beetle" names herself "Alyce" after being mistaken for a young woman of the same name, a young woman who reads. After this case of mistaken identity, "Beetle" wonders about it and realizes a truth about herself. "This face," she said, "could belong to someone who can read. And has curls. And could have a lover before nightfall. And this is me, Beetle." She stopped. Beetle was no name for a person, no name for someone who looked like she could read. As a result, Alyce christens herself anew—really for the first time—and here the pace of emotional growth gains momentum.

Names, it seems, have everything to do with who we are, where we come from, the power to read the world and the power to read ourselves. When we name ourselves—with a first name, a title, a degree, or even as "father" or "mother"—we change our perspective on the world. We see more, we see differently, and we see with a purpose. Without a perspective from which to see, we see everything that is to say, we see nothing. . . .

From the moment Alyce names herself—like Catherine's growth as a writer discovering herself in the writing—in *The Midwife's Apprentice,* Alyce's growth as an emotional and intellectual woman takes off. Extending the power of naming, not unlike some latter-day Eve in the garden, she names her nameless cat "Purr." Rather than run or hide, she defends herself from the boys who torment her in the village. She takes some gentle revenge on the villagers who tormented the girl called "Dung" and "Beetle." And rather than merely serve Jane Sharp, the village midwife, she begins to pay attention to the art of midwifery, and her skills—and her confidence—as a midwife's apprentice begin to develop.

Cushman's interest in the process and power of naming speaks to the power and process of historical fiction and it's cousin, history. What we see is, really, up to us and the sense we make of it depends on who we are, the information we have at our disposal and the values and cultural morays by which we determine which parts of that information are important and which parts might be disregarded. Historians and historical fiction writers work this problem out according to their own goals, but both share a similar desire to get to the truth about things. Both order their historical information in a way that best suits their ends. Does Cushman tell the "whole truth" about the relationship between the village and the manor, between the peasant and the lord? Probably not. Perhaps this might best be left to the historian. Nevertheless, Cushman persuasively draws a medieval world not so much to provide facts about medieval England, but rather, to help us remember the truth about who we were as people, and as a result, help remind us of who we are right now. Cushman's *A Midwife's Apprentice* remembers the past in order to help us recover the present. . . .

Literature offers a way to remember the past and live more passionately in the present. It helps us remember ourselves. Those in medicine and psychiatrics have concluded that, yes, the repression of memories does occur. In many cases repression is a type of psychic safeguard. It helps the abused and traumatized to stay alive in the midst of unspeakable cruelty and suffering. In other words, repression can be a good thing for a while. It acts as a defense mechanism in the face of suffering. We can shut it out, shut it off, and go on somehow. Nevertheless a lifestyle of repression, science also tells us, leads to unhealthy habits, even disease. We store memories in our bodies on a cellular level—and if the memories are traumatic enough they come out, some say, as a physical disease. These outbreaks of memory testify to the traumas we have repressed and that our bodies—when we break out in stress, illness, and disease, ask us to remember.

Cushman marks Alyce's growth and development as a woman and as a human being not so much by the skills she learns as a midwife's apprentice or the babies she helps birth—though these are important details to consider—but rather, by her ability to feel her emotions. At the outset of the tale Alyce, known as Dung, is numb to the cold, to her hunger, and most of all to her emotions. As Alyce gains a measure of physical security in her life—i.e., food, shelter, and a kind of surrogate mother in the guise of Jane Sharp, the midwife—she begins to remember inchoate memories that mark her as human: she remembers how to make a song after helping Tansy the cow give birth to twins. Soon after, Alyce helps the Bailiff's wife give birth after the midwife had given the baby up for lost. So grateful are the Bailiff and his wife that they name their daughter Alyce Little. Never before has Alyce felt so complimented, appreciated, and respected by her community. That night, for the first time, she "lay down on her straw mat by the fire, and had a dream about her mother."

After a later, second attempt to act as midwife ends in failure,

> Alyce backed out of the cottage, then turned and ran up the path to the road, she didn't know why or where. Behind her in that cottage was disappointment and failure. The midwife had used no magic. She had

delivered that baby with work and skill, not magic spells, and Alyce should have been able to do it but could not. She had failed. Strange sensations tickled her throat, but she did not cry, for she did not know how, and a heavy weight sat in her chest, but she did not moan or wail, for she had never learned to give voice to what was inside her. She knew only to run away.

Alyce finally gains enough experience and confidence that she can experience loss, shame, and disappointment. Nevertheless, though the sensations "tickled her throat" she cannot mourn nor give voice to her pain and so she runs away. Only after meeting the young boy, Edward, and finding him safe and happy does she discover how much she has missed him, her life in the village and her role as the midwife's apprentice. Yet before she can go back she must give voice to what is inside her. After Edward helps her identify and experience her maternal feelings, she finds a voice for the sadness and loss she experienced as a child.

> She would not be bringing Edward back with her to make her heart content, but she knew she had not failed him, and she breathed a heavy sigh of sadness, disappointment, and relief. It felt so good that she did it again and again until her sighs turned to sobs and she cried her first crying right there in the hen house . . .

Soon after this she masters her fear and feelings of worthlessness and helps a woman birth a baby. From this experience Alyce recovers another part of her emotional life: she learns to feel joy in her own abilities, and pride in herself as a woman. "And then she laughed, a true laugh that came from deep in her gut, rushed out her mouth, and rang though the clear night air. And that was the true miracle that night, the first of June—the month . . . named for Juno, the Roman goddess of the moon, of women, and of childbirth." Soon after Alyce discovers her desire to return to the village and take up again her role as midwife's apprentice.

Catherine, Called Birdy and *The Midwife's Apprentice* represent stunning examples of historical fiction because *history* and the malleable—and contentious—process of history-making plays such a large role in the reader's experience of these texts. Cushman's *Catherine, Called Birdy* and *The Midwife's Apprentice* foreground Catherine's and Alyce's "becoming" and in the process, foreground the notion of history itself as one that is always becoming. From one perspective Cushman's historical fiction does not offer her audience historical figures from which we can draw a "true" experience of medieval England. We cannot. It is this among other things that separates her from the likes of *Johnny Tremain*. And yet, Cushman's handling of historical figures—and her view of women in thirteenth-century England—provokes a kind of crisis of knowing in the reader: what do we know of the past but the stories we tell of it? From this unmooring of our surety, and through the personally familiar yet historically overlooked Catherine and Alyce, we gain a broader understanding of our own society, and of our own sense of how we construct ideological notions of "woman," "child," and "self." Cushman teaches us, and we learn a little about how we too tell stories, sometimes whoppers, to justify our own ideological assumptions; she provides us with the opportunity to read her historical fiction the way her work reads us: as historians, as poets, as truth-makers.

TITLE COMMENTARY

CATHERINE, CALLED BIRDY (1994)

Kirkus Reviews

SOURCE: A review of *Catherine, Called Birdy,* in *Kirkus Reviews,* Vol. LXII, No. 6, March 15, 1994, p. 395.

Unwillingly keeping a journal at the behest of her brother, a monk, Birdy (daughter of a 13th-century knight) makes a terse first entry—"I am bit by fleas and plagued by family. That is all there is to say"—but is soon confiding her pranks and troubles in fascinating detail. Her marriage must suit her drunken father's financial needs, and though the 14-year-old scares off several suitors (she pretends to be mad, sets fire to the privy one is using, etc.), in the end she's "betrothed and betrayed." Meanwhile, she observes Edward I's England with keen curiosity and an open mind, paints a mural in her chamber, evades womanly tasks whenever possible, reports that—ladylike or no—"I always have strong feelings and they are quite painful until I let them out," and chooses her own special profanity, "God's thumbs." At year's end she makes peace with her family and acquires, beyond hope, a possibly compatible betrothed (they have yet to meet). Birdy's frequent saint's day entries begin with pithy summaries of the saints' claims to fame; their dire deaths have a uniquely medieval tang, as do such oddities as St. Bridget turning bathwater into beer. Much else here is casually earthy—offstage bedding among villagers, home remedies, pissing out a fire—while death is commonplace. The period has rarely been presented for young people with such authenticity; the exotic details will intrigue readers while they relate more closely to Birdy's yen for independence and her sensibilities toward the downtrodden. Her tenacity and ebullient naiveté are extraordinary; at once comic and thought-provoking, this first novel is a delight.

Bruce Anne Shook

SOURCE: A review of *Catherine, Called Birdy,* in *School Library Journal,* Vol. 40, No. 6, June, 1994, p. 147.

This unusual book provides an insider's look at the life of Birdy, 14, the daughter of a minor English nobleman. The year is 1290 and the vehicle for storytelling is the girl's witty, irreverent diary. She looks with a clear and critical eye upon the world around her, telling of the people she knows and of the daily events in her small manor house. Much of Birdy's energy is consumed by avoiding the various suitors her father chooses for her to marry. She sends them all packing with assorted ruses until she is almost wed to an older, unattractive man she refers to as Shaggy Beard. In the process of telling the routines of her young life, Birdy lays before readers a feast of details about medieval England. The book is rich with information about the food, dress, religious beliefs, manners, health, medical practices, and sanitary habits (or lack thereof) of the people of her day. From the number of fleas she kills in an evening to her herbal medicines laced with urine, Birdy reveals fascinating facts about her time period. A feminist far ahead of her time, she is both believable and lovable. A somewhat philosophical afterword discusses the mind set of medieval people and concludes with a list of books to consult for further information about the period. Superb historical fiction.

Rebecca Barnhouse

SOURCE: A review of *Catherine, Called Birdy,* in *Voice of Youth Advocates,* Vol. 17, 2, June, 1994, p. 81.

The year is 1290 and Edward I rules England. In the tiny village of Stonebridge in Lincolnshire, a thirteen-year-old girl named Catherine, but called Birdy by her family, is plagued by fleas, by her father, who wants to marry her to a horrible rich nobleman, and by her own testy temper and hasty tongue, which keep her in constant trouble with both her parents and her nurse. On the orders of her brother, a monk who has taught her to read Latin and to write, Birdy keeps an account of a year in her life, written on parchment left over from her father's household accounts. The details she includes illustrate life on a small manor in the Middle Ages in all of its rich earthiness: food, farting and privies, sickness, spinning and sewing, death, the church and its ceremonies, and endless chores command much of Birdy's consciousness, and always in the background is the threat of marriage to the odious Shaggy Beard. Her comments on her father, "the beast," and the long line of suitors he haggles with, her Uncle George the Crusader, on whom she has a crush, her friends Aelis and Perkin the goat boy, and her abominable brother Robert reveal a girl likable for her stubbornness, her fondness for a joke, and her mixture of wisdom and naiveté. In the year recorded here, Birdy learns and matures, leaving behind some of her selfishness as she nurses her mother during a frightening difficult childbirth, and as she comes to realize that she will never escape her approaching marriage. The narrative style of her journal is amusing and believable.

Cushman's knowledge of life in the Middle Ages is broad; readers will not get a misty view of a pleasant fantasy-land. Instead, the details will remind them of the harshness of life in a period that had few creature comforts and only the most rudimentary understanding of medicine. The pervasive presence of Christianity as a part of daily life is accurately presented, and Birdy's recording of the days by noting the feasts of saints underscores this pervasiveness. (A useful bibliography about life in the Middle Ages appears at the end of the novel.) Only Perkin the goat boy seems out of place; it is hard to believe that the daughter of the lord of the manor would have much to do with a smelly, flea-bitten boy with one leg shorter than the other; even harder to believe is Perkin's desire to become a scholar. Nevertheless, the novel succeeds because of the attention to detail in both the historical setting and in the development of the delightful character of Catherine, called Birdy.

Ruth France

SOURCE: A review of *Catherine, Called Birdy,* in *The School Librarian,* Vol. 44, No. 4, November, 1996, p. 168.

A humorous novel in diary form which differs from others of this ilk in that it is set in 1290! Catherine, or Birdy as she is called, is in trouble but she is not your usual damsel in distress. Her boorish father is determined to sell her off as a wife to the highest bidder but Birdy is equally determined to stay single, for she is only 14, and sets out to repel her suitors by fair means and foul. She seems, however, to be on the brink of defeat when old Shaggy Beard appears. Will she marry this revolting suitor whom she describes as a "dog assassin whose breath smells like the mouth of Hell, who makes wind like others make music?"

The description of medieval life is lively and absorbing, full of colour, danger, hardships and romance. We read of bawdy villagers, travelling minstrels, hangings, childbirth, great fairs and festivals, drunkenness, swearing, flatulence and flea bites! But despite its setting, there is much that a modern teenager can empathise with. An off-beat novel which may have a limited appeal but which gives a good flavour of life in the Middle Ages.

Anne Scott Macleod

SOURCE: A review of *Catherine, Called Birdy,* in *The Horn Book Magazine,* Vol. LXXIV, No. 1, January, 1998, pp. 30-1.

Catherine, Called Birdy, by Karen Cushman, is a brave excursion into medieval social history through the diary of a fourteen-year-old who questions nearly everything that governed the lives of medieval people in general and of women in particular. Birdie's world seems real enough—it is rough and dirty and uncomfortable most of the time, even among the privileged classes. Her feisty independence is perhaps believable, as is her objection to being "sold like a parcel" in marriage to add to her father's status or land. However, those were the usual considerations in marriage among the land-holding class-es, for sons as well as daughters, and Birdie's repeated resistance might have drawn much harsher punishment than she got. The fifteenth-century Paston letters record what happened to a daughter who opposed her mother about a proposed match: "She has since Easter [three months before this letter] been beaten once in the week or twice, sometimes twice in one day, and her head broken in two or three places." As the historian of the Paston papers points out, "The idea that children . . . had any natural rights was almost impossible to a medieval mind. Children were just chattels . . . entirely at the direction and disposal of their fathers." If this attitude applied to sons, it applied even more to daughters.

Cushman sticks to historical reality while Birdie considers and discards the few alternatives to marriage she can think of—running away, becoming a goatkeeper, joining a monastery. But once her heroine agrees (for altruistic reasons) to her father's final, awful choice for her, Cushman quickly supplies an exit. The intended husband dies, so Birdie can marry his son, who, fortunately, is heir to the land and thereby meets her father's purposes. The son is, of course, young and educated where his father was old, ugly, and illiterate. Even granting that life is unpredictable, so fortuitous an escape strains the framework. In fairness, I think Cushman knew this; she just flinched at consigning her likable character to her likely fate.

THE MIDWIFE'S APPRENTICE (1995)

Publishers Weekly

SOURCE: A review of *The Midwife's Apprentice,* in *Publishers Weekly,* Vol. 242, No. 9, February 27, 1995, p. 104.

Having focused on a well-born young heroine in her Newbery Honor debut novel, *Catherine, Called Birdy,* Cushman returns to a similar medieval English setting, this time to imagine how the other half lived. The strengths of this new, relatively brief novel match those of its predecessor: Cushman has an almost unrivaled ability to build atmosphere, and her evocation of a medieval village, if not scholarly in its authenticity, is supremely colorful and pungent. The protagonist here first appears asleep in a heap of dung; the "rotting and moiling" of the refuse give forth heat enough to compensate for the stench. Homeless and nameless, she can remember no time when she did not wander from village to village. She is rescued from the dung heap by a sharp-tongued local midwife, who feeds her in exchange for work. Gradually the girl forges an identity for herself and learns some timeless truths. Some of the characterizations lack consistency (particularly that of the midwife), the plot depends on a few too many conveniences and the development of the themes seems hurried—but no matter. The force of the ambience produces more than enough momentum to propel the reader from start to finish in a single happy sitting.

Kirkus Reviews

SOURCE: A review of *The Midwife's Apprentice,* in *Kirkus Reviews,* Vol. LXIII, No. 6, March 15, 1995, p. 380.

During the Middle Ages, an itinerant girl of about 12 or 13 who knows "no home and no mother and no name but Brat" finds refuge one night by burrowing into a village dung heap where the warm, rotting muck will protect her from the bitter cold. In the morning she is taken in by a sharp-tongued woman who turns out to be Jane, the midwife. Brat is such a hard worker that before long she is accompanying Jane to birthings, where she cleans up after the work is done and acts as the midwife's "gofer" whenever necessary. Jane begins to trust her with some of the secrets of her trade, but when Brat is asked to help with a difficult birth and fails, she runs away ashamed not only of her lack of knowledge, but for her belief that she was ever worthy of learning.

How Brat comes to terms with her failure and returns to Jane's home as a true apprentice is a gripping story about a time, place, and society that 20th-century readers can hardly fathom. Fortunately, Cushman does the fathoming for them, rendering in Brat a character as fully fleshed and real as Katherine Paterson's best, in language that is simple, poetic, and funny. From the rebirth in the dung heap to Brat's renaming herself Alyce after a heady visit to a medieval fair, this is not for fans of historical drama only. It's a rouser for all times.

Deborah Stevenson

SOURCE: A review of *The Midwife's Apprentice,* in *Bulletin of the Center for Children's Books,* Vol. 48, No. 9, May, 1995, p. 303.

She starts out as Brat, aged twelve or thirteen; the midwife finds her hiding in a dungheap, christens her Beetle (short for dungbeetle), and takes her on as a slavey and gofer. As Beetle begins to grow in confidence and in knowledge, she names herself Alyce, and although she suffers setbacks (a crisis in confidence when attempting to deliver a baby on her own), she eventually realizes that midwifery is her destiny and becomes a full-fledged apprentice. As she did in *Catherine, Called Birdy,* Cushman blends earthy realism with a certain pastoral coziness in her picture of early England, which, added to an appealing heroine, make the story an absorbing tale of another time. Her depiction of inarticulate Alyce's gradual blossoming remains credible, never demanding too much of her heroine or her readers. The book's brevity and simplicity also commend it to older readers who find the era intriguing but are intimidated by more epic tales of medieval life. Cushman adds an historical note about midwifery, which includes mention of the maternal and child mortality that never appears in the story itself. This is an offbeat, well-crafted story; fans of the author's first book will enjoy it.

Sara Miller

SOURCE: A review of *The Midwife's Apprentice,* in *School Library Journal,* Vol. 41, No. 5, May, 1995, p. 118.

With simplicity, wit, and humor, Cushman presents another tale of medieval England. Here readers follow the satisfying, literal and figurative journey of a homeless, nameless child called Brat, who might be 12 or 13—no one really knows. She wandered about in her early years, seeking food and any kind of refuge and, like many outsiders, gained a certain kind of wisdom about people and their ways. Still, life held little purpose beyond survival—until she meets the sharp-nosed, irritable local midwife, which is where this story begins. Jane takes her in, renames her Beetle, and thinks of her as free labor and no competition. Always practical but initially timid, the girl expands in courage and self-awareness, acquiring a cat as a companion, naming herself Alyce, and gaining experience in the ways of midwifery. From the breathless delight of helping a boy to deliver twin calves, to the despair of failure during a difficult birth, to the triumph of a successful delivery, Alyce struggles to understand how she can allow herself to fail and yet have the determination to reach for her own place in the world. Alyce wins. Characters are sketched briefly but with telling, witty detail, and the very scents and sounds of the land and people's occupations fill each page as Alyce comes of age and heart. Earthy humor, the foibles of humans both high and low, and a fascinating mix of superstition and genuinely helpful herbal remedies attached to childbirth make this a truly delightful introduction to a world seldom seen in children's literature.

Ann A. Flowers

SOURCE: A review of *The Midwife's Apprentice,* in *The Horn Book Magazine,* Vol. LXXI, No. 2, July, 1995, pp. 465-66.

In a sharply realistic novel of medieval England by the author of *Catherine, Called Birdy,* a homeless, hungry orphan girl called Beetle is discovered trying to keep warm in a pile of dung by the village midwife. The midwife, Jane Sharp, takes Beetle in to work as a servant for little food, barely adequate shelter, and cutting words. To Beetle, however, it is a step upward. The midwife is far from compassionate, but she is, for her times, a good midwife. Beetle becomes interested in the work and watches Jane covertly as she goes about her business. Beetle also adopts a scraggly cat that she has saved from the village boys' cruel mistreatment, and she feeds it from her own inadequate meals. As Beetle grows and learns, she begins to gain some hard-won self-esteem, and renames herself Alyce. She becomes more accepted by the villagers and is sometimes asked for advice. On one occasion she employs her common sense and compassion to successfully manage a difficult delivery when Jane Sharp is called away. Jane is far from pleased; she wants no rivals and is angered when a woman in labor asks specifically for Alyce. But Alyce finds she knows less than she thought, and Jane must be called in to save the mother. Alyce, in despair and humiliation, takes her cat and runs away. She spends some time working at an inn, where she learns a good deal more about herself and the world. At last she admits to herself that what she wants most is to become a midwife, and she returns to Jane. The brisk and satisfying conclusion conveys the hope that the self-reliant and finally self-respecting Alyce will find her place in life. The graphic and convincing portrayals of medieval life and especially the villagers—given to superstition, casual cruelty, and duplicity—afford a fascinating view of a far distant time.

Kenneth L. Donelson

SOURCE: A review of *The Midwife's Apprentice,* in *English Journal,* Vol. 85, No. 7, November, 1996, pp. 131-32.

I just recently learned the importance of the term "chapter books" as a way of identifying books for little kids that look like books for grown-ups. The term came to mind when I first glanced at *The Midwife's Apprentice.* It's short, only a bit more than 100 pages, and it seems episodic, that is until you begin to read it. Then you discover that it's a delightful and wise and witty story of a nameless young girl. She keeps warm by staying in a dunghill in the dangerous, noisy, dirty world of medieval England. The village midwife reluctantly takes the girl in and names her Beetle and trains her in the delivery of babies. Later, Beetle renames herself Alyce and befriends a cat. Alyce achieves some successes but runs away after one miserable failure. Then she learns something about herself and the world and picks herself up and starts over again.

Cushman has a wonderful ability to capture characters in only a few words. Early on, she writes about the midwife: "She did her job with energy and some skill, but without care, compassion, or joy." Cushman makes Beetle/Alyce a real child of misery who slowly gains confidence in herself and in her ability to win friends. When Alyce is at an inn two-thirds of the way through the book, she is asked, "What, inn girl, do *you* want?" She thinks for a while and answers, "I know what I want. A full belly, a contented heart, and a place in this world." That is what Alyce has at the end of the book.

This might be a good book to read aloud to late junior high or early high school students. It's a simple book, but it has humor and compassion for its characters and its time. A couple of my students loved its earthy language and earthy wit.

A couple of other students who read Cushman's *Catherine, Called Birdy* (1994) wondered why that book had been named a Newbery Honor book while *The Midwife's Apprentice* received the Newbery Award. Maybe this is another case of an author getting an honor a year later after critics and readers recognize their mistake of a year ago. Perhaps. But *The Midwife's Apprentice* is as strong as *Catherine* and in some ways is a more compact and better told story.

Maybe the answer to this puzzle—if it is a puzzle—is for teachers and librarians and students to read both books. Between the two, Cushman presents a marvelous portrait of the stench and wonder of medieval England.

Robert Dunbar

SOURCE: A review of *The Midwife's Apprentice,* in *Books for Keeps,* No. 105, July, 1997, p. 25.

"From someone who had no place in the world, she had suddenly become someone with a surfeit of places." This is the transformation achieved by the young woman whom we met as Brat and leave as Alyce in this highly readable and always engaging novel. Set in the England of the fourteenth century, it belongs to that genre of historical fiction which places its emphasis on the everyday lives of ordinary men and women (here, mainly women) as distinct from the doings of the mighty and privileged. As we follow Brat's progress from abandoned orphan to young midwife a vivid picture emerges of a world characterized by harshness and cruelty and a desperate struggle to survive. It is her combination of humour, resilience and adaptability which enables her to come through, to learn to live with disappointment and, above all, to understand the gap which exists between dream and reality. Cushman brilliantly incorporates these themes of personal growth within a fascinating frame of medieval social (and medical) history, the erudition being lightly and entertainingly displayed.

THE BALLAD OF LUCY WHIPPLE (1996)

Publishers Weekly

SOURCE: A review of *The Ballad of Lucy Whipple,* in *Publishers Weekly,* Vol. 243, No. 28, July 8, 1996, p. 84.

In a voice so heartbreakingly bitter that readers can taste her homesickness, California Morning Whipple describes her family's six-year stay in a small mining town during the Gold Rush. Her mother, a restless widow with an acid tongue, has uprooted her children from their home in Massachusetts to make a new life in Lucky Diggins. California rebels by renaming herself Lucy and by hoarding the gold dust and money she earns baking dried apple and vinegar pies, saving up for a journey home. Over years of toil and hardship, Lucy realizes, somewhat predictably, that home is wherever she makes one. As in her previous books, Newbery Award winner Cushman proves herself a master at establishing atmosphere. Here she also renders serious social issues through sharply etched portraits: a runaway slave who has no name of his own, a preacher with a congregation of one, a raggedy child whose arms are covered in bruises. The writing reflects her expert craftsmanship; for example, Lucy's brother Butte, dead for lack of a doctor, is eulogized thus: "He was eleven years old, could do his sums, and knew fifty words for liquor." A coming-of-age story rich with historical flavor.

Sally Lodge

SOURCE: A talk with Karen Cushman, in *Publishers Weekly,* Vol. 243, No. 35, August 26, 1996, p. 46.

When she was interviewed for *PW*'s "Flying Starts" feature just two years ago, no one realized how high Karen Cushman would soon soar. Her first novel, *Catherine, Called Birdy,* was selected as a 1994 Newbery Honor Book, and the very next year the 54-year-old author won the Newbery Medal for her second work of fiction, *The Midwife's Apprentice.* Both titles are published by Clarion, which this month is releasing Cushman's third book, *The Ballad of Lucy Whipple.*

Though Lucy Whipple, like her prior stories, centers on a girl grappling with her destiny, it differs in a significant way. Cushman fast-forwarded her setting hundreds of years, from the medieval England of Catherine and Midwife to a California mining town during the Gold Rush. Twelve-year-old Lucy unwillingly moves with her siblings and her widowed mother from Massachusetts to a place called Lucky Diggins, which, as the girl, writes in a letter to her grandparents back East, "isn't much of a town—just tents and rocks and wind."

Asked what inspired this dramatic change of scenery, Cushman muses that it may well have come from the anger she felt one day standing in the gift shop of a historical society, looking at flap copy on books about the Gold Rush. "I read that the Gold Rush was a 'movement of men'—that 90% of those who came to California at that time to make their fortunes were male," she recalls. "And I though that was a quick dismissal of the other 10%—a sizable population. What about the women who accompanied and kept house for the prospectors? What if there were a 12-year-old girl who didn't want any part of the Gold Rush but had no choice? And then Lucy's whole story came."

Cushman remarks that this era was more difficult to research than the Middle Ages, since there was a dearth of information on the specifics she was interested in. "Most of what we have on these years we know from miners' journals and letters," she explains. "There is virtually nothing about the experiences of women or children. So I ended up extrapolating from the miners' writings—and making some things up."

The author is grateful that she had finished Lucy Whipple before learning she had won the Newbery. "I probably wouldn't have gone back to writing it for a long time after that," she says. Has this high honor changed her life significantly? Cushman has a mixed response:

"I'm still the same person who has to empty the cat box and do the dishes, and it's strange to me that people are standing in line to have me sign my book. On the other hand, I feel pride and I feel a certain responsibility. People are now going to seek out my books. And they will come to talks that I'm giving with pens poised above pads of paper, ready to write down what I say. It's a bit scary"

The award has also brought a change in the Oakland, Calif., author's daily routine. "Ideally, I'd like to dedicate each day to writing, reading or thinking about my work," she says, "but life gets in the way. Since winning the Newbery I've been writing in snatches and have spent quite a bit of time giving interviews and speeches. I try to tell myself that life will soon normalize and I'll feel lonely and neglected—but at least then I'll be able to devote more time to writing." Cushman fans will be happy to learn that she has, however, found the time to begin another novel, which returns to medieval days.

Though the demands on her time are many, Cushman has made a point of keeping up her visits to school and bookstores. In her words, "Writers and young readers feed each other in an important way. As a writer, I whisper in children's ears. And they talk back. One day when I was signing books I met a family with three girls. Their mother had read my first two novels aloud, and the youngest child began telling me the story of *The Midwife's Apprentice* as though I'd never heard it. And I began to realize that in her mind, this was not Alyce's story, but the story of the cat that appears in the novel. I realized then what a collaborative effort writing is: not only am I writing the book I think I'm writing, but I'm also creating a story that kids will see in their own special way."

Though her craft gives her enormous pleasure, Cushman didn't launch her career as a novelist until her daughter, Leah—now 23—left home for college. "I'm not sure that I could have done this earlier," she says. "I believe my life up to now has been preparation for my writing. I spent 10 years teaching in a graduate museum studies program. I taught about material culture and researched artifacts to discover the details of life that I was later able to put into words. The teaching and writing came from the same place.

"But I couldn't have written these novels while Leah was still at home and so much a part of my life," she continues. "The space she left when she went away to school freed me up and allowed me to concentrate on Catherine, Alyce and Lucy—my other girls I've been living with these past few years."

Kirkus Reviews

SOURCE: A review of *The Ballad of Lucy Whipple,* in *Kirkus Reviews,* Vol. LXIV, No. 12, June 15, 1996, pp. 896-97.

The recent Newbery medalist plunks down two more strong-minded women, this time in an 1849 mining camp—a milieu far removed from the Middle Ages of her first novels, but not all that different when it comes to living standards.

Arvella Whipple and her three children, Sierra, Butte, and 11-year-old California Morning, make a fresh start in Lucky Diggins, a town of mud, tents, and rough-hewn residents. It's a far cry from Massachusetts; as her mother determinedly settles in, California rebelliously changes her name to Lucy and starts saving every penny for the trip back east. Ever willing to lose herself in a book when she should be doing errands, Lucy is an irresistible teenager; her lively narration and stubborn, slightly naive self-confidence (as well as a taste for colorful invective: "Gol durn, rip-snortin' rumhole and cussed, dad-blamed, dag diggety, thundering pisspot," she storms) recall the narrator of *Catherine, Called Birdy,* without seeming as anachronistic. Other characters are drawn with a broader brush, a shambling platoon of unwashed miners with hearts (and in one case, teeth) of gold. Arvella eventually moves on, but Lucy has not only lost her desire to leave California, but found a vocation as well: town librarian. With a story that is less a period piece than a timeless and richly comic coming-of-age story, Cushman remains on a roll.

Bruce Anne Shook

SOURCE: A review of *The Ballad of Lucy Whipple,* in *School Library Journal,* Vol. 42, No. 8, August, 1996, p. 142.

Following the death of Lucy's father, her mother moves her family from Massachusetts to the gold fields of California. Their home is now the rough-and-tumble gold-mining town of Lucky Diggins. Lucy feels distinctly out of place and longs for her grandparents and home. She tells of traveling west and settling down in this lonesome place, occasionally relating incidents through letters to her grandparents. She is a dreamy, bookish girl, not interested in the harsh life of the gold camps and California wilderness. Still, she makes unusual friends and has some adventures. Her brother, Butte, 11, dies; her mother works hard in a boarding house for miners and falls in love with a traveling evangelist. Lucy matures considerably over the course of the book, in the end choosing to remain in California rather than return to Massachusetts or follow her sisters, mother, and her mother's new husband to the Sandwich Islands. Cushman's heroine is a delightful character, and the historical setting is authentically portrayed. Lucy's story, as the author points out in her end notes, is the story of many pioneer women who exhibited great strength and courage as they helped to settle the West. The book is full of small details that children will love. Butte, for example, collects almost 50 words for liquor; listing them takes up half of a page. Young readers will enjoy this story, and it will make a great tie-in to American history lessons.

Linda Perkins

SOURCE: A review of *The Ballad of Lucy Whipple,* in *The New York Times Book Review,* February 16, 1997, p. 25.

Some very fine writers labor in obscurity for years with little or no recognition, but not Karen Cushman. Her first novel, *Catherine, Called Birdy,* was named a 1994 Newbery Honor Book. Her second, *The Midwife's Apprentice,* won the 1996 Newbery Medal for Children's Literature. Both books portray young women struggling to establish their identities in an oppressive medieval society. Catherine rails against a father who seeks a wealthy husband for her. In *The Midwife's Apprentice,* a young woman with no given name rises from a dung-hill to learn midwifery and to earn a proper name and self-respect.

With this kind of initial success, one might expect Ms. Cushman's next novel to be more of the same: another story of a young woman coming of age in medieval England. It would make a fine trilogy at a time when historical fiction for girls is attractively packaged and marketed by series. Like her heroines, however, Ms. Cushman breaks with convention. *The Ballad of Lucy Whipple* does feature a young woman, but this time the setting is gold-rush California, and it's clear that Ms. Cushman's early honors were not just beginner's luck.

When the Whipples, including a 12-year-old named California Morning, sell the family business in Massachusetts and migrate west, they wind up in Lucky Diggins, a Sierra hamlet of tents, shacks and lean-tos. In this hardscrabble mining camp, the Whipples—the widowed mother, Arvella; California; her 10-year-old brother, Butte; and her younger sisters, Prairie and Sierra—run a boarding tent for miners and other rough-and-tumble types.

At first, these grimy strangers, with their dreams of gold and their colorful "dag-diggety" turns of phrase, frighten California. She longs for the comforts, culture and "snug spaces" of the East, and decides to change her name to Lucy because it isn't beautiful but ordinary, "a very Massachusetts name." When her mother rhapsodizes over the natural beauty of the Sierra, "the color of the grass, the light trapped in the cracks of the mountains, the sun setting over the peaks," the homesick Lucy points out what's missing: a school, a library, books, which she especially regrets.

An extraordinary cast of eccentric characters parades through Lucky Diggins. Some, like the "sunken-eyed, scar-faced, pinch-mouthed" Mr. Coogan, suddenly disappear. Others, like Snowshoe Ballou, the mail carrier, speak tenderly with their actions, bringing not words but gifts, like an eagle's feather. When the hulking Brother Clyde Claymore, a minister "preaching the benefits of prunes and proverbs," arrives on an undersized mule, Lucy and her mother quickly brush him off, but learn not to judge this man by his ludicrous first impression.

Hungry for security and stability, Lucy finds California's climatic conditions formidable. Cold, drenching winters alternate with searing summer droughts. Fire ravages the town, followed by an equally devastating flood, and death is a constant presence. People mysteriously arrive and disappear, and to Lucy's horror, boarders openly court her mother. Worse, her brother falls gravely ill. Despite her stubborn resistance, Lucy changes her attitudes.

Lucy is not one to suffer in silence. Letters to her grandparents, full of self-pity and wistful whining, vividly describe "living with a bunch of men who never wash or change their clothes . . . in a space so small I can lie in bed and stir the beans on the stove without getting up. . . . No one has a book or a new dress or flowers growing outside the door." In this print-starved town, Lucy generously lends her few precious books to the filthy but voracious readers.

Lucy's observations and idiom belong to the gold rush, but in spirit and temperament she reflects the thoughts of contemporary young women as well. Her change of name is just the first rebellious step toward independence. Why can't her mother treat her like an adult, and why is she so demanding? Just who is Lucy Whipple, and what does she intend to do with her life? Follow her mother as a missionary to the Sandwich Islands? Return east? Stay in Lucky Diggins?

In an afterword, Ms. Cushman cites an 1850 census indicating that 90 percent of the gold-rush population was indeed male, but the other 10 percent included "wives, mothers, sisters, daughters and sometimes women like Arvella Whipple who came without a man." Meticulously researched right down to the slang of the era, including some 50 terms for liquor, Lucy's story is packed with more history than many textbooks. Deftly and unobtrusively integrated into Lucy's narrative, this background information never overshadows the characters or distracts from the story.

As in her earlier books, Ms. Cushman re-creates a time and place in gritty detail. Through Lucy's eyes one observes the streets of "mud and dust, littered with oyster tins, ham bones and broken shovels." Noting the constant reek of privies in Lucky Diggins, Ms. Cushman holds the reader's nose up to the stench of history. Such particulars bring a breath of fetid but authentic air to a genre too frequently sanitized for young readers.

In contrast to the vivid gold-rush tableau, there are few clues about Lucy's physical appearance. This is highly unusual in historical fiction about girls, a genre prone to dwell on looks, fashion and romance. In an interesting twist, it's Arvella Whipple who finds romance, not her daughter. Instead, Karen Cushman takes the reader inside Lucy's heart and mind, and dag diggety, that girl opens a library!

Additional coverage of Cushman's life and career is contained in the following sources published by The Gale Group: *Authors and Artists for Young Adults,* **Vol. 22 and** *Something about the Author,* **Vol. 89.**

Donn (J.) Kushner

1927-

Canadian author of fiction and picture books.

Major works include *The Violin-Maker's Gift* (1980; U.S. edition, 1982), *Uncle Jacob's Ghost Story* (1984; U.S. edition, 1986), *A Book Dragon* (1987; U.S. edition, 1988), *The House of Good Spirits* (1990), *The Dinosaur Duster* (1992).

INTRODUCTION

Kushner is best known for challenging elementary graders with his strong, thought-provoking story lines presented in a uniquely creative style. Although his rich characterizations and multilayered narratives have occasionally left reviewers wondering in which age group to place his fictions, his imaginative writing primarily appeals to mature child readers who enjoy complex, engaging adventures. "No one could criticize Donn Kushner's writing for patronizing young readers," wrote Mary-Ann Stouck in her review of *The House of Good Spirits*. She added, "More than most, his books demand thoughtful and informed reading. But the rewards are rich for those willing to pursue them." Similar to traditional fairy and folk tales, Kushner's stories present narrative-within-a-narrative structures populated with fantastically original, multi-faceted characters, such as a philosophical dragon, a fortune-telling bird, a dinosaur-bone cleaner, and two stage-struck ghosts. Reviewers have consistently recognized Kushner's fertile imagination, praising the dimension and scope of his plots as well as the "uncommon aura" of his descriptions, which combine supernatural elements with touching moments of humanity. As both a writer for children and a research scientist, Kushner finds parallels between the scientific and the literary imaginations, as he explained in *Emergency Librarian*: "One thing in science which is very valuable, indeed one of the most valuable, is imagination. And the imagination in science can often be like the imagination in literature in that you connect things which weren't necessarily there before." Kushner's works characteristically have moral messages and illuminate traditional values such as love, freedom, and family integrity. He also has addressed such issues as racism, desire for power, the role of the past and memories, and death and dying, adding a dollop of humor to lighten the tone. Reviewer Mary-Ann Stouck noted that "one of the distinctive features of Kushner's writing is his profound humanitarian concern for society." Although publishers often have been reluctant to target his books at children, and his stories have sometimes been criticized for being difficult for children to follow, there is little debate that Kushner's works, as Patricia Morley once commented, "instruct and delight 'children' of all ages who respond to beauty, fantasy, fun, and more than a little wisdom."

Biographical Information

Kushner was born in Lake Charles, Louisiana, but has made his home in Ontario, Canada. Kushner ascribes his motivation for moving to "a feeling of wanting to go to foreign places," as he stated in an interview with *Emergency Librarian*. "Canada wasn't all that foreign. I just stayed in Canada. I found it very much to my taste." As a child he was an avid reader, particularly of folk tales, and developed a fondness for telling stories, as he explained in *Emergency Librarian:* "I found, somehow, that I have a gift of imagination. I could think of stories. . . . Stories kept coming." He earned a bachelor of science degree at Harvard University in 1948 and a master of science and Ph.D. at McGill University in Montreal, Quebec, in 1950 and 1952, respectively. While studying in Canada, he met Eva Milada Dubska and the two were married in 1949. Kushner took a job as a research scientist with the Forest Insect Laboratory in Sault Sainte Marie, Ontario, and later with the National Research Council of Canada in Ottawa. In 1965 he accepted a position as a professor of biology at the University of Ottawa. He has been a visiting scientist at the National Institute for Medical Research in London and is currently a visiting professor at University of Toronto in the Department of Microbiology and the Institute for Environmental Studies. Although Kushner has been writing stories since he was fifteen, his first book for children, *The Violin-Maker's Gift*, was not published until 1980. In addition to his fiction, Kushner has also written 130 scientific papers and is the North American editor of *Archives of Microbiology,* a monthly publication based in Germany. He and his wife have three sons.

Major Works

Kushner wrote in *Something about the Author* (SATA), "I aim towards the contrapuntal in my writing (I am a keen amateur musician and have played the violin and viola in chamber music groups for years), so that a major theme may be under the surface, in the mind of the main character. Thus in *The Violin-Maker's Gift*, Gaspard, the violin-maker, silently expresses his love and feeling of loss for the little bird he gave away even after he realizes it is a magical creature." Kushner's first book for children, *The Violin-Maker's Gift,* tells of a lowly violin-maker, Gaspard, who lives in the French Pyrenees near the border of Spain. One day Gaspard rescues a small bird and gives it as a gift to Matthias, a toll-keeper who he passed daily on his way to the village market to sell violins. To Gaspard's amazement, his gift grows into a beautiful, rare bird that not only talks, but predicts the future as well. As the bird brings Matthias fame and fortune, Gaspard grows jealous until he realizes that Matthias has been exploiting the bird for his own gains. Gaspard steals the creature back and gives it the greatest gift of all—its freedom. In return, the grateful bird tells the violin-maker the secret he had always longed to know. In his review of the story, Dave Jenkinson wrote: "the book offers a richness of layered characterization which transcends that normally found in folk literature." Zena Sutherland noted that the story "has a mellow, almost nostalgic quality and a quiet humor that, combined with the twin appeals of magic and justice, may be enjoyed by readers who can appreciate the nuance of the writing."

Kushner's second book, *Uncle Jacob's Ghost Story*, "departs in style from that usually found in children's literature" and is "quite sophisticated in its structure," according to Dave Jenkinson. In the story, young Paul is anxious to know more about his great-uncle Jacob, the mysterious outcast of the family. Spending a day in a senior citizen's home with his grandfather and his grandfather's roommate, Paul learns of Jacob's early life in Poland, and of his two friends Simon and Esther, who had glorious dreams of becoming actors in New York. When Simon and Esther die of typhus, Jacob emigrates to New York, where he runs a newsstand in Times Square and earns a reputation for his kindness. There he meets two street musicians, who turn out to be the ghosts of Simon and Esther. Jacob chooses not to join them until one day he sees the police brutally beating a crowd of poor, hungry people in the Square. During the night

Jacob deliberately freezes to death in his newsstand and joins his traveling musician ghost friends. A *Kirkus Reviews* critic commented, "This haunting book is beautifully written, with vivid descriptions of the characters inhabiting Times Square in the early 1900s. Strong themes of love and memory, destiny and individuality run through the story. For the unusual child who would grasp the layers of meaning in the narrative, or for the adult." Ellen Mandel writes, "Though this setting is hardly the stuff to rivet most youngsters, the supernatural events, the moments of humor, the touching human relationships, and a provocative moral message will reward special readers for their persistence."

In *A Book Dragon*, "Kushner hits his stride and establishes what may prove to be the trademark of his beautifully crafted longish fictions: an inspired mix of imagination, history, and ethical values," noted Patricia Morley. Opening in medieval Britain, the story focuses on the life of a young and very philosophical dragon named Nonesuch. Nonesuch spends his early days in a cave listening to his grandmother's stories and guarding his family's treasures. When his grandmother dies, he sets out to search for his own treasure and adventures. He eventually meets Brother Theophilus, a monk who draws pictures of Nonesuch for his illuminated *Book of Hours*. Nonesuch is inadvertently packed away with the book when it is stolen, and journeys through time with his treasure, eventually waking up in a twentieth-century rare-book shop. "*A Book Dragon* is a refreshingly different fantasy," remarked Mary-Ann Stouck. "Broader than most in the scope of its concerns, it resists the current fashion to ask children to concentrate upon their own psyches and instead opens up to them a wider world of social issues experienced through a great range of colourful characters, both animal and human. Its stylistic innovations function solidly as essential vehicles of theme and plot; they do not merely call attention to their own cleverness, and the non-human characters are never sentimentalized. This book should establish Kushner clearly in the forefront of children's fantasy writing in Canada."

Similar to *A Book Dragon*, *The House of Good Spirits* is complex in theme, style, and plot and rich in characterization. The story features an 11-year-old boy, Amos, who has traveled with his family from Nigeria to Port Jordan, Ontario, where he encounters various forms of racial prejudice. His experiences with contemporary racism are interwoven with the racism of the past in the "house," a former storage space for alcoholic spirits smuggled during Prohibition. The house sits on land once occupied by a church built by runaway slaves. As Amos enters the house, he is haunted by the spirits of former slaves who were once trying to reach freedom in Canada. With Amos's help, the spirits move on to their final destination. "Kushner is a master of surrealistic invention. . . ," marveled Mary-Ann Stouck. "Far from escapism, this fantasy is a sometimes terrifying transformation of the real worked in such a way as to illuminate its true significance. . . ."

Kushner's first picture book, *The Dinosaur Duster,* tells

of Mr. Mopski, who is responsible for cleaning two dinosaur skeletons for a museum exhibit. Mr. Mopski's habit of singing while dusting the bones causes one of the skeletons to speak up one day. Tired of the same view day-in and day-out, the dinosaurs crave a change of scenery. So Mr. Mopski switches their heads, thus transforming the stegosaurus and triceratops into a "tricerosaurus" and "stegatops," the unknowing experts say. The new species go on a world tour, but are delighted to return to their own museum. Bernie Goedhart remarked that *The Dinosaur Duster* "boasts an engaging and intelligent text . . . Kushner's sly sense of humour is evident throughout the carefully-crafted text and gives *The Dinosaur Duster* a quality all picture books should have: it's as appealing for the adult reading it aloud as for the child who is listening." Marion Scott further hailed the story as "a whimsical, off-beat tale and a new twist on the ever-popular dinosaur theme. . . Kushner's narrative is warm and humorous, yielding new enjoyment and discoveries with successive readings. . . Mr. Mopski's character succeeds as a lovable eccentric, and the dinosaurs have distinctive personalities. The museum and scientific worlds are gently spoofed, and comic details and dialogue abound."

Awards

In 1981, Kushner received the Canadian Library Association Book of the Year for Children Award for *The Violin-Maker's Gift*. Short listed for the 1988 Governor General's Prize for Children's Literature, Kushner's third juvenile title, *A Book Dragon*, won the IODE National Chapter Award which, since 1985, has been given annually to the best English-language book written for children thirteen and under.

GENERAL COMMENTARY

Bernie Goedhart

SOURCE: "Renaissance Man Donn Kushner a Delightful Challenge for Children," in *Books for Young People*, Vol. 1, No. 6, December, 1987, pp. 1, 3.

The trouble with clichés is that they sometimes offer the best way to express a concept, but through glib overuse, they have lost their punch. A "Renaissance man", for example, is defined by *Webster's* as "a person who has wide interests and is expert in several areas"—surely an apt description of Donn Kushner, a biology professor, research scientist, and musician who has just published his third children's book. Add the fact that he is also extremely well read and appears to be interested in virtually everything, and you have a Renaissance man who personifies the cliché.

It helps to have a nimble mind when conversing with

Kushner. He is not a relaxed, gentle conversationalist; his delivery is rapid-fire, almost urgent at times, and his thoughts often take sudden twists and turns. "When you're talking to Donn, if you see his eyes darting in the middle of a conversation then you know he's come up with another idea," says Macmillan's managing editor Pat Kennedy, who worked on *A Book Dragon*, Kushner's latest novel. "He has an incredibly fertile imagination and an editor's job is always to cut back—to stop him from taking off on a new, imaginative tangent that strays from the plot."

A Book Dragon is the story of Nonesuch, a dragon who learns to survive by making himself as tiny as an insect. Any self-respecting dragon has a treasure to guard, and the one in Nonesuch's care is an illuminated manuscript that brings him from England to North America—and through five centuries. Another well-crafted foray into fantasy, *A Book Dragon* follows the critically acclaimed *Uncle Jacob's Ghost Story* and the award-winning *Violin-Maker's Gift*, all three reflecting the author's love of fairy tales.

A Book Dragon serves almost as a paean to the wonders of literature and literacy. Books, in this story, serve as keys to the past and links with the future. They afford Nonesuch with very real travel opportunities; they give safe haven when he needs it, and they connect him to his grandmother after her physical departure from earth. Books aid in the dragon's spiritual growth—a growth that Kushner says is the essence of this story.

Not surprisingly, the 60-year-old author, who says he began writing stories when he was 14, considers reading an integral part of life. All the members of his family, he says, are avid readers. Dr. Eva Kushner, his wife, was a professor of French literature at McGill University in Montreal before her recent appointment to the presidency of Victoria College at the University of Toronto. The couple has three sons: Daniel, 37, a management consultant in Toronto; Roland, 32, who works with the Bethlehem Bach Choir in Bethlehem, Pennsylvania and is the father of Nathan, six, and Benjamin, four; and Paul, 21, a physics student at McGill.

With little prompting, Kushner launches into an animated discussion about literacy that tempts one to view him as something of an unassuming intellectual. The surroundings—Kushner's tiny, cluttered, book-filled office off a laboratory in the University of Ottawa's biological-sciences building—only add to this impression, as do his academic credentials. He holds a bachelor's degree in chemistry from Harvard and a doctorate in biology from McGill, and for many years he has been researching "the molecular biology of halophilic archaebacteria"—or, more simply put, "strange creatures who live in high concentrations of salt".

But later, over Mexican food in a small campus restaurant, the image of Kushner as intellectual suddenly shifts when he quotes a cartoon seen in *Mad* magazine. ("I like *Mad* magazine," he says, surprised that anyone might find this incongruous.) The cartoon showed young boys discussing the intricacies of various types of aircraft. "They knew all the complicated names and facts," explains Kushner. "Then they went to school, opened their books, and started reading: 'Run, Spot, run. See Spot run.'"

No one could ever accuse Kushner of writing down to children. In fact, one of the criticisms leveled at his books—*Uncle Jacob's Ghost Story* in particular—has been that they are difficult for some children to follow. *Uncle Jacob's Ghost Story,* the tale of a disgraced family member and his attachment to long-dead friends from the old country, is told on several levels and concerns friendship, the world of theatre, family relationships, spirits, death and dying—much of it played out from the vantage-point of a newsstand on Times Square in the early 1900s.

"*Uncle Jacob* was a mature book for children and a children's book for adults," says Kennedy. "I don't think booksellers quite knew what to do with it." They weren't alone. The staff at Macmillan had difficulty knowing how best to market *Uncle Jacob,* and the author, too, was uncomfortable with the book's placement on the children's literature list. Nevertheless, it won the hearts of those who read it with the care it deserved. One of Kushner's favourite reviews, in the December 1984 issue of *Jam* magazine, quotes one Patrick Braithwaite, age 12, as saying in part: "I recommend it to people 10-503 years of age who like to read books that make you think."

A Book Dragon offers as much food for thought as its predecessor, but both author and editor feel it will have wider appeal. "It's not that I wrote down to anyone," says Kushner, "but I think a dragon (as central character) has immediate appeal." Kennedy agrees. "I think *A Book Dragon* is a bit more accessible. It has a stronger story-line."

Illustration also helps. The woodcuts by Nancy Jackson echo the style of Nonesuch's illuminated manuscript—and they offer almost as many surprises as Kushner's text. On page 18, for example, a tiny archer in the top margin has shot an arrow into the 18, causing the numerals to tumble. On pages 100 and 101, tiny bees buzz around the flowers that highlight several paragraphs. And on page 160, a cat at the foot of the page eyes some birds perched on the margin line at the top; the same cat appears contentedly curled up on page 166, while mama bird chirps frantically in the top margin for her three lost offspring. . . .

Meanwhile, Kushner reports with obvious pleasure that his grandson Nathan grabbed a copy of *A Book Dragon* "and won't give it up". Kushner has already written the text for his next book and says he created it for Nathan.

"It's called *The Dinosaur Duster,* and it's about Mr. Mopski, who dusts dinosaur bones in a museum." One night, Mr. Mopski ("my wife suggested his name; he

started out as Murgatroyd . . . ") starts singing one of the Carpathian folk-songs of which he is so fond ("they have names like When Will Uncle Dimitri Finally Go To Bed and The River Dluda Is Flowing Backwards and The Czar's Third Son Has Only One Leg . . . ") when he hears a voice complain: "Oh, that old thing again."

It turns out that Stegosaurus and Triceratops can speak. But the skeletons are in separate rooms, and Mr. Mopski thinks it would be nice if they could have a change of scenery. He's not strong enough to move them, so he simply switches their heads. "This turns them into Tricerosaurus and Stegatops," says Kushner, and the museum officials are thrilled by these so-called new discoveries. The dinosaurs go on exhibit at museums throughout the world, with Mr. Mopski along as their caretaker. Ultimately, of course, they grow homesick and a simple solution on Mr. Mopski's part results in their being sent back to resume a more settled existence.

The text is brief, compared with Kushner's other books, and he thinks it should be profusely illustrated. Kennedy says that the text has already been sent to Henry Holt in hopes of another co-publication.

Never at a loss for ideas, Kushner says he is now working on a story about a mysterious grey duck. It's a tale that began to develop during a visit to Zurich last year, when Kushner was on a year's sabbatical from the University of Ottawa, working in Paris with a Japanese scientist, Dr. Masamichi Kohiyama.

In addition to stories about dragons and ducks and multi-leveled tales of death and dying, Kushner has also written 130 scientific papers and is the North American editor of *Archives of Microbiology,* a monthly publication based in Germany. He sees no incongruity between his roles as scientist and creator of children's books. His ideas, he says, come from "a general world view", and he admits that his view has been described as quirky. "I guess that's right, if it means that it pleases me when unexpected things happen that turn out to be the right things to have happen."

Then he adds, in typically quirky fashion: "Robertson Davies says, 'I don't get ideas; ideas get me', and Dr. Seuss has said, 'I get my ideas from a six-foot-high bird that lives in the desert and I don't know where *he* gets them . . . '"

Kushner's résumé also lists, under hobbies, the fact that he plays violin and viola, with chamber music his primary focus. But he also plays folk-music and has been a square-dance fiddler at times. While some might consider this real Renaissance-man material, Kushner sees nothing unusual in his transitions from science to music to literature. The connection between science and music, he suggests, is perfectly natural. "Many scientists tend to go in for amateur music. Maybe it's the form—the discipline—that's attractive. When I play here in Ottawa, it's usually with scientists." And during his sabbatical in Paris, his colleague Dr. Kohiyama turned out to be a cellist.

As for science and literature, "they both require two things, imagination and discipline. In science, the most valuable people are those who make the leaps of imagination. They're the 'what-if' people. . . . Granted, the uses of language are different. Scientific writing employs an expository prose in which the meaning must be clear. But the kind of weight that words carry—the kind of resonances words have—exists on many levels in both science and literature."

Kushner's love of words exhibits itself in a fondness for unusual, often humorous names—as evident in *A Book Dragon* as it was in *Uncle Jacob*. ("I named that character Mr. Eisbein because it sounded like 'ice' and 'bone' and that seemed right for a ghost story," he told a school group shortly after *Uncle Jacob*'s publication. "Then I found out that it really means a bone from a pig's foot. If I had known that, I might have given him another name.")

In *A Book Dragon,* the dragons have names such as Schatzwache ("treasure watcher" in German) and Feuerschlange ("fire snake"). Nonesuch's disreputable cousin, the only one of the family to still eat humans, is called Cauchemar ("nightmare" in French).

As for Nonesuch himself? The central character's name, Kushner says, should not be construed as a tongue-in-cheek reference to dragons as mythological and, therefore, non-existent creatures.

"On the contrary. It means there's no dragon like that one. As dragons go, he's unique. There's none such as he!"

Dave Jenkinson

SOURCE: "Donn Kushner: Ghosts and Dragons," in *Emergency Librarian,* Vol. 17, No. 2, November-December, 1989, pp. 67-72.

A research scientist who has authored over 100 scientific papers and who works on the physiology of microorganisms that live in such extreme environments as cold, heat, or high salt concentrations seems an unlikely creator of award-winning children's fiction. Nevertheless, Donn Kushner is such a person, and he sees a relationship between what may appear to be the dichotomous roles of scientist and author of creative works.

"One thing in science which is very valuable, indeed one of the most valuable, is imagination. And the imagination in science can often even be like the imagination in literature in that you connect things which weren't necessarily there before. There are always facts in science, and of course, you have to learn the facts like you have to learn the language. You need to know the facts, or at least you should have people around you who have

the specialized knowledge and with whom you can work. I tend to do a lot of collaborative work. Often, I've been able to ask questions whose answers are illuminating; that's one of my stronger points. You also must have discipline; you often have to learn techniques, or at least read and help others learn techniques."

Donn Kushner was born March 29, 1927, in Lake Charles, Louisiana. The double "n" in his given name is not a misprint; Donn was his mother's maiden name. After earning his B.Sc. in Chemistry at Harvard in 1948, Kushner emigrated to Canada where an M.Sc. and a Ph.D., both in Biochemistry, from Montreal's McGill University followed in 1950 and 1952. The motivation for moving Kushner ascribes to "a feeling of wanting to go to foreign places. Canada wasn't all that foreign. I just stayed in Canada. I found it very much to my taste. I also met my wife, Eva, in Canada." Dr. Eva Kushner, a former professor of French Literature at McGill University, is President of Victoria College on the University of Toronto campus.

First a research scientist with the Forest Insect Laboratory in Sault Saint Marie, Ontario, between 1954 and 1961, and then with the National Research Council of Canada in Ottawa, Kushner joined the University of Ottawa in 1965 as a professor of biology. In July, 1988, Kushner moved to the University of Toronto. "I'm a Visiting Professor there in the Department of Microbiology and the Institute for Environmental Studies. I also have a lab at the University of Ottawa with graduate students finishing off work." The Ottawa lab necessitates Kushner's commuting weekly to the nation's capital.

Regarding his development as a writer, Kushner recalls, "I blush to say that they never made us write in any English courses in high school. We just did grammar. We never did any actual writing and that was a great loss compared with what I saw my three sons do in Ontario schools. My parents always had lots of books around and my mother had an old friend, very well educated, and she took an interest in me and encouraged me quite a bit. But I've always been a storyteller. When I was 10-years-old, I got a book called *Jokes for All Occasions,* and I just inflicted them on my poor parents. I still tell jokes.

"I read a great deal. Growing up in Louisiana, as a person who read much more than most of my school mates, I tended to be quite lonely. Very often, somebody who has intellectual interests will find him or herself relatively alone. I always liked telling stories, and I found, somehow, that I have a gift of imagination. I could think of stories. I was writing at 15. Stories kept coming. Some of them were 'light', and it took me awhile to realize the difference between a substantial story and something which was just a 'sketch'. Most of the adult fiction I've done is published in *The Witnesses and Other Stories.* I've not done very much adult fiction since I started publishing children's books. I seemed to have found what I could do better."

Reading a Kushner juvenile title can leave the impression of having read a piece of traditional literature, but such a response is not surprising for Kushner claims a strong link to such material. "I've been reading folk tales all my life. I like reading and rereading them because they have so much in them. Often so much is not stated, just implied. This is just the way I seem to write. My writing tends to be very descriptive, even too descriptive. Sometimes when I look it over later on, I think maybe I could have made it move a little faster. It's something I'm trying to watch out for in other things that I'm doing. An editor once said I have a very 'painterly' style."

Kushner's first children's book, *The Violin-Maker's Gift,* won the 1981 Canadian Library Association Book of the Year for Children Award. In addition to American and British editions, the book has been published in France, Holland, Germany and Poland. The book's plot essentially follows the common folk pattern wherein a poor but honest person performs an altruistic act and is later rewarded for that action; however, the book offers a richness of layered characterization which transcends that normally found in folk literature.

Set in the early nineteenth century, *The Violin-Maker's Gift* tells the story of Gaspard l'Innocent, a violin-maker, who, while on his way to market to sell his modest instruments, accidentally overlooks the local custom of tipping Matthias, the toll-keeper. On his return trip, Gaspard, having forgotten his intention to purchase something for Matthias, arrives at the toll-bridge empty-handed. While in the village, Gaspard had climbed the brick wall of the church to rescue a young, flightless bird. Lacking the needed tip and recognizing Matthias' ability with animals, Gaspard gives Matthias the bird. Later, Gaspard seeks the bird's return, but Matthias requests a price that Gaspard considers exorbitant. As the bird matures and its plumage increases in beauty, Matthias exhibits the bird and charges admission. Matthias comments on his good fortune. "Just to think that a simple act of kindness on my part, in taking the little bird off your hands, should turn out so well! It shows that one should never hesitate too long before doing an unselfish deed—some benefit may come from it."

The bird's value seemingly increases greatly when it begins to talk and is able to foretell the future. "Sometimes the bird predicted good events, sometimes bad, sometimes important ones and sometimes trivial, but it always told the truth, and its fame spread." Unfortunately for Matthias, the bird only responds when it wishes to do so. Because of the bird's unpredictability, Matthias is forced to display the bird in shabby inns where people risk a small fee that the bird will answer their future oriented questions. Gaspard sees the bird in such a setting, and, noting its dulled plumage, he worries about its health.

Gaspard imagines how *he* would treat the bird if it were his again. "'He (the bird) would have a room to himself,' Gaspard said." Gaspard would also display the bird, but "the price would be high; only rich wealthy people could afford it." Possibly pricked by his conscience, Gaspard reconsiders his intentions. "But why should only rich people consult him? That would be selfish of me . . . No, four days each month poor people could ask him questions free." Momentarily comfortable with what he is about to do, Gaspard takes the bird from the inn. Unwilling to label himself a thief, Gaspard rationalizes, "I saved the bird first. Is it right that I should have no part in it?"

Later, Gaspard, recognizing the bird will die if kept in captivity, releases it. The bird, prior to flying away, addresses Gaspard, "Since you are the only one who ever spoke to me without making a request, though you would have been most justified in asking—I will tell you something you may want to know." The bird reveals the location of a rare plant, which, when added to Gaspard's violin, yields instruments "that sing with a human voice." Earlier, Gaspard had confessed that he wanted to be able to construct violins like those of the great masters. "If I could make such violins I would not be a simple peddler at this fair." Gaspard's listener prophetically responds, "You might be no better off than you are now." Gaspard's violins became known for their excellent sound, but "the pressures of business worried him; his uncertainty whether he could find the plant again the following spring made him anxious and his face took on a drawn, peaked look. The days he spent each spring in the cold mountain rains and wet snow damaged his health." The concluding chapter reveals that "as the violins grew older their human voices gradually disappeared."

Kushner acknowledges *The Violin-Maker's Gift,* though published in 1980, had been written years before. "I actually wrote it in 1967, and then it hung around. The first publisher I sent it to said, 'Well, you know, it is a fantasy, but the language is complicated.' And they didn't know what to do with it. Then I kind of put it aside. Around 10 years or so later, I began taking it out again and sending it out, and somebody at Macmillan's saw it and liked it. Eventually, after a couple of years, it got published."

"The book underwent a lot of reworking in the hands of the editors, and some very good reworking. For example, when the book first started, I didn't have Babette, Matthias' wife, in it. They said, 'There should be a female figure.' Babette sort of came out and made a big difference in the way the story is told. Having her there, in the beginning foretelling something, catches the reader's attention, I think. I found the editors, by and large, to be helpful. I don't always agree with them, but if they say, 'I like it, but this and that is too long or seems to drag,' I take it very seriously. You realize that you don't want to sell your soul to the devil by losing integrity, but, on the other hand, sometimes you *can* say things in shorter and livelier ways. You have to think of your audience who are actually going to read this stuff."

Kushner's second book, *Uncle Jacob's Ghost Story,* departs in style from that usually found in children's literature. The story is told by two old men to a young boy, Paul, and the story's central character is an adult. During the day Paul spends with his grandfather at a New Jersey senior citizens' home, Grandfather's roommate, Mr. Eisbein, joins the pair, and the two old men tell Paul of his Great Uncle Jacob, the black sheep of the family, who had lived in eastern Poland, near the Russian border at the end of the nineteenth century.

Jacob's childhood friends had been Simon and Esther, brother and sister, and Jacob's relationship with the latter had matured into a romance. All three longed to go to America. Jacob, who "considered himself a 'rationalist'; that is a person who believes in the power of reason," sees America as a place where "they know how to live: a great, free, hopeful nation. They are not bound by old men and superstition, as we are— . . . There, if you work hard, if you use your intelligence, you have a good chance for a useful, happy life . . . There, when they have problems, they solve them scientifically." Simon's and Esther's reasons for emigrating were more specific. "They loved the stage: to them, an actor's life was the most glorious on earth. Where could they lead such a life better than in America?"

Jacob and Simon were drafted into the army, with Jacob serving in the Russo-Japanese War. Upon returning to his village, Jacob finds both friends dead from typhus. Emotionally adrift, Jacob emigrates to America, but he has lost the drive to succeed. A succession of jobs occurs before Jacob purchases a newsstand in New York's Times Square.

At this point, the second part of the story begins. After learning that three mannequins had been stolen from Macy's department store, Jacob encounters three street musicians, but one is a mannequin. "Their faces seemed familiar but he was sure he had never spoken to them." When he next encounters the trio, "the mannequin was not the short young man but the tall one! . . . There must be some natural, rational explanation, Jacob told himself. After all, this was America." Following his third encounter with the dancers, Jacob realizes that two of them are Simon and Esther. Jacob, once separated from them and ever the rationalist, doubts the evidence of his eyes. "But next morning the clear light made everything seem different. Jacob had to be convinced all over again."

Confirmation of Simon's and Esther's altered state is offered Jacob by Mr. Stephen Spangler, ostensibly a theatrical agent, who miraculously restores the sight of Times Square's blind beggars. Spangler, whose original name was Shternen Shpringer, Yiddish for "star-jumper," is an angel, or, as Grandfather says, "It's better to say 'messenger,' a messenger from heaven." Spangler's task is to shepherd Esther and Simon about this world until they are ready to go "above." Esther had been given the choice of remaining on earth or going above. Simon, by deserting the army to nurse typhus-struck Esther, "an unorthodox action that disturbs the moral balance of the universe," was forced to remain behind. When Jacob hears his friends are "leaving," he expresses the wish that they could stay. Following the one avenue of behavior available to make his wish possible, "Jacob froze to death in his newsstand"; the *Times* reported the "Sad death of a well-known figure in Times Square"; and the third mannequin "walked towards the girl dancer, who took its arm until they had joined her brother."

Imbedded in the storyline are several other themes. One involves the notion that the "angels" gamble for amusement with humans and their behaviors being the subject of their wagers. As Mr. Eisbein says, "I think they bet on what all of us will do; it's a game there." Spangler bets on the causes of World War I, and Jacob's decision about joining his spirit friends is even the subject of a "celestial" wager. A second theme involves the concept that stories seemingly have a life of their own and, to live, they must be told. Paul, emotionally reflecting on the day's happenings, says, "They (the ghosts) were so lonely: they wanted to have their story told." He realizes that "some day, only I will know it, and it must be told."

Paul's sense of obligation to story reflects Kushner's own feelings. "What motivates me to write is that I very often get ideas of stories which I think are very good ones. Often, I don't know any stories like them. This is true of the stories in my books. Perhaps they are not as unique as I think since other people have written about dragons and the immigrant experience, though not in the same way. In one of my stories, there is a writer who feels a certain responsibility to stories. If nobody tells them, they will sort of be lonely out there in the world. Somebody once said I have a feeling of responsibility towards the stories that I think about so that they should be told."

Of his second book's creation, Kushner says, "*Uncle Jacob's Ghost Story* took about three years to write from when I got the idea. It started off simply. I have a nephew who is an artist and a playwright. We'd even talked about his illustrating *The Violin-Maker's Gift.* I said, 'I have an idea. I'll write a simple story for you to illustrate. There's this man in a newsstand in Times Square, and he sees these three dancers but only two are alive, not the third one. It's a mannequin. The next day again he sees the three dancers and only two are alive, but not the same two.' That was the original idea. Then, where they came from and everything like that, it all got worked in afterwards. It worked out partly in my head, partly in discussion. I knew that the three dancers were spirits, but where did they come from? At one point I thought they were people who tried to make it in the theater and couldn't so they killed themselves. I mentioned this to one of the editors and she made a face and I thought, 'No!'

"The whole story of immigrants coming over struck me. In fact, people think the book's autobiographical. I mean my father was one of seven children and so was my mother, and the character Jacob was the middle of seven boys. There was no Jacob in the family like that even though, in point of fact, I did have an Uncle Jacob. He wasn't at all like the Jacob here. My father's name was Sam, and I had an Uncle Abe; those are the two old men in the story. The family I was writing about, a Jewish family with all their anxieties and all their worries, that's like my family."

Uncle Jacob's Ghost Story is quite sophisticated in its structure. One of the techniques Kushner utilized involved having the ghosts appear in the present as musicians performing in a bandstand across the river from the home. Kushner says this device "caused one of the difficulties in the story. Not all of the editors who saw it liked it. Some people worried about a story within a story idea, having it told by two old men. I think the main reason I did it that way was to have the ghosts across the river, urging on by those songs, to have their stories told. That was putting on another layer, of course. Maybe it wasn't necessary, but I kind of liked to do it that way. In some ways, Uncle Jacob's book is, to me, a successful story, but it is the one which has not sold as well as the others."

Short listed for the 1988 Governor-General's Prize for Children's Literature, Kushner's third juvenile title, *A Book Dragon,* won the IODE National Chapter Award which, since 1985, has been given annually to the best English-language book written for children 13 and under. The central character is a dragon, Nonesuch, who "was—and still is, for that matter—the last of a family of dragons that lived over five hundred years ago in a limestone hill . . . near the south coast of England." Today Nonesuch still dwells somewhere in North America where he continues to guard his treasure, a fifteenth century "Book of Hours." How and why Nonesuch came to make this object his treasure are the plot's foci.

Nonesuch's grandmother, whom Kushner describes as "the closest thing you'll find to a Jewish grandmother amongst dragons," is initially the most important living thing in the young dragon's life. "Teller" of the family's history, Grandmother also passes on such "truisms" of dragon life as, "Guard your treasure. A dragon without a treasure is nothing but an ugly flying reptile, with even less dignity than a salamander!" Over time, dragons had lost their ability to breathe fire and most no longer ate human flesh because, as Grandmother explained, "They mistrusted it." She arrived at that conclusion after observing that, "since humans killed, but did not eat each other, there must be something terribly wrong with their flesh."

At a mere 50 years of age, Nonesuch was 30 feet from nose to tail. Although Nonesuch would have continued to grow, "he was beginning to understand that strength and size, and even skill, were not enough, so long as humans existed in the world" for "humans could make something bigger, or at least stronger." After Grandmother deliberately follows a tunnel that "had become a

volcanic vent, leading down to the molten rock in the center of the earth" and disappears, Nonesuch hides her treasure and goes out into the world, "a dragon without a treasure." When he stops eating for a period, Nonesuch discovers he has shrunk. His smaller size, he observes, brings advantages. "He found that he hunted with more vigour, that he was more agile for being smaller." Coming to the conclusion "that there was little profit in being a very large dragon," Nonesuch continues "dieting" until he reaches the size of large insects.

The smaller Nonesuch is haunted by his grandmother's words, "A dragon without treasure has part of his soul missing: his heart is hollow." Though Grandmother's treasure had been gold and jewels, she defined treasure as those things valued by humans. Nonesuch happens on his "treasure" when he enters the scriptorum of a fifteenth century church where Brother Theophilus, a scholar and scribe, is writing and illuminating a "Book of Hours" which he refers to as "my treasure." When a thief steals the book, Nonesuch, who has been accidentally locked in the book's box, is transported along as well. A series of incidents ultimately culminates in the box and its unknown contents being purchased at an auction and brought to North America by Mr. Gottlieb, the owner of a secondhand bookshop, who realizes what a treasure he has found. The book's security is threatened, however, by Abercrombie, an unscrupulous businessman, who wants the shop's location for a hotel. When Gottlieb spurns Abercrombie's purchase offers, Abercrombie suggests that fire could accidentally destroy the shop. Among Grandmother's sayings was, "A true dragon always remains with what he loves; if he can." To guard his treasure, Nonesuch resumes eating, grows in size, and confronts the threat. "Eating Mr. Abercrombie was the hardest action of Nonesuch's life." Devouring Abercrombie, Nonesuch discovered "the reason dragons should not eat people . . . was that they took in the people's thoughts along with their flesh." And, until he diminishes in size, Nonesuch must experience Abercrombie's malevolent thought patterns.

For Kushner, getting the idea was the easy part of writing *A Book Dragon.* "The idea just came to me. I started with an idea which I thought was strong enough to carry it." Unlike the earlier books which flowed largely from Kushner's imagination, this title required research. "The dragon took about two years. There's a book called *The Book of the Dragon,* written by a couple of ladies. It describes dragons guarding bodies of water, dragons guarding treasures, dragons in alchemy, cosmic dragons which create and destroy universes, and I threw that all in. I read about life in monasteries to some extent. I knew a little about the different "hours" by reading *Name of the Rose.* The history? I knew about the Great Plague in London and the fire in London, and then I read a good deal about the chap books they had at the time. A lot of it I put in and took out again at the editors' insistence who found it too complicated. I have friends in Ottawa who run a used bookshop, and actually they made some useful comments. They quite liked my picture of the bookshop, but they said if they had a valuable book like that they could never keep it. I even had thought, if I ever wanted to do a dragon sequel, the book might be sold to a museum or something and the dragon would go along with it."

Kushner plays the violin and the viola, mainly in chamber music groups, and he has also been a square dance fiddler. Sometimes he accompanies his readings with the violin. Kushner's music background can be seen in his writing via his incorporation of contrapuntal structures wherein a major theme is under the surface. "There's counterpoint in *Uncle Jacob* with the two stories going on at once. In *The Violin-Maker's Gift,* it's the unstated feelings of Gaspard. About *The Book Dragon,* I'm not sure of the counterpoint. I guess the theme of finding treasures and losing homes is there."

As an active researcher, Kushner must find time in his schedule for his creative writing. "I take time at odd times—sometimes in the evening, sometimes on weekends, half an hour in the morning. I walk to work now, and I think about my writing while I'm walking. I write at odd times when I'm not doing other things that I'm supposed to be doing: these include scientific reading; writing and editing—I'm North American editor for *Archives of Microbiology*—and, of course, my teaching in microbiology. And I write when I travel. I go back and forth to Ottawa on the train every week. I find it really works pretty well."

"I usually write by hand first, then I do the retyping on a mechanical typewriter so it doesn't 'push' me too much. Then I go to the computer. My stories may go through several drafts. I usually do the first two by handwriting, often in pen and ink, then I type the next one out. I find it better to take my time over it. If the computer is blinking at me, the cursor seems to push me. It doesn't bother me to write non-fiction and letters on a computer."

As his own critic, Kushner observes, "It's hard to say if I'm widely read. I've been told that some people like my stuff very much and read it over and over again, but it's not read by great numbers of people. Probably my books would be for advanced or enriched children. I don't know if the language is complicated. I've been told my books are well written. I like language. As a musician, I like the rhythm of language. I like words to carry weight. I don't think my stuff can be read very, very rapidly. It can't just be skimmed through. Although my books aren't very long, there's a certain 'time' involved in reading them."

As to the future, "retiring and going full-time into writing is something that I've been thinking about. I would like to do less teaching. I would like to keep myself active with one thing and another. I could see myself going full-time into writing. Whether it would be all fiction or not I do not know."

"My colleagues in science usually accept my writing for children in quite a friendly way. They've been quite proud of it, actually. I've been worried about that a little bit because they might say, 'Is he a scientist if he's writing so much?' Fortunately, my research has one of the higher rates of support in the country by NSERC, the Natural Sciences & Engineering Research Council of Canada. Nevertheless, it does take time to write children's books, and it takes intellectual energy. A lot of thought goes into those books. I would say that there is no question that it does take away from other activities. If I put all that energy into science, I would be further ahead in science. But writing was a choice. If I hadn't made that choice, I'd be a different person too."

TITLE COMMENTARY

📖   *THE VIOLIN-MAKER'S GIFT* (1980; U.S. edition, 1982)

Publishers Weekly

SOURCE: A review of *The Violin-Maker's Gift,* in *Publishers Weekly,* Vol. 221, No. 15, April 9, 1982, p. 51.

Kushner, a professor at the University of Ottawa, bows with his first book for children. The story is original, related in spirit to folktales and moving as well as subtly humorous. Panton's fine, strong drawings illustrate the story of Gaspard l'Innocent who carves violins in his cottage near the French Pyrenees Mountains. Gaspard gives the fledgling he has saved from death to Matthias, the toll collector, but regrets the gift when he hears that Matthias is mistreating the bird. It grows into a fabulous creature who can speak and foretell future events. Its owner works the bird hard so Gaspard steals and sets it free, receiving a strange reward. With all the story's charm, it's too bad to report that the finished book contains inexcusable errors like "after he," (instead of after him), "all dead but she," and more.

Denise M. Wilms

SOURCE: A review of *The Violin-Maker's Gift,* in *Booklist,* Vol. 78, No. 17, July, 1982, p. 1445.

A spectacularly plumed bird that can both speak and foretell the future irrevocably changes the lives of the two men who are responsible for its welfare. Gaspard the violin maker has rescued the bird as a stranded, bedraggled waif, whose gold-and-blue-flecked feathers contain only a hint of its future splendor. He gives it to Matthias the toll-bridge keeper, who knows best how to nurture it but becomes seduced by the bird's revealed talents and shamelessly exploits it. A disturbed Gaspard rescues the bird, setting it free to return to its altitudinous domain; in return he's given the secret of making his violins sing as no others can. The story has a haunting quality that underscores its themes of love and self-interest. And although the telling is essentially formal, there are emotional undercurrents that ensure sufficient tension.

Anne Scott MacLeod

SOURCE: A review of *The Violin-Maker's Gift,* in *The Washington Post Book World,* May 9, 1982, p. 23.

This small book tells the story of Gaspard l'Innocent, a simple craftsman who lives alone and contented in the French Pyrenees. Every two weeks, he travels to the local town market to sell his worthy but unremarkable violins to buyers of unexacting taste. One day, while at the market, Gaspard, driven by an impulse he doesn't understand, climbs a brick wall to rescue a young bird stranded high up on the town cathedral. On the way home, he gives the bird to Matthias, the toll collector. He soon regrets the decision, for the bird quickly grows into a marvelous creature, large and beautiful, capable not only of human speech, but of prophecy. It foretells the future, in riddles, but always truthfully.

Matthias sets about improving his fortunes by exhibiting the bird around the countryside until Gaspard, unhappy over the bird's confinement and exploitation, steals it from him and sets it free. In princely gratitude, the bird tells Gaspard how to make his instruments "sing with a human voice," which knowledge brings the violin maker fame and fortune for the remainder of his life.

The story wears the air of a fairy tale or legend, though both characterization and setting are realistic rather than symbolic, as folk tales are. The prose style is graceful and straightforward; the narrative mixes reality and fantasy without blinking or blushing. There is a good deal of description, little dialogue, no child character and no humor. The nearest comparison is with some of Julia Cunningham's semi-fantasies, though Kushner is less pretentious than Cunningham about weighting his story with moral significance.

According to the book jacket, this, the author's first writing for children, won the 1981 Canadian Library Association Book of the Year for Children Award. It is a somewhat puzzling choice, I think, since it is not clear that the book will readily find an audience among children. While the wholly adult cast of characters does not automatically put the story outside a child's interest, neither does it help to draw a reader into a tale whose concerns (the sound of a violin, for example) and references (to Napoleonic battles, peasants and gypsies) are likely to be unfamiliar. Moreover, the message of the narrative has none of the simple clarity of the fairy tales it resembles in other ways.

Gaspard is obviously on the side of virtue when he decides not to exploit the bird, as Matthias has done (and as he considers doing himself), but to set it free. Yet the bird's gift in return, while it makes Gaspard's fortune, also destroys his simple life and, with it, his

peace of mind. "The pressures of business worried him . . . (he became) anxious and his face took on a drawn, peaked look." It is a grayed conclusion which has neither the triumphant closure of a fairy tale nor the firm, plain morality shared alike by children and folk literature. Kushner's blend of the real and the symbolic blunts the point of the tale.

I would guess that the story is best read aloud by an adult, which the author's care with language would make a pleasant task, to listeners about 7 to 9 years old.

The pen and ink drawings by Doug Panton are detailed but unsatisfactory overall. I like the sense of the terrain they convey, but the human figures are stiff and amateurish. The picture of Gaspard as he climbs down the wall after rescuing the bird shows him apparently floating in the air in front of the wall; contrary to the text, there is not a foothold in sight. As for the bird, repeatedly referred to as "small" at this point in the story, he works out to being about as long as Gaspard's arm, if the drawing is to be believed. Adults may not notice, but children will.

Zena Sutherland

SOURCE: A review of *The Violin-Maker's Gift,* in *Bulletin of the Center for Children's Books,* Vol. 35, No. 10, June, 1982, p. 191.

Winner of the 1981 Canadian Library Association Book of the Year for Children Award, this is a gentle fantasy in the folk tradition, illustrated by heavily hatched black and white drawings. The setting is the French Pyrenees, where Gaspard the violin-maker lived in contented isolation with his patient donkey, leaving his hut only to take his instruments to market in the town nearby. It was there that he rescued a young bird trapped in the church belfry, later giving the bird to the keeper of the toll gate, Matthias, as a tip for his services. Gaspard began to hear rumors that the bird could not only talk but also predict the future; when he saw the bird, which had grown large and beautiful (looking, in the illustrations, like a lyrebird) and realized that Matthias was exploiting the creature, he stole it and set it free. Before it left, the bird told Gaspard a great secret, so that from that time on the violin-maker's instruments sang as though they had a soul. This may not appeal to readers who crave action and excitement, but it has a mellow, almost nostalgic quality and a quiet humor that, combined with the twin appeals of magic and justice, may be enjoyed by readers who can appreciate the nuance of the writing.

Holly Sanhuber

SOURCE: A review of *The Violin-Maker's Gift,* in *School Library Journal,* Vol. 29, No. 1, September, 1982, p. 123.

The violin-maker Gaspard l'Innocent rescues a wondrous

bird from a perilous perch on the town cathedral and then gives him to Matthias the crusty toll-keeper. Soon it is seen that the bird can talk and is able to foretell the future. Seeing the bird maltreated, Gaspard determines to rescue it once again. Although this literary fairy tale is beautifully told, in simple language wherein every word seems inevitable, the book's appeal to children must be questioned. There is a curious remoteness about the story, as though the author did not wish to get too involved. There is nothing compelling or even likable in any of the characters, but then neither is any character fully realized. Awarded the 1981 Canadian Library Association Book of the Year for Children Award, this book, like many another award winner, may be doomed to life on the shelf.

UNCLE JACOB'S GHOST STORY (1984; U.S. edition, 1986)

William Blackburn

SOURCE: A review of *Uncle Jacob's Ghost Story,* in *Canadian Children's Literature,* No. 43, 1986, pp. 69-70.

C. S. Lewis once called children's stories "the best art-form for something you have to say." Unfortunately, Lewis's remark has reached those whose grim duty it is to flog new books for children; hence, season after season, the guarantees festooning dust jackets, promising "universal themes," and pledging "appeal to readers of all ages." On rare occasions the promise is justified. We are assured, for example, that *Uncle Jacob's Ghost Story* is such a book; and—*pace,* honest cynicism—it is certainly true that Donn Kushner (whose *The Violin-Maker's Gift* won the Canadian Library Association's 1981 Book of the Year for Children Award) has now given us another novel worthy of serious attention.

Uncle Jacob's Ghost Story deals with our idealism and our desire for power, and with the gulf dividing our glorious vision of what might be from the sordid fact of what is. The author brings these themes home through the story of Paul's Uncle Jacob. Eager to know more about the man denounced by his relatives as a "completely impractical person" who "went his own way . . . the family disgrace," Paul learns of his uncle's early life in a village in Poland, and of his two stage-struck friends, Simon and Esther, who dream of acting careers in New York. Jacob too dreams of America, and after watching some Cossacks exercising their ingenuity on three old men he longs for America a land "where the soldiers don't make the old men dance." Simon and Esther die in a typhus epidemic; Jacob emigrates to New York. At his newsstand in Times Square, he meets two street musicians, who turn out to be the ghosts of Simon and Esther (for bodies they use mannequins stolen from Macy's). Jacob's friends are actors still; now they perform in the streets, offering wry and incisive commentary on American mores. Jacob refuses their invitation to join them until he sees mounted police brutally clear

the Square of a crowd of the poor and the hungry. Then he dies, his lost hopes for America tempered by his reunion with those he loves.

There is much to commend and enjoy in *Uncle Jacob's Ghost Story.* Its sense of humour is robust but subtle. Jacob's disillusionment with his chosen land is handled delicately and—mercifully—altogether without stridency. Furthermore, the novel's anatomy of America-as-Bonbon is part of a larger inquiry into our dreams and our limitations. Power is most emphatically not the answer to our problems; Simon and Esther know so much more now than they knew when they were alive and thought the actor's magic could change the world—but now they also know how weak they really are, their powers restrained by inexorable law.

Finally, then, the best thing about *Uncle Jacob's Ghost Story* is the way in which it honours Jacob's dream without succumbing to a chic cynicism or a cheap assurance that the dream must some day be realized in this world. It deserves praise too for its refusal to confuse worldly prosperity with spiritual maturity. In the eyes of society, those of its characters who truly possess moral integrity look like hopeless failures, like Jacob, who "never had to meet a payroll" and consorted with "street people." In adroit puncturing of our smug assumptions, *Uncle Jacob's Ghost Story* has much to offer thoughtful readers.

Kirkus Reviews

SOURCE: A review of *Uncle Jacob's Ghost Story,* in *Kirkus Reviews,* Vol. LIV, No. 7, April 1, 1986, pp. 550-51.

Paul has tried to discover the truth about his mysterious great-uncle Jacob. At last, his grandfather and Mr. Eisbein, his companion, tell him the fantastic story.

When his dearest friends died of typhus, nothing was left to keep Jacob from joining his successful brothers, who had emigrated from Poland to America. But Jacob did not become wealthy in his new country; he ran a newsstand in New York City's Times Square, where he was well-known and loved for his kindness. Jacob's life was transformed when he discovered that two familiar street musicians were the ghosts of his dear friends, Esther and Simon, who had died in Poland. Jacob's story seems to end one winter night when he freezes to death inside his newsstand. But the story comes full circle when an adult Paul, prompted by three traveling musicians (Esther, Simon, and Jacob?), feels compelled to pass on Jacob's story.

This haunting book is beautifully written, with vivid descriptions of the characters inhabiting Times Square in the early 1900s. Strong themes of love and memory, destiny and individuality run through the story. For the unusual child who would grasp the layers of meaning in the narrative, or for the adult.

Zena Sutherland

SOURCE: A review of *Uncle Jacob's Ghost Story,* in *Bulletin of the Center for Children's Books,* Vol. 39, No. 9, May, 1986, pp. 170-71.

More mystical than spectral, this is the story of three friends, two of whom died in a typhus epidemic that struck their Jewish village in Poland, and the other of whom immigrates to America and sets up a newsstand. There, he's visited by his friends as ghostly street singers who inhabit the bodies of mannequins and finally spirit Jacob away after he dies one night in the cold. It's an odd story, oddly told. The narrators are an old man talking to his grandson, Paul, and the old man's friend reminiscing on a park bench outside their nursing home. What's vivid is the sense of continuity between past, present, and future as connections among family and friends bind life and death into one cycle. What's confusing is the weaving in and out of too many characters whose roles are obscure and a splicing of events that will lose the average reader; a protest parade at the end of the book seems to come out of nowhere and go nowhere. There are, however, many levels to the book, and for the special or gifted reader interested in extrasensory experiences, this has an uncommon aura.

Catherine van Sonnenberg

SOURCE: A review of *Uncle Jacob's Ghost Story,* in *School Library Journal,* Vol. 32, No. 9, May, 1986, p. 94.

Paul has heard some elusive information about his mysterious Uncle Jacob—family outcast, renegade, a man with a peculiar, and possibly shameful, past and an unknown present. Paul wants the truth, and his relatives either don't know or aren't telling but refer him to his ailing grandfather in a nursing home. Grandfather recounts his truths about Uncle Jacob's life back in Poland, emigration to the United States and life in New York City. It is a past of touching and magical relationships, to which Paul responds with alternating satisfaction and puzzlement. Mysteries and questions remain with readers as well, many of whom will find this story that incorporates mystical elements as it spans from shtetl to Times Square too removed and incredible to be particularly compelling. The extensive descriptive details of the magical musicians and actors may be accurate, but the same descriptive detail is too often tedious. Respectable writing with some of the ethnic color of Singer and Potok still doesn't bring a weak story with esoteric characters the richness it needs.

Ellen Mandel

SOURCE: A review of *Uncle Jacob's Ghost Story,* in *Booklist,* Vol. 82, No. 21, July, 1986, p. 1614.

Uncle Jacob was the pariah of Paul's family—no relative spoke of him except Grandfather, who told how Jacob was called to serve in the czar's army and returned home to a village decimated by typhus. Included among the victims were Jacob's dearest friends, Simon and Esther, a brother and sister who had longed to be actors in New York. Jacob, too, harbored dreams of the New World, and it was there, overlooking the city's theater district, that Jacob was eventually reunited with Simon and Esther. The ultimate goal of these ghosts' mission was to recruit Jacob to their street performing act. Though literally living in another world, Jacob remained devoted to his friends, and one frigid winter night, he deliberately froze to death, thereby joining Simon and Esther forever. Told with sophistication by the author of *The Violin-Maker's Gift,* this bizarre tale is haltingly framed in the contemporary realm of the senior citizens' home where Grandfather resides. Though this setting is hardly the stuff to rivet most youngsters, the supernatural events, the moments of humor, the touching human relationships, and a provocative moral message will reward special readers for their persistence.

📖 *A BOOK DRAGON* (1987; U.S. edition, 1988)

Patricia Morley

SOURCE: "Guard Your Treasure": Donn Kushner's Fiction for Older Children," in *Canadian Children's Literature,* No. 49, 1988, pp. 68-71.

"Guard your treasure." Or could we say, "Defend your values"? This maxim, the motto of dragons from ancient times, is one of many moral lessons that children (and adults) will imbibe painlessly along with great dollops of fun, excitement and fantasy in Donn Kushner's *A Book Dragon.*

In this, his third book for older children, Kushner hits his stride and establishes what may prove to be the trademark of his beautifully crafted longish fictions: an inspired mix of imagination, history, and ethical values. *Values:* does the word make us uneasy? Twentieth-century critics have managed to turn the concept of didacticism into a pejorative. Perhaps it is time to restore it to its rightful place. All great novelists are didactic, but not *simply* didactic: technique is all. Witness the work of Dickens, Tolstoy, and our own Margaret Laurence. Kushner's work, like that of the masters, teaches children to value love, freedom, family ties, and integrity. To these universals we can add *books,* the particular treasure featured in his third novella.

Something of Kushner's own attitude to writing seems to be implied in a speech made by the golden bird in his first novella, *The Violin-Maker's Gift* (1980), set in the French Pyrenees just after the Napoleonic Wars. The prophetic bird tells its benefactor: "Poetry and parables are all very well when you're a captive and have to hide your meaning or when you're feeling very elated. . . . But for the ordinary business of life, give me direct prose." Kushner's prose is indeed direct, and strong, but not without its poetic side. Witness part of the description of the magical bird: "The golden bars on its wings had spread, and their colours were so intense that the wings seemed to be encased in a living network of metal. . . . The crest of golden feathers on his head had grown to a comb that shone like wheat in the autumn sun."

As a young dragon of some fifty years, Nonesuch discovers that his size depends on his food intake. He suspects that the great heat to which he had been exposed in following his grandmother far down the tunnel has worked a change in his tissues. He is now unique among his kind. There are (he decides) advantages to being small: the air tastes better, colours look brighter, he can think more quickly. He therefore embarks on the adventure of growing smaller. Kushner plays with size much as Swift does, in *Gulliver's Travels*. The resulting conceits are full of fun and wit.

After a leisurely start, the story moves into high gear when Nonesuch discovers the Abbey of Oddfields, with a Scriptorium where Brother Theophilus is illuminating a Book of Hours. Such books often show a detailed picture of life in their time. Kushner's knowledge of ordinary life in medieval times finds whimsical ways to express itself. Nancy Jackson's beautiful woodcuts and illustrated capital letters (in the manner of an illuminated manuscript) also add to the medieval flavour.

The monk and the tiny dragon become friends. Soon there is a dragon, or part of one, on every page of the precious manuscript: "He would paint a wing with its individual scalloping just emerging from behind the figure; a head peeping out of the bushes; or a tail flying away. . . . Only their colors varied. Some were red, some gold, several green, one deep-black with red eyes."

Traditionally, dragons are guardian spirits. By now, Nonesuch has found his own treasure to guard: the book whose loose pages are kept in a sturdy oaken box. He sleeps on it at night. The precious book is stolen, then lost. Two hundred and fifty years pass, during which time Nonesuch lives on insects. This diet has the double advantage of keeping the pages safe and himself small. By 1666, a hole in the box permits him to go in and out. He learns to read from a rat who has listened to an old man teaching children.

Lodged in the cellar, the box survives the Great Fire of London. It is used for a time as a block for a flask in a private laboratory, then bought at auction by a North American bookseller who shrewdly suspects the treasure inside. Intriguing lore concerning off-beat areas of history is used effectively.

Nonesuch, and the reader, now find themselves on the eastern coast of North America in the late twentieth century. The unnamed city could be Halifax. Here he discovers his grandmother, sprightly and happy in flame. Her opinion of humans has never been high, and has not improved with the passage of five centuries: "They're of little account, really," she advises Nonesuch. Our hero, who had found a friend in Brother Theophilus, defends humans in a curious debate. Humans are often kind to one another ("So are rabbits"); "they work together" ("Usually for no good purpose"); they make beautiful things such as cathedrals ("If you like that sort of thing"). His final defense comes down to the point that humans make books, and that this particular book is the most beautiful thing in the world.

Thus far, the novella has been part romantic quest, part SF and fantasy—solidly grounded in daily life, as good fantasy always is. Once the action has been brought back to our own time and place, however, it becomes a thriller, with a satisfying villain and some very likeable humans, the keepers of the book.

The Gottlieb family name means "lover of God," as does "Theophilus." They sell used and antique books in a store called "Distant Voyages." Nonesuch realizes that old Mr. Gottlieb guards the book as jealously as he. Many of the books tell of intrepid journeys or quests. Nonesuch is addicted to reading bits, as his time permits. The story of Scott of the Antarctic increases his admiration for humans:

> He came to Scott's words: "We are weak, writing is difficult, but for my part I do not regret this journey, which has shown that Englishmen can endure hardships, help one another, and meet death with as great fortitude as ever in the past. We took risks, we knew we took them; things have come out against us, and therefore we have no cause for complaint, but bow to the will of Providence, determined still to do our best till the last. . . ." No, Nonesuch thought, carrying on a silent conversation with his grandmother, this was the way in which a dragon might speak. These humans seemed worth saving after all, even if one of them had not written his special *Book of Hours*.

Trouble looms. A wealthy developer decides that the bookstore and its adjacent properties are occupying the perfect site for his new hotel complex. After the owners have refused to sell, they become the target of mysterious threats and attacks. The pace quickens, the plot thickens, and the villainous developer—you guessed it—is eventually killed by Nonesuch, who has gone on an eating binge in order to grow back to a size suited to his role as Avenger. Greed meets its comeuppance. The man who prides himself on being an agent of change, who loves power for its own sake ("It was better to be one of those who called the tune, not one of those who danced") and who studies Machiavelli's *The Prince* is consumed by a dragon whose reality he denies.

Suspense is handled well in all three of Kushner's fictions. In *The Violin-Maker's Gift*, he makes us care about the safety and well-being of the precious bird, which is twice rescued by the violin-maker. In *Uncle Jacob's Ghost Story* (1984), curiosity is whetted by the descriptions of the boy's Great-Uncle Jacob, who is variously described (long before he enters the action) as the family disgrace, a completely impractical person, and an idealist searching for his own kind of truth.

Kushner himself plays the violin, and has poured his love of music into his story of the golden bird and the rare violins which speak with a human voice. He is Professor of Microbiology at the University of Ottawa, and has slipped some of his knowledge in this area into Nonesuch's experience in *A Book Dragon.* His first three novellas are destined to become classics, to instruct and delight "children" of all ages who respond to beauty, fantasy, fun, and more than a little wisdom.

Nancy Black

SOURCE: A review of *A Book Dragon,* in *CM: A Reviewing Journal of Canadian Materials for Young People,* Vol. XVI, No. 3, May, 1988, pp. 88-9.

This is a fascinating fantasy adventure about the life and times of a young dragon, Nonesuch. The story opens with Nonesuch's early life in a cave, complete with his grandmother and dragon treasure, in medieval Britain. This period of his life is secure and content. The hours are filled with his grandmother's stories. With the death of his grandmother, Nonesuch feels the need to leave the cave and search for his own treasure to guard. It is this quest that leads him to a monastery and the discovery of a very special book. For a time, he is trapped in a box with this book (an earlier incident has changed his body so that he can shrink or grow as necessary) and he sleeps undisturbed, guarding the book for many years while the box changes hands several times. Eventually, the box is bought by an American bookseller, who, upon opening the box, discovers the wonderful book and displays it in his bookshop. Thus, Nonesuch arrives in the twentieth century to guard this treasure and the bookshop from those with questionable intentions.

A Book Dragon is an absorbing, well-written book that should appeal to a wide audience, especially those who are fascinated by dragon lore. While it moves a little slowly in the beginning, the pace soon picks up as action, dialogue and characters become more interesting. Readers should be intrigued by description of dragon life and glimpses of British history: monasteries, the Black Death, and the pastimes of a well-to-do eighteenth-century gentleman.

The concluding chapters are an exciting, appropriate culmination of events and leave the reader satisfied with the outcome. *A Book Dragon* is on the list of titles being considered for the Saskatchewan Library Association's Young Adult Canadian Book Award.

Kirkus Reviews

SOURCE: A review of *A Book Dragon,* in *Kirkus Reviews,* Vol. LVI, No. 9, May 1, 1988, p. 695.

An engaging and truly original fantasy—600 years in the life of a dragon, from medieval England to present-day "eastern North America," by the author of *The Violin-Maker's Gift.*

Nonesuch's ancestors were traditional dragons—hoarding treasure, indiscriminately devouring livestock and maidens—although his father died a deliciously satirical death as a result of his gourmet tastes. But Nonesuch develops a philosophical bent, thanks partly to his own curiosity and partly to his grandmother—who warns him early on that since humans kill but don't eat each other, "there must be something terribly wrong with their flesh." When his family dies out, Nonesuch chooses to abandon their treasure and to eat sparingly, so that he gradually shrinks to insect size; in this form, he meets Brother Theophilus, who incorporates Nonesuch in his illustrations for a marvelous *Book of Hours.* With some intermittent adventures, Nonesuch sleeps away centuries tucked into this beloved book, only to later find himself in the shop of a benevolent rare-book dealer—threatened by the 20th-century equivalent of a robber baron. Enlarging himself once more, just enough to save the day, Nonesuch discovers what his grandmother meant about human flesh before returning to his benignly bookish existence.

Wise as well as amusingly whimsical, Nonesuch's story is beguilingly embellished with occasional marginal designs and chapter headings. Try reading aloud, or including some of the splendidly funny passages in a book-talk.

Publishers Weekly

SOURCE: A review of *A Book Dragon,* in *Publishers Weekly,* Vol. 233, No. 23, June 10, 1988, p. 8.

This new novel by the author of award-winning *The Violin-Maker's Gift* and *Uncle Jacob's Ghost Story* follows the life of a dragon, Nonesuch, from his birth during the Dark Ages up until the present day. Nonesuch survives the changes of history (the War of the Roses, the great fire of London, etc.) by becoming as small as a large insect. He forsakes his family treasure of gold—though his dragon nature demands that he guard something—and finds treasure of his own: a *Book of Hours* lovingly illuminated by a monk during Nonesuch's youth near the end of the Middle Ages. He learns to read from a rat during the Black Plague. Centuries later, Nonesuch and his book are in the New World. How he becomes enmeshed in human affairs is at the center of Kushner's quiet, intelligent book. His matter-of-fact treatment of history and philosophical discussions makes this a thought-provoking work.

John Peters

SOURCE: A review of *A Book Dragon,* in *School Library Journal,* Vol. 34, No. 6, June-July, 1988, p. 118.

Dragons are scarce these days, but they can still be found if you know where to look. Young Nonesuch, seeing his proud family wiped out by brutish humans during the Wars of the Roses, shrinks down to the size of a large insect to escape notice and sets out to learn more about people, and to find treasure—as his grandmother always said, "a dragon without a treasure is nothing but an ugly flying reptile." Something draws him to a gloriously illustrated *Book of Hours,* and he accompanies it on its bumpy journey through the centuries. It comes to rest at last in the back room of a quiet bookstore on this side of the Atlantic, and Nonesuch guards it there still; a small, ferocious presence, seldom seen but comforting nonetheless. Plenty of lively characters help animate this rather leisurely story, from Lopped Cedric the one-legged bandit to the nameless rat who teaches Nonesuch to read and Abercrombie, the suave, ruthless real estate developer who learns that dragon justice is sudden and simple. Historiated initials and occasional small, sprightly drawings in the text and margins give the book [illustrated by Nancy Ruth Jackson] a slightly antique look. As with Kushner's other books, this treasure house of dragon lore will appeal most to patient readers.

Ann A. Flowers

SOURCE: A review of *A Book Dragon,* in *The Horn Book Magazine,* Vol. LXIV, No. 5, September-October, 1988, p. 627.

Nonesuch the dragon is raised mainly by his grandmother, a formidable creature with a large store of useful precepts, among them, "Guard your treasure." Nonesuch appreciates his grandmother's tutelage and is quite upset when she deliberately disappears down a tunnel into the hot central core of the earth. Nonesuch attempts to follow her but eventually turns back; the immense heat, however, permanently alters his physical nature. He finds that the less he eats, the smaller he grows. Being a curious creature, he decides to sample life as a very small dragon. Living as he does in medieval times, he soon makes his way to a monastery, where he finds shrewd, kindly Brother Theophilus illuminating a *Book of Hours* and frequently including dragons in the illustrations. Nonesuch is inadvertently packed in a box when the book is stolen and spends several centuries in a cellar. He becomes mixed up in alchemical experiments and finally ends up in modern times with his *Book of Hours* in a bookstore. Along the way he has amusing philosophical discussions with such creatures as turtles, rats, bats, and parrots. Fascinating historical characters flicker in and out of the story, and many subjects are lightly touched upon—history, religion, physics, chemistry, warfare, and the stupidity of human beings. Charming little pen-and-ink diversions appear from time to time in the margins of the pages. Although the story moves a trifle slowly at times, we cannot help admiring Nonesuch for his inquiring mind and adherence to the finer values.

Mary-Ann Stouck

SOURCE: "Dragon Wise," in *Canadian Literature,* No. 121, Summer, 1989, pp. 194-96.

Donn Kushner's third book for children is a refreshing reversal of the dominant convention of psychological fantasy, in which the supernatural aids the child hero in overcoming the problems of everyday living. In Kushner's book there is no single child hero, and the normal perspective is reversed: the real world, not the supernatural, is "out there," and we focus upon its problems from the point of view of a supernatural hero, the dragon of the title. Archetypally, dragons are of course a source of evil; their function is to be slain by the prince. This dragon, however, explicitly abandons the violence and homicide associated with his kind and adopts an unusual set of values: a respect for life in its smallest manifestations, a love of wisdom acquired from books, and an appreciation for all truly humanitarian forms of endeavour.

By manipulating the conventional elements of fantasy, Kushner gives new impact to the theme of the supernatural: his characters ignore the vital importance of the spiritual and intellectual qualities of life only at their risk. Nonesuch, the dragon hero, recognizes these values when he abandons the traditional family treasure hoard of armour, weapons and gold and sets out, the last survivor of his race, in search of a treasure worth guarding in the post-medieval world. That treasure turns out to be an illuminated *Book of Hours* made by Brother Theophilus, a medieval monk, and we follow Nonesuch's adventures down through the ages to the present time as he tenaciously guards this symbol of learning and wisdom, and the human beings who come into contact with it.

The human characters though secondary are vital to Nonesuch's quest; he encounters a great variety of them in his journey down through time, and though at first their abrupt and short-lived appearances are disconcerting, we soon realize that as types of human nature, they are repeated in the cycles of history. Brother Theophilus reappears later as Mr. Gottlieb, antiquarian book lover and owner of a bookstore in a small eastern town in the U.S.A.; Simon, the young stone sculptor of the medieval monastery, reappears as Samson, the avid young American book-reader; and Hubert, the thief, as Mr. Huberman, the relentless materialist and agent of the villain Mr. Abercrombie, himself a counterpart of the sinister Sir Ambrose. Through this innovative handling of time in the story, Kushner's characters achieve both depth and a thematic significance beyond their immediate natures. At the same time, the rich variety of deftly drawn secondary characters—amusingly literate animals as well as human figures—prevents the book from being overly schematized.

And that is important, for Kushner's vision of the role of the spiritual-supernatural in society is explicitly moral, more than is currently fashionable in children's fantasy. The book is brilliantly imaginative at times (as in the early stories of Nonesuch's eccentric relations), but the didactic element is evident both in the third-person narration and in the extended conversations between Nonesuch and the animals he encounters. While these are entertaining in themselves, a child might well feel that they do little to advance the action (as opposed to the meaning) of the story. But these dialogues are balanced by the rich variety of Kushner's moral concerns, by the fact that he is mostly willing to show them rather than prescribe what should be done about them, and because they are presented through the eyes of such a likeable creature as Nonesuch.

One of the distinctive features of Kushner's writing is his profound humanitarian concern for society, and many of the maladies of civilization come under Nonesuch's eye: religious intolerance, carelessness of the ecology, disease, technological pragmatism, materialism and the violent abuse of power. That the story does not founder on these themes is a tribute to the strength of Kushner's imagination, his sense of humour, and his timing. In Kushner's prose the supernatural intervenes in the real world with an effect simultaneously matter-of-fact and surrealistic: ultimate proof of the power of things unseen.

A Book Dragon is a refreshingly different fantasy. Broader than most in the scope of its concerns, it resists the current fashion to ask children to concentrate upon their own psyches and instead opens up to them a wider world of social issues experienced through a great range of colourful characters, both animal and human. Its stylistic innovations function solidly as essential vehicles of theme and plot; they do not merely call attention to their own cleverness, and the non-human characters are never sentimentalized. This book should establish Kushner clearly in the forefront of children's fantasy writing in Canada.

THE HOUSE OF THE GOOD SPIRITS (1990)

Dave Jenkinson

SOURCE: A review of *The House of the Good Spirits,* in *Quill and Quire,* Vol. 57, No. 2, February, 1991, p. 23

Kushner's fourth juvenile novel, his most complex in theme and style, will offer middle-grade readers many challenges. The title, like much of the book, operates on more than one level. During Prohibition, the "house" was a storage space for alcoholic spirits being smuggled into the United States, but the now-deserted building, on land where a church built by runaway slaves once stood, also contains still-restless spirits of the dead.

The book's central character, 11-year-old Amos Okoro, has come from Nigeria to Port Jordan, Ontario, with his Great-Aunt Naomi and his parents, both doctors, who are doing a residency in nearby Kingston. From the

moment of the Okoros' arrival in Canada, Amos encounters various forms of racial prejudice. His experiences with contemporary racism become intertwined with the racism of the past via a dream/fantasy sequence that fills over half the book. When Amos "enters" the house, he meets the spirits of former slaves, and by means of a "picture show," he observes three slaves' struggle to reach freedom in Canada while being pursued by slave catchers. Sharing his biblical namesake's concern with social justice, Amos becomes the catalyst that allows the house's spirits to complete their journey to freedom.

Appropriately, readers will be left wondering whether Amos really experiences the events in the house or whether they are a dream that incorporates distorted elements of things he had seen, heard, or read. The book's complexity demands rereading for a full appreciation of how Kushner's plot repeats and reworks details. For example, Amos's present-day tormentors are Henry Stiggs and Norman Glanders, while in the past he finds the slave-catching Brimston brothers, who temporarily adopt the names Henry and Norman Blessington. The commonality of given names will likely go unnoticed in a first reading.

The House of the Good Spirits is not the sort of book that will enjoy a wide readership, but it deserves to be made available to those special students who will give the work the thoughtful attention it merits.

B. Henley

SOURCE: A review of *The House of the Good Spirits,* in *CM: A Reviewing Journal of Canadian Materials for Young People,* Vol. XIX, No. 2, March, 1991, pp. 105-06.

Donn Kushner's fourth book for young people is a fascinating read, full of a wealth of historical information woven throughout the plot.

The House of the Good Spirits takes place just outside Kingston, Ontario, during the present. Amos, his mother and father (who are both doctors), and his great aunt Naomi have just arrived from Nigeria to spend a year. One of few black families in the town, their presence creates curiosity, and Amos is subjected to some ridicule in his new school. However, Amos soon becomes familiar with two or three of the town's more eccentric individuals, who share with him stories of the town's past.

He learns firsthand from old Mr. Prewitt about the rum runners who used to smuggle spirits across Lake Ontario to the United States during Prohibition. He also learns the fascinating story of the slaves who attempted to escape into Canada after the Fugitive Slave Law was passed in the U.S. in 1850. In the past, both of these groups used the same site for their activities—originally as a church haven for fugitive slaves, and later as a house used to store liquor. It is in this house, many years later, that the main part of the story unfolds as Amos enters its "haunted" interior.

At this point, the story becomes spellbinding. Amos enters another dimension and meets many of the characters from the past he has just learned about. In this world, the House of the Good Spirits is a purgatory for a group of people, including some slaves who drowned in Lake Ontario on their route to freedom. With the help of Amos and the wisdom he has learned from African folktales told to him by his Aunt Naomi, the group of spirits manages to journey on to their final destination.

The story deals not only with prejudice and conflict (in the U.S. Civil War, the War of 1812, Nazi Germany during World War II, the civil war in Biafra, and even in Amos's new schoolyard) but also with tolerance and understanding gained through wisdom. The treatment of these themes is very imaginative. As complex as the plot may sound, the story unfolds easily and flows smoothly.

The House of the Good Spirits will appeal to a wide range of people, but especially to students in grades 7 to 10.

Mary-Ann Stouck

SOURCE: A review of *The House of the Good Spirits,* in *Canadian Children's Literature,* No. 65, 1992, pp. 81-3.

Early in Donn Kushner's book, *The House of the Good Spirits,* the eleven-year-old protagonist wonders "Why does everybody want to teach me things?" His mother consoles him, "It's because you're such a good listener," and adds "But you have to learn some things by yourself." These words describe the book's structure (Amos both listens, and finds out for himself), but the question—really a complaint—is also a possible criticism of any book that deals explicitly with issues of broad moral and social significance. In this new book Kushner takes up the theme of human rights previously explored in *A Book Dragon* (winner of the I.O.D.E. Book Award-National Chapter), this time focusing directly upon racial prejudice. And fortunately, he handles the issue with enough subtlety and complexity to allay most complaints.

The risk of preaching on such a theme is great; indeed, hardly avoidable, one might think. But Kushner does avoid heavy-handed didacticism without sacrificing moral content, first of all by the creation of an admirable and likeable protagonist. Amos Okoro, an eleven-year-old Nigerian boy, comes with his great aunt Naomi to spend a year in a small town near Kingston, Ontario, while his parents, medical doctors, study at the nearby hospital. As Amos attends the local school and meets the townspeople, he encounters a variety of racist attitudes, from the well-meant slurs of Mr. Bidcup ("It's like a little jungle. . . . You'll be right at home here," he comments genially on the neglected garden of Amos's new home), to the deliberate hostility of some of his new schoolmates. The range, variety and penetrating analysis of racist attitudes Kushner gives us is impres-

sive. Children and adults display the whole gamut, from the unthinking to the brutally international: a boy who at first sees in Amos the stereotypical black athlete concludes "Well, I guess *some* of you aren't such good ball players;" a teacher deliberately provides the other children with a theme for harassment when he calls Amos's parents "witch doctors;" a child remarks, perhaps innocently, that he knows why Amos is not afraid of ghosts: "Because he's used to spooks already. That's what my dad calls blacks: spooks. He says in some streets in Toronto you can't see anything else."

Kushner's choice of the black child's point of view for his story risks the alienation of the white reader, but this does not happen. Children, whether racially stigmatized or not, are often the victims of prejudice, teasing and threats; Amos, who is intelligent and clever, fearful and courageous by turns, is an empathetic guide through these experiences. His understanding, and ours, is furthered by the reflections of Aunt Naomi whose cultural sophistication, disguised beneath her native dress, makes her the obvious superior of Amos's tormentors. We sympathize with Amos also because the ignorance of some (by no means all) of the "whites" in the story is made to look ludicrously funny, or just plain pitiable. Naomi "teaches" unobtrusively and entertainingly by means of African legends, and her wisdom merges with that of the clever tortoise who becomes Amos's emblem and guide into his fantasy adventure.

The first half of the book moves slowly and somewhat confusingly: there is not much action, and we are introduced to numerous characters who are hard to remember. But after Amos enters a fantasy world through the door of a reputedly haunted house, the book becomes a compelling read. Kushner is a master of surrealistic invention. Here he draws together themes of black slavery and its history in the United States, the adventures of slaves escaping to Canada, and finally the terrors of the Nigerian civil wars of this century, to which Amos has his own family connections. Far from escapism, this fantasy is a sometimes terrifying transformation of the real world in such a way as to illuminate its true significance: a television set is morally empowered to show a series on black slavery; Lake Ontario becomes the setting for an odyssey through the islands of temptation; the local inhabitants of Port Jordan introduced earlier in the book are reincarnated as types of good and evil, leading us to an understanding of the history of slavery.

The thread that holds all these together is Kushner's awareness that fear is the central cause of racism, and that racism exists everywhere, including among competing black peoples. Amos's courage in the schoolyard is given its true significance when he performs an act of great bravery in the fantasy world. But Kushner does not fob us off with soft psychological explanations either: in his two schoolyard bullies, reincarnated as adults in various stages of the fantasy odyssey, he presents the profound wickedness that underlies racial discrimination.

No one could criticize Donn Kushner's writing for patronizing young readers; more than most, his books demand thoughtful and informed reading. But the rewards are rich for those willing to pursue them.

📖 *THE DINOSAUR DUSTER* (1992)

Bernie Goedhart

SOURCE: A review of *The Dinosaur Duster,* in *Quill and Quire,* Vol. 58, No. 11, November, 1992, p. 33.

Just when you think there can't possibly be anything new to say about dinosaurs, along comes Donn Kushner.

The Dinosaur Duster is Kushner's first picture book and, like his novels for young people, it boasts an engaging and intelligent text. But where his novels tend to be complex, this book is within reach of even the youngest child.

It tells of Mr. Mopski, who is in charge of cleaning two dinosaur skeletons that are the museum's prize exhibit. While dusting, Mr. Mopski sings Carpathian folk songs—a practice that prompts one of the skeletons to speak up. Both the stegosaurus and triceratops, it turns out, can talk. And both are fed up with their lot in life; they're bored, and they want a change of scenery.

Mr. Mopski, in a flash of brilliance, switches their heads so they can get a different view on life. But in so doing, he seems to have created two new species: Tricerosaurus and Stegatops! They're launched on a world tour and eventually come to the same discovery as Dorothy in *The Wizard of Oz:* there's no place like home.

Kushner's offbeat story is complemented by the equally offbeat illustrations by Marc Mongeau, who joins a growing list of Quebec artists enlivening children's books in English Canada. . . .

[Kushner's] sly sense of humour is evident throughout the carefully-crafted text and gives *The Dinosaur Duster* a quality all picture books should have: it's as appealing for the adult reading it aloud as for the child who is listening.

Sandy Odegard

SOURCE: A review of *The Dinosaur Duster,* in *Canadian Children's Literature,* No. 71, 1993, pp. 82-3.

It is especially true of children's fiction that it should give pleasure during repeated readings. *The Dinosaur Duster* passes this test through combining an ingenious plot and amusing details, such as the titles of imaginary Carpathian folk songs like "A soldier boy loves sour cabbage," with interesting information about Paris, Florence, and London. A teacher or parent could readily use this book as a springboard into geography or history, or for language skills such as writing some of the 24 verses of "When will uncle Dimitri finally go to bed?" Even without such guidance, the young reader will naturally absorb broadening ideas about how the large cities of Europe are both different from, and the same as, the large cities of North America.

The story, about talking dinosaur skeletons, gives a whole new meaning to the idea of knowing something in your bones. The stegosaurus and triceratops mounted in a North American museum not only can speak and learn, but were able to hear and learn folk songs while buried for millennia in the Carpathian mountains. They complain to their caretaker, Mr. Mopski, about being confined to only one view of the world. The stegosaurus is bored with his view of a city park; the triceratops is annoyed by the bustle of a city street. When Mr. Mopski resolves their problem by switching their heads, experts declare them to be new discoveries, a Tricerosaurus and a Stegatops. Such obtuseness, of course, gives delight to the knowing reader. (Kushner's assumption that all seven-year-olds know the difference between a stegosaurus and a triceratops is, I believe, well-founded.) Mr. Mopski, the Tricerosaurus, and the Stegatops are sent on a world tour during which they learn about other people and other ways and, ultimately, that there's no place like home. Once the dinosaurs are returned home as scientifically unimportant (after Mr. Mopski re-switches their heads), the dinosaur duster has his friends mounted on wheels, so they are happily able to learn about the world they live in.

The text's richness in entertainment and information is enhanced by Marc Mongeau's cartoon-like illustrations. His lively scenes are full of intriguing details including some great bone jokes, some of which involve their association with dogs. Unlike the text, his pictures include actively participating females. He depicts a cheerful and peaceful multiracial and multicultural world that most children would be glad to inhabit.

Marion Scott

SOURCE: A review of *The Dinosaur Duster,* in *CM: A Reviewing Journal of Canadian Materials for Young People,* Vol. XXI, No. 1, January, 1993, p. 22.

Award-winning children's writer Donn Kushner turns to the picture-book format with this latest work. The result is a whimsical, off-beat tale and a new twist on the ever-popular dinosaur theme.

The dinosaur duster is Mr. Mopski, an ingenious museum guard entrusted with dusting the museum's two dinosaur skeletons. As he discovers, the skeletons can talk—and not only that, they are bored, tired of the same view day in and day out. To provide a change of scene, Mr. Mopski switches their heads, unwittingly creating a scientific incident: scientists announce the discovery of two new dinosaur species! A tour of Europe follows, but the dinosaur skeletons soon long for home. Mr. Mopski switches the heads back, ensuring an instant loss of celebrity and a quick return to their own museum. But best of all, he has a permanent solution to dinosaur discontent—wheeled display platforms that easily allow for a change of venue.

Kushner's narrative is warm and humorous, yielding new enjoyment and discoveries with successive readings. It is relatively long, but has a conversational flavour and flows well. Mr. Mopski's character succeeds as a lovable eccentric, and the dinosaurs have distinctive personalities. The museum and scientific worlds are gently spoofed, and comic details and dialogue abound.

Mongeau's illustrations complement the story beautifully, and an attractive layout cleverly frames the text. Like Kushner, Mongeau uses amusing and plentiful detail to extend both plot and character, and his cartoonish art style, off-balance perspectives, and bright colours fit the story's off-beat character. Particularly memorable are the dinosaur heads with their smug-cum-leering grins and the European museum scenes.

All in all, this is a delightful book, sure to be among the more popular and successful of the 1992 publishing season. I would recommend it for children aged four to eight, and for school and public library collections.

Diane Schoemperlen

SOURCE: "Adventures with Colour," in *Books in Canada,* Vol. XXII, No. 1, February, 1993, pp. 36-7.

The Dinosaur Duster is a wonderful book sure to be enjoyed, as they say, by adults and children alike. Written by Donn Kushner (not only an award-winning author, but also a world-famous microbiologist and an accomplished violinist), this book is both funny and intelligent.

Two dinosaur skeletons, a stegosaurus and a triceratops, are the pride and joy of the museum where they are displayed. They are lovingly tended by old Mr. Mopski who, like the dinosaurs, is from the Carpathian Mountains and is always singing old folk songs from his homeland while he works. The dinosaur skeletons get to reminiscing with Mr. Mopski. They admit that they are both unhappy with their views from the museum windows. The stegosaurus, who looks upon a peaceful park, longs for excitement and action. The triceratops, who looks upon a busy city street, longs for peace and quiet. The solution is obvious: they should switch places. But they are much too big for Mr. Mopski to move. He comes up with an innovative compromise: he switches their heads. The next morning three visiting dinosaur experts discover what they think are two new species, a tricerosaurus and a stegatops. Immediately the skeletons and Mr. Mopski are sent out on a world tour, and exhibited at famous museums in Paris, Florence, and London. But they are too homesick to enjoy themselves, and so Mr. Mopski must come up with another innovative solution to get them all home safe and sound. Of course the moral of the story is "There's no place like home," but Kushner is not heavy-handed or didactic.

A THIEF AMONG STATUES (1993)

Phyllis Simon

SOURCE: A review of *A Thief among Statues,* in *Quill and Quire,* Vol. 59, No. 9, September, 1993, p. 69.

This short fantasy novel is set in the early years of the 20th century in the town of Merchantville, Ontario. The main character is Brian Newgate, a British waif and a petty thief. Worried about his ability to survive in Ontario, he seeks refuge in the Merchantville church. While hiding in the church, Brian watches in fascination as two wooden Nativity statues talk to each other. Joining in the conversation, he learns that the other statues were removed 20 years earlier and distributed among the Merchantville townspeople. The remaining two had, in fact, been waiting all these years for Brian himself to show up and reunite them. To do that, he must sneak the statues out from under the noses of their current owners.

There are a number of problems with this odd fantasy. The story is quite complex, and the development of the plot requires very close attention. Kushner's short, choppy sentences often lack dramatic tension, and some conversations are disjointed. Occasionally, the language seems at odds with the historical setting.

The wood engravings [by Nancy Jackson] used as illustrations, however, are beautiful. They are entirely appropriate for the book, and further the reader's understanding of the story. The accompanying note on the history and art of wood engraving is also of interest.

A Thief among Statues is recommended with some reservations. As a bit of Canadiana for Christmastime, it is suitable for fireside read-alouds.

Dave Jenkinson

SOURCE: A review of *A Thief among Statues,* in *CM: A Reviewing Journal of Canadian Materials for Young People,* Vol. XXII, No. 2, March-April, 1994, pp. 44-5.

Kushner's Christmas fantasy has the potential to become a seasonal classic.

Shortly after World War I, Brian Newgate, a parentless, thieving lad from London's streets, is sent to Canada as one of the "Home Children," who were put to work on farms short of adult help. After two unpleasant experiences on Ontario farms, Brian runs away and ends up Christmas Eve taking secret refuge in a church in the town of Merchantville, where he encounters two "talking" statues carved into wooden pillars.

The pair, Kings Caspar and Melchior, inform Brian that they were once part of a nativity scene carved twenty years before by Jabez Lignum, but that the other free-standing statues had been sold by the "pious" congregation because the now deceased Lignum had used real and "unsavoury" people from the community as models for his statues' faces. For example, Mary was an unwed parlourmaid, while Joseph was a freethinking, evolutionary-teaching schoolmaster. Since the parishioners "never would have welcomed the originals in the church . . . naturally they didn't want to look at the statues."

Brian's quest, given him by the kings, is to reunite the nativity scene by "stealing" the statues of people and animals, which are scattered throughout Merchantville. Aided by Lignum's "ghost," Brian is ultimately successful, and he is given the choice of leaving, or staying and learning how the carver does his work. As Brian was offered a choice, readers can choose between a prosaic or magical conclusion to the book.

Jackson's ten full-page black-and-white woodcuts, which are scattered throughout the work, perfectly mirror the story's mood and theme.

A Thief among Statues can be enjoyed by a wide readership with younger readers simply appreciating the moving storyline and older readers recognizing and exploring the biting satire that flows through this slim volume. Kushner's superb use of language would also make the book a fine read-aloud.

📖 THE NIGHT VOYAGERS (1995; U.S. edition, 1997)

Mary Beaty

SOURCE: A review of *The Night Voyagers,* in *Quill and Quire,* Vol. 61, No. 12, December, 1995, p. 37.

The Sanctuary Movement of the 1980s was led by U.S. church groups who provided a network of safe houses and immigration counselling to families fleeing right-wing dictatorships and death squads in Central America. Because U.S. refugee admissions were less than one percent in the United States but a liberal 70 percent in Canada, many of these networks shepherded refugees all the way from Mexico to our border. (Things changed in the '90s as Canada's admissions tightened and U.S. regulations eased.) Like *The Return,* Sonia Levitin's novel about Operation Hope among the Falashas in Ethiopia, or Barbara Smucker's *Underground to Canada,* Donn Kushner has recreated tensions and personalized politics, following one family's flight from the Mexican border to the Thousand Islands in the St. Lawrence River.

When village doctor Luis Cardenas becomes a *desaparecido*—those whose very existence is mysteriously and violently erased—his sons Manuel and Pepe and their mother Sonia are warned by friends to escape. Teenage

Pepe is impetuous and political, but young Manuel is mute, traumatized by scenes of horror he cannot understand or assimilate; his interior life is convincingly populated by the spirits of his murdered father and two street children who accompany the family on their journey. These beneficent presences engage Manuel in a battle of wits with the Mayan Lords of the Land of Death, who can take on the personas of paramilitary border guards, immigration informers, pickpockets and other forces threatening the family.

Good political fiction involves the reader in the emotional lives of believable characters while weaving exposition unobtrusively into the narrative, as in Kit Pearson's successful WWII series. Kushner's mix of Mayan mythology and the odyssey theme is sensitive and creative, and Manuel's encounters with the Dark Lords are brilliantly integrated with the realistic dangers facing stateless refugees. Despite a few minor flaws in voice and syntax and an over-abundance of commas, it's a dramatic and sensitive piece of writing which reads well aloud. It would enrich grade 6-9 curriculums on North American political and social history, literature, and mythology. The clear visual scenes should also appeal to kids comfortable with storytelling on film. Indeed, this book would make a tremendous movie.

Martha J. Nandorfy

SOURCE: A review of *The Night Voyagers,* in *Canadian Children's Literature,* No. 81, 1996, p. 60-1.

The Night Voyagers follows a Central American family on their journey to freedom in the North, after the military slaying of the young protagonist's father. The brutality of military dictatorship, torture, and killing by death squad is formidably handled by Donn Kushner through indirect representation, from the emotional and psychological point of view of Manuel. In an age when video games, comics, movies and all their related money-making and propaganda-generating machines promote lust for violence, a novel based on the contemporary historical fact of human rights abuses serves as a sobering and thought-provoking antidote to the glamorizing of war and death so prevalent in mainstream children's culture.

Donn Kushner seems to agree with other children's writers that the absence of myths in children's lives produces disorientation and anxiety. This novel incorporates elements from the *Popul Vuh,* one of the sacred books of the Maya, thereby associating evil with the Lords of Xibalba, the Land of Death, of which Manuel's father had told him stories. While the combination of historical and supernatural events works well to express Manuel's repression and later resolution of the traumatizing memory of his father's death, and also situates the family's struggle in a cultural context, two problems arise: the author's representation of pre-Columbian cosmology reveals an obvious Judeo-Christian bias, and the universalizing force of myth depoliticizes the concrete and historical causes of human rights abuses.

Pre-Columbian cosmology shares the Judeo-Christian division of the world into zones of good and evil, life and death, but departs radically from the hierarchical Western world view, according to which evil ultimately must be annihilated. The Pre-Columbian vision accepts death and war as the necessary complements of life and peace, the two sides of this opposition held in a dynamic struggle ensuring the very continuity of existence. The cosmic notion of complementarity, however, should not be confused with historical situations that have tangible political causes and therefore merit such activism as the Sanctuary movement represented in *The Night Voyagers.*

It is understandable that Manuel would associate all characters who seem to embody evil or somehow perpetuate it (the murderous soldiers, the immigration officials and informants in the U.S.) with the metamorphosing creatures of the mythical stories his father told him, but while myth appears to help Manuel make sense of the dangers surrounding his family, it actually confuses him and extends the force of abstract and universal evil into the contemporary context. This universalizing aspect of myth may provide people with a philosophical concept of evil, but the historical thrust of the text would seem to demand political solutions to what is represented not as an abstract form of evil, but rather a complex social and political problem. While Kushner draws relevant connections between the current genocide in Central America and similar actions in Canadian history, by relating these injustices to the universalizing force of myth, he seems to suggest that evil is abstract and inevitable, a message that young readers may find fatalistic and depressing despite the novel's happy ending.

Janice M. Del Negro

SOURCE: A review of *The Night Voyagers,* in *Bulletin of the Center for Children's Books,* Vol. 51, No. 3, November, 1997, pp. 89-90.

Manuel flees a small Central American village with his mother and older brother after his schoolteacher father "disappears." Refugees befriended by the sanctuary movement, the three flee north, first, to the United States, then to Canada. Manuel refuses to talk—it is clear that he has witnessed something terrible related to the disappearance and probable death of his father—but his fantasy life teems with active dialogue, for he is accompanied on his journey by the possibly ghostly manifestations of his father and two homeless children. These comforting shades are present to protect Manuel from the Lords of Xibalba, the underworld denizens of the Popul Vuh who have only his destruction at heart. Journeys are important in mythic tales, and after a somewhat disjointed beginning Kushner gets his characters on the chronological and actual road and keeps them there, revealing their inner lives through their actions and reactions. The magical realism of Manuel's double life is convincingly well-integrated into the chase-and-escape suspense as the family flees the *migras* (immigration

officials). Manuel's silence, his brother Pepe's anger, and his mother's desperate dignity provide the emotional hook necessary to hold readers, with the added attraction of insight into the nature of Mayan mythology. This is an issue-oriented novel that is not issue driven. The emotional truth of the main characters is never far from the action, and even politically naïve readers will be drawn in by the emotional suspense. A foreword and afterword give some political and social context to the novel; a glossary and list of sources are also included.

LIFE ON MARS (1999)

Lisa DuMond

SOURCE: A review of *Life on Mars,* at <http://www.sfsite.com/03a/life52.htm>, SF Site Reviews, 1999.

It isn't often that you can describe a book in one word, but through every page of *Life on Mars* a single thought kept surfacing: *charming.* The illustrations [by D.J. Knight] are certainly. Kushner's prose is quite charming. The whole package will have adults—young and old—under its spell.

Suppose those far-reaching Viking missions just missed the real story on Mars. There was life all right, but it had the good fortune to escape detection. And for that very reason, it is still there.

The Martians of Kushner's creation resemble nothing so much as big-eyed versions of *Fantasia*'s dancing mushrooms. Or, perhaps, the unlucky inside-out umbrellas after a big storm. They are quiet, guileless creatures, spending their days soaking up sunlight and playing the games they based on a few moments of garbled television transmissions from Earth . . . The gentle Martians spend their nights resting and dreaming of things that may or may not have been. And watching over them all is their Chief, unseen but involved in every aspect of their lives.

Life on Mars is the kind of story that takes you back to the books you adored while growing up. These are the books you search for now for your little guys, only to find they went out of print before you got your learner's permit. When we were about 11, we would have inhaled this book in one sitting. Of course, when we became teenagers, a charming little tale like this would have been far too babyish for our tastes. One of the great gifts of life is outgrowing that self-depriving phase and returning to the things that simply bring us wonder and joy.

Why is it more fun to pick out books for my nieces and nephews than for myself? Maybe because their books are just more fun.

Then again, maybe it's the hidden messages that lie within such pages. Chances are, a young child is not going to pick up the subtle point of the story, but the adult reading them will hear it clearly and, hopefully, pause to think about the moral. It's worth mulling over. Then again, maybe kids already know the message. They usually come out of the womb with more common sense than we retain.

Go on! Get out there and find a copy of *Life on Mars* for your children. Or pretend to have kids. Or, just have the confidence to waltz in and openly buy it for yourself. Like all genuinely enriching works for children, it ought to be required reading for all of us.

Additional coverage of Kushner's life and career is contained in the following sources published by The Gale Group: *Contemporary Authors New Revision Series,* **Vol. 35 and** *Something about the Author,* **Vol. 52.**

Fredrick L(emuel) McKissack
1944-

Patricia (L'Ann) C(arwell) McKissack
1939-

African-American authors of fiction, nonfiction, retellings, and picture books.

Major works include *Sojourner Truth: "Ain't I a Woman?"* (1992), *Christmas in the Big House, Christmas in the Quarters* (1994), *The Royal Kingdoms of Ghana, Mali, and Songhay: Life in Medieval Africa* (1994), *Red-Tail Angels: The Story of the Tuskegee Airmen of World War II* (1995), *Rebels against Slavery* (1996).

For information on Patricia McKissack's career prior to 1990, see *CLR*, Vol. 23.

INTRODUCTION

Finding a need for nonfiction that reflects the African-American experience, the McKissacks have amply filled that void, although they contend there is plenty of room for more. The McKissacks are recognized for their histories, biographies, and information books for elementary graders and young adults that focus on individuals and movements that have influenced the development of African-American history and culture. Praised by reviewers for their timely subjects, thorough research, provocative writing, and strong narrative style, the McKissacks make their subjects come alive for young readers with their clear, enjoyable prose and exciting stories. The idea of writing biographies occurred when Patricia was looking for material to teach her class about the poet Paul Laurence Dunbar and found that there were no books about him. She solved this problem by writing a biography, and the McKissacks have continued to work in the genre ever since. Although Patricia had been a successful, published writer for several years, she began collaborating with Fredrick, a stickler for detailed research, and together they have produced over 100 biographies and historical accounts for children about celebrated African Americans. Researching and writing together, the McKissacks have supplied inquiring students with information about persons such as Frederick Douglass, Louis Armstrong, Langston Hughes, Sojourner Truth, and Madame C. J. Walker. They have also illuminated the stories of the Negro Baseball League, the Tuskegee air pilots of World War II, and the Civil Rights movement of the 1960s.

The depth and candor of their writing, embellished with primary documents and photographs, has garnered recognition for their works as authoritative histories. Building on family traditions of story telling, the McKissacks are further acknowledged for bringing historical awareness to African-American children by returning to them their often overlooked past, and thereby enriching Americans of every color. Coming of age in the 1960s when segregation was finally beginning to lose its hold and doors were just starting to open for African Americans, the McKissacks found inspiration in their common experiences and acquaintances from the vanguard of the Civil Rights movement. Their approach is multicultural, based on a belief that people from different backgrounds have more in common than they have differences, and that all people can learn to live together if they respect each other. In an interview for *Many Faces, Many Voices*, Patricia stated, "Find a way, find a way. You know, that's the real struggle, isn't it? It's a struggle for all of us, and I think to me that's the key to what we call multiculturalism, because that's one of the ways in which we all become a parallel culture. . . . " Fredrick added, "We do things more alike than we do them differently. The more you talk to people, the more you find that out." The McKissacks have enriched the body of American literature and contributed to America's heritage by making many vital and important pieces of the nation's history available and accessible to children.

Biographical Information

Both Patricia and Fredrick McKissack were born in Nashville, Tennessee. Although Patricia moved to St. Louis, Missouri as a small child, she returned to Nashville while still a young girl. She later attended Tennessee State University (formerly Tennessee Agricultural and Industrial State University), where she became reacquainted with Fred, five years her senior, who entered college after a three-year stint in the Marine Corps. Fredrick and Patricia had grown up in the same neighborhood and had known each other most of their lives, so they decided to get married almost immediately, a decision their families regarded as foolish. Patricia received a bachelor of arts degree in English in 1964, and continued her education at Webster University in St. Louis, where she received a master of arts degree in 1975. Shortly after, she began writing children's books. Fredrick graduated in 1964 with a bachelor of science degree and worked as a civil engineer for the city and federal governments, then started his own general contracting company in St. Louis. Patricia taught English, first at a junior high school, then at Forest Park College and the University of Missouri in St. Louis before becoming a children's book editor at Concordia Publishing House. She eventually left that job to become a freelance editor, writer,

writing teacher, and storyteller. Despite the reservations of family and friends, the McKissacks' marriage has become stronger over the years, as has their writing partnership. Drawn together by a common philosophy and shared experiences during the Civil Rights movement, the McKissacks have maintained a mutual social conscience born of that era. As Patricia explained in *Something about the Author* (*SATA*), "Writing has allowed us to do something positive with our experiences, although some of our experiences have been very negative. We try to enlighten, to change attitudes, to form new attitudes— to build bridges with books." Together they own a company called All-Writing Services, through which they conduct educational workshops and speak as consultants on minority literature for children. They have three sons.

Major Works

The biography for which the McKissacks have received the most praise is *Sojourner Truth: "Ain't I a Woman?"* It was welcomed as a riveting account not only of the life and career of this famous anti-slavery and women's rights advocate, but as a cogent description of the institution of slavery and the residual racism of the nineteenth century. A reviewer for *Publishers Weekly* called the book "a

great deal more than a biography of a remarkable woman. The forceful narrative also offers a startling portrayal of a pivotal yet appalling era in American history." A *Kirkus Reviews* critic regarded the work as "a valuable contribution, well-balanced and broad-minded." *Christmas in the Big House, Christmas in the Quarters* provides a fascinating multi-level view of the last Christmas preparations and celebrations on a Virginia plantation before the outbreak of the Civil War. Descriptions of the festivities alternate between the master's house and the slaves' quarters, with evident contrasts between traditions, resources, and lifestyles in both locations. Whispered undertones anticipate the changes to come and hint to readers that the holiday is not as joyous as it appears to be on the surface. A reviewer for *Publishers Weekly* commented, "The McKissacks carefully and convincingly delineate the discrepancies between the two milieu—from the physical settings to the people's differing appreciations of the holiday's riches. The contrast is startling and stirring. This is a book of significant dimension and importance, and could be read at any time of year."

The McKissacks turned to a more scholarly style with *The Royal Kingdoms of Ghana, Mali, and Songhay: Life in Medieval Africa*. In an attempt to correct the impression that Africa was void of culture during the Middle

Ages, the McKissacks present a history of the three societies that thrived in medieval West Africa, societies that are usually ignored by world history books. Using a variety of sources, the McKissacks describe these kingdoms and their legacy in Africa. Hazel Rochman commented, "The history of medieval Africa, long ignored and distorted, is here given full attention. The McKissacks are careful to distinguish what is known from what is surmised; they draw on the oral tradition, eyewitness accounts, and contemporary scholarship." Betsy Hearne also recognized the need for such a book, noting, "[T]his will be extremely useful as a springboard to books and articles that offer more depth but are less accessible to students."

Not all of the McKissacks' nonfiction is about individuals. *Red-Tail Angels: The Story of the Tuskegee Airmen of World War II* recounts the history of the first squadron of African-American airmen, trained at Tuskegee Air Base, who flew dangerous missions during World War II. Most telling are the accounts of blatant racism, insults, and degradation that these dedicated men suffered while serving their country and taking part in its defense. Richard Gereoff commented that *Red-Tail Angels* was "authoritative and admirable in its integration of social, political, military, and racial history," while a critic for *Social Education* noted "the many opportunities throughout the text for students to examine incidents from multiple perspectives." In a similar vein, *Rebels against Slavery* dispels the idea that slaves were passive about their situation, waiting helplessly for white abolitionists to garner their freedom. There were many instances of slaves rising up against their masters, protesting their condition, and freeing themselves, or trying to do so. *Rebels Against Slavery* presents the stories of some of these rebellions, both violent and subtle, and the men and women who led them. "The authors' careful research, sensitivity, and evenhanded style reveal a sad, yet inspiring story of the will to be free," noted Carol Joan Collins, while a *Kirkus Reviews* critic recognized the tales as "gripping."

Awards

The McKissacks twice received the Coretta Scott King Award, in 1990 for *A Long Hard Journey: The Story of Pullman Porter* and in 1993 for *Sojourner Truth: "Ain't I a Woman?"* The latter also received the AIM Children's Book Award in 1993.

AUTHOR'S COMMENTARY

Anthony L. Manna and Carolyn S. Brodie with Patricia and Fredrick McKissack

SOURCE: "A Conversation with Patricia and Fredrick McKissack," in *Many Faces, Many Voices: Multicultural Literary Experiences for Youth*, Highsmith Press, 1992, pp. 29-49.

[Manna and Brodie] How did you come to write for children?

P.Mc.: Need, just need. Need, in big bold letters. And I will write as long as there continues to be a need. I wanted to introduce my own children to the poetry of Paul Laurence Dunbar, so I went to the library, but there was not one single book in our library about Paul Laurence Dunbar. I wondered, "Why isn't there one?" Dunbar was a great African-American poet who gave us beautiful poems. Instead of complaining and moaning about what's not there, I decided to write his biography myself. And so I did.

M/B: How long ago was that?

P.Mc.: 1971.

M/B: You were teaching at that point.

P.Mc.: Yes, I was still teaching. I wrote about Dunbar because there was a need. There was also a need for picture books with children of color. As a child I read a lot, but I was always searching for myself and I didn't find myself in books, and that bothered me. I didn't want that situation to bother other young readers as well. If children don't see themselves in books or have anything that relates to them, soon they won't like to read; that soon becomes *I can't read,* and I can't read means doom.

So I write because there's a need to have books for, by, and about the African-American experience and about how we helped to develop this country.

F.Mc.: Talking about need again, Pat likes Dunbar's "Little Brown Baby" because it's one of the few early instances where a black father and a child are shown in such a positive experience.

P.Mc.: And very playful and loving, too. You don't see that image often in children's books. You know, words give us images. What images are our young people getting from television, radio, movie, tapes? How are we writers counteracting that? What are we doing to create positive images so that when children close their eyes they see themselves in positive ways. Too often words like violence, underachiever, poverty—and welfare have become synonyms for African Americans. That's horrible. We need to inspire a generation of writers and illustrators who create positive images. We also need a generation of readers who are going to read to their children.

M/B: Why did you start to read?

P.Mc.: My grandfather. He couldn't read but he loved the idea of reading. And he provided reading material for his family. He bought the newspaper every day, and read it by looking at the pictures and making out what they might mean. He also loved his Bible. He held it. Through the years he had memorized many of the passages. So he quoted it a lot. I loved to hear him quote I John. That's 1st John, but he called it "I John."

M/B: Memory seems important to your life as a writer.

P.Mc.: Memory is very important. Sometimes I start with just a small memory and then embellish it by adding bits and pieces from other events in my life. My own strength comes from my grandparents who were very strong. That's where some of my bad habits come from, too.

M/B: Would you talk about the oral tradition in your own background and how that figures into your writing.

P.Mc.: Writing is an outgrowth of my love of books and words. I heard stories all my life, and I also read stories. People often ask what I read as a child. My favorite book was a collection of mythology. I read Bullfinch long before I was supposed to be able to read and understand those stories. But I read them because I enjoyed them. It was one of the few places where I felt like I was connecting with something. In a lot of the stories I was reading I was looking for an experience that I could relate to and I couldn't do this in the contemporary novels that were being written in the fifties. So I read old stories. I have always loved the way the words were put together.

When Fredrick and I were growing up, the Nashville Public Library was never segregated. It was one of the few places in Nashville that wasn't. We went in and out of it. We had a respect for books because the librarian respected us. We could go right in the front door. That was quite a thing to be able to do in the South, to go into a large, imposing Carnegie Library as ours was and use the books. So, that was where the love affair with books started. Add all of that to my grandfather's telling tales, my reading to him, and his rich language—all of those things made words very special to me.

M/B: Is it difficult to try to capture the oral feel of a story on the page?

P.Mc.: I had to get beyond language restrictions. As an English major, I was taught to appreciate standard English, e.g., where to put question marks, how to make a complete sentence, verb-subject agreement. I had to throw all of that out and write the way my grandfather talked, in fragments, made-up words, etc. It wasn't easy, but it was fun and much more realistic in my stories.

M/B: You have said the tape recorder is another one of your tools.

P.Mc.: We tape and listen and tape and listen. *A Million Fish . . . More or Less* came out of that experience. That story is actually one Fredrick told me.

F.Mc.: It was a joke that I had heard, but Pat changed it. It was actually about a catfish that weighed 500 pounds.

Leb and Eb caught a catfish down in the old slough that weighed 500 pounds. So that is what Leb was telling Eb, and Eb didn't want to call Leb a liar. He just said, "What a funny old slough that place is. I was down there and I found a lantern that Ponce de Leon used in 1492 and it was still burning." Well, Eb didn't want to call Leb a liar so he said to him, "I'll take a few pounds off the catfish, if you put the lantern out."

P.Mc.: He told me that joke and I loved it.

F.Mc.: She recognized it.

P.Mc.: That's the kind of tall tales Daddy James, my grandfather, and Mr. Tinstey, his friend, used to tell all the time. One might say, "He was so strong, he could pick that heavy thing up with one hand." Just exaggerated tales, but then they'd start backing off of them after they made them so wide and so deep; they'd start subtracting some of the pounds. "Did it really weigh 500 pounds?" "Well, give or take a pound." "Was that lantern still burning?" "Well, let's just say it was flickerin' a bit." So what I did was to use Fred's story and by changing it a bit it worked as an introduction to Hugh Thomas's adventure.

M/B: Do you always collaborate in this way?

P.Mc.: Yes, all the time. We talk all the time.

F.Mc.: We have fun with it. We get up at eight o'clock in the morning and we go back to bed at ten or eleven and we tell stories the whole day long. We've come up with an answer for kids who ask us about how stories are created. We tell them that there are two creative processes which come out of literature itself. There's a process where a story literally pops out of your head, just like Athena popped out of the head of Zeus. This is instantaneous creation.

The other one we have named the Mustard Seed type of creation. You get a flicker of an idea—the size of a mustard seed—but it has to grow from an idea to a story or to a book. The idea is there and you just need to keep going back over it. You're driving along and it pops into your head and it grows and grows and grows, and then somewhere along the way you put it down on the word processor and it changes some more.

P.Mc.: *Messy Bessey* was one of those Athena-like ideas that just popped out of our heads fully grown.

F.Mc.: It never was a child.

P.Mc.: It took about an hour to write. We're constantly telling stories to children. Fredrick and I always told our own kids stories, too, which is part of the African tradition. They taught with stories. They communicated with the great kings with stories, because they couldn't very well tell a king outright that he was wrong. They couldn't tell a ruler that he had made a mistake, and so the storytellers used story to instruct, to influence, to convince, among other things. That's what we try to do with stories.

M/B: And to entertain.

P.Mc.: Oh yes. First to entertain. That's how you get people to listen in the first place.

F.Mc.: We went down to Alabama to Pat's family home-place for a reunion around 1974 or 1975 or somewhere in that area. One of the old codgers there, who grew up without radio or television, told us stories one night. They were barbecuing in an old-fashioned pit in the ground and everybody sat around the fire. He told his stories there. On our way home we talked the whole time about Uncle B.J.'s stories. We noticed that three-year-olds were smiling and laughing, and so were ten-year-olds, at twenty, and at eighty, too. He told those stories in such a manner that everybody got something out of them.

I think in a sense, Pat tries to tell that type of story where there is a little something for everybody to think about. So a little kid might think of *Flossie and the Fox* in one way and an older person might think of it in another way, but they'd all be entertained. And I think that's important to understand about our history, because that was the way stories were told in slavery times.

P.Mc.: We try to tell our non-fiction in a story voice as well.

M/B: What's your method for doing that?

F.Mc.: I don't think there is a method. The first thing is to pick topics that are of high interest in our community. One of the things that we've talked most about was the 1960s, the era of the sit-ins, the stand-ins, and the wait-ins. Pat and I were part of those events, so we are interested in giving a clear picture of that era. One of the things the reviewer said about *Martin Luther King, Jr.* was that we had overdone the book. We had looked at every word and every phrase to make sure that we were recording and telling the truth.

Pat's office is right next to my office, and we still run from one room to another saying, "Look what I found." We research a lot. First it's the library. We not only go to the public library, we've also built an extensive li-brary of our own on African-American issues. Another thing we do is to call old friends to talk about the subjects. Then we have to tie it all together.

P.Mc.: I think it's substance and feeling. We dig con-stantly, we read constantly. When we go to cities and have a moment, we try to go to museums and libraries and gather bits and pieces of information there. We've found that working on one project gives us an idea for another book.

So a lot of the books we have written are rooted in the civil rights movement. The idea for the James Weldon

Johnson book came when we were at the Coretta Scott King breakfast in Chicago. The ceremony started off with "Lift Every Voice" and we looked around and all of the people over forty were singing. They knew the words and seemed to enjoy them. But all the people under forty, and practically all of the whites, couldn't sing the song. They didn't know the words. "Lift every voice and sing, 'till earth and heaven ring, ring with the harmonies of liberty." I said, "Oh Fred, we've got to do a book."

M/B: In that book the hymn has become the structure. That's a beautiful way to go about it.

P.Mc.: That song is an important part of our history. I was speaking with someone yesterday and we laughed about how "Lift Every Voice and Sing" was so impor-tant to us, because she lived in one part of the country and I lived in another part of the country, yet our school days started off exactly the same way. We sang "The Star Spangled Banner" and said "The Pledge of Alle-giance." Then we said the Lord's Prayer or the Twenty-Third Psalm. And then we sang "Lift Every Voice and Sing," followed by a poem from some great poet. That was the way we started the day.

M/B: Lucky for you, too, because that gave you the rhythm of the language. So many children don't get that because poetry is often considered a special thing for special kids.

F.Mc.: James Weldon Johnson and Paul Laurence Dun-bar were good friends.

P.Mc.: Dunbar wrote beautiful poetry in standard En-glish and in black dialect. Johnson was inspired by Dunbar to write "Sence You Went Away," his first dialect poem.

F.Mc.: Dunbar had died when James Weldon Johnson wrote that poem. James Weldon Johnson and his brother were the first, among the first, that is, to write down the black spirituals, or the Negro spirituals, as they were called at the time. In that book he dedicated each and every song to people like Booker T. Washington, W. E. B. Du Bois, and Paul Laurence Dunbar. When you pick up that book and look at the songs you see so many connections.

P.Mc.: Ideas beget ideas. Most of our books come from work that we did on other books. When we did our biography of W. E. B. Du Bois we were led to Booker T. Washington. They came out of the same era, but they were in conflict with each other.

F.Mc.: And here again, the connections. Dudley Ran-dall, a very famous black poet, wrote about that con-flict. We used his poem in *The Civil Rights Movement in America from 1865 to the Present*. And if you listen to this poem, you'll hear an ongoing conversation in the black community from 1619 to the present day. . . .

[P.Mc.] You have some blacks who are currently saying, "Hey, we don't need the civil rights movement, it's passé. We don't need affirmative action, we don't need social reform, we don't need those things." Then you have other people who are saying, "Wait a minute, wait a minute, we do need those things." Within the African-American community there is conflict and that's why it bothers me when people try to say one black leader represents all black people. We have many, many different leaders and we try to show that in the books we write.

M/B: When you're writing a book like *The Civil Rights Movement in America* what particular angle do you take? This has been done so much, so how do you approach it?

F.Mc.: You've got to keep readers interested in order for them to read anything. In the civil rights book we tell our readers that man's quest for justice didn't begin in the twentieth-century United States. Actually, the story of civil rights has no beginning or end. From ancient times to present, the struggle for rights has been at the core of countless social and political conflicts. But even though the concept for rights is constantly being re-evaluated, life and freedom are universally accepted as a basis for human rights. Human rights are the foundation upon which our entire democracy is based. We tell our readers that America itself is founded on the subject of rights which goes back to the time of David and further back still to the story of Adam and Eve. We try to make a connection because the day will come when they will be asked to choose. They'll have to stand up; the trick of it is to stand up for what is right.

P.Mc.: And the best way to know is through reading and gathering information, sorting information, and then coming to conclusions. We felt that our book should not focus entirely on civil rights in African-American history. We tried to include the Native American story, we tried to include the Hispanic and Asian story, as well. The struggle for rights among women and immigrants, too, because all of them in turn have had to struggle for their rights. We even included children's stories, because child labor laws were not passed in this country until we had a woman as Secretary of Labor under Roosevelt in the 1930s. Frances Perkins was the first to help push through child labor laws because up until that time children were forced to work in terrible conditions for as little as a dime a day.

M/B: One of the things you remind us of is the split between the spirit and the word.

P.Mc.: What we bring to our subject is the spirit and I think the spirit is what makes the words sing. A lot of people have knowledge of these subjects, they know them very well, but they have difficulty making them interesting to children. And children will not read what they do not enjoy. Let's face it. We can shove it at them, we can test them, we can make it mandatory, we can put it on reading lists from now until forever, but young readers will not read a book if they do not like

it. I taught eighth grade English for nine years, and I had trouble trying to get my students to read biography. Then I read some biographies myself and I thought, "No wonder they don't like to read this material. It's awful. It's just listing one dry fact after the other." Very academic and very well researched, but—there was no story, and the people didn't seem real.

Fred's too modest to say, but he digs for the stuff that makes children want to read. I don't like research. Research is tedious. If I can get in the ballpark of the year, that's close enough for me. I'll say, "It happened in 1917." Fredrick will see 1917 sticking up like a sore thumb and he'll say, "We've got to add some detail to that." So he will go out and find the day, the date, the hour if possible, and he'll even check the weather report and find out if it was raining or sunny that day. So what readers get in our books is that fine detail that you don't usually get in a book, because a lot of people like me would just quit at 1917.

M/B: How did the Pullman Porter book evolve?

P.Mc.: Theirs was a story that needed to be told. You see, it's a wonderful story about a group of men who fought for their rights and made it possible for all black workers to have a little dignity in the jobs they held. It gave other people a reason to stand up later.

M/B: There's a powerful photograph on page 95 of *A Long Hard Journey* of A. Philip Randolph with William Green, who is president of the American Federation of Labor, AFL.

P.Mc.: That's a very important picture because the Brotherhood of Sleeping Car Porters was the first African-American union to be recognized by a major corporation and the first to be an independent brotherhood within the AFL. That's history. It was a fourteen-year struggle. It was incredible what the founding porters went through. They almost lost everything. E. J. Bradley lost his wife because she couldn't take the pressure. She divorced him, and he had to move the Brotherhood office to the trunk of his car. The second Mrs. Bradley is the woman who helped us secure so many of the good photos. . . .

P.Mc.: This has never been in any published book before. But just look at the history here. Adam Clayton Powell and Eleanor Roosevelt; that's a civil rights movement right there.

F.Mc.: It didn't die there either. When they were tearing down the wall in Germany they were singing "We Shall Overcome." Would you have guessed that? Did you know that the first Pullman car was in Abe Lincoln's funeral? Just the crazy connections that you really can never make any sense of, but they are there all the time.

P.Mc.: There are connections in our fiction, too. One of the sections in an upcoming book, *Christmas in the Big*

House, Christmas in the Quarters, which will be out in 1993, contains big connections. One of the Christmas foods was "Sweet Potato Pie;" we give the recipe.

Take two sweet potatoes grown in the garden patch outside. Add two cups of sugar. If sugar's not available, use one cup of molasses or honey. One-fourth pound of butter scraped from the inside of the butter churn. Two tablespoons vanilla, one tablespoon of cinnamon, one tablespoon of nutmeg, but if you can't get spices then use a tablespoon of rum. One-fourth cup of milk, if you get to milk a cow. And four eggs. Send the children to gather eggs in the hay. And then you mix them together and make your pie. When I found this recipe I was in tears, because to make a sweet potato pie, it wasn't like just going out, gathering or buying the ingredients, and making it. They pieced it together, the way black people have always had to piece their lives together from shattered hope and lost dreams. That's the way the cake was made for the cakewalk, too. That's what made the cake the prize. Kids who know *Mirandy and Brother Wind,* wonder about the cake. Why not another prize? You have to show them why that cake is so special, because you had to pilfer, you know, eggs, butter, sugar, from the big house.

F.Mc.: And that's the prize.

M/B: Now we understand that much better, to tell you the truth. Now we understand the social significance of the cake. And who would ever think that there could be a whole world of history in a cake?

P.Mc.: But you know, this is how books happen. I look down at this recipe, and I'm saying, whoa, what a part of history I could do with recipes. Maybe I'll look up more recipes and have a time with story recipes. There are stories in those recipes. The potato pie was the validation for the cakewalk. Because this is how they made the pie, that's how they made the cake. You know, one by one you dig up these things. *Christmas in the Big House, Christmas in the Quarters* tells how Christmas was celebrated in 1859 in Virginia. Now the reason why we chose 1859 is because that's the last time that Christmas would be celebrated in the antebellum South as it was, as it had been, because in 1860 secession would start, and the war would begin, of course, in 1861. The South would never be the same again. So that Christmas had to be a very special one for both slave and master.

F.Mc.: It was also the Christmas of Harpers Ferry.

P.Mc.: Robert E. Lee defeated John Brown, so naturally there would have been a lot of talk in Virginia about that incident. Of course, the underground railroad was very active at that time. It's the changing of history, changing from the old South to the coming of freedom. The reason why we chose the state of Virginia is because Virginia is the mother of the American Christmas. Christmas was first celebrated in Virginia. The eastern colonies didn't celebrate Christmas. In fact, it was for-bidden among the Puritans, and a person could be fined for even feasting at Christmas.

But the Virginians always celebrated Christmas, both slave and master. Many of our present-day traditions come from the big house. The drinking of eggnog, for example. The Christmas tree which came from Germany was first brought to Williamsburg, Virginia. There were also the slave traditions of celebrating Christmas, using red and green for example. Those were slave colors, because red was an easy dye to make, and greenery came from the woodland.

F.Mc.: There are some personal connections in *The Dark Thirty,* another new book of ours.

P.Mc.: When I was growing up and we were playing in the yard, [at the end of the day] we would look up at the sky at the twilight hour, and call it the *dark-thirty,* because we had thirty minutes to get home before it got dark and the monsters came out. So these are stories that have an odd twist to them. Again, I've taken historical events and written around them.

In **"Woman in the Snow"** I created a ghost that haunts a local bus at about the time of the Montgomery Bus Boycott. There's another story that happens during the death of Martin Luther King, that horrible period when King was killed, and then Robert F. Kennedy was killed within months. All of the stories are based on historical events. Perhaps you'd like to hear one of the stories to give you a flavor of the way they sound. This is called **"The Chicken Coop Monster."**

When I was nine my parents' ten-year marriage dissolved. Nobody really wanted to talk about divorce in those days. They whispered about it in hushed tones, so I had to define it my own way. I defined divorce to mean if my parents didn't love each other, then they didn't love me. I carried all my hurt and anger and frustration inside.

My parents shipped me off to Nashville to be with my grandparents, and I hated the whole idea. As soon as I walked onto their place I knew that a monster lived in the chicken coop. I knew that he was there, because I could feel his hot red eyes watching me when I played. When I got too close to that old coop I could smell its foul breath, so I knew it was there. One evening my grandmother said to me, "Pat, the chicken coop door is open, would you please go out and close it?" It was at the hour called the dark thirty. It was neither light nor dark. It's when things change and the mind plays tricks on the eyes and you think that it's a tree branch, but it could be the arm of a monster reaching out. I wasn't about to go near that chicken coop at that hour because that's when the monster is strongest. So I stood there frozen in terror and my grandmother said, "Pat, haven't you gone and shut that door for me?" and I said, "No, I'm not going out there." "What do you mean," she said, "you're not going out there; of course you're going out there to close that door." "No," I said, "There's a monster out there." "Oh, girl, don't be silly. There's no such thing as a monster." You see, that's how monsters work, they fool adults. They make you think that they don't exist. Well she said, "If you don't go close that door, something will get in and trouble my chickens." I hated to be the one to tell her but there was already something in there and that's why I didn't want to go.

She was going to drag me out there. I broke away from her, ran into the house, screaming and crying. That's when I felt strong—very, very strong—arms patting me on my back. It was my grandfather, Daddy James, and he said, "What troubles you so about that old chicken coop?" And I said, "It's a monster in there." "Oh? Tell me about your monster," he said. Aha, my grandfather didn't say there's no such thing as a monster. He asked me what my monster looked like. Was he a believer? I had to check it out. "Daddy James, do you believe in monsters? Mama Frances says they don't exist." He said, "Oh, you know monsters are like that, they try to make you think that they don't exist, but, oh yes, I know they do." He had asked me to describe my monster. Of course, I had never seen my monster. I didn't know what he looked like really, but I guess if it lived in the chicken coop, it must look like a chicken, right? It must have big claws, clawed feet, it must have a long beak that was pointed, and instead of having just the regular feathers on its back, it had scales. And big red eyes. So I described my monster.

My grandpa said, "You know, there used to be a monster that lived in the crawl space under my house, too. And that old monster used to just scare me to death. Had me so scared I couldn't even play in my own front yard." "You did?" And he said, "The only way I could get rid of him was to call him out." "To call him out? You called out a monster?" "Yep." "Did you win?" "Yep, I whipped him good and sent him right back to monsterland." "Well, good, will you go and do something about the monster that lives in your chicken coop?" "No," he said, "I can't do that. That's your monster and you've got to call out your own monster." "But I'm just a little girl," I said. "Well, I was just a little boy. Now with some monsters you can face them, you have to be strong and just believe that you can beat them. And you know the stronger you get, the weaker that monster will get."

Well armed with the only thing I had I went out to face my monster and I called him out. And the creaky old door swung open and I thought, nope, this is not a good decision. I started to run, but then I thought about what my grandfather said. If I stayed strong the monster would leave, so I called him out and I said, "Monster, come on out, it's me and I'm not afraid of you." Of course, I was terrified. "Come on out," I said. "I am the oldest granddaughter of James Leon Oldham and he loves me and I know it." That monster left. The point is that if we create our own monsters, we also have to face them.

M/B: In your presentation at the Virginia Hamilton Conference you said that your female characters are the

daughters you always wanted, considering that your children are males.

P.Mc.: Those are my daughters, all right. They are the outgrowth of me. They can't be me totally because I never did all those wonderful things, like catch the wind or outsmart a fox, but if I had daughters, that's how I would want them to be able to react to problems, that's how I'd want them to make decisions and solve problems. Now, naturally, I have set them in very tight situations, but I think you can guess the kind of upbringing they had by the way they act. So in a way that's me and that's where the "me" comes through.

M/B: They're all survivors.

F.Mc.: There's a statement in the black community that you hear all the time. It says, "Keep on keepin' on."

M/B: That's central in all of your books.

F.Mc.: Keep on keepin on.

P.Mc.: I love that. We never give up, we find a way.

M/B: That's a beautiful message to give to people, in general, and to children, in particular.

P.Mc.: Find a way, find a way. You know, that's the real struggle isn't it? It's a struggle for all of us and I think to me that's the key to what we call multiculturalism, because that's one of the ways in which we all become a parallel culture, as Virginia Hamilton says.

F.Mc.: We do things more alike than we do them differently. The more you talk to people, the more you find that out.

GENERAL COMMENTARY

Phyllis Stephens

SOURCE: A review of *Ida B. Wells-Barnett: A Voice against Violence, Marian Anderson: A Great Singer, Martin Luther King, Jr.: Man of Peace,* and *Ralph J. Bunche: Peacemaker,* in *School Library Journal,* Vol. 37, No. 11, November, 1991, p. 111.

The McKissacks present their subjects in language that is simple, clear, and matter-of-fact. Fictionalizing is kept to a minimum. Incidents of racial bigotry appear as a matter of setting with almost no attempt at explanation or detail. The result is a short, barebones biography of each person. These are not extraordinary individuals who transcend the limitations of racism. Instead, they are people of such drive and determination that not even a racially biased society could provide effective obstacles to deter them from their goals. Accuracy, style, and content are consistent throughout; the abundance of exclamatory statements and questionable glossary entries are minor annoyances. Generous black-and-white photos with informative captions and pen-and-ink drawings augment as well as illustrate the texts.

Hazel Rochman

SOURCE: A review of *Mary McLeod Bethune: A Great Teacher, Frederick Douglass: Leader against Slavery,* and *Louis Armstrong: Jazz Musician,* in *Booklist,* Vol. 88, No. 9, January 1, 1992, p. 832.

The writing is undistinguished in this "Great African Americans" biography series. The attempt to have illustration [by Ned O] on every page makes an odd juxtaposition of fine documentary photographs and dull drawings. Still, there's not much else available for beginning readers about these extraordinary people whose life stories will be of great interest to children.

Laura Culberg

SOURCE: A review of *Paul Robeson: A Voice to Remember* and *Booker T. Washington: Leader and Educator,* in *School Library Journal,* Vol. 38, No. 10, October, 1992, pp. 105-06.

Two biographies that are brief, informative, and fill a need for materials on noted African-Americans for primary-grade readers. Both touch on the childhood, education, careers, and family life of these men. Their determination to achieve and the obstacles they had to overcome are emphasized. Black-and-white photographs, usually from their adult years, appear throughout. Some of the captions in *Robeson* are short on details. (One photo shows Robeson receiving an award in France, but the caption does not give a date, the reason for the award, or the name of the man presenting it.) Hazy, undistinguished pencil drawings [by Michael Bryant] illustrate the subject's early years in *Washington;* the pen-and-ink drawings [by Michael David Biegel] in *Robeson* are far more expressive. However, in the glossary of that book, the authors define words such as "slave" and "concert," but then they use the term "Allies" in a definition of World War II and do not explain who the Allies were. These comments aside, the books will find an eager audience among beginning readers because of their bold, easy-to-read texts, wide margins, and short chapters.

Susan Knorr

SOURCE: A review of *Langston Hughes: Great American Poet, Jesse Owens: Olympic Star, Satchel Paige: The Best Arm in Baseball,* and *Sojourner Truth: A Voice for Freedom,* in *School Library Journal,* Vol. 39, No. 1, January, 1993, pp. 116, 118.

Short sentences, large, well-spaced text, and a blend of black-and-white photographs and sketches serve as accessible introductions to the highlights in the lives of these African Americans. Each book tells of their early childhood, adversity, and adult achievements. However, the brevity of the coverage leaves out much of the detail and excitement in their lives and allows for little amplification or emotion. Owens's victories in the 1936 Olympics naturally dominate the coverage of his adult life, but many of Hughes's accomplishments and travels from the 1930s until his death are quickly glossed over and his political involvement is covered not at all. *Paige* may introduce readers to the segregation of baseball that hampered the player's career, while *Truth* will give an overview of that great woman's achievements. While several biographies of her are available, including Ferris's *Walking the Road to Freedom* (1988), most are for older readers.

TITLE COMMENTARY

📖 *TAKING A STAND AGAINST RACISM AND RACIAL DISCRIMINATION* (1990)

Roger Sutton

SOURCE: A review of *Taking a Stand against Racism and Racial Discrimination,* in *Bulletin of the Center for Children's Books,* Vol. 43, No. 9, May, 1990, p. 222.

While the cover pictures four hands colored to represent the major racial groups, this book is primarily concerned with discrimination in regard to black Americans. This is still a large topic for any single book, and many of the topics covered, *Brown v. Board of Education,* for example, are given sketchy treatment. On the whole, however, the McKissacks have provided a cogent and provocative discussion of racism and civil rights from sociological, historical, legal, and personal perspectives. Students will particularly appreciate the portraits of young activists such as Portland Birchfield, who wrote a play about racism in her high school, and George Sakaguchi, who recalls his internment at age seventeen in a U.S. concentration camp for Japanese Americans. Advice on getting involved in civil rights issues, including information on national organizations, is helpful, and could have been expanded. A bit too text-bookish in style, organization, and coverage to encourage independent reading, this will still be a useful primer for social studies classes.

JoEllen Broome

SOURCE: A review of *Taking a Stand against Racism and Racial Discrimination,* in *Voice of Youth Advocates,* Vol. 13, No. 4, October, 1990, p. 248.

This book is valuable because it is well written and probes a sensitive issue in an honest way devoid of "preachiness." It moves swiftly through the major incidents of racism in our history and the legal statutes that supported it or tried to redress it. The reader is taken right up to the Reagan Administration. The heroines and heroes of the Civil Rights Movement and their predecessors are given their due recognition. The most impressive story is about a black high school student named Portland Birchfield who was bused to a predominantly white high school. She wrote a play that was produced and presented to parents, teachers, and students that discussed racism and discrimination in the day-to-day world of high school. It moved, outraged, and entertained, serving as a vehicle for starting honest discussions on the topic. It was her way of coming to terms with her troubling observations of what was taking place in her own environment. It has a strong message of empowerment for other young people who are in this situation. Something can always be done. There are some other good ideas on what can be done in the here and now to solve problems as well as what others have done in the past. More in-depth discussion of the subtle ways racism and racial discrimination insinuate themselves into our lives will be helpful to young readers. The most flagrant evidence of the horror is the discussion of the death of 19-year-old Michael Donald at the hands of two Ku Klux Klansmen in 1981. Such incidents were more common in the earlier part of the 20th century, but the fact that it erupted again in the more tolerant 1980s is a frightening reminder that the hatred has not been banished. What changed was the legal redress that the mother was able to obtain in a southern state but she still had to be very courageous to pursue the case.

This is a most worthwhile book. There is a concern that those who might be most helped or startled into self-examination by this book are the least likely to pick it up. Teachers need to promote it. Very well researched, the book includes black and white photographs and a list of civil rights organizations to contact if the reader or a class is motivated to get involved.

JAMES WELDON JOHNSON: "LIFT EVERY VOICE AND SING" (1990)

Denise M. Wilms

SOURCE: A review of *James Weldon Johnson: "Lift Every Voice and Sing,"* in *Booklist,* Vol. 87, No. 1, September 1, 1990, p. 54.

The McKissacks introduce James Weldon Johnson and the well-known song "Lift Every Voice and Sing," which he co-authored with his brother, Rosamond. As important as the surface facts of Johnson's life is the social context of that life; the authors explain the segregation policies and the violence used to intimidate blacks who stepped outside the bounds of acceptable behavior. This then becomes history as much as biography, especially when one considers the photographs reproduced here.

They picture not only Johnson and his family, but also key events of his time. A slim and very accessible introduction.

Jeanette Lambert

SOURCE: A review of *James Weldon Johnson: "Lift Every Voice and Sing,"* in *School Library Journal,* Vol. 37, No. 2, February, 1991, p. 79.

A biography that succeeds in highlighting the life of a talented individual whose legacy has been an inspiration to many, and makes Johnson come alive for young readers. Although "Lift Every Voice and Sing" is acknowledged as the African-American national anthem, less commonly known is that it was written in 1900 by Johnson, a principal in Florida, and his brother for a celebration of Abraham Lincoln's birthday. Johnson excelled in areas beyond song writing, as well. He was the first African American in Florida to pass the bar, the principal of the first black high school in Jacksonville, a consul to Venezuela and Nicaragua, and an executive secretary of the NAACP. The book's layout is appealing; black-and-white photographs, which enhance the text by depicting Johnson's era, and highlighted lyrics are attractively arranged. Although brief, this title captures the essence of a remarkable individual.

IDA B. WELLS-BARNETT: A VOICE AGAINST VIOLENCE ("Great African Americans" series, 1991)

Kirkus Reviews

SOURCE: A review of *Ida B. Wells-Barnett: A Voice against Violence,* in *Kirkus Reviews,* Vol. LIX, No. 7, April 1, 1991, p. 474.

Wells-Barnett (1862-1931) was a journalist whose life-long fight against discrimination began at age 16. A founder of the NAACP, she was most effective in speaking and writing against the horror and injustice of lynching. Her story is outlined here in simple yet lively prose.

Like the others in the new "Great African Americans" series this serves as an introduction, the didactic feel not helped by boldfaced terms defined in a glossary and by the utilitarian line drawings that, with b&w photos, appear as illustrations. These will be more effective in the classroom than as additions to juvenile collections.

MARIAN ANDERSON: A GREAT SINGER ("Great African Americans" series, 1991)

Roger Sutton

SOURCE: A review of *Marian Anderson: A Great Singer,* in *Bulletin of the Center for Children's Books,* Vol. 44, No. 10, June, 1991, p. 245.

While there is a great need for biographies at the primary grades level, this entry in a new series is adulatory, oversimplified, not always accurate, and stodgily designed. Anderson had a temper as well as temperament, but in this book she is only "sad" and "not for herself" (twice) when confronting racial prejudice. There is no clue that Anderson was a contralto, nor, in fact, is there any indication that she sang classical music: aside from spirituals, all the book says is that she "sang the high notes, the low notes, and all the notes in between." The year of Anderson's disastrous Town Hall recital was 1924, not 1922; the year of her famous triumph over the DAR and subsequent concert at the Lincoln Memorial was 1939, not 1943. Although the print is large and readable, the format is 50s-primer, and the pen-and-ink drawings look like advertising art from the same era (the several photographs are better). The cover painting gives the singer a halo.

📖 CARTER G. WOODSON: THE FATHER OF BLACK HISTORY ("Great African Americans" series, 1991)

Cherry A. McGee Banks

SOURCE: A review of *Carter G. Woodson: The Father of Black History,* in *Social Education,* Vol. 58, No. 5, September, 1994, p. 318.

Contents, words to know and index sections, and interesting black and white photographs and illustrations [by Ned O] help to make this a "big girl-big boy" book for young elementary students. The McKissacks pack a great deal of information about Woodson and events such as "Negro History Week" into a few pages. Three positive and powerful messages, 'it is never too late to learn,' 'read everyday,' and 'pride,' are repeated throughout the text.

Carter's father, James Woodson, a runaway slave who was freed near the end of the Civil War, could not read or write. However, James Woodson always made sure his seven children knew it was never too late to learn. Even though Carter worked on the family farm and later on the railroad and in a coal mine, he learned to read and developed his vocabulary by reading daily. Patricia and Fredrick McKissack have made it possible for young readers to learn about African Americans who have done great things for our country.

📖 A MILLION FISH . . . MORE OR LESS (written by Patricia McKissack, 1992)

Kirkus Reviews

SOURCE: A review of *A Million Fish . . . More or Less,* in *Kirkus Reviews,* Vol. LIX, No. 24, December 15, 1991, p. 1595.

Out fishing on the Bayou Clapateaux, young Hugh

Thomas listens with delight when Papa-Daddy and Elder Abbajonto happen by to tell him a tall tale concerning a 500-pound turkey, a Spanish conquistador's lantern that's still burning, and "the longest, meanest cottonmouth I ever did see." After they leave, Hugh Thomas catches just three small fish—and then imagines an even taller tale to tell the men: he catches a million fish, but the crocodiles demand half, and he's able to keep only half of the remainder by winning a jumprope contest with some piratical raccoons on his way home. Most of the rest disappear while he's talking to his friend Miss Challie Pearl: Did her cat get them? Still, he has those first three fish, just enough for supper.

Though it doesn't have quite the enchantment of the author's *Flossie and the Fox* (1986), this lively, well-cadenced tale makes a good African-American counterpart to Seuss's classic *And to Think That I Saw It on Mulberry Street.* In her picture book debut, [Dena] Schutzer provides freely rendered oil paintings with bold strokes of vibrant color that are especially effective at a distance—fine for groups.

Publishers Weekly

SOURCE: A review of *A Million Fish . . . More or Less,* in *Publishers Weekly,* Vol. 239, No. 6, January 27, 1992, p. 97.

Down in Louisiana, young Hugh Thomas has heard many a tale of the extraordinary goings-on in the Bayou Clapateaux—"a mighty peculiar place." Given the stories of 500-pound turkeys, lamps that never burn out and snakes that take to their legs and run, it is only natural that Hugh, catching three small fish, should land "a million more! Big ones, little ones, all sizes." Told with verve and a sly wit, this exuberant Bayou tale admirably captures the captivating regional cadences and comedy of the intrepid fisher boy's adventures. Each unlikely event is topped by the next, and despite the snapping gators and sneaky raccoons, Hugh Thomas lives to tell his tale with glee. Similarly ebullient and evocative is the Gauguinesque artwork; Schutzer's rainbow palette of thickly daubed paint both portrays and extends the absurdity and vivacious spirit behind the storytelling. This splendid collaboration is a perfect blend of two distinct styles—text and art trying to outdo each other, it seems, with joyous results.

Betsy Hearne

SOURCE: A review of *A Million Fish . . . More or Less,* in *Bulletin of the Center for Children's Books,* Vol. 45, No. 10, June, 1992, pp. 270-71.

The clue here is purple alligators and mauve fish, and the tone is tall: in Bayou Capateaux, say the two fishermen to young Hugh Thomas, they once caught a wild turkey weighing five hundred pounds, were chased by a cottonmouth with legs, fought off an attack by giant mosquitoes, and found a Spanish lantern from 1542—still burning. But that's nothing like what happens to Hugh after the two men leave. If listeners don't quite believe the million fish that Hugh catches, and the fate of all but three, they'll be all the wiser to yarns and how to spin them. The play between fantasy and reality is neatly handled, with action following exaggeration in an ambiguous way that leaves the ending open as to who's telling the truth and who believes what. The African-American characters and swamp setting swirl across the pages in thick, rounded strokes of brazen-hued paint, well-matched with the story's brassy flash.

📖 *MADAM C. J. WALKER: SELF-MADE MILLIONAIRE* ("Great African Americans" series, 1992)

Kirkus Reviews

SOURCE: A review of *Madam C. J. Walker: Self-Made Millionaire,* in *Kirkus Reviews,* Vol. LX, No. 13, July 1, 1992, p. 858.

One of seven new entries, all by the McKissacks, in the "Great African Americans" series. The text here is condensed almost to outline form and delivered in short, easily read but often choppy sentences. Still, the McKissacks are reliable researchers who manage to pack a substantial amount of information into their brief account, deftly setting this 19th-century entrepreneur in the society of her time and providing all the proper accouterments of nonfiction, including historical photos to supplement [Michael] Bryant's serviceable drawings. Workmanlike and sure to be useful.

Cherry A. McGee Banks

SOURCE: A review of *Madam C. J. Walker: Self-Made Millionaire,* in *Social Education,* Vol. 58, No. 5, September, 1994, p. 318.

Patricia and Fredrick McKissack have produced this award-winning elementary book in simple understandable language and with what is usually termed textbook-type formatting (Table of Contents, Index, Words To Know).

Madam C. J. Walker: Self-Made Millionaire was born Sarah Breedlove on Grand View Plantation. Louisiana. Her parents, Owen and Minerva, were freed slaves, and Sarah was the first of their children to be born free. The McKissacks guide the young reader systematically through eight states and simultaneously through the phases of Sarah's entrepreneurial journey toward another first—achieving millionaire status via the development and marketing of hair products for the African-American woman under her married name, Madam C. J. Walker. Readers are told about Madam Walker's philanthropy and civil rights interests. They meet many of her acquaintances and her daughter A'Lelia through interesting

sketches and actual photographs at intervals throughout the book. This book, a testament to Mrs. Walker's journey from daughter of freed slaves to "one of the richest women in the United States—black or white," will provide inspiration to all who read it.

📖 *THE DARK-THIRTY: SOUTHERN TALES OF THE SUPERNATURAL* (written by Patricia McKissack, 1992)

Kirkus Reviews

SOURCE: A review of *The Dark-Thirty: Southern Tales of the Supernatural,* in *Kirkus Reviews,* Vol. LX, No. 20, October 15, 1992, p. 1313.

McKissack invites readers to gather in the "dark-thirty"—the eerie half hour when dusk darkens to night—for ten shivery tales inspired by African-American folklore and history. The historical links are especially potent: in the **"The Legend of Pin Oak,"** a free mulatto and his family escape re-enslavement by leaping from a cliff; in **"We Organized"**—written in free verse and based on an actual narrative—a cruel owner is forced by magic to free his slaves. An African-American lynched by the KKK, and another left by a white bus-driver to freeze to death, return to haunt their tormentors; when a dying Pullman porter hears **"The 11:59,"** he knows it's time to go. Each tale is told in a simple, lucid style, embellished by a few deftly inserted macabre details and by one of [Brian] Pinkney's dramatic, swirling scratch-board illustrations. A fine collection that teaches as it entertains.

Betsy Hearne

SOURCE: A review of *The Dark-Thirty: Southern Tales of the Supernatural,* in *Bulletin of the Center for Children's Books,* Vol. 46, No. 4, December, 1992, p. 117.

The author's brief introduction bills this as "a collection of original stories rooted in African-American history and the oral storytelling tradition"; what she doesn't mention is that, after the first two slave tales, the remaining eight have a contemporary, urban-legend tone that makes them all the spookier for being more immediate. In terms of development, this is more fiction than folklore, and kids looking for short stories that are fast-moving and easy to read will find the ghosts a bonus. **"The Woman in the Snow"** about a haunted bus route, **"The Conjure Brother"** about a girl's misguided wish, **"Boo Mama"** about a mother and child taken by Sasquatch, or **"The Gingi"** about an evil Yoruban spirit's possession of a house could all happen any minute (especially after dark). Every once in a while, McKissack's style starts skimming the surface of both action and characters, but she knows how to tell a good story and isn't afraid to dramatize scary details, on the one hand, or throw in some history, on the other. Every story gets a context-setting introduction, and Brian

Pinkney's black-and-white scratchboard illustrations serve to heighten the suspense without overdramatizing it.

Kay McPherson

SOURCE: A review of *The Dark-Thirty: Southern Tales of the Supernatural,* in *School Library Journal,* Vol. 38, No. 12, December, 1992, p. 113.

Ten original stories, all with a foundation in African-American history or culture. Some are straight ghost stories, many of which are wonderfully spooky and all of which have well-woven narratives. There is a tale from slavery times; a story set among the Brotherhood of Sleeping Car Porters; and one from the 1940s segregated South, in which a black man's ghost brings revenge upon the white klansman who murdered him. Strong characterizations are superbly drawn in a few words. The atmosphere of each selection is skillfully developed and sustained to the very end. Pinkney's stark scratchboard illustrations evoke an eerie mood, which heightens the suspense of each tale. This is a stellar collection for both public and school libraries looking for absorbing books to hook young readers. Storytellers also will find it a goldmine.

Janice Del Negro

SOURCE: A review of *The Dark-Thirty: Southern Tales of the Supernatural,* in *Booklist,* Vol. 89, No. 8, December 15, 1992, p. 738.

McKissack identifies these 10 tales as "original stories rooted in African-American history and the oral story-telling tradition." She prefaces each with a short introduction explaining the historical incident or custom from which it grew—for example, slavery, belief in a psychic ability known as "the sight," or the Montgomery, Alabama, bus boycott that began in 1955. The most successful of the stories have the structure and style of traditional folktales as well as the shiver-up-the-back feeling of "real" ghost stories. In **"Justice,"** an innocent black man lynched by the Klan comes back to haunt the man who engineered his death; the sad tale of **"The Woman in the Snow"** shows prejudice and cruelty overcome; and in the semi-autobiographical story **"The Chicken Coop Monster,"** a young girl becomes secure in the knowledge that love casts out fear. An accessible collection on a popular topic, easy to booktalk to a wide range of readers.

📖 *SOJOURNER TRUTH: "AIN'T I A WOMAN?"* (1992)

Publishers Weekly

SOURCE: A review of *Sojourner Truth: "Ain't I a Woman?"* in *Publishers Weekly,* Vol. 239, No. 48, November 2, 1992, p. 73.

This work by the authors of *A Long Hard Journey—The Story of the Pullman Porter* is a great deal more than a biography of a remarkable woman. The forceful narrative also offers a startling portrayal of a pivotal yet appalling era in American history. Born a slave in Ulster County, N.Y., in 1797, "Hardenbergh's Belle" (so named after her first owner) had been bought and sold by several masters by the time she was a teenager. In 1826, betrayed by an owner who reneged on his promise to free her if she "worked extra hard," Belle made the first of many intrepid moves, and escaped with her youngest child. After living for some time in New York City, in 1843 the deeply religious woman followed what she interpreted as a directive from God and, assuming the name of Sojourner Truth, went off "to do the Lord's work." For the rest of her long life, the indefatigable abolitionist and feminist journeyed from one state to another, delivering her impressively articulate message at anti-slavery and women's rights conventions—often to hostile, jeering audiences. The authors' meticulously researched account describes Truth's relationships with such noted figures as William Lloyd Garrison, Frederick Douglass, Harriet Beecher Stowe and Abraham Lincoln, underscoring the book's value as a chronicle of not just one, but many courageous individuals' battles against injustice.

Kirkus Reviews

SOURCE: A review of *Sojourner Truth: "Ain't I a Woman?"* in *Kirkus Reviews,* Vol. LX, No. 22, November 15, 1992, p. 1446.

Presenting the dramatic life of one of slavery's staunchest opponents, the McKissacks illuminate the most important issues of 19th-century American politics. Born a slave in upstate New York, Belle Hardenbergh struggled to survive, to create and hold together a family, and to be free. Her children grown, she answered a spiritual call to preach against slavery, using her own experiences to win over hostile audiences and choosing a new name, Sojourner Truth, to reflect her commitment. Many other leading lights joined her campaigns for the welfare of African-Americans and women. In describing the effects of her ministry, the authors clearly convey her differences of opinion with other abolitionists and fairly depict other important actors in her life—including her former master, who actually became an abolitionist. Though they don't document the thoughts and feelings they attribute to Sojourner Truth (they appear to be drawn from other biographies), these emotions and ideas do ring true. A valuable contribution, well balanced and broadminded.

Deborah Stevenson

SOURCE: A review of *Sojourner Truth: "Ain't I a Woman?"* in *Bulletin of the Center for Children's Books,* Vol. 46, No. 5, January, 1993, p. 152.

For those familiar only with Sojourner Truth's famous "Ain't I a Woman" speech, this biography is an eyeopener, describing the eventful life of a woman who took part in some of the most important movements in American history. After a brief historical note explaining the slavery laws in New York, the book follows Sojourner's life from her birth in slavery in 1797 to her troubled path to freedom, her renaming of herself, and her long career as an abolitionist and feminist. A pioneer even before her remarkable speaking career, she was one of the first black women to make successful use of the law, suing to gain possession of her son and, later, for damages against the authors of a libelous pamphlet. Although the writing is sometimes awkward or unclear ("If people had bothered to notice, there was a change in Belle"), the many quotes from Sojourner Truth herself convey her wit and eloquence (she marketed a postcard with her likeness on it, bearing the caption "I sell the shadow to support the substance"). The McKissacks supply historical context for both pro-woman and anti-slavery movements, and Sojourner Truth's life as a feminist and former slave is a unique one for following them both. Period photos, engravings, and historical documents scattered thickly through the book keep it visually lively; an index, bibliography, and brief biographies of important persons mentioned are included.

Ellen Fader

SOURCE: A review of *Sojourner Truth: "Ain't I a Woman?"* in *The Horn Book Magazine,* Vol. LXIX, No. 2, March-April, 1993, p. 221.

Born into slavery in New York in 1797, Sojourner Truth began life with the name Isabella—Belle to her parents and the other slaves. It wasn't until she endured the separation of her family, was bought and sold several times, and, after having been tricked by a man who promised her freedom in exchange for extra work, ran away with her youngest child, that Belle achieved freedom. In 1843, at the age of forty-six, she assumed the name Sojourner Truth and began the period of her life which was to bring her fame. In her travels, she brought a strident abolitionist and feminist message to many parts of the country, often facing considerable opposition while delivering her speeches. The authors do a particularly fine job relating the major incidents in Sojourner Truth's life, as well as establishing the political climate in the country at the time she lived. A final section provides brief biographical sketches of the many people Truth knew and worked with until her death in 1883, among them women's rights advocates Susan B. Anthony, Lucretia Mott, and Elizabeth Cady Stanton and abolitionists Frederick Douglass, Harriet Tubman, and William Lloyd Garrison. The photographs are well placed and used liberally to bring a sense of immediacy to the narrative. A fine contribution to the body of work about this remarkable and articulate activist.

THE ROYAL KINGDOMS OF GHANA, MALI, AND SONGHAY: LIFE IN MEDIEVAL AFRICA (1994)

Kirkus Reviews

SOURCE: A review of *The Royal Kingdoms of Ghana, Mali, and Songhay: Life in Medieval Africa,* in *Kirkus Reviews,* Vol. LXI, No. 24, December 15, 1993, p. 1593.

Calling on both contemporary travelers' accounts and songs of the griots, the McKissacks reconstruct the history of three West African empires, each of which flourished in turn, only to be nearly buried by time and scholarly prejudice. Supported by trade in gold, salt, and, later, slaves, all three enjoyed long stretches of prosperity and peace between the 6th and 18th centuries AD, practicing religious toleration and giving women enough freedom to shock visiting Muslims. Mansa Kankan Musa I of Mali (d. 1332) "governed an empire as large as all of Europe, second in size only to the territory at the time ruled by Genghis Khan in Asia." Ironically, and typically, the very location of Musa's capital is disputed today. The McKissacks shed light on the area's enduring social structures and family customs as well as its political history; they present different sides of controversies, sometimes supporting one of them (e.g., the contention that an African expedition crossed the Atlantic during Musa's reign). A final chapter, about two 19th-century slaves from West Africa, one of whom eventually returned to his homeland, probably belongs in another book, but it does help to narrow the gap between today's young readers and this glorious, obscured era in African history.

Hazel Rochman

SOURCE: A review of *The Royal Kingdoms of Ghana, Mali, and Songhay: Life in Medieval Africa,* in *Booklist,* Vol. 90, No. 10, January 15, 1994, p. 914.

This history challenges those old myths of "darkest" Africa waiting to be opened up by the "civilizing" Europeans. While parts of Europe struggled to emerge from the Dark Ages, trade and culture flourished in great cities of West Africa, where artisans crafted sumptuous gold objects and scholars attracted students to centers of learning. The history of medieval Africa, long ignored and distorted, is here given full attention. The McKissacks are careful to distinguish what is known from what is surmised; they draw on the oral tradition, eyewitness accounts, and contemporary scholarship; and chapter source notes discuss various conflicting views of events. Nor is the history all glorious: the authors are candid about widespread slavery in the old African kingdoms and about brutal conditions in the salt and gold mines that provided the wealth for the cities; they depict even great leaders such as Sundiata, the warrior-king of the Mali, as fully rounded people rather than as mythic heroes. Unfortunately, however, this is not easy reading. The facts are dramatic, but the prose is boring. Parts read like research notes, with little of the strong narrative style that distinguishes the best of the McKissacks' work.

Betsy Hearne

SOURCE: A review of *The Royal Kingdoms of Ghana, Mali, and Songhay: Life in Medieval Africa,* in *Bulletin of the Center for Children's Books,* Vol. 47, No. 6, February, 1994, p. 194.

An ambitious introductory survey, this is much needed to counter the persistent under-representation of African history in U.S. children's literature, but it has some of the problems of an encyclopedia article in trying to organize huge amounts of material under general headings such as "Ghana's Government," "Ghana's Kings," "The Military," "Ghanaian Justice," etc. In a section called "Daily Life," for instance, the text leaps from a paragraph describing family relationships among the Mande to an example of poetry that seems unrelated except for broad connections of time and place. What stands out most clearly from the names, dates, and political complexities are leaders such as Sundiata, whose stories have an unforgettable epic quality. Indeed, the authors make a point of balancing Arabic and European accounts with the oral narrative of griots, whose records they strongly credit and whom they say still function importantly in West African society today. Despite the textbook tone, this will be extremely useful as a springboard to books and articles that offer more depth but are less accessible to students. Maps, black-and-white photographs, and clearly marked sections open up the format, while a time line, notes, a bibliography, and an index will prove helpful to readers involved in researching specific topics.

Susan Giffard

SOURCE: A review of *The Royal Kingdoms of Ghana, Mali, and Songhay: Life in Medieval Africa,* in *School Library Journal,* Vol. 40, No. 6, June, 1994, pp. 140-41.

The McKissacks describe the West African civilizations that flourished between the years 700 C.E. to 1700 C.E. A chronological account is given of each successive kingdom, and there is also substantial information about the social history of Mali and Songhay, e.g., education, the treatment of women, religion, and arts and crafts. The relationship between Islam and politics, and the interplay between traditional and Islamic customs in Mali and Songhay are highlighted. The authors have attempted something unique with their inclusion of indigenous and contemporaneous historical accounts (by such historians as Leo Africanus and Ibn Battuta), as well as in their substantial use of oral history. While this makes for an interesting perspective, it prevents the line between history and mythology from being clearly drawn.

For example, in the story of Sundiata, visits from a powerful king in the magical form of an owl are not distinguished from the factual dates that Sundiata ruled Mali. This might limit the usefulness of the book to situations in which adults are able to help students think critically about the text. Adequate but uninspired photographs of ancient artifacts and modern people with traditional life styles illustrate the text. Unfortunately, the maps do not make clear the geographical relationships among the three kingdoms (they existed at different times, and in each case the territory of the earlier kingdom was wholly or partly subsumed under the later kingdom). The helpful notes discuss the validity of certain bibliographical sources. The informative time line links events in Africa to those in other parts of the world, and the bibliography is impressive. In spite of its limitations, this title will be an important addition to most collections.

AFRICAN-AMERICAN SCIENTISTS (1994)

Lois F. Anderson

SOURCE: A review of *African-American Scientists,* in *The Horn Book Guide to Children's and Young Adult Books,* Vol. V, No. 2, January-June, 1994, p. 387.

Characterized by ingenuity and determination, the African-American scientists presented in the collection made achievements in spite of the obstacles they faced as African Americans. Not only do the McKissacks provide documented, fascinating portraits of well-known figures such as Benjamin Banneker and George Washington Carver, but they also consider the remarkable contributions of persons rarely written about, including outstanding women scientists. Black-and-white photographs and artwork illustrate the text.

Doug Carmichael

SOURCE: A review of *African-American Scientists,* in *Science Books & Films,* Vol. 30, No. 9, December, 1994, p. 271.

This short book (aimed at third graders and above) superficially describes the scientific contributions of some African-American scientists. Several of these (Benjamin Banneker, George Washington Carver, and Percy Julian) are given special attention, while others are simply listed with a short summary of their achievements. The result is, at best, a glancing look that fails to reveal these scientists as real people. Reporting the degrees, honors, and major milestones of the scientists' work may be sufficient to present them as role models for young people, but the book is not likely to draw the young reader in. The usual perception of science as stuffy or inaccessible is not dispelled here. Some illustrations are uninformative, but the index is complete, and the excellent bibliography should prompt readers to explore this topic elsewhere.

The Reading Teacher

SOURCE: A review of *African-American Scientists,* in *The Reading Teacher,* Vol. 48, No. 8, May, 1995, p. 712.

Patricia and Fredrick McKissack have written a well-researched book for young children, **African-American Scientists,** that includes some very interesting and little-known information about African-American women who made outstanding contributions in science. Drawing on the work and research of sociologist Dr. W. E. B. DuBois and historian Dr. Carter Woodson, they tell about women in the medical profession from conjure women and granny doctors to Dr. Mae C. Jemison, the first African-American physician to serve as an astronaut. The McKissacks also write about Dr. Shirley Ann Jackson, the first African-American woman to earn a Ph.D. in theoretical physics from the Massachusetts Institute of Technology. Photographs accompany the text, and a bibliography of books and articles is included.

📖 BLACK DIAMOND: THE STORY OF THE NEGRO BASEBALL LEAGUES (1994)

Mary Harris Veeder

SOURCE: A review of *Black Diamond: The Story of the Negro Baseball Leagues,* in *Booklist,* Vol. 90, Nos. 19-20, June 1 & 15, 1994, p. 1795.

This book goes far beyond the few familiar photographs and names most readers associate with the Negro Baseball Leagues, and it makes the trip in style. We discover, for example, that George Washington's troops were "batting balls and running bases" and that the nineteenth-century relationship between baseball and race was more diverse than many young readers may realize. The McKissacks carefully record the differences of opinion about some events and the difficulty of finding source material. Oral histories from surviving players add startling depth to descriptions of conditions of play and travel, and Jackie Robinson's entry into major league ball becomes a richer and more complicated moment because the authors show where Robinson came from (and how) in addition to where he went. A player roster will be helpful to students, and a time line carefully weaves together the sports world and the world of lynchings, race riots, the Civil War, and the incandescent electric lamp.

Tom S. Hurlburt

SOURCE: A review of *Black Diamond: The Story of the Negro Baseball Leagues,* in *School Library Journal,* Vol. 40, No. 9, September, 1994, pp. 251-52.

Books for children about Negro League Baseball were virtually non-existent until last year when two titles on the subject were published. The McKissacks begin their presentation with a brief discussion of baseball's origins and then take a look at the early role of blacks in the sport. The main body of the text portrays the various Negro Leagues' teams, their players, organizers, and owners. Emphasis is placed on the many injustices the ballplayers faced due to segregation and prejudice. Black-and-white photographs appear throughout. Appendixes include brief player profiles and a list of league players who have been enshrined in baseball's Hall of Fame. **Black Diamond** is similar in scope to Robert Gardner and Dennis Shortelle's *Forgotten Players,* but it lacks the documentation found in that book and doesn't read quite as smoothly. Michael Cooper's *Playing America's Game,* while less in-depth, provides more of a photo-essay account of the same era. Consider **Black Diamond** for purchase where the aforementioned titles are popular.

Janet Mura

SOURCE: A review of *Black Diamond: The Story of the Negro Baseball Leagues,* in *Voice of Youth Advocates,* Vol. 17, No. 4, October, 1994, p. 233.

If you are a baseball fan and interested in the history/politics of the game this book offers an easy and breezy view. This doesn't have quite the depth as *Only the Ball Was White,* but it is informative and enjoyable. Each chapter has a catchy title: The Shutout (Introduction) on through the Winning Season. The book describes the ups and downs of the black players, teams and leagues. The late 1860s saw the first documentation of black baseball teams—records tell of a "champion of colored clubs" game in October 1867 between the Uniques of Brooklyn and the Excelsiors of Philadelphia. The first major league was formed in 1871 and by mutual consent of the white owners all black teams were rejected.

From this point to the signing of Jackie Robinson on October 23, 1945 by the Brooklyn Dodgers, blacks had to form and run their own teams and leagues. Many blacks played "south of the border" during the off-season where their color was accepted and they were able to play with and against white players. In these leagues their abilities and talents were recognized, written about in the white press (which usually ignored the black U.S. teams) and some were considered heroes. Ty Cobb, a renowned player and racist, said in 1910 he would never play with blacks after a six-game series where Havana played Detroit and Ty was unable to steal any bases and hit only .369.

After 1945, with Robinson in the major leagues, the NL and the AL started recruiting blacks. This fact began the end of the black teams and leagues. The debates over the power of early black players is on-going. Each enthusiast has his/her own ideas if they were as good as or better than the early white players and some of these arguments are given. Also included is a list of black Hall of Famers. The photos are very nice and add to the text.

📖 *CHRISTMAS IN THE BIG HOUSE,*
    CHRISTMAS IN THE QUARTERS (1994)

Carolyn Phelan

SOURCE: A review of *Christmas in the Big House, Christmas in the Quarters,* in *Booklist,* Vol. 90, No. 22, August, 1994, p. 2052.

This unusual book shows life on a Virginia plantation in 1859. Beginning after the harvest is in, the narrative describes the preparations for the Christmas season and the celebrations that follow. The differences in resources, lifestyles, and traditions between the plantation owner's family and the slaves provides a continuous contrast. Although the slaves' hardships are evident, they are not sensationalized, and the slaves' relationships with Massa and Missus in the big house are drawn with more subtlety than in many other children's books on the period. The final scenes use ironic foreshadowing: the master tells his young daughter that she'll be old enough to have her own slave in 1865, and in the quarters, a mother tells her son not to speak of running away, because she has heard rumors of freedom coming. Dramatic, full-color illustrations [by John Thompson] throughout the book offer windows on the period, showing individualized portraits of the characters at work, at rest, and at play. Some may find this a romanticized picture of slavery, but appended notes provide background information and show the authors' research on the period.

Publishers Weekly

SOURCE: A review of *Christmas in the Big House, Christmas in the Quarters,* in *Publishers Weekly,* Vol. 241, No. 38, September 19, 1994, p. 32.

On a Virginia plantation in 1859, the slaves work hard to get the Big House ready for Christmas, and to prepare their own Quarters for the "Big Times" also. As they describe the goings-on during the weeks before Christmas as well as the actual rituals of the day, the McKissacks carefully and convincingly delineate the discrepancies between the two milieus—from the physical settings to the people's differing appreciations of the holiday's riches. The contrast is startling and stirring. This is a book of significant dimension and importance, and could be read at any time of year. The authors also add riddles, rhymes, recipes and copious notes. Rendered in acrylic on board, Thompson's remarkably realistic paintings are charged with emotion and masterfully tie together the book's diverse contents.

Roger Sutton

SOURCE: A review of *Christmas in the Big House, Christmas in the Quarters,* in *Bulletin of the Center for Children's Books,* Vol. 48, No. 2, October, 1994, pp. 56-7.

It's a delicate job, eliciting the joys of Christmas and the sorrows of slavery in the same book, but, by and large, the McKissacks have managed it. Their fictionalized account of a Virginia Christmas in 1859 on the eve of the Civil War flows smoothly between the elaborate preparations in "Massa's" plantation mansion and the homelier observances in the slave quarters. While the former are more deluxe, it's the latter that have the spirit, echoed by the authors' segues from formal prose to a more relaxed phrasing: "Reckon it won't hurt to hang yo' stockings by the fire." The tensions of race and slavery are never forgotten, at least by the slaves; they show up in the ritual of the Mistress's handing out presents to the slaves ("graciously given and humbly received") and the favor returned ("humbly given and graciously received") as well as in the slaves' relief when the whole charade is finished. There's plenty of detail of the kind that kids will like: how they decorated, what kinds of gifts were exchanged, and what was eaten, including a slave recipe for sweet potato pie. Sometimes the tone is little too sweet ("Happy boys and girls skip and dance; happy voices shout and sing") and Thompson's full-page acrylic paintings are photo-realistically attractive but somewhat glamorized, with the cozy firelight of the slave cabins as welcoming as the glowing Christmas candles of the Big House. That may be the point, but the illustrations . . . uncomfortably teeter into the picturesque. The text is more balanced, ending with forebodings of war and emancipation, and explanatory notes and a comprehensive bibliography add historical legitimacy.

Lois F. Anderson

SOURCE: A review of *Christmas in the Big House, Christmas in the Quarters,* in *The Horn Book Magazine,* Vol. 71, No. 1, January-February, 1995, p. 68.

Hardly a detail is missed in this vivid description of a traditional Christmas on a Virginia plantation in 1859—the "last Yuletide celebration before the Southern Rebellion." The authors view the holiday from the perspectives of both the slaveholder and his household in the "Big House" and the slaves in the "Quarters." Rich descriptions of preparations fill the text—recipes and menus from both groups are provided—and colorful paintings reflect the antebellum period. Sprinkled throughout the book are lyrics of traditional spirituals, carols, and poetry. The joyful spirit of the holiday is prevalent; but lurking underneath the gaiety in the Big House is fearful talk of black insurrection, abolitionists, and the possibility of war, while the blacks secretly speak of emancipation rumors, Frederick Douglass, the Underground Railroad, and escape. Use of authentic language of the time helps the narrative flow, and carefully documented notes illuminate the interesting text. An extensive bibliography is included in this well-researched history of contrasting celebrations.

📖 *AFRICAN-AMERICAN INVENTORS*
(1994)

Janet Hamilton and Gregory Cote

SOURCE: A review of *African-American Inventors,* in *Appraisal: Science Books for Young People,* Vol. 27, No. 4, Fall, 1994, pp. 35-6.

LIBRARIAN [Janet Hamilton]: This is a very interesting introduction to African-American inventors that puts their history in the context of slavery. Beginning with an introduction to patents and inventions, the book moves through African-American history, from slave and free inventors to those who worked in the automotive and railroad industries to the present. Such historical events as the Dred Scott decision are described and used to place inventors in an historical context. The book is well-illustrated with photographs of the inventors and their inventions and diagrams from their patents. Unfortunately, no women are included, but otherwise this is a very good introduction to African-American invention.

SPECIALIST [Gregory Cote]: Normally, I would return a book of this nature with the comment that, since it is more history and sociology than science, it should not be considered in a review of science books. However, once I started reading it, I found it so interesting (indeed, fascinating in some places) that I felt compelled to let my opinion be known. This volume tells about African-American inventors from the early days of our history until the mid-20th century. Taken by themselves, the stories may serve as role models for young African-American students. However, this book goes far beyond just that. The authors have done an excellent job of considering the inventors and their inventions in the greater context of American history and the technology and social situations of the times. The way in which they tie together history and technology is commendable. In most instances, the transitions are smooth and the connections are clear. The book gives us a coherent history of many aspects of our technological development and of the human aspects thereof. Strictly speaking, of course, there is a difference between scientific discovery and technical invention. They are so closely tied together, however, that they cannot be easily separated. The process of innovation is much the same in either endeavor. Therein lies the connection between this book and science.

The stories give us an idea of how some people have looked beyond the limitations imposed upon them, whether they be scientific dogma or racial bias, to come up with new ways of looking at problems and finding novel answers to old questions. Although more illustrations might make the book more appealing to younger readers, this is a very minor point. I do think the publisher should be less modest in recommending the age appropriateness of the book; it should be expanded to ages 9 to 18, if not more. I'm sure many adults would find it good reading as well.

Susan Dove Lempke

SOURCE: A review of *African-American Inventors,* in *Bulletin of the Center for Children's Books,* Vol. 48, No. 3, November, 1994, pp. 94-5.

The McKissacks have done a creditable job of presenting the somewhat sparse information available on African-American inventors. In the introduction, they quote a Maryland politician who said that "not one black person [has] ever yet reached the dignity of an inventor" and contrast this with the fact that in 1900 a four-volume series had been published listing hundreds of patents granted to black inventors. This book is clearly their own attempt to set the record straight and to highlight a few of the particular inventors. They give an excellent background on patents, explaining the five different types available, and continue with a basically chronological survey. The section on inventions by slaves is of necessity the skimpiest, since the Dred Scott Decision said that black people were not citizens and therefore could not apply for patents; their work was often presented as that of their white owners. After the Civil War, a flood of patents was issued to African Americans, and the authors rush through some of these inventions very quickly, with those of black women taking only one paragraph. Other inventors are given more space: Norbert Rillieux, Jan Matzeliger, Lewis Latimer, Elijah McCoy (whose work may have inspired the phrase "The Real McCoy"), and Granville T. Woods are thoroughly discussed. A more in-depth treatment of modern inventors would have been interesting to young readers, especially those looking for inspiration, but the clear writing, clean book design, and ample black-and-white photographs and drawings make this a good choice for filling an important gap in American history collections.

Margaret M. Hagel

SOURCE: A review of *African-American Inventors,* in *School Library Journal,* Vol. 40, No. 11, November, 1994, p. 115.

An attractive, well-organized series entry. After presenting a brief history of the patent process and the law, the McKissacks provide an overview of African-American inventors throughout the 19th and 20th centuries, including those who were free born and those who were slaves. Some of their innovations, such as those connected with the railroad and automobiles, are grouped together. Individual chapters are devoted to Lewis Latimer, Granville T. Woods, and Norbert Rillieux and Jan Matzeliger. Contributions of contemporary inventors are outlined as well. Good quality black-and-white photographs and reproductions, along with the drawings that accompanied the original patent applications, appear throughout. This title fills a real need; its readable text gives information not often found in books on inventions or on U.S. history.

RED-TAIL ANGELS: THE STORY OF THE TUSKEGEE AIRMEN OF WORLD WAR II (1995)

Publishers Weekly

SOURCE: A review of *Red-Tail Angels: The Story of the Tuskegee Airmen of World War II,* in *Publishers Weekly,* Vol. 242, No. 49, December 4, 1995, p. 63.

The McKissacks add to their distinguished explorations of African-American history with a well-researched, informative look at the only all-black flying unit to serve in WW II. Established in 1941, the pilot-training program at Tuskegee, Ala., had been designed as an "experiment," without full military support to ensure its success and with many officers predicting utter failure. Despite segregated facilities at the base, hostile reactions from the locals and other demoralizing conditions, the aviators trained at Tuskegee went on to fly hundreds of missions over North Africa and Europe. They were known as Red Tails for the designs on their planes; they earned the nickname Red-Tail Angels with their reputation for staying with the bomber planes they escorted. The pilots of the 332nd division, the McKissacks point out, never lost a bomber—a record unmatched by any other group in the Army Air Force. As the McKissacks outline the history of the squadron, they also tell the larger story of racial tension and bigotry in the U.S. Numerous photos, from both military archives and individual fliers, depict the pilots and their deeds.

David A. Lindsey

SOURCE: A review of *Red-Tail Angels: The Story of the Tuskegee Airmen of World War II,* in *School Library Journal,* Vol. 42, No. 2, February, 1996, p. 119.

The prolific McKissacks have collaborated once again to produce yet another well-crafted, thoroughly researched account of a little-known facet of African-American history. *Red-Tail Angels* is much more than just the story of the black "Tuskegee Airmen" who served with distinction in segregated squadrons and bombardment and fighter groups under white commanding officers during the Second World War. The authors also present necessary background information that delineates the black experience in the military from the Revolutionary War through World War I. Readers learn that, "Despite their performance and character, black soldiers were not accepted by the military or by the civilian communities to which they returned." The narrative continues with historical information about flight in the U.S., women and blacks in aviation, and West Point cadets who faced tremendous odds in their struggle to become commissioned officers in the army. The rest of the coverage moves year-by-year from 1940-1945 with an epilogue for the years 1946-1948. It was, conclude the authors, the Tuskegee Airmen and their predecessors, who helped create more "open doors" for the black airmen and air-

women of today and the future. This attractive book has a wonderful collection of seldom-seen historical photos and an extensive bibliography of secondary and primary sources (interviews). A lively, compelling addition to any collection.

Richard Gercken

SOURCE: A review of *Red-Tail Angels: The Story of the Tuskegee Airmen of World War II,* in *Voice of Youth Advocates,* Vol. 19, No. 1, April, 1996, p. 56.

This readable book about a famous group of African-American flyers combines history and collective biography. With numerous illustrations, bibliography, index and glossaries, it makes an important moment in our history accessible to young readers in an attractive, easy-to-read format.

The 99th Fighter Squadron known as the Red-Tail Angels were black pilots trained at Tuskegee Army Air field in Alabama during World War II. The many brief biographies reveal competence, dedication and spirit, pointing up the contribution this group made to the U.S. war effort in Europe. The structure of the well-organized material and the intelligent transitions integrate the Tuskegee story into the mainstream of U.S. history, the black struggle, and the facts about blacks in the military. Young readers can learn that from the beginning of aviation history there have been women flyers, even black women flyers. Regularly citing black firsts, the text treats along the way such topics as black flying clubs, flying shows, and commercial air services. Flying became a full-fledged reality before most people had seen an automobile.

Without preaching, the book makes clear that the Red-Tail Angels, who never lost a bomber and earned 150 Distinguished Flying Crosses and Legions of Merit, did it all with the kind of constant battle against prejudice which has marked every forward step taken by African-Americans in our history.

There are glossaries of terms, of insignia and of types of aircraft. The index does not always do justice to the text. For example, it gives two page references for *sexism,* one for a page on which the word itself is used, another for a page where *sexist* appears. But several unindexed pages nearby deal with sexist issues.

While the style never exhibits the "joy and enthusiasm" with which the McKissacks claim they wrote in their authors' note, the book is authoritative and admirable in its integration of social, political, military and racial history.

[T]he book should interest not only young people who need information on this topic and era but also those who, encouraged, would read about them for fun. It is more accessible to young readers than flyer Davis, Jr.'s autobiography and is longer and fuller than the juvenile book about Davis and the Angels by Catherine Reef.

Social Education

SOURCE: A review of *Red-Tail Angels: The Story of the Tuskegee Airmen of World War II,* in *Social Education,* Vol. 61, No. 4, April-May, 1997, p. 217.

This book tells the story of how the Tuskegee airmen were able to perform as pilots during World War II—a time when racist attitudes in this country were condoned by law and by daily practices. The text does not glorify war. Rather, it discusses how members of the black community struggled to participate actively in the history of this nation by serving in the Army Air Corps. To use this book merely as a way to incorporate black experiences into U.S. history classes would be to minimalize the power of the text, which has been meticulously researched. The authors share with readers both stories which they have been able to confirm as true from multiple sources, and stories that are not as easily confirmed. They explore alternative explanations, involving both racist and non-racist factors, as to why Tuskegee Institute was chosen as the site for training black airmen. There are many opportunities throughout the text for students to examine incidents from multiple perspectives. Two of the central characters in this book are relatives of the authors, whose black architectural and construction firm, McKissack and McKissack of Nashville, Tennessee, built the Tuskegee Army Air Field. This book offers a rich field for students to discuss institutional versus individual responses to the success of the Tuskegee airmen, and whether or not the power vested in civilian officials was abused to uphold racist actions within the U.S. Army during World War II.

📖 *REBELS AGAINST SLAVERY* (1996)

Kirkus Reviews

SOURCE: A review of *Rebels against Slavery,* in *Kirkus Reviews,* Vol. LXIII, No. 23, December 1, 1995, p. 1705.

Stories of African-Americans, some slaves and some free, who fought against slavery both in the U.S. and the Caribbean, including Nat Turner, Harriet Tubman, Toussaint Louverture, and Denmark Vesey. Many of their stories have been told before, but the McKissacks perform the important service of bringing them together in one volume. The book highlights that slaves were not—as some myths hold—passive suffers awaiting freedom wrought by white abolitionists; many fought their oppressors with every available means, through minor inconveniences and full-scale revolts, taking leading roles in the abolition movement. The writing here is occasionally awkward—readers may have difficulty distinguishing among facts, opinions, and rationalization—but these are gripping tales, in a solid volume about the slavery era.

Ilene Cooper

SOURCE: A review of *Rebels against Slavery,* in *Booklist,* Vol. 92, No. 12, February 15, 1996, p. 1015.

The McKissacks present a fascinating cast: the men and women who led slave revolts in the Americas. Among those introduced are Toussaint-Louverture, a skillful general who led a revolt in Haiti; Gabriel Prosser, a Virginia slave who was inspired by Toussaint-Louverture; and Cinque, who gave captured Africans a face and a name, as well as more familiar names, such as Harriet Tubman and Nat Turner. There is also information about day-to-day resistance and alliances between African and Native Americans, especially those between runaway slaves and the Seminole tribe in Florida. Acknowledgment is given to the white people, especially the Quakers and Methodists, who helped the cause of abolition, but the McKissacks make it clear that numerous blacks, known and unknown to history, took their fate into their own hands by securing their freedom and rescuing others. The writing itself is informative, though occasionally garbled; sometimes it's hard to know to what a pronoun refers.

Carol Jones Collins

SOURCE: A review of *Rebels against Slavery,* in *School Library Journal,* Vol. 42, No. 3, March, 1996, p. 228.

The McKissacks explore slave revolts and the men and women who led them, weaving a tale of courage and defiance in the face of tremendous odds. Readers learn not only about Nat Turner and Denmark Vesey, but also about Cato, Gabriel Prosser, the maroons, and the relationship between escaped slaves and Seminole Indians. The activities of abolitionists are described as well. The authors' careful research, sensitivity, and even-handed style reveal a sad, yet inspiring story of the will to be free. Black-and-white reproductions of paintings, drawings, and documents appear throughout. A fine contribution to a growing body of literature about the African-American experience.

📖 *MA DEAR'S APRONS* (written by Patricia McKissack, 1997)

Publishers Weekly

SOURCE: A review of *Ma Dear's Aprons,* in *Publishers Weekly,* Vol. 244, No. 3, January 20, 1997, p. 401.

If Ma Dear puts on her blue apron, "the one with the long pocket across the front," then young David Earl knows it must be Monday, wash day. Tuesday's yellow apron means it's ironing day; the green apron says it's Wednesday, when the laundry gets delivered to "the rich people." And so goes the rest of the week until Sunday, a special day when Ma Dear doesn't do any work—and needs no apron at all. McKissack writes with fondness and respect about an African-American widow who takes on exhausting work in order to support her son, and the early-20th-century setting—an era that knew few household appliances—renders her story all the more poignant. Her imagery ("a wind-dried sheet that smells of peach blossoms") is as bright and crisp as the "snappy-fresh" aprons. With Ma Dear's gentle words and attentiveness to David Earl, even in the face of her obvious weariness, the author offers a lesson in strength and kindness. One caveat: the story, so polished throughout, drops off abruptly on the final page. [Floyd] Cooper's always luminescent oil washes here radiate the warmth of a loving mother-son relationship. His work abounds, too, with period details (non-electric irons, wash tubs, huge laundry baskets). A tender tale of love and sacrifice.

Maeve Visser Knoth

SOURCE: A review of *Ma Dear's Aprons,* in *The Horn Book Magazine,* Vol. 73, No. 3, May-June, 1997, p. 310.

Inspired by the life of her own great-grandmother, McKissack tells the story of a single mother and her son David Earl. The homely reminiscence is aptly illustrated with Cooper's soft oil wash paintings. David Earl's mother wears a different apron for each day of the week; the various aprons tell David Earl what work lies ahead for them. One day he accompanies his mother as she cleans house for a wealthy family; on another, they deliver freshly washed and ironed laundry to earn money for groceries. The week is filled with both work and love. The narrator describes the routine for each day, focusing on David Earl's part in it. Along with the work, the days bring small treats and plenty of time together. Ma Dear tells David stories about his father—who died in the army—and they have time to play string games and have picnics down by the creek after Sunday church services. There is little plot, but there is plenty of emotion and many details to attract a child. The love between the mother and son is palpable, and the composition and colors of the illustrations emphasize the strength of the relationship; Ma Dear leans toward or touches David Earl in each picture. Text and illustrations together create a portrait of a family working hard to survive but also finding much to be joyful about.

Janice M. Del Negro

SOURCE: A review of *Ma Dear's Aprons,* in *Bulletin of the Center for Children's Books,* Vol. 50, No. 10, June, 1997, p. 367.

In this tribute to her great-grandmother, McKissack tells the story of Ma Dear, African-American single mother and domestic worker in the turn of the century South. Her son David Earl always knows what day it is by the "clean, snappy-fresh apron Ma Dear is wearing—a different one for every day of the week." Divided into aprons and days of the week, the story follows Ma Dear as she accomplishes the jobs that support them: laundry on Monday, ironing on Tuesday, etc., until finally it reaches

Sunday, the one day there are no chores and no aprons. Interspersed with Ma Dear's back-breaking jobs are brief, warm scenes that illustrate the obvious affection between mother and son, as Ma Dear tells David Earl stories of his father, takes him to hear the music of Madam Pearlie, and saves hard-earned money for his schooling "come next year." The ending, however, is perplexingly abrupt, and readers may turn the page looking for some more obvious closure. While the compositions are uneven and the scenic renderings are generic, Cooper's oil wash paintings have a golden glow, and the close-ups of mother and son have a remarkably loving aspect.

RUN AWAY HOME (written by Patricia McKissack, 1997)

Publishers Weekly

SOURCE: A review of *Run Away Home,* in *Publishers Weekly,* Vol. 244, No. 34, August 18, 1997, p. 93.

In this intriguing historical novel, which was inspired by the author's research into her own ancestry, an African-American family in Alabama takes in an Apache runaway teenager in the late 1800s. The story centers on 12-year-old Sarah Jane Crossman, her father (a former slave turned farmer) and her part-Seminole mother. Although slavery has ended, old attitudes die hard in the South, and the three struggle daily to protect their land from prejudiced and greedy Sheriff Johnson (who relentlessly pesters them with unfair share-cropping propositions). One day they find a 15-year-old Apache named Sky in their barn, sick with a fever. They nurse him back to health and convince the authorities to release him into their care. McKissack's multi-dimensional storytelling chronicles the complex relationship between Sky, the Crossmans, the African-American community and the white community, resulting in an exciting, tension-packed page-turner. The novel's climax scene, in which Apaches, white Army soldiers, and African-American neighbors join together to defend the Crossmans' property, seems a bit Utopian for the era, but readers will cheer for Sky as he leads the defense of "his family's land" against a white supremacist group. McKissack's skillful presentation of the obstacles confronting minorities after the Civil War makes this not only a captivating tale, but a comprehensive introduction to a pivotal period in U.S. history.

Cindy Darling Codell

SOURCE: A review of *Run Away Home,* in *School Library Journal,* Vol. 43, No. 11, November, 1997, p. 122.

It's 1888 in Alabama, and Sarah Crossman, the 12-year-old daughter of a Seminole woman and a freed slave, finds herself shielding an Apache boy who has escaped federal troops during the transport of Geronimo's followers to Mount Vernon. Her mother immediately sides with her and proceeds to nurse the unconscious Sky, but her father remains opposed. Mr. Crossman has already invited attention because he owns land coveted by others, refuses to be a sharecropper, and assists other blacks in passing nearly impossible voter registration tests. He relents when George Wratten, army scout and interpreter for the Apaches, gives an unofficial consent for the boy to remain until he is well enough to travel. As Sky begins to recover, his fierce, independent demeanor lessens as he warms to the girl's parents, but Sarah doesn't like sharing their attention with someone who is so aloof from her. Other challenges arise when boll weevils destroy the cotton crop, the sheriff calls in the note of debt on the farm, and a hooded white supremacist group arrives on the scene. Based on Wratten's papers and other historical sources, as well as the oral tradition of McKissack's family, the story evolves exquisitely. Attention is even given to the debate about what is most important for the empowerment of an oppressed people: political rights or economic progress. Grabbing readers with wonderful characters, an engaging plot, and vital themes, McKissack weaves a compelling story of cultural clash, tragedy, accommodation, and ultimate triumph.

Mary M. Burns

SOURCE: A review of *Run Away Home,* in *The Horn Book Magazine,* Vol. 73, No. 6, November-December, 1997, pp. 681-82.

Although a work of fiction, this story of the young Apache who escaped from the train transporting Geronimo and his companions-in-exile from Florida to Alabama is rooted in the author's family history. The narrator is eleven-year-old Sarah Jane Crossman, who first befriends Sky when, sick and friendless, he seeks shelter in her family's barn. At first sympathetic to his plight, which she compares to that of the slaves seeking freedom, she later begins to resent the affection and approval that her parents show him. Ultimately, she learns to appreciate his strength of character, the pivotal role he plays in the family's economic survival, and the emotional support he offers to all. McKissack knows how to pace a story, create suspense, and interweave period details of the late nineteenth century into a coherent narrative. As a result, the persecution of the blacks, the conflicting attitudes toward the conciliatory approach urged by Booker T. Washington, and the sad treatment of Native Americans are all elements in a book sophisticated in content yet tuned to the understanding of a middle-school audience—no small accomplishment.

☐ *A PICTURE OF FREEDOM: THE DIARY OF CLOTEE, A SLAVE GIRL* (written by Patricia McKissack, for "Dear America" series, 1997)

Melissa Hudak

SOURCE: A review of *A Picture of Freedom: The Diary of Clotee, a Slave Girl,* in *School Library Journal,* Vol. 43, No. 9, September, 1997, p. 220.

Clotee is an orphan living on the plantation of "Mas' Henley" and "Miz Lilly." Her owners have put her to work fanning Miz Lilly and her young son William during tutoring sessions. William may not be keen to learn, but Clotee is. She has learned to read while looking over the boy's shoulder and eventually she teaches herself how to write. She practices her new-found skills by writing in a makeshift, secret diary, which is found by William's new tutor. Luckily, he turns out to be an abolitionist. Through his work, Clotee helps some of her friends escape to the North, but she herself chooses to stay behind on the plantation as a conductor on the Underground Railroad. Clotee is such a vibrant, fully rounded character that it is almost painful to think of her left on the plantation while her friends and fellow slaves go to freedom. McKissack brings Clotee alive through touching and sobering details of slave life, told in such a matter-of-fact way that their often brutal nature is made abundantly clear. However, this is in no way a depressing book. In fact, it is an inspiring look at a young girl coming of age in terrible circumstances who manages to live life to the fullest.

☐ *YOUNG, BLACK, AND DETERMINED: A BIOGRAPHY OF LORRAINE HANSBERRY* (1998)

Anne O'Malley

SOURCE: A review of *Young, Black, and Determined: A Biography of Lorraine Hansberry,* in *Booklist,* Vol. 94, No. 12, February 15, 1998, p. 995.

Hansberry once noted that she was sent to kindergarten on Chicago's South Side too well dressed for the Depression years. "The kids beat me up; and I think it was from that moment I became a rebel." The youngest child of successful, politically involved parents who encouraged their children to succeed, Hansberry grew up in a spirited, intellectual atmosphere in which the likes of Paul Robeson, Langston Hughes, Jesse Owens, and others were entertained in her home. From an early age, she was aware of the tensions of racism that divided American society. Her father was party to a major Supreme Court case, *Hansberry v. Lee,* which invalidated a racially restrictive housing covenant. She studied briefly at the University of Wisconsin but left for the livelier confines of New York City in the early 1950s, where she wrote for *Freedom,* a monthly commentary founded by Robeson. She married Robert Nemiroff and began to write the play that became *A Raisin in the Sun,* and that work, of course, went on to make dramatic history. The McKissacks' biography sparkles with the energy and passion that characterize their subject. Readers can drink in the whole civil rights history of much of this century and an in-depth treatment of Hansberry's major play, along with her fascinating life, which cancer ended prematurely in 1965. The playwright's sister, Mamie, provides abundant material for this highly recommended biography.

Kirkus Reviews

SOURCE: A review of *Young, Black, and Determined: A Biography of Lorraine Hansberry,* in *Kirkus Reviews,* Vol. LXVI, No. 4, February 15, 1998, p. 271.

A playwright who is well known to readers through *A Raisin in the Sun* is given fair tribute by the McKissacks, who also provide a window into the times in which Hansberry lived.

Born in 1930, the fourth child of a prosperous family living on Chicago's South Side, Hansberry played childhood games and reported mixed views about her role as baby of the family. The McKissacks make clear, however, that from Hansberry's earliest days, her parents were raising her to "advance the cause of African-American equality through intelligent and articulate leadership." She grew up "listening to NAACP lawyers planning legal strategies in her living room"; surrounded by influential adults, she learned to express herself, seeking comfort in the aftermath of the bombing of Pearl Harbor by writing about "clouds, flowers, and music." After college graduation and marriage to Robert Nemiroff, she took up residence in Greenwich Village, New York City, where a windfall from her songwriter-husband's efforts allowed her to concentrate on her writing. Her death at age 34 comes through as a decisive loss to the American theatre; the authors cull from her short, high-impact life a thorough, very readable, work.

Marilyn Heath

SOURCE: A review of *Young, Black, and Determined: A Biography of Lorraine Hansberry,* in *School Library Journal,* Vol. 44, No. 4, April, 1998, pp. 148-49.

This well-written biography brings its subject to life by successfully capturing that unique spark that makes Hansberry noteworthy and interesting. Writing in an engaging style, the McKissacks follow the woman's life chronologically. The daughter of influential, black upper-class parents, her early childhood in Chicago was studded with visits from African-American notables, such as W. E. B. DuBois, Langston Hughes, Jesse Owens, and Duke Ellington. However, from an early age, she identified with those of her race who suffered the effects of poverty and discrimination. After she left college prematurely, she moved to New York where her writing career began in earnest. Throughout her life she was dedicated to the cause of civil rights and made her unique mark as a writer, a speaker, and an activist. This biography is divided into three long chapters, each covering a specific period of Hansberry's life. The text has been researched extensively and is well documented. It includes several references to telephone interviews with Hansberry's older sister Mamie and excerpts from the playwright's personal journal. The black-and-white photographs are well reproduced and do a fine job of supplementing the text. A time line and index are helpful reference aids. Whatever their purpose for using this volume, readers will find it lively and engaging.

MESSY BESSEY'S SCHOOL DESK (1998)

Sharon R. Pearce

SOURCE: A review of *Messy Bessey's School Desk,* in *School Library Journal,* Vol. 44, No. 8, August, 1998, p. 144.

Another "Messy Bessey" story, this title covers a familiar topic in a friendly way. After assessing the condition of her own desk, Bessey cleans out the useless things. She then helps her classmates to straighten their desks as well. In the end, her leadership is recognized and she is elected class president. Although the impending election is not specifically mentioned in the text, posters for it are shown in the full-page, cartoon illustrations [by Dana Regan]. The limited sentence structure and vocabulary do not diminish the authors' ability to tell a good story. In addition, readers see a strong African-American character who is recognized for her organizational and communication skills. A winning selection.

LET MY PEOPLE GO: BIBLE STORIES TOLD BY A FREEMAN OF COLOR TO HIS DAUGHTER, CHARLOTTE, IN CHARLESTON, SOUTH CAROLINA, 1806-16 (1998)

Janice M. Del Negro

SOURCE: A review of *Let My People Go: Bible Stories Told by a Freeman of Color to His Daughter, Charlotte, in Charleston, South Carolina, 1806-16,* in *Bulletin of the Center for Children's Books,* Vol. 52, No. 4, December, 1998, pp. 137-38.

Charlotte Jeffries Coleman, a fictional African-American abolitionist, writes of the Bible stories her father told her when she was a child in South Carolina. Incidents in the young Charlotte's life—the death of one young slave, the escape of another, the story of her parents' courtship—all are catalysts for Price Jeffries' retelling of a familiar Old Testament Bible story to the young Charlotte in order to enlighten her about both the injustices and the beauty she sees around her. The incidents that set up the Bible stories (Cain and Abel, Moses and the Exodus, Ruth and Naomi, etc.) are deliberately constructed as thematic mirrors and they at first seem cumbersome, but the relationship between Charlotte and her father overcomes the somewhat programmatic quality of the frame. Simply stated, the retellings of the Bible stories shine. Price Jeffries' language rolls with a surprising, fierce splendor that embodies the solid faith he passes on to his daughter. The spot art for each title heading is graceful and delicate, and the full and half page paintings reflect and amplify the text. If occasionally the drafting of the figures and the articulation of their expressions is a bit awkward, the sweep of the illustrations overall is still dramatic. The McKissacks include notes on each incident in the fictional Charlotte's life, relating it to the historical events or persons that inspired it; there is a bibliography for both the opening stories and the Bible stories. This is an unusual combination of history, commentary, and Bible story that will lend itself to a wide variety of uses within curriculums and collections.

Additional coverage of the McKissacks' lives and careers is contained in the following sources published by The Gale Group: *Contemporary Authors,* Vols. 118, 120; *Contemporary Authors New Revision Series,* Vols. 38, 49; *Contemporary Literary Criticism,* Vol. 23; *Junior DISCovering Authors; Major Authors and Illustrators for Children and Young Adults;* **and** *Something about the Author,* Vol. 73.

Cornelia Lynde Meigs

1884-1973

(Also wrote as Adair Aldon) American author of fiction, nonfiction, and plays.

Major works include *The Trade Wind* (1927), *Clearing Weather* (1928), *Swift Rivers* (1932), *Invincible Louisa: The Story of the Author of "Little Women"* (1933), *Jane Addams: Pioneer for Social Justice: A Biography* (1970).

INTRODUCTION

Although Meigs has written over forty works of historical fiction, mystery, drama, and biography for primary graders and young adults, she is best known to contemporary readers as the author of *Invincible Louisa: The Story of the Author of "Little Women,"* and as the editor of *A Critical History of Children's Literature*, a critical retrospective of literary works for children. Considered to be the best biography of Louisa May Alcott ever written for youth, *Invincible Louisa* has been praised by reviewers for its meticulous research and factual accuracy, and lauded as a highly entertaining and pleasurable story. Combining her enthusiasm for history, her interest in Alcott, and her astute scholarship, Meigs fashioned a children's literary classic that has remained popular and in print for generations. In a similar vein, *A Critical History of Children's Literature*, published in 1953 and updated in 1969 to correct minor factual errors, has been regarded as a required reference for anyone who is interested in children's literature. Edited by Meigs and combining the work of three other established authorities on books for children—Anne Thaxter Eaton, Elizabeth Nesbitt, and Ruth Hill Viguers—*A Critical History of Children's Literature* traces children's literature from early folk and fairy tales and nursery rhymes, through primers and tracts, up to the Golden Age. As a critical compendium, the work has never been matched.

Meigs's historical fiction, though initially well-received, is not as well-known to contemporary readers. Written during the early twentieth century when children's literature was first coming into its own as a recognized genre, Meigs's historical works such as *The Trade Wind* and *Clearing Weather* have been praised for their accuracy, detail, strong themes, and evocation of the conditions of the period. They typically feature exciting plots, life-like historical backgrounds, and wholesome themes such as reverence for land and home, pride, responsibility, and awareness of the interdependence of humanity and nature. Examining the development of the United States, these books typically take place during the early seventeenth through mid-nineteenth centuries in New England, the mid-Atlantic states, the Midwest, and on

the seas. Meigs's protagonists are typically children and teenagers who face extraordinary difficulties and conflicts—walking across hundreds of miles of uninhabited territory, rafting timber down the Mississippi River, surviving harsh weather, creating a homestead, and making friends with enemies. Solving their problems with moral courage, hard work, and ingenuity, Meigs's characters often serve as inspirations to young readers. Historic figures such as Nathan Hale, William Penn, and Benjamin Franklin often appear in these stories to offer words of wisdom and lend both physical and moral support. While Meigs is occasionally criticized for her lack of character development, reviewers have generally described her writing as clear and fluid, her adventures exciting, and her historic settings well-researched and impeccable.

Meigs believed that children should have access to interesting books written for their understanding, yet without condescension. This philosophy is evident in the books she produced, as well as in the way she produced them, welcoming the opinions and advice of young relatives and students. She was, moreover, a true scholar who balanced quality writing with historical accuracy. Meigs once told *Something about the Author*, "I came to realize, in those years just before the First World War, how few good books were being published for children. As time went on and I went more fully into writing, I began to understand that I was at the beginning of a great movement to recognize and remedy that lack. . . . I went forward on the wave of that exciting development, finding that teaching and writing went well together and that the American history that I was interested in gave me endless material for stories."

Biographical Information

The fourth of five daughters, Meigs was born and raised in Keokuk, Iowa, where her father, a civil engineer, worked to improve navigation on the Mississippi River. After her mother died, seven-year-old Meigs was raised by her father and older sisters, to whom she was devoted. Meigs came from a family of storytellers. With navy and army officers in her father's family and frontierspeople in her mother's family history, tales of romantic adventure and the thrill of history were familiar in the Meigs household. Meigs often listened to her father's stories about seamen, pioneers in the Midwest, the War of 1812, and the Civil War; one of her older sisters also told her many tales learned from their mother, and Cornelia did the same for her younger siblings. She especially loved stories about adventures at sea. While growing up, she spent time in New England, where both sides of her family originated, and gained great affection for the people and the region.

In 1908 Meigs received a bachelor of arts degree from Bryn Mawr College and went on to teach English at a boarding school in Iowa. She loved to tell stories to the younger students, and learned much from their reactions. Experimenting with different kinds of tales led to the writing of her first book, *The Kingdom of the Winding Road* (1915). She continued to write, and produced at least one book almost every year, with the exception of the World War II years. In 1932 she took a position as instructor of English composition and creative writing at Bryn Mawr College, eventually attaining the status of professor emeritus. Although Meigs never married, choosing instead to keep house for her father, her home was continually filled with nieces and nephews to whom she gave much credit for the success of her stories. "There are twelve of them," Doris Patee once wrote, "and some have lived with her since they were children. (She says they used to sit by the typewriter and watch the story come out, and tell her very frankly what they thought of it.)" Meigs keenly felt the need for quality books for children, and was pleased to be a part of the upsurge of literature written expressly for them. She wrote a steady succession of children's stories and, after the publication of her first book, she never stopped writing. Her last two books, *Jane Addams: Pioneer for Social Justice* and *Louisa May Alcott and the American Family Story* (1970), were published three years before her death in 1973 at the age of 89.

Major Works

Meigs's fiction is noted for its settings and historical relevance, beginning with the publication of *The Trade Wind*. Although Meigs's earlier publication, *Rain on the Roof* (1925), takes place in historic New Bedford, Massachussets, it primarily contains stories similar to those Meigs had been told as a child. *The Trade Wind*, an original tale set in the United States just prior to the Revolutionary War, recounts the conditions of the era. Eighteen-year-old David Dennison, dreaming of adventure, stows away aboard the schooner *Santa Maria* with his father's old shipmate, who is charged with a secret mission against the British. The two men engage in many escapades and misfortunes as they follow the path of the trade winds, exchanging flour, rum, and tobacco for Eastern goods. They encounter pirates, smugglers, the British navy, and natives, until at last they return to the New England coast. Jacqueline Overton noted: "Here is excellent writing—the description of the British man-of-war 'Pegasus' that passes close by them under full rig 'sails away with David's heart,' and the reader's too." Admiring Meigs's penchant for adventure tales, a critic for *The Saturday Review of Literature* acknowledged, "The period is fascinating: life on the ocean never held more circumstantial picturesqueness than in the pirate-chasing, buccaneering, revenue-running days directly before the Revolution. There is no dull adventure in this book . . . no verbiage, no bunk, and the characters are solidly executed."

After a sojourn to mid-nineteenth-century America in *As the Crow Flies* (1927), Meigs returned to colonial times in *Clearing Weather*. In this book, Meigs examines the aftermath of the Revolutionary War: its poverty, unemployment, and devastation, as well as the influx of trade and commerce. Readers witness the design, building, launching, and first voyage of the *Jocasta*, which after many escapades on the high seas, returns to home port. Dudley C. Lunt commented, "[Meigs] has cultivated to a high degree the art of spinning a yarn well-spiced with excitement and intrigue," while Dudley Nichols remarked that "Miss Meigs can tell a story and no boy will lay down the book once he sets his teeth in it."

Swift Rivers revisits the American Midwest in 1835 at the time of the Louisiana Purchase. Meigs's story begins on the Goose Wing River in Minnesota, the home of young Chris Dahlberg, grandson of an old Swedish pioneer. To save his farm, Chris harvests timber from his land and, during the spring floods, rafts it down the Mississippi River to the lumber market in St. Louis. As readers follow Chris down the Mississippi, they experience the beauty and power of the river's currents and embark on adventures with the pilots and other rafters Chris meets on his journey. Ann Thaxter Eaton remarked that *Swift Rivers* is "[a] book that has poetry and out-of-doors in it, and a background typical of this country, as well as daring and adventurous deeds that any boy and girl will enjoy." Writing in *Scribner's Magazine*, Bertha A. Mahony praised *Swift Rivers* as a "story so truly American and so perfect a piece of writing that if it does not win the one established laurel wreath, a special garland should be made for it."

Published during the year-long commemorative celebration of Louisa May Alcott's one-hundredth birthday, *Invincible Louisa* is Meigs's most popular and acclaimed book. With its clear, straightforward prose and its fine photographs and portraits of Alcott's contemporaries, such as Ralph Waldo Emerson and Nathaniel Hawthorne, *Invincible Louisa* is considered a definitive biography of Louisa May Alcott and the best work for young readers about Alcott's life. A 1934 Newbery Medal winner, the biography follows Alcott's life in great detail from birth to death, showing great compassion for her family relationships and the many obstacles, including her own skepticism, she had to overcome to complete and publish her work. Praised for avoiding fictionalization, speculation, and stilted dialogue—common flaws in biographical works of Meigs's time—*Invincible Louisa* has become a classic children's biography.

Over twenty-five years later, Meigs wrote a similar biography of Jane Addams, America's first social worker. *Jane Addams: Pioneer for Social Justice* primarily relates the story of Hull House, yet also includes accounts of Addams's struggles over such issues as child labor, building inspections, and the health and welfare of the poor. It further touches on Addams's travels to Washington and Europe in support of peace and international cooperation. Cecelia Zelman recognized *Jane Addams* as ". . . a very good source of information for students researching the period of rising industrialism—its evils and its reformers."

Awards

The Trade Wind received the Beacon Hill Bookshelf Prize in 1927. Three of Meigs's books were named Newbery Honor Books by the American Library Association: *Windy Hill* in 1922, *Clearing Weather* in 1929, and *Swift Rivers* in 1933. *Invincible Louisa* received the Newbery Medal in 1934, as well as the Lewis Carroll Shelf Award in 1963. In 1943, *Mounted Messenger* received the Spring Book Festival middle honor. In 1971, Meigs received the Jane Addams Award for *Jane Addams: Pioneer for Social Justice*.

AUTHOR'S COMMENTARY

Cornelia Meigs

SOURCE: "Acceptance Paper," in *Newbery Medal Books: 1922-1955*, The Horn Book, Inc., 1955, pp. 122-24.

[The following is Cornelia Meigs's acceptance speech for the 1934 John Newbery Medal for Invincible Louisa: The Story of the Author of "Little Women."*]*

It is with the greatest and most complete appreciation that I have heard all the kind things said of *Invincible Louisa* and that I receive this very high honor at the hands of the American Library Association. I say complete appreciation, for I have long understood how fully librarians know about books and whether or not they are fulfilling their real purpose. Library work does not allow the cherishing of many illusions or the survival of false values. Writers, publishers and general critics have little opportunity to see what the librarian can observe constantly at close hand, namely the actual impact upon the mind it was intended to reach. It is in that impact, I think, in the question of how long and how deeply it touches its reader, that the worth of a book really lies. For this reason I believe that librarians become very wise indeed concerning the human values of what has been written and what is being written today.

Mark Twain has defined a classic as something which everybody praises—and doesn't read. It is thanks to the librarians that we now have a distinction between the classics to which that definition applies and those to which it does not; between, say, *Rasselas, Prince of Abyssinia,* which once was put forward as improving reading for the young, and *Treasure Island.* Further, when certain of their number undertake constructive criticism, like the work of Miss Moore and Miss Jordan, and many others whose writing happens to be less familiar to me, they speak from a very deep experience, and have that to say which makes for the building up of all writing. Therefore, it is a singularly happy event to any one when such commendation as theirs falls upon the fruit of his or her own toil, when they see in it what she, faintly and remotely, hoped to put there.

Also it is a pleasure to me to have this occasion for offering public thanks for the kind of help which librarians always afford to writers in process of producing a book. It is something we all grow to expect, not from one or two friendly souls, but from all librarians alike. Their good will and cordiality and enthusiastic cooperation are so universal that one begins to think of them as interchangeable parts of a great and kindly system. I have lived most of my life in a small town where library service is informal and very complete, and the general public knows enough to make the most of it. It has been known to happen that someone will call up the head librarian in great haste and ask her to look up a good recipe for gingerbread, because there is company coming for supper and Mother's old recipe has been mislaid. As a householder, I have not made just this use of the library, but as a writer, I, and those like me, have certainly done so. We develop passionate desires to know whom the second wife of Governor John Jones married after she became a widow, and how many horses it takes to draw a Conestoga wagon, and how tall was Henry the Eighth. The librarians retire into some lair of information of their own and always come out with a volume containing the right answer. Nor do they inquire why we ask so many foolish questions, as they must surely be tempted to do.

It is my feeling that this is a specially happy and important presentation of the Newbery Medal. It is because the laurels, this time, do not all go to one person, but are shared. I am deeply sensible of what this honor means to me, but no one sees more clearly than myself, how large a share Louisa Alcott had in making the book which you have commended, just as it was the essence of Miss Alcott herself who made *Little Women.* It has been a most congenial task to put down the record of that heroic spirit, but it was the spirit, and not the putting down, which has given the book many of the qualities which you see in it. From the time I was first able to read freely to myself, I have loved the volume of *Louisa Alcott's Life, Letters and Journals,* and I have read it over and over again through my growing years. There have been times in my life, as there are in every life, when difficulties and perplexities seemed almost too many to face. At such moments I have deliberately got down the *Letters and Journals* and read a page or two, for the stimulation of courage which such reading never fails to bring. Such courage as hers, which was a compound of a naturally bold and intrepid spirit with a very sensible philosophy of life and an unswerving belief in the goodness of God, makes an unforgettable contribution to man's knowledge of how to live.

Her life, and what she accomplished in it, was worthy of every possible reward. She got money for what she did, for which she cared very little except as a measure of what she could do for her beloved family. She got fame, for which she cared very much less than nothing. But of literary honors, such as we think of them today, she did not have very many. In her era there was no generous Mr. Melcher with his scheme for stimulating and encouraging workers in the field of junior letters. But it is one of the pleasant things of life that what cannot be done at one time can still be done at another. So it seems to me, and I take delight in its so seeming, that what you have done today is, in effect, to bestow the Newbery Award upon Louisa Alcott. She has deserved it for a very long time. I think my publishers cannot object to this division of the honors, for we are both, as it were, daughters of the same house. If I could stretch my voice across the years, I would say, "Louisa, this medal is yours," and I do assure you that Louisa and I both thank you from the bottom of our hearts.

TITLE COMMENTARY

📖 *THE KINGDOM OF THE WINDING ROAD* (1915)

The Spectator

SOURCE: A review of *The Kingdom of the Winding Road,* in *The Spectator,* Vol. 115, December 18, 1915, pp. 881-82.

Every year brings us some good modern fairy-tales, and *The Kingdom of the Winding Road,* by Miss Cornelia Meigs, is worthy of a place in this pleasant company. These stories are quiet, we might even say pensive, in tone, and form a strong contrast to those of the roistering Jacks and Giants. . . . Here character is of more importance than strength, and the monsters to be overcome are spiritual rather than material. The stories are hung on the ribbon of the winding road which runs through all the kingdoms of this Fairyland, and on it wanders a beggar happily playing on a silver flute, who is the good genius of the princes and people of the land. "'The winding road is my kingdom,' he said, 'and is the way I shall follow always. . . . You can offer me no wealth nor honours that will tempt me from my narrow realm, that stretches out and away across the world, and brings me adventures at every turn.'" The pictures, black-and-white and coloured, are by Frances White. The landscapes about the winding road are attractive, and carry us back in fancy to those castle-crowned hilltops or mountain streams and villages that may be seen out of a train window, but of which we never know more, however much we resolve some day to stop and explore them.

The Bookman

SOURCE: A review of *The Kingdom of the Winding Road,* in *The Bookman,* Vol. L, No. 295, April, 1916, p. 26.

The perfect parable appeals by its story to the child that lives in every man's heart, while its moral touches the man already present in the waking conscience of the child. If Miss Meigs, in this collection of twelve stories, does not attain to the level of the great masters, she follows closely in their footsteps. The scene of her book is laid in *The Kingdom of the Winding Road,* whose lord, though he appears in every story in the guise of a beggar, lame and poorly clad, is possessed of very marvellous powers and great wisdom. All who travel through the kingdom, fall in with him at some time or another, and those who are wise enough to take his advice and march to the music of his slender silver pipe meet with the most exciting and wonderful adventures out of which they come laden with spoil of many sorts. Miss Meigs knows the geography of the Kingdom intimately and is at home in such places as Twopenny Town, the Palace of Bubbles, and the Garden of Tears and Smiles, and other equally famous and interesting places. The style is terse and restrained. Miss White's illustrations are quaint and good. Altogether a delightful book, somewhat out of the common run.

📖 *THE STEADFAST PRINCESS* (1916)

The Booklist

SOURCE: A review of *The Steadfast Princess,* in *The Booklist,* Vol. 12, No. 8, May, 1916, p. 389.

A play for young people, simple in spirit and often poetic, above the average in idea, treatment and style. Tells the story of a little princess, who is discovered helping a toymaker in his shop and who is brought to her kingdom, where she finds it a difficult task to remain true to her ideals and her people's best interests. Won the prize in a contest conducted by the Drama League of America.

THE NEW MOON (1924)

Anne Carroll Moore

SOURCE: "The New Children's Books," in *The Bookman,* Vol. LX, No. 2, October, 1924, pp. 162-69.

A romantic story of American pioneering is told by Cornelia Meigs in *The New Moon.* You are held in Ireland by the first four chapters of the book, and then you cross in a sailing vessel with a flock of sheep, and land in Philadelphia. "We will cross the state of Pennsylvania which is bigger than Ireland and as green," says Thomas Garrity. "It might seem a tedious journey to walk at a sheep's pace across the whole state of Pennsylvania," says the author; but no more than the boy who came over with Thomas Garrity do we find it tedious to follow beyond the Mississippi, for there is beauty and authenticity on every page, and a light that does not shine on many stories drawn from American history. Miss Meigs has pioneered in a field of writing which holds rich possibilities for the historically minded who have the artist's sense of values in the selection and blending of their material.

The Saturday Review of Literature

SOURCE: A review of *The New Moon,* in *The Saturday Review of Literature,* Vol. I, No. 20, December 13, 1924, p. 385.

His youthful brain filled with wild, sweet tales of The Little People, and a silver sixpence for good luck in his pocket, motherless Dick Martin emigrated from Ireland. A new moon foretokened luck. Apprenticed to Garrity, a sheep raiser, and accompanied by his collie, Dick reaches America.

Garrity seeks the Iowa lands for his sheep, and on the toilsome journey discovers the invaluable services of the dog and his young master. They settle beyond the Mississippi, not far from an Indian village. Dick becomes fast friends with Mateo, an Indian boy of his own age. This cements an everlasting friendship with the tribe.

Striking examples illustrate Dick's bravery and loyalty through pioneer hardships and thrilling dangers. A wholesome story, interesting and inspiring.

RAIN ON THE ROOF (1925)

Alice M. Jordan

SOURCE: "A Few Children's Books," in *The Independent,* Vol. 115, No. 3937, November 14, 1925, p. 560.

Cornelia Meigs's chosen field is American history, but in her new book she has gone outside of America to include related episodes from the European past. *Rain on the Roof* does not reach the high level of *The New Moon,* which she published last year, but it does show Miss Meigs's power to discern forgotten and romantic elements in the lives of everyday people and little towns. It is filled, too, with reflections of her love for our great ship-building past; her feeling for the graceful lines of the old clippers and for the happiness and serenity that comes with the fashioning of beautiful ship models. The story centers in an old New England seaport. John Selwyn, the crippled maker of ship models, is a rare story-teller and shares with a young audience of three the tales he has dug out of neglected town annals and dull-looking sheepskin volumes. A story of his own invention is that of the possible first book for children—made at the monastery of Saint Martin by understanding Brother Nicholas for Jehan and Yvette. There is mystery, too, in the book and a brave adventure connected with the launching of the model of the *Great Michael.* Altogether, this is a book of substance and charm.

The Saturday Review of Literature

SOURCE: A review of *Rain on the Roof,* in *The Saturday Review of Literature,* Vol. II, No. 18, November 28, 1925, p. 353.

Rain on the Roof, besides having one of the most delectable titles in the world, is one of those rarely encountered juveniles that does not seem to be written down to children. The author takes it for granted that they will enjoy atmosphere as well as action, and the result is a book to delight both boys and girls, particularly those in the difficult stage between fairy tales and fiction. From the very first chapter, in which a boy finds shelter in an old house at the edge of a New England harbor and there listens to old tales told by a remarkable story teller and maker of ships to the accompaniment of rain on the shingles outside, there is enchantment. People out of the past wander through the stories—Mary, Queen of Scots and a loyal Scotch sailor lad; Brother Nicolas and his Monastery; Pilgrims in the East; and Indians of the Western Plains. But this is not all, there are strange adventures and dark doings in the old seaport town; doings in which the three children who have listened to the story teller in the little attic room, have important parts to play. We feel sure this volume will need constant rebinding when it takes its place in the children's room of the public library.

Leonore St. John Power

SOURCE: A review of *Rain on the Roof,* in *New York Herald Tribune Books,* November 29, 1925, p. 6.

Not while Cornelia Meigs can grasp a pencil is she going to allow her heroes to be without adventure, "tethered like a goat," to use her own expression, for the tame prospects of boys who come from herding sheep in the wild highlands of Scotland to tending geese on the countryside. As the rain pours down on the quaint old roof which covers the attic room where Mr. John fashions ship models and tells stories out of the old romances that line his book shelves, one feels that the author is herself chock full of the spirit that sent heroes out into the world. That she has a generous gift in weaving romances out of bits of history and creating characters to act out the stories is evident in her earlier volumes, *Master Simon's Garden* and *The New Moon.*

In *Rain on the Roof* the atmosphere of an old New England town with streets that skirt the harbor, wharves, yachts and fishing schooners sets the stage for a number of stories held together by the characters—the boy Christopher, a summer visitor; Phyllis, of the "big house"; Peter Timmy, possessed of freckles, red hair and a lively spirit; old Mrs. Corydon, and John Selwyn, host to all those who climb the stairs to his attic. The children are all young; the stories are not. They tell of cavaliers who fought on Scottish ground and of heroes who came to the New World, of Peter's grandfather, crotchety Mr. Toby, of the Duke of Gloucester's men, of Indians, ships and sailor men. There is perhaps in Miss Meigs's work a carefulness of style, a refinement and prescience that a little dims the vigor of the stirring events and makes her a romancer for girls rather than for boys.

Marcia Dalphin

SOURCE: "Christmas Cargoes by Reindeer, Ltd.," in *The Bookman,* Vol. LXII, No. 4, December, 1925, pp. 457-63.

Stories of distinction are hard to come by, but Cornelia Meigs's *Rain on the Roof* has all the literary quality that we have learned to expect from this author, and is a good story as well. The scene is laid in a seaport town in New England. There is an element of mystery in it, and a villain, and there is also a particularly fascinating workshop where ship models are all about underfoot, in process of being built or painted or rigged, and stories at large are being told by the nice man who makes them. There are at least three excellent short stories told within the long story, one of mediæval times, one of Scotland in the days when Queen Mary was a little girl, and one of the Pilgrims at Plymouth.

📖 *THE TRADE WIND* (1927)

Dudley C. Lunt

SOURCE: A review of *The Trade Wind,* in *New York Herald Tribune Books,* September 4, 1927, p. 8.

The enterprise, adventure, and dangers that marked the rise of the maritime glory of the American colonies and nation form a splendid field for tales for boys. Trade was the pursuit that solidified the front of the thirteen colonies, widely separated in their geographical aspects, their points of view and their interests.

As the resources of the West called to the men of the East they forsook their ships and the carrying trade slowly died away. However, in the early months of 1917 the shipyards on the Atlantic Coast awoke from a century of slumber and for a few fleeting years the American flag again was seen on the seven seas.

One wonders if this awakening prompted the writing of *The Trade Wind.*

If you like a good story, well spiced with exciting adventures, you will find it in this book by Cornelia Meigs. Although the author experiences some difficulty in getting her tale under way, before one is wholly aware of it, David Dennison has shipped as supercargo on the Santa Maria and has shoved off on a long cruise. David goes forth a youth of eighteen and returns a man. On this cruise there ensues, in swift succession, an escape from a British brig; a stop at Half Moon Island, where dwells old Adam Applegate, pirate, sorcerer and patriot, all rolled into one; an unsuccessful attempt to discharge their cargo in the West Indian ports; an attack on the ship by Carib Indians; cruising in the paths of trade from all quarters of the globe, and Yankee bartering with the crafts they bespeak; a visit to Mediterranean ports; encounters with Algerine pirates, and, finally, picking up in a most astounding manner—but that is the high point in the tale.

David does not want for good, hearty companions. There is Andrew Bardwell, kindly yet stern, in command; Master James Babcock, a spirited and adventurous gentleman; Anthony Churchill, divinity student and patriot. There is also a fine girl in the book, Janet Harris, who accepts the news of David's going away without clamor and "simply, as became a sensible girl."

To the writing of this book the author has brought more than the tools of superior workmanship. She has given to it the creative results of a long and honorable tradition of the sea of which she is the fortunate possessor. This tradition took its rise in her great-great-grandfather, Commodore John Rodgers, onetime commander of the U. S. S. Constitution, a man who participated in the revolt, sailed on such cruises and touched at the ports which she has described. It has been perpetuated by son after son of the same name until it was terminated within our own day by the untimely death of Commander John Rodgers, the naval flyer.

As a result there lives again in the pages of **The Trade Wind** the glamour of the carrying trade that once was ours. It was this traffic that kept the hammers ringing in the shipyards and gave rise to that swift swallow of the sea, the American clipper ship, that carried forth for barter with the world the produce of an incipient nation—lumber, tobacco, dried fish, flour and "sparm"—and that made familiar in the ports of the Indies, West and East, in the Levant and in the maritime centers of Europe the figure of a bronzed and clear-eyed fellow, the American sailor.

Furthermore, the author's work bespeaks familiarity with ships and ports. Her pictures are not obscured by the technical detail that so often mars a story of the sea. The reader is left with striking conceptions of Yankee schooners, the brigs, frigates and ships of the line of the Royal Navy, the Dutch East Indiaman, the high-pooped ships of Spain and the feluccas of the Barbary pirates that festered about the Anna Maria "like a flock of black bats." As Ben Turner, an old sailor, says to David, "You can read a nation's history in the build and rigging of her ships."

A waterfront is a fringe of the human pattern where men and men's manners mix in strange and varied hues. It is a fortunate person who can evaluate the peculiar individuality of a port. In **The Trade Wind** you may tread the ennobled quays of Kingston beneath a tropical sun and witness the melange of squalor and color that characterizes a West Indian port.

Miss Meigs's work is characterized by some fine bits of descriptive writing. A single instance suffices:

> He stood in the bow of the Anna Maria and watched, with agony in his eyes, how the mighty ships careened slowly, then, with a rush and a roar, went down. Her stern dropped first and her bow rose high, with the great horse rearing far aloft, spreading his broad wings in the semblance of a last wild defiance of that towering, white-capped wave which was reaching up for him. David had to look away, as in a final plunge the flying horse went under and was drowned forever in a smother of green water and white foam.

The format of this book deserves comment. It is a pleasure to review a book which lends itself so readily to enjoyable reading as does this one. The type is clear and well spaced on the page. Although the volume has been bound for permanency, yet it possesses a nice degree of flexibility. It contains eight full-page illustrations in colors by Henry Pitz. In his work Mr. Pitz has caught with sympathy and understanding the background of Miss Meigs's endeavor. Furthermore, his portrayal of some of the several dramatic scenes in the tale is apt and convincing.

The Saturday Review of Literature

SOURCE: A review of *The Trade Wind,* in *The Saturday Review of Literature,* Vol. IV, No. 12, October 15, 1927, p. 212.

This book now rests securely on the Beacon Hill Bookshelf, chosen from almost four hundred manuscripts submitted for the Bookshelf's prize—all of which means much thought on the subject of literature for the young. The $2,000 was finally awarded to **The Trade Wind** because of its "vibrant atmosphere, its picturesque life, and its strong appeal to the creative imagination." Indeed, if the imaginative pitch of the first fifty pages could have been sustained the growing girl (for girls like adventure) or boy would have had a lasting thrill. Our first thought was accompanied by a thrill: "Here is a book that equals *Drums!*" We rejoiced that a book for youth should fly straight, free of the arbitrary limits of the imagination that usually cramp a juvenile writer's material and style. The young mind is superior to ours in the power of transmuting life. Perhaps it is a sneaking inferiority-complex that ties our thought in didactic knots in the presence of youth. In the first chapter a boy with a mind full of sea-romance passed down from his father, who returned to the sea and was lost in it after years on shore, looks out of his window above the bay on a night of rain and thinks sadly that nothing ever happens. Presto! A flash of lightning reveals "six or seven men coming along the path which slanted across the garden, men with sea-beaten faces, this one with a red handkerchief tied around his head, that one with an unsheathed cutlass in his hand. The noise of the rain drowned the crunching of their heavy boots. . . . " Immediately the spirit of David's father urged me to read as it urged David to run the seas.

Alack! When David is actually off on the bounding wave, he becomes no longer the wistfully expectant David we know well already, but a boy on an adventure, any boy. Not any adventure. For this tale passes skillfully through outlandish fleets and about unfriendly harbors below the equator. The period is fascinating: life on the ocean never held more circumstantial picturesqueness than in the pirate-chasing, buccaneering, revenue-running days directly before the Revolution. There is no dull adventure in this book. Also, it may be added, no verbiage, no bunk, and the characters are solidly executed. Nevertheless, in company with David we do not get quite the thrill that the first chapters led us to expect; and only at the end do we recapture first-hand romance, when the gorgeous *Pegasus* sinks, and the winged horse, her figurehead, "in a final plunge, went under and was drowned forever in a smother of green water and white foam." To our mind at least, the appeal to the creative imagination, which after all comes from a creative imagination vividly at work, is not any too strong.

In short, **The Trade Wind** will be outstanding in the juvenile year because of its entire soundness and its partial vibrancy. But it misses the place in the ranks of books in general which any book, for young or old, that lives all through its being, can claim! However, we are more than grateful to writer and publisher and Bookshelf for giving our children an interesting and able piece of work, and such criticism as we offer is in fact a compliment.

The Nation

SOURCE: A review of *The Trade Wind*, in *The Nation*, Vol. 125, No. 3254, November 16, 1927, p. 546.

The Trade Wind, by Cornelia Meigs, won a $2,000 prize offered by Little, Brown and Company. We are told that it was chosen from nearly four hundred manuscripts submitted and was the choice of experts in children's tastes. Yet it seems a dull and clumsy piece of work. It is the very apotheosis of the romantic novel synthetically achieved. If the prize had been frankly offered for the nearest approach to the Stevensonian formula this tale with its heavy paraphernalia of pirates, privateers, and gun-runners would have better deserved it.

Jacqueline Overton

SOURCE: A review of *The Trade Wind*, in *The New Republic*, Vol. LII, No. 676, November 16, 1927, p. 363.

The Trade Wind, by Cornelia Meigs, which won the Beacon Hill Bookshelf prize, blows straight out of the days when revolution was brewing between England and her colonies in America. A chain of rapid-moving circumstances sends David Denison off as a supercargo aboard the schooner "Santa Maria" (or "Anna Maria" as they later call her), with his father's old shipmate, Andrew Bardwell.

The "Santa Maria" was unlucky from the start (some said her keel had been laid on a Friday). Her captain and crew fail in their secret mission, and before seeing the New England coast again they meet with pirates and smugglers, tilt with the King's officers and are boarded by Carib Indians. As they follow the path of the trade winds, exchanging flour, rum, tobacco, for Eastern goods, one adventure follows another.

Here is excellent writing—the description of the British man-of-war "Pegasus" that passes close by them under full rig "sails away with David's heart," and the reader's too.

Anne Carroll Moore

SOURCE: A review of *The Trade Wind*, in *New York Herald Tribune Books*, November 27, 1927, p. 8.

The Trade Wind is no mere prize story. It has the quality and value of a story rooted in sound research and

good writing. This accounts, perhaps, for its appeal to men as well as to boys. It may be of interest to other readers of the book, as it was to me, to know that Miss Meigs spent three or four years in the preparation and writing of this book, only to lay it aside for a year or two before bringing it to completion. A refreshing thing to contemplate in midst of the superabundance of made-to-order boy and girl books with American background which flood the market. For a dozen years or more Cornelia Meigs's work in this field has been quietly taking a permanent place in public and school libraries. Better typography, adequate illustration and more attractive format would have widened the audience for *Master Simon's Garden, The New Moon* and *As the Crow Flies*. The good form of *The Trade Wind* gives this author for the first time her rightful place among the writers of distinctive books of the year, and we trust it may point the way to more satisfactory editions of her earlier work.

AS THE CROW FLIES (1927)

Bray Hammond

SOURCE: A review of *As the Crow Flies*, in *The Saturday Review of Literature*, Vol. IV, No. 20, December 10, 1927, p. 438.

This is a story of Lieutenant Zebulon Pike's first trip of exploration, and of the reaction of the Indians to his efforts at racial reconciliation. There is accordingly nearly as much idealism in the book as adventure, but it is pretty clearly objectified in the actions of the two principal characters, Natzoon, the Indian boy, and the young Zebulon Pike himself. Without being skillfully done, the book is nevertheless interestingly done, and though the characters never seem very real, there is yet a persuasive recognition of what was dramatic in the first relationships between the Indian possessors of this continent and the aggressive white men, good and bad, who relentlessly supplanted them. Just what the Indian thought as he felt the pressure of our westward expansion, and experienced indiscriminately the good and evil of white contacts, we cannot know, but we can profitably imagine. Similarly we cannot know the emotions of the first whites who penetrated the wildernesses of immemorial savagery, but it is profitable for us to try to imagine that too. Both states of feeling are presented in this story, and any reader adolescent or even older is bound to find in it an impressive historic sense of events that have had more than merely national import.

CLEARING WEATHER (1928)

Dudley C. Lunt

SOURCE: A review of *Clearing Weather*, in *New York Herald Tribune Books*, October 28, 1928, p. 8.

Ships, trade and adventure—these three lead in swift succession from one to the other in an endless cycle of interest and form the spindle on which many a good yarn has been spun. The course of maritime history has been a ceaseless struggle for sea power. Individuals, communities, nations and empires have, for the brief moment of their glory, written the record of their achievement in the trackless expanse of the seven seas. Such a moment came to New England when the clipper ship was mistress of the seas.

In those days the little towns by the sea teemed with creative activity. Shipyards, rope walks and sail lofts were alive with busy men. They plied trades known to-day only by name and a few rusty tools in some marine museum. There were riggers, caulkers, block makers and ship carpenters. In the drafting room native shrewdness, combined with a flair born of wide experience, conceived the plans and fashioned the models of ships that for the combined qualities of grace and beauty and of speed and utility are unequaled in the annals of the sea. Of such were the Flying Dutchman and the Flying Cloud.

Heavy teams rumbled over cobbled streets and discharged their loads of bales, boxes and bundles into the cool, cavernous depths of waterfront warehouses—cargoes for voyages, barter for trade. In the counting-houses, back of roll-top desks, pigeonholed with papers and documents, sat the merchants. Here voyages were planned, masters were interviewed and handsome profits reckoned. Beyond the paned glass partition sat the clerks on high stools who bent over huge ledgers, tallied figures, and made up long cargo lists.

In the tavern over mugs of grog and hot toddy the talk was of ships, voyages and trade. The women folk were at it the day long in the steady replenishing of larders subject to constant attack by the hearty appetites of the men. In their spare time there was the homespun and the knitting that kept a body warm on a night watch in midwinter. In every home a father or a brother followed the sea.

The life of every soul in the community, from the richest merchant to the water boy in the shipyard, was a cog in the wheel of these ventures. Apart from the fruits of their labor many a family put its small savings into a share in the ships and the cargo. Every household had its accumulated treasure of bits of carved jade and exquisite shawls from China, the rich folds of Cashmere and Chuddah from the East Indies and queer gimcracks and priceless objets d'art from all the ports of the globe. Stately houses were planned by the same minds and built by the same hands that created beauty in ships and sought for profit in far ports. With increasing wealth grew up a society long since lost, in which a lady clad in rustling silks had two black boys to carry her train and served China tea in China cups from a carved chest filled to the brim with gold coins garnered in outlandish places by a seafaring uncle. From keelson to truck and from the launching to the homecoming ships and their voyages were the very life blood of these communities.

And the cruises they went on. To this day the mention of "rum, sugar and molasses" will bring a gleam to the eye of the oldest inhabitant. This was the West Indian trade. Then there was whaling out of Nantucket and New Bedford, for generations a source of profit, and fishing off the Banks, to-day the sole relic of departed glory. Forbidden the English ports, Yankee skippers courageously struck out for far countries. Their brigs, snows and clippers rounded the Horn and touched on the West Coast to barter with the Indians for hides and furs. They forged across the Pacific and had their share in the Far East. It was a Yankee ship that opened Oriental Japan to the Occident. They rode at anchor in the port of the Indies, and the Mediterranean came to know the sheer beauty of a clipper's bow.

Chronicled in the scrawls of many an old log are exciting events and strange adventure. The Yankee skipper and his crew were fighters. They fought then with the Indians and with Malay, the Barbary and the pirates of their own and kindred faces as they are prone to do this day in foreign ports. Their stout ships ran through full many a gale and storm. And then there were the ships for which the owners waited patiently through tedious months and finally gave up hope. The laconic record "Lost at sea with all hands" was entered on the books after her name. In a score or more homes there were those who did not give up hope so easily and waited patiently in vain.

In *Clearing Weather* there is fashioned by a sure hand an excellent tale of adventure. Cornelia Meigs knows intimately this background of Colonial trading days. She also knows ships and can write well of them. She has cultivated to a high degree the art of spinning a yarn well spiced with excitement and intrigue. Those readers who liked her earlier book, *The Trade Wind,* will find this story of the building, the launching, the voyaging and the homecoming of the Jocasta of absorbing interest. The tale was worth the telling and the book, in an attractive format, is well worth the reading and the owning.

Dudley Nichols

SOURCE: A review of *Clearing Weather,* in *The Saturday Review of Literature,* Vol. V, No. 16, November 10, 1928, p. 350.

This title, though pleasant sounding, is inapt, for it rather intimates a book of verse, which the volume is not, than a fast moving adventure story, which the volume is.

Miss Meigs (surely Cornelia is not a male?) has brought to this yarn all the stirring ingredients—patriotism, three heroes, conflict between heroic lads and villainous men, an old inn, a seaport, ship and a venture to Cathay, Indians, pirates, cannon and muskets, love romance; and in the fade-out comes the fulfilment of dreamful wishes. Miss Meigs can tell a story and no boy will lay down the book once he sets his teeth in it. (The jacket does wrong to synopsize, even for the sake of lazy reviewers.)

In a manner of speaking all such stories are *clichés.* However varied the plot there is no originality, it is an endless weaving of used threads. There may be invented actions but there are no new feelings, no new air for us to breathe. We know the atmosphere of this old attic thoroughly. It is the genius who coins the phrase and a hundred following generations *cliché* it. Picking up books on this pattern we can never forget [Robert Louis Stevenson], for he did the thing to perfection: the Admiral Denbow, Jim, the good and evil characters, and Long John who was both and therefore true. Nothing could be remoter from reality than *Treasure Island,* yet because it was genuinely imagined and perfectly wrought the thing seems indestructible. If it cannot exist in reality, very well: the tale makes its own world, then, and in that created *milieu* exists as a "real" thing.

However Miss Meigs has written no *Treasure Island,* even though there is a kinship sensed. Perhaps it is not so strange a thing, this girl's writing a pirate story. You cannot have your adventure romance and live it too. There was a good deal of the woman in Stevenson; maybe that is why men hold him in such deep affection. And it is noteworthy that after he had set out to live his sea adventure he ceased writing it with that old glamour of inexperience. For if you are going to imagine unreal things perfectly, you must steer off reality.

As for the manner of the present book, if an unadventurous male may venture to take Miss Meigs up on anything, he would beg her to obey her good demon of directness and economy, whom she always hearkens to when her characters have been marshaled into action but ignores when her fancy is in calm. Thus ignoring him she can launch her book with:

> The bent plum trees set in the square of rough grass behind the Blackbird Inn, were as white on this mild February day as though it was May. Ordinarily their branches were as black with age as they were twisted by sea winds; for beyond the hawthorn hedge was the marsh, across which gales from the north and east could sweep unhindered; and beyond the marsh was the sea. It was neither blossom nor snow which covered the wide-reaching boughs in that hazy sunshine, but a gossamer-light veil of frost which lay upon every branch and twig, and penciled each with a delicate tracery of white . . .

And so on and so on. Why couldn't we have had simply: "The bent plum trees behind the Blackbird Inn were white with frost"?

Mary Graham Bonner

SOURCE: A review of *Clearing Weather,* in *The New York Times Book Review,* December 2, 1928, p. 6.

Cornelia Meigs, whose **The Trade Wind** of last year

was a prize winner—and an excellent story—has written a book this year entitled *Clearing Weather.* Again the sea is the background. The period of the story is that following the Revolution with its forlorn poverties, its wretchedly scant opportunities for work, its discouragements and its need for courage. Vividly, Miss Meigs tells her story, interspersing mystery and piratical episodes with such facile sureness that they are inevitably a part of the story rather than merely being dragged in for book plot virility. And the reader who loves the sea and ships feels a welcoming glow for the weather-beaten Jocasta as she comes back from her brave travels.

> She was not now that proud, untested beauty which had set out with all their hearts and hopes aboard her; she was a worn and weather-scarred ship of world-wide voyaging. Her sails were no longer snowy white as those two had last seen them; they were gray and some of them patched. What breezes had filled them, what storms had torn them asunder? Ah, how little it mattered now, since there had been winds to waft her home!

THE WONDERFUL LOCOMOTIVE (1928)

Anne T. Eaton

SOURCE: A review of *The Wonderful Locomotive,* in *The Saturday Review of Literature,* Vol. V, No. 23, December 29, 1928, p. 558.

Peter, a small boy who "loved no sound quite so well as the puff-puff of a steam engine," makes friends with Nels Stromberg, once an engineer, but who now spends his time helping to mend engines and doing other repair work in his house near the railroad yards. Many happy hours does Peter spend in this little one-room house, full of bits of machinery, nuts, bolts, and screws, and other delightful playthings. Most wonderful of all, in the yard, close to Nels's doorstep, stands a real locomotive, the remnant of former glory. The railroad men said that "44," once a fine engine, had made its last run and would stand on the side track until Nels sold it for junk, but Nels and Peter thought differently. Old "44" was the delight of Nels's heart, and while Peter watched him, he tinkered away hopefully, insisting that some day "44 would show them all what she could do." Then one night—and here the story really begins—Peter is waked from a sound sleep; Nels is calling him and "44" is ready to start. Alone, except for the puppy he rescues on the way, Peter makes a dashing journey from coast to coast, across the desert, over the mountains, helping a circus to reach a town on time, rescuing a party of children from a forest fire, and then triumphantly home again to tumble into bed.

This is one of the books that will find its readers from six to sixty. Out of curiosity I sent the story to a young railroad man who, fourteen or fifteen years ago, was another Peter, and I quote from his letter in reply. He says: "Miss Meigs has written a book that fills a long empty space in the children's libraries. I only wish she had written it years ago. She has taken a wonderful plot and made the most interesting story about railroads for little children that I have ever read. It carries out the ideas, rules, and the true spirit of railroads. It is as near perfect in the details of railroading as could be to make the engine 'magic.' It is geographically correct."

Adults need not be disturbed because of the combination of real and unreal, for it will not disturb the child reader. The locomotive is a real locomotive, and what the youthful engineer does is what the child who loves engines dreams of doing. Fairy tales, which supply the element of wonder, that most necessary element in a child's experience, are not always concerned with elves and dragons. In the fairylands of some children their places are filled by trains and shops, glorified but still actual and practical. This book will not conflict with the books of information, but will provide an outlet for the imagination along other lines than those of giants and fairies. The illustrations by Berta and Elmer Hader are delightfully satisfactory; they have caught the "go" and zest of the story.

THE CROOKED APPLE TREE (1929)

Mary Graham Bonner

SOURCE: A review of *The Crooked Apple Tree,* in *The New York Times Book Review,* October 6, 1929, p. 34.

The ingredients of this story are rather familiar but always have a human appeal. The trials of an orphan boy and his sister who cannot bear separation have been told many a time in story, but Miss Meigs has invested them with warm, human affection, and has made the crooked apple tree itself loved by the readers as certain trees can be loved by those who dwell near them. The reader goes out-of-doors with Miss Meigs's characters. "The apple tree was almost ready to bloom. Every twig held a bunch of tightly rolled buds, deep rose in color and as yet quite unopened. From where Jane and Anthony sat, they could look directly into its branches with their new leaves of palest green and their dull pink promise of abundant bloom."

Is there any wonder that Jane, watching the completion of their house, should almost wish that the roof and walls need not be finished. The reader sits there too, with Jane, and almost says with her, "It is so glorious to look right through them and see the whole world."

The Saturday Review of Literature

SOURCE: A review of *The Crooked Apple Tree,* in *The Saturday Review of Literature,* Vol. VI, No. 18, November 23, 1929, p. 462.

A charming story of two orphans, Anthony, aged thirteen, and Jane, eleven, and Nora-Who-Lives-With-Us,

which will be a delight for both boys and girls. The two children, after the death of their father and mother and the loss of much of their money, have come to live at Winstead, a lovely old town on the Mississippi, which was Nora's and their mother's former home. They discover with joy a real friend, Matthew Ballantine, who tells them the history of the old cabin on Apple Creek Hill, where grows the crooked apple tree, many years old. Matthew is a delight to the children in contrast to their niggardly guardian, Jarvis, who, as they go on to discover, was formerly Matthew's business partner. Jarvis almost wrecks their happiness, but the children's wish to build a house on Apple Creek Hill for Nora finally comes true.

The author has created a lovable character in Anthony, whose devotion to his Irish setter, Brian Boru, makes him a real boy. His accepted responsibility for Jane and Nora is almost manlike. Jane is a precocious little child, timid, but with great confidence in Anthony.

The book is full of thrills and surprises such as children love, all interestingly told. There are many fascinating illustrations in black and white by Helen Mason Grose.

THE WILLOW WHISTLE (1931)

Anne T. Eaton

SOURCE: A review of *The Willow Whistle,* in *The New York Times Book Review,* October 4, 1931, p. 25.

Here we have an Indian story for children from 7 to 10. True to Indian customs, it also describes with truth and charm the little girl Mary Anne, her playmate Eric, son of the Norwegian settler who is their neighbor, her father and mother John and Jane Seabold, fine pioneer types, and the individual Indians, some friendly and others not so friendly, who influence in one way or another the course of events for the settlers. Miss Meigs writes in her usual fine and distinguished style and the pictures by E. Boyd Smith illustrate the exciting events in the story, presenting Indians, buffaloes and ponies in a way that will be highly satisfactory to young readers.

SWIFT RIVERS (1932)

Constance Lindsay Skinner

SOURCE: A review of *Swift Rivers,* in *New York Herald Tribune Books,* October 23, 1932, p. 9.

Chris Dahlberg lived on Goose Wing River, in Minnesota. He was one of a scattered colony of Swedish immigrants, farming the wild lands. His parents were dead and he worked early and late for the bread and bit of roof which his uncle grudgingly allowed him. His only source of companionship was his grandfather, a spry, sympathetic old man who had taught Chris all he knew.

So far, Chris was just such a boy as thousands of those older boys for whom Miss Meigs has written this story: a boy who worked, helped keep the household going, knew responsibility and didn't grouch because his position in life demanded that he be intelligent and manly. But there was something more in Chris than the qualities required to keep Uncle Nels's fields and livestock in shape—and this involves a contradiction of the statement that grandfather was his "only" companion. Chris was companioned by his fields. The companionship had begun long ago, when he was too young to realize it, as he followed grandfather's scythe through the meadow and listened to grandfather talking of the habits of growing things and of wild creatures scurrying through and flying above. At seventeen, his age when the book begins, Chris was conscious of this intimacy. Swinging his scythe or watching the wheeling flight of eagle or hawk, his body was deeply aware of its identity with earth and sky.

It would appear that Chris was rooted in that meadow as firmly as the grass. But sudden change can come to rooted lives, and then comes also the test of what the years of deep thrusting into the soul have bred. A break with Uncle Nels, recognition that grandfather was no longer a strong man, inspired Chris to seek his fortune. All about him were tall, smooth timbers; below him, the running tide which passed through that gap in the hills and in time found the Father of Waters. On the Mississippi many huge rafts floated yearly down to the mills at St. Louis. There was money in logging for men who could bring their timber safely to market.

So almost the whole book about this boy, whom the Minnesota meadows taught to know himself, deals with Chris on the raft, his life attuned to the long, swinging rhythm of the rivers. Inevitably be met dangers, some from ruffians and others from moods and tricks of the rivers. The story has plenty of incident, all of it natural. Its dramatic peak is the wrecking of the raft and its laborious reassembling.

As a storyteller Miss Meigs has the peculiar charm of those whose tales begin "Once upon a time there was a prince." Period, type of life, persons of her books seem to be magically lifted out of an actual world into the realms of story. Her artistry weaves her selected elements into a pattern harmonious and beautiful, true with art's truth, not necessarily nature's. It is a cut crystal, not a mirror, with which she catches life's reflections. As in a fairy tale, tree or bird may talk and its talking seem natural to the reader; so in *Swift Rivers* cultured English speech such as no French Chippewa would even understand comes from the lips of Pierre Dumenille without jarring one's sense of fitness. By keeping all speech in the key of her own limpid, softly growing prose, she preserves the special illusion—that is, the storied reality—which she seeks. The result of her transmutation of actualities into another, illusory, form of experience is enchantment for young readers—and for readers not so young.

Anne T. Eaton

SOURCE: A review of *Swift Rivers,* in *The New York Times Book Review,* November 13, 1932, pp. 9, 15.

A beautifully written book, in which unusual material and a period in the history of this country about which little has been written, have been used in a picturesque and absorbing tale. Christian Dahlberg, a boy of Swedish descent, lives with his grandfather in Northern Minnesota on the Goose Wing River in 1835. Difficulties arise in Chris's life, he feels that he must be ready to take care not only of himself but of his grandfather and that he must be entirely independent of the uncle who has helped him only grudgingly and with no real affection. So Chris and his grandfather cut some of their trees and Chris floats them down the Mississippi in the Spring floods to the lumber market at St. Louis. His adventures with river pilots and raft hands, his association with Pierre Dumenille, his friendship with Stuart Hale, the healing of the feud between Dumenille and the other great pilot, Joe Langford, and Chris's return to his grandfather, make an interesting and convincing narrative. Chris himself is alive and appealing, but the real characters of the story, however, seem to be the rivers, the floods of Spring, the great logs of walnut, spruce and pine, floating down slowly and not without danger, under the sun by day and the brightness of the stars by night. A book that has poetry and out-of-doors in it, and a background typical of this country, as well as daring and adventurous deeds that any boy and girl will enjoy.

INVINCIBLE LOUISA: THE STORY OF THE AUTHOR OF "LITTLE WOMEN" (1933)

May Lamberton Becker

SOURCE: A review of *Invincible Louisa: The Story of the Author of "Little Women,"* in *New York Herald Tribune Books,* June 4, 1933, p. 7.

Let us one day take up seriously this matter of year-long commemorative celebrations and see what they do to the popularity of their subjects. It took the Pilgrims at least ten years to recover from their Tercentenary. By the middle of last March, with months of glory yet to go, it was clear that the one American hero most likely to be remembered with a shudder by the American school child would be George Washington. But look at the other side of the goodwill ledger. Throughout this same year we celebrated something we would never have believed if some one had not told us—the fact that it was 100 hundred years since Louisa Alcott was born. And it seems to have done her no harm. No wonder Miss Meigs calls her *Invincible Louisa;* she prevailed even against her own centenary.

The amazing feature of Miss Meigs's book is that it overcomes two unusually heavy handicaps. The first is that Ednah Dean Cheney's *Life and Letters* is as good an arrangement of source material as we have for an

American author, and the interest of children in these sources has always been so great that the book is to be found wherever Miss Alcott is on a library shelf. Yet it is now no longer possible to say you have the standard life of Miss Alcott unless you possess *Invincible Louisa,* which will be read more readily and rapidly than its predecessor. The second is that with the spotlight of newspaper and magazine publicity playing for a year, not ruthlessly, but with the searching power of affection, upon the Alcotts and their circle, one would think it impossible for a book coming out now to provide the new material justifying the appearance of a new life and its claim to be taken seriously. But there really is such material, new at any rate to children. The last turn of the screw in the tragic episode of Fruitlands, the one unbearable, unbelievable possibility whose very thought made the Alcotts determine forever to forget it, may have appeared elsewhere in print, but I never read it till I found it here.

It is the touch needed for that picture. Perhaps it came out of the "verbal information" from those carrying on the Alcott tradition, to which acknowledgment is made in the foreword; at any rate, this verbal information evidently brightens the general tone. All documentary sources have been also consulted, but the book is written in that steady creative flow that shows they were consulted far ahead of actual writing.

We have been lately hearing a good deal about "the American dream" and how it has been suffering at the hands, first of our prosperity, and then of our depression. It may be reassuring—or otherwise—to find it in full bloom in this book, and to find it was no more popular in the forties than it is today. The Alcotts had it. It was largely because they asked so little from the material world that they were not permitted to get that. Plain living and high thinking: there it is: both of these by choice and a sort of spiritual compulsion, and from both of them, joy. This is why photographs in this book have so high a documentary value in our social history; they are for the most part interiors showing rooms in the Alcott house, not at their time of greatest financial stress, but when they could have spent money on the things everybody with money was buying. See how beautiful these rooms are today: clear in an age of clutter, dignified in the face of *Godey's,* sure and self-contained against the flutter of fashion. There will never be many people in any period who live in rooms serene as that and in a like serenity of mind. There were mighty few in Emerson's day, and there are mighty few now.

Anne T. Eaton

SOURCE: A review of *Invincible Louisa: The Story of the Author of "Little Women,"* in *The New York Times Book Review,* June 11, 1933, p. 11.

Louisa May Alcott and Cornelia Meigs are an ideal combination. Sir Sidney Lee has somewhere said that the aim of biography is the truthful transmission of personality. No one could be better fitted than Miss Meigs to make the personality of *Invincible Louisa* real and vivid and to show how Miss Alcott's books grew inevitably out of her life and experience.

Cornelia Meigs is herself the author of a number of excellent and well-loved books for young people; in their pages the reader finds the same integrity that characterizes Louisa Alcott's writing. Back of each author's work one senses a certain fine reserve and dignity and Miss Meigs's books, like those of the earlier writer, have a very definite American quality.

Louisa May Alcott has always seemed very much alive in her *Life, Letters and Journals,* edited by Mrs. Cheney. In this volume she seems even more so because of the imaginative understanding which enables Miss Meigs to make the reader see the Louisa of different periods from the "unquenchable baby who would never stay where she was put and who, as soon as she could really walk, loved nothing so much as to run away," and the 6-year-old hoop-rolling champion of Boston Common, to the successful and very modest author of whom Ellen Terry wrote when they were guests of honor at the same luncheon, "My ambition is gratified: I sit at the same table and behold with my own eyes, the authoress of *Little Women.*"

Interesting and enlightening for readers of any age is the clarity with which the members of the Alcott family are drawn and their influence on the life and books of the author of *Little Women* described. Even very young readers have an inkling that much of *Little Women* is true; here is a fascinating opportunity to find out what was real and what was imaginary and how a character in the story has his or her origin in one or perhaps more than one of the characters that Louisa Alcott knew in real life.

Miss Meigs's book, however, does still more than this. Her story of the life and wanderings of the Alcott family, their various homes, Germantown, Philadelphia, Boston, Concord, "Fruitlands," Walpole, Concord again, each change dictated not by their personal choice but because of the father's loyalty to an idea and because of his heroic wife's loyalty to him, her account of the unselfishness which the children began to practice very early in life and quite as a matter of course—through these she interprets *Invincible Louisa* herself, shows why her life and writing took the course they did and explains the quality that the reader feels underlying all her books.

Especially fine and understanding is Miss Meigs's picture of Bronson Alcott, a unique character and one not without influence in his own day and later, in spite of apparent failure during his lifetime.

One of the most interesting portraits in the book is that of Ralph Waldo Emerson as the Alcotts knew him; the Emerson who gave the young Louisa the privilege of his library, where she could choose anything from the tall mahogany shelves that reached the ceiling, could curl herself in a corner of the comfortable sofa and read to her heart's, content; the Emerson who attended Anna Alcott's wedding, eliciting the comment in Louisa's diary, "Mr. Emerson kissed Anna, and I thought that honor would make even matrimony endurable"; the Emerson who many a time stood by his friend Bronson Alcott with very practical help and encouragement.

Other well-known names figure in the book: Theodore Parker, William Lloyd Garrison, Nathaniel Hawthorne, [Henry David] Thoreau, William Ellery Channing, making it not only a record of the Alcott family's friendships but a picture of a famous New England group in the nineteenth century.

The volume has a chronology and a well-made index, and it is illustrated by twenty-one admirable photographs showing the Alcott family and the houses where they lived. It is a book for every school and children's library and one that adult readers as well as young people will enjoy.

The Catholic World

SOURCE: A review of *Invincible Louisa: The Story of the Author of "Little Women,"* in *The Catholic World,* Vol. CXXXVII, No. 822, September, 1933, p. 761.

Certainly it was a wise choice which brought together Cornelia Meigs and Louisa Alcott in this wholly satisfying book about the dauntless and beloved author of *Little Women.* Miss Meigs has interpreted her subject with admirable understanding and sympathy and a remarkable correlation of technique and matter. Wholly truthful and not at all mawkish, this biography illumines for us the Alcotts and their brilliant circle so many members of which achieved lasting fame. The author tells her story with a sprightly simplicity in a stream of well-blended visualizations, engrossing to old and young. *Invincible Louisa* may well be a rallying cry to the timid or discouraged of our disheartening day. To lovers of Miss Alcott's work the identification of her characters with people of real life, the exposition of how inevitably her writings grew out of her circumstances and environment, and the photographs of persons and places enlivened by her pen will be a matter of satisfaction and delight.

Elizabeth Janeway

SOURCE: A review of *Invincible Louisa: The Story of the Author of "Little Women,"* *The New York Times Book Review,* September 29, 1968, p. 46.

Invincible Louisa won the Newbery Medal when it first appeared in 1933, and it is to be praised still for its straightforward account of a life of struggle and success, which was no less intense because it took place within narrow boundaries and against severe limits. If you want

to know about Louisa's external life, and trace there the events which gave rise to the internal urges and passions that produced *Little Women,* this book will serve well. It will give an excellent idea too of that vanished New England culture which, a century ago, was already hardening into rigidity but which contributed an ineradicable strain to the American ethos.

WIND IN THE CHIMNEY (1934)

Elinor Whitney

SOURCE: A review of *Wind in the Chimney,* in *The Horn Book Magazine,* Vol. X, No. 6, November, 1934, pp. 378-79.

Wind in the Chimney, by Cornelia Meigs, is a story [set during the late eighteenth century]. Washington is President and Cherry Hill near Valley Forge seems to the Moreland family a comfortable, peaceful place to settle near their Quaker cousins when they come to America. There even seems to be a little house waiting just for them, a little house in a square garden space with a wide chimney in which the wind sings a friendly song. The highway to Lancaster leads past their house and over it rumble steadily wagons carrying goods to western Pennsylvania. Here comes the Conestoga wagon drawn by eight horses bearing on their collars iron hoops each with its row of jingling bells. Richard Moreland takes to the road with Marcus Horner and his wagon, and has a memorable journey to Pittsburgh, bringing back to his sister Debby the quilt pattern which is the means of making the house which they have all come to love their permanent home, and gaining for himself faith in his own courage and manliness. As in all of Cornelia Meigs's stories there is in this, a strong fibre of unselfishness and simple heroism. The values are clear and true. There is never a touch of sentimentality or pointing of a moral, but only sureness and strength in the author's handling.

Constance Lindsay Skinner

SOURCE: A review of *Wind in the Chimney,* in *New York Herald Tribune Books,* November 11, 1934, p. 12.

In *Wind in the Chimney,* Miss Meigs has written another of her tenderly conceived and sweetly cadenced books for younger children. The period is during Washington's Presidency, and the scene Pennsylvania, not far from Philadelphia. Little Debby, her sister Ann and her brother Dick and her widowed mother arrive from England and take possession of an empty house near some Quakers. The mother, Elizabeth Moreland, is a weaver, and hopes to support her family by making cloth and linen. Dick presently joins a sturdy trader who is on the road to the Indian country with his Conestoga wagon and his train of pack horses. Debby has her mother's own talent for weaving and helps at the loom, when she is not at the little school or poking about amid the fairy-like wonders of Cherry Hill. The only cloud on her horizon is the fact that the house on Cherry Hill is not theirs, and the rich gentleman who owns it will not say positively that they may continue to live in it.

The cause of his vacillation is his willful, arrogant sister, who dominates him and who wants him to give Cherry Hill to her daughter as a wedding present. Sister Susannah has another desire as strong: to find a quilt woven in the Wheel of Fortune pattern. She had one, an heirloom, which she intended to give to her daughter, and it was destroyed by fire. Dick is bidden to search for this pattern among the settlers along his route. He finds it at last, and Debby and her mother weave the quilt and present it to Susannah. They are rewarded for the gift by being allowed to remain at Cherry Hill, where the wind sings a special song in the broad chimney. The book is illustrated with full pages in black and white and a colored frontispiece by Louise Mansfield.

Anne T. Eaton

SOURCE: A review of *Wind in the Chimney,* in *The New York Times Book Review,* November 25, 1934, p. 10.

Wind in the Chimney, the story of an English mother and her three children who come to Pennsylvania as pioneers during the years when Washington was President in Philadelphia, has a freshness and genuineness that is entirely convincing. Mrs. Moreland, Roger and Ann, and particularly 8-year-old Debby, are very real; so too are the friendly neighbors, the schoolmaster, the Morelands' landlord, and Marcus Horner, the wagoner, with whom Richard takes the road and, helping with the great Conestoga wagon and the train of pack horses, makes an adventurous journey to Pittsburgh and back. And then there is also Cherry Hill, one of the most delightful little houses ever found in a book. Debby, looking through a gap in the hedge, sees it standing in a square garden space, "with a low, shingled roof and thick walls of yellow stone, and beyond it a row of old black-trunked cherry trees."

It might have been built for the Morelands, for there were three rooms below and a steep little stair going to twin attic chambers. There was a chimney oven and cupboards and closets and a little iron pot with legs to stand among the coals. As the children explored there came to them a deep singing murmur that Debby recognized as the wind in the chimney. No wonder the family from England longed to settle down for good at Cherry Hill. How what seemed at first an impossible dream became a reality makes up a story of unflagging interest. It was not chance that brought a happy ending, but their own fine qualities of courage and loyalty and generosity that gave the Morelands permanent possession of the home they had come to love so dearly. Most of all, perhaps, the reader rejoices with Debby—Debby, who was a practical little girl but who felt a part of all the gay beauty of the upland meadow as she ran along to school, and who could "always bear things better out of

doors"; Debby, in whom Miss Meigs has drawn a fine portrait of a brave and sensitive child.

There are excellently managed glimpses of President Washington, where we see him through the eyes of his contemporaries, and delightful descriptions of the countryside. A book with a strength and beauty that give it the rank of real literature. The illustrations in color and in black-and-white are charming and thoroughly in keeping with the story.

📖 *THE COVERED BRIDGE* (1936)

New York Herald Tribune Books

SOURCE: A review of *The Covered Bridge,* in *New York Herald Tribune Books,* November 15, 1936, p. 14.

Vermonters, native or adoptive, put this book into your libraries, for your ten-year-old children—perhaps younger—and for yourselves. It is a pioneer story, but it has the spirit of the state today, the spirit that makes so many summer Vermonters wish they could claim kin with the old stock.

This covered bridge crosses Hebron Brook—then, as now, having the Vermont brook's capacity for acting on occasion like a river—on the road that leads to Sarah Macomber's farm. Sarah was a vigorous, reticent and warm-hearted grandmother who cooked the meals for a rich Boston family, stayed in their kitchen and preserved about her an aura of social integrity, by sheer force of being somebody. She owned a farm in Vermont—which southern New England then considered pretty wild country, calling it, indeed, The Wilderness. For years Sarah had been saving to get enough to join forces with her grandson, a boy of twelve at work on another farm, and set her home place going again. When something had suddenly to be done with little Connie, niece of her employers, while they were forced to go South, Sarah instantly made up her strong mind that now was the time to leave Boston for good, take the little girl with her to Vermont, recall her grandson and take up the responsibilities of what she believed the right kind of living, running one's own farm.

So little Connie, used to the purple and fine living of post-Revolutionary Boston, set out in the fall of the year, with the approval of her relatives, as a fellow-worker with the "help" who had now resumed her independent status. One who knows Vermont will feel the thrill with which Sarah comes back to her own, where everybody is a farmer, where animals have rights sometimes before those of folks, because if folks profit by them they owe them support. Connie is soon to learn that there are crises in which animals are people so far as dealing by them is concerned. She is to learn that because your neighbor is close-fisted he may not be unjust, and because he exacts the last penny of your debt to him is no reason why you should not pay it. She is to find—best of all—how much depends upon a neighbor, how much one has a right to expect and be ready to give on demand. She is to learn that the sparsely settled region has become a community because this neighborliness creates a nervous system that functions for miles around. All these things and more she is to learn in action and through the involuntary, instinctive decisions of Sarah and her young grandson. Moreover, she is to meet Ethan Allen, who comes to life in these clear, snow-lit scenes.

A child could still see much that happens in this story by spending a winter on a one-man farm up-country. The sword of Damocles still hangs over many a mountain settlement in the roaring landslip: such rescues of cattle on icy hills must still be made; no Vermonter living is likely to forget when gentlerivers rose to flood such as set this covered bridge, just after the War of Independence, in peril of destruction. I don't see how Connie could get a letter every week in those days from parents as far away as the Virgin Islands, but I agree to all the rest. The scene and the people are Green Mountain from the heart out.

Here is Ethan Allen as they still believe him to be, not only on the islands in Lake Champlain whose names show forth his praise but wherever they read "The Green Mountain Boys."

Anne T. Eaton

SOURCE: A review of *The Covered Bridge*, in *The New York Times Book Review*, January 24, 1937, p. 9.

Cornelia Meigs may be depended upon to provide a story that has not only interest but a fine integrity, and her books, with their authentic pictures of American life, shed a light over many periods of this country's history. In **The Covered Bridge** she has turned to the Green Mountain country in the days of Ethan Allen. One day the big kindly man visited the school and, striding down the aisle between the benches, wrote on the blackboard. "Today is a holiday," the master consenting, for, as he said, "you can have your way wherever you go, Ethan Allen, for every person in Vermont owes you a debt of gratitude." Then, as the children shared their luncheons with their friendly visitor around the fire, the school master explained how this man had given Vermont everything she had, and had stood for her rights against those who would have oppressed her on every side. As the reader follows the story there comes to him a realization of the gratitude and affectionate admiration that the people of Hebron and the surrounding country felt for a neighbor whom they loved and trusted.

Constance, a little girl of Gloucester, Mass., goes to spend the winter in Vermont with Sarah Macomber, her aunt's old housekeeper. The Green Mountain country was rough country in 1800, and Constance's visit was not without its excitements. She has Peter, Sarah's grandson, as companion and playmate, and with him shares some real adventures. There were long snowstorms when the care of the stock and the keeping up of the fires were real problems; there was a barn raising; a flood, and a flock of sheep saved, in part, by the children's prompt action. Most exciting of all was the day when Hebron brook became a foaming yellow torrent, and but for Peter's courageous efforts, seconded by Connie and Sarah, the covered bridge would have been swept away.

The Vermont country which the author knows and loves is in the book, snowy fields and blue mountains cutting into the paler blue of the sky, pastures where Spring came suddenly, bringing hepaticas and bloodroot and days like nothing else in the world. Though Connie rejoiced when her father came to take her home,there was regret, too, for the work, the adventures, the beauty that these months had brought to her. But she would return to all of it, of that she felt sure, and, as the stage rolled away, she was content to realize that "you could always think about coming back to a farm. That was the last beautiful thing to think about, that the valley and the mountains and the long slope of the hill would always be there, would always be the same."

Marguerite de Angeli's charming drawings in black and white and the frontispiece in color have caught the spirit of the text. A book that boys and girls from 9 to 12 will thoroughly enjoy.

THE SCARLET OAK (1938)

May Lamberton Becker

SOURCE: A review of *The Scarlet Oak*, in *New York Herald Tribune Books*, November 13, 1938, p. 8.

Boys and girls in the eager age of ten-to-fourteen need books like this, and seldom get one that blends so well a true feeling for early American life and a strong sense of the dramatic, expressed in rich, melodious English. As it opens, two American boys have just returned from France with their widowed mother to live with their grandfather in the family mansion at Bordentown, N.J. It has taken their sailing ship but thirty-five days to cross the Atlantic in 1817, now that the long wars are over, but in this time the last stroke has fallen on their grandfather's crumbling fortunes: they find him strangely preoccupied and his old servant prepared to hold off any messenger who may bring the bad news he dreads to hear. The older boy is seventeen; the tumult through which he has passed has strengthened a sound nature. He faces the situation and shoulders the burdens of a man. The family's last ship has been taken as prize of war, but may be recovered if the case is personally presented. Jeremy goes back to Europe to do this; twelve-year-old Hugh gets a job as gardener's boy at the finest place in Bordentown. An elderly Frenchman lives there, a Mr. Joseph Bonaparte, for a brief interval King of Spain and still wearing—to himself and his servants at least—the aura of royalty.

Mr. Stephen Girard, the boys' guide and friend in their

business affairs, is far more of a hero to them, and Hugh's adjustments to pseudo-royalty show an American spirit already sharply defined. An element of mystery soon appears: the reader becomes aware that a refuge is being planned in America for the exile of St. Helena. It is Jeremy, returning with his case won, who brings news that preparations will be in vain.

In the country between Bordentown and Philadelphia enough of the architecture and general surroundings of this period still remains to give this story a special welcome there, but it will be an outstanding addition anywhere to the collection of this author's books that every wise library has been making. The Napoleonic legend in relation to the life of the young republic seldom figures in fiction.

Florence Bethune Sloan

SOURCE: A review of *The Scarlet Oak,* in *The Christian Science Monitor,* November 17, 1938, p. 8.

Cornelia Meigs never disappoints us in her books, for first of all she writes a capital story well; secondly, she brings to her writing a fine appreciation of what young people like; thirdly, her books are sound all the way through and, where historical scenes and events are part of the story, they are faithfully drawn and accurately set down.

The Scarlet Oak has all these qualities and is another in her long list of fine tales with American backgrounds.

Hugh and Jeremy Armond arrive from England with their mother to make their home with their grandfather, a shipping merchant living outside Bordentown, New Jersey. They find him in serious business troubles, for it is the time when men and nations were working to restore stability and order out of the discord the world had been thrown into during the Napoleonic wars. How Jeremy is advised to return and work abroad for the American shipping interests, and the part played by Hugh, the real hero of the story, when he becomes gardener's boy at Point Breeze, the estate of Joseph Bonaparte, makes good reading.

While there, Hugh witnesses and plays an important part in the exciting events that happen in the household of the brother of the great Napoleon, then in exile. Some of the important people of the period are characters in the story, and Miss Meigs provides another picture of early America and makes us appreciate the courage, skill, and spirit that went into its building.

Anne T. Eaton

SOURCE: A review of *The Scarlet Oak,* in *The New York Times Book Review,* December 11, 1938, p. 10.

A spirited story touching on events and characters in American history not so far used in books for boys and girls. Hugh and Jeremy Armond come with their mother from France in 1817 to make their home with their grandfather in Bordentown, N.J., not far from Philadelphia. Stephen Girard is their grandfather's friend. Ships belonging to their grandfather and to Girard have been seized by the British during the Napoleonic Wars and are held in Denmark. Since the charge that the ships were carrying unlawful goods is false, Girard hopes by bringing the matter up in the law courts to get the vessels back, and when his agent goes to Denmark on this business, Jeremy, who is 18, is sent with him to help.

Hugh, the younger of the two boys, is the real hero of the story. Wishing to do his share toward helping the family's fallen fortunes, he finds work at Point Breeze, the estate of Joseph Bonaparte. The old French gardener is Hugh's good friend, but other members of the household are not so kindly disposed toward him. A mysterious stranger appears and reappears and Hugh finds himself involved in unforeseen and exciting adventures.

There are well-drawn portraits of Joseph Bonaparte and of Girard, and the period and the countryside are suggested in convincing fashion. Like all Miss Meigs's books, *The Scarlet Oak* has sincerity and a fine four-square quality that make it a welcome addition to stories based on American history. Elizabeth Orton Jones has drawn some excellent pictures successfully suggesting the atmosphere of the time.

📖 *CALL OF THE MOUNTAIN* (1940)

Ellen Lewis Buell

SOURCE: A review of *Call of the Mountain,* in *The New York Times Book Review,* November 10, 1940, p. 10.

"If the valley has no place for a man there are always the mountains," so Nathan Lindsay thought as he turned his back on his heritage and climbed in the bitter cold of a Vermont Winter night in 1830 to the deserted mountain farm he had chosen. He had inherited from his benefactor the valley farm which he had loved and worked and thus he had incurred the hate of Hamilton Bemis, who thought it should have been his, a hatred which festered until Nathan was accused of falseness and finally of murder. This is the story of a young man's double fight to clear his name and to wrest from the wilderness, singlehanded and without money, a place he could call his own.

It was a hard-fought battle against cold, privation and unremitting labor, and against malice too, but it has its rewards in the loyalty which Nathan found among his friends. Indeed the best element of this fine novel for young people is its portrayal of a New England community with heart-warming friendliness pitted against the suspicion of people less malicious than bored.

It is an inspiring story of courage for youth to read in a troubled period. The fresh winds of Vermont sweep through it and the sensitive descriptions of farm and wild animals will delight those who love the outdoors. James Daugherty has illustrated it with true understanding in pictures which are less restless than most of his work but just as vigorous.

Alice M. Jordan

SOURCE: A review of *Call of the Mountain,* in *The Horn Book Magazine,* Vol. XVII, No. 1, January, 1941, p. 31.

The boy of nineteen who made for himself a home in a lone cabin on a farm on "Height of Land," between the Green Mountain range and the Champlain valley, needed courage and strength. He had to meet not only the hardships of the wilderness, the raid by wolves, the savage onslaught of the wild boar, but also the hostility of a man to whom he had done no wrong. Here were the elements to develop the fine traits that Cornelia Meigs loves to present in her stories for young people. Here again she has drawn a boy with vision and integrity. The vigorous pictures by James Daugherty are well suited to the rugged Vermont scene in the second quarter of the last century.

📖 *VANISHED ISLAND* (1941)

Alice M. Jordan

SOURCE: A review of *Vanished Island,* in *The Horn Book Magazine,* Vol. XVII, No. 6, November, 1941, p. 461.

The background for this stirring story of a boy and his job is the varied and exciting life along the Mississippi River. Cornelia Meigs knew this locale well in the time of which she writes. She draws the river steamboat with its shining engine room, its watchful and resourceful pilot, with a sure hand. She makes her readers feel the power of the great river, its floods and currents, its sandbars, and greedy devouring of the land. The plot of the story has to do with a boy under a cloud whose determination to make good was awakened by his year on a steamboat. As in all the books by Miss Meigs the young people, of whom there are several, are convincingly and sincerely pictured.

I. S.

SOURCE: A review of *Vanished Island,* in *The New York Times Book Review,* November 2, 1941, p. 30.

The Mississippi River in the 1890s is for this story a proving ground, where Don Perry had the chance to outlive his bitterness and find himself through hard work. When he was dismissed from school the boy felt that his family too, in his time of need, deserted him, so that tensions developed on both sides. Working aboard the proud steamer Mary Morton, Don Perry gained understanding of others at the same time he was regaining his own self-respect and the right to return to school.

This is a story of river-boating at the height of its glory, of river life along the shores, and of the Mississippi itself, whose changing course shaped the destinies of travelers, traders, adventurers and crew. The narrative progresses with rather less assurance than Miss Meigs usually exhibits, and lacks somewhat in suspense and vitality. Yet the characterizations emerge naturally, stemming straight from the well-proportioned background. Destructive flood waters and the doom of Amaranth Island provide an artistic finish to a story in which the river is after all the chief actor.

📖 *MOUNTED MESSENGER* (1943)

Alice M. Jordan

SOURCE: A review of *Mounted Messenger,* in *The Horn Book Magazine,* Vol. XIX, No. 3, May, 1943, p. 175.

At last someone has written a book showing the romantic beginning of the United States postal service. Fortunately for us, the someone is Cornelia Meigs, who has such genuine sympathy with each significant step in American history. In *Mounted Messenger,* Benjamin Franklin, King's Postmaster of all the colonies, in 1755, envisions the consequences to the thirteen colonies of frequent exchanges of ideas among the different leaders. He sees the coming of national unity through the faithful delivery of mail. Tom Wetherall, the boy chosen as messenger, carries mail east to Boston, where he sees John Adams, and west from Philadelphia just during Braddock's fateful campaign. The story centers around Tom and his sister Prudence. It abounds with exciting episodes and gives a fine sense of American feeling before the Revolution.

Alice M. Jordan

SOURCE: A review of *Mounted Messenger,* in *The Saturday Review of Literature,* Vol. XXVI, No. 20, May 15, 1943, p. 27.

Books dealing with phases of American history are to be found both in biographical form and in fiction. Cornelia Meigs has added another fine book to her lengthening list covering a wide range of periods. In *Mounted Messenger,* she shows Benjamin Franklin, Colonel Washington, and John Adams, honored leaders in 1755, intent upon bringing the best minds of the colonies into closer accord through frequent exchange of letters. Franklin was Postmaster of the thirteen colonies, and his sixteen-year-old messenger, carrying the mail over difficult routes, east and west, has a share in knitting the sections together. In stressing the leaders' vision of unity among the colonies, Cornelia Meigs inevitably foreshadows the move toward world unity of the wisestminds of today. Sound historical research always goes into the writing of her good stories, which are essentially true in facts and spirit.

Ida Tarbell

SOURCE: A review of *Mounted Messenger,* in *The New York Times Book Review,* June 20, 1943, p. 7.

Cornelia Meigs in her thoughtfully written, carefully authentic stories has described many significant periods in American history. This latest story begins in 1755, just as Mr. Franklin of Philadelphia, "head postmaster for all the colonies," was planning the first western mail route on which the post riders would carry the mail and bring news to the settlements along the Susquehanna. Already messengers were riding the northern route to New York and Boston.

The story catches something of the excitement of those early days when change was in the air and when men like Franklin, Colonel Washington and John Adams of Boston were seeking, through better means of communication, to unify the interests and decisions of the colonies.

Eleven-year-old Prudence and her 16-year-old brother Tom lived in the colony of Pennsylvania, and it was Tom, eager to do a man's work in the world, whom Franklin hired as the first rider of the western mail route. When the French and Indian War broke out, Tom played his part in getting horses and men to General Braddock. The girls, Prudence and her friend Gertrude, found themselves sharing in the growing tension when they offered to help Mr. Franklin in his print shop, preparing the copies of *The Pennsylvania Gazette* and the bills which were to be distributed along the post routes in order to bring to the scattered settlers the news of the day. They also wrote letters at Mr. Franklin's dictation and once, indeed, they found themselves copying reports and records for young Colonel Washington.

The story shows clearly what the difficulty of communication meant to the colonists and suggests the atmosphere of that stirring period just before the Revolution. For boys and girls from 9 to 12.

THE VIOLENT MEN: A STUDY OF HUMAN RELATIONS IN THE FIRST AMERICAN CONGRESS (1949)

Helen Fay

SOURCE: A review of *The Violent Men: A Study of Human Relations in the First American Congress,* in *The Horn Book Magazine,* Vol. XXV, No. 4, July, 1949, pp. 297-98.

In a book so clear and simple as to be read eagerly by a young student, Cornelia Meigs presents a penetrating study of the Continental Congress from its inception in May, 1774, until July 4, 1776. The reader moves with the patriots representing the thirteen colonies in a drama that begins as a protest against unfair taxation but ends with a vote for independence and final union. The contrast in background and aims between the homespun, radical John Adams of Massachusetts and the rich, conservative Pennsylvania Quaker, John Dickinson, is perhaps the sharpest of all the many differences. Miss Meigs shows how logically "the violent men" overcame most of these differences by their knowledge of words and their ability to express their ideas clearly to each other, by their integrity and their growing recognition of the importance of freedom. How refreshing is the humor in the picture of the "worthy gentlemen of Boston" who went home from the Tea Party "looking innocent but with their shoes full of tea" and in the wooing of the undecided South Carolina delegates through their pleasure-loving wives, caught up in Philadelphia society's gay whirl! Miss Meigs puts us on speaking terms not only with the well-known patriots who formulated the Declaration of Independence, but also with many of the "lesser lights" who at times were as important as those who made the headlines.

Merrill Jensen

SOURCE: A review of *The Violent Men: A Study of Human Relations in the First American Congress,* in *The Saturday Review of Literature,* Vol. XXXII, No. 35, August 27, 1949, p. 15.

This is history in the romantic tradition. There are heroes and villains. Caesar Rodney arrives at the deliberations of the Continental Congress on a foaming horse in time to break the Delaware deadlock and throw the vote of his colony for Lee's resolution just as he does in the old poem. We are given men's innermost thoughts as they faced one crisis after another. Thus John Dickinson sits in his study sorting papers on the night of July 1 after he has made his last speech against independence. The next day he goes forth to lead his troops into battle. It might have been thus, but we cannot know, however pleasant and plausible the reconstruction. Such things make for a rich story of the First and Second Continental Congresses between 1774 and 1776, but the very richness hides the fact of an oversimplified pattern of interpretation of men and events.

When the First Congress met it soon divided into two opposed groups. One group wanted reconciliation with Great Britain; the other group, the "violent men," were driving in the direction of independence. Those who wanted to stay within the empire were led by men like Joseph Galloway, James Duane, and, later on, by John Dickinson. The "violent men" were led by Samuel and John Adams, Richard Henry Lee, Patrick Henry, and others. This basic division is recognized but its roots are not, and it is overlaid with the story of personal animosities and friendships, with charming accounts of how men looked and acted, of the social life of Philadelphia, and so on. This discursiveness is well illustrated in a fifteen-page chapter called "Between Hawk and Buzzard," which covers nearly twenty topics ranging all the way from a private conference between John Adams and John Jay through an account of the Canada expedition, the examination of Richard Penn by the House of Lords, the debate between Burke and Wedderburn in the House of Commons, the funeral of Peyton Randolph, the treachery of Benjamin Church, the problems of army supply, and the memorial service for Richard Montgomery.

The emphasis on the role of individuals makes for good reading, but it also raises the question of what that role really was. Thus I do not think it an adequate explanation of Joseph Galloway to write of him only in terms of a man with an overweening ambition for whom the First Congress was a "fertile field in which to work," and who planned to play a "high role" in his plan of Union. The Galloway plan had a long history behind it. It was supported by Americans who had long hoped for some constitutional means of settling the disputes between Britain and the colonies. Galloway was as much spokesman as leader of this group, and his plan was certainly not one of "appeasement." The problem was not to overcome Galloway in the First Congress, but to overcome perhaps a majority of the members who felt as he did, even before they arrived in Philadelphia. . . .

Among these "violent men" it is surprising to find Samuel Adams given a minor role. It is said that he was underrated and that he needed the notoriety of a position in Congress to support his prestige. No contemporary would have given this superb strategist so low a mark, however little they might like him. It was Sam who broke the deadlock in the First Congress by having the Suffolk Resolves brought in. It was he who outmaneuvered those who wanted to stay in the Empire and they knew it. True, men like his cousin John Adams and Richard Henry Lee did most of the talking, but it was "Adams and his crew" who were given credit for the results of the First Congress. By the winter of 1775-76 he was known as "Judas Iscariot" by many a horrified if fascinated opponent.

The value of this book therefore lies in its excursions into the byways of history, its portraits of men and women, its accounts of the social life of Philadelphia. It does not lie in its interpretation of the basic issues between 1774-76 and of the men who debated them.

📖 *THE TWO ARROWS* (1949)

Frances C. Darling

SOURCE: A review of *The Two Arrows,* in *The Christian Science Monitor,* December 8, 1949, p. 17.

It has been a long time since we have had a story by Cornelia Meigs, but this Christmas there is *The Two Arrows,* written for ages 10-14. The title makes it sound like a tale of Indian adventure, but these arrows refer to the yearly token sent from Maryland to the King, as promised in the original charter. This payment is worked into the story in charming fashion.

The time is 1745, when the first of the great plantation houses were being built along the Tidewater, and when the colonists were beginning to take real pride in the new land. The feeling for the beauty of the country is one of the nicest things in the book and the description of the way in which the life there changes the character of the settlers. The two boys, Ronald and Jan, deported from England and forced to work as indentured servants, had various adventures with smugglers, pirates and a scheming overseer before they earned their freedom and decided to stay in the colony where there was opportunity for all.

Louise S. Bechtel

SOURCE: A review of *The Two Arrows,* in *New York Herald Tribune Book Review,* December 18, 1949, p. 8.

From the day when she published **Master Simon's Garden,** Cornelia Meigs's wide public has been assured. With books like **Mounted Messenger,** and **Invincible Louisa,** which won the Newbery Medal, for older boys and girls, and **The Wonderful Locomotive** and **The Willow Whistle** for younger children, she has brought many aspects of the American scene to their attention in imaginative ways, combining history with good storytelling. Hers is an outstanding contribution to well over twenty-five years of children's book-making.

Now she tells an adventure story which begins in England in 1745; its teen-age heroes are captured as indentured servants and taken to the new colony of Maryland. There many still are loyal to the Pretender. The brother, who is already an able architect, finds himself in an interesting job, but his spirit is broken. The younger brother soon comes to love the new, wild land. After much excitement, it is he who shares the task of taking Maryland's two Indian arrows as tribute to the King at Windsor.

But it wouldn't be a Cornelia Meigs book were there not an idea along with all the excitement. Here it is the earliest thinking toward a land with no king. It is a fine book for boys and girls of around twelve.

📖 *THE DUTCH COLT* (1952)

Virginia Kirkus' Bookshop Service

SOURCE: A review of *The Dutch Colt,* in *Virginia Kirkus' Bookshop Service,* Vol. XX, No. 17, September 1, 1952, p. 553.

In a story that carries with it a good deal of the idealism

of the times, Cornelia Meigs writes of a boy and girl who lived as caretakers' children on William Penn's manor. During Penn's years in England to re-fortify finances, young Hugh and Gertrude Andrews fall prey to the maneuverings of Jonas Bonner who takes the colt, Dapple, one of the last horses on Penn's impoverished estate. There's adventure in Dapple's recovery and Hugh's satisfying recounting of events to Penn himself when he returns to the colony.

Sarah Chokla Gross

SOURCE: A review of *The Dutch Colt,* in *The New York Times Book Review,* November 9, 1952, p. 52.

Hugh and his younger sister, Gertrude, lived at Pennsbury, where their cousin, James Harrison, was the manager. So much did they love the property that they too felt as if they were stewards of the place. When the horses had to be sold to meet Penn's debts, it was they who managed to save and hide the valuable Dutch colt, Dapple. But Dapple disappeared and it was only Hugh's persistence that tracked down the thief and retrieved the colt in time for William Penn's return from England. In the process a "bound girl" is enabled to get back to her mother, and Gertrude's prize possession, an antique doll bed, becomes an important figure in this exciting story.

The drawings by Doris and George Hauman, especially of the night scenes, heighten the interest in this Quaker narrative of colonial Pennsylvania.

New York Herald Tribune Book Review

SOURCE: A review of *The Dutch Colt,* in *New York Herald Tribune Book Review,* November 16, 1952, p. 6.

Hugh lived at Pennsbury, the house built by Mr. Penn by letters from England, with his mother and younger sister, and the uncle who was its caretaker. He loved the horses and wept when three of them had to be sold to help the great man far away to pay his debts. But then came the new colt. Could they keep it from being sold? Hugh helped to hide it, but through his fault it was stolen. His determination to rescue it and courage in doing so, make a fine story; with a vivid setting of the early Pennsylvania country and of Philadelphia as a very new city.

Miss Meigs writes with all her old skill at weaving indescription with the action she knows children like. Both boys and girls of around nine to twelve will enjoy Hugh and Gertrude. The book is fairly short, of the length of those fine earlier books, *The Willow Whistle, Wind in the Chimney,* and *The Covered Bridge.* It is more modest in format with a very few indifferent black-and-white pictures, but the price is fortunately low, so it may lure a new audience to Miss Meigs's many fine books for these younger readers.

A CRITICAL HISTORY OF CHILDREN'S LITERATURE (edited by Meigs, with Anne T. Eaton, Elizabeth Nesbitt, and Ruth Hill Viguers, 1953; revised, 1969)

Louise S. Bechtel

SOURCE: "Of Children and the Books They Love," in *New York Herald Tribune Book Review,* June 21, 1953, p. 4.

The publication of this imposing volume is an event of importance. Carefully planned by the publisher with one of America's best-loved authors as supervising editor and co-author, discussed by the collaborating writers, all of whom have had long experience in the field of children's books, it stands as a unique achievement, a job that has long needed doing.

For, as Miss Meigs says in her cogent foreword, it still remained to be proved to the world at large that there is a body of writing, part of the main stream of English and American literature, which can justly be called "children's literature." Its aims also include "an attempt to capture the essence of that experience of delight which children have enjoyed in exploring their own literature from the beginning of remembered history onward," "to offer a critical analysis of what has endured and why," and "to discuss what is best in that bewildering supply now available for young people's reading."

A book of this scope is of special interest to children's librarians, and its publication is timed to meet the opening of the American Library Association convention at Los Angeles. Its wider audience should include teachers, students, booksellers, writers and publishers. The work is dedicated to "three great leaders in the knowledge and understanding of children's literature": Anne Carroll Moore, Bertha Mahony Miller and Frederic G. Melcher. The stories of their contributions are told at fitting points on the way, and several chapters give valuable outlines of the growth of children's library work in this country.

It consists of four sections: 1. "Roots in the Past Up to 1840," by Cornelia Meigs. 2. "Widening Horizons: 1840-1890," by Anne [T.] Eaton. 3. "A Rightful Heritage: 1890-1920," by Elizabeth Nesbitt. 4. "The Golden Age: 1920-1950," by Ruth Hill Viguers.There are twenty-six pages of index.

This is a book about books and writing, about authors and the creative impulses which led to their writing for children, about certain books originally written for adults but gradually adopted by children. It is not a book of advice, nor is it one of facts and figures about children's reading, libraries, bookshops, sales. The word "critical" in the title implies what it would in writing of adult books, an attempt to evaluate, to compare and record, to relate the books discussed to their eras. Each author, besides pointing out high spots, establishes the trends of her times and indicates the shifts of children's own interests, as affected by social, economic and literary developments. The matter of a possible philosophy underlying the American attitude toward children's reading is cleverly forecast for the whole book by Professor Henry S. Commager.

Miss Meigs's section is a brilliant compression of the influence of the great past of English literature, from the days before print, the days of the shaping of folklore, up to the earliest American books. "The New England Primer," the works of Samuel Goodrich and Jacob Abbott. She is as excellent a guide to the past as she must have been as an English teacher, for she offers a procession of living portraits of writers, and with well-chosen quotations lets us feel the quality of their writings. Her historic backgrounds are vivid, and she does not neglect the changes in education brought about by Locke and Rousseau. However often you may have read such historic material, you will find her pages fresh and stimulating. Like the seafaring ancestors who inspired many of her own fine historic stories, Miss Meigs keeps a firm hand on the helm and shows us the two great routes still being traversed today: adult literature as it affected children and was adopted by them, and ways of writing specifically for children.

Her section ends with a delightful chapter on poetry, as does each of the other parts. These four chapters are high points in the book. Perhaps they give us extra pleasure because the literary values of poetry are those on which we all can most easily agree. . . .

We would have liked to see a conclusion by Miss Meigs which pulled all the themes together. But, as her foreword says, any such survey is spade work, an exploration, not a definition. Surely this volume has proved that the best writers for children deserve a place in the sun, and that there is a body of literature for children worthy of that word.

Elizabeth Gray Vining

SOURCE: "Lit with the Freshness and Vigor of Childhood Itself," in *The New York Times Book Review,* June 21, 1953, p. 7.

The history of children's literature from its earliest, unrecognized beginnings to the present day has an element of struggle and conflict that makes it dramatic reading. Furthermore, it is lit with the freshness and vigor of childhood itself, for though it deals with books it is concerned also, and primarily, with the child, his wonder, his imagination, his power of growth, his sense of play, his innate taste and discrimination.

There are two main threads in the drama. One is the conflict between the children's own choice, the books they accept and appropriate, and the adults' inveterate determination to ply them with instruction and admonishment. The second is the struggle of children's literature as such to achieve recognition as a field of writing with dignity and importance of its own.

First of its kind, *A Critical History of Children's Literature* is a major undertaking and an important achievement. Though divided chronologically into four sections, each by a different author, it has unity, and through its long sweep the threads of the drama are evident and the fascinating story moves with swiftness and interest.

Part One, "Roots in the Past," is the work of Cornelia Meigs, herself a writer of note for children. Her section is marked by beauty of style, by humor, by her appreciative understanding of children, and her love and knowledge of books.

In the earliest period, children listened with their elders to stories of Celtic and Anglo-Saxon origin, followed by the medieval romances and the ballads. With the institution of printing in fifteenth-century Europe, the battle was joined between the choice of the children and the desire of the grown-ups to edify. The *Book of Curtasye* and *The Babee's Book* and other manuals of behavior, the first books written expressly for children, lost the first round to "Reynard the Fox" and Aesop's "Fables," the delight of the children themselves.

Two centuries and more later the children pounced upon *Pilgrim's Progress, Robinson Crusoe* and *Gulliver's Travels,* and made them their own. After John Locke's liberal and understanding *Thoughts on Education* prepared the way for attractive books designed especially for children, John Newbery (1713-1767) began to publish his gay little sixpenny books in his shop called the Bible and Sun, and children's books, as Miss Meigs says, "finally stood on their own feet."

From then until 1820 the story continues with the three kinds of books then available for children; books thrust upon them, like Foxe's *Book of Martyrs* and the *New England Primer,* books written for their pleasure as well as improvement, like Abbott's *Franconia Stories* and Maria Edgeworth's *Parent's Assistant,* and books appropriated by them, like those of Scott, Cooper and Irving. . . .

A Critical History of Children's Literature is a book not solely for those who deal professionally with children and their reading (including parents), though certainly not one of them can afford to miss it, but it is for all who are interested in literature. Perhaps most of all it is for those who remember their own enchanted childhood hours with books, when books were the very stuff of magic and adventure.

Helen Ferris

SOURCE: A review of *A Critical History of Children's Literature,* in *Saturday Review,* Vol. XXXVI, No. 34, August 22, 1953, pp. 18-19.

With the publication *A Critical History of Children's Literature,* literature for children takes its long merited place in the written history of literature as a whole. Against a richly realized historical and sociological background is presented the emergence among English-speaking peoples of a body of writing for the young more comprehensive and significant than anywhere else in the world.

Edited by a distinguished author of books for young readers, Cornelia Meigs, [and] published under the direction of Doris Patee, able editor of the children's book department of the publisher, it is the work of four recognized authorities and critics of children's literature, each of whom has enjoyed years of intimate association with children and their books.

This *Critical History,* writes Cornelia Meigs in her foreword,

> is written in an attempt to capture the essence of delight which children have enjoyed in exploring their own literature from the beginnings of remembered history onward, the adventure of childhood itself in finding, pursuing, and even helping to shape the course of that reading which has grown up to be theirs in their own right. This book, moreover, sets out to refute the idea that children's literature has had only a brief and unimportant record. And, finally, it undertakes to offer a critical analysis of what has endured and why, of how time and circumstances have affected the progress of children's literature as it has shaped that of adults, and to discuss what is best in the bewildering abundance of supply which is now available for young people's reading, and where are the contemporary books which, in their turn, may endure.

It is a purpose brilliantly achieved, to which is added a further significance, pointed out by Henry Steele Commager in his stimulating introduction: "Because the record is so long and rich . . . we have in literature not only a continuous record of childhood but . . . of the ideals and standards that society wishes to inculcate into each new generation." The result is a book not only for parents, authors, librarians, and teachers and students of children's literature but for all to whom children are of special concern.

With the sensitive perception by which Miss Meigs has recreated the past in her books for young readers, she brings vividly alive, in the book's first section, "Roots in the Past Up to 1840," the period from the days before the invention of printing to those of Sir Walter Scott and James Fenimore Cooper. We see the children pressing eagerly forward in the crowd around the ancient story-tellers, "young persons who hearkened and remembered and told the same stories to their children in their own time." We feel the drama of the first printed books and rejoice to find among them Caxton's *Aesop's Fables* and, later, the gay little volumes issued by John Newbery, first publisher for children, *Goody Two-Shoes, Mother Goose.*

But the generations during which children delightedly

appropriated *Robinson Crusoe* and *Gulliver's Travels* brought forth as well, in both England and America, "grim representations of the Age of Admonition," with their "doctrines of election and original sin, awareness of possible early death and the necessity of laying up treasures in Heaven." And there arose the clash of philosophies between those adults who held that moral, didactic lessons were of single urgent importance and those who would bring to children books vibrant with life, richness, and beauty.

We applaud Locke's defense of each child's right to his own individuality; Rousseau's insistence that *Robinson Crusoe* is the only "suitable" book for the young. And there is more than one chuckle in the sight of the children imperturbably going their preferred reading way, in the midst of the contention, taking for their own "the true literature . . . which was cherished in their hearts always."

Marguerite Archer

SOURCE: A review of *A Critical History of Children's Literature,* in *School Library Journal,* Vol. 17, No. 8, April, 1971, pp. 35-7.

The field of the history of children's literature has not fared so well, though several excellent studies were published in England during the past 80 years. Virginia Haviland's *Children's Literature: A Guide to Reference Sources* lists only one comprehensive history including American children's literature: *A Critical History of Children's Literature.* It is alone in its category, and has dominated as the standard textbook in the fieldsince it originally was published in 1953.

Reviewers lauded both the original and revised edition. High praise is merited. The authors—Cornelia Meigs, Elizabeth Nesbitt, Anne [T.] Eaton, and Ruth Hill Viguers—attempted a gigantic task to meet an obvious need and should be given full credit for their vision, enthusiasm, organization, grasp of the subject, and above all, critical ability and high aim.

Unfortunately, the book had one serious flaw, soon discovered by a small group of people, though probably overlooked by most users. In 1954 Earle Walbridge and a committee of the Bibliographical Society of America itemized over 150 errors in the Society's *Papers* (v. 48, second and third quarters). Appalled at the number of mistakes in what was surely destined to become a major reference work, Walbridge told a friend he had written to Macmillan offering his services in correcting the book, but never received a reply. Perhaps the letter went astray.

Few corrections were made in the second printing (also 1953). It no longer had Mayne Reid dead at age four, but otherwise the errors remained.

Of course errors inevitably occur, though proofreading

usually eliminates typographic ones. Submitting a manuscript to expert readers also helps. But if there is urgency to publish to a rigid deadline, errors are far more likely to remain. The book was published just before the 1953 ALA meeting and immediately hailed. It was lengthy, and the errors so numerous that it is unlikely the publishers wanted to change the plates. The book had, after all, cost a great deal of money, and no profit had yet been shown. With accumulating praise and perhaps no further adverse criticism in print, it would be easy to overlook the entire matter. Also, the juvenile editor thought the criticism inconsequential and "nit-picking."

The issue is one of scholarship. Does anyone care whether or not a history of children's literature be correct? Teachers of children's literature and its history probably care a great deal. Scholarship is as essential in this academic area as it is in English or American literature. Inaccurate history is mere opinion.

Some 126 errors (my own rough count) have been corrected in this revised edition. Sometimes material containing errors was omitted, and in a few instances the decision has apparently been made that the book is correct. A very careful job—at last. . . .

If you have the old edition and ever expect to use it, you should surely buy the revision. Despite the smaller print, it is a marvelous improvement—a superb book, fascinating to read, and in the latter sections brilliantly updated by the late Ruth Hill Viguers.

One question does arise about format. One is impressed with the clear print, attractive spacing, and handsome illustrations in *Children and Their Literature*. It is a pity that *A Critical History* . . . was not as well treated. Yes, it would cost more. Perhaps the next edition should be two volumes. . . .

One hopes any remaining errors—probably very few—will be corrected in the next edition; the public and the authors are certainly due this courtesy. Seventeen more years would be too long to wait. . . .

Next edition? Eventually, there will have to be a third edition incorporating new scholarship: new references, updated bibliographies for each chapter. It is a pleasure to see instances of bibliographic improvement in the present revision. Credit is given to Richard L. Darling's *The Rise of Children's Book Reviewing in America, 1865-1881* (1968) for pointing out the informed and constructive literary criticism of that time. . . .

Time alters perspective on many books (as one quickly sees by perusing old copies of *The Horn Book* or other reviewing magazines). The revision of a page on biographies is an excellent example of facing this fact. The section on Africa is a fine updating of perspective in another field, as is a passage on fairy tales and fantasy. The old material on Lucy Fitch Perkins should have been moved to the past tense, (*e.g., were* favorites) and

her books might be faulted (from today's viewpoint) for their stereotypes. The revision should have acknowledged the fact that Joseph Altsheler's historic novels are no longer very popular. As time goes on some works recede into obscurity; this truism accounts for the wise omission of any mention of Nathaniel Cotton and another lesser author.

Attitudes toward social conditions change. A paragraph on *The Story of Little Black Sambo* has been deleted in the revision. An added section on "Stories about Negro Children" is short but effective. *Durango Street* is justly applauded, though violence in realistic juvenile fiction was taboo a dozen years ago.

As children's literature changes, material written about it will change too. In both editions Charles Kingsley's long-popular book *The Water-Babies* is given due credit for changing a social condition, the forcing of children to clean out soot-filled chimneys. *Labour* has become *labor* in the revised edition. A third edition might show this as more than an "unjustifiable form of child labor," since boy chimney sweeps developed a dreadful occupational disease—cancer of the scrotum.

A constant effort should be made to update and perfect this extremely valuable book, without embarrassment or tactful silence about any shortcomings. *A Critical History of Children's Literature* is so important that it should be the responsibility of the profession as well as all the authors, editors, and publishers to make such a work as fine as possible. . . .

In all probability, *A Critical History of Children's Literature,* will continue to be the leading work in its field, especially now that accuracy has been tacitly acknowledged as a necessary requisite to historical scholarship in children's literature.

📖 *FAIR WIND TO VIRGINIA* (1955)

Virginia Kirkus' Service

SOURCE: A review of *Fair Wind to Virginia,* in *Virginia Kirkus' Service,* Vol. XXIII, No. 17, September 1, 1955, p. 656.

A well-paced story of pre-Revolutionary War Williamsburg tells of Hal and Peggy Morrow, two youngsters from England, and relates a segment of American history with the sense of sympathy in Cornelia Meigs's other historical novels (*The Mounted Messenger, The Two Arrows*). Mr. Morrow, a member of parliament, has been speaking against the King's colonial policies, he has had to flee to France. This leaves Hal and Peggy with the open choice of going to Virginia in the hope that their parents may be able to join them there sometime. In Williamsburg, the youngsters have a double set of connections—those loyal to the King, and the others—Jefferson among them—who want a freedom from tyranny. But when Hal gets a job in Jefferson's law office, all of the Morrow loyalties are soon with the colonists and when they also find land for the whole family to settle on there is a sense of unity with the new country and a satisfying end to the story.

Louise S. Bechtel

SOURCE: "Stories of Lively Young Americans," in *New York Herald Tribune Book Review,* November 13, 1955, p. 24.

When their father was suspected of treason and hustled off to France, two English children were sent to Virginia, where the family was to be reunited. Eleven-year-old Peggy and thirteen-year-old Hal found the small capitol at Williamsburg not so different from England, and others more friendly than the Governor who was supposed to care for them. As messenger boy for the famous lawyer Wythe, Hal helped to foil a plot against the Aldgates; he also traced the location of land across the mountains that belonged to his father. On a wonderful journey by horseback, the children found this inheritance of a home in the new country. As the Revolution began, at last their parents arrived.

Miss Meigs has described Colonial Williamsburg with skill. She makes its people, homes, shops, Governors' palace, church and capitol, really vivid and alive. Even better is the contrast of the newly settled wilderness in the "Valley of Virginia," the rich, beautiful land which took hold of the hearts of these English country children. At the point in her story where the villain disappears, the tension preceding the Revolution takes his place. The portrait of the young lawyer Jefferson is very interesting.

The book gives a picture of the well-to-do, cultivated, intelligent English people who stood forth early for America's freedom. It will illuminate the visits of children to the Williamsburg of today but is also fine reading for boys and girls of about eleven to fourteen, anywhere in America.

WILD GEESE FLYING (1957)

Miriam James

SOURCE: A review of *Wild Geese Flying,* in *The New York Times Book Review,* April 21, 1957, p. 20.

The Milton family, after years of wandering, settled lovingly into the gracious Vermont home that Grandfather Devon left to them. While father is away on business the others find that grandfather has left a mystery which affects their reception in Jefferson Village. The townspeople doubt the Miltons' right to the house and will not accept their presence. Twelve-year-old Dick and his warmhearted family slowly surmount the rigors of a New England winter and New England ethics. By

June, when the mystery is unraveled, their own value as people already has triumphed over suspicion.

Cornelia Meigs's easy-rolling book has the quiet understanding of hills and valleys, of wild geese flying over a secret pond, and of the likenesses and diversity of people. It's a good book for children entering that age when relationships command so much thought and time.

Saturday Review

SOURCE: A review of *Wild Geese Flying,* in *Saturday Review,* Vol. XL, No. 19, May 11, 1957, p. 55.

The Milton family were baffled by the unfriendly attitude of the Vermont villagers when they arrived to live in the house they recently inherited. Learning that money left with their late grandfather by a young war veteran had disappeared, the Miltons were determined to solve the mystery or relinquish the house. In the meantime, because of their kindliness, industry, and initiative—qualities so admired in this New England village—the Miltons were accepted and invited to take part in community activities.

Again Cornelia Meigs has written a story with depth and perception, with warm family relationships, a well-knit plot, and good description of life in a New England village today. It will appeal to boys and girls aged ten to twelve.

MYSTERY AT THE RED HOUSE (1961)

Ruth Hill Viguers

SOURCE: A review of *Mystery at the Red House,* in *The Horn Book Magazine,* Vol. XXXVII, No. 5, October, 1961, pp. 441-42.

In a reversal of the usual order this story *begins* with the finding of a treasure of rare jewels. How the jewels happened to be in the old well where eleven-year-old Nina found them and what they had to do with the sudden disappearance of a family that everyone in the little New England village respected and loved were mysteries that took many weeks to solve. Full of intriguing events, pleasant people, and a variety of interests, this should find a ready public; but it does not approach the quality of some of Miss Meigs's truly memorable stories.

JANE ADDAMS: PIONEER FOR SOCIAL JUSTICE: A BIOGRAPHY (1970)

Janet Harris

SOURCE: A review of *Jane Addams: Pioneer for Social Justice,* in *The New York Times Book Review,* May 10, 1970, p. 26.

Cornelia Meigs's *Jane Addams: Pioneer for Social Justice* should be a winner. Miss Meigs is a distinguished author, and Jane Addams (1860-1935) was probably the most important woman in the history of American social reform. Her influence extended into every sphere, from founding modern methods of social work, to influencing legislation concerning child labor and trade unionism. At once a radical and a great lady, she shook up political and social structures, and the effects of her work are still felt. Nevertheless, this biography is disappointing. Despite a wealth of detail, it is not a complete presentation—a point the author herself concedes. It concentrates on Jane Addams's work at Hull House. But why are her contributions to world peace—for which she shared the Nobel prize in 1931—given such short shrift? A second failing is that the mood of Chicago'steeming, polyglot ghetto is not conveyed. The writing here is graceful, but the book leaves the reader uninvolved.

Cecilia Zelman

SOURCE: A review of *Jane Addams: Pioneer for Social Justice,* in *School Library Journal,* September, 1970, Vol. 17, No. 1, p. 174.

Cornelia Meigs concludes this sober, thorough biography with the idea that youth today needs someone like Jane Addams, who loved young people, helped and protected them. She and her co-workers at Hull House opened new vistas to young immigrants by providing recreation to leaven their long work week. She also crusaded for many, often unpopular, causes: against child labor; against intolerable sweatshops; for woman suffrage; etc. While the story is inspiring, average readers will probably find the style too heavy for leisure-time reading. It will be a very good source of information for students researching the period of rising industrialism—its evils and its reformers.

Additional coverage of Meigs's life and career is contained in the following sources published by The Gale Group: *Junior DISCovering Authors; Major Authors and Illustrators for Children and Young Adults;* **and** *Something about the Author,* **Vol. 6.**

Bernard Waber
1924-

American author and illustrator of picture books.

Major works include *The House on East 88th Street* (1962; British edition as *Welcome, Lyle*, 1969), *An Anteater Named Arthur* (1967), *A Firefly Named Torchy* (1970), *Ira Sleeps Over* (1972), *Do You See a Mouse?* (1995).

INTRODUCTION

Waber is best known for his series of picture books devoted to a delightful, whimsical, and lovable crocodile named Lyle. Capturing the hearts and imaginations of primary graders for nearly 30 years, Lyle was brought to life in Waber's second book, *The House on East 88th Street*, has been the subject of over seven books, and has inspired several plays and animated musicals. Reviewers praise Waber's sketchy and jubilant watercolor-and-ink illustrations, which make his fanciful, spirited characters like Lyle so beloved by children, and which make his farfetched situations seem plausible and perfectly natural. Skating at Rockefeller Center, doing handsprings in the park to please a crowd of children, sharpening pencils in an office, or practicing frightening expressions in a mirror are just a few examples of Lyle's diverting shenanigans. In the spirit of his highly regarded Lyle books, Waber has written and illustrated comical fantasies for children about other charming anthropomorphic animals such as mice, bears, and lions. He is also recognized for his use of wordplay and rhyme, and for his characteristically "droll, understated wit," noted a *Kirkus Reviews* critic. Waber's exuberantly playful language, combined with a subtle wickedness, shrewd understanding, and comforting warmth, appeal to child as well as adult readers. An observant parent, he incorporates the anxieties, concerns, and dreams of children into his picture books, using a gentle, yet meaningful voice.

Many of Waber's works present serious themes from a child's perspective, and offer suggestions for loving responses from parents. *A Firefly Named Torchy* touches on the theme of being yourself; *Lovable Lyle* (1969) deals with overcoming prejudice; *But Names Will Never Hurt Me* (1976) explores a child's response to teasing; *Mice on My Mind* (1977) spoofs obsession; and *Ira Sleeps Over* and *Ira Says Goodbye* (1988) present several childhood fears and anxieties. Whatever the creature or situation, Waber has a certain talent for enlivening and ennobling his characters with humor, life, and feeling. As Hanna B. Zeiger of *Horn Book* asserted in her review of *Do You See a Mouse?*: "Bernard Waber's characterizations are full of sly humor, and readers of all ages will have to smile at the antics of the little rascally rodent who successfully bamboozles one and all in his comic adventures."

Biographical Information

The son of immigrant parents, Waber grew up in Philadelphia, PA. He had an itinerant childhood, his family moving frequently during the Depression in pursuit of business opportunities and in flight from bill collectors. At each new home, young Waber's two priorities were to locate the nearest cinema and to find the neighborhood library. Movies and books helped him to survive the constant upheavals in his home life. At age eight he took a job as an usher in a local movie house, where he had opportunities to catch the final ten or fifteen minutes of the daily feature films. This, he claims, was when he began making up stories, reconstructing the beginning and the middle for the film's ending he had just seen.

After serving overseas during World War II, Waber returned to Philadelphia and enrolled at Philadelphia College of Art and then the Pennsylvania Academy of Fine Arts. He later married, and he and his wife moved to New York City where Waber began working as a commercial artist for Conde Nast, publisher of fashion magazines. He became a graphic designer for *Life* magazine, and then for *People*. Waber fell in love with children's books when he began reading aloud to his own children. He told *Something about the Author* (*SATA*): "I am afraid my enthusiasm for their books began, in fact, to cause my children occasional discomfort. 'Daddy, why don't you look at the grown-ups' books?' they once chided as I trailed after them into the children's room of our local library." He further added, "What impressed me most was the great and unlimited variety of expression afforded to writers and illustrators of children's books. Before long, I was writing and submitting." Waber was nudged into the illustrating of children's books by encouragement from his colleagues. After suggestions by several art directors that the drawings of children in his portfolio were very suitable for children's books, Waber launched a career of writing and illustrating his own picture books. He published his first work for children, *Lorenzo*, in 1961.

Major Works

Waber's best known books star the affable crocodile named Lyle. In the first of these, *The House on East 88th Street*, Lyle meets the Primm family, who discovers him in the bathtub making "Swish, Swash, Splash, Swoosh" noises when they move into their new home. Lyle has been left behind by Hector P. Valenti, the previous owner of the house, who could not support Lyle's expensive appetite for Turkish caviar. The crocodile proves to be a talented acrobat and natural performer, and becomes so popular that Mr. Valenti comes back to reclaim him and take him on a world tour. All goes well until Lyle begins to miss the Primms, and Mr. Valenti finally has to cancel the tour and return Lyle to his family. George A. Woods called this book a "lightly amusing extravaganza," while Virginia Haviland asserted, "The sketches of the great, green creature in all his fantastic endeavors will delight any child."

In *Lyle, Lyle, Crocodile* (1965), Lyle has many friends, but the neighbor cat, Loretta, goes into fits every time she sees him. Her owner, Mr. Grumps, has Lyle committed to the zoo. Lyle, however, escapes in order to save Mr. Grumps and Loretta from a house fire, showing them that he is "the bravest, kindest, most wonderful crocodile in the whole, wide world." *Lyle and the Birthday Party* (1966) finds Lyle going into a jealous sulk when Joshua Primm has a birthday party. Thinking that Lyle is ill, Mrs. Primm calls the doctor and Lyle lands, by mistake, in the hospital where he loses his bad mood by cheering up others. In *Lovable Lyle* (1969) the reptile receives nasty pen notes from someone who claims to hate him. The distressed Lyle tries his best to be kind and amusing, exhausting himself by his efforts. The perpetrator is revealed to be Clover Sue Hipple, whose mother is prejudiced towards crocodiles. When Lyle saves Clover from drowning, however, the crocodile becomes a hero.

Hector P. Valenti reappears in *Lyle Finds His Mother* (1974). Having fallen on hard times, Mr. Valenti con-

vinces Lyle to return to the road by promising him that they will search for Lyle's mother. When Lyle's mother finally appears, she is not the sweet, comforting woman—like Mrs. Primm—who Lyle has envisioned, but is more like Lyle himself, a bouncy, cheerful performer. Continuing the story in *Funny, Funny, Lyle* (1987), Lyle's mother Felicity, whose name is "of her own choosing," comes to live with the Primms in New York and gets herself into trouble by collecting bottles of perfume while on a shopping trip. She is sentenced to community service at the hospital, and is so good at nursing that she proves quite helpful when Mrs. Primm gives birth to her new baby. In *Lyle at the Office* (1994), Lyle visits the advertising agency where Mr. Primm works. The amiable reptile charms his new audience, especially in the day care center; yet, when Mr. Primm refuses to allow Lyle's picture to be used on a cereal box, both are kicked out of the office and Mr. Primm loses his job. All is well again, however, when Lyle saves Mr. Primm's boss from an injury. Mr. Primm returns to work and Lyle retains his privacy. Of *Lyle at the Office,* a *Publisher's Weekly* reviewer noted, "Lyle has aged exceptionally well since his first appearance some 30 years ago: he is as winsome as ever, and this new tale combines the charm of the first, somewhat quaint stories with a contemporary freshness."

An Anteater Named Arthur contains numerous conversations between a mother anteater and her young son that parallel similar interactions of human parents and their children. When Arthur tells his mother that his room is untidy because he has been playing magician, she offers to go away while he makes the mess disappear. When Arthur refuses to eat nutritious red ants, even with sugar or lemon, his mother eventually gives in and allows him to eat the brown ones. When Arthur cannot find anything to do, his mother's suggestion that he share the housework sends him outdoors to seek a friend. A reviewer in the *New Yorker* commented, "Children and mothers will recognize themselves in this book, which casually pokes fun at the way things are but also suggests, in the easy and good-humored relationship that exists between mother and son, and in the air of comfort and contentment that prevails in the household, that they really aren't so bad."

When Waber published *A Firefly Named Torchy*, critics were most enchanted by the artwork. A reviewer for *Publishers Weekly* declared, "His firefly flies through pages of Jackson Pollack skies and forests, finger-painting type illustrations add to the drama of his firefly's dilemma." Torchy's dilemma is that his light is too bright. The other forest creatures complain; they think it is day when it is night. Torchy is delighted to discover the city, where his light fits in beautifully with the spectacular flashes of night lights. After an evening of giving his all, Torchy comes home to find that he has little energy left, and his light is now the modest twinkle of a normal firefly. A *Kirkus Reviews* critic called this book "a dazzler," while George A. Woods declared, "Mr. Waber . . . really lets loose here with his technique to give us sights far beyond the ordinary."

Ira Sleeps Over follows a young boy as he prepares for his first sleepover at his best friend's house. Ira is excited about the activities his friend Reggie has planned for the sleepover, from examining his junk collection to telling scary stories. However, Ira must decide whether or not to take his teddy bear, which he has slept with for years. Confused by his obnoxious older sister's taunts that Reggie will think he is a baby, Ira finally decides not to take his bear. After an evening of fun, Reggie sneaks *his* teddy bear out of a drawer, so Ira goes home to get his, and finds Reggie asleep when he comes back. A reviewer for *The Booklist* called *Ira Sleeps Over,* "An appealing picture book which depicts common childhood qualms with empathy and humor. . . ."

Twelve years later, Waber returned to another story of Ira in *Ira Says Goodbye* (1988). Reggie is moving away, and Ira is hurt and angry at his best friend's excitement and apparent happiness at leaving his friend behind. When it is time to go, Reggie bursts into tears, and Ira realizes that Reggie has been hiding his feelings and is just as upset as Ira about the move. After Reggie leaves, he phones Ira to invite him over for the weekend. David Gale noted the universality of the book, commenting, "Ira's concerns reflect those of any child in a similar situation, but its humor is even more universal, so there should be a wide and responsive audience for this funny and moving book." A *Kirkus Reviews* critic further remarked, "Waber deftly conveys a true friendship and the mixed, unmatched emotions at parting, with plenty of entertaining, realistic detail. His cheerful, cartoon-like illustrations are pleasantly full of life and humor."

Do You See a Mouse? contains very little text except the frequently asked question, "Do you see a mouse?" Someone has reported seeing a mouse at the ultra-chic Park Snoot Hotel. Laurel and Hardy look-alikes Hyde and Snide, who specialize in "elegant pest management," search the hotel from top to bottom, asking each hotel worker and guest if he or she has seen a mouse. Hyde and Snide never find the cheeky little devil, and eventually certify the hotel to be mouse free. Readers, however, can see the mouse in each scene, smugly hiding in plain sight of the posh detectives. Mary Lou Burket commented, "Pre-readers, of course, will chant the question and spot the wily creature as he peeks from beds and flower pots and hitches a ride with an unsuspecting porter. In one amusing scene, we see him lounging atop the hotel's framed certificate of excellence. Could anyone give the whereabouts of such a mouse away?" Trev Jones observed: "The uncluttered pictures with lots of white space make finding the endearing rodent challenging but not frustrating, and are a perfect accompaniment to the simple text."

Awards

Waber has won awards for both his writing and his illustrations. In 1962, *The House on East 88th Street* won the Children's Spring Book Festival picture book honor from the *New York Herald Tribune*. *An Anteater Named Arthur* was selected as an American Institute of Graphic Arts Children's Book for 1967-68. *A Firefly Named Torchy* was named a Notable Book in 1970 by the American Library Association and a *Boston Globe-Horn Book* Honor Book for illustration in 1971. *Ira Sleeps Over* was included in the Children's Book Showcase of the Children's Book Council in 1973. *But Names Will Never Hurt Me* was selected one of Child Study Association's Children's Books of the Year in 1976. *Lyle, Lyle Crocodile* received the Lewis Carroll Shelf Award in 1979. *The Snake: A Very Long Story* was selected as an International Reading Association's Children's Choice for 1979.

AUTHOR'S COMMENTARY

Bernard Waber

SOURCE: "Voices of the Creators," in *Children's Books and Their Creators,* Houghton Mifflin Company, 1995, p. 667.

In my book **Nobody Is Perfick,** a little girl doing homework tries desperately not to slip into daydreaming. She resists daydreaming with gargantuan will. She gulps down glasses of water. She chews bubble gum furiously. She stands on her head. She somersaults. But in the end she succumbs to a perfectly lovely daydream.

True confession: That was me, or in the words of Flaubert's reference to *Madame Bovary,* "C'est moi." I was that kid, a hopeless, chronic daydreamer. Everyone told me it was bad—bad, bad, bad—to daydream. "Wake up! Snap out of it!" These were the admonitions of my childhood. And don't think I wasn't worried. I tried everything to cure myself of this pernicious affliction. If a support program were available to cure daydreaming, I would have rushed to sign up. The problem deviled me all through my maturing years. Even in the army, sergeants constantly bellowed at me to wake up.

True confession: I still suffer from the same affliction. The only difference is, now I'm encouraged to do it. Now, it's quite proper for me to do it. Now, I'm even expected to do it. So, when I am asked where I get my ideas, I'm tempted to say, "I'm only doing what I've always done—daydreaming."

True confession: Wordplay tops my list of greedy pleasures, just after fudge sundaes and M&Ms. The idea and plot for **But Names Will Never Hurt Me** came to me while shaving one morning. The story has nothing to do with shaving; it has to do with a little girl named Alison who has the unfortunate surname of Wonderland. Get it?

Alison Wonderland. Often, my ideas begin with just such musings. An absurd name like Alison Wonderland tickled me. But digging deeper, I was moved by the burden of troublesome names, and that burden became the central theme. Similarly, in *Ira Sleeps Over,* a little boy's dilemma on whether or not to take his teddy bear along on his first sleepover seemed like a funny idea. But probing the idea's underside revealed tantalizing complexities—peer pressure, separation, self-belief, even sibling rivalry.

True confession: Among the really pleasurable dividends of writing for children are the letters children send to authors. In their letters, children talk freely about family, friends, school, pets, sports, everything crucial to their lives. They also want to know about their authors—absolutely everything. Sometimes I think kids want more personal information than my health insurance plan. My age and other vital statistics are matters of keen interest. I always tell the truth about my age because I love to astonish children. A frequent question from children is, "What made you become a writer?" Early environment had much to do with it. My siblings, a sister and two brothers, all older and all artistic, were a major influence. My sister played piano and wrote poetry. She also wrote love letters, in the fashion of Cyrano de Bergerac, for love-stricken, but less poetically expressive, friends. She read her love letters to the family for critical comment and hearing them made us all fall in love just a little. My brothers wrote and drew, and I spent a major chunk of my childhood hanging over their shoulders, observing words and pictures emerge on paper.

True confession: I did not set out to be an author. I began professionally as a designer and illustrator for magazines. My illustrations tended toward whimsy, and my love of drawing animals led to this fatal attraction—children's books. Quality time, for me, meant hanging out in bookstores—looking, looking, looking at picture books. And looking wasn't all that easy way back then. Unlike today's mammoth book chains, where one could literally spend the day reading *War and Peace* unnoticed and unmolested, back then I could scarcely begin browsing without an overzealous clerk offering unsolicited assistance. I did, however, buy lots of children's books, mostly as gifts, but many for myself to satisfy an insatiable appetite for them. Children giggle when I tell them I fell in love with picture books. One even asked, "Did you marry one?"

Later, as the father of three, I had three compelling reasons for giving children's books close scrutiny. I loved reading aloud and, as many parents do, began inventing stories. I probably caused my children some self-consciousness as I constantly trailed after them into the children's room of our library. Once, they suggested that I might find more appropriate books in the grown-ups department. True confession: It was too late to change a habit—especially one so possessing. Besides, I had already begun to write my first children's book.

TITLE COMMENTARY

📖 *LORENZO* (1961)

Virginia Kirkus' Service

SOURCE: A review of *Lorenzo,* in *Virginia Kirkus' Service,* Vol. XXIX, No. 3, February 1, 1961, p. 99.

An over-developed curiosity always takes Lorenzo, the fish with the red spotted tail, on personal explorations. The wonders of a sunken ship win his interest but lose him his companions. How funny Lorenzo looks swimming among the sardines; thus, we are relieved when one day he spies a red spotted tail and rejoins his own family. A humorous little story with few words and many picture clues that will appeal to the perceptive in the picture book fraternity.

Zena Sutherland

SOURCE: A review of *Lorenzo,* in *Bulletin of the Center for Children's Books,* Vol. XIV, No. 7, March, 1961, pp. 117-18.

A small picture book about a small fish named Lorenzo who was more curious than all the other fish in his family—fish with red spots on their tails. Lorenzo, loitering about a sunken ship, was separated from all the others; he swam about, leading a lonely life until the happy moment when he saw a tail with a red spot. A nice touch of humor appears in the ending: Lorenzo has rejoined his family, and the reader is asked if he can single out the hero; the next page shows the school of absolutely identical fish, one of which is circled. The illustrations, in black and white with touches of red, have a reiteration that is well suited to the humor of the story and the stress on family resemblance.

📖 *THE HOUSE ON EAST 88TH STREET* (1962; British edition as *Welcome, Lyle,* 1969)

Virginia Kirkus' Service

SOURCE: A review of *The House on East 88th Street,* in *Virginia Kirkus' Service,* Vol. XXX, No. 6, March 15, 1962, p. 279.

"Swish, Swash, Splash, Swoosh," echoed through the Primms' new house on East 88th Street—an ordinary house except for its one eccentric resident—Lyle the crocodile. Warned by Hector P. Valenti, down-and-out star of stage and screen and erstwhile owner of Lyle, to be kind to his pet, the Primms are amply rewarded by the most elegant display of crocodile friendliness. The sweet smell of Lyle's success brings Hector back to claim him and back once again to deposit him, when Lyle sheds a river of crocodile tears for the Primms.

Fancy and funny pictures by the author in full color and black and white.

George A. Woods

SOURCE: A review of *The House on East 88th Street,* in *The New York Times Book Review,* June 3, 1962, p. 18.

Once you get over the initial shock, crocodiles and alligators make perfectly acceptable house guests. In *The House on East 88th Street* the Primm family finds Lyle—that's a croc—left behind by former tenant Hector Valenti who couldn't afford Lyle's taste for Turkish caviar. A talented performer, Lyle endears himself to the family doing domestic chores and grows famous as a crowd pleaser. Crocodile and human tears come when Mr. Valenti reclaims his pet and goes on a tour that begins with high hopes and ends sadly, though with good results for Lyle and the Primms. The reader should have good results, too, from Mr. Waber's persuasive, lightly amusing extravaganza. Unlike his previous book, *Lorenzo,* this one has illustrations bolstered with lots of color and pleasing background details of faded elegance.

Alice Dalgliesh

SOURCE: A review of *The House on East 88th Street,* in *The Saturday Review,* Vol. XLV, No. 28, July 21, 1962, pp. 35-6.

When the Primms and their young son, Joshua, moved into the house on East 88th Street strange sounds came rumbling through it. SWISH, SWASH, SPLASH, SWOOSH. There it came again. "Joseph!" cried Mrs. Primm, "there's a crocodile in our tub." Sure enough, there was—a large green crocodile. Although we seem to have had an unusual number of crocodile-in-the-home books recently, Lyle will amuse children because of the many absurd things he does. It is sad when his owner reclaims him, but the ending is most satisfactory. The pictures are of a modified cartoon type.

Virginia Haviland

SOURCE: A review of *The House on East 88th Street,* in *The Horn Book Magazine,* Vol. XXXVIII, No. 4, August, 1962, p. 367.

Tried out with a picture-book group, this tale of a demesticated crocodile named Lyle proved consistently captivating. In his story, Lyle wins the hearts of new residents of a New York City house where an actor has left him with a note, "Please be kind to my crocodile. He is the most gentle of creatures and would not do harm to a flea . . . " He proves most helpful and engaging as a companion, performing various housekeeping tasks (" . . . when he sets the table there is always a surprise"), doing tricks, playing in the park, and perform-

ing in a parade. The sketches of the great, green creature in all his fantastic endeavors will delight any child.

The New York Times Book Review

SOURCE: A review of *The House on East 88th Street,* in *The New York Times Book Review,* September 8, 1974, p. 38.

First they hear "SWISH, SWASH, SPLASH, SWOOSH." Then the Primm family finds Lyle—who's a large, green crocodile—smiling up at them from their bathtub. He had been left behind by a former tenant who couldn't afford Lyle's taste for Turkish caviar. Thus the Primms gained an amiable, affectionate pet, and children's literature, a character. On Lyle's appearance 12 years ago, George A. Woods noted that Lyle was a "crowd pleaser" and his tale an "amusing extravaganza." This appearance in paperback should give Lyle a huge audience to please—and that's as it should be.

HOW TO GO ABOUT LAYING AN EGG (1963)

Virginia Kirkus' Service

SOURCE: A review of *How to Go about Laying an Egg,* in *Virginia Kirkus' Service,* Vol. XXXI, No. 2, January 15, 1963, p. 58.

Taking a level (but never hard boiled) view, the author outlines the serious business of egg production. A sharp questionnaire establishes whether or not you are a chicken. This is followed by 8 rigid rules of procedure—(#2—you must really *want* to, #8—concentrate). Illustrated by the author, the swiftly scratched line drawings exactly convey the air of outraged determination followed by blank astonishment that marks the effort of the dedicated hen. The combination of picture, tone and text is very amusing and let's face it—the whole idea of laying an egg is funny to children of all ages (we won't go into *why*). Readable books on poultry science are not easy to come by.

Zena Sutherland

SOURCE: A review of *How to Go about Laying an Egg,* in *Bulletin of the Center for Children's Books,* Vol. XVI, No. 8, April, 1963, p. 135.

A small book of elaborately bland nonsense, giving, in humorous illustrations and text, some sensible advice to hens. Rule [1] asks, "Are you all feathers? . . . When taking a walk, do you sometimes catch yourself flying? . . . If your answer has been yes to each of the above questions, it is safe to say you are a hen. CONGRATULATIONS!" and later, "Bring along books, puzzles and games to while the time away." Slight but amusing; one set of pictures, needing no caption, show the hen looking frowning and intent—in the next drawing, she is startled at her achievement.

📖 *RICH CAT, POOR CAT* (1963)

Virginia Kirkus' Service

SOURCE: A review of *Rich Cat, Poor Cat,* in *Virginia Kirkus' Service,* Vol. XXXI, No. 13, July 1, 1963, p. 596.

Poking about in the opposing worlds of rich felines and a scraggly alley cat, Mr. Waber digs up many striking, comical contrasts. There are those named Abigail, Tasha or Ernestine,—and then there is Scat. There are those who "look out of picture windows" and "sleep on downy pillows"—and then there is Scat whose "pillows are the coarse cobblestones" of the city street. The fresh illustrations in color boast a rare combination of good humor, fine design, and pleasing simplicity. A more than satisfying stroll through catdom by the author of *How to Go about Laying An Egg.*

Virginia Haviland

SOURCE: A review of *Rich Cat, Poor Cat,* in *The Horn Book Magazine,* Vol. XXXIX, No. 5, October, 1963, p. 498.

The creator of Lorenzo the fish and Lyle the crocodile may win yet more of an audience with this wittily true comparison of the lives of two kinds of cats. In elementary and humorous terms he has depicted the hard contrasts of luxury and alley life. "Some cats have names like Ernestine, Abigail, Coco, Tasha, and even Cherie. Everyone knows Scat's name. Whenever people see her coming, they always say SCAT! SCAT!" And so, too, there are other differences—in food, housing, beauty care, and playtime. But, at last, Scat herself gains a stylish name. A companion in format to that similarly straight-faced and jolly *The House on East 88th Street,* with much to be discovered and examined on each lively page.

Zena Sutherland

SOURCE: A review of *Rich Cat, Poor Cat,* in *Bulletin of the Center for Children's Books,* Vol. XVII, No. 9, May, 1964, p. 148.

A picture book that has humor in text and in illustrations but is so drawn-out that it loses impact. The first part of the book has no plot, but moves back and forth contrasting the luxurious lives of coddled pets and the paw-to-mouth existence of Scat, an alley cat that has no owner, no home, no affection given her. In the last five pages, the text suddenly moves from present to past tense—confusing in itself—and describes the little girl with whom Scat finds a home. The ending would be

From Lyle at the Office, *written and illustrated by Bernard Waber.*

abrupt even if the tenses were reversed; after forty-three pages of, "Scat also climbs trees . . . There isn't anything very special in Scat's life . . . Scat is mousy gray," it is jarring to read, "One day, in the market place, Scat met a little girl."

📖 *JUST LIKE ABRAHAM LINCOLN* (1964)

Virginia Kirkus' Service

SOURCE: A review of *Just Like Abraham Lincoln,* in *Virginia Kirkus' Service,* Vol. XXXII, No. 13, July 1, 1964, p. 594.

Lincoln liked a good laugh. This might be one of the few biographies of himself that he would enjoy. It is told by a little boy who had a neighbor named Mr. Potts who looked just like Abraham Lincoln. Lincoln was Mr. Potts' hobby and he told the narrator a good deal about the great man. At the boy's suggestion he even grew a beard. As a surprise, he came to the boy's school and recited the Gettysburg address to the assembly on Lincoln's Birthday. "Suddenly we were in Gettysburg . . . one hundred years ago." It's a shame to lose a neighbor who shared all Lincoln's best qualities, but Mr. Potts had to move away shortly after that. However, someone named Mr. Pettigrew was going to move in. "I wonder what he's like," our narrator ponders while the illustration shows the spit and image of the Father of his Country and the next big birthday coming up. The illustrations are a swift, bold wash, done with humor. Teachers in the early grades will like this for its lighthearted approach and its manageable vocabulary.

Zena Sutherland

SOURCE: A review of *Just Like Abraham Lincoln*, in *Bulletin of the Center for Children's Books*, Vol. XVIII, No. 7, March, 1965, p. 111.

An engaging story in which a boy describes an adult neighbor who looks like Lincoln and has many of his finest qualities. Mr. Potts is a hospitable man who loves children, who reads a great deal, and who—aware of his resemblance to Lincoln—collects Lincolniana in a modest way. Mr. Potts dresses as Lincoln for a school program; some time later he moves away and his home is purchased by a Mr. Pettigrew. The last page of the story shows the moving-in; the comment is, "I wonder what he's like." The moving men are carrying a portrait of George Washington. Although the text rambles a bit, it achieves a conversational, mulling-over quality that is natural and warm. In the double description of Mr. Potts and Abraham Lincoln, there is enough (but not too much) information for primary-age children.

📖 *LYLE, LYLE, CROCODILE* (1965)

Ethel L. Heins

SOURCE: A review of *Lyle, Lyle, Crocodile*, in *The Horn Book Magazine*, Vol. XLI, No. 5, October, 1965, p. 496.

The benign and amiable crocodile who lives a life of incongruous contentment in the Primms' Victorian home becomes the center of controversy when he frightens a neighbor's cat. Poor Lyle is taken downtown where his day's activities—frolicking in the park, skating at Rockefeller Center, browsing in antique shops, and finally creating a commotion in a department store—make hilarious picture-book sequences but fail to help him out of his difficulties. Only Lyle's great heroism in a middle-of-the-night fire establishes him as a desirable citizen and restores neighborhood harmony. In design and format, similar to *The House on East 88th Street*.

George A. Woods

SOURCE: A review of *Lyle, Lyle, Crocodile*, in *The New York Times Book Review*, October 3, 1965, p. 56.

Where else but in a picture book would you find a big, green crocodile playing skip rope on the city streets or gliding over the ice at Rockefeller Center without any

eyebrows being raised? Never mind how he got to Manhattan—that story was told in Bernard Waber's *The House on East 88th Street*. In the author-illustrator's new book, *Lyle, Lyle, Crocodile,* the presence of Lyle is very unsettling to a neighbor, Mr. Grumps, and his cat. An impromptu vaudeville performance in a department store gets Lyle banished to the zoo from where he goes on to prove that he is—in Mr. Grumps's words—"the bravest, kindest, most wonderful crocodile in the whole, wide world." There's no quarrel with that statement. The easy naturalness of the illustrations make it all seem perfectly plausible.

Ruth P. Bull

SOURCE: A review of *Lyle, Lyle, Crocodile*, in *The Booklist*, Vol. 62, No. 7, December 1, 1965, p. 366.

Lyle the crocodile hero of *The House on East 88th Street* wants desperately to win the friendship of the cat Loretta two doors away but every time Loretta catches a glimpse of him she flings herself into a nervous fit. Her furious owner insists that something be done about "that crocodile." Whether he is frightening the cat, helping in the kitchen, shopping, sleeping with other crocodiles in the zoo, or rescuing Mr. Grumps and his cat from a fire, Lyle is as lovable as ever and the story and colored pictures as nonsensical.

The Junior Bookshelf

SOURCE: A review of *Lyle, Lyle, Crocodile*, in *The Junior Bookshelf*, Vol. 31, No. 2, April, 1967, p. 109.

If Bernard Waber could draw like [Roger] Duvoisin, *Lyle, Lyle, Crocodile* might be on the way to the kind of immortality enjoyed by Petunia and the Happy Lion. Maybe he will still make the grade, for this nonsense is of a highly memorable kind. Lyle, who lives with the Primms in Hudson Road, is a helpful crocodile about the house and on the whole a good neighbour. The plot of this story is rather better than the telling, and the idea behind the pictures much better than the drawing. Nevertheless Mr. Waber has his moments, notably in two adjacent pictures of Lyle being sociable to the other crocodiles in the zoo.

📖 *"YOU LOOK RIDICULOUS," SAID THE RHINOCEROS TO THE HIPPOPOTAMUS* (1966; reprinted, 1979)

Virginia Kirkus' Service

SOURCE: A review of *"You Look Ridiculous," Said the Rhinoceros to the Hippopotamus*, in *Virginia Kirkus' Service*, Vol. XXXIV, No. 4, February 15, 1966, p. 178.

The lion, the leopard, the elephant, the monkey, the giraffe, the tortoise, and the nightingale all confirmed that opinion. Then the hippopotamus had a vision of herself with all the plumage the others had recommended to her—a rhinoceros horn, a mane, a spotted coat, etc. and decided *that* was ridiculous. Very young children will think so too, and that picture of the composite hippo will draw plenty of laughs from them. The moral is easy to share—that it's best to be yourself even if you are "a big, fat, wonderful hippopotamus." The pictures, done in an interesting technique with inks and stamps in dulled gray, green, and orange, show a happy, lumpy view of the jungle beasts.

Virginia Haviland

SOURCE: A review of *"You Look Ridiculous," Said the Rhinoceros to the Hippopotamus,* in *The Horn Book Magazine,* Vol. XLII, No. 2, April, 1966, p. 190.

The title of the rollicking tale suggests perfectly the nature of the fun. It develops freshly from the fable motif of a discontented animal who at length learns to leave well enough alone. Bold, free drawings extend the humor of the words in picturing the self-deprecating hippo, whose dream showed her a ridiculous image of her remodeled self, equipped with the various unique appendages of her jungle associates. She will go on being "just what she is—a big, fat, wonderful hippopotamus."

The Junior Bookshelf

SOURCE: A review of *"You Look Ridiculous," Said the Rhinoceros to the Hippopotamus,* in *The Junior Bookshelf,* Vol. 31, No. 6, December, 1967, p. 371.

Bernard Waber has a conventional idea in ***"You Look Ridiculous"*** of the animal who aims to please all and pleases none, but he develops it in an original and highly pleasing manner. The repetitive text is a model of its kind, and a gift to the oral story-teller, and what charming colours in his jungle pictures.

Publishers Weekly

SOURCE: A review of *"You Look Ridiculous," Said the Rhinoceros to the Hippopotamus,* in *Publishers Weekly,* Vol. 215, No. 21, May 21, 1979, p. 70.

Colorful stencils and paintings decorate and illustrate Waber's heartening tale. With no obvious moralizing, he encourages little kids who are different and encapsulates a lesson for those who put them down. The rhino declares that the hippo, with no imposing horn like his, is ridiculous. The poor beast goes to consult other candid "friends," all of whom point out that she would be greatly improved if she were more like them. Slumping

back to her mudhole, the hippo falls asleep and dreams she has acquired a lion's mane, a giraffe's neck, a nightingale's sweet song, etc. She catches a glimpse of the creature she has become and discovers what ridiculous really means and is enormously relieved to awaken as herself.

LYLE AND THE BIRTHDAY PARTY (1966)

Virginia Kirkus' Service

SOURCE: A review of *Lyle and the Birthday Party,* in *Virginia Kirkus' Service,* Vol. XXXIV, No. 13, July 1, 1966, p. 621.

Lyle the crocodile is lovely this time again at (***The House on East 88th Street***). He lives with the Primms and when their son Joshua had a birthday party, Lyle helped with the preparations, joined the guests in party games but all the time the wish to have a party of his own was growing on him. Lyle was reluctantly coming down with a major case of jealousy. Mr. Waber shows the only crocodile you'd care to have around the house sliding into the sulks in a way every child will be able to recognize. Lyle goes from pensive to the mean-eyed glance of indifference to putting his foot (intentionally?) through Joshua's drum. Since Lyle can't talk, he couldn't tell the Primms next day that he was suffering from continuing envy and painful shame. Mrs. Primm decided to call a doctor and, because she inverted the first and last names of the recommended croc specialist, she wound up with a regular doctor who ordered Lyle into the hospital. It's the sort of mix-up that children find terribly funny and while Lyle works of his guilt serving the patients, they'll be learning all the symptoms of chronic covetousness and lingering conscience. Lyle in the grip of the green-eyed monster can be used as a miracle cautionary cure.

Zena Sutherland

SOURCE: A review of *Lyle and the Birthday Party,* in *The Saturday Review,* Vol. L, No. 11, March 18, 1967, p. 35.

One of the fine arts in writing fanciful stories for the picture book age is knowing just how far to go in exploiting a ridiculous situation. Lyle is a crocodile who lives with a fond family in New York City, and he behaves almost like a human being—but the human beings in the story never forget that Lyle is a crocodile. Well, hardly ever. When Lyle, suffering familiar pangs of jealousy at somebody's birthday party, acts gloomy and loses his appetite, Mrs. Primm is so worried that she calls a doctor. By mistake Lyle is taken to a hospital for people, where his normal attitudes of good humor and helpfulness return as he trots about in a hospital gown, doing good deeds for the bed-bound. Nice nonsense, blandly told and illustrated with engagingly silly pictures.

Zena Sutherland

SOURCE: A review of *Lyle and the Birthday Party,* in *Bulletin of the Center for Children's Books,* Vol. 20, No. 8, April, 1967, pp. 130-31.

One of the accompaniments to many a child's birthday party is the sulking of a jealous sibling. Here the smitten one is Lyle, the amiable crocodile of *The House on East 88th Street* and *Lyle, Lyle, Crocodile.* Worried by his unusual fretfulness, his mistress calls a doctor; she gets confused and calls the wrong one, however, so Lyle is admitted to an ordinary hospital. The staff is slightly baffled, but they process and admit Lyle, who proceeds to improve in disposition and health in direct proportion to the amount of help he gives other patients. The writing is straightforward, in contrast to the nonsensical situation; all of the expressed humor is in the lively illustrations.

S. M. Askew

SOURCE: A review of *Lyle and the Birthday Party,* in *Children's Book News,* Vol. 3, No. 1, January-February, 1968, p. 13.

Lyle is a delightful crocodile who lives with the Primm family. When Joshua has a birthday party, poor Lyle finds all the fuss too much for him to bear. He becomes desperately jealous, sulks and broods, and finally the family, thinking he must be ill, ring up a crocodile doctor. Unfortunately, the wrong doctor is contacted and Lyle finds himself whipped off in an ambulance to a hospital for humans. He soon leaps out of bed and starts exploring the hospital, makes himself useful to the patients, enjoys himself, and thus becomes once again his old lovable self. Mr. Waber tells his story with such ease and naturalness it is a pleasure to read, and the expressions on the face of Lyle are so full of feeling one can't help but feel for him in his jealous despondency.

AN ANTEATER NAMED ARTHUR (1967)

Kirkus Service

SOURCE: A review of *An Anteater Named Arthur,* in *Kirkus Service,* Vol. XXXV, No. 17, September 1, 1967, pp. 1043-44.

"Most of the time Arthur is . . . (an) altogether wonderful son." BUT . . . *Sometimes Arthur doesn't understand; Sometimes Arthur has nothing to do; Sometimes Arthur's room is more than I can believe; Sometimes Arthur is choosy; Sometimes Arthur forgets.* In five little-bearish episodes, Arthur, who has a similar insouciance, variously exasperates his mother, is sometimes outwitted but generally emerges a little bit ahead: *Sometimes Arthur is choosy* about his food, especially when red ants are the main dish for dinner; neither the prospect of growing up as big and strong as his father nor the reminder

that "red ants aren't exactly easy to come by" moves him—he prefers brown ants. Arthur's little eyes and long nose are perfect for expressing puzzlement, boredom, disdain, determination—and for giving mother a good-by kiss. A funny physiognomy for a lot of little boys named Tom, Dick, Harry—or Arthur.

The Booklist

SOURCE: A review of *An Anteater Named Arthur,* in *The Booklist,* Vol. 64, No. 7, December 1, 1967, p. 452.

The author-artist of *The House on East 88th Street* has created a new character equally as endearing as Lyle the crocodile. According to his mother, Arthur the anteater is an altogether wonderful son but he can also be a problem. At times he is forgetful, messy, inquisitive, and so choosy that he refuses nutritious red ants, even with sugar and lemon. Not surprisingly, his goodbye kiss, delivered as he leaves for school, quells his mother's exasperation. Droll illustrations in pink and brown portray the gamut of Arthur's emotions entirely through eyes set in a mouthless face.

Janet Malcolm

SOURCE: A review of *An Anteater Named Arthur,* in *The New Yorker,* Vol. XLIII, No. 43, December 16, 1967, p. 157.

An Anteater Named Arthur, by Bernard Waber, is told from the point of view of Arthur's mother, who discourses, in five brief chapters, on aspects of life at home with her small son. For some reason, she is dressed in a long Victorian dress and apron (perhaps simply because Mr. Waber, who also did the illustrations, did not want to tangle with a female anteater's legs), but there is nothing Victorian about the way she deals with her child. She has obviously read Gesell and Ilg, and she shows a fine grasp of a technique they style "developmental discipline," of which the chapter entitled "Sometimes Arthur's Room Is More Than I Can Believe" gives a very clear illustration. The mother comments mildly on the untidiness of Arthur's room, and when he explains that "I was playing magician," she neither nags him nor lets him leave the mess but humors him into tidying his room by suggesting that he perform a magic trick for her and make certain things appear and other things disappear. In the next chapter, which is set at the breakfast table, the dialogue goes like this:

> "What are we having?" he asks.
> "We are having ants," I answer.
> "What kind of ants?"
> "The red ones," I tell him.
> Arthur makes a face.

The mother tells him the ants are beautiful ("Arthur looks and makes another face"), next suggests that he sprinkle sugar on them, or would he like a twist of lemon peel ("more head shaking from Arthur"), then shifts ground and reminds him that "red ants aren't exactly easy to come by!" ("Arthur begins playing with his spoon"), and finally has the sense to give up and ask him what he will eat instead (brown ants). Children and mothers will recognize themselves in this book, which casually pokes fun at the way things are but also suggests, in the easy and good-humored relationship that exists between mother and son, and in the air of comfort and contentment that prevails in the household, that they really aren't so bad.

Zena Sutherland

SOURCE: A review of *An Anteater Named Arthur,* in *Bulletin of the Center for Children's Books,* Vol. 21, No. 6, February, 1968, p. 103.

Arthur's mother, describing her son, is less plaintive than she is resigned—a woman (that is, a female anteater) who has been through the mill of living with a young male. Arthur gives a long and rational explanation of why he has nothing to do: friends away, toys broken, books read. Mother suggests household chores; Arthur promptly disappears. The illustrations are attractive in a sedate way, a quality also present in the writing. For example, one section is headed "Sometimes Arthur's room is more than I can believe." Next page: "'Arthur!' I exclaim. 'Your room is more than I can believe!'" The understated humor is a nice foil for the solemn, beaked faces and the familiar patterns of child behavior.

📖 *A ROSE FOR MR. BLOOM* (1968)

Kirkus Service

SOURCE: A review of *A Rose for Mr. Bloom,* in *Kirkus Service,* Vol. XXXVI, No. 7, April 1, 1968, p. 389.

The rose that grows out of Mr. Bloom's left ear wafts him out of his ordinary routine and makes him someone special all summer: his boss asks his opinions, children stop him on the street, Mrs. Bloom dances with him after dinner. Comes the fall, the rose droops and dries up . . . but after a long dismal winter, he begins to feel a tickling—in both ears. *Scent*imental silliness.

Sherry Petchul

SOURCE: A review of *A Rose for Mr. Bloom,* in *The Christian Science Monitor,* May 2, 1968, p. B3.

Back on land, where Mr. Bloom like a good many men rides the train to work every morning, and every evening comes home to his good wife, the preposterous can still happen. *A Rose for Mr. Bloom* sprouts in Mr. Bloom's left ear and changes his life as only a rose in a man's left ear can.

"Delicious!" said the train conductor as he punched Mr. Bloom's ticket and smelled his rose. "Let us smell your rose!" called the neighborhood children to Mr. Bloom when he came home from work. "Your rose is so grand, it makes me want to have dinner by candlelight," announced Mrs. Bloom shyly.

But as the days grew cooler, the rose began to droop and one morning it was gone. Mr. Bloom missed his rose.

Bernard Waber's cartoon-like illustrations are ridiculously right for his rightly ridiculous story, which ends happily the next spring.

📖 *LOVABLE LYLE* (1969)

Kirkus Reviews

SOURCE: A review of *Lovable Lyle,* in *Kirkus Reviews,* Vol. XXXVII, No. 4, February 15, 1969, p. 174.

Lyle the crocodile, loved by one and all, is dismayed to discover that he has an enemy: who can be sending those poison pen notes? "Hoping somewhere, somehow, his 'enemy' would see what a nice crocodile he really was," he exhausts himself trying to be amusing and kind and helpful—but to no avail. Then Clover Sue Hipple, who keeps popping up, is caught slipping a note under the door and Mrs. Primm pries out her reason: her friends run off to play with Lyle and she's "not allowed to play with crocodiles." What has been rueful and funny (*vide* Lyle looking out the window and thinking "Somebody out there hates me") becomes at this point, a tract on tolerance (call him Charley). Mrs. Primm's attempt to convince Mrs. Hipple that Lyle is harmless fails until, one day at the beach, Lyle saves Clover from drowning and, in becoming a hero, becomes a desirable companion. Children who love Lyle for himself will rise in indignation, so will adults who've had enough of minding manners and making nice, to make friends.

George A. Woods

SOURCE: A review of *Lovable Lyle,* in *The New York Times Book Review,* February 23, 1969, p. 22.

Ordinarily I don't like crocodiles. They're reptilian and slithery and bumpety all over. And they've got teeth— wow *have* they got teeth—inside of jaws that yawn wide, and unless you've got a stick to prop them open they close with a WHOOMPF! Then you're nothing, man, nothing. Besides, they were always after Tarzan like he was pigmeat, and Tarzan would pull out his big stabber, and they would be thrashing around in the lagoon with froth and bubbles coming up, and I couldn't look because it was too gruesome.

But I like Lyle. He's of a different stripe—urbane, cosmopolitan, one of the family, a charmer. This fourth book featuring Lyle is almost an affectionate catalogue of his gallantries on which he's working hard, trying to improve his image, because someone has been sending him poison-pen notes—"I hate you so much I can't stand it"—and chalking "Down With Crocodiles" on walls. Yet when the culprit is discovered, Lyle makes it worse by tumbling out of a clothes closet where he had hidden away out of shyness and embarrassment. The poor guy has to prove his worth all over again. This much is sure: here, in story and illustration, he's worth more than any pair of shoes, handbag or belt.

Zena Sutherland

SOURCE: A review of *Lovable Lyle,* in *The Saturday Review,* Vol. LII, No. 19, May 10, 1969, p. 54.

That most amiable of crocodiles, Lyle, is now firmly entrenched in the hearts of his readers, so it may come as a shock to them when Lyle starts getting messages saying, "I hate you." Trying to be more lovable than ever, Lyle runs himself ragged doing good deeds, but only when he saves Clover Sue Hipple from drowning does he win over this jealous child and her mother, who has been prejudiced against crocodiles. More contrived than the three earlier books, this still has a raffish charm in its bland style and vigorous, funny pictures.

Ruth P. Bull

SOURCE: A review of *Lovable Lyle,* in *The Booklist,* Vol. 65, No. 20, June 15, 1969, p. 1179.

Though less spontaneous than the earlier Lyle books the present picture-book story is fun nonetheless and the amiable crocodile is as winning as ever. Lyle, who loves the whole wide, wonderful world, is terribly distressed to learn, via letters surreptitiously slipped under the door, that somebody out there hates him, and he exhausts himself trying to be extraordinarily nice to impress the unknown enemy. The secret enemy is a little girl who hates him because the other children run off to play with Lyle and she is not allowed to play with crocodiles. Lyle, of course, wins over both the child and her prejudiced mother.

A FIREFLY NAMED TORCHY (1970)

Publishers Weekly

SOURCE: A review of *A Firefly Named Torchy,* in *Publishers Weekly,* Vol. 198, No. 6, August 10, 1970, p. 56.

Bernard Waber, who has to his credit the contribution of a new character to the select crowd of fictional characters children love, his crocodile Lyle, as well as that endearing character, *An Anteater Named Arthur,* has

gone off on a totally new tangent in his latest book. His firefly flies through pages of Jackson Pollack skies and forests, finger-painting type illustrations add to the drama of his firefly's dilemma (too bright a light). A different kind of technique for a different kind of story. And a deserved round of applause to Bernard Waber for leaving his safe, established country to fly into a new world.

Kirkus Reviews

SOURCE: A review of *A Firefly Named Torchy,* in *Kirkus Reviews,* Vol. XXXVIII, No. 17, September 1, 1970, pp. 947-48.

Snappy repartee and spectacular effects hook up in Times Square (or its equivalent anywhere) where a wistful little firefly who can't twinkle shines his bright light happily . . . so happily "that on his way home without even thinking, he began to twinkle." From the outset the text sparkles—the sleepy animals shout in unison "TURN OFF THAT LIGHT," Torchy's mother advises him to "think happy, twinkly thoughts"; but at the outset the swirling, bursting, splattering art seems to be showing off. That is until Torchy, muttering to himself "Why shouldn't I twinkle . . . Fireflies are supposed to twinkle . . . Besides it's nice to twinkle," sees in the distance dancing lights that "must be millions of fireflies" and goes to join them. You know the rest: big lights, little lights, bright lights, dim lights, yellow, blue, green, orange, red, purple and white lights, dazzling, zooming, zipping, zigzagging lights. "It's true," says Torchy, "there are many kinds of lights in this world. Why should I hide mine?" A dazzler.

George A. Woods

SOURCE: A review of *A Firefly Named Torchy,* in *The New York Times Book Review,* September 27, 1970, p. 30.

How did that song go—"light up the sky with love"? Bernard Waber lights up the night-sky pages of his newest picture book with some pretty spectacular displays. There are bursts and curls and Pollack-like swirls, clusters of color that you might see in a 4th of July night sky. And the source of all this—other than Mr. Waber? Torchy, a firefly, starts out as a little flicker but when he grows and glows his brightness has all the nocturnal woodland animals thinking they're on the day-shift. Even nightcrawlers scramble for cover when Torchy turns on. Happiness is "twinkling," but Torchy's output is just too much. Against a background of city lights—and here is Mr. Waber's peak performance—Torchy has a fling at not hiding his light under a bushel and gets it all out of his system.

The story's not exactly incandescent, but it's good enough. Mr. Waber, having worked in picture books since 1961 with fish, anteaters and crocodiles as characters, really lets loose here with his technique to give us sights far beyond the ordinary.

Zena Sutherland

SOURCE: A review of *A Firefly Named Torchy*, in *Bulletin of the Center for Children's Books*, Vol. 24, No. 8, April, 1971, p. 131.

Misfit-finds-niche stories are not rare, but to have a firefly's maladjustment solved by a factor inherent in urban environment is. Blithely told, the story has humor in style and concept, and the illustrations erupt with flashing color and vitality. Torchy's problem is that his light is too bright. He just can't produce a moderate, normal twinkle. "Nonsense," says his mother. "Any one can twinkle. All you must do is take your time about it." "Nobody is perfect," Owl says. "Look at it this way. There are many kinds of light in the world. You should be proud of yours . . ." But it is in the night lights of the city that Torchy finds his metier; exhilarated by the dazzling lights, he exceeds himself—and finds, homeward bound, that all he has energy left for is a modest, run-of-the-mill twinkle.

NOBODY IS PERFICK (1971)

Kirkus Reviews

SOURCE: A review of *Nobody Is Perfick*, in *Kirkus Reviews*, Vol. XXXIX, No. 17, September 1, 1971, pp. 939-40.

[*Nobody Is Perfick*] except for Peter Perfect, antihero of the final sketch in this original set of drawings and dialogues that most closely resemble junior Jules Feiffers. Peter is projected through testimonials by mother, father, teacher, grandparents, even the soda fountain man ("Peter Perfect's straws do not get bent or mushy at the ends"), and through less enthusiastic comments by his peers. ("Peter Perfect's mother never has to raise her voice." "How does he know when she means it?") At the end, the children try with mixed results to "Say three times fast: PETER PERFECT'S PAPA PICKED A PERFECT PETER!" But the last page, which shows Peter from behind, reveals him to be a wind-up toy: "If only you were real, Peter Perfect!" Another vignette begins with a girl making a list of the ten best days of the year. ("I have lots of other lists. It's one of the ten best things I like to do.") When her friend calls her "the silliest person I ever met in my whole life," the punishment is fitting: "Just for that I'm going to cross you off my ten-best-friends-of-the-year list." The pictures for each "strip" are varied for interest, thanks largely to roller skates, gestures, and facial expressions; the backgrounds, though sparse, are unmistakable: a brownstone stoop, a few haphazard lines suggesting grass. Words and pictures together make childlike fun that is never coy or condescending; they appeal to children and adults alike, and at the same level.

Natalie Babbitt

SOURCE: A review of *Nobody Is Perfick*, in *The New York Times Book Review*, October 3, 1971, p. 8.

This rueful and funny little book comes very near to being a minor masterpiece, so sure is its understanding of the ingredients which make up life's more humble, quiet desperations. It is a child's book but the eight truths it catalogues are universal in their implications. They deal, for instance, with the sun that always shines on a new raincoat, the disloyalty of a best friend and the fragile nature of good intentions, and all are told in red type face with pen-and-ink drawings which are so relaxed and charming that only after two or three readings do you realize that every segment ends in frustration, tears, rage or all three: the rumple-haired owner of the new raincoat laments: "I know I will have to face another AWFUL, TERRIBLE, MISERABLE, ROTTEN, MEAN, NASTY beautiful new day." But the tears and the rage are the only appropriate reactions. It could not be otherwise.

Of the eight, the title segment is the least successful because it departs from the pattern of the other seven by offering asides from children in the margins which smack just a little of Peanuts, and closes the book with the statement, "If only you were real, Peter Perfect!" Surely nobody wishes that, the children in the book least of all.

There are no black faces in any of the pictures, and all of the girls but one are in skirts and hair ribbons, while on one page where a large group of children are shown pursuing various activities, the girls are all flowers and dolls and butterflies while the boys do the tree-climbing, kite-flying and so on, which goes to show that Mr. Waber is out of touch with a few realities.

But these are for once excusable oversights because the children and the situations are thoroughly real and, like all true humor, it is the sadness on the other side of the comedy that gives this book its final satisfying flavor.

Zena Sutherland

SOURCE: A review of *Nobody Is Perfick*, in *Bulletin of the Center for Children's Books*, Vol. 25, No. 4, December, 1971, p. 66.

A series of daft little stories designed as a book for the preschool child seems more appropriate for the eight and nine year olds. The type of humor, the fact that some of the joke is in the style of the writing, and the fact that much of the humor depends on visual appreciation indicates the independent reader as prime audience. The stories are exemplified by "Say Something Nice," in which a boy and girl are having a conversation: he tosses "Slimy, crawly, creepy things," at her; she responds, "Oh, how terrible! Stop it, Arthur!" and she protests more and more as his comments elaborate on the theme. Called indoors by her mother, the girl says brightly, "This was fun. Let's do it again tomorrow." Alone, he makes a horrible grimace of disappointment. There is a basis of truth to most of the pieces, but the purpose is entertainment, and—in varying degrees—entertaining it is.

Ethel L. Heins

SOURCE: A review of *Nobody Is Perfick,* in *The Horn Book Magazine,* Vol. XLVIII, No. 1, February, 1972, pp. 42-3.

Considering the range of subject matter, style, and design in the author's recent books—*An Anteater Named Arthur, You Look Ridiculous, A Firefly Named Torchy,* and the Lyle stories—one cannot say that he has sunk into his own stereotype. The shape and the feel of the new book are exactly right: small and squarish, with red-ink text beautifully balanced by the scrappy, black-line drawings. The eight wholly childlike sections—consisting of the kind of giddy monologue and dialogue that seem like aimless nonsense to an eavesdropping adult—

deal with such crucial subjects as a secret diary, an absurd dream, and a catalogue of favorite days in the year. The final chapter, "Peter Perfect: The Story of a Perfect Boy," clearly echoes a child's mind bent on silly, sweet revenge.

IRA SLEEPS OVER (1972)

Publishers Weekly

SOURCE: A review of *Ira Sleeps Over,* in *Publishers Weekly,* Vol. 203, No. 2, January 8, 1973, pp. 64-5.

Ira is invited to spend the night with a friend, for the first time. And what adventures friend Reggie has planned: the two boys will examine Reggie's junk collection, have a wrestling match and a pillow fight, play checkers. Best of all, according to Reggie, they will outscare each other with ghost stories. Ira's only problem is what his friend will think if he brings his teddy bear to sleep with. A delightful story and one little boys should especially enjoy. The cartoon pictures are just as much fun as the story.

From Do You See a Mouse?, *written and illustrated by Bernard Waber.*

Zena Sutherland

SOURCE: A review of *Ira Sleeps Over,* in *Bulletin of the Center for Children's Books,* Vol. 26, No. 6, February, 1973, p. 98.

Ira had never stayed overnight with a friend before, and was delighted at the prospect of sleeping at Reggie's until his sister said that if he didn't take his teddy bear along there might be problems. That started Ira worrying, since he'd never slept without his bear. Would he miss it? But he couldn't take it, Reggie would laugh. Ira vacillates as the hour approaches—opts against it—can't sleep—steals home and returns to find that Reggie is asleep, clutching *his* teddy bear. The dialogue is natural, the plot explores a familiar stage in childhood as well as the delights of comradeship, and the text and illustrations have a cozy humor—as in the picture in which Ira departs for the night, going all the way to the house next door.

The Booklist

SOURCE: A review of *Ira Sleeps Over,* in *The Booklist,* Vol. 69, No. 12, February 15, 1973, p. 575.

A small boy's joy in being asked to spend the night with a friend who lives next door is unrestrained until his sister raises the question of whether or not he should take his teddy bear. Torn between fear of being considered babyish and fear of what it may be like to sleep without his bear, Ira has a hard time deciding what to do. His dilemma is resolved happily, however, when he discovers that his friend Reggie also has a nighttime bear companion. An appealing picture book which depicts common childhood qualms with empathy and humor in brief text and colorful illustrations.

Joan W. Blos

SOURCE: "Getting It," in *School Library Journal,* Vol. 25, No. 9, May, 1979, pp. 38-9.

The thing about young children is that they are so young! Many books look as if they're meant for young children but prove to depend on attitudes or knowledge which their intended audience does not yet possess. Consider one gifted preschooler's suggestion that the seeds of seeded rye bread be planted so "we could have more bread." Then recall the Lawson drawing for Munro Leaf's *Ferdinand* in which grape-like clusters of wine-bottle corks hang from a cork tree's branches. Since apples, peaches, and other fruits hang from appropriate fruit-bearing trees, it is as logical as it is wrong to show the corks this way. The humor depends on the logic and the wrongness; a matter of A and B again, and a small child wouldn't get it.

We might ask how it is that some of these books have been used with children with evident success? It appears that when the story is right, children can miss the in-

tended humor and enjoy the story straight. Bernard Waber's *Ira Sleeps Over* is a popular book with three to five year olds. They hear it as a suspenseful account of a sleep-over visit with a resolution well worth the wait. Likely to be missed (but no matter if it is) is the heavy sarcasm of Ira's older sister. ("Who's worried?" she asks at one point, when Ira plainly is).

📖 *LYLE FINDS HIS MOTHER* (1974)

Kirkus Reviews

SOURCE: A review of *Lyle Finds His Mother,* in *Kirkus Reviews,* Vol. XLII, No. 15, August 1, 1974, p. 800.

Our favorite crocodile is still living contentedly with the Primms on East 88th Street but his impoverished former partner Hector P. Valenti is "up to tricks again" scheming to lure Lyle back to the stage. Promising him a meeting with his "dear sweet mother" ("P.S. Bring along a snack"), Hector then announces that they will have to perform together to earn the fare to her jungle home. To Hector's surprise Lyle actually does find his mother—what other crocodile would greet him with those fancy somersaults, handsprings, twirls and leaps?—and though she's not quite as Lyle had pictured her (that is, not at all like Mrs. Primm) . . . "a mother is still a mother." And, being Lyle's, she's lovably at home here.

Zena Sutherland

SOURCE: A review of *Lyle Finds His Mother,* in *Bulletin of the Center for Children's Books,* Vol. 28, No. 5, January, 1975, pp. 86-7.

Save perhaps for Paddington the Peruvian bear there is no animal character in contemporary picture books who is so happily ensconced in a family's affections as Lyle the crocodile. Here he is disturbed in the happy pattern of his life by the calculating Hector P. Valenti who has come on hard days and wants to lure Lyle back into a theatrical life that will benefit Valenti; as bait he uses the thought that Lyle might meet his "dear, sweet mother." Lyle's never thought about it before but it occurs to him that he must indeed have had a mother, and eventually he gets Valenti to fly him down to the "land of the crocodile." Naturally, they immediately meet Lyle's mother. She doesn't turn out to be the sweet, solicitous, indulgent mommy he's envisioned—but she and Lyle prove to have much in common. The familiar characters, the combination of bland style and nonsensical situation and the conflict-resolution of the plot, however silly it is, are as fetching as they are in earlier books about the amicable crocodile of 88th Street.

M. Hobbs

SOURCE: A review of *Lyle Finds His Mother,* in *The Junior Bookshelf,* Vol. 40, No. 3, June, 1976, pp. 148-49.

The saga of Lyle the Crocodile continues with Hector P. Valenti, Lyle's erstwhile stage partner, scheming to relieve his penury by luring Lyle back to the stage with the bait of a letter inviting him to meet his own mother. It works: the smiling, chubby crocodile finds his kind hosts, the Primm family, can no longer substitute for his own flesh and blood. They try everything to interest him, even local-election campaigning, but he returns to the stage. Even Hector is not proof against Lyle's dumb pleading, however, and has at last to go through the motions of looking for the mother he invented. In the tropics, to his surprise, they find her, just like Lyle only more so, and they bring her back to New York to see the Primms. The publishers apologise endearingly for retaining the American spelling.

Margery Fisher

SOURCE: A review of *Lyle Finds His Mother,* in *Growing Point,* Vol. 15, No. 2, July, 1976, p. 2924.

In the fifth anecdote about the amiable crocodile, [Lyle] is persuaded by Hector Valenti, his one-time trainer, to join him in a vaudeville show, ostensibly to earn money to find his "dear, sweet Mother". In fact, in the land of the crocodiles, while he is disporting himself in the water, he encounters an athletic animal who proves to be his mother indeed, and they return together to the hospitable Primms. Hard, casually disposed colour and comic attitudes suit the given character of Lyle and the mildly amusing portrait of a middle-aged crocodile standing erect and wearing a flowery hat and a fur neck-piece.

I WAS ALL THUMBS (1975)

Denise M. Wilms

SOURCE: A review of *I Was All Thumbs,* in *The Booklist,* Vol. 72, No. 4, October 15, 1975, p. 306.

Legs, an octopus about to be returned to sea after spending most of his life in a tank, is understandably apprehensive. Not that life was perfect with his keeper, Captain Pierre, who wrote a best-selling book on octopuses without crediting Legs and who persisted in calling him Legs when in fact he had arms. But Legs' new environment initially offers none of the serene comforts he enjoyed as a laboratory captive; he elaborates on the difficulties posed by his new freedom. "I was in trouble from the start—and all thumbs. I turned red when I should have turned yellow. I squirted my ink . . . in the wrong direction. I tripped all over myself . . . I felt just like crawling into a hole . . . which I did . . . the wrong hole." Such a misfit needs a mentor, and so Knuckles, coincidentally a former resident at Pierre's, conveniently turns up to instruct Legs in life at sea. He rapidly adjusts, so much so that he has never stopped being curious about the ocean and "wouldn't dream of living anywhere else." Legs' remembrances are colored with a tone of quaint propriety and peppered with wit and

wordplay. And Waber's reliance on mock melodramatic coincidence reinforces the humorous charm of the memoir, illustrated in loose watercolors.

Maie Wall Clark

SOURCE: A review of *I Was All Thumbs,* in *School Library Journal,* Vol. 22, No. 4, December, 1975, p. 50.

A whimsical and engaging new story by a reliably funny author. Legs the octopus is a happy laboratory dweller, living high on crab and lobster, until his friend, Captain Pierre, decides it is time for him to return to the sea. Dumping Legs rudely into his natural habitat, he sails away, leaving the octopus to fend for himself amidst a sea full of hidden disasters and unsettling experiences. In slyly sophisticated digs at society, Waber tells of Legs' self-probing, "Perhaps I should get out, be sociable, join a group." Legs will immediately gain readers' sympathy because his first attempts at fitting into the ocean-bottom scene are disastrous—his protective ink squirts in the wrong direction, and he turns the wrong color when he tries to camouflage himself. Just when he most needs a friend, however, he meets Knuckles, another former laboratory inmate, and is introduced to "all the many magnificent things that make for true octopus happiness." The illustrations are splashy delights done with wry good humor, and the underwater impression is heightened by use of blues in wavy, watery effects.

Paul Heins

SOURCE: A review of *I Was All Thumbs,* in *The Horn Book Magazine,* Vol. LII, No. 1, February, 1976, p. 43.

The inventor of Torchy the firefly, Arthur the anteater, and Lyle the crocodile has created another anthropomorphic success. Legs the octopus tells his own story—of how he had been living happily in a tank in Captain Pierre's laboratory and how one day he had been stuffed into a jar and cast, against his will, into the ocean. Although Legs never had to decide whether to sink or to swim, he did have to learn how to adjust himself to a strange, new milieu. He found the multi-colored denizens of the deep, to say the least, startling, forgot to squirt his protective ink in the right direction, and erroneously joined a school of fish—a crowd too fast for him. But after a while he learned to live like a successful octopus and finally realized he wouldn't dream of living anywhere but in the sea. The ingenuous humor of the story is accompanied by full-color, iridescent watercolors in which black outlines, prints, and washes reflect the wonders of the ocean floor.

Zena Sutherland

SOURCE: A review of *I Was All Thumbs,* in *Bulletin of the Center for Children's Books,* Vol. 29, No. 9, May, 1976, pp. 150-51.

Legs is a small octopus who has never known any home except a laboratory tank. He's told he will be happy in the sea, and Legs is apprehensive. "Why complain, I thought. Why make waves. Leave well-enough alone." So Legs is taken to the sea and sent crashing down into a new, strange world. Everyone stares, and poor befuddled Legs does all the wrong things, like squirting ink in the wrong direction. He finds a hiding place but suspects it might be better to be sociable and join a group. (Somehow he doesn't fit into a school of fish, a "very fast crowd.") Life improves, however, with the advent of a friend and the conviction that the sea offers more action and variety than the dear old tank. The illustrations have color, movement, and a merry quality; the story has a felicitous blend of bland treatment of a silly situation and a witty use of cliché phrases when they are delightfully inappropriate to the situation.

📖 *BUT NAMES WILL NEVER HURT ME* (1976)

Kirkus Reviews

SOURCE: A review of *But Names Will Never Hurt Me,* in *Kirkus Reviews,* Vol. XLIV, No. 4, February 15, 1976, p. 196.

Names will never hurt me . . . even when my name is Alison Wonderland? Unlike the first person title, most of the story is in the second, in the manner of someone (a parent?) explaining to Alison—"It began with your Voonterlant grandparents . . ."—how she came to be stuck with the, name that set her up for endless teasing at school. "Just remember, Alison," "your" mother finally advises, "this was a name given to you with oh, so much love." With its small size, limited color range, plotless text and quiet wit, this could be seen as either a model for or a gentle spoof on all those tender, dull stories dispensed to help "you" deal with a new sibling, parental divorce, etc. And if the concluding shift to the first person is curiouser yet and momentarily disconcerting—"I should know. Because you grew up to be me" (someone who talks to herself?)—we're pleased, and amused, to see Dr. Alison Wonderland, now a veterinarian, dealing so knowingly with rabbits. As prescription, this makes more therapeutic sense than Martha Alexander's *Sabrina* (1971)—but it's Waber's drollery that finally persuades us to label this READ ME.

Marjorie Lewis

SOURCE: A review of *But Names Will Never Hurt Me,* in *School Library Journal,* Vol. 22, No. 8, April, 1976, pp. 66-7.

An adoring mother, who loves the name Alison, gives it to her baby girl. The only trouble is her last name is Wonderland (changed from Voonterlant long ago by an immigration officer). Although the kids tease Alison as she grows up ("Hey, Alison Wonderland, watch out for rabbit holes!") she weathers it all just fine to become a happy, well-adjusted veterinarian who doesn't mind helping out a rabbit now and then. The line drawings, tinted in green and yellow, are exuberant and jolly. Children who hate their names and kids who want to know why great grandpa's name was different from theirs will like this. Young listeners, however, may not get the pun and may need an explanation as to why such a pretty name should be the source of so much unhappiness.

Denise M. Wilms

SOURCE: A review of *But Names Will Never Hurt Me,* in *The Booklist,* Vol. 72, No. 15, April 1, 1976, p. 1119.

Alison Wonderland's unusual and problem-causing name began with her grandparents, the narrator tells her, when an immigration official decided that their surname Voonterlant sounded better as Wonderland. Grandmother reasons, "We are happy to be here. Let it be Wonderland." "No problem," Grandfather accedes. Alison's first name is decided when her pregnant mother fixes on the appellation despite the fact that "It sounds too much like . . . " As the months go by, Father finally decides he's become used to it, so "Maybe it's not such a problem." But of course, when Alison starts school, it is. Mother responds to her tears and accusations by admitting that the name choice may have been wrong but recalls that it was chosen with "oh, so much love." The final pages disclose (smoothly) that the narrator is, in fact Alison, who has grown up to be a veterinarian. "Well, come right in," she reassures a small girl holding—guess what? "I know all about rabbits." Scruffy brown line drawings washed with greens and yellows illustrate the story.

Zena Sutherland

SOURCE: A review of *But Names Will Never Hurt Me,* in *Bulletin of the Center for Children's Books,* Vol. 29, No. 11, July-August, 1976, p. 184.

A busy immigration official had changed "Voonterlant" to "Wonderland," and that was Alison's last name. Teased by her classmates when a family move brought her to a new school, Alison protested unhappily to her parents. So they told her the story of how they had named her, and she did feel better. In fact, when she grew up she could joke about it. The story is amusing and ruefully tender, but Waber makes a point: name-calling can wound a child.

📖 *GOOD-BYE, FUNNY DUMPY-LUMPY* (1977)

Kirkus Reviews

SOURCE: A review of *Good-bye, Funny Dumpy-Lumpy,* in *Kirkus Reviews,* Vol. XLV, No. 3, February 1, 1977, p. 94.

In the easy-reading mode, Waber gives us five homey scenes from the life of a happy, middle-class pre-WW I family of cats. There is a funny little sketch called "Everybody," with Monroe and Eudora getting ready for school and explaining to their parents that "Everybody wears their hats backwards" and "They don't carry schoolbags anymore"; there is a visit from "Great-Grandfather" whom they all must kiss though he doesn't remember their names (when he takes out his teeth at bedtime, Octavia asks if he can take his tongue out too); and there is a glimpse of someone else's sadness in "Picnic" which begins with kites and games and ends with Aunt Effie in tears and Uncle Wally falling into the lake after too much wine. In contrast, the saddest moment for the family is saying good-bye to their lumpy old sofa when a new one arrives; and the biggest problem at the "Outdoor Concert" is, as Mother puts it, "three children and only two laps." Likable.

Pamela D. Pollack

SOURCE: A review of *Good-bye, Funny Dumpy-Lumpy,* in *School Library Journal,* Vol. 23, No. 7, March, 1977, p. 138.

The era is Edwardian and the family feline, but the home truths easily transfer to their modern human counterparts. In the title story the family pays its last respects to a sofa on its last legs and learns to make do with a less "lived-in" model. "Everybody," as in "Everybody is outside without a jacket and a hat," plays on that most commonly marshaled childhood defense. The humor in "Great-Grandfather" isn't at the expense of the senile centenarian but in the children's guileless interest in his second childhood. Her "Picnic" spoiled by a soused spouse, tearful ex-teacher Aunt Effie conducts an unplanned lesson in grown-up vulnerability. On an upbeat note, "The Outdoor Concert" turns into a round of musical laps as siblings compete for parental affection. Pointedly observant without being obvious, the stories are carried nearly on natural dialogue alone with the characters affectionately rendered in the line-and-wash sketches.

Virginia Hamilton

SOURCE: A review of *Good-bye, Funny Dumpy-Lumpy,* in *The Horn Book Magazine,* Vol. LIII, No. 3, June, 1977, p. 309.

The creator of the beloved Lyle the Crocodile and of Arthur the Anteater introduces a feline family with three offspring, who live in the village of Whitetip Corners. Monroe, the eldest, and Eudora are of school age, and little Octavia is too young for school. Dressed in the early-in-the-century fashion, the three are actively engaged in such human activities as attending a band concert in the park (the mood of a moonlit summer night nicely projected) and picnicking with Aunt Effie and wine-loving Uncle Wally, who falls into the lake. The

gray wash drawings supply nostalgic details of family life and Waber, like H. A. Rey, catches the spirit of real children by artless anthropomorphism in every spontaneous move, in animated, harmless bickering, and in humorous responses to adults. When father has fruitlessly attempted to mend "the funny dumpy-lumpy" sofa, which everyone has loved, Octavia asks how long "will it take for the new sofa to grow lumps?"

Donnarae McCann and Olga Richard

SOURCE: A review of *Good-bye, Funny Dumpy-Lumpy,* in *Wilson Library Bulletin,* Vol. 52, No. 3, November, 1977, p. 257.

Goodbye, Funny Dumpy-Lumpy is an exceptional group of narratives and sketches, yet it will be harder to use than picture books designed for an obvious age-group. Librarians will have to thrust this into the hands of ten-year-olds who can enjoy a retrospective glance at family life and a view of themselves as part of the human comedy. The book contains five anecdotal vignettes about such simple things as a visit from Great-Grandfather, a family picnic, a dispute over who sits on whose lap, the problem in getting a child to wear his jacket, and the sorrow over discarding "funny Dumpy-Lumpy," the old sofa.

These events are enacted by a nineteenth-century family of cats; and although children will tell you that they don't think of them as cats, the book needs this fantasy to underline its humor. The episodes are plotless, but appealing through their verisimilitude and affectionate evocation of the domestic scene.

The inclusion of senile grandparents is a tiresome stereotype in children's books generally, but the approach here is to spoof elderly tendencies and problems, just as other chapters satirize childish behavior.

Waber's illustrations are an enormous asset, but the page design hampers their visibility. He has created a painterly quality of color in his tones of gray, using an animated surface upon which objects are sketched in shades of gray and black. About 30 additional pages, though, should have been added to the book to provide sufficient white space around each drawing. They are really worth seeing, but the printed text interferes with the quivering black-and-white richness that characterizes this style. By blending the print and the picture, the designer has produced a feeling of clutter.

📖 *MICE ON MY MIND* (1977)

Laura Geringer

SOURCE: A review of *Mice on My Mind,* in *School Library Journal,* Vol. 24, No. 1, September, 1977, p. 117.

A cat, pillar of the community, reveals his obsession

with mice, mice, mice. Cold showers, hot baths, jogging, deep breathing exercises, reading—are all distractions insufficient to turn his mind from its rut. Inviting friends over (cocktail conversation revolves around the inevitable theme) and going to see a shrink (he has the same problem) also fail to bring relief to the haunted mouser. Indignation ("It's so unfair!"), self-pity ("I ask for so little . . . "), petulance ("I think I deserve a mouse."), martyrdom ("Oh, how I have tried!"), self-doubt ("Do I believe in mice?") all wreak comic havoc on the hero's highly mobile feline face until one day it lights up over a newspaper item—Upper Transpopolis has a rodent over-population problem—and the sufferer stops brooding and hops a plane bound for greener fields. Nimbly illustrated, Waber's droll, contemporary monologue with its can't-go-against-nature theme is sure to strike funny-bones.

Joyce Milton

SOURCE: A review of *Mice on My Mind,* in *The New York Times Book Review,* October 30, 1977, p. 34.

"I try so hard not to think about mice. I take cold showers. I soak in hot tubs. I jog." So says Mr. Cat as he dresses up in a dinner jacket for an unsuccessful attempt to seduce mice out from the baseboards of his living room, then fills his psychiatrist's office with visions of the luscious rodents that have eluded him. The adult who can steer his mind away from the obvious analogy is more pure-minded than I. However, the object of this cat's obsession is incidental to Bernard Waber's sly satire on the accouterments of middle-class anxiety: a succession of compulsively pursued hobbies; cocktail-party small talk; a leering shrink (also a cat) in expensive tweeds and a full beard. Waber's puckish cartoons are right on target as usual; this time, I suspect, they're aimed over the heads of the picture-book set.

Zena Sutherland

SOURCE: A review of *Mice on My Mind,* in *Bulletin of the Center for Children's Books,* Vol. 31, No. 6, February, 1978, p. 103.

Although Waber's books are usually for the picture book audience and this is in picture book format, it would be a rather sophisticated pre-reader who'd appreciate the latent content and sly innuendo of **Mice on My Mind.** The characters are all cats, the protagonist an adult male, and the problem the absence of mice. "I jog . . . I took up needlepoint . . . I pay my taxes . . . I give at the office . . . " He tries everything to rid himself of the obsession, but all he can think about is mice, mice, mice. Why aren't there any? Scattering cheese about the house and drilling holes in the baseboards produce only a smelly house and drafts. A psychiatrist doesn't help; in fact, he gets carried away along with his patient. Clever and sprightly in style, the book could well become a favorite of older readers.

THE SNAKE: A VERY LONG STORY (1978)

Publishers Weekly

SOURCE: A review of *The Snake: A Very Long Story,* in *Publishers Weekly,* Vol. 214, No. 9, August 28, 1978, p. 395.

It's always true to say of Waber that he's up to his new tricks again. His latest picture story is more evidence that he never repeats himself. The top half of each page shows a traveling snake, slithering along, while an economical text explains that he plans to make a trip and how he fares. The bottom halves of the pages show the path the tourist takes around the world, starting from his home under a brazen yellow sky in Africa. As he pushes on, the colorful scenes reveal mountains, bucolic settings gay with flowers, neon-lit streets with shrieking signs commanding attention to traffic laws—inspired vistas of various countries. Finally, the exhausted snake arrives and gets a jolt, like the one the reader feels in the funny bone. The book is sly, original and absorbing.

Kirkus Reviews

SOURCE: A review of *The Snake: A Very Long Story,* in *Kirkus Reviews,* Vol. XLVI, No. 17, September 1, 1978, p. 948.

Though it contains scarcely more than 100 words, this "very long story" does extend around the world as Waber's snake journeys across the long, low pages. First, his head appears on the left and works its way along the double page until all you see is an undulating green band—and then "at last the end was in sight." But as that end wiggles off the right hand edge—"Oh, dear . . . (more turns, blank pages) I am back where I began"—with his head peeking in from the left. Visually boring? Not when the traveler's passage through lands of domes and minarets, snow, flowers, tall buildings, and traffic signs is represented along the bottom of the pages in ever-changing style (and sometimes two combined, as in the freight-crate stencils over Gorkey-esque blobs and squiggles). Miles of fun.

Zena Sutherland

SOURCE: A review of *The Snake: A Very Long Story,* in *Bulletin of the Center for Children's Books,* Vol. 32, No. 6, February, 1979, p. 108.

The wider-than-tall pages of this silly but engaging book are used nicely to show a snake that carries over for pages and pages, its rippling green body moving over an assortment of running friezes at the foot of each double-page spread. There are a string of telephone poles and wires (with conversation), a blurred photograph of night traffic, a pattern of road signs, one of flowers, one of snowflakes, etc. The text is simple: the snake travels for days and nights and months; it's the longest trip ever undertaken by a snake and it wonders if it will ever reach its destination. Wiggling with joy, it sees the end ahead. Alas, the snake discovers it is right back where it started. Not much there? Yes, there is: the concepts of time and distance, the appeals of exaggeration and humor, and the visual variety of the pages.

📖 *YOU'RE A LITTLE KID WITH A BIG HEART* (1980)

Mary B. Nickerson

SOURCE: A review of *You're a Little Kid with a Big Heart,* in *School Library Journal,* Vol. 26, No. 9, May, 1980, p. 63.

Octavia Blisswink, seven and very redheaded, happens upon a magic kite stuck in a tree. When she frees it she is granted a wish, and without much consideration she asks to be old enough to do what she wants. The next thing she knows she's thirty-nine and fully grown. Her parents are dismayed but Octavia is pleased to see that they don't boss her at suppertime or tell her when to go to bed. Staying up late to watch television and gorging herself are fun, but being shunned by all her old friends is awful. She decides to find a job, but fails to impress the employment agency when she confides that her best skills are spelling and cutting out pictures ("My favorites are horses"). Loneliness and boredom set in, and when one day Octavia sees the magic kite again, she is after it like a shot. Luckily it gets snagged once more, and Octavia demands the return of her childhood. As her parents tuck her into bed that night, Octavia declares that she doesn't ever want to grow up again, but her father assures her that in time she will be ready. Where the title came from is anyone's guess, but the turnabout is drolly done. With limited color (red, green, yellow) and a loose, splotchy style Waber creates a gently humorous, warmly unfashionable setting for Octavia, who wears glasses as still too few story children do.

Publishers Weekly

SOURCE: A review of *You're a Little Kid with a Big Heart,* in *Publishers Weekly,* Vol. 217, No. 20, May 23, 1980, p. 77.

Waber again displays his rare ability to balance nonsense and pathos in his new book, the story of seven-year-old Octavia (Tavie) Blisswink. She rescues a kite, stuck in a tree, and the magic toy grants the kind child one wish. Tavie says she'd like to be old enough to live her own life, so the next instant she is 39. Mr. and Mrs. Blisswink are flabbergasted at having a daughter older and bigger than they but Tavie is thrilled, at first. She spends hours indulging in grownup privileges but then realizes she has lost not only friends (they call her "ma'am" and won't play with her) but also the childhood she realizes now is precious. When Octavia gets a chance at another wish, she doesn't flub it. Brightly colored cartoons do justice to the cunning cautionary tale.

Paul Heins

SOURCE: A review of *You're a Little Kid with a Big Heart,* in *The Horn Book Magazine,* Vol. LVI, No. 3, June, 1980, pp. 289-90.

When Octavia Blisswink, aged seven, rescued a kite entangled in the branches of a tree, she was granted a magic wish. Desiring to be old enough to decide for herself what she wanted to do, she discovered that she had become thirty-nine years of age. Octavia soon found out that her new status in life entailed some distinct disadvantages: Her mother took her toys away, her best friend would not play ball with her, and her elementary school had not prepared her for a job. The rough-and-ready line drawings patterned and washed with strong color provide the comic visual equivalent for Octavia's preposterous experiences and metamorphoses—from little girl to woman, from woman back to little girl—and for her ultimate tender acceptance of childhood.

📖 *DEAR HILDEGARD* (1980)

Publishers Weekly

SOURCE: A review of *Dear Hildegarde,* in *Publishers Weekly,* Vol. 218, No. 17, October 24, 1980, p. 49.

A talented and versatile author-illustrator has written a delectable anthropomorphic tale with kernels of commonsensical counseling mixed with the amusement. Hildegarde the wise old owl gives advice to readers of her column, telling "Stuck-up," a giraffe accused of snootiness, that she should be herself, never stoop to the level of spiteful animals. A bird signing herself "Who" asks who made the rules her mate Gus obeys, meaning that he sits on a branch and whistles all day while she slaves away at nest-building, etc. Hildegarde says rules can be changed, also Gus's tune. "You try whistling while he works." Scratchy pen drawings of Hildegarde at her typewriter on a sturdy roll-top desk and other details representing her male and female clients' dilemmas do full justice to the unusual entertainment.

Kirkus Reviews

SOURCE: A review of *Dear Hildegarde,* in *Kirkus Reviews,* Vol. XLIX, No. 1, January 1, 1981, p. 4.

Dear Hildegarde as in "Dear Abby"—except that Hildegarde is an owl (motto on wall: "Better to be wise than otherwise") and her troubled correspondents are animals of various sorts. A dog objects to the name Bernard ("Why couldn't I have been given a decent dog name—something interesting like: Rover, Spot, Champ, or Prince?"). A giraffe's problem is, of course, "I am extraordinarily tall." A pig protests "insulting remarks like . . . dirty pig"; a spider has trouble spinning a neat web; a female bird complains that her mate does nothing but whistle—and then calls it work. Some of these, like the giraffe's, are old plaints that elicit standard answers with a verbal twist (to the giraffe: "Just continue being your own sweet uplifting self.") Some, most notably the bird's, reflect current, topical gripes—and get a properly up-to-date, also word-juggling reply (re mate Gus: "Ask Gus if he ever heard of whistling while you work"). And there's an element of parody throughout. But that, together with the verbal hijinks and some of the plaints, seems altogether geared to an older child than the picture-book format suggests—however amusingly Waber's black-and-white sketches convey the animals' problems.

Ann A. Flowers

SOURCE: A review of *Dear Hildegarde,* in *The Horn Book Magazine,* Vol. LVII, No. 1, February, 1981, p. 54.

Hildegarde is the Ann Landers of the animal world, and her correspondents are creatures with heartbreaking problems—a tall giraffe whose friends accuse her of being uppity, a dog named Bernard who feels he is really a "Prince," a spider who cannot spin a normal web. Two of the saddest cases are the bird whose mate does not help her prepare the nest—he only whistles—and the moth irresistibly attracted to light bulbs. But wise old Hildegarde gives thoughtful, helpful answers. To the moth she replies, "I am still in the dark about this light bulb disturbance. But I can see where your life needs brightening. I would advise that you switch to new outlets." The black-and-white drawings of the pained and pathetic animals, not to mention Hildegarde's scruffy office walls covered with wise maxims, are full of humor which should appeal to both children and adults.

Hara L. Seltzer

SOURCE: A review of *Dear Hildegarde,* in *School Library Journal,* Vol. 27, No. 6, February, 1981, p. 60.

Hildegarde, an owl, writes a "Dear Abby" column for animals who write and tell her their problems. There is a bird whose mate is no help at nest building. A beaver works nights and his days are disturbed by forest noises. A moth complains of his light-bulb obsessions; a pig protests anti-pig remarks. Hildegarde, at desk and in tree, is maternal, but cute. The spoof is modest and pleasant, and young children may enjoy hearing it or attempting to read it themselves. The pen-and-ink line drawings are an engagingly humorous accompaniment.

BERNARD (1982)

Publishers Weekly

SOURCE: A review of *Bernard,* in *Publishers Weekly,* Vol. 221, No. 26, June 25, 1982, p. 118.

This is a masterpiece by the author-illustrator of *Ira*

Sleeps Over, Lyle the Crocodile adventures and many more best-selling books. Bernard is a dog sorely tried when the man and woman he loves quarrel and announce their separation. Each claims ownership of Bernard, but he runs away rather than hurt either by his choice. Action-filled scenes in summery tones depict the waif as he trots along city streets and park paths and tries to ingratiate himself with strangers he hopes will give him a home. Bernard even helps stop a bank robbery to show he's a good citizen but nobody takes him in. Everyone feeds the nice dog, pats him and plays with him. But they all leave him lonely and lost. So artfully does Waber end the story that the reader will be caught up in speculations about the fate in store for Bernard.

Kirkus Reviews

SOURCE: A review of *Bernard,* in *Kirkus Reviews,* Vol. L, No. 13, July 1, 1982, p. 731.

Poor Bernard! His home is breaking up and the original bitter quarrel has now become a dispute over whether Bernard will live with the man or the woman. Unable to choose between them, Bernard runs away. When he's found, the frantic couple realize their mistake and agree—not to reconcile, that would be unrealistic, but to work out a way to share Bernard. "And however we decide will be—must be—what is best for Bernard." Topical therapeutics unworthy of Waber? It would be, except that Bernard is not a child but a dog, the pet of the splitting couple. With this small switch Waber makes it an amusing story, filling the interval between lost and found with Bernard's beguiling attempts to adopt another family. As these involve him in playground games, a parade, a van burglary, and lots of feedings, there's no sense here of a drab, doctor-ordered scenario.

Zena Sutherland

SOURCE: A review of *Bernard,* in *Bulletin of the Center for Children's Books,* Vol. 36, No. 5, January, 1983, p. 99.

Bernard, a thoughtful dog, is disturbed by the quarreling of his owners (a couple who are about to separate) about who gets custody. Bernard just can't choose, when invited to do so, and runs off. He has a series of encounters in which he tries to show that he is quiet (watching a parade), a good watchdog (catching a robber), and gentle with children—but, while he's appreciated, Bernard's never invited to go home with anyone. Caught in a torrential rain, Bernard is picked up by his worried owners; they take him home and agree that whatever is done will be for their dog's good. This leaves the custody question unanswered, but it satisfies Bernard. The line and wash drawings are bright and are replete with action and humor, and the story is told with a recurrent pattern that should appeal to the read-aloud audience, with a brisk pace and light style.

FUNNY, FUNNY LYLE (1987)

Publishers Weekly

SOURCE: A review of *Funny, Funny Lyle,* in *Publishers Weekly,* Vol. 232, No. 29, July 24, 1987, p. 185.

Readers may be somewhat mystified by this latest installment in the saga of Lyle the lovable Crocodile, who lives with the Primm family on Manhattan's Upper East Side. In Waber's convoluted tale, clear narrative is sacrificed in the name of playful atmosphere. Lyle's mother Felicity has journeyed from the Land of Crocodile to join Lyle; they are happiest by day, when it is "just the two of them doing their chores." In the pivotal episode, Mrs. Primm takes Felicity shopping at a department store. Felicity, who innocently stocks her shopping bag with perfume bottles, lands in jail. Sentenced by a lenient judge to perform community service, Felicity gets the necessary training to care for the Primm's new baby. The story is carried on the strength of the warm illustrations, rendered in blotted ink line and soft watercolor washes. Whether this is a story of naturalization or cultural inculcation is unclear and perhaps unimportant, when irresistible scenes include one of Lyle, mirror in hand, practicing his best crooked-grin grimaces.

Ilene Cooper

SOURCE: A review of *Funny, Funny Lyle,* in *Booklist,* Vol. 83, No. 22, August, 1987, p. 1753.

Lyle, that lovable crocodile, makes his sixth appearance in a story that stars his mother, Felicity. Last time out, Lyle found his mother in the jungle. Now, she is happily ensconced with the Primms in the house on East 88th Street, taking bubble baths and arranging the guest towels. But Felicity isn't entirely in tune with the ways of the world. During a visit to a department store she not only sprays herself with perfume samples but also takes the bottles. Poor Felicity is picked up for shoplifting, but a kind judge sentences her to community service. In the hospital she finds her true calling in being a nurse, and when Mrs. Primm has a baby, Felicity is ready to help the family care for little Miranda. Warm and witty, the book's multi-level text gets plenty of help from the colorful pictures in Waber's familiar style, which are a joy in themselves. Felicity, always neatly outfitted in a hat and pearls, will especially provoke chuckles. There's no doubt Lyle's (and his mother's) legion of fans will say, "Welcome back!"

Ethel R. Twichel

SOURCE: A review of *Funny, Funny Lyle,* in *The Horn Book Magazine,* Vol. LXIII, No. 5, September-October, 1987, p. 604.

Lyle's mom is now comfortably settled in the house on East 88th Street, where she has endeared herself to the Primm family, made friends in the neighborhood, and even been given a new name, Felicity. Those who have enjoyed Lyle's antics in earlier books will find the same cheerful adaptability to human surroundings and amiable innocence in the scaly twosome's adventures. Lyle tries to protect the family with an unconvincing show of fierceness; Felicity lands in jail; and Mrs. Primm is expecting a baby. Felicity's getting out of jail and into a job as a nurse's aid provides wonderful opportunities for Waber's bright, cartoon-like drawings to blend a deadpan acceptance of the two large animals in the community with the humor stemming from their amphibian characteristics. An ingenuous good nature flavors all the illustrations, but is particularly engaging in those depicting a delighted Lyle as he imagines himself cradling and feeding the new little baby and shares, with the rest of the family, her safe arrival.

Marcia Hupp

SOURCE: A review of *Funny, Funny Lyle,* in *School Library Journal,* Vol. 34, No. 4, December, 1987, p. 78.

Lyle the Crocodile is back and, with him, his charming, if socially naive mother, Felicity ("a name of her own choosing"). Less focused than others in the series, this begins with Felicity settling happily into life with the Primm family and her beloved son, Lyle. Meanwhile, Lyle is developing his anti-burglar technique; Mrs. Primm announces she will soon have a baby; and Felicity, "new to our ways," is arrested for shoplifting and sentenced to six months of public service. Felicity chooses hospital work and proves to be a superb nurse. And, of course, this is a great help to the Primms when their new baby, Miranda, is finally born. Waber has a facility with language and rhythm that accounts, at least in part, for the enduring charm of his reptilian hero. It establishes a tone of innocence and earnestness where anything might happen, but everything is bound to turn out all right. His colorful watercolor cartoons show a fine sense of family and place and an energetic use of composition, line, and design. Lovers of Lyle—and they are legion—will take this latest chapter in his eventful life immediately to heart.

IRA SAYS GOODBYE (1988)

David Gale

SOURCE: A review of *Ira Says Goodbye,* in *School Library Journal,* Vol. 35, No. 1, September, 1988, p. 175.

Best friends Ira and Reggie, whom readers will remember from *Ira Sleeps Over,* are back—but not for long. Reggie is moving out of town. With much humor and a clear sense of what is important to children, Waber portrays the range of feelings and emotions that accompanies this move. At first both boys are upset at the prospect, then Reggie gets excited about his expectations of his new town ("In Greendale, all people do is have fun," watching a killer shark that snorts and riding the thriller rides in the park), making Ira even more upset, and angry. As Reggie is about to leave, though, he bursts into tears and the two boys reconcile. Later that afternoon Reggie calls from Greendale to invite Ira for a weekend visit. Cheerful full-page and vignette watercolors on large white pages bring Ira's first-person narrative alive with style. Ira's concerns reflect those of any child in a similar situation, but its humor is even more universal, so there should be a wide and responsive audience for this funny and moving book.

Ilene Cooper

SOURCE: A review of *Ira Says Goodbye,* in *Booklist,* Vol. 85, No. 1, September 1, 1988, pp. 85-6.

Ira, the teddy bear—loving star of **Ira Sleeps Over,** is sad to learn in this sequel that his best friend, Reggie, is moving away. Ira remembers all the fun they've had together—starting a club, putting on a magic show—but Reggie hides his distress behind a display of bravado.

He informs Ira what a great new town he's moving to, complete with an amusement park and a football team. Not until Reggie says good-bye does he show his true feelings, and Ira, who's been irked by Reggie's good humor, finally realizes just how sad Reggie is to be leaving. A phone call and an invitation for a weekend sleepover add a satisfying ending to the poignant story. Although the text could use a little trimming, kids will respond to the familiar circumstances. And while Ira will be welcomed back, Waber does a particularly nice job with the character of Reggie, who'd rather cover up than admit his feelings. As in his other books, Waber's thick pen-lined drawings, dabbed in color, are filled with nuances that children will pick up on and enjoy.

Kirkus Reviews

SOURCE: A review of *Ira Says Goodbye,* in *Kirkus Reviews,* Vol. LVI, No. 1, September 1, 1988, pp. 1329-30.

Like its predecessor, **Ira Sleeps Over,** this is a warm-

Everyone was silent.
But then, after a little while, Bearsie Bear said,
"Porkie Porcupine, if you are very careful about it,
and if you are very careful not to thrash about,
you may come back to bed."
"Hooray!" said Porkie Porcupine.

So, Porkie Porcupine climbed into bed.
And he was very careful about it.
And he was very careful not to thrash about.

From Bearsie Bear and the Surprise Sleepover Party, *written and illustrated by Bernard Waber.*

hearted picture of one of childhood's classic dramas: in this case, having a best friend move. Reggie and Ira are such good friends that they even keep their turtles in the same tank; but when Reggie turns out to be pleasantly excited by the prospect of his own departure, Ira is understandably miffed. Still, when Reggie comes to pick up his turtle, Ira gives it to him—and on moving day, it's Reggie who bursts into tears. Waber deftly conveys a true friendship and the mixed, unmatched emotions at parting, with plenty of entertaining, realistic detail. His cheerful, cartoon-like illustrations are pleasantly full of life and humor. The long text makes this appropriate for use as a transitional young reader.

Roger Sutton

SOURCE: A review of *Ira Says Goodbye,* in *Bulletin of the Center for Children's Books,* Vol. 42, No. 2, October, 1988, pp. 56-7.

A few years older than when he worried about taking his teddy to Reggie's house in *Ira Sleeps Over,* Ira has just found out that Reggie is moving away. The news is delivered by Ira's sister, who is just as entertainingly obnoxious as she was in the first book: "Far, far away. Oh, I would hate it to pieces if my best friend were moving away. What will you do when your best friend in the whole wide world moves away? Hmmmmmm?" Reggie himself is more excited about the move than is seemly ("Reggie just went on talking about Greendale, as if he had never heard about best friends"), and doesn't even blink when Ira pointedly tells him to take both their pet turtles, rather than split up Felix and Oscar, friends "who are used to being together." Friendship does win in the end, but in the meantime Waber again demonstrates a keen ability to score psychological points through funny and natural dialogue. The illustrations have an offhand air that is similar to the first book, but more spare of line and in full color. The cover art neatly mirrors the first book as well, with a bigger Ira going *up* the stairs (to pack for a visit to Reggie's).

📖 *LYLE AT THE OFFICE* (1994)

Ilene Cooper

SOURCE: A review of *Lyle at the Office,* in *Booklist,* Vol. 90, Nos. 19-20, June 1, 1994, p. 1846.

Lyle, that lovable crocodile, returns, and now he's spending some time at Mr. Primm's office. There seems to be no particular reason for the trip downtown; it's not like it's Take-Your-Crocodile-to-Work Day or anything, but once he's in the office, Lyle meets the staff, sharpens pencils, enjoys lunch in the cafeteria, and spends time in the company's day-care center surrounded by kiddies (if he weren't green, you might mistake Lyle for Barney). But when Mr. Primm's boss, Al Bigg, wants to use Lyle in Krispie Krunchie Krackles' new advertising campaign, Mr. Primm protectively says no and loses his job for his

trouble. Some of this is rather silly, and it all gets resolved, amicably, of course, but that's one of the pleasures of the series. The action is recognizable and not very threatening (the family breezes right through unemployment), yet there is never a dull moment in these books. Also noteworthy is the art. Waber seems at the top of his game here. The pictures are delightful, very busy, with lots of bits that can be looked at again and again. It's hard to go wrong with Lyle, and libraries may have to order enough copies to go around.

Publishers Weekly

SOURCE: A review of *Lyle at the Office,* in *Publishers Weekly,* Vol. 241, No. 27, July 4, 1994, p. 61.

The much-loved crocodile of Manhattan engages in a quintessential venture: visiting a grown-up (in Lyle's case, Mr. Primm) at work (an advertising agency). Affable Lyle has a grand time delivering memos, working the copy machine, sitting in on "a very important meeting" and, most of all, playing with the children in the day-care center. But when the boss, Mr. Bigg, sees Lyle as a potential product promoter and Mr. Primm balks ("Lyle will never say, 'Yum, Yum, Yummy Yum, Yum,' nor will his picture be on a cereal box"), both Mr. Primm and Lyle are shown the door. When Halloween rolls around, Lyle heroically rescues Mr. Bigg from a mishap in the "haunted house" Bigg is renovating, and in due course Mr. Primm is reinstated in his job—as long as Lyle promises to pay frequent visits to the office. Lyle has aged exceptionally well since his first appearance (*The House on East 88th Street*) some 30 years ago: he is as winsome as ever, and this new tale combines the charm of the first, somewhat quaint stories with a contemporary freshness. The art is, if anything, brighter than that in the previous books. An enticing reappearance on all scores.

Joy Fleishhacker

SOURCE: A review of *Lyle at the Office,* in *School Library Journal,* Vol. 40, No. 9, September, 1994, p. 200.

Crocodile fans rejoice! Lyle is back and ready to take on the work world. When he visits Mr. Primm at his advertising office, he is an instant success. He sharpens pencils, delivers memos, and makes many friends. After listening to him munch his way through a box of Krispie Krunchie Krackles, Mr. Bigg, the big boss, attempts to recruit Lyle as a spokesreptile for the cereal. Mr. Primm refuses to allow his friend to pose for the ad and is fired. On Halloween night, while answering a desperate cry for help coming from an abandoned house, the family discovers Mr. Bigg hanging from a ceiling fixture. Lyle picks up the ladder and helps their new neighbor climb down. The happy ending is complete when Mr. Primm is invited to return to the agency. This is another appealing installment in the adventures of lovable Lyle.

Contemporary touches, such as a pair of working moms (Mrs. Primm and Lyle's mother) and a company day-care center, bring this classic crocodile into the '90s. Although the plot unfolds a little bit like a sitcom, the text reads smoothly and builds to a neat conclusion. Waber's trademark watercolor and crayon illustrations are filled with warmth and humor. Lyle's always expressive face shines with pride while showing baby pictures of the youngest Primm, clouds with worry while listening to pleas for help, and smiles with contentment when everything turns out right. Totally satisfying.

Mary M. Burns

SOURCE: A review of *Lyle at the Office*, in *The Horn Book Magazine*, Vol. LXXI, No. 1, January-February, 1995, p. 56.

Lyle's fans will not be disappointed by his latest escapade, in which the agreeable crocodile narrowly eludes unwanted fame in the glitzy world of advertising when his guardian, Mr. Primm, takes him for a field trip to his office. There, Lyle's good manners and helpful nature quickly win the affections of the staff, particularly the supervisors of the company day-care center. But events take an unfortunate turn when Mr. Bigg, a CEO with dollar signs for ethics, attempts to force the Primms into making the talented but privacy-loving saurian into an advertising gimmick for "Krispie Krunchy Krackles." The situation is resolved happily as Lyle triumphs once again. What separates Lyle's stories from more mundane excursions into animal fantasy is Waber's uncanny ability to induce a willing suspension of disbelief in his audience. The great green crocodile dominates every scene, at ease in all sorts of situations, perfectly acceptable to the crowds who surround him. Like the nursemaid dog in Barrie's *Peter Pan,* he has a believable persona. Through carefully orchestrated detailed illustrations and a marvelously insouciant text, supported by a rather substantial theme focusing on values rather than wealth, Lyle has his own reality—and we love it!

📖 DO YOU SEE A MOUSE? (1995)

Publishers Weekly

SOURCE: A review of *Do You See a Mouse?*, in *Publishers Weekly*, Vol. 242, No. 4, January 23, 1995, p. 70.

"What a scandal! What a calamity!" Someone has spotted a mouse in the ultra-chic Park Snout Hotel. Everyone else says it ain't so. Says Simon the doorman, "Do you see a mouse? I do not see a mouse"—a refrain echoed by other hotel employees and guests. Delighted youngsters, however, will squeal "Yes!" as they spy the mouse on the subsequent pages of this predictable yet engaging tale by the creator of the Lyle Crocodile books. The mouse can be seen riding atop a pile of luggage on the bellman's cart, nibbling a piece of cheese in the kitchen, peeking out from a napkin on a waiter's tray, helping the conductor direct the hotel orchestra, etc. Though the hotel owner, too, denies the existence of the rodent, he decides to put everyone's mind at ease and hires the world's foremost mouse-catchers to "look into this beastly matter." In lively slapstick style, Waber shows the debonair mouse looking on as the identically mustachioed, bowler-hatred Hyde and Snide search high and low, finally certifying (and double certifying) that there is no mouse in the hotel. Even more than his lighthearted text, Waber's droll cartoon art delivers the humor here.

Hanna B. Zeiger

SOURCE: A review of *Do You See a Mouse?*, in *The Horn Book Magazine,* Vol. LXXI, No. 4, July-August, 1995, p. 454.

The Park Snoot Hotel, an obviously posh New York establishment, has had an incredible complaint—someone has seen a mouse. How can that be? Impossible. As a considerable cast of employees and guests emphatically affirms, "No, no, no, there is no mouse here," the mouse gazes calmly out from a variety of vantage points. He rides Emil the bellman's baggage cart, nibbles cheese in Gaston the chef's kitchen, and helps to conduct the hotel orchestra. Neither Sir Horace Morris, world-famous explorer, nor Madame Eevah Deevah, the opera singer, sees the jaunty little fellow. But just to be sure, Mr. Josh Posh, the hotel owner, engages the services of Hyde and Snide, who specialize in "Elegant Pest Management." The two gentlemen arrive looking as though they've stepped right out of a silent comedy film and, with butterfly nets at the ready, engage in such an inept and fruitless search that even our ubiquitous friend, the mouse, can't believe his eyes. In a grand finale, the two experts deliver their report of "no mouse" to all the assembled characters—including the mouse; and, as they leave the hotel, the mouse waves good-bye. Bernard Waber's characterizations are full of sly humor, and readers of all ages will have to smile at the antics of the little rascally rodent who successfully bamboozles one and all in this comic adventure.

Trev Jones

SOURCE: A review of *Do You See a Mouse?*, in *School Library Journal,* Vol. 41, No. 9, September, 1995, p. 188.

When a mouse is spotted at the highbrow Park Snoot Hotel, all of the employees and guests emphatically deny its existence. But, just to put everyone's mind at ease, the exterminator team of Hyde and Snide is brought in, and then the fun really begins. Very easy to read, with lots of repetition ("Do you see a mouse? I do not see a mouse"), the book is ideal for beginning readers, who will love their own miniature, less complicated version of "Waldo." The uncluttered pictures with lots of white space make finding the endearing rodent challenging but not frustrating, and are a perfect accompaniment to the simple text. The adult characters are amusing in their denial of the presence of varmint, but it's the impish little mouse who steals the show here.

Mary Lou Burket

SOURCE: A review of *Do You See a Mouse?*, in *The Five Owls*, Vol. X, No. 1, September-October, 1995, p. 21.

Bernard Waber pays a visit to the Park Snoot Hotel, where there's a rumor of a mouse. As we tour this fine establishment, room by room, every person we encounter asks the title question, Do You See a Mouse? And no one does. Not even the arrival of a vaudevillian pair of pest "managers" causes the mouse to be detected. Pre-readers, of course, will chant the question and spot the wily creature as he peeks from beds and flower pots and hitches a ride with an unsuspecting porter. In one amusing scene, we see him lounging atop the hotel's framed certificate of excellence. Could anyone give the whereabouts of such a mouse away?

📖 *GINA* (1995)

Publishers Weekly

SOURCE: A review of *Gina*, in *Publishers Weekly*, Vol. 242, No. 33, August 14, 1995, p. 83.

Gina is understandably disappointed when she discovers that no other girls her age live in her new apartment building. "Yet, and more oddly still, / there were boys, boys, boys galore, / boys, boys, boys—Gina's age, / on every floor." After a lengthy, breezily illustrated roll call of the young males in Gina's building, Waber shows how they all have a grand time hanging out together, while "Day after day, Gina played all alone. / No friends rang her bell, or called on the phone." One day, Gina mentions that she "could throw" and the boys give her a chance to prove it. She does that handily and goes on to show her prowess in batting, biking, climbing trees— and even standing up to bullies. "Gina made many friends that day. / Her whole life changed in every way. / Moving to the apartment was no longer a bummer. / Gina began having fun, fun, fun that summer." Waber offsets the randomness of his rhythms and his frequently forced rhymes with the domesticated daffiness of his action-packed watercolors, served up here in panels, whole pages and quick vignettes.

Hazel Rochman

SOURCE: A review of *Gina*, in *Booklist*, Vol. 92, No. 2, September 15, 1995, p. 176.

With a lively rhyming text and energetic line-and-water-color pictures, the author and illustrator of *Ira Says Goodbye* offers another book about moving. When Gina moves to an apartment in Queens, there are no girls her age in the neighborhood. just boys everywhere: At first she's lonely, but she loves sports, and when she shows that she can slam the ball right over third base, she's part of the crowd. Still, she clings to her dream "of someday seeing other girls play on her team." The story's a bit purposive, but Waber has fun with names and rhymes ("Yusuf, Yakov, Laird, and Sonny. If it weren't so weird, it could have been funny"). The pictures show that the guys on the street may all be boys, boys galore on every floor, but they come in all shapes and sizes, colors and crews.

Virginia Opocensky

SOURCE: A review of *Gina*, in *School Library Journal*, Vol. 41, No. 10, October, 1995, p. 123.

Gina has just moved into a new apartment building in Queens, NY. There are no girls her age, but boys galore, none of whom wants to be her friend. In lilting rhyme and funny, full-color cartoons, dozens of boys are named and personified: "Kyle, Lyle, Vic, and Stu, Tom, John, and Zbigniew." Families, gaggles, and gangs of boys ignore Gina who, day after day, draws and reads books about sports. "One day—/ was it Nate or was it Joe?/ Well, anyway, Gina told one of them/ she could throw." Henceforth, she becomes friends with them all. In a quatrain for equity, the author states: "Although her life was full,/ Gina clung to the dream/ of someday seeing other girls/ play on her team." Another winner from the redoubtable Waber.

📖 *A LION NAMED SHIRLEY WILLIAMSON* (1996)

Ilene Cooper

SOURCE: A review of *A Lion Named Shirley Williamson*, in *Booklist*, Vol. 93, No. 1, September 1, 1996, p. 128.

Because of a telephone mix-up between a woman at the Wildlife Trading Company and the zoo director, the new lion at the zoo is named Shirley Williamson. This delights the zoo-going public, but the other lions are put out. Why are they always taking a backseat to Shirley? Shirley's biggest booster is zookeeper Seymour, but he fuels the other lions' ire by feeding Shirley her raw meat on a tray with a rose. Finally, the zoo director fires Seymour and renames Shirley, Bongo. The other lions love it, "Bongo! It's a scream!" Shirley, who misses Africa anyway, sneaks out when the new zookeeper leaves the door open and winds up at Seymour's house. She plays at being a pussycat, but Seymour convinces her she must return to the zoo, though how to get her there unnoticed is a problem. Dressing Shirley up in his late wife's clothing, Seymour finally gets Shirley to the zoo, where an insistent public demands she get her name back. And to placate them, the other lions get names, too: Ralph Weinstock, Harvey Johnston, and Sylvester J. Hotchkiss Jr. Waber is back in full form with a story that is both hysterical and poignant. It succeeds at every level, offering a plot that prances along, characters that show the inevitable tangle of emotions life elicits, and artwork that is so funny yet sly that adults and children can both relish it. Shirley, take your place alongside Waber's perennial favorite, Lyle the crocodile.

Kirkus Reviews

SOURCE: A review of *A Lion Named Shirley Williamson,* in *Kirkus Reviews,* Vol. LXIV, No. 18, September 15, 1996, p. 1409.

A lionness bound for a zoo is dubbed Shirley Williamson due to a bad phone connection. It's a name that draws attention (hordes come to view her), special privileges from Seymour the zookeeper (his deceased wife's name was Shirley and the memories are strong), and resentment from the lions—Goobah, Poobah, and Aroobah. The attention is nice, but what Shirley really pines for is her home on the African savannah. The zoo director renames Shirley Bongo and fires Seymour; the director's incompetent first cousin gets Seymour's job and leaves Shirley's door open, allowing her to flee to Seymour's Brooklyn apartment. Seymour, not a little concerned by the hungry look in Shirley's eye, knows that to keep her as a pet would be impractical. Together, they head zooward. With the same tristful humor he brought to the stories of Lyle Crocodile, Waber makes the best of an imperfect situation, a slice of life without the whipped cream and a cherry on top: Shirley gets her name back—but also her cage. Humor with bite, as it were, given substance by the playful artwork.

Publishers Weekly

SOURCE: A review of *A Lion Named Shirley Williamson,* in *Publishers Weekly,* Vol. 243, No. 39, September 23, 1996, p. 75.

The newest perky animal character from the creator of Lyle the Crocodile is a lion with an unlikely moniker. The big cat's name earns her preferential treatment from Seymour the zookeeper: he serves her meals on a tray adorned with a rose and decorates her cage with a patterned rug and a potted palm. She quickly becomes the zoo's star attraction (although there are problems: people named Shirley Williamson "didn't like sharing their name with a ferocious animal"). A consummate crowd-pleaser, Shirley loves the limelight, but nonetheless grows homesick for the wilds of Africa and for her freedom. Oddly, Waber leaves this issue hanging; next thing the reader knows, zoo officials fire Seymour and change Shirley's name to Bongo because the other lions are jealous of the attention she receives. A madcap sequence involves Shirley's escape, her reunion with Seymour in his Brooklyn apartment, and his resourceful plan to return

her to the zoo. Shirley gets back her original name and Seymour is reinstated, but kids may well fret that the heroine winds up beyond bars, her dreams of freedom unresolved. Waber's waggish cartoons and comical dialogue are as enjoyable as ever, but the loose ends bar this entry from the top of the list of his largely first-rate offerings.

Selene S. Vasquez

SOURCE: A review of *A Lion Named Shirley Williamson,* in *School Library Journal,* Vol. 42, No. 12, December, 1996, pp. 108-09.

Waber's characteristic sly humor and droll, watercolor-and-ink cartoon art bring to life the hilarious mishaps that befall a lion named Shirley Williamson. Because of her unusual name, Seymour, the zookeeper, indulges her with beautiful roses; admiring fans send her flattering letters; and the director of the zoo proclaims an official "Shirley Williamson Day." The other lions, Goobah, Poobah, and Aroobah, growl in jealous rage over Shirley's exceptional status. Then, one ill-fated day, much to the wicked satisfaction of the envious pride, Shirley is stripped of her name and simply becomes Bongo. Miserable and homesick for Africa, she escapes from her cage and hunts down Seymour in Brooklyn. In the end, she regains her special name and accepts the fact that the zoo is her home. A delightful adventure for reading aloud in humorous tribute to one of nature's most majestic creatures.

📖 BEARSIE BEAR AND THE SURPRISE SLEEPOVER PARTY (1997)

Kirkus Reviews

SOURCE: A review of *Bearsie Bear and the Surprise Sleepover Party,* in *Kirkus Reviews,* Vol. LXV, No. 18, September 15, 1997, p. 1464.

A humorous cumulative tale that makes a great read-aloud for the very young. A wintry scene shows an isolated house so deep in snow that the road can't be seen. A moose plods its way to the door and knocks; a bear sleeping cozily near his blazing fireplace opens one eye and asks who it is. "'It's me, Moosie Moose,' said Moosie Moose. 'Moosie Moose?' said Bearsie Bear. 'Yes, Moosie Moose,' said Moosie Moose." The repetition of the already repetitive names continues as more animals join the bear and moose in a wide bed; mild joking transpires as unlikely bedfellows are added: cow, pig, fox, goose. The generosity of the host is strained when a porcupine joins in, and everyone leaves. But the sad faces at the snowy window melt Bearsie Bear's notably large heart, and all find peaceful sleep away from the elements. Waber's familiar watercolors find humor in every scene while warmth and security are the backbone of the story. The reading of the accumulated names every time the animals settle down results in a book that may be too raucous for bedtime, but ideal for story hours.

Publishers Weekly

SOURCE: A review of *Bearsie Bear and the Sleepover Party,* in *Publishers Weekly,* Vol. 244, No. 38, September 15, 1997, p. 75.

The creator of the affable **Lyle, Lyle Crocodile** is as playful as ever in this cumulative caper that uses repetition and alliteration to rollicking effect. On a cold evening as "the wind hissed and howled," a chilly Moosie Moose knocks at Bearsie Bear's door to ask if he may sleep over. Five other animals in turn make the same request, each time the most recent arrival answers the door for the newcomer, who then leaps joyously into Bearsie's increasingly crowded bed. Waber's effervescent watercolors depict the wide-eyed gang, with only heads and paws (or claws or hooves) showing from under the bedspread, until Porkie Porcupine shows up and the six sleepy creatures wisely chime "Uh-oh." Waber's precisely timed splashes of slapstick (twice the remark, "You can say that again" brings on a repetition of what was just said) adds to the comedy of the tale. A great pick for both beginning readers and for reading aloud in a variety of voices, this comical nocturnal tale is especially suitable for a bedtime giggle or two.

Ann A. Flowers

SOURCE: A review of *Bearsie Bear and the Surprise Sleepover Party,* in *The Horn Book Magazine,* Vol. LXXVIII, No. 5, September-October, 1997, p. 565.

On a cold winter night when the wind is howling and Bearsie Bear is just warmly tucked in and falling asleep, there comes a knock at the door. It is Moosie Moose wanting to sleep over. Just this once, says Bearsie Bear, and they retire to their cozy slumber. But subsequent knocks reveal Cowsie Cow, Piggie Pig, Foxie Fox, and Goosie Goose, all bent on the same errand. Kindly Bearsie Bear adds them one by one to the now-crowded bed. But when Porkie Porcupine arrives, all the other guests depart in a prickly hurry, and Bearsie Bear exiles Porkie to under the bed. But finally all are reconciled, with Porkie Porcupine in bed with the others— "and he was very careful not to thrash about." A splendid read-aloud, extremely repetitive ("'It's me, Piggie Pig,' said Piggie Pig. 'Piggie Pig?' said Cowsie Cow. 'Piggie Pig?' said Moosie Moose. 'Piggie Pig?' said Bearsie Bear. Yes, 'Piggie Pig,' said Piggie Pig") and very funny, too: the reader-aloud will undoubtedly be joined by a chorus of

listeners happily helping the story along its cumulative way. The line-and-watercolor illustrations are funny and homey, with a generous use of white space that gives the story plenty of room.

Hazel Rochman

SOURCE: A review of *Bearsie Bear and the Surprise Sleepover Party,* in *Booklist,* Vol. 94, No. 3, October 1, 1997, p. 339.

With droll repetition Waber retells the old cumulative story about the animals who knock at the door, one by one and ask for room in the bed. Laid-back line-and-watercolor cartoon drawings capture the farce and coziness of being snuggled up warm together when the wind is storming outside—and when your bedfellows are not exactly of your choosing. Each time someone wants to come in, there is the ritualized question and answer and repetition ("Who is it?" said Bearsie Bear. "It's me, Piggie Pig," said Piggie Pig. "Piggie Pig?" said Cowsie Cow. "Piggie Pig?" said Moosie Moose). The climax comes when Porkie Porcupine jumps into the bed and everyone runs, but they work it out, and finally they all get to sleep. Young preschoolers will love acting out the elemental scenario and joining in the solemn, silly refrains. There is a lesson about acceptance here, all the more effective because it is part of the wonderful nonsense

LYLE AT CHRISTMAS (1998)

Kirkus Reviews

SOURCE: A review of *Lyle at Christmas,* in *Kirkus Reviews,* Vol. LXVI, No. 18, September 15, 1998, p. 1391.

Mr. Grumps's "down-in-the-dumps" approach to the Christmas holiday leads to the disappearance of Lyle's favorite feline friend in this reassuring tale about the love of family and friends. When Loretta, the cat, disappears, the Primm family at East 88th and Mr. Grumps know exactly what they want for Christmas—her safe return. Prunella, the Cat Lady, takes Loretta in; an out-of-work actor, Hector, happens to know both the Primms and Prunella and provides the means (and requisite misunderstandings) to a happy resolution. Waber demonstrates again an uncanny ability to convey a multitude of emotions in a few strokes, giving each character in the Primm household a distinct personality. Especially charming are the scenes of Lyle engaged in the household chores of washing dishes, making the beds, scrubbing, dusting, sweeping, and waxing. Fans of the big green crocodile will welcome this holiday adventure.

Additional coverage of Waber's life and career is contained in the following sources published by The Gale Group: *Contemporary Authors,* Vol. 1-4R; *Contemporary Authors New Revision Series,* Vols. 2, 38, 68; *Major Authors and Illustrators for Children and Young Adults;* and *Something about the Author,* Vols. 47, 95.

Paul O. Zelinsky

1953-

(Full name Paul Oser Zelinsky) American illustrator and author/illustrator of picture books, fiction, and retellings.

Major works include *Hansel and Gretel* (retold by Rika Lesser, 1984), *Rumpelstiltskin* (retold by Zelinsky, 1986), *The Wheels on the Bus: A Book with Pictures that Move and Occasionally Pop Up* (adapted by Zelinsky, 1990), *Swamp Angel* (written by Anne Isaacs, 1994), *Rapunzel* (retold by Zelinsky, 1997).

INTRODUCTION

One of the most highly acclaimed American illustrators in the field of contemporary children's literature, Zelinsky is recognized for bringing fresh interpretations of familiar stories, songs, and games to the books that he has created and for providing pictures of exceptional quality to works by other authors. Noted for turning ambitious projects into tours de force, Zelinsky has written and illustrated stories featuring human and animal characters, several of which are adaptations of folktales with European sources. He is perhaps best known for his versions of *Rumpelstiltskin* and *Rapunzel,* familiar stories drawn from the fairy tales collected by the Brothers Grimm. As an illustrator, Zelinsky is perhaps best known for creating the art for *Hansel and Gretel,* a retelling by Rika Lesser, and for *Swamp Angel,* an original tall tale by Anne Isaacs. His illustrations have also graced the stories, folktales, poetry, and retellings of such authors as Avi, Beverly Cleary, Carl Sandburg, E. Nesbit, Jack Prelutsky, Mirra Ginsburg, David Kherdian, and Lore Segal.

In both his own books and works by other authors, Zelinsky is noted for creating illustrations in a variety of styles—most prominently those inspired by the Old Masters and American folk artists—that reflect his originality, imagination, thorough research, and exceptional technique. His pictures are composed with mediums such as ink and gouache, charcoal and chalk, and black line; however, the artist is considered to have made his reputation with his oil paintings, sumptuous works that are compared to classic painters such as Botticelli, Vermeer, and Velázquez. Zelinsky is also acknowledged for his use of perspective and attention to detail, as well as for his skill with both page design and paper engineering. As a writer, Zelinsky favors spare texts praised for their economy, directness, and smoothness; he is also praised for creating retellings that reflect both his understanding of his source material and his willingness to depart from standard versions. Although his art is occasionally criticized as self-conscious and extravagant and his books are sometimes thought to be too sophisticated for children, Zelinsky is celebrated as a particularly

gifted artist and author whose works are both elegant and emotionally satisfying. Ilene Cooper stated, "Zelinsky is equally adept at drawing in the style of the Italian Renaissance or with the flamboyant rhythms of the American folktale. It is this remarkable talent for creating such varied worlds, as well as his meticulous and innovative attention to design and detail, that gives Zelinsky his special place in the world of children's literature." In her review of *Rumpelstiltskin*, Mary M. Burns concluded, "Reviewing a book illustrated by Paul Zelinsky is both a pleasure and a challenge. Because of his versatility, each book is an entity in itself; each is a new work, distinctive but not necessarily reminiscent of a total *oeuvre*. . . . Zelinsky is at heart a storyteller—one of the most important distinctions between an artist and the artist who is an illustrator."

Biographical Information

Born in Evanston, Illinois, a suburb of Chicago, Zelinsky grew up in a nearby town. His father, a college mathematics professor, taught both nationally and internationally, so Paul was often the new student in school.

"My drawing, though," he remarked in *Sixth Book of Junior Authors and Illustrators,* "was a constant; it could never be left behind. . . . And I drew easily, and always." Zelinsky drew on everything—even on his exams. He noted, "When it got really bad I tried to hide my pen from myself, but that never quite worked." In high school, Zelinsky made etchings and linoleum cuts to accompany the stories he was reading in English class as well as for poems by friends. While attending Yale University, Zelinsky took a course on the history and making of children's books taught by noted author/illustrator Maurice Sendak. This experience convinced Zelinsky, who was also interested in science and architecture, that he should become an art major and that he might be able to make a living making picture books. After graduating from Yale, Zelinsky took some of his drawings to the art director of *The New York Times,* who gave him his first illustration assignment. An early collaboration with a writer friend from Yale led to the acceptance of his first book, but the project was shelved when the publishing house dissolved. After earning his master's degree in painting from Tyler School of Art, Zelinsky tried teaching art, but found that he was not suited for it. He shopped his portfolio around New York City and was hired to provide the pictures for *Emily Upham's Revenge,* a story with a Victorian setting by Avi that was published in 1978. The success of this book cemented Zelinsky's reputation as an illustrator. In 1981, Zelinsky married musician Deborah Hallen—the couple have two children, Anna and Rachel—and published his first retelling, *The Maid and the Mouse and the Odd-Shaped House.* He found the text that inspired this book, a school exercise designed for the blackboard, in a notebook owned by the grandmother of his editor, Donna Brooks. Since that time, Zelinsky has continued to be inspired by a variety of sources—for example, seventeenth-century Dutch genre paintings for *Hansel and Gretel* and Italian Renaissance art for *Rapunzel*—and to look for new ways of expanding his interests into books for children.

In his Caldecott Award acceptance speech, Zelinsky queried, "[W]hat makes a child respond to a picture in a book? . . . It might be an instinctual button being pushed—bright colors, cute animals—but it's also compelling form that works." Writing in *Sixth Book of Junior Authors and Illustrators,* he stated, "I've been able to illustrate books that are so different from one another that I always get to learn new things, new materials and ways of drawing, and all sorts of information. . . . It's a great deal of fun, this work. I learn things. I make things. And I feel I get to change my mind all the time about what I want to do—my mind changes with every new book I take on. And when I realize that there are people around the country who will read my books and (I hope) enjoy the pictures, I think: How could I have been so lucky?" He added in an interview in *The Horn Book Magazine,* "Instead of a style I have a chain, a continuous chain, of ways that I work. From my point of view, I do what I do. I try to make the book talk, as it talks to me. . . . I do my books mainly for myself. It seems to work that way. If the narrative has a childlike feeling, it should come through."

Major Works

Zelinsky's first self-authored book, *The Maid and the Mouse and the Odd-Shaped House: A Story in Rhyme,* is a cumulative participatory tale in verse. Based on a humorous poem used by a Connecticut teacher in 1897 to get her students to draw their representations of the text, the book describes how a small, thin maid and a fat mouse move into what they assume is a strangely designed house. When the maid trips and falls, the pair realizes that their new domicile is actually a very large cat, so they run off to settle in another place. The story, which is actually a puzzle, is illustrated with line drawings colored in pastels that are noted for their distinctive use of space and color. Sally Holmes Holtze commented, "Zelinsky creatively uses the pages of a picture book the way a director uses every inch of the stage," while Elaine Edelman concluded that Zelinsky is "an artist with ideas and great gifts." In the next book that he wrote and illustrated, *The Lion and the Stoat* (1984), Zelinsky describes how the title characters—both artists—compete with each other for an exhibition before having each of their paintings hung in the new town hall; however, at the end of the story, the artists begin to play an intense game of tic-tac-toe. A satire on rivalry and conceit that is based in part on two tales by Pliny the Elder, *The Lion and the Stoat* is illustrated with comic pictures that draw on clichés from the art world. According to Kathleen Birtciel, the book has "child appeal and insight into human nature"; a critic in *Kirkus Reviews* added that Zelinsky "displays the assurance here of a much older pro."

Zelinsky first received acclaim for his pictures for *Hansel and Gretel,* the story of a brother and sister who defeat a wicked witch. He illustrates this work, a tale that has haunted him since childhood, with rich paintings in the style of French, Dutch, and German artists of the seventeenth century. Filled with drama and the interplay of darkness and light, Zelinsky's pictures are noted for their impact and evocative quality. Ethel L. Heins remarked that much of the art work, which favors panoramic landscapes and other outdoor scenes, "constitutes an extraordinary display of skill, composition, and beauty." Kenneth Marantz further commented, "Zelinsky's vision is such that he adds fresh nuance to the well-worn story. . . ." With *Rumpelstiltskin,* Zelinsky retold and illustrated another favorite folktale; in this story, a miller's daughter prevents an imp from taking her first-born child by guessing the imp's name. Set in the Middle Ages, Zelinsky's retelling is noted for its less violent conclusion: the title character runs off rather than tears himself in half, as he does in the traditional version of the tale. Zelinsky's textured oils are credited with presenting viewers with riveting close-ups and interior shots as well as fascinating architectural details. Mary M. Burns called Zelinsky's approach a "brilliant adaptation of techniques employed by masters of the Flemish school," while Susan H. Patron concluded that Zelinsky's "smooth retelling and glowing pictures cast the story in a new and beautiful light."

The Wheels on the Bus: A Book with Pictures That Move and Occasionally Pop Up is considered a departure for Zelinsky as well as a particularly ingenious and well-executed toy book. In his adaptation of the popular children's participation song, Zelinsky, who adds a number of visual subplots to his pictures and shows the library as the bus's final destination, illustrates the book in swirling pinks and purples that have been compared to the works of regionalist American painter Thomas Hart Benton; he also creates moving parts for the bus, such as doors and windshield wipers. John Peters noted that "the art and engineering are woven together seamlessly, and the book will lose little of its appeal after the moving parts have run their race." *Swamp Angel* is a tall tale by Anne Isaacs about the giantess Angelica Longrider, the greatest woodswoman in Tennessee. Angelica, who got her nickname at the age of twelve when she rescued a wagon train stuck in the mud, is a heroine in the tradition of Paul Bunyan and John Henry. Zelinsky illustrates the story in American-primitive oils set against a background of birch, cherry, and maple veneers. Hazel Rochman stated that "Zelinsky's detailed oil paintings in folk-art style are exquisite. . . . They are also hilarious, making brilliant use of perspective to extend the mischief and the droll understatement." Wendy Lukehart called *Swamp Angel* "an American classic in the making." Zelinsky won the Caldecott Medal in 1998 for *Rapunzel,* his adaptation of the classic fairy tale. Basing his retelling on the German and French versions of the tale as well as the original in Italian, Zelinsky outlines how a young woman shut up in a tower uses the power of her love to save her beloved—a prince who has given her twins—from a sorcerer's curse. Zelinsky studied paintings by Italian Renaissance artists, such as Giovanni Bellini and Filippo Lippi, and Dutch masters to create his illustrations in oil; several of the pictures in *Rapunzel* are based on well-known paintings such as "The Jewish Bride" by Rembrandt and "Madonna and Child with the Young St. John" by Raphael. A reviewer in *Publishers Weekly* claimed, "Zelinsky does a star turn with this breathtaking interpretation of a favorite fairy tale," while Jane Connolly noted, "This is a book to be owned and cherished." Mary M. Burns concluded, "[I]t takes a scholar's mind and an artist's insight to endow the familiar with unexpected nuances—which Zelinsky does with passion and dazzling technique. . . . Simply put, this is a gorgeous book; it demonstrates respect for the traditions of painting and the fairy tale while at the same time adhering to a singular, wholly original, artistic vision."

Awards

In addition to the 1998 Caldecott Medal for *Rapunzel,* Zelinsky was presented with three Caldecott Honor Book designations: for *Hansel and Gretel* in 1985, for *Rumpelstiltskin* in 1987, and for *Swamp Angel* in 1995. *How I Hunted the Little Fellows* was selected to appear in the American Institute of Graphic Arts Book Show in 1980, as was *The Maid and the Mouse and the Odd-Shaped House: A Story in Rhyme* in 1982. In the same year,

Three Romances was selected to appear in the Society of Illustrators Show, as was *Rumpelstiltskin* in 1986. *The Sun's Asleep behind the Hill* was selected to appear in the Bratislava Biennale by the International Board on Books for Young People in 1983, as was *Rumpelstiltskin* in 1987. *Hansel and Gretel* was selected to appear in the Bologna International Children's Book Fair exhibition in 1985. In the same year, *The Story of Mrs. Lovewright and Purrless Her Cat* received an America's Children's Books of the Year Award from the Child Study Association. *Rumpelstiltskin* won the Redbook Award and the White Raven Book Award, International Youth Library, both in 1987. *The Wheels on the Bus* received the Redbook Award in 1990. In addition, several of Zelinsky's works have received awards from children's literature reviewing sources such as *The Horn Book Magazine, Publishers Weekly, The New York Times,* and *School Library Journal,* as well as several child- and parent-selected awards.

ILLUSTRATOR'S COMMENTARY

Sylvia Marantz and Kenneth Marantz

SOURCE: "Interview with Paul O. Zelinsky," in *The Horn Book Magazine,* Vol. LXII, No. 3, May-June, 1986, pp. 295-304.

Born and raised in a quiet suburb of Chicago, Paul O. Zelinsky now lives in New York City. To visit him you must first endure the physical affront to the senses generated by the subway: a clattering cacophony amplified by the long tunnel under the East River, odors to make you gasp, and the shrieking intimidation of the spray-painted graffiti. The climb up into the light and air of Brooklyn Heights is a spiritually cleansing experience that brings you onto narrow streets lined with old but apparently well-maintained apartment buildings. You turn onto his street and are suddenly confronted with lower Manhattan's skyline almost within reach across the active harbor. Zelinsky lives in a modest brick apartment building with a very alert, vocal, active, and adorable toddler named Anna and her alert, active, and charming mother—a full-time music teacher and part-time graduate student. We entered a multi-purpose living room, a room obviously very much lived in. A piano, harpsichord, shelves of books, and paintings competed for space with the more typical social furniture. After the usual greetings we asked him about his work.

Marantz: What are your early memories of picture books?

Zelinsky: The Little Golden Book *The Tawny, Scrawny Lion* with Tengren's illustrations. And I liked *The Story of Ferdinand.* It wasn't long ago that I looked at it again, the first time since childhood, and saw the corks hanging from the trees. I never knew that was a joke! I liked Margaret Wise Brown's *The Color Kittens.* But beyond these impressions, I don't have a good recollection of other books from my childhood.

M: Then how did you start doing children's books?

Z: I would look at them in stores, but it didn't occur to me that I could create them for a livelihood until I took a course at Yale with Maurice Sendak, a seminar initiated by a student who had convinced him to teach it. He seemed to be making a living at creating books. At that point I had already decided to be an art major, so I wouldn't have any means of making a living. I thought that making picture books would be something I could do.

M: You were more level-headed about your future than many young art students we know. But how did you go about breaking into this competitive field?

Z: I have an uncle who works for *The New York Times*. He suggested I show some of my drawings to their art director. Because I was an art major and did real paintings, I didn't feel as if my ego was at stake. I showed drawings to the art director. He liked them, and I went home with an assignment. The real possibility of a career in illustration fell into my lap, more or less.

I went on painting and thought I might teach. Then I got my master's in painting and got a short-term teaching job. I found out that I was a lousy teacher and that teaching wasn't what I wanted to do. In the meantime I had been visiting publishers with a portfolio, feeling all the while that I didn't have anything personal at stake because I was really a painter. In my art education the word *illustration* had been a term of criticism. I was embarrassed to tell my painting teachers for some time what I was doing. I was actually taken aback when I found that William Bailey, one of my favorite painting teachers at Yale, had seen some of my books and thought they were *wonderful*—a word he used for almost nothing.

M: When we see the illustrations in your books, it's clear that your approach to the way you depict characters is so varied. Is there a Zelinsky style?

Z: Instead of a style I have a chain, a continuous chain, of ways that I work. From my point of view, I do what I do. I try to make the book talk, as it talks to me, and not worry about whether it is in my style or not. In my different books, I may have covered the range that I can work in: from extremely detailed, rounded images in real space, such as the almost photographic images in *How I Hunted the Little Fellows,* to *The Maid and the Mouse and the Odd-Shaped House.* It seems to me that everything else I've done fits somewhere on a continuum between the two.

I would worry more if I were doing what my art school training taught me—to do one thing again and again, hone in on a particular image. I get a kick out of doing each book differently. I've been pleased that people like the fact that there's a lot of variation in what I do, because I expected to be called on the carpet for not

having a style—the pictorial equivalent of a voice for an author. I figure a style will come on its own.

I was first given *Emily Upham's Revenge* because there was something in my portfolio that looked Victorian. When I did the *Little Fellows* which is set in the 1890s, I got worried that I would be typecast as working in the nineteenth-century style. I guess I didn't really want to be pegged. I would never want to do any book in the same style. Different books offer different things. I have a lot of loyalty to the text. I don't think any book is a "Zelinsky." When I look at a text, I don't usually know how it should look right away, but I often know what it shouldn't look like, and that's enough to start with.

For Cleary's *Ralph S. Mouse* I visited a real classroom to see how big fifth-graders actually are. I bought a mouse. I named him, or her, Ralph. She posed pretty well, didn't run around too fast. The next day she ran around even slower. After a couple of days, she was barely moving. Then she died. I had to buy Ralph II, who just wouldn't stay still. I returned Ralph II to the store with instructions to tell anyone who bought him that he was soon going to be famous.

M: *The Maid* was our introduction to your work, and her depictions immediately challenged and amused us. Where did she come from?

Z: The text came from a school notebook in the editor's grandmother's house. It was pretty crude and dated and took a lot of changing. It sounded like an 1890s idea of a funny rhyme. I didn't know where the old maid came from. From the start I thought of the book as a sort of board game, very flat and ornamental. At first I thought I was inspired to know just when to set the book, but later I realized that I was just thinking along the lines of Mother Goose. The maid is thin, and she wears that dress because of the time period. I tried lots and lots of maids. The size and the extreme nature of her character were deliberate. I had just recently looked at Sendak's *Hector Protector* and saw the size of the woman's bonnet and the period costume and found it funny. The editor later thought of the old maid character in the card game. I do remember that I played "Old Maid." She could have come from there.

M: Do you work in sequence?

Z: I try always to work out of sequence because I tend to learn how to do what I'm doing better as I do the book, and the later drawings are generally better than the first ones—if not aesthetically better then technically more facile. So the book would start out crudely and become facile at the end. I jump around, so people won't know.

M: How do you decide on the particular scenes in a story that you want to illustrate? Do you have them all in mind before you start creating anything on paper?

Z: If a picture book is an art form, the art happens at

the stage when you are choosing what you will illustrate. That's when the rhythm is set and when the general emotional impact, if there is any, gets set up. Choosing the scenes to illustrate is the first thing that I do. I start out knowing the number of pages, which makes an enormous difference, and with a text that seems to break in certain places. Maybe a surprise in the text really needs to be accompanied by a visual surprise at the exact moment. Sometimes it has to be a double-page spread or a single-page. Just dealing with the text from the beginning sets a lot of constraints on what is and is not going to be pictured.

Telling the story through the pictures means: how do you get from one picture to the next in a visual and logical progression? There may or may not be changes in the scale or scheme. Selecting the pictures is making the whole book into what you want it to be.

M: What made you choose such a demanding visual setting for *Hansel and Gretel*?

Z: From the time I started illustrating children's books I've always wanted to do *Hansel and Gretel.* I was disappointed that everyone else was doing it, too. I hadn't seen any *Hansel and Gretel* book that expressed the story for me, that seemed remotely right. The story is very serious. I don't mean that it's not happy. But it's deep; it's rich emotionally and deals with very basic fears. It's about how infants become their own people, how they come to realize that they're not an outgrowth of their parents.

Before I did the book, I made a concentrated effort not to look at other versions because I didn't want to be responding or reacting to them. I was trying to put down the very intense response I've always had to the story. When I remembered it, the image I first thought of wasn't the house; it was the children lost in the woods: how big the woods are and how small the children are. The idea of thousands of birds in the vast forest eating up all the crumbs is an operatic idea that I responded to when I first heard the story as a child.

M: Did you choose a winter setting to make a more compelling book?

Z: I thought about the season and about the fire the father builds, so it's not very warm out. Actually my vision was affected by the painting my great-grandmother did of *Hansel and Gretel.* My great-grandmother started painting when she was in her mid-seventies, a sort of Grandma Moses. Actually, I showed her painting, the painting I grew up with, on the wall in the witch's house. I cleaned up the painting a bit. You can't see it too well in the tapestry. It has a glowing, light greenish, creamy white roof and a very intense blue sky with black trees against it. The whole thing has a glow to it; the light doesn't seem to come from anywhere. I suppose that's why I would even think of the glowing light that illuminates the house and illuminates the children and not the woods.

M: Did her painting or other factors lead you to a kind of pastiche of seventeenth-century painting styles?

Z: I was looking at seventeenth-century Dutch genre paintings—like Steen's—that are full of characters. I went to the Metropolitan Museum of Art. Strangely enough, nobody offered to pay my way to see the paintings in Europe. When I was thinking of an approach, I had a closer, heartfelt feeling towards those paintings. Genre paintings don't have the kind of emotional distance that some other classical paintings have. You can look at them more as illustrations—really look at the people, get involved in what they're doing, be amused by them, and not have a layer of great art come between you and the painting. I turned to that source when I thought of *Hansel and Gretel,* which speaks directly.

Rika Lesser's text was almost finished by the time I started the pictures. I was dividing it into pages while the story was still in a rough form. Then Rika actually did make some changes based on the pictures, which is a nice way to work. After that, I had to break the text up into even portions.

I don't know if there was any idea of tradition in what I was doing, when I selected the scenes to illustrate. I hadn't looked at other picture books. It might just be the way the text is; you're left with certain necessary ways of telling certain scenes. Sometimes the text might dictate a certain composition.

M: Do you do items more for illustration purposes than for painting design—such as the chamber pot in the bedroom scene?

Z: I hope that they come together in their purpose. The fact that there's a chamber pot doesn't bear on the character of the people in particular, but it does fill out the world of that household. They would have had a chamber pot. The scene of the parents in bed really had to be a one-page picture. It's very difficult to fit the objects into such a vertical shape. The very large footboard of the bed would have left a lot of dead space in that spot, and the cut-off chamber pot does bring the foot-board much closer to the reader and does make the base of the picture more alive. The curve in the handle refers in some ways to other curves in the picture: the curves in the brim of the man's hat and also the shape of the woman's nightcap.

M: Did you do a dummy first?

Z: I did pencil drawings which I tore out of the sketch book as I did them, so I could flip through them. The drawings were fairly detailed. Because of time constraints, I ended up taking slides of those pencil sketches and projecting them onto stretched paper. Then I could make changes. The dummy had been done before I knew the exact proportions of the book and how much space the text would take. With the slides I could project the paintings onto the paper at an angle and change the proportions and squash them sideways. In the first forest scene the trees are actually twenty per cent thicker than the sketch because there was more text than I had anticipated. I wanted to make the woods very big and the children very small. Sometimes I had to keep exerting an effort because the children got bigger and the woods smaller. I went walking in the woods of western Connecticut to prepare myself. Without those walks in the woods, I wouldn't have thought there would be so many large fallen trees.

M: Where did the witch come from?

Z: I think I made her face up. She doesn't really remind me of anything outside the book. The picture where Hansel is sticking the bone outside the cage was one of the first ones I did. When I was visiting my grandmother, I suddenly realized that the witch's costume—the whole picture and composition—was really from a little bronze set of figures that my grandmother had, a little scene of Persian shoemakers about four inches high with their turbans and robes. It had a little light bulb inside it, and when I visited my grandmother as a child, I would have her turn it on.

Suddenly it was time for Anna's nap and for us to walk several blocks to Zelinsky's "safe house," a studio on the second floor of a somewhat seedy old building on a store-lined street. On the way Zelinsky told us about his notebook full of story ideas and his possible interest in doing board books now that he has his own customer for them. "I wouldn't if Anna hadn't come. The idea of books that are like catalogues with a word and an object are not that interesting for me. I would like to do a board book if I could do more than just a catalogue. I do my books mainly for myself. It seems to work that way. If the narrative has a childlike feeling, it should come through."

Upstairs, beyond the multi-locked door, were the room and work tables. While not chaotic, the scene gave no evidence of the kinds of order found in Zelinsky's paintings or drawings. Tubes of paint reminded us that before the printed illustration there was a hand-produced object.

M: Are you satisfied with *Hansel and Gretel* as you look at it now?

Z: The longer I spend without looking at the originals, the more satisfied I get. The second printing was better. The book was printed in Hong Kong with nobody from the publisher there. I don't know if the artwork could have been reproduced better. The sense of light is vastly changed.

M: We noticed when comparing one of your paintings with the printed version that some parts of the original were cut off. Were you consulted first?

Z: No, I wasn't. That's the way the book came back from the printer. There were all sorts of little disappointments and mistakes. There always are. The pictures were many different shapes. I tried to do them all in exactly the right proportion, but a couple of times I miscalculated or was given the wrong figures. Generally I don't like to publicize the flaws.

M: But we see only the books, not your artwork, and reviewers respond to the pages produced by your printer. How do you handle reviews?

Z: I exercise my critical facility on reviews and decide what I think of the reviewer. When the review is good, I have a higher opinion of the reviewer. There's a lot of reviewing that could be done on a higher level of intelligence. Sometimes reviews, such as some of *Hansel and Gretel,* seem to be negative for reasons that are personal to the reviewer. Something about the book really sets them off, so much so that I can't believe it's just the book. I must have hit a chord with that person.

Clearly he had hit several of our responsive chords. But it was time to return to the streets and to retrace our steps to the subway and the return journey to Manhattan. Somehow we didn't seem to notice the dirt and noise as much this time as we reflected on the hours we had filled listening to this quiet artist and gentle father tell us about his books.

Paul Zelinsky

SOURCE: "Voices of the Creators," in *Children's Books and Their Creators,* Houghton Mifflin Company, 1995, p. 708.

I fell short in my art school training because I never quite believed in Quality of Edge or Color Relationship as a painting's only reason for being; I was, and still am, happier trying to put these abstract qualities in the service of something else, such as a story.

Every story is a different experience, carries its own feelings and associations. When I read a story to illustrate it, I want to capture the feelings—grab them and hold on, because they can be fleeting—and figure out how to make pictures that support and intensify them. This problem demands abstract solutions (a quality of line, a kind of space, a color relationship), which often means playing with new and different mediums: pencil, pastel, oils, on paper, canvas, drafting film, wood. But increasingly, I spend time just thinking about the feelings in the story.

Often these feelings come to me as a sort of flavor. I know that when I call up my earliest memories, what I remember seeing and hearing is accompanied by a flavor-like sense of what it felt like to be *there* and see *that.* It is usually a wonderful sense, belonging to the whole experience the way the smell of a room can become the whole experience of the room. Some years ago I was reading my daughter a Babar book for the second or third time when suddenly an illustration (of the monkeys' tree-houses) sparked a lost memory. It was simply the memory of that same page, but as I had seen it as a young child. Not only did the crudeness of the drawing fall away in this child's-eye view, and the sketchy detail blossom into something incredible, but the whole scene was enveloped in a kind of air, had a particular quality. Suddenly I could breathe, smell, and taste this world. So, too, with each new text I take on, I want to grasp what its taste is, and bring it out in the pictures.

When I first learned the song "The Wheels on the Bus" I knew I wanted to illustrate it some day (I was well out of kindergarten, and already illustrating books). My literal-minded mind immediately suggested a book where the bus's moving parts would really move. But what should the pictures look like? The song reminded me a little of bubble gum: it was sweet and bouncy. The pictures needed plenty of rhythm, and the sense of sinking your teeth into something. I thought thick oil paint might give that chewy feeling. And the palette of colors I eventually came up with does, I think, give some of the same kind of pleasure as sweets. There was also a physical pleasure in the laying down of paint and the way colored pencil lines would sometimes plow through the wet oils. Altogether the flavor is strong and full of energy. I hope the pictures are more nutritious, though, than bubble gum.

Lore Segal's marvelous ear for language gave *The Story of Mrs. Lovewright and Purrless Her Cat* a tangy quality. I think perhaps of dill pickles, which are sour, deliciously flavorful, and somehow unintentionally funny. Looking for ways to make these feelings visual, I saw all stretched-out shapes and sharp angles. (Not how a pickle looks, certainly, but how I think the *taste* of a pickle would look.) Mrs. Lovewright was so uncomfortable a person—a chilly woman, trying vainly to make things cozy by cuddling with an unwilling cat. The drawings were in colored pencil; its line has a fittingly edgy quality, unlike, say, watercolor.

I used watercolor as well as opaque watercolor and pastels for Mirra Ginsburg's good-night book *The Sun's Asleep behind the Hill.* This chant-like text seemed to breathe the smells of a summer night. Soft and darkening by degrees, the watercolor pictures took on a filmy haze of color, consisting of pastels rubbed onto the thumb and smeared over the paper. The best pictures were done while house-sitting for friends in the country, where night came on slowly and I was alone to sense the changes of color and the sounds and smells in the air. That was an attempt to bring some real-life experience into the illumination of a text. Drawing *Rumpelstiltskin* was an effort to create a purely imagined world. It called for a sort of perfect beauty: smooth surfaces placed in a clear light, reminiscent of the paintings of the Northern Renaissance. These were painted in many transparent layers of carefully applied oil paint, and I worked out my own version of the technique. I would have liked to paint what it's like on the inside of a jewel—bright and still, perhaps with no smell at all.

It seems I give myself the task, with every book, of

inventing a new way of working toward a different effect. Three-quarters of the way through each project, I wonder why it has taken so very long before the drawing started to flow. It is hard to remember after the fact how much trial and error—and error and error—goes into the earliest stage of the work of illustrating: sensing the flavor of a text, and figuring out how to capture it for the eyes.

Paul Zelinsky and Ilene Cooper

SOURCE: "The Booklist Interview," in *Booklist,* Vol. 94, Nos. 19-20, June 1 & 15, 1998, pp. 1776-77.

BKL: *You've illustrated two Caldecott Honor Books,* **Hansel and Gretel** *and* **Rumpelstiltskin,** *and other terrific books that have been mentioned for the Caldecott Medal. Did you think* **Rapunzel** *would be the one that would win?*

ZELINSKY: I really didn't. I thought there was no chance this would be it.

BKL: *Why not?*

ZELINSKY: There were various reasons I gave myself. I had already done two Grimm tales, and both were Caldecott Honor Books, so it was reasonable to think my efforts in that arena had been sufficiently recognized. Also, there are several other fine versions of *Rapunzel* out there. I wasn't sure people would feel the world needed another one.

BKL: *So what drew you to the story of Rapunzel? You have said that Hansel and Gretel was a story that haunted you since childhood, especially the image of little children in a big forest. But Rapunzel is a much more adult story.*

ZELINSKY: Yes, it is. At least in the sense that it doesn't have as many obvious routes of entry for children. I don't have a clear understanding of why I was so drawn to *Rapunzel.* I grew up with a picture of Hansel and Gretel that my great-grandmother painted, so that image is very personal. But *Rapunzel* also struck a chord with me, and I have memories and associations about it from way back.

BKL: *You have made the story even more adult by having the sorceress discover that Rapunzel is pregnant. As you say in your author's note, this element appears in early versions of the tale. However, in most modern retellings, the sorceress learns about the prince when she is alerted by others or when Rapunzel lets down her hair, draws the woman up, and notes how much heavier she is than the prince.*

ZELINSKY: I don't think most people are familiar with this version of the story. I discovered the pregnancy element when I was doing my research; the pregnancy was in the French version that preceded the Grimms. To me, it makes the story stronger, it makes more sense, and it was one more reason I wanted to do another version of a familiar story.

BKL: *Because of the sophistication of the art and story, this seems like a picture book for older children.*

ZELINSKY: I never really get involved with thinking about a particular age level when I make a book. Instead, I try to put the story through my own mind at a certain age. I don't want to do stories I would have been bored with at age five or six.

BKL: *The book you did before* **Rapunzel** *was* **Swamp Angel,** *written by Anne Issacs. Can you tell us about the difference between being an illustrator of someone else's work and doing the whole project yourself?*

ZELINSKY: When I received the manuscript of *Swamp Angel,* it was essentially done, so that work was not intensively collaborative. When I did *Rapunzel,* the text also came first. I can't juggle two things at the same time, so I wanted to get the text done before I moved on to the art. Because writing the text is such a separate function, when I go to work on the art, I don't feel terribly different than I do when I'm the illustrator receiving someone else's text. Except, of course, I have less compunction about manipulating the text when it's my own writing. I'll shorten a paragraph to make room for a character's elbow.

BKL: *How easy is writing for you?*

ZELINSKY: I feel pretty comfortable with the writing. In the case of *Rapunzel,* I was much more concerned about the pictures than I was about the text.

BKL: *How come?*

ZELINSKY: The goal, a lofty one, was to have the pictures look like Italian Renaissance art. While doing the research on the history of *Rapunzel,* I got the strong impression that there was no original version. So I decided I could set the story where I pleased, and that's how I wound up in Italy.

BKL: *Did you literally wind up in Italy? Did you go there to study Renaissance artwork?*

ZELINSKY. I went to Italy, but after the book was almost done.

BKL: *Do you wish you had gone earlier in the book-making process? Or would it have inhibited you?*

ZELINSKY: When I look at great art, I'm inspired more than intimidated. But it was wonderful to be in Italy after the book was mostly finished. I kept bumping into pictures I had pored over in my art-history books. It was fantastically exciting. I felt like I was personally related to these paintings.

BKL: *How pleased are you when you finish the art for a book in general and this book in particular?*

ZELINSKY: In general, I'm not very pleased. With *Rapunzel,* I guess I felt what might be called a satisfied despair. The art didn't look the way I wanted it to look, but I had tried so hard I don't think I could have done it much better—or much of it better—unless perhaps I had five more years to work it out.

BKL: *How does the work of your editor, in this case Donna Brooks, figure into a project like* **Rapunzel,** *which is your text and your vision?*

ZELINSKY: The first input came while I was working on the text. After I did the research and made my first attempts at writing, Donna had a lot of reactions [laughs]. I got the first draft very marked up. As far as the art goes, Donna and I go way back. We worked together at Dodd, Mead, where there was really no art director who had time for children's books. So when I came along and said I wanted to write some bang-up, four-color picture book, it was up to me and Donna to pull it off. We decided on the design and selected and placed the type, though I think we had someone who could do the actual cutting-and-pasting. So we have a history of working together on all phases of making a picture book, and that's continued. On *Rapunzel,* we were lucky to have the input of the Dutton art director, Amy Bernicker. In general, it is wonderful to be able to bounce off someone whose instincts you trust and who has that editorial eye for detail—Rapunzel's wearing a necklace on page six, why isn't she wearing it on page nine?

BKL: *One impressive thing about* **Rapunzel** *is that it does what a good picture book is supposed to do—it extends the story, it goes beyond the words on the page. I'm thinking particularly of the picture where the sorceress is taking baby Rapunzel away. On the previous page, the woman is horrific, but here on this wordless spread, she is transformed, as she looks so lovingly at the child.*

ZELINSKY: A picture will say things about the character, just as the text does. I knew from early on, probably as soon as I resolved the question of the pregnancy, that the sorceress was a complicated person. She wasn't an ugly old witch who just unaccountably punishes a girl. I saw her as a mother figure who couldn't let go. She causes Rapunzel to be isolated just because she is so intense.

BKL: *On a technical point, how long did you work on the spread where the sorceress takes the baby?*

ZELINSKY: It's hard to pin down a time span for one picture because it goes back beyond the finished piece. The length of time from when I started working was especially long on this spread because of the detailing in the rug. I really got into that rug.

BKL: *Do you work from beginning to end, or do you sketch one picture while making the finishing touches on another?*

ZELINSKY: I'm happiest if I can do the whole book in rough first and then go back and do a finished version. I certainly don't begin doing any finished art until I know what the whole book is going to consist of. I prefer not to do the paintings in the order of the story because I generally get better over the course of the book, and of course, I don't want all the good stuff at the back.

BKL: **Swamp Angel** *was a lighthearted piece and* **Rapunzel** *much more serious. Does your mood differ depending on the sort of work you're doing?*

ZELINSKY: My mood is the function of how successfully the images appear in front of me on the paper. I can be elated by having an easy time with the world's darkest subject, but I'll be devastated if I can't get anywhere on a cartoon.

BKL: *When you were in college, you took a course on the picture book from Maurice Sendak. How much influence did that have on your choice of career?*

ZELINSKY: When I took the course, I didn't know I wanted to do picture-book illustration, but I felt it was a possibility. The course was wonderful. It was the first time Sendak had taught, and I think everyone in the course knew that we were privileged to be taught by him. I was a sophomore the year I took that course, and at the end of that year, I had to declare a major. There were lots of things I was interested in, not just art. But I did declare art as my major because I thought I would be a better artist than I would be a scientist. I was not sure, though, that I was more interested in art than science.

BKL: *If you weren't illustrating picture books, what kind of artwork would you be doing?*

ZELINSKY: My schooling was for an academic art career—college teaching. People who do that get shows in galleries, and they build careers as fine artists. Since I've graduated from college, what I've seen in the world of fine art has become so depressing that I'm very happy I went in the direction I did.

Paul O. Zelinsky

SOURCE: "1998 Caldecott Medal Acceptance Speech," in *Journal of Youth Services in Libraries,* Vol. 11, No. 4, Summer, 1998, pp. 346-52.

[*The following is Paul Zelinsky's acceptance speech for the Randolph Caldecott Medal for illustration, which he delivered at the annual conference of the American Library Association in Washington, D.C., on June 28, 1998.*]

Members of the Caldecott Committee, librarians, publishers, and all who have wished me so well and who make me feel so welcome and happy and important here today: what a day this is for me and my family! I—we—are so proud to be given this great honor.

I have a confession to make: this is a moment I have staged in my imagination, any number of times, when I've needed cheering up. I stand at a podium in a vast room. Surrounding me, a festive crowd fills a sea of round tables and disappears off into the misty distance. The image of this transcendent scene, I'm embarrassed to say, has lulled me to sleep during troubled times that accompanied more than one book. The best part of my vision was that I didn't even have to write a speech! The scene began and ended before I opened my mouth.

But here I stand, in real time, with my mouth open in no small disbelief. It's hard enough to believe that I actually finished *Rapunzel.* I started thinking about this book long ago. Something in the story kept pulling at me. For years those fertile images—of garden, tower, wilderness, hair, and more hair—were taking root in my mind. I talked about a "Rapunzel" with my editor, Donna Brooks, as far back as 1987, when *Rumpelstiltskin* was in progress. The two books would clearly be related in style. But when the *Rumpelstiltskin* paintings came out in a way that surprised and pleased me, I had no confidence that I could paint at that level again. I found myself extremely reluctant to try. Intriguing projects came up and came first: *The Wheels on the Bus, Strider, The Enchanted Castle, More Rootabagas, Swamp Angel,* and other books allowed me to put off *Rapunzel* again and again. It was eight years before I felt ready to approach the girl with the long hair. By then, signs had been gathering: in the window of a top floor apartment across the street from us, someone set a wig stand with a long blond wig on it. I found myself trying to memorize all the cupolas and turrets I saw on the tall buildings around me. And altogether too many people, appreciative of my work in *Rumpelstiltskin,* came to me and said, "I loved your book *Rapunzel.*"

So I set out to discover what my book *Rapunzel* was going to be. Soon I uncovered Rapunzel's colorful past: how in France, under the name of Persinette, she had resided luxuriously in a fairy's silver tower; how before that, as Petrosinella, she'd carried on wildly in Naples with her prince, right under the nose of a live-in witch; and how in both places she was named after parsley, not *rapunzel.* (It was the whim of a German translator to rename her for the salad herb known in English as rampion.) My first challenge was to find a way to tell the strong story I felt lurking among these versions, a many-leveled story about children and mothers, about coming of age, about home and the world outside. After many attempts, and with lots of help from the intrepid Donna, *Rapunzel*'s text gradually pulled its strands together. We brushed and braided them and they began to look like writing.

My *second* first challenge was to figure out the pictures. Ever since the paintings for *Rumpelstiltskin* came out looking a little less Northern European and a little more Southern European than I had intended, I knew that something Italian in me was trying to show itself. Evidently, it was this *Rapunzel.* The story was like a many-layered onion. And a nice onion, with its elegant, round shape and lustrous surface, embodies most of the qualities I cherish in Italian Renaissance painting. Such a solid, symmetrical shape, the onion. Set in a pure light, it defines a clear space with its simple geometry, like the simple geometry of Perugino, or Raphael. This would be the perfect space in which to set my "Rapunzel." And then the tower, that staple of Italian architecture, could be a thing of beauty like the marble campanile of Tuscany. It seemed inevitable: my "Rapunzel" pictures would have to look like painting from fifteenth- or sixteenth-century Italy.

If I had let myself think realistically about what I was getting myself into, I might have put *Rapunzel* off for another decade. The list of what I couldn't do was endless, if I hoped to emulate even the least of the Renaissance painters. Could I quickly learn how they painted cloth? Or, harder still, faces? How they laid down paint so smoothly, yet with such form and shape? (When I try to smooth brushstrokes away, my shapes lose all definition.) Not to mention the bigger picture: the simplicity and grandeur of the images. I had set myself a goal I had no prospect of achieving.

So I moved hesitantly, wrestling with my limitations. When figures refused to come out right in my sketches, I would make another trip to the Metropolitan Museum, buy another Renaissance art book, spend more mornings at Minerva Durham's figure drawing and anatomy workshop in Soho to whip my fingers into shape. Sketch by sketch I crept forward, but there was always that odd detail needing research: the shape of a sixteenth-century scissors, or the underside of a cuckoo in flight. In most of my books there is a moment after which the work starts to come easily. I never reached that point here. At least, thank goodness, most of the attempts I made to improve the pictures seemed to help. But they helped— oh, so slowly.

Keeping a picture book interesting in all the right ways is a little like keeping four or five juggling balls in the air. You have to follow them all with your mind's eye. I constantly struggled not to get too distracted by any one of them. Technique, for example: I had to limit the time I spent trying to make leaves on bushes and trees as patterned, yet as leaf-like as Raphael's (did his oak leaves always go: one up, three across, two down?). Obsessing on technique, I'd risk losing sight of whether the pictures work to tell the story, and whether the story flows as you turn from page to page. There should be no forgetting that on each page the feeling must be the right one, that it be expressed through literal means, such as facial expressions and body language, as well as abstract means—the way the picture is constructed, its colors, its shapes. When these means combine to tell a vivid story, that's good illustration. But the abstract elements operate on another level as well: a structural level where something other than storytelling takes place, something that can turn illustration into art.

The storytelling in pictures is more natural to me than the art. This dawned on me during my first drawing course at Yale with my great teacher, Bernard Chaet. He looked at the pen-and-ink pictures I had brought to show him and said, "You can already do what those guys at *Esquire* do, but, Paul, you really have to learn how to draw." I was shocked to hear this. I most certainly could not do what those guys at *Esquire* could do—slick, deft work—and what did he mean I couldn't draw?

You can't really draw or paint, said my teachers, Mr. Chaet and William Bailey, unless you can make pictures "work formally." You have to "make the form work." And what on earth does that mean? I would wonder. What is form, and how does it work? Here is what I've come to believe: form is what you would see if you had brand new eyes and no names, no real-life associations for things. Form is what your retina takes in before your brain starts recognizing. You see colors and shapes. You see lights and darks, textures, lines, patterns. You see indications of depth, of space. Everything drawn has form. And form creates motion, speed, influence. Shapes and colors act on each other. Dramas are played out in the realm of form. Beauty—pictorial beauty—arises from form. I have never been sensitive enough or creative enough to completely get through to it. But when form works very well, I have faith that everyone who can see, children as well as adults, will respond to it. When shapes perform dances with other shapes, when colors play up and down scales, when they fall into chords, when lines move in patterns that look inevitably right, we will all feel it.

When form works, something profound happens. Art happens. All stories move us with the emotions they provoke. We feel sad when Rapunzel and the prince suffer in the wilderness, and happy when they reunite. But art moves us on another, complementary level as well. My friend Rika Lesser, the poet and translator who wrote the words for my *Hansel and Gretel,* and also helped me with *Rapunzel*'s text, told me a Swedish neologism for the part of us that responds to art: *tänke-hjärta.* I think it's wonderful; in English it would be the "thought-heart." Not the heart that fills with sentiment, and not the mind that judges ideas; this is a separate organ. It gives us the emotion of thought and the logic of feeling. It lies deep inside all of us, I am certain. Hoping to sense its pulse, I sit in my studio day after day, and strive to make my pictures engaging as form. When I need to show how intrusively a prince bursts into the ordered life of a Rapunzel, I want to make the shapes show it along with the characters: the prince's straight lines jutting forward and Rapunzel's curves wheeling out of their way. To the degree that I succeed, form and content of the picture will become one thing, and you'll feel it in your thought-heart.

I've been convinced that classical artists thought about their creations just as formally as Mr. Chaet does ever since I saw one drawing by a pupil of Rembrandt in an exhibition at the Chicago Art Institute. A group of figures were clustered at the bottom of the drawing, and an angel filled the upper left corner. Rembrandt himself had marked up this composition with a bold line to show his pupil how the angel's wing should look. And the difference made by that one line was beyond remarkable: it not only gave strength to an unstable little pen-scratch, it made an empty, formless space around the wing into a shapely compartment of air. It made the wing a better wing, it charged the angel with a sense of direction, and the drawing with a spirit it hadn't had before.

It made a better angel's wing. Who here has ever seen, much less judged, an angel's wing? How do I know a better one when I see it? What was it but perfect form at work, making me think I knew, assuring me that this was right. Children, especially little children, have never seen many things. To them, so much of the world is no different from angels' wings. And what makes a child respond to a picture in a book? Is it accuracy of depiction? Is it photographic realism? No! It might be an instinctual button being pushed—bright colors, cute animals—but it's also compelling form, form that works. Then, after that, it's what's particular to the child, whatever happens to appeal to her or him, as with any person of any age.

Many artists in children's books are masters of form. Maurice Sendak, my first and only illustration teacher, is one. He raised a curtain for me on the workings of the picture book when he applied the word rhythm to it. Others whose work has helped me to see in new ways are Garth Williams, Marc Simont, Evaline Ness, Margot Zemach, Irene Haas, Robert Lawson. I'm leaving out so many whose drawings get me in my thought-heart.

I, too, was aiming for the thought-heart one Monday morning last January, working and reworking an old sorcerer's right hand for a paperback book cover. I was also aware that the ALA was meeting then, but I can never remember days or dates. I asked my wife Deborah, who always can, if she remembered what day of the week the call had come telling me that *Swamp Angel* had won a Caldecott Honor. It was a Tuesday, she said.

So I went to work Monday morning concerned with other things. I was eager to check for e-mail, and maybe look into the Internet, a brand-new treat for me. My new computer had been failing to go online through two weeks of grueling phone calls for technical support from AT&T, my service provider, but on Friday, things had seemed to work. First thing Monday, the software couldn't locate the modem. Which was the reason I was working on a painting that morning, and my telephone line was clear.

It's about 9:15 a.m. The phone rings. A male voice asks for Paul Zelinsky. Now, this can mean one of two things: someone hawking financial services, or a salesman for a long distance phone company. "Who's calling?" I ask,

not admitting to my name, and ready to bite the head off of anyone connected with AT&T.

"This is John Stewart," the man seems to say. I know of no John Stewart. "What is this about?" I ask, icily.

Then came the words, "I'm calling for the Caldecott Committee here in New Orleans"—and the world reshaped itself around me. My heart went to my throat; my throat went to my head. I think I said "Oh!" And John Stewig said, "Is Paul Zelinsky there please?" Oh, yes, that's me after all. And suddenly there was only one thing more I wanted to know, which John was about to reveal. "We're happy to tell you," he continued, "that we've voted *Rapunzel* the book of the year." A magnificent thrill and a cheer welled up inside me, but didn't quite make it out of my mouth.

Instead, I burbled, "I don't believe it!" This, after all, was the wrong day!

But when I heard the entire committee cry "hooray" in the background, I had to believe it. I think I thanked them, hung up, and out came the cheer. "YOWEE!" Immediately, I called Deborah at P.S. 8. "Interrupt her class," I told the school secretary, "it's urgent: *Rapunzel* won the Caldecott Medal!" Deborah says that when she saw the secretary enter her classroom, pink message-paper in hand, she started to cry. She had known all along that Monday was the day; she had wanted to give me an easy weekend. My weekend had been just fine, but hers hadn't. She had prayed and stewed and tossed and turned. I thank her for the kind deception she played on me.

After the fact, the signs all seem to have shown that *Rapunzel* was marked for something special. Mind you, I am not a superstitious person. I'm as rational as they come. But I like the attitude of Niels Bohr, the father of quantum theory, who kept a horseshoe over the door of his country house. When guests saw it, they would say, "You of all people don't believe in this primitive superstition, do you?" And he would answer no, he didn't, but he understood that it's supposed to work even if you don't believe in it. In this spirit, I would like to tell you some of the indications that *Rapunzel* might have been specially blessed.

The first sign happened just before the ALA Annual Conference last year. I had managed to buy rapunzel seeds by mail, and Deborah raised the plants on the roof deck of our apartment building. I wanted to portray the plant and its flowers accurately, and also to know what it tasted like. (Knowing the flavor, I thought, would help me in some indefinable way with the illustrations.) Rapunzel is a biennial; in its first year it grows only leaves; in its second year, mainly flowers; and then it dies. I started to work on the book in 1995. That summer we ate lots of rapunzel salad. It was crisp and spicy. I hadn't gotten nearly far enough along in the painting by the summer of '96, but we had plenty of rapunzel flowers. The following summer was last summer, 1997, and we planted other plants in the rapunzel pots. I was supposed to have finished *Rapunzel* long since, but I hadn't. There had been a deadline, then an urgent deadline, then a dead-and-buried-line and a brutally-murdered-line, and I missed them all. I completed the book in a sustained rush the likes of which I hope never to repeat. Not for the first time, I put my family and myself through quite an ordeal.

The rush lasted right up until the ALA Annual Conference itself. Deborah and I were to leave for San Francisco on a Saturday, and not until Thursday did I finish the back of the book jacket, the last piece of art. I delivered it to Dutton, then returned home half dazed. In the elevator I met our neighbors, ninety-three-year-old Janet and her daughter Nancy, both avid roofdeck gardeners, who said, "Have you been to the roof today? We think your rapunzel is blooming."

I said, "No, there is no rapunzel this year. It's a biennial."

Nancy said, "Well, why don't you come up and look? We thought it was your rapunzel." So instead of getting off on eight, we all went up to the penthouse. There on the roof deck, in the center of a large clay pot full of marigolds, one slender stalk of rapunzel was poking up, with four purple flowers, newly opened, nodding on their stems. What a sign that was, don't you think?

And what am I to make of the fact, which I perceived during a bout of procrastination three-quarters of the way through the *Rapunzel* oil paintings, that my full name, Paul Oser Zelinsky, is an anagram for "Rapunzel's key oils?"

By the way, is this related to the fact that in the Library of Congress cataloging code, the call numbers for children's stories all begin with PZ? How could I have gone into any other line of work?

Clearly I belong with you, the children's librarians who have taken so enthusiastically to the books I have been lucky enough to work on. My gratitude belongs to you. And it belongs to my dear friend and longtime editor—we have collaborated for almost half my life!—Donna Brooks, to whom I owe more than I can say, starting with *How I Hunted the Little Fellows* and *The Maid and the Mouse and the Odd-Shaped House* and going on and on. And it belongs to my glamorous wife of almost equal tenure, whom I love. Deborah, a teacher of uncanny understanding, bestows beauty and order on the life of our family, and makes it rich with her love of music. And my gratitude goes to our children, Anna and Rachel, for being so terrific. I know they can't help that, but they did put up with a sometimes-absent and distracted father in exchange for seeing their cat Skimbleshanks made a supporting actor in a picture book. I'm prouder of them than of any product of my hand. And if my parents had not brought me up with a love of the arts, I would surely not be here tonight. I am thankful to them for a childhood full of trips to the Art Institute,

among other things. And I wish to thank Amy Berniker for being a patient collaborator on all questions of *Rapunzel*'s design, and Laurence Tucci for conjuring a magical tower of a production schedule: somehow he squeezed more stages of proof into this book's preparation than there was space on the calendar to fit them in. And thank you, Alissa Heyman, for doing so much of the extra work brought on by my tardiness, and many others at Dutton Children's Books.

The Caldecott call has made me feel like the prince at the end of the French Rapunzel tale, "Persinette," when the sorceress rescues the prince's little reunited family from certain death in the wilderness. John Stewig and the committee play the part of the sorceress to my prince. Imagine that you're hearing courtly seventeenth-century French:

> She transported herself to the place where they stood; she appeared in a chariot resplendent with gold and precious stones. She had them climb in, placing herself between the fortunate lovers, and setting their lovely children on magnificent cushions at their feet. And in this manner she drove them to the palace of the king, father to the prince. It was there that joy burst all bounds: the prince, who had for so long been thought lost, was received as if he were a god. And he was so happy to find himself at peace after having been so agitated by the storm that nothing in the world was comparable to the felicity in which he lived with his perfect spouse.

I think that nothing in the world is comparable to this. Thank you very much.

GENERAL COMMENTARY

Sally Lodge

SOURCE: "Paul Zelinsky's Surprising Debut," in *Publishers Weekly*, Vol. 245, No. 13, March 30, 1998, p. 27.

Though he wasn't aware of it until very recently, the winner of the 1998 Caldecott Medal—for *Rapunzel*, a Dutton title—was a published artist at the age of four. Actually, Paul Zelinsky was a tot of only three when he drew the impressively sophisticated picture of a fan-waving Geisha, which appeared in *Highlights* magazine's November 1957 issue, in a section showcasing youngsters' art and poetry.

Several weeks ago, Tim Moses, director of publicity for hardcover books for Penguin Putnam, received a call "out of the clear blue sky" from *Highlights*'s senior editor, Marileta Robinson. While poring over vintage copies of the magazine more than a year ago, Robinson, a longtime fan of Zelinsky, spotted the drawing and put it aside. Only after the January announcement of Zelin-

From Rapunzel, *retold and illustrated by Paul O. Zelinsky.*

sky's Caldecott win did she pick up the phone to ask Moses if, by any chance, the 1950s preschool artist from Princeton, N.J., could be the very same Paul O. Zelinsky.

Indeed it is. Living in Princeton during the 1955-56 academic year, which his father spent at the Institute of Advanced Studies, Zelinsky spent a good bit of time drawing Geishas. "Our family had lived in Japan the prior year," he explained, "where I remember being captivated by Geishas. I don't really recall drawing them when we returned, but according to my mother, I definitely did."

How the picture came to appear in *Highlights* is a mystery to both Zelinsky and his mother, who never knew of its submission or publication until Robinson's discovery. They suspect it may have been sent in by the artist's nursery-school teacher, whom they are now trying to track down. "We had moved away from Princeton by the time the drawing was published," Zelinsky said, "and at the time we did not subscribe to *Highlights.* Coincidentally, years later, when we did, the kids' submission page was the first I turned to each month. I'd immediately want to check out the drawings and see how old the kids were—and try to figure out if I could draw as well as they could."

Now the Caldecott Medalist realizes that he must revise

his autobiographical trivia. "For years I've been telling people that my first published work was a picture I drew in high school for a math textbook my father wrote," he said. "All along I was certain that was my first published art. Little did I know I was 10 years off."

Donna Brooks

SOURCE: "Paul O. Zelinsky: Geishas on Tractors," in *The Horn Book Magazine,* Vol. LXXIV, No. 4, July-August, 1998, pp. 442-49.

[*In the following article, Donna Brooks, editorial director of the trade list at Dutton's Children's Books, a division of Penguin-Putnam Books for Young Readers, shares some insights about Paul O. Zelinsky and his art.*]

When Paul's elder daughter, Anna, was thirteen months old, Paul made a "Dictionary of the Anna Language" for her great-grandparents on their sixtieth anniversary. A little book, carefully hand-lettered on marbled paper from India and bound in leather (from an old briefcase he found in the garbage), it contained fifty-five entries for twelve letters. Except for a colophon drawn on the title page (a small rubber duck with the word *dah* under it), the dictionary was unillustrated. It is a tender example of the considerate attention with which Paul enters into the world of another person, and of the delicacy and humor he brings to bear on what he finds there. Here are a few entries.

> Bub·buh (bŭ′bə) *n.* button. *interj.* "Get me something to drink!" (*lit.,* bottle).

> Dad·dy *n.* (də′dē) 1. Daddy 2. doggie; dog 3. donkey.

> Mom·my (mŏ′mē) *n.* Mommy; *occas.,* Daddy.

> Nnononono (nōnōnōnō) *interj.* 1. no 2. yes.

> Pap·pa·doo (păpä dōō) *interj.* meaning obscure.

> Ta(t) (tâ-) *n.* cat; also chihuahua.

> Tah·toe (tä′tō) *interj.* "Take this away from me!" (*lit.,* thank you).

> Tup·py·tup·py·tup·py (tŭ′pē-tŭ′pē-tŭ′pē-) *interj.* expression denoting a cheerful mood and the desire to kill time.

Such faithful, amused appreciation of a baby's utterances has to please a children's book editor. Anna's wants, her confusions, her economies, her delights—here they all are, given to us with gentle wit, orderliness, grace.

The dictionary reminds me of Paul's own personal gentleness, which you can hear in his voice as well as feel when you are with him, and which permeates his studio and heightens the perceptions of anyone who spends time there. I have seen this quality persist under great pressure, when he is exhausted, even suffering from illness, painting to meet a deadline that has passed. His gentleness takes his less gentle impulses and casts them as humor. Given an assignment to build a box in seventh-grade woodshop, he created a small guillotine with a storage area underneath. The weight of the dropping blade (a thick piece of stainless steel that he sawed and filed) opened the lid. I asked him if he ever cut anything with this guillotine. "No," he replied sadly. "I didn't have the strength to make it really sharp."

I first watched Paul draw when he was working on the pen-and-ink illustrations for *How I Hunted the Little Fellows* by the Russian author Boris Zhitkov, translated by Djemma Bider. But I didn't realize how much everything he drew was infused with character until I looked at a page of doodles in his studio. Whether a goblin head resting in a goblet or a cat playing its own fiddle-body, each had a distinct energy and personality, each seemed to suggest an invisible world behind it. "How do you do this?" I asked, unable to draw even an apple myself and make it look round. He shrugged. "It just comes out that way."

Perhaps this ability to animate is simply innate. Some years back Paul told me that when he was two and his family lived in Japan, he fell madly in love with geishas. He drew them over and over. "Their white, white faces; their black hair; the rich colors of their costumes—their otherworldliness." Perfect, I thought, seeing my vague idea of geisha beauty and Japanese art in some of the geometrical forms that I love in Paul's work. This spring *Publishers Weekly* reproduced a geisha drawing of Paul's (age three years) that *Highlights* had unearthed from the pages of their November 1957 issue. The drawing was tiny, but I've seen a larger one of similar vintage. This geisha, too, is holding open the sleeves of her kimono, a delicate motion implied in the lines of her arms and the tilt of the fan she holds. She's looking at us and her face is lovely, with wide-set eyes, a sweet, modest smile, no nose, and a hair ornament slanted just right. Sure enough, even in this drawing by a not-yet-four-year-old illustrator, a person—poised, appraising, friendly—is peeking out.

As the geisha drawings surfaced, I learned more of their story. After the year in Japan, Paul's family moved to Princeton, New Jersey, where they lived across the street from a construction site. Again Paul fell madly in love, this time with tractors and steam shovels. Did he desert the geishas? By no means. In his new, obsessive drawings of tractors and steam shovels, the geishas were the drivers.

Even then, Paul brought together what gave pleasure to his eye and mind. He is a maker of things, an assembler of worlds. At Yale, he thought about becoming a set designer, and you can see that interest in his books. Costumes, furnishings, buildings, interior space, landscapes—the set of elements represents coherent choices yielding drama and beauty. He has something of the

director in him as well. I've seen this in the way he works with models or revises his sketches, feeling out the possibilities in their poses, expressions, compositions.

I often go to Paul's studio when we are working together. Early on, his studio was his apartment—a large, high-ceilinged unit in a brownstone in Brooklyn Heights. His drawing table, surrounded by doodles, supplies, and a radio, stood near the window in a tiny room that served as his bedroom. In the main room were his easel, a few paintings, a small table and chairs, and a big oak book-case with intricately carved molding that Paul had patiently stripped of paint using a sharp-pointed instrument the size of a crochet hook. Against the wall lay a round, reflective blue glass tabletop, suggesting magic and sorcery. And indeed, it seemed to me, over the years, that Paul was a conjurer. "As adults we have lost that equality of belief in what we see and what we don't," he once wrote in a piece about a fellow painter. For Paul, illustrating a book must summon up that lost belief. Projects begin to develop a power that recasts the physical world around him, drawing whatever or whomever is useful toward the studio. A friend from college, the poet Rika Lesser, was pressed into service—between pillows—as a model for a grandmother. I was recruited to wear a tablecloth as a skirt and lead my children briskly into the forest; and another time to stand hunched over and, thinking like a witch, hold my hand out to an imaginary Hansel. A lovely young woman Paul spied in a Chinese restaurant visited the studio to model for the miller's daughter in *Rumpelstiltskin*. (Paul's wife, Deborah, assured her of his honorable intentions.) Fresh from class, Alexandre Proia, a ballet dancer, trekked downtown to be tucked into a tunic held together with staples and masking tape, crowned with an inside-out beret, and made to emerge and reemerge from Paul's bathroom as the king coming into a room full of gold. From time to time his family might lend a hand, an ear, a pair of legs, or whatever else had to be drawn.

Often Paul constructed what he needed to see—a boat of papier-mâché, a grandmother's head in clay, a tiny Swamp Angel out of bent wire wrapped in paper tape. He built the front half of the top quarter of Rapunzel's intricately patterned tower out of cardboard. (Later, at a party, he reproduced the tower as a table-long arrangement of different cheeses.) And if he could not make what he needed to look at, he journeyed to find it: to the woods to examine lichen, the Museum of Natural History to look at drawers full of cuckoos, Coney Island to find the perfect Russian boy. Or he brought what he needed back: grass to dry into straw; rapunzel; seeds to grow; books of all sorts; a live mouse, which he attempted to coax onto a toy motorcycle. Somehow Paul would assemble these homemade objects, improbably draped models, and piecemeal, jerry-built sets and transform them into a seamless and ravishing new world. When enough illustrations had been completed—a kind of critical mass—a moment would arrive that never failed to stagger me. The effects of the separate pieces would suddenly express their coherence, and I would finally grasp the power of the book (and the world) that was emerging. That it was once again a new and different look, that Paul had been struggling toward this all along, and that I had blithely "helped out" without realizing what was underway, all fueled my feeling of amazement. If I expressed my astonishment and regard to him in terms that suggested he had been painting what he saw in his mind's eye, he was careful to correct me. He didn't necessarily know what he was doing, he worked his way moment by moment, and it could be wonderful and flow, or it could go nowhere.

The streak of scientist in Paul (he might have majored in physics, but "I liked it better than I could do it") and his fascination with ingenious construction allow him to face down complicated technical challenges. He charged intrepidly into the paper engineering for *The Wheels on the Bus.* For *Swamp Angel* by Anne Isaacs, he experimented until he had systematized a way to prepare cherry veneer for oil paints. (Getting the veneer was another story.) And in the olden, budget-conscious days of pre-separated art for all but the most famous illustrators, Paul figured out how to use silk-screened gray paper to achieve flat background colors—a lot harder than it looks—for *The Maid and the Mouse and the Odd-Shaped House.* It doubled his work, but it came in at the right cost.

All of this research and pursuit of precision rarely derails Paul's nimble sense of humour. He has an elastic wit that stretches from the sublime to the silly (or worse). A sly bathos always brings things down to earth. One day when he was cross-hatching the illustrations for *How I Hunted the Little Fellows,* a story set in nineteenth-century Russia, I showed up to see the drawings. There, amidst all the carefully researched and finely rendered details of the grandmother's room—wallpaper, rugs, door-handles, picture frames—stood Mickey Mouse, waving out at the reader from between the plates on Grandmother's armoire. Paul explained that it was a joke; Mickey was carefully positioned to disappear into the gutter when the book was side sewn. I instantly fantasized reviewers ripping the binding apart, finding Mickey Mouse on a shelf in a St. Petersburg apartment in 1896, and writing damning reviews about smart-aleck illustrators and their publishers. Or worse—thinking we didn't know better! Finally my mind went to the printers. What if they thought Mickey was *supposed* to show, and actually cut and split the art so as not to lose him? That possibility held sway with Paul, and the mouse was sanded away.

I love getting birthday cards from Paul. Often these cards are little books themselves, sardonically recapitulating our most recent project together. Here he can express all the inevitable feelings of aggravation, frustration, and yes, even rage, that he never lets loose in the actual working process. His cards offer me a side-splitting view of the ridiculous extremes that go into making a children's book. The birthday card I received after *Hansel and Gretel* (where much effort had been expended to find the earliest Grimm versions) bore these words on the title page: "Three hitherto undiscovered very early and even more authentic versions." The illustrations were colored pencil in a smart-looking Bauhaus style. In the first version, the children were eaten by wild animals in the forest. From behind a tree a little bearded man peeked out, saying, "Ach, Wilhelm—perhaps dis ist too harsch? Mebbe ve try again." At the end of the second version, Gretel shoved the witch into the oven, and "when they reached home their father said, 'Your mother is dead and this is one great story. Sell the rights and we can live happily and prosper to the end of our days.' Early the next morning, they set off into the forest. They walked and walked. Finally they reached Frankfurt. A gnarled old man came out from behind a desk, 'I'm sorry, folks,' he said, 'You're in the public domain.'" In the third version, the mother turned nice, the children stayed happily at home, and Wilhelm cried, "Dis time I tink I got it."

After *The Maid and the Mouse and the Odd-Shaped House,* a picture book adapted from an old tell-and-draw story, Paul made me a small tell-and-draw book called "The Cat" as a birthday card. In the actual book, a maid and a mouse make improvements in their odd-shaped house, unwittingly "drawing" a cat's face (the new chimneys become ears; the windows, eyes; and so on). The body of the cat is created by the path the maid takes when she goes looking for the source of a hissing sound. Once she realizes what their house has become, she races back to snatch the mouse from the jaws of this now animated feline. "Matter enough, my mouse so fat! / Oh, dear! Alas! It is the CAT!" The book works as a kind of puzzle; though the viewer can tell that something is being constructed, the full picture of the cat is withheld as long as possible for maximum surprise.

The card Paul made has illustrations that are simple, energetic, and dead-on funny. The whole thing mimics the real book—its meter, its pacing—with a few significant plot alterations. The maid's roommate is not a mouse but a rat, and the two live not in a pentagonal house but a cat's stomach. "The rat was young, the maid was old. / The Cat, of course, was rent-controlled." The maid and the rat get busy taking their revenge on the cat—lopping off its head, disguising the stump of a neck, stretching out its legs like rubber bands. Then the maid goes out to investigate a bothersome noise. "'It sounds,' announced the little hag, / 'like paste extruding from a bag.'" Again, what all this decapitation and transmogrification amounts to is withheld from the viewer until the very last, when the maid hurries back inside. "What she had seen to prompt her flight / was this most unexpected sight: / The Cat, expressive in its looks, said" . . . and here you turn the page to a picture of what the cat has finally become—a big beautiful birthday cake with frosting letters spelling out . . . "Happy Birthday, Donna Brooks!"

In my own tell-and-draw story, had I Paul's clever command of line and form, a gold-colored cat would by some means be squashed into a perfectly round, flat shape except for a slight feeling of embossment left over from its bones. The maid and the mouse would have gone out to investigate a loud noise. Upon discovering that the source of the sound was a cheering crowd, the maid would exultantly return on mouseback, riding side-saddle across the golden circle. The last lines of my story would go something like, "And so, dear Paul, a cat it's not./ *This* time it's the Caldecott."

TITLE COMMENTARY

📖 *HOW I HUNTED THE LITTLE FELLOWS*
(written by Boris Zhitkov; translated by Djemma Bider, 1979)

Publishers Weekly

SOURCE: A review of *How I Hunted the Little Fellows,* in *Publishers Weekly,* Vol. 216, No. 12, September 17, 1979, p. 146.

The late, renowned Russian author undoubtedly express-es a rueful mea culpa in this story, translated by Bider who loses no whit of the original's flavor. Zelinsky's magnetic drawings provide more haunting realism in scenes of a long-gone Russian town where little Boria (the narrator) visits his grandmother. Generous and lov-ing, the woman nevertheless forbids Boria to touch her treasure, a marvelously complete miniature steamship—her "dear memory." But the boy is obsessed by finding tiny sailors he envisions inside the ship. When he's alone, he pulls the graceful thing apart and can't put it together again. The story ends before Boria's grandmother dis-covers the wreck but should make any reader think twice about the need to respect people's property.

Marjorie Lewis

SOURCE: A review of *How I Hunted the Little Fellows,* in *School Library Journal,* Vol. 26, No. 3, November, 1979, p. 72.

Boria, a small boy in turn-of-the-century Russia, spends several weeks with his grandmother longing to see in-side the magnificent ship-model that sits on a shelf over the table. Warned by Grandmother not to touch it be-cause it holds precious memories for her, Boria becomes obsessed by the beauty of the intricate, realistic details and is certain that "little fellows" are aboard hiding from the world of big people. Left alone one day, he is powerless to control his curiosity and rips the ship apart in an effort to find the tiny people. Devastated as much by what he has done as by the realization that his fantasy is just that—no more, he is desolate. A first-person memoir, this is a poignant story with an open-ended climax excellent for motivating discussions about conse-quences and self-control or for stimulating creative writ-ing. It reads aloud well in language that echoes earlier

times in far off places, and the design of type, lightly boxed in the gracefully detailed and dramatic sketches, reinforce this low-key remembrance of a piece of a long-ago childhood when imagination transcended reality.

Kirkus Reviews

SOURCE: A review of *How I Hunted the Little Fellows,* in *Kirkus Reviews,* Vol. XLVII, No. 22, November 15, 1979, p. 1328.

In Grandmother's house is a model of a steamship, which looks absolutely real and is "a dear memory" to her, and which the little boy who tells this is forbidden to touch. But he becomes fascinated, then preoccupied, with the little fellows he imagines inhabit the ship; and he makes up all sorts of excuses so he'll be in a position to catch them moving about on deck. (He's afraid and needs the night light on; he has a fever and can't go out with her.) Finally on the day he plays sick and Grand-mother is gone, he determines to overturn the ship and shake the little fellows out. No luck? They must be sitting on the benches inside, "tucking their legs in under the boards and holding on with all their strength." The outcome is inevitable—a wrecked and devastatingly empty ship, and a little boy sobbing with guilt when Grand-mother returns. As that's the end of the story really, Zhitkov doesn't condescend to tell what happens next—though children who must be told can read in the ap-pended biographical sketch of an unpublished sequel in which the little boy runs away in remorse and his grand-mother forgives him. The story itself is a perceptive, unmanipulated picture of a child's single-minded secret passion. Bider's use of the term "little fellows" gives it a properly quaint but not too quaint distance, and Zelin-sky's fine-line drawings, though they overdo the lighting effects to the point of hokiness, do convey the quiet but intense subjectivity of the experience.

Paul Heins

SOURCE: A review of *How I Hunted the Little Fellows,* in *The Horn Book Magazine,* Vol. LVI, No. 1, Febru-ary, 1980, p. 58.

Encouraged by Kornei Chukovsky to become a writer, the author made a number of contributions to Russian children's literature. Boria tells how he was taken to stay with his grandmother when he was a little boy and forbidden to touch a miniature steamship on a shelf. Fascinated by the perfection of its construction, he imag-ined that the vessel was manned by tiny mariners who kept themselves in hiding; and one day when his grand-mother went out, Boria took the steamer apart and dis-covered that his imagination had not only led him astray but had caused him to disobey the old lady. In addition to skillfully suggesting the motif of little people fre-quently found in children's books, Boria's story astutely reveals the intenseness of the child's experiences and his emotional relationship with his grandmother. The narrative, however, ends abruptly and somewhat inconclusively, but it is interesting to note that the author wrote a sequel, which was lost in a Leningrad editorial office. The carefully detailed and shaded hatched drawings on practically every page evoke a mood of late nineteenth-century domesticity and successfully portray the steamship and its imaginary little crew; but occasionally the exterior architectural details appear to be more symbolically than authentically Russian.

Denise M. Wilms

SOURCE: A review of *How I Hunted the Little Fellows,* in *Booklist,* Vol. 76, No. 13, March 1, 1980, p. 985.

This evocative story of a boy who becomes obsessed with a fantasy and destroys his grandmother's beloved ship model is at once riveting and problematic. The unnamed narrator, visiting his grandmother, notices the lifelike steamship on her mantel and wants to play with it, but she forbids him; he gives his word of honor that he won't touch it. But the ship's presence provokes tantalizing images of a tiny crew who are people-shy, and the boy settles in to an unending watch to catch them at work. Ultimately, the power of his vision takes complete hold; he violates his word and takes the ship down for a look, which ends with his dismantling and destroying his grandmother's prized possession. Zhitkov uses the first person to set a mood of quiet intimacy that reinforces his tale's psychological dimensions. The bleak finish is open-ended and powerful as far as it goes, but still abrupt; children of an age to respond to the picture-book format will want a more explicit ending, especially if they've been confused over the hinted reality of the boy's fantasy (what really took the crumbs he left aboard ship to entice the crew out?). Jacket copy tells that Zhitkov later wrote a sequel. It's an example of storytelling that, though artful and aimed at children, may involve adult retrospection rather than child sensibilities. It will certainly provoke discussion among its young readers. Accompanying black-and-white illustrations are masterful in their meticulous creation of a cozy, old-fashioned house and profoundly real characters. The web of refined cross-hatching develops unending nuance and a hushed mood that is palpable and in absolute accord with the story's picture of irretrievable damage.

WHAT AMANDA SAW (written by Naomi Lazard, 1981)

Publishers Weekly

SOURCE: A review of *What Amanda Saw,* in *Publishers Weekly,* Vol. 219, No. 7, February 13, 1981, p. 94.

Lazard's reputation is based on her distinguished poetry for adults. Now she offers her first children's book, written with imagination and grace. The haunting fantasy harmonizes with Zelinsky's atmospheric drawings, skillful representational figures in real and dream landscapes, the difference emphasized by a wash of gold over the former and misty blue over the latter. Amanda is sleepless after a day of searching futilely for her cat Bubble. The child and her parents are leaving their country home in the morning; what will she do if Bubble is still missing? Slipping from bed, Amanda walks across a field to where she hears sounds of conviviality. Peeking through a fence, she beholds Bubble as guest of honor at a going-away party given by all the local animals, even mice and birds. Lazard's awareness of the feline's imperial posture contributes to the quietly humorous finale.

Janet French

SOURCE: A review of *What Amanda Saw,* in *School Library Journal,* Vol. 27, No. 7, March, 1981, p. 133.

It is the last night at their summer cottage, and Amanda goes to bed troubled because Bubble, the family cat, has not come home. At last she slips outside to find him and is rewarded by a remarkable sight: the neighborhood animals are having a farewell party for Bubble, complete with a cake and fancy hats. Amanda watches the festivities for a while and then tiptoes back to bed, satisfied that Bubble is safe. In the morning she shares her knowledge of the night's events with the now returned Bubble and smiles knowingly when he curls up beside her in the car to sleep "all the way home." No speculations on its origin as a dream mars the mood of the fantasy. Zelinsky's charcoal-and-chalk drawings sustain the mood. Nicely done, the best of them recall the tender realism of Symeon Shimin.

Virginia Haviland

SOURCE: A review of *What Amanda Saw,* in *The Horn Book Magazine,* Vol. LVII, No. 3, June, 1981, p. 296.

In a familiar situation a family cat disappears as its owners are ready to leave their summer home to return to the city. Fantasy, however, mixes with realism, for during the night the child Amanda sees her cat Bubble being given a farewell dinner party by the animals who live in the nearby countryside. As well as the chickens and the squirrels, there are the goat ("Amanda never did catch his name"); Carmen, the pony; and Whipper, the mongrel dog. Next morning the inscrutable Bubble gives Amanda only a piercing look in response to her "Did you have a good time last night, Bubble?" Charcoal drawings capture the softness and fluffiness of fur and of the downy breasts of birds; in addition, anthropomorphism endows faces with expressions of pleasure and excitement, enhanced by party-favor hats. The assemblage around the table of squirrels, geese, hen, horse, sheep, and others reminds one of the famous nineteenth-century McLoughlin picture book *The Dog's Grand Dinner Party.*

THE MAID AND THE MOUSE AND THE ODD-SHAPED HOUSE: A STORY IN RHYME (adapted by Zelinsky, 1981)

Publishers Weekly

SOURCE: A review of *The Maid and the Mouse and the Odd-Shaped House,* in *Publishers Weekly,* Vol. 219, No. 16, April 17, 1981, p. 62.

Used in "tell and draw" exercises by a teacher during the late 1800s, the jingly verses in this book have been animated in Zelinsky's version and blithely illustrated in extremely pretty paintings. The skinny maid and the fat mouse move into a house and happily improve the place. The fireplace draws well, the new windows give the householders a view of the outdoors and things are fine until the maid trips and falls: "Oh, no! She tripped and fell again!/ And *then* she heard a dreadful roar." Zelinsky begins to reveal his dandy secret by shapes showing the path the wee maid takes in her tumbles. Gradually, readers discover that the odd couple's odd house is a cat, an angry fellow they escape from, to settle down elsewhere.

Sally Holmes Holtze

SOURCE: A review of *The Maid and the Mouse and the Odd-Shaped House,* in *School Library Journal,* Vol. 27, No. 9, May, 1981, p. 61.

Zelinsky has adapted a "tell and draw" story from folk literature, crediting the Connecticut teacher who used it in 1897. The rhyming tale is of how a "wee maid" and a mouse lived in a house, first shown as a hexagonal border around them; as the maid makes improvements like sweeping dirt out the door, modifications are made (the dirt becomes cat whiskers) until the structure slowly takes the shape of a watchful, omnipresent cat. The maid finally sees the danger (after readers do) and rescues the mouse, running off to a more civilized, less animated abode. Zelinsky creatively uses the pages of a picture book the way a director uses every inch of the stage. There is much finely drawn activity in and out of the house and, like Joyner and Charlip in *Thirteen,* Zelinsky uses line, space and color in a unique way.

Barbara Elleman

SOURCE: A review of *The Maid and the Mouse and the Odd-Shaped House,* in *Booklist,* Vol. 77, No. 21, July 1, 1981, p. 1397.

Pale shades of yellow, lavender, peach, and blue provide an appropriately whimsical background for this nonsensical old folk rhyme, across which finely drawn characters race in well-paced rhythm. Used as a "tell-and-draw" piece in a Connecticut teacher's 1897 classroom, the tale features an oddly shaped house that gradually takes on the appearance of a cat as a wee maid and a plump, pink-eared mouse make various changes in it. Unusual composition results from the small, thin-lined characters placed against open space and the offstage action that unfolds on the sidelines. Children will delight in the appearance of the eyes, ears, whiskers, body, and tail; even after a first reading takes away the surprise, the inventiveness and humor remain.

Kirkus Reviews

SOURCE: A review of *The Maid and the Mouse and the Odd-Shaped House,* in *Kirkus Reviews,* Vol. XLIX, No. 13, July 1, 1981, p. 799.

In the tradition referred to here as a "tell and draw" story, this old rhyme puts a "wee maid" and a fat mouse in a new five-sided house; then adds two chimneys (a dead giveaway for readers who've seen this trick in a simpler version); has the maid take off on a stumbling walk and then rush home again; and *then*—with a few clever touches (dirt swept out of the house becomes cat whiskers; a swept-off walk becomes a tail)—steps back to reveal house, path, and trimmings as the outline of a giant cat. In a sort of contrapuntal border, humans and animals parade sedately or dash by in predatory chase. Zelinsky gives the tale an antic elegance. (The "wee maid" is not a little girl, as that term suggests, but a spaghetti-thin, white-haired lady in 18th-century costume.) The overall effect is quaint, but spry.

Elaine Edelman

SOURCE: A review of *The Maid and the Mouse and the Odd-Shaped House,* in *The New York Times Book Review,* September 27, 1981, p. 36.

While this odd, intriguing book will drive anyone who tries to explain it (such as adults and reviewers) batty, it will probably entertain many children and may even inspire a few to try similar stories on their own. It's based on a draw-and-tell concept that comes from American folk literature and here allows Paul O. Zelinsky to create the "purest" kind of picture book, one that requires you to read words in order to get hold of its story.

For the story is really a puzzle, and it takes pictures and words in counterpoint to piece it together. If you miss the visual cues, you'll be as befuddled as the wee, 19th-century maid and her pal, the saxophone-playing white mouse, who don't see that their attempts to remodel their odd-shaped house are making a pattern on the pages around them. We do, if we look. We see that the windows these two put in seem a lot like eyes, and the trail drawn by the maid's tumbles when she goes outside to check on a strange hissing noise outlines part of a figure—just what figure isn't clear at first, but page by page it's slowly, suspensefully revealed.

Thus, through handsomely colored and cleverly designed

pages, go a heroine and hero who can't let well enough alone, whose repeated efforts to fix their house are actually creating (without their knowing it) the figure of their enemy. At last, we see it: The odd-shaped house has become the face of a cat! Panic, terror, skedaddle! The maid (drawn as an "old maid," her body as skinny as a question mark, barely holding up her large, quizzical face as she looks out through rimless spectacles on a world she doesn't see) and the mouse escape to safety, to another house where "nothing is odd at all," to live, we assume, happily ever after.

Paul Zelinsky obviously has an odd head of his own. While his antique cartoon style in this book is less emotionally forceful than the realism of his earlier *How I Hunted the Little Fellows,* he's an artist with ideas and great gifts.

Zena Sutherland

SOURCE: A review of *The Maid and the Mouse and the Odd-Shaped House,* in *Bulletin of the Center for Children's Books,* Vol. 35, No. 2, October, 1981, p. 40.

Based on a cumulative participatory tale in rhyme found in late-nineteenth-century school notebooks, this was originally designed so that children would, each in turn, draw their representations of the text. Here it is presented in an oversize book, with mixed media illustrations (ink and gouache) making good use of the page space, with graceful, intentionally disproportionate figures against pastel backgrounds. The mouse-companion is as long as the Maid's head, for example, and several times as wide. There is some inventiveness in the illustrator's use of the story to create a graphic menace, yet the scale and pace of the gradually-achieved dénouement make it lose the focus that might give the story impact, as the Maid's path is traced to create a huge and frightening cat.

David Macaulay

SOURCE: A review of *The Maid and the Mouse and the Odd-Shaped House,* in *The Horn Book Magazine,* Vol. LXII, No. 6, November-December, 1986, p. 722.

The Maid and the Mouse and the Odd-Shaped House grew out of a "tell and draw" story read aloud in a nineteenth-century Connecticut classroom. At various places in the story each child added a piece to a growing picture on the chalkboard, piquing the curiosity of the others.

Zelinsky's large format book with flat, highly-designed drawings, pastel colors, and whimsical line work captures all the playfulness of the original experience. From the beginning, despite its odd shape, the house appears comfortable and secure. In the center of the page it is counterbalanced by text on the facing one. Straight lines that divide the house into rooms and create floor pattern,

fireplace, and chimneys are parallel with the edges of the page. The colors are unthreatening. Less certain elements are shown beyond the safe perimeters of the building—smoke curls, vegetation, people pursued by a bull, a rabbit threatened by an owl. But what is the mysterious hiss, and where does it come from? Outside surely? The maid searches, tracing a path that adds lines to a picture we never see completely. Meanwhile, a frog chases butterflies and distracts us as the maid sweeps the house, adding more lines. Eventually the completed drawing is revealed in its entirety. The house has become the head of a large cat, its body drawn by the lines of the maid's earlier movements. Lines once straight now curve and swell as the cat comes to life. Danger lies in the place we least expect it. The mouse is still inside. We turn the pages quickly now, anxious to know the outcome. No text slows us down. As the cat gradually runs from the page, the maid and mouse flee to a new house, which is far from odd and happens to be placed securely on the center line of the final page. With superb design and masterful pacing, Zelinsky carefully builds an illusion of safety in order to shatter it with an unexpected reality.

THE SUN'S ASLEEP BEHIND THE HILL
(adapted by Mirra Ginsburg, 1982)

Patricia Dooley

SOURCE: A review of *The Sun's Asleep behind the Hill,* in *School Library Journal,* Vol. 28, No. 7, March, 1982, p. 132.

The day winds to a close here in a wonderfully rhythmic and reassuringly orderly fashion. The sun grows tired and goes away "to sleep behind the hill": the breeze, the leaves, the bird, the squirrel and finally, inevitably, the child, also grow tired and seek their rest. The moon comes out, recapitulates the series, and takes possession of the nighttime world. This diurnal drama is set in a vast and rolling park: the artist first draws the scene from a great height, and the subsequent depth of field is interestingly varied throughout, right down to intimate close-ups of the bird and the squirrel in their nests. A kite flown by the small boy provides continuity, appearing on many pages, including the last, wordless image of the full moon shining on the sleeping child (the only indoor scene). The style Zelinsky employs here is as different as possible from that of *The Maid and the Mouse and the Odd-Shaped House* (1981). Color and volume dominate line, and the warm light of a summer evening, the rough underside of a leaf, the softness of a bird's throat are lovingly and realistically painted.

Kirkus Reviews

SOURCE: A review of *The Sun's Asleep behind the Hill,* in *Kirkus Reviews,* Vol. L, No. 6, March 15, 1982, pp. 341-42.

From Rumpelstiltskin, *retold and illustrated by Paul O. Zelinsky.*

"The sun shone/ in the sky all day./ The sun grew tired/ and went away." With those quiet, arresting lines begins an Armenian lullaby reconceived here in spacious, deep-toned pictures—with insets at alternate openings to illustrate the refrain ("The sun shone/ in the sky all day./ The sun grew tired/ and went away/ to sleep behind the hill"). As the twilight deepens, the leaves, the bird, and the squirrel each grows tired and seeks rest; and when the little boy (glimpsed from the first flying his kite) grows tired in turn, his mother carries him homeward—while the moon rises from behind the hill, sings its solitary song, and, on the last wordless page, shines into the little boy's room (where the kite hangs on the wall). That particular scene, potentially a children's-book cliché, has instead a wondering, timeless feel. Altogether a simple, reverberating entity.

Denise M. Wilms

SOURCE: A review of *The Sun's Asleep behind the Hill,* in *Booklist,* Vol. 78, No. 15, April 1, 1982, pp. 1017-18.

Zelinsky's impressive paintings are luxurious interpretations of the fading day, as personified breeze, leaves, and animals all make contingent decisions to rest. Leaves, for example, say, "The breeze blew / in the trees all day./ The breeze grew tired, / The breeze is still./ Now we can also rest.'" Near the end comes a tired child whose mother urges him home; the picture of her carrying him home asleep over her shoulder toward cozy lighted windows is immensely comforting and a suitable lead-in to a finale of moonlit fields and a peaceful bedroom. In fact, the pictures make this poetic mood piece. There is some dramatic sense in the repeated declarations of time for rest, but this would founder were it not for the compelling aura of the darkening scenes.

Zena Sutherland

SOURCE: A review of *The Sun's Asleep behind the Hill,* in *Bulletin of the Center for Children's Books,* Vol. 36, No. 1, September, 1982, p. 9.

Soft paintings of outdoor scenes grow more dark and quiet as the book progresses, a soothing visual accompaniment to Ginsburg's adaptation of an Armenian lullaby. The text has a pattern that gives it shape: the sun goes to sleep behind the hill, and the breeze comments on this and adds, "It's time that I was still," then the leaves comment on the retirement of the breeze (each comment is framed to set it apart from the linking text) and say, "Now we can also rest." A mother brings her child home as the park grows still and dark, the moon comes out, and the last picture shows the child sleeping in the moonlight. A gentle, peaceful book for bedtime reading-aloud.

📖 *ZOO DOINGS: ANIMAL POEMS* (written by Jack Prelutsky, 1983)

Holly Sanhuber

SOURCE: A review of *Zoo Doings: Animal Poems,* in *School Library Journal,* Vol. 29, No. 8, April, 1983, p. 116.

The animal verses from three of Prelutsky's books, *A Gopher in the Garden, Toucans Two* and *The Pack Rat's Day,* are gathered in this single volume. Clever wordplay, these verses are like jellybeans: gobbled quickly as a snack, they offer little in the way of long-lasting nourishment. The rhymes are well constructed, but silly, without being either rib-ticklingly funny or elegantly witty. Line drawings by Paul Zelinsky are a suitable accompaniment to the drollery.

Zena Sutherland

SOURCE: A review of *Zoo Doings: Animal Poems,* in *Bulletin of the Center for Children's Books,* Vol. 36, No. 9, May, 1983, p. 175.

Deft, comic line drawings illustrate a collection of the animal poems from three earlier books by Prelutsky. The subjects are appealing, the verse bouncy and lilting, with strong rhymes and meter. Although not new, the poems are witty, and the book can also be used for reading aloud to younger children.

THE LION AND THE STOAT (1984)

Kirkus Reviews

SOURCE: A review of *The Lion and the Stoat,* in *Kirkus Reviews,* Vol. LII, Nos. 1-5, March 1, 1984, p. J-13.

Three sneaky episodes in the competitive life of rival artists, a lion and a stoat—and a showcase for the elegant wit of author/illustrator Zelinsky (who displays the assurance here of a much older pro). We first meet the pair as, lion in top hat and tails, stoat in scarf and beret, each critically studies a painting by the other (great-art spoofs) at the local museum—where the observant child will not only take in the rivalry at a glance (from the artists' posturings), but also spot the amusing details that Zelinsky distributes sparingly (and all the more tellingly) in his spacious compositions. Episode I has the lion and the stoat agree to a painting contest, at the marketplace. When birds peck at the lion's painted grapes, he claims victory—and challenges the stoat to unveil his painting. "There is no curtain," says the stoat. "Your still life may have fooled the birds, but my painting has fooled you." Episode II is not a guffaw, it's a gasp. (Both, we're told, are from Pliny.) Alone in the stoat's studio, the lion leaves a message—"a very thin, straight line across the middle of the canvas." The stoat, returning, leaves a message in turn—in a different color, "another, even thinner line over the one the lion had made." The lion, coming back, pronounces the result "not bad." But it's his third line, "so thin it was almost invisible," that decides this second contest—as we see the stoat rushing to congratulate the lion at his sidewalk-café dinner. (Slightly Gallic or Pène-du-Bois-ish, yes; whimsical or satiric, not really.) Episode III finds each painting a picture, again in competition, for the new Town Hall—and both painting self-portraits. The mayor, disconcerted, has no choice but to hang both. Meanwhile the two artists, agreeing no-more-contests, head for lunch—and a game of tic-tac-toe on the checked table-cloth. Affectionate and sparkling.

Susan Roman

SOURCE: A review of *The Lion and the Stoat,* in *Booklist,* Vol. 80, No. 19, June 1, 1984, p. 1402.

Zelinsky does an excellent job of illustrating three episodes in the rivalry of two artists, a lion and a stoat. Smugness, surprise, and clever conniving are clearly evident in the animals' faces as they play out the short tales that, according to the author, are based in part on *Natural History* by Pliny the Elder. In the first effort to determine which of the two artists is the best, they arrange for a public contest, which the stoat wins. The

second incident finds the stoat conceding the best line drawing to the lion. By the third go-around, the stoat and the lion understand that each is a fine artist and that they both should forget about competing, bringing the book to a very satisfying ending for the lion and the stoat, as well as for lucky readers and listeners absorbed in the comic, full-color illustrations.

Kathleen Birtciel

SOURCE: A review of *The Lion and the Stoat,* in *School Library Journal,* Vol. 30, No. 10, August, 1984, p. 67.

Zelinsky's lion and stoat are two brilliant and competitive artists who meet in three contests. In the first, the lion's painting of some grapes is so real that it fools the birds into trying to eat it, but the stoat's painting of a red curtain covering a non-existent painting fools the lion and wins the contest. In the next episode, the lion wins a line-drawing contest, and in the third both artists paint self-portraits for the city council. When both are declared winners, they agree to forget about contests, but, in keeping with their competitive nature, are seen in the final illustration engrossed in a game of tic tac toe. The illustrations, reminiscent of William Pène DuBois, depict all the emotions of those involved in a struggle for one-upmanship: pride, vanity, hostility, self-doubt and victory. These bright, four-color illustrations, combined with the economical, subtly humorous text, fill the stories, two of which are based on anecdotes from Pliny's *Natural History,* with child appeal and insight into human nature.

Margery Fisher

SOURCE: A review of *The Lion and the Stoat,* in *Growing Point,* Vol. 24, No. 4, November, 1985, p. 4532.

Two anecdotes of Pliny the Elder are the basis for an engaging duel of ambition between two artists, a lion and a stoat, whose technical achievements are as comical as their egotism. The satire on overweening conceit is carried in a simple, direct text and the personalities of the two animals are confirmed in pictures of dashing colour and mannered shapes in which sundry clichés of the art world are used to comic effect. A picture-book for older boys and girls who can see and apply the point.

HANSEL AND GRETEL (retold by Rika Lesser, 1984)

Kirkus Reviews

SOURCE: A review of *Hansel and Gretel,* in *Kirkus Reviews,* Vol. LII, No. 21, November 1, 1984, p. J90.

An odd, static work for Zelinsky—composed of painterly, Old Master paintings. But these have the eerie, haunting quality of German Romanticism (or, sometimes, of Balthus)—with intimations of real malevolence in the mother who'd leave the children in the forest, truly Wagnerian visions of the forest at sundown and in moonlight, distorted perspectives and drastic foreshortenings in the scenes of imminent danger, and even a welcome-home from their father that works in the same gestural mode. The telling is also stern, unadorned. (Lesser's appended Note explains the omission of the familiar, "Nibble, nibble, little mouse/ Who's that nibbling at my house?") For anyone who wants a cruel and joyous, dire and tender *Hansel and Gretel,* this is it—with the screaming old witch visible through the door of the burning oven as Gretel slams it shut. But be warned: it's the story of good triumphing over evil, not a fairy tale with a happy ending.

Kenneth Marantz

SOURCE: A review of *Hansel and Gretel,* in *School Library Journal,* Vol. 31, No. 4, December, 1984, p. 73.

What, yet another version? And why not! There seems to be at least as much reason to reset some of our classical folk tales as there is for recording a Mozart symphony again and again. Although many attempts are potboilers, others add significantly to the aesthetic delight. Zelinsky's vision is such that he adds fresh nuance to the well-worn story of resolute siblings who courageously fight against their unwholesome social situation. Lesser's telling reflects the earliest, clean-lined versions and leaves out the psychological embellishments frequently included in other settings. The mother (not stepmother) sees the economic impossibility of their poverty and convinces her husband to abandon the children. All the bare bones of the story remain. The pebble gambit works the first time; the crumbs don't pan out the next. The emotional impact is carried out by the paintings. Zelinsky has chosen a painterly style that suggests the naturalistic genre works of the 17th-Century Dutch or German. The paintings are rich in detail of forest and architecture and consistent in the costuming. There is the sharp contrast between the rugged plainness of beds in the woodcutter's cottage (complete with half-hidden chamber pot) and the ornate canopied beds in the witch's house. The scene of the family on the forest's twisting path, the mother and child aproned and capped reminds one of Bruegel's peopled landscapes. The first scene at the cottage's open door has luminosity associated with de Hoach or perhaps Vermeer. In other words, the artist has done a great deal of visual research in order to create convincing stage sets that both carry the necessary information and, much more, that stimulate the emotions. But although naturalistic, there is yet a crudeness, rather than slickness, to the painting that suits this telling. The emphasis is on the solidity of the figures and their gestures and on the design of the details of each picture. In sum, the book evokes a sense of com-

passion and concern rather than horror and retribution. It's a strong reason for continuing to reconceptualize old favorites.

Zena Sutherland

SOURCE: A review of *Hansel and Gretel,* in *Bulletin of the Center for Children's Books,* Vol. 38, No. 7, March, 1985, p. 126.

A simplified retelling of a favorite tale is weakened by the occasional use of language that seems jarringly contemporary, as when the children's mother says, "Just get going!" and by the device of having Gretel ask the witch to demonstrate: "If you get on the board, I'll push you in," whereas the witch in standard versions offers to show Gretel how to get on the board but does not suggest that she be pushed into the oven. The fact that it is the mother (not the stepmother of the standard version) is because Lesser has based her text on an early transcription which apparently was later changed. The full-color paintings on the oversize pages have a dark, old-fashioned look (not inappropriate) on most pages; they tend toward Victorian romanticism.

Ethel L. Heins

SOURCE: A review of *Hansel and Gretel,* in *The Horn Book Magazine,* Vol. LXI, No. 2, March-April, 1985, p. 176.

The folkloric motifs in *Hansel and Gretel* are found in many stories throughout Europe, and even among the numerous German editions of Grimm there is no definitive version. Thus, the present story is not a translation of a single text; direct and unembellished, however, it resembles that of the earliest edition, published in 1812, before the ferocity of the mother had been softened by the term *stepmother* and without the later addition of the final episode of the duck. Every illustrator, of course, has his or her own individual perception of a favorite story and of the essential idea of the picture book. A visual feast, the illustrations frequently recall Flemish and French genre painting of the seventeenth century, while the idyllic woodland scenes reflect a later Romantic mood; much of the artwork constitutes an extraordinary display of skill, composition, and beauty. But the sumptuous, painterly pages and the artist's fascination with elaborate detail, especially in depicting the witch's house, tend to overwhelm the unadorned text and leave too little to the child's imagination.

Barbara Keifer

SOURCE: A review of *Hansel and Gretel,* in *Booklist,* Vol. 83, No. 2, September 15, 1986, p. 139.

Richly detailed paintings evoke the German origins of

this Grimm tale and recall northern Renaissance painters such as Peter Brueghel. Carefully detailed endpapers set the scene and the interplay of light and dark values heightens the drama.

THE STORY OF MRS. LOVEWRIGHT AND PURRLESS HER CAT (written by Lore Segal, 1985)

Publishers Weekly

SOURCE: A review of *The Story of Mrs. Lovewright and Purrless Her Cat,* in *Publishers Weekly,* Vol. 228, No. 16, October 25, 1985, p. 67.

No one will disagree with the statement from Maurice Sendak, who sees the collaboration of author and illustrator as "the essence of an original picture book." Segal adds to her laurels as a novelist, translator and writer of prized children's books with this lark, and so does Zelinsky. His full-color, hilarious pictures are as splendid as his award-winners in **Hansel and Gretel** et al. The story of chilly, unsociable Mrs. Lovewright starts tamely when she asks Dylan, who delivers her groceries, to find a cat, little and cute, to purr on her lap. Dylan delivers, all right, and the kitten is little and cute but he was born with the proud, intransigent character of his kind. He will not purr. He will not curl up cozily on Mrs. Lovewright's lap. The story becomes funnier and more surprising as Purrless and his adversary get into furious battles for supremacy, with Dylan as the interested onlooker, until the wistfully comic resolution.

Betsy Hearne

SOURCE: A review of *The Story of Mrs. Lovewright and Purrless Her Cat,* in *Bulletin of the Center for Children's Books,* Vol. 39, No. 4, December, 1985, p. 78.

Very thin and always cold, Mrs. Lovewright decided that in order to achieve Total Cosiness she needed a cuddly, purring kitten when she sat toasting her toes in front of the fire. The hulking young man who delivers the groceries and who appears periodically to toss in a laconic comment brings a tiny kitten that Mrs. Lovewright immediately names Purrly. Alas, as this saga of a battle of wills progresses, it is clear that Purrly won't purr, won't sit in a lap, and will bite and scratch. As he grows, Purrly becomes harder to evict from the exact center of the footstool or the bed when he establishes squatter's rights. This very funny story has no turnabout ending; it's Purrly Victorious and Mrs. Lovewright who's tamed, although she does rename her obdurate pet. The artist has that happy combination of just-this-side-of exaggeration to achieve humorous effect and a firm control of line and space; he endows each of his characters with a distinct personality that is in judicious accord with the text.

Xenda Casavant

SOURCE: A review of *The Story of Mrs. Lovewright and Purrless Her Cat,* in *School Library Journal,* Vol. 32, No. 4, December, 1985, p. 82.

Spindly, pinched-faced Mrs. Lovewright is a "chilly person." She is also a rather lonely one, and so she decides to get a cat. Her desire for companionship heralds her doom. When Purrless (originally named Purrly) arrives via the delivery boy, he is little and cute, but he steadfastly refuses to purr or even sit upon Mrs. Lovewright's lap. What ensues is a grueling and prolonged battle of wits. As Purrless grows from a small kitten to an enormous cat, children see Mrs. Lovewright scratched, beaten, tumbled out of bed and bombed with a variety of common household objects. Neither character ever grasps the importance of compromise or mutual respect. In the end they are pictured in a tenuous truce with Mrs. Lovewright still lamenting her pet's lack of coziness and Purrless' twitching tail foreshadowing the possibility of future attacks. Although Segal should be commended for her attempt to demonstrate poorly motivated pet ownership and its potential for dire consequences, this story's execution is marred by excessive and inappropriate violence. Jarring transitions further detract from the text and add annoyance. The strongest point is Zelinsky's illustrations, which are both witty and satirical. Each of the characters gains clarity and personality under his sure hand. Textures and subtle colors blend well to portray this quiet home turned battleground. Unfortunately, they do not salvage this unpleasant story of on-going strife.

RUMPELSTILTSKIN (retold by Zelinsky, 1986)

Publishers Weekly

SOURCE: A review of *Rumpelstiltskin,* in *Publishers Weekly,* Vol. 230, No. 8, August 22, 1986, p. 92.

One of the most exquisite picture books of the season, Zelinsky's **Rumpelstiltskin** will have strong appeal for children and for adult picture-book collectors alike. The artist has illustrated numerous award-winners, including **Hansel and Gretel** (a Caldecott Honor Book) and **The Story of Mrs. Lovewright and Purrless Her Cat** (a *New York Times* Best Illustrated Book of the Year).

Here Zelinsky has retold the fairy tale himself; he has captured its magic and frightening wonder while incorporating elements from a number of 19th century Grimm versions. The spare story flows beautifully, and the illustrations are extraordinary. Incredibly detailed full-color paintings show the influence of careful study of styles and techniques of European portrait and landscape painters. In **Hansel and Gretel,** the tale's dark side was communicated principally through Zelinsky's depiction of a powerful and frightening background. But here the interior scenes—heaps and heaps of straw, and baskets of empty spindles, with rooms suddenly full of golden thread—carry the story. The little man Rumpelstiltskin is by turns mysterious, comforting, devious, furious and pathetic. And Zelinsky shows dramatically the love that the miller's daughter has for her child, and the terror she feels when she realizes she may have to give him up.

Rumpelstiltskin is a tour de force by an immensely talented artist. Zelinsky is that rare creative spirit who can produce sophisticated work that adults will marvel at, and that children will joyfully embrace.

Ilene Cooper

SOURCE: A review of *Rumpelstiltskin,* in *Booklist,* Vol. 83, No. 1, September 1, 1986, p. 69.

Those who admired Zelinsky's artistic interpretation of *Hansel and Gretel* will find his *Rumpelstiltskin* very different and even more exquisitely wrought. *Hansel and Gretel* was notable for its panoramic overviews with individual characters taking a backseat to the sweeping development of the tale. Here the artwork grips with its riveting close-ups. The paintings feature a realistic miller's daughter who gets unexpected help in turning her bunches of hay into shimmering gold thread from a gnomelike little man outfitted in medieval garb. Zelinsky makes thoughtful use of composition and provides strong interplay between light and shadow. His jeweled tones and precise renderings give his pictures a museum-quality look. Special attention is given to architectural details—windows, posts, beams, and doorways all have significance and yet are well integrated. The care of each brush stroke is apparent in every piece of hay and thread of gold. A detailed author's note explains that the artist based his text primarily on the 1819 version of "Rumpelstiltskin" found in the Grimms' *Children and Household Tales.* However, Zelinsky's story uses an earlier, less-violent ending in which the little man runs off rather than tearing himself in half when his name is discovered. The tale also has subtle feminist overtones—it is the miller's daughter and a female servant who outwit Rumpelstiltskin. A lush and substantial offering.

Kirkus Reviews

SOURCE: A review of *Rumpelstiltskin,* in *Kirkus Reviews,* Vol. LIV, No. 18, September 15, 1986, p. 1447.

After comparing several of the original Grimm variants, Zelinsky has selected and retold to make his own version. Graceful and lucid, it differs from the familiar in having the imp overheard crowing about his name by a servant rather than by the king, and by having him ride about and ultimately depart forever on a cooking spoon, a non-violent conclusion.

Zelinsky's illustrations are opulently painted, full of classical architectural detail, fantastic distant landscapes, and that early use of perspective which gives a raked stage effect. Rumpelstiltskin is a bug-eyed, spindle-legged Machiavelli of an imp, dressed as a courtier. The miller's daughter/queen has the face of a madonna, although her expressions are contemporary enough to interest modern children in her plight. The king (not a savory character, since he was prepared to murder his wife if she failed to spin straw into gold) stays in the background.

A distinguished edition of one of Grimms' favorite tales.

Susan H. Patron

SOURCE: A review of *Rumpelstiltskin,* in *School Library Journal,* Vol. 33, No. 2, October, 1986, p. 168.

Zelinsky's painterly style and rich colors provide an evocative backdrop to this story. The medieval setting and costumes and the spools of gold thread which shine on the page like real gold are suggestive of an illuminated manuscript. Without overpowering the text, the illustrations give depth and background, providing exquisite texture and detail: the castle interior; subtle facial expressions; the foreboding landscape when Rumpelstiltskin is overheard to reveal his name. The imp himself is deeply fascinating, with his bird-like features, tiny agile body, and Rackhamesque hands and feet. This retelling is based on the 1819 Grimm version. Zelinsky's ending, in which Rumpelstiltskin flies away on his wooden spoon, is a departure from the source, wherein he stomps one foot deep in the ground, grabbing the other foot and tearing himself in half. . . . Zelinsky's smooth retelling and glowing pictures cast the story in a new and beautiful light.

Mary M. Burns

SOURCE: A review of *Rumpelstiltskin,* in *The Horn Book Magazine,* Vol. LXII, No. 6, November-December, 1986, pp. 751-52.

Reviewing a book illustrated by Paul Zelinsky is both a pleasure and a challenge. Because of his versatility, each book is an entity in itself; each is a new work, distinctive but not necessarily reminiscent of a total *oeuvre.* *Rumpelstiltskin* is no exception, for Zelinsky has decided to present his version of the familiar Grimm story as fine art through large scale, richly hued oil paintings, notable for careful composition and exquisite rendering of detail. But these paintings are first and foremost illustrations and not simply a gallery of pictures in the grand tradition, for the emphasis on the characters—gestures, expressions, posture—are visual clues to attitudes suggested by the narrative, making the personalities come alive. The appended "Note on the Text" indicates the care with which the artist researched variant tellings before creating "a text best suited for a picture book." Consequently, this retelling of the beautiful miller's daughter who succeeds in overcoming the greed of the various male figures who dominated her life becomes a new and stimulating experience. The emphasis on setting as well as on characters places the story within a specific framework, challenging the artist to suggest, but not slavishly imitate, the style of the period: landscapes glimpsed through doors or windows give a sense of depth and distance found in portraits from the Italian school; the use of light and shadow to emphasize the luster of gold, the shimmer of fabric, the richness of the palace's furnishings is a brilliant adaptation of techniques employed by masters of the Flemish school; the figure of Rumpelstiltskin could have been conceived by Velázquez. Yet, for all their elegance, the illustrations are comprehensible, dynamic, compelling, and unforgettable, imbued with human—and humorous touches: a large winged insect drowses on the stone column of the first straw-filled room; the triumphant Rumpelstiltskin rides on a wooden cooking spoon; and the Queen smirks with unroyal pride as she banishes her would-be nemesis. Even the endpapers with panoramic views of the countryside are integrated into the design of the whole, for Zelinsky is at heart a storyteller—one of the most important distinctions between an artist and the artist who is an illustrator. This book is truly a *tour de force*.

Marcus Crouch

SOURCE: A review of *Rumpelstiltskin,* in *The Junior Bookshelf,* Vol. 51, No. 3, June, 1987, pp. 119-20.

Paul Zelinsky has worked hard on his version of **Rumpelstiltskin,** not only in the superbly detailed and finely crafted illustrations but also in establishing a text based on variants of the familiar story. He provides a note on his sources at the end of his book. Whether the results justify his labour may be in doubt. His text is adequate but unexciting, and the ending may seem tame to children brought up on the robust brutality of the traditional version. About the pictures there is unlikely to be much dissention. Paul Zelinsky has an impeccable technique and a consistent viewpoint. The miller's daughter makes a most convincing queen, gravely beautiful and dignified, and all the architectural and decorative details of her palace are put before us. The final effect may be a little too lush—this story after all offers a peasant's view of the high life—but it is beyond question impressive.

📖 ***THE RANDOM HOUSE BOOK OF HUMOR FOR CHILDREN* (edited by Pamela Pollock, 1988)**

Kirkus Reviews

SOURCE: A review of *The Random House Book of Humor for Children,* in *Kirkus Reviews,* Vol. LVI, No. 21, November 1, 1988, p. 1609.

A splendid collection of 34 stories, many of them excerpts from familiar children's books by such favorite contemporaries as Byars and Cleary and from classics like those by Twain and T. H. White. The book starts with an all-time winner that also illustrates a problem: Fudge swallowing the turtle in Blume's *Tales of a Fourth Grade Nothing* is not *quite* as funny taken out of context, although it is still funny enough to whet appetites (if that's necessary!) for the whole (book, not turtle). The short stories (Kipling, Natalie Babbitt) stand better on their own; some nontraditional inclusions (Saki, Shirley Jackson) are among the best offerings. All are in the comic tradition, though there are more chuckles than belly-laughs here; more important, all have proven appeal, and most are of good literary quality.

Though libraries already have most of these selections in other forms, Zelinsky's illustrations make it an essential library purchase—and a winning one for the home. Each of the soft black-and-white drawings, many of them full-page, is an inspired new slant on an old favorite, without intruding on beloved preconceptions. Full of the movement and tension born of masterful design, burgeoning with humor and delightful characterizations, they represent an unusual achievement in illustration. Even Zelinsky's Homer Price is a worthy rendition (though his reverential treatment here uncharacteristically lacks the vitality of the original). Grand for browsing, sharing aloud, or as inspiration for further reading.

John Peters

SOURCE: A review of *The Random House Book of Humor for Children,* in *School Library Journal,* Vol. 35, No. 4, December, 1988, pp. 110-11.

This fresh, substantial prose anthology of modern humor will send middle-grade readers scurrying to the library shelves for more. The table of contents reads like a roll-call of popular authors—Judy Blume, Richard Peck, Robert Newton Peck, Betsy Byars, Beverly Cleary, Roald Dahl, Thomas Rockwell, and more—with a few surprises thrown in: Garrison Keillor, Delia Ephron, even a Bob & Ray script. Episodes vary greatly in length, from two to about two dozen pages; the print is comfortably large; and Zelinsky's rubbery, expressive drawings not only bind the collection together while setting individual moods for each story, but also, where appropriate, subtly evoke the original illustrations. Although most of the extracts stand alone, Pollack adds an introductory sentence or two where needed. Several tried-and-true entries ("The Elephant's Child," for instance, and Thurber's "The Moth and the Star") provide historical depth. Outstanding booktalk material, too.

Mary M. Burns

SOURCE: A review of *The Random House Book of Humor for Children,* in *The Horn Book Magazine,* Vol. LXV, No. 2, March-April, 1989, pp. 211-12.

Thirty-four selections, including excerpts from novels, short stories, and a radio script dialogue, guarantee that there is something in this volume to satisfy a variety of intermediate and older readers. Some are staples in the humorist's repertoire: "The Elephant's Child" by Rudyard Kipling and the doughnut machine episode from *Homer Price* by Robert McCloskey. Many are selections from well-known books by popular contemporary authors: for example, *Tales of a Fourth Grade Nothing* by Judy Blume, *The Midnight Fox* by Betsy Byars, and *Beezus and Ramona* by Beverly Cleary. What adds spice and depth are the passages from books originally intended for adults but accessible to younger readers, such as Garrison Keillor's description of the nervous fourth-grade teacher from *Lake Wobegon Days* and the wickedly delicious parody "Prodigy Street" from *Write If You Get Work: The Best of Bob and Ray*. Nor are the popular titles of earlier years forgotten. Pollack is to be commended for her prodigious efforts in securing adequate representation from past and present, from the slapstick to the sophisticated, from the poignant to pure exaggeration. A superb resource for reading aloud as well as for introducing the originals, the book is a thoughtfully produced anthology which belongs in every library, school, and home. It would make a perfect traveling companion, as the selections are short enough to finish at one sitting and sufficiently universal to reach a wide range of listeners and readers. Paul Zelinsky's illustrations, executed in modulating grays, are designed for visual unity; redefined in bright colors, they transform the endpapers into decorative invitations. In a few instances, however, notably in the images of Ramona and her family, the newer illustrations cannot quite compete with their predecessors, now firmly impressed on the collective memory of generations of fans.

📖 THE WHEELS ON THE BUS: A BOOK WITH PICTURES THAT MOVE AND OCCASIONALLY POP UP (adapted by Zelinsky, 1990)

Publishers Weekly

SOURCE: A review of *The Wheels on the Bus: A Book with Pictures that Move and Occasionally Pop Up,* in *Publishers Weekly,* Vol. 237, No. 39, September 28, 1990, p. 100.

In an ingeniously designed, deftly executed lift-the-flap (and pull-the-tab) book, Zelinsky elaborates on the well-known and much-loved children's song. Not only do its wheels go round and round, but the bus here also has doors that open and shut, windshield wipers that move back and forth, and so on. The text consists of the lyrics of the song itself, but Zelinsky has neatly inserted a number of visual subplots that flesh out the story—one involving a boy with a boxful of adventurous kittens, another a motorcyclist and her runaway puppy, a third a young man with a guitar. The music and refrain are included on the back cover, and those unfamiliar with the song may well want to bone up in order to sing the book's praises to the most appropriate tune.

Roger Sutton

SOURCE: A review of *The Wheels on the Bus: A Book with Pictures that Move and Occasionally Pop Up,* in *Bulletin of the Center for Children's Books,* Vol. 44, No. 2, October, 1990, p. 50.

The wheels on this bus really do go round and round, the wipers swish-swish-swish, and, funniest of all, the babies waah-waah-waah while their mothers' eyes roll with frustrated dismay. And, oh joy, this bus is on its way to the library. There's inherent wit in the joining of repetitive chant with the push-and-pull tabs of a pop-up book, but Zelinsky is not content to let the gimmick alone do his job for him. His colors are post-modern pinks and purples while the woozy perspectives are post-office WPA and Thomas Hart Benton. The last picture is magnificent, sprawling paint and perspectives and pop-ups across a double-spread to reprise the entire song. A real trip.

John Peters

SOURCE: A review of *The Wheels on the Bus: A Book with Pictures that Move and Occasionally Pop Up,* in *School Library Journal,* Vol. 36, No. 10, October, 1990, p. 106.

The wheels on the bus literally go 'round in this brilliantly designed and produced pop-up edition of the familiar participation song. The realistic special effects use pull-tabs plus a few lifted flaps; doors open and close, wipers swish, babies comically "WAAAH!," and mothers "Shh!" as the bus bounces its way "all over town," arriving at last at the Overtown Public Library in time for a musical program. A compressed, undulating perspective and swirling colors animate each vigorously busy scene. Figures are rendered with slightly exaggerated but individual gestures and expressions, and there's plenty of detail and byplay for readers to pick out. The song, with its repeated but contained gestures, is a perfect choice for a pop-up, for the art and engineering are woven together seamlessly, and the book will lose little of its appeal after the moving parts have run their race. Music is included on the back cover.

Elizabeth S. Watson

SOURCE: A review of *The Wheels on the Bus: A Book with Pictures that Move and Occasionally Pop Up,* in *The Horn Book Magazine,* Vol. LXVII, No. 1, January-February, 1991, p. 80.

Fresh, lively, and imaginative, this adaptation of the traditional rhyme and song beloved by thousands of preschoolers rollicks along to the familiar tune depicted on the back cover. Not only does a man with a guitar board the city bus, bound to perform his folk songs at the public library, but so does a boy carrying a box of curious kittens, a lady carrying overstuffed bags of groceries, and lots of mothers and babies. As if a fine old song and Paul Zelinsky's new interpretation were not enough, the book also features paper engineering—flaps, fold-outs, and other items to manipulate. Wheels that spin, windows that move up and down, windshield wipers that go "swish, swish, swish," and a last double-page spread that reviews the whole trip will enthrall youngsters. Some of the tabs don't pull as smoothly as one would wish, but the construction is very sturdy, and the whole product, enchanting.

Kristina Lindsay

SOURCE: A review of *The Wheels on the Bus: A Book with Pictures that Move and Occasionally Pop Up,* in *Magpies,* Vol. 6, No. 4, September, 1991, p. 25.

Adapted from the traditional song and rhyme, **The Wheels on the Bus** is a creative and delightful new picture book with parts that move. Children will enjoy spinning the wheels round, sliding the windows up and down and pulling the wipers back and forth on the bus while chanting the expressive, rhythmic text.

The illustrations are amusingly clever and bright. The book is ideal for the very young child as well as appealing instantly to the older child with all its enjoyable features. The only disadvantage for a book such as this one is it's durability—how long will it last in the hands of children? I doubt it would last very long in a busy library, but if you are prepared to use it with adult supervision it should survive! For example the book will make an excellent storytelling tool where you can sing the traditional rhyme and then show the picture book. The movable parts of this book have been creatively designed and to finish off it is nice to see the destination of this bus—the local public library!

THE ENCHANTED CASTLE (written by E. Nesbit, 1992)

Carolyn Phelan

SOURCE: A review of *The Enchanted Castle,* in *Booklist,* Vol. 89, No. 8, December 15, 1992, p. 738.

Originally published in 1907, this book concerns four likable English children and their adventures with a magic ring. It's hard to imagine a more appealing showcase for Nesbit's fantasy than this handsome volume, which features paper of fine quality, pages with generous margins, and a dozen plates with full-page illustrations. With fine, cross-hatched lines tinted in luminous colors, Zelinsky's artwork is as lively as the story and very much of the period. While the novel is not one of Nesbit's best, this beautiful book is recommended for larger fiction collections.

MORE ROOTABAGAS (written by Carl Sandburg, 1993)

Publishers Weekly

SOURCE: A review of *More Rootabagas,* in *Publishers Weekly,* Vol. 240, No. 41, October 11, 1993, p. 88.

In his foreword, George Hendrick explains that Sandburg, searching for bedtime stories for his three daughters, lamented the lack of fairy tales native to this country. So the Pulitzer Prize-winning poet and biographer of Abraham Lincoln wrote three volumes of his own, which he described as "tales with American fooling in them." There is indeed "fooling" and whimsy aplenty in the 10 previously unpublished tales collected in this cleverly designed, exquisitely illustrated book. In several (but disappointingly few) spots, the type is manipulated playfully around Zelinsky's wondrously inventive art, rendered colored pencil on plastivellum drafting film. Alliteration and clever—if decidedly unorthodox—word usage and sentence structure abound, as do such curious character names as Peter Potato Blossom Wishes, Dippy the Wisp and Sweeter Than the Bees Humming. This all makes for mellifluous, ear-pleasing passages when read aloud, though beginning readers may have trouble tackling some of the text-heavy pages, and may need help deciphering sentences such as "You give the horses many thoughtfuls, it seems to me." Few readers—or listeners—will easily forget Sandburg's unique characters—among them five whispering blue cats that seem to disappear when held up to the sky, a three-legged hat dancer and a green hat-eating horse. And visions of Zelinsky's magical renditions of each will linger equally long.

Kenneth Marantz

SOURCE: A review of *More Rootabagas,* in *School Library Journal,* Vol. 39, No. 12, December, 1993, p. 116.

Sandburg's poetic talents invest these 10 stories with sounds and rhythms that will make readers' imaginations dance. Characters with names like "Ax Me No Questions," "Silver Pitchers," and "Hoboken Kitty-Kitty" will tickle children's funny bones. Words like "slimpsing," "huck bug," and "mooches," and phrases like "sleepy songs soft" and "you snoof of a snitch" will make them realize the potential of language to rise above the mundane. Zelinsky complements the stories with colored-pencil drawings that echo their emotional content while maintaining a more naturalistic array of images. The title page of each piece shows a rootabaga with some subtle but intriguing hints of what's to come. Other illustrations depict bits of action or portraits of characters, piquing interest and eliciting sympathy. The designer has woven text and pictures into a seamless sequence of pages that allows Sandburg's witty wisdom and Zelinsky's artistic inspiration to sing in unison.

Carolyn Phelan

SOURCE: A review of *More Rootabagas*, in *Booklist*, Vol. 90, No. 7, December 1, 1993, p. 691.

Culled from Sandburg's unpublished papers, these 10 Rootabagas appear in print for the first time, plucked and scrubbed and beautifully packaged. Though little read by children today, the stories in the older volumes (*Rootabaga Stories*, *Part* 1 and *Part* 2) are still beloved by some readers. Like the previous Rootabaga stories, Sandburg's "American fairy tales," these work best when read aloud so that their words, cadences, and repeated sounds can cast their dreamy, hypnotic spell. Besides Sandburg's name, this collection's main selling point is Zelinsky's artwork. Fresh, energetic, and well composed, the colorful shaded pencil drawings illustrate the tales with originality and wit. Recommended for larger collections and those with a demand for Rootabagas.

SWAMP ANGEL (written by Anne Isaacs, 1994)

Publishers Weekly

SOURCE: A review of *Swamp Angel*, in *Publishers Weekly*, Vol. 241, No. 40, October 3, 1994, p. 69.

Zelinsky's stunning American-primitive oil paintings, set against an unusual background of cherry, maple and birch veneers, frankly steal the show here. Their success, however, does not diminish the accomplishment of Isaacs, whose feisty tall tale marks an impressive picture-book debut. Her energy-charged narrative introduces Angelica Longrider. "On August 1, 1815," Isaacs begins, "when [she] took her first gulp of air on this earth, there was nothing about the baby to suggest that she would become the greatest woodswoman in Tennessee. The newborn was scarcely taller than her mother and couldn't climb a tree without help. . . . She was a full two years old before she built her first log cabin." The story continues in this casually overstated vein, explaining how Angelica got the appellation Swamp Angel at the age of 12 after rescuing a wagon train mired in the mud. But the larger-than-life girl's reputation grows to truly gargantuan proportions when she bests an even larger bear, throwing him up in the sky, where "he crashed into a pile of stars, making a lasting impression. You can still see him there, any clear night." This valiant heroine is certain to leave youngsters chuckling—and perhaps even keeping a close watch on the night sky.

Hazel Rochman

SOURCE: A review of *Swamp Angel*, in *Booklist*, Vol. 91, No. 4, October 15, 1994, p. 424.

Forget those images of angelic maidens, ethereal and demure. Angelica Longrider is the greatest woodswoman in Tennessee. She can lasso a tornado. She can toss a bear into the sky so hard that it is still on the way up at nightfall. She snores like a locomotive in a thunderstorm. Isaacs tells her original story with the glorious exaggeration and uproarious farce of the traditional tall tale and with its typical laconic idiom—you just can't help reading it aloud. The heroine was nothing special as a newborn baby ("scarcely taller than her mother and couldn't climb a tree without help . . . She was a full two years old before she built her first log cabin"). Zelinsky's detailed oil paintings in folk-art style are exquisite, framed in cherry, maple, and birch wood grains. They are also hilarious, making brilliant use of perspective to extend the mischief and the droll understatement. Sweet-faced Angelica wears a straw bonnet and a homespun dress, but she's a stalwart savior who comes tramping out of the mist on huge bare feet to lift a wagon train from Dejection Swamp. She is bent over in many of the pictures as if too tall to fit in the elegant oval frames. Pair this picture book with [Julius] Lester and [Jerry] Pinkney's *John Henry* for a gigantic tall-tale celebration.

Jack Zipes

SOURCE: "Power Rangers of Yore," in *The New York Times Book Review*, November 13, 1994, p. 30.

It is a joy to read tall tales and legends that revise American folklore in provocative ways and are just as interesting for adults as they are for children. . . .

In the case of *Swamp Angel* we have [a] poignant [example] of how contemporary writers and illustrators use fabulous stories to suggest that we still have a lot to learn from folk heroes, even if they may not have existed.

Anne Isaacs begins her tale by simply stating that a certain Angelica Longrider was born on August 1, 1815. Immediately thereafter, however, we discover that Angelica was almost a giant at birth and became the greatest woodswoman in Tennessee. "Although her father gave her a shiny new ax to play with in the cradle, like any good Tennessee father would, she was a full two years old before she built her first log cabin." It is Ms. Isaacs's dry, tongue-in-cheek style, moving us from possibility to impossibility, matched by the stunning primitive and burlesque-style oil paintings done on wood veneers by Paul O. Zelinsky, that makes this book one of the most intriguing and hilarious tall tales to be published in recent years.

Angelica becomes known as Swamp Angel after she saves a wagon train mired in Dejection Swamp, but her fame is ultimately based on her struggles with a ferocious bear named Thundering Tarnation, which ravages homesteads in Tennessee. So powerful and cunning is this bear that a huge reward is offered for anyone who can kill it. Despite the valiant attempts of many brave men, it is only Angel who is savvy and strong enough to take on the critter. In several striking full-spread illustrations, Mr. Zelinsky depicts a wrestling match that covers the Tennessee landscape and is reminiscent of the great celestial combat of the Greek gods. Angel and Tarnation continue to wrestle in their sleep, snoring so loudly that they bring down the trees around them. She finally defeats the bear by snoring down one last tree, which accidentally knocks the bear dead, and there is a great celebration. All the folks in Tennessee enjoy a feast of bear meat and dance away the night to commemorate Angel's victory. The next morning she drags Tarnation's enormous pelt toward Montana, creating the Great Plains along her way.

There are very few tall tales about extraordinary women in American folklore compared to those that extol the virtues of men, and this comic rendition about a gifted, powerful and helpful woman is in all ways superb.

M. P. Dunleavey

SOURCE: "The Bedeviled *Swamp Angel*," in *Publishers Weekly*, Vol. 241, No. 48, November 28, 1994, pp. 30-1.

Asking illustrator Paul Zelinsky—or anyone at Dutton—to talk about his latest picture book, *Swamp Angel*, written by Anne Isaacs, is a bit like getting *Titanic* survivors to recall the iceberg. While they're willing to preserve their story for posterity, they're really just thankful to be alive.

"I don't even want to remember the anxiety," shudders Donna Brooks, executive editor of Dutton Children's Books. "There was a curse on this book from the moment I started it," agrees Zelinsky. But to look at the serene, golden-hued landscapes in the book that was just named a *New York Times* Best Illustrated Book of the Year, no one would ever know that the ordeal was on the Paul Bunyanesque scale of the Swamp Angel herself. So fraught with mishap it makes Murphy's Law seem optimistic, the tale of how *Swamp Angel* started as an unsolicited manuscript and emerged a Caldecott contender is the story of a bad day that lasted for two years.

The manuscript, from a completely unknown writer, arrived on Brooks's desk in early 1991. It recounted the legend of one Angelica Longrider, destined to become the "greatest woodswoman in Tennessee. The newborn was scarcely taller than her mother and couldn't climb a tree without help," Isaacs's tall tale begins.

Brooks sent the story to Zelinsky, who liked it so much that even though he had other projects on his plate, he committed to a fall '93 delivery, for publication in fall '94. Unfortunately, he fell behind and couldn't begin work on *Swamp Angel* until May '93. That was all right with Brooks. She had very simple artwork in mind. With the story taking place during frontier days, Brooks imagined something straightforward in pencil or crayon. She recalls thinking, "This will be so easy."

And with another illustrator, it might have been. But Dutton's art director, Sara Reynolds, is now convinced Zelinsky draws his inspiration from a good stiff challenge. "He takes on projects other illustrators would shy away from," she says. "That tendency to push himself is what makes his work so spectacular."

That said, Reynolds admits that in 15 years in the business she has never seen a picture book "quite so ambitious or with quite so many opportunities for things to go wrong."

The first thing to go wrong was the paper. In these days of high-tech wizardry, a casual observer thumbing through *Swamp Angel* might think that the wood surrounding the images was somehow computer-generated. In fact, they are painted on very thin wood veneer paper that cost $12 a sheet. Zelinsky was inspired by a 19th-century American folk painting by Linton Park, "The Flax Scutching Bee," that had been executed on mattress ticking. Zelinsky felt that a particular cherry-colored, wood-grained paper he had seen months before in an art supply store would make a perfect folk-like background.

It was now mid-summer 1993, and the distributor for that particular paper was going out of business. Though the fall '93 delivery date by now was out of the question, Zelinsky says Dutton took the delay in stride, understanding that the paper was fundamental to the project. When a shipment arrived in late August, Zelinsky bought 10 of the best sheets, and, he says, "I became a scientist." He prepped and primed until he found the perfect way to prepare the wood so it wouldn't curl and could take the paint. These pieces he sent to Hong Kong for a test shoot.

Though color reproduction is a complicated process that involves wrapping the art around special cylinders, called drums, it didn't occur to Brooks that the thickness of the wood veneer might be a problem. "I think I was in denial," she says. But the test went fine, the wood was flexible enough and the color reproduced nicely. In the meantime, Zelinsky had made some sketches and dummies, and all systems were go. Except for one thing: he needed more paper, and the store was fresh out. And the distributor was completely out of business. So, by hook and by crook (and the promise of a very large order), the store manager somehow procured 30 sheets of the wood-grained paper by November 30.

By now, having materials to show at the 1994 ABA convention was out of the question. Dutton decided to print a blad, a 16-page preview of the book. But Zelinsky was having trouble getting his paper to uncurl, because the wood's paper backing was so thin. He took it to a framer to have it drymounted (for a mere $13 a sheet), and finally began to paint. "This was December," Zelinsky says, "and at Dutton they were biting their nails. They desperately wanted at least two finished paintings for their sales conference." He commenced 100-hour work weeks, painting until 2 a.m. and rising early to get his daughters to school, trying to get paintings ready for the January sales conference and for the blad, due in February. All was going well, but "the hex had not lifted," he says.

The framer charged with uncurling the unruly paper and mounting it had bent it the other way, and the entire batch was ruined. "We had a joke," Brooks recalls grimly, "that there was another angel besides Swamp Angel—the Dark Angel."

In his studio building in Brooklyn, Zelinsky says, tenants circulate old magazines rather than throwing them away. He had saved a copy of a woodworking magazine, which happened to have an ad for a maker of flexible wood veneer. "My heart lifted," he says. He ordered the 4 x 10 sheet sight unseen and had them send it via UPS.

But UPS was on strike. The strike ended the next day, but then a series of snowstorms struck the Northeast. The sheet of maple finally arrived on February 15. "I was worried for months," Brooks confesses, "but I had complete faith in Paul." Brooks, who has worked with Zelinsky since 1977, edited his first picture book, *How I Hunted the Little Fellows* (1979) and both of his Caldecott Honor books, *Hansel and Gretel* (1984) and *Rumpelstiltskin* (1986). "It wasn't so much that Paul was late, but that we were being dogged by some outside force," she says.

The Dark Angel entered the picture again. The new sheet of maple wood veneer was thick. "But I was so happy to have gotten the paper that I put the thickness of it right out of my head," Zelinsky admits ruefully.

The pages, sent to Hong Kong for the blad printing, would not fit on the drum, a fax informed Dutton. Fortunately, only two paintings were affected and Zelinsky set to work sanding them down. It was March 1994. "I was grinding from the back of the painting, hoping I wouldn't go through the front or crack it into pieces," he says. "It was nerve-wracking," Reynolds recalls, "because we didn't want him to ruin what he'd already done."

Somehow, the paintings survived. Zelinsky resumed his round-the-clock schedule; he finished all but the last three paintings by May 23 and shipped the art to Hong Kong. The end was in sight, but the worst was yet to come.

Like the assassination of JFK, everyone remembers exactly where they were and what they were doing when the fax rang out from Hong Kong with the news. "Hong Kong said there seemed to be little white fibers stuck in the varnish of all the painting," Zelinsky recalls. "And we didn't know if they were being cautious or it really looked terrible. So there was nothing to do but have it all shipped back." Once it arrived the damage was far worse than anyone had imagined. "It looked as though huge swaths of the covering paper had gotten stuck to the paintings," Zelinsky says. "We all lost it," says

Brooks. "That was when we began to wonder if we'd ever get out from under."

Reynolds sent the art, with Zelinsky in tow, to an art conservator who chastised him for not letting the oil paint dry the recommended six months before varnishing. The problem was that the varnish had melted, interacting with the paint and sticking to the tracing paper, clouding the finish. The conservator had a week to dissolve the varnish by reapplying a new and different varnish to every page, with everyone praying that the paintings would become visible through the new layer. It was now June.

"I was verging on apoplexy," says Zelinsky. "But with each thing that happened I felt that much more determined not to let it stop me."

The varnish trick worked, and the art, miraculously, was unscathed. The conservator built a special box so that nothing would come near the surface of any of the paintings, and they were packed off, gingerly, to Hong Kong in mid-June. At last, says Zelinsky, "the hex was off."

Though the printing wasn't exactly easy ("We lost an extra day and night somehow," says Zelinsky), *Swamp Angel* was printed more or less without incident in Massachusetts in August. And Zelinsky admits, "I was more pleased than I usually am."

The book has earned reviewers' praise (in addition to the *New York Times* award, it was named one of *PW*'s Best Books of 1994). The few cracks and flaws that remain in the artwork, says Reynolds, "enhance that American primitive style." Indeed, there is a museum-like quality to *Swamp Angel,* a feeling of familiarity to the images, in part because they look old enough to suggest a legend that has been told again and again. And as the tale of the book's harrowing creation is told and retold, perhaps it too will become the stuff of legend.

Wendy Lukehart

SOURCE: A review of *Swamp Angel,* in *School Library Journal,* Vol. 40, No. 12, December, 1994, p. 76.

Newborn Angelica Longrider, "scarcely taller than her mother," was a "full two years old before she built her first log cabin." Thus begins Isaacs's original tall tale, and she captures the cadence of the genre perfectly with its unique blend of understatement, exaggeration, and alliteration. Set in Tennessee, it is the story of a resourceful young woman who rescued wagon trains "mired in Dejection Swamp." Now she has set her sights on saving settlers from an enormous black bear named Thundering Tarnation and beating the lineup of male competitors in the process. Zelinsky paints his primitive views of Americana with oil on veneer, a choice that gives each page a grainy border, well suited to this backwoods tale. A master of composition, he varies readers' perspectives by framing the portrait of the newborn and, later, the series of male hunters with small ovals. He uses double-page lunettes to depict the massive bear and woman sprawled across the pages, and places the menacing beast lunging over the frame in another memorable scene. The pictures and words cavort across the page in perfect synchronization, revealing the heroine's feisty solution. Buy for a great guffaw in small groups or one-on-one. It's an American classic in the making.

📖 *RAPUNZEL* (retold by Zelinsky, 1997)

Paul O. Zelinsky

SOURCE: "Artist's Notes on the Creation of Rapunzel," in *Journal of Youth Services in Libraries,* Vol. 11, No. 3, Spring, 1998, pp. 214-17.

"Rapunzel" has a rich and surprising history. Although Wilhelm and Jacob Grimm included it in their famous collection of German folktales, *Children's and Household Tales,* their "Rapunzel" was hardly the rustic story of "folk" origin that they implied it to be. It was actually their own adaptation of a rather elegant story of the same name, published in Leipzig some twenty years earlier. That "Rapunzel" was a loose German translation of a much older French literary fairy tale, which itself drew heavily on a story published in Naples, a story that did have a local folktale as its source.

Il Pentamerone, or *The Tale of Tales,* written in the Neapolitan dialect by Giambattista Basile and published in 1634, was a colorful and sometimes ribald collection of stories-within-a-framing-story, in the manner of *The Thousand and One Nights.* One of its tales was "Petrosinella."

In this story a pregnant mother, craving her witch-neighbor's parsley (called *petrosine* in Neapolitan), is caught in the act of stealing it. Seven years later the witch collects on her debt, taking the young, long-haired Petrosinella to live with her in a tower. After some time, a prince happens on the tower, climbs the braids hanging from its window, and falls in love with Petrosinella. A neighbor sees his nighttime visits and warns the witch that Petrosinella may soon run away. The witch brags that the girl is held by a charm and cannot flee. But Petrosinella and her prince elope, using a rope and the witch's own amulets: magic acorns that allow them to evade her fierce pursuit.

When a vogue for fairy tales swept Europe in the late seventeenth century, *Il Pentamerone* inspired a French noblewoman, Charlotte-Rose de Caumont La Force, to write her own *Tale of Tales*. Published in 1697, these stories were written in a nunnery—La Force had been banished from Louis XIV's court for her scandalous satirical novels. *La Conte des Contes* included "Persinette," an elaborate tale based in part on "Petrosinella."

Here a newly wed and pregnant young wife urges her husband to steal parsley *(persil)* from the neighboring garden of a fairy. The husband is caught, and the fairy claims the child, Persinette, at birth. Twelve years later the fairy moves the long-haired girl into a magical silver tower deep in the woods. There, in its many glowing rooms, Persinette lives amidst great luxury; there she is discovered by, and soon married to, the handsome prince. In time, her pregnancy scandalizes the fairy, who cuts the girl's hair, banishes her (to a lovely seaside cottage), and tricks the prince, resulting in his blindness. After a year, when Persinette's tears heal the prince's eyes, the reunited family must still undergo some terrible ordeals—food turning into stone, birds into dragons and harpies—before the fairy takes pity and saves them.

Among the translations of "Persinette," one by Joachim Christoph Fredrich Schulz, in his 1790 *Kleine Romane,* found favor with the German public. Schulz dealt freely with La Force's text (to which he gave no attribution), altering phrases and adding details, such as the tight dress that betrays the girl's pregnancy to the old woman. And for parsley he substituted the altogether unrelated herb called rapunzel in German and, in English, rampion.

(Rampion is both an ornamental flower and a salad green, edible in its leaf and tuberous root, with a flavor somewhere between watercress and arugula. It is not related to the wild onion known as rampion or ramp, a traditional dish in some parts of the United States. In this book I have chosen to refer to the herb only as "rapunzel.")

The Grimms wrote in the appendix to the first edition of their collection (1812) that Schulz's "Rapunzel" was "undoubtedly derived from an oral tale." Apparently they were unaware of its French provenance, though they did mention its similarity to "Petrosinella." For their own version of the tale, they shortened and recast Schulz's story in the harsher style of their other tales. So La Force/Schulz's newlyweds became a couple burdened with infertility; the magical tower turned into a prison tower, in which no marriage ceremony occurred; and Rapunzel's place of exile became an inhospitable wilderness. In the Grimms' first edition, Rapunzel's tight dress gave away her secret trysts, but by the second edition it was now her familiar slip of the tongue: "Why are you so heavy to pull up, while the prince is here in the blink of an eye?"

Although the Grimm brothers purportedly created their collection to preserve ancient stories in a pure state, untouched by literary influence, the history of "Rapunzel" shows how far from this goal the reality actually fell. In recent years, scholars of folklore have traced the confluence of oral traditions and literary invention; indeed, "Rapunzel" is a prime example of this intermingling.

My retelling of "Rapunzel" takes its shape from both the Grimms and earlier versions of the tale. I have tried to combine the most moving aspects of the story with the most satisfying structure, and to bring out its mysterious internal echoes. In selecting a setting, too, I considered the story's three countries of origin. The formal beauty of Italian Renaissance art seemed to fit well with a tale centered on the beauty of a young girl and a mother figure whose own youth is gone. Also, for me, the very image of a tower evokes the Italian landscape, where the campanile, or bell tower, plays a prominent role in architectural tradition. (The closeness of this word to *Campanula,* the name of the bellflower genus to which rapunzel belongs, helped me to believe I was setting out on the right track.)

As an interloper in the August tradition of Italian Renaissance painting, I have been humbled by my own attempts to achieve effects that any Renaissance painter's apprentice could have tossed off as though it were nothing: billowing drapery or the glint from a fingernail or light falling on tree leaves. The picture-making for this *Rapunzel* included a great deal of gazing at Italian Renaissance paintings (almost all, alas, in books) and trying to figure out "how they did that," both technically and expressively. I also took many details of costume and architecture directly from these paintings by Giovanni Bellini, Vittore Carpaccio, Filippo Lippi, Domenico Ghirlandaio, and others.

In a number of scenes I based my central figure or figures on rather well-known paintings. This reuse of poses, in the tradition of Renaissance art, was not considered plagiarism or failure of creativity; it was standard practice. Poses and compositions were the common currency of art, and they were used to add a layer of understanding, another level of meaning to a painting. As I was working on sketches for Rapunzel, trying to express my characters' feelings through their bodies, I thought about certain great paintings that gave form to these feelings in a powerful way. I decided to do what a painter might have done five hundred years ago, and use, or reuse, these images. I hope that people who recognize my sources will see my use of them as meaningful, too.

The couple in the book's first picture, for instance, comes from a painting by Rembrandt called *The Jewish Bride.* There could hardly be a finer, deeper portrayal of a couple's love and tender concern than in this painting. Sketching Rapunzel's parents, I tried many poses of my own invention before taking Rembrandt's, which was conveniently adaptable: the husband's right hand could be moved only slightly into a natural gesture of belly patting, feeling for an unborn child.

One of my first inspirations for the character of Rapunzel—not her looks but her spirit—was another Rembrandt, a commissioned portrait of Agatha Bas. I can't look at the painting without feeling the woman's presence, and responding to the uncertain gesture of her hand, raised to the edge of the window that separates her from us. This sense of separation, and the knowing, feeling gaze, are exactly what I would expect to see in Rapunzel,

framed by the window of her tower, and separated from the world by an over-protective sorceress.

Another picture in the book called for the prince to stumble off into the woods, blind, and, even worse, devastated at having lost Rapunzel. The image in my mind was a fifteenth-century fresco by Masaccio—the intensely tragic figure of Adam from *The Expulsion from Paradise.* Every part of this figure, from the covered eyes to the heavy footfall, shows what it is like for Adam to face the loss of his perfect life in Eden. So it is, too, with the prince; his life with Rapunzel, somehow artificial and untenable, seeming to be gone forever.

The last picture in the book may be the most likely to ring a bell with viewers; Raphael's *La Belle Jardiniere,* or *Madonna and Child with the Young St. John,* long one of his more popular paintings, was indeed my source. It is a compelling expression of maternal love, and I felt a certain pleasure in adapting it into my composition; I was rather happy with the way my own prince added on to it.

These and some other quotations from art history are now part of my *Rapunzel.* I did not want to mention the fact in my note at the end of the book. Doing so, I thought, would have reduced the pictures in the book to some sort of hiding place for the answers to a puzzle. I've had doubts about divulging the fact of these sources at all; I would not like this intermediary issue to get in the way of people's direct experience of the story. But in a presentation about *Rapunzel* at an ALA convention, I showed some slides of my sources anyway, and was convinced that it would be appropriate to present this information in some venue apart from the book. . . .

It has also occurred to me that the connections between the pictures in the book and the art they descend from might be interesting to any children who come to know and like these illustrations—might, in fact, help spark an interest in that art. So my scruples about publicizing my sources for *Rapunzel* at all have been outweighed by the prospect that my quotations could be used by educators to foster a feeling for the beauty of Renaissance art.

Publishers Weekly

SOURCE: A review of *Rapunzel,* in *Publishers Weekly,* Vol. 244, No. 40, September 29, 1997, p. 89.

Zelinsky does a star turn with this breathtaking interpretation of a favorite fairy tale. Daringly—and effectively—mimicking the masters of Italian Renaissance painting, he creates a primarily Tuscan setting. His Rapunzel, for example, seems a relative of Botticelli's immortal red-haired beauties, while her tower appears an only partially fantastic exaggeration of a Florentine bell tower. For the most part, his bold experiment brilliantly succeeds: the almost otherworldly golden light with which he bathes his paintings has the effect of consecrating them, elevating them to a grandeur befitting their adoptive art-historical roots. If at times his compositions and their references to specific works seem a bit self-conscious, these cavils are easily outweighed by his overall achievement.

The text, like the art, has a rare complexity, treating Rapunzel's imprisonment as her sorceress-adopted mother's attempt to preserve her from the effects of an awakening sexuality. Again like the art, this strategy may resonate best with mature readers. Young children may be at a loss, for example, when faced with the typically well-wrought but elliptical passage in which the sorceress discovers Rapunzel's liaisons with the prince when the girl asks for help fastening her dress (as her true mother did at the story's start): "'It is growing so tight around my waist, it doesn't want to fit me anymore.' Instantly the sorceress understood what Rapunzel did not." On the other hand, with his sophisticated treatment, Zelinsky demonstrates a point established in his unusually complete source notes: that timeless tales like Rapunzel belong to adults as well as children.

Kirkus Reviews

SOURCE: A review of *Rapunzel,* in *Kirkus Reviews,* Vol. LXV, No. 19, October 1, 1997, p. 1540.

Exquisite paintings in late Italian Renaissance style illumine this hybrid version of a classic tale.

As Zelinsky explains in a long source note, the story's Italian oral progenitor went through a series of literary revisions and translations before the Brothers Grimm published their own take; he draws on many of these to create a formal, spare text that is more about the undercurrents between characters than crime and punishment. Feeling "her dress growing tight around her waist" a woman conceives the desire for an herb from the neighboring garden—rendered in fine detail with low clipped hedges, elaborate statuary and even a wandering pangolin—that causes her to lose her child to a witch. Ensconced for years in a tower, young Rapunzel meets the prince, "marries" him immediately, is cast into the wilderness when her own dress begins to tighten, gives birth to twins, and cures her husband's blindness with her tears at their long-awaited reunion. Suffused with golden light, Zelinsky's landscapes and indoor scenes are grandly evocative, composed and executed with superb technical and emotional command.

Betsy Hearne

SOURCE: A review of *Rapunzel,* in *Bulletin of the Center for Children's Books,* Vol. 51, No. 5, January, 1998, p. 182.

Just as Donna Jo Napoli has elaborated "Rapunzel" fictionally in *Zel,* Zelinsky has elaborated the fairy tale visually, with a sequence of paintings that reflect Italian Renaissance art in their refined modeling of feature and drapery, antique burnish of hues, and idealized drafting of landscapes and interiors. Rapunzel's tower, for instance, combines the effects of marbled mosaic and intricate cloisonné, projecting a seductive safety rather than an ominous detention. The sorceress herself, like Trina Schart Hyman's witch in Paul Heins's *Snow White,* is a portrait of aging elegance rather than an unattractive crone, lending psychological force to the interpretation of generational conflict. Graphically articulated with lavish attention to detail, this is strongly balanced with a formal but flowing text that shows a depth of familiarity with the tale's history (summarized in an extensive author's note). There's a fine echo in the wife's dress tightening from pregnancy at the tale's opening and Rapunzel's asking the sorceress to help her with her tightening dress after the prince's nightly visits; this is a version in which Rapunzel gives birth to twins in the wilderness before her reunion with the prince and her healing his blindness with tears. Although romantic, the overall tone is distant, appropriate for a story with action and implications as traditionally forbidding as these.

Mary M. Burns

SOURCE: A review of *Rapunzel,* in *The Horn Book Magazine,* Vol. 74, No. 1, January-February, 1998, p. 85.

Reduced to its plot, the story of **Rapunzel** is the ultimate melodrama: a hapless child, because of her mother's longing for a particular herb, is given to a sorceress to be raised in a formidable tower until an undaunted prince breaches the defenses. Pregnant, she is banished; he is blinded by a fall. Both must wander through a desolate wilderness until their final triumphant reunion. But, as Zelinsky's extensive notes reveal, the tale is far more than a folktale version of a long-running soap opera. Dating back to Basile's *Il Pentamerone* (1637), it underwent several metamorphoses before being included by the Brothers Grimm in the first edition of their *Household Stories* (1812). Various retellers obviously knew a good story when they found one—and **Rapunzel,** with its roots in the human psyche, is all of that. But it takes a scholar's mind and an artist's insight to endow the familiar with unexpected nuances—which Zelinsky does with passion and dazzling technique. Given the story's Italian origins, his choice of a Renaissance setting is inspired, allowing for many allusions to the art and architecture of the fifteenth, sixteenth, and seventeenth centuries. Yet these are not slavish imitations of masterpieces; rather, he has assimilated the sources and transformed them, giving depth to the characters and endowing the story with an aura of otherworldliness that enlarges upon the historical references. There is both love and menace in the sorceress's face; the landscape through which Rapunzel and the prince wander is both beautiful and desolate. Simply put, this is a gorgeous book; it demonstrates respect for the traditions of painting and the fairy tale while at the same time adhering to a singular, wholly original, artistic vision.

Jane Connolly

SOURCE: A review of *Rapunzel,* in *Magpies,* Vol. 13, No. 4, September, 1998, p. 30.

Winner of the 1998 Caldecott award, this version of the age-old fairytale is a work of visual and literary art. Adopting a Renaissance style, Zelinsky's richly detailed paintings are like a fresco on which this tale of possessiveness, confinement and the enduring power of love is played out.

Because of the very nature of traditional literature, the story's origins are as mysterious as they are intriguing. Included in Grimms' collection of eighteenth century folktales, *Rapunzel,* it appears, is a much older tale originating in Italy in 1634 only to be retold in French a century later. To what extent the more familiar Grimms' translation varies from the original is unknown. This retelling has elements of the dark and forbidding nature of many of Grimms' tales and is certainly not a 'Disneyesque' version for very young children. Indeed to fully appreciate the complex elements of the story and the stunning artwork a measure of literary maturity is required of the reader. In his comprehensive notes, Zelinsky traces a little of the story's history and justifies his choice of artistic medium. Basing his retelling on the older Italian version of the story, he creates an Italian setting of ordered, walled gardens, and cities distinguished by the terracotta tiled rooftops. In keeping with this setting, the tower in which Rapunzel is imprisoned becomes not the forbidding lonely place of exile suggested by the brothers Grimm, but a magnificent example of Renaissance architecture, a richly patterned campanile. The witch who imprisons Rapunzel is presented as a sorceress, a mother figure whose care of the girl is prompted by a desire to protect her from the world. Her anger at a perceived betrayal is a powerful and very human response. The face of the sorceress reveals both her love and despair.

Each canvas illustrates the unfolding drama of the story in vivid and authentic detail. The richness and texture of patterned mosaics and parquetry, marbled walls, brocaded costumes, the luxuriant waves and curls of Rapunzel's hair, the interplay of light and shadow are all testament to Zelinsky's artistic skill. This is a book to be owned and cherished for it truly is, as its blurb proclaims, *a work of rare endeavour.*

Additional coverage of Zelinsky's life and career is contained in the following sources published by The Gale Group: *Contemporary Authors New Revision Series,* Vol. 38; *Major Authors and Illustrators for Children and Young Adults;* and *Something about the Author,* Vols. 49, 102.

CUMULATIVE INDEXES

How to Use This Index

AAYA = *Authors & Artists for Young Adults*
AITN = *Authors in the News*
BLC = *Black Literature Criticism*
BLCS = *Black Literature Criticism Supplement*
BW = *Black Writers*
CA = *Contemporary Authors*
CAAS = *Contemporary Authors Autobiography Series*
CABS = *Contemporary Authors Bibliographical Series*
CANR = *Contemporary Authors New Revision Series*
CAP = *Contemporary Authors Permanent Series*
CDALB = *Concise Dictionary of American Literary Biography*
CDBLB = *Concise Dictionary of British Literary Biography*
CLC = *Contemporary Literary Criticism*
CMLC = *Classical and Medieval Literature Criticism*
DAB = *DISCovering Authors: British*
DAC = *DISCovering Authors: Canadian*
DAM = *DISCovering Authors: Modules*
    DRAM: *Dramatists Module*; *MST*: *Most-Studied Authors Module*;
    MULT: *Multicultural Authors Module*; *NOV*: *Novelists Module*;
    POET: *Poets Module*; *POP*: *Popular Fiction and Genre Authors Module*
DC = *Drama Criticism*
DLB = *Dictionary of Literary Biography*
DLBD = *Dictionary of Literary Biography Documentary Series*
DLBY = *Dictionary of Literary Biography Yearbook*
HLC = *Hispanic Literature Criticism*
HW = *Hispanic Writers*
JRDA = *Junior DISCovering Authors*
LC = *Literature Criticism from 1400 to 1800*
MAICYA = *Major Authors and Illustrators for Children and Young Adults*
MTCW = *Major 20th-Century Writers*
NCLC = *Nineteenth-Century Literature Criticism*
NNAL = *Native North American Literature*
PC = *Poetry Criticism*
SAAS = *Something about the Author Autobiography Series*
SATA = *Something about the Author*
SSC = *Short Story Criticism*
TCLC = *Twentieth-Century Literary Criticism*
WLC = *World Literature Criticism, 1500 to the Present*
WLCS = *World Literature Criticism Supplement*
YABC = *Yesterday's Authors of Books for Children*

CUMULATIVE INDEX TO AUTHORS

Author Index

Author Index

Author Index

CUMULATIVE INDEX TO NATIONALITIES

Nationality Index

CUMULATIVE INDEX TO TITLES

Title Index

Title Index

Title Index

Title Index

Title Index

Title Index

Title Index

Title Index

Title Index

Title Index